Linux! I Didn't Know You Could Do That™..., Second Edition

by Nicholas D. Wells

ISBN 0-7821-2935-8
448 pages
$24.99

Turn your Windows-using friends green with Linux envy! Using this completely updated and revised book, you can take all you know about Linux and do it faster, easier, and better! Learn how to soup up your Linux box to suit your own personal style. Boasting over 70 pages of new material, this book has easy-to-follow instructions, tips, tricks, and valuable software that will allow you to run your home office on Linux, set up a crash-free web server, manage your finances, automate everyday tasks, blast your MP3 tunes, and more!

Linux Apache Web Server Administration (Craig Hunt Linux Library)

by Charles Aulds

ISBN 0-7821-2734-7
640 pages
$39.99

With more than 40 percent of the purchase-based server market, Apache is renowned as the most powerful and capable web server available—and the toughest to master. In this detailed guide, expert Linux professional and Webmaster Charles Aulds tackles the issues that Linux administrators and Webmasters need to know to build stable and hackproof web servers for intranet, extranet, and Web use. Includes in-depth treatment of configuring, maintaining, and troubleshooting Apache in the real world.

LINUX COMPLETE
SECOND EDITION

SYBEX®　SAN FRANCISCO ▸ LONDON

Associate Publisher: Joel Fugazzotto

Acquisitions and Developmental Editor: Ellen L. Dendy

Compilation Editor: Mark Lierley

Editor: Loren E. Redding

Production Editor: Leslie E.H. Light

Technical Editor: Jesse Patterson

Book Designer: Maureen Forys, Happenstance Type-o-Rama

Electronic Publishing Specialist: Interactive Composition Corporation

Proofreaders: David Nash, Yariv Rabinovich, Nancy Riddiough

Indexer: Nancy Guenther

Cover Designer: Design Site

Cover Photographer: Jeffery Coolidge/ImageBank

ACKNOWLEDGMENTS

This book is the work of many, both inside and outside Sybex including the publishing team members Joel Fugazzotto and Ellen Dendy, and the editorial/production team of Loren Redding, Leslie Light, Jesse Patterson, Nancy Guenther, and Stacey Loomis at Interactive Composition Corporation.

Mark Lierley deserves particular thanks for pulling together all of the chapters in this book and making sure it all flowed together. Linux experts Nick Wells, Roderick Smith, Janet Valade, and Steve Suehring revised chapters to make sure all of the material was as up to date as possible.

Finally, our thanks to those contributors who agreed to have their work excerpted into *Linux Complete:* Nick Wells, Arman Danesh, Ramón J. Hontañón, Roderick Smith, Vicki Stanfield, Charles Aulds, Craig Hunt, Bryan Pfaffenberger and Mark Minasi.

CONTENTS AT A GLANCE

CONTENTS

Part II ▶ Learning the Basics   61

PART IV ▸ Security   409

Chapter 21 ▫ GUI Configuration Tools and the *smb.conf* File   607

INTRODUCTION

Linux *Complete, Second Edition* is a one-of-a-kind computer book—valuable both for the breadth of its content and for its low price. This thousand page compilation of information from some of Sybex's very best books provides comprehensive coverage of Linux. This book, unique in the computer book world, was created with several goals in mind, among them:

▶ To offer a thorough guide covering all the important features of Linux at an affordable price

▶ To acquaint you with some of our best authors, their writing styles and teaching skills, and the level of expertise they bring to their books—so that you can easily find a match for your interests and needs as you delve deeper into Linux

Linux Complete is designed to provide you with all the essential information you'll need to get the most from Linux and your computer. At the same time, *Linux Complete* will invite you to explore the even greater depths and wider coverage of material in the original books.

If you have read other computer "how to" books, you have seen that there are many possible approaches to effectively using the technology. The books from which this one was compiled represent a range of teaching approaches used by Sybex and Sybex authors. From the expansive, soup-to-nuts coverage of *Mastering Red Hat Linux 7.1*, to the singular focus of *Linux Apache Web Server Administration*, you will be able to choose which approach and which level of expertise works best for you. You will also see what these books have in common: a commitment to clarity, accuracy, and practicality.

In these pages, you will find ample evidence of the high quality of Sybex's authors. Unlike publishers who produce "books by committee," Sybex authors are encouraged to write in their individual voices, voices which reflect their own experience with the software at hand and with the evolution of today's personal computers, so you know you are getting the benefit of their direct experience. Nearly every book represented here is the work of a single writer or a pair of close collaborators. Similarly, all of the chapters here are based on the individual experience of the authors, their first-hand testing of pre-release software, and their subsequent expertise with the final product.

In adapting the various source materials for inclusion in *Linux Complete*, the compilation editor preserved these individual voices and perspectives. Chapters were edited to minimize duplication, omit coverage of non-essential information, update technological issues, and cross-reference material so you can easily follow a topic across chapters. Some sections may have been edited for length in order to include as much updated, relevant, and important information as possible.

Who Can Benefit From This Book?

Linux Complete is designed to meet the needs of a wide range of computer users working with Linux. Linux provides an extraordinarily rich environment, with some elements that everyone uses, as well as features that may be essential to some users but of no interest to others. Therefore, while you could read this book from beginning to end—from installation, to file management and using applications, and on to network administration—all of you may not need to read every chapter. The contents and the index will guide you to the subjects you're looking for.

Beginners   Even if you have only a little familiarity with computers and their basic terminology, this book will start you working with Linux. You'll find step-by-step instructions for installation, desktop navigation and file management, running application programs, and working with multimedia and graphics. You'll want to start at the very beginning of this book, Parts I and II, which cover the basics.

Intermediate Users   If you already know how to do routine tasks in Linux you're more than likely aware that there is always more to learn about working more effectively. Throughout this book, you'll find nuggets of knowledge from which you can benefit.

Power Users/Network Administrators   If you've mastered all the basics and are ready to try Linux out as a network operating system, you'll find plenty of material in this book to get you on your way to becoming a well-rounded Linux network administrator. This book discusses everything from e-mail administration, to security, to running Linux on a Windows server.

NOTE

Red Hat Focus — All chapters of this book were written based on the standard edition of Red Hat Linux 7.1. For more information about Red Hat Linux 7.1 and the packages it includes, please visit http://www.redhat.com/.

How This Book Is Organized

Here's a look at what *Linux Complete* covers in each part:

Part I: Installation   The first three chapters cover basic installation, as well as special issues that crop up during installation.

Part II: Learning the Basics   In this part, you'll learn how to do basic tasks such as manage files, use and understand X Windows, navigate the differences between the GNOME and KDE desktops, run various applications, and work with multimedia and graphics.

Part III: Basic System Administration and Network Address Services   Part III covers user accounts, TCP/IP networking, hardware issues, connecting to the Internet, and setting up a web server.

Part IV: Security   Security is more important than ever. This part introduces you to basic network security within the Linux environment.

Part V: Samba   Learn how to use Samba to make your Linux machines operate seamlessly as part of your Windows network in Part V.

Part VI: Apache and Sendmail   Apache is the most widely used Linux web server. Part VI provides an overview of Apache's features and configuration tools. You'll also learn how to install Apache and how to extend Apache with add-on modules. Installation and configuration of Sendmail, the key program for routing and delivering mail on Linux systems, is covered in two separate chapters.

Appendix: Recompiling the Linux Kernel   Hundreds of option settings are available as part of the standard kernel configuration utilities. This appendix describes how to use the kernel configuration tools to select options that you want included with your running Linux system and then shows how to recompile the kernel source code based on those options.

A Few Typographic Conventions

This typeface is used to indicate the contents of configuration files, messages displayed at a text-mode Linux shell prompt, filenames, and URLs.

Boldface type is used whenever you need to type something into a command line or text box.

You'll find these types of special notes throughout the book:

TIP

You'll see a lot of these Tips—quicker and smarter ways to accomplish a task, which the authors have based on many hours spent testing and using Linux.

NOTE

You'll see Notes, too. They usually represent alternate ways of accomplishing a task or some additional information that needs to be highlighted.

WARNING

In a few places, you'll see a Warning like this one. Pay attention to it.

YOU'LL ALSO SEE SIDEBAR BOXES LIKE THIS

These sections provide added explanations of special topics that are referred to in the surrounding discussions, but that you may want to explore separately in greater detail.

For More Information

See the Sybex website, www.sybex.com, to learn more about all of the books excerpted to *Linux Complete*. On the site's Catalog page, you'll find links to any book you're interested in.

We hope you enjoy this book and find it useful. Happy computing!

PART i
INSTALLATION

Chapter 1

GETTING READY TO INSTALL RED HAT LINUX 7.1

In this chapter, you'll learn how to install Red Hat Linux 7.1. Most of this chapter is concerned with decisions that affect the installation process, rather than with the actual installation process itself, but this decision-making is an essential step to ensure that your Linux installation goes smoothly and that you end up with a well-configured system.

This chapter starts with a brief discussion of the minimum Linux system. What hardware is necessary to run a useful Linux system? It is possible to boot Linux from a single floppy disk, but the resulting system will be so limited that it will be useless for most purposes. This chapter describes what equipment you need in order to make Linux a useful tool in your computing arsenal.

Adapted from *Mastering Red Hat Linux 7.1*
by Arman Danesh
ISBN 0-7821-2927-7   1008 pages $49.99

From there, this chapter discusses a crucial issue: hardware compatibility. Even in the Windows world where vendors quickly provide drivers for almost every conceivable piece of hardware, things go wrong, and hardware incompatibility can be the cause of long, sleepless nights trying to get the Windows operating system to work. In Linux, there is equal potential for problems, especially if you try to use hardware for which there is currently limited or no support.

WHAT YOU NEED

Before you can install Linux, it is important to step back and consider exactly what type of computer you need. Linux can be installed on a wide range of hardware, including the following:

- ► ARM processors
- ► Motorola 68000 series processors
- ► Alpha processors
- ► SPARC processors
- ► MIPS systems
- ► PowerPC-based systems
- ► S/390-based servers
- ► Acorn computers
- ► Power Macintoshes
- ► Intel and Intel-compatible PCs

By far, though, Intel-compatible PC hardware is the most common Linux platform. It generally provides the lowest cost/performance ratio for Linux and is the primary development platform for most Linux tools. Intel Linux offers the best selection of device drivers for peripheral hardware, the largest body of available applications (both commercial and free), and the strongest user community on the Internet to turn to for support and assistance.

The Minimum PC for Linux

As an operating system, Linux has amazingly modest requirements for computer resources. It is possible to get Linux up and running on a 386-based computer with only 4MB of RAM. Of course, such a machine is limited in the following ways:

- ▶ It can't run X Windows (so, no GUI).

- ▶ The number of programs it can run simultaneously is limited by the amount of physical RAM.

- ▶ Its performance is slow enough to prevent its use in most mission-critical applications (for instance, as a mail server or web server).

Given these limitations, a system like this can still play a role in an organization as:

- ▶ A terminal to another Linux or Unix server where applications are running

- ▶ A low-end server for services such as Domain Name System (DNS), which helps computers translate hostnames such as www.yahoo.com into actual numeric Internet Protocol (IP) addresses or as an authentication server for a small network

In fact, Linux can provide a better way to use this type of old hardware than DOS can. DOS has limited networking capabilities and cannot handle the server duties described.

If you want to try to run this type of minimalist Linux system, turn to the Small Memory Mini-HOWTO at http://www.linuxdoc.org/HOWTO/mini/Small-Memory for some basic tips to help you get Linux up and running in a system with limited memory.

A Good PC for Linux

Needless to say, just as you wouldn't want to run Windows on the type of machine described in the previous section, you need a more robust PC to fully enjoy the features and benefits of Linux.

Linux actually requires far fewer resources to perform far more functions than the average Windows 98 or Windows NT/2000 system. For instance, a functional workstation can be put together with a

486-100MHz processor and 16MB of RAM. This system will be able to run X Windows (for a graphical interface), access the Internet, run a graphical web browser, and all the while perform as a low-end server on a network.

Still, the average user will want a somewhat more powerful Linux system. A respectable Linux workstation needs the following specifications:

A Pentium-class CPU   Even a Pentium 133 will do just fine for most users. It is wise to avoid certain clone chips, such as the Cyrix 686 line, because of some reported difficulties people have had running these chips. Generally, though, most Pentium-class systems work well. Of course, if you are buying a new PC today, you won't be able to find a standard Pentium, so choose a Pentium IV, Celeron, Athlon, Duron, or Itanium-class system.

32MB of RAM   Linux is exceptionally good at taking advantage of any extra memory you throw at it. 32MB is enough for the average workstation, but you will notice the difference if you add 64MB or more of RAM.

A 3GB hard disk   You can get away with a 1GB (or even smaller) hard disk, but a roomier disk is preferable. Larger disks tend to perform better than the older, smaller ones. In a number of cases, you won't be able to install all of the features associated with Red Hat Linux 7.1 unless you have at least 3GB of hard disk space.

A supported video card   See the section "Checking Your Hardware for Compatibility," later in this chapter.

With a system like this, you will have more than sufficient resources to run Linux as a desktop operating system. You don't need to go out and buy the latest 1.7GHz Pentium IV system with all the bells and whistles to get Linux up and running at a respectable speed. In fact, you may want to avoid the latest hardware, especially if it was just released in the past few weeks.

Added Bonuses

Of course, in today's computing environment, you will probably want to extend your PC's capabilities into areas such as multimedia and the

Internet. There are a few add-ons that greatly enhance any Linux system, and you should consider them as a way to round out your workstation:

A CD-ROM drive   If you are going to install one, consider an IDE/ATAPI CD-ROM drive or, if you can afford it, a SCSI CD-ROM drive. Generally, it is best to avoid proprietary CD-ROM drives that work with their own interface cards or connect directly to special interfaces on sound cards. These CD-ROM drives are usually poor performers and difficult to configure in Linux.

A sound card   Most Sound Blaster®–compatible cards are supported in Linux; check the hardware compatibility section of this chapter.

A modem   In terms of speed, the same rules apply here as with Windows: It is generally best to get the fastest modem you can that will be able to connect at its top speed to your Internet service provider (ISP).

Two caveats, though: First, it is generally wise to opt for external modems in Linux. This is especially true for ISDN modems, because there is limited support in Linux for internal ISDN modems. The advantages of external modems (ISDN or analog) are that they are easier to configure and they offer external indicators so you can more easily debug configuration problems.

Second, it is generally wise to avoid "winmodems," which are modems that use Microsoft Windows driver library files. Linux supports only a few winmodems without difficulty.

Although a CD-ROM, a sound card, and a modem are fairly standard equipment on newer PCs, if you plan to use Linux as a small server on your intranet, you should consider the following add-ons:

A SCSI card   SCSI offers much better performance for hard drives than the IDE interface and has better support for multiple devices. If you plan to run any type of multiuser system (for instance, file server, web server, or applications server), you really need to use a SCSI card. Be sure to consult the hardware compatibility section before selecting a SCSI card and, if possible, choose a card with Ultra-Wide SCSI support.

Part I

SCSI hard drive(s)   One function of the SCSI card is to be able to use the faster SCSI hard drives. If possible, use Ultra-Wide SCSI drives for the best performance. You may want to consider multiple disk drives. For instance, if you estimate that you need 8GB of space for your users' data as well as the operating system and all installed applications, you may want to consider two 4GB drives (one for the user data and the other for the system and software). By splitting the software and the data, you will probably find that performance improves because the same disk is not being accessed for both.

A tape drive   If you plan to run a server, you will want to do backups to ensure that your data is safe from system failure and other disasters. While it is possible to use some tape drives that connect through the floppy disk bus, you will find that life is a lot easier if you opt for a SCSI tape drive, if you can afford one. They are faster and better supported by Linux.

CHECKING YOUR HARDWARE FOR COMPATIBILITY

As with a Windows (especially Windows NT/2000) system, it is important to check that hardware you intend to buy will work with your Linux operating system and with the rest of the hardware in your computer before buying. Hardware incompatibility with the operating system and other hardware can be the cause of endless difficulty and time spent trying to debug and reconfigure a computer.

This issue is especially important in the Linux community. Although support for Linux is growing among hardware vendors, many vendors still do not provide Linux drivers for their hardware, and their support staff may be unable or unwilling to work with users to debug hardware conflicts and problems in a Linux environment. This means that the hardware needs to be supported by drivers included in the user's Linux distribution or by add-on software that provides drivers for the hardware in question. In addition, users must rely on the Linux community for help when problems arise.

Although a vast majority of hardware is supported in some way by Linux, it is wise to do some research before installing Linux or before purchasing new hardware for a Linux-based system. Here's what you can do:

▶ Try consulting the Red Hat Hardware Compatibility List at `hardware.redhat.com`. This contains a searchable database of compatible hardware for the most current Red Hat distributions.

▶ Consult the Linux Hardware Compatibility HOWTO. This document, authored by Patrick Reijnen, contains extensive lists of hardware known to work with Linux, hardware known not to work with Linux, and issues related to both types of hardware. If you purchase hardware that has the stamp of approval from this HOWTO guide, your life will be easier. You can find the latest version of this guide at `http://www.linuxdoc.org/HOWTO/Hardware-HOWTO.html`.

▶ Consult the `comp.os.linux.hardware` newsgroup. This is a good source of information about hardware issues as they relate to Linux. If you are unsure whether your intended hardware purchase is wise, post a question to the group asking if anyone has had any experience with the hardware in question. You will usually find that others have tried what you are considering, and their collective wisdom is an invaluable resource in making informed purchase decisions. Alternatively, search through newsgroup archives at `http://groups.google.com`.

▶ Try to evaluate the hardware before purchasing it. If you are considering making a corporate purchase of hardware from a vendor you use regularly, it may be possible to borrow the hardware to test it with Linux before actually purchasing it. Of course, this is the only way to be certain that the hardware will work the way you want it to.

RECORDING YOUR HARDWARE INFORMATION

Once you have put together your target Linux PC, you need to collect the hardware-related information necessary to get your hardware working. This section briefly looks at the information you should be aware of in order to get your hardware working quickly with Linux.

Video Cards

If you install Linux without X Windows (the graphical user interface for Unix systems), you will probably have no difficulties with any video card. However, with X Windows, you need to take care and pay attention to detail to get your card working. Record the following information about your video card before installing Linux:

- ▶ Vendor and model of the card.
- ▶ Video chipset used on the card. (Sometimes X Windows might not provide explicit support for a particular card but will offer general support for the chipset used in the card.)
- ▶ Amount of video memory on the card.
- ▶ Type of clock chip on the card. (If there is one; many common cards do not have clock chips.)

All of this information should be available in the documentation that came with your card or in Linux-related archives, HOWTOs, or the card manufacturer's website if you no longer have the documentation.

Sound Cards

Sound cards require that you supply very specific information in order to get them working. The following information is critical to configuring most sound cards:

- ▶ Vendor and model of the card
- ▶ IRQ(s) of the card
- ▶ I/O address(es) of the card
- ▶ DMA address(es) of the card

You may have to set the IRQ, I/O address, and DMA address manually, using jumpers or DIP switches. Depending on your card, not all of this information may be required. Refer to the card's documentation for instructions.

Monitors

As with your video card, it is important to record the technical specifications of your monitor in order to get it working optimally with X Windows. If you don't have this information or use the wrong information, there is a risk that your monitor will be damaged. Record the following specifications after consulting your monitor's documentation:

- ▶ Vendor and model of the monitor
- ▶ Top resolution of the monitor
- ▶ Top refresh rate of the monitor when running at its top resolution
- ▶ Horizontal sync range of your monitor
- ▶ Vertical sync range of your monitor

Mice

In order to get your mouse working, both in Linux's character-based console mode and in X Windows, you need to note the following information:

- ▶ Vendor and model of the mouse.
- ▶ Number of mouse buttons.
- ▶ Protocol of the mouse. (Consult the mouse's documentation for this; common protocols include the Microsoft protocol, USB, the Mouse Systems protocol, and the PS/2 protocol.)
- ▶ Port where your mouse is connected to your computer. (In DOS terms, this is generally COM1:, COM2:, or the PS/2 mouse port.)

Hard Drives

If you plan to use Linux to repartition your hard drive during installation (see the section about arranging your hard disk's partitions, "Arranging Your Hard Disk," later in this chapter), you may need the following information:

- ▶ Total storage capacity of the hard disk
- ▶ Number of cylinders
- ▶ Number of heads
- ▶ Number of sectors per track

Generally, you will not need to provide this information because Linux will successfully auto-detect it when the system is booted.

Modems

If you have a modem, you should record the following information:

- ▶ Vendor and model of the modem

- ▶ Speed of the modem

- ▶ Port that your external modem is connected to or that you have configured your internal modem to use (in DOS terms, this is generally COM1: or COM2:) or with internal modems, the IRQ, I/O address, as well as the port

Network Cards

If you have a network card, you should record the following information:

- ▶ Vendor and model of the network card

- ▶ IRQ(s) of the card

- ▶ I/O address(es) of the card

- ▶ Specialized drivers, if available

- ▶ Compatibility with Novell 1000 or 2000 network card drivers

Some network cards include driver disks with Linux drivers. Alternatively, if your card is compatible with Novell 1000 or 2000 network card drivers, you may be able to use these drivers to install your network card on Linux. Consult your network card's documentation for more information.

USB

Several Linux distributions include partial USB support, primarily for keyboards and mice. These distributions include SuSE 6.4, Red Hat 7.0, Mandrake 7.1, and Corel Linux Second Edition (and above). As of this writing, Linux support for USB hardware within the 2.2.x kernel is limited to static configuration.

However, Red Hat 7.1 is based on the 2.4.x kernel, which allows nearly the full available range of USB support. As shown in the Linux-USB device database at http://www.qbik.ch/usb/devices, Linux USB support is available at some level for just about every type of USB device, from modems to web cameras.

If you're interested in "hotplugging," installing a USB device while your computer is in operation, refer to the Linux Hotplugging website at `http://linux-hotplug.sourceforge.net`. This site includes downloadable scripts in `.rpm` format that are designed to work with Red Hat Linux.

Considerable work on USB for Linux is in progress. If you can't install your USB hardware on your distribution, you can review the Linux USB project at `http://www.linux-usb.org` for additional drivers and utilities.

Other Peripherals

Many other peripherals have specific requirements for configuration. The number and types of possible peripherals are too varied to list here. Generally, additional hardware such as specialized serial cards, specialized PCMCIA or PC cards, and tape drives is not configured and installed at the time Linux is installed but rather after you have a running Linux system.

CHOOSING AN INSTALLATION METHOD

Generally, Linux is distributed on CD-ROMs because of its size. Although Linux can be downloaded from the Internet, it is too large for most people to download unless they have access to a high-speed, dedicated Internet connection.

A CD-ROM, then, is usually at the core of installing Linux, as it is in the case of the Red Hat Linux 7.1 distribution. While it is theoretically possible to install Linux directly off the Internet, this method is too time-consuming or too expensive to be practical for most Linux users.

This section will consider different approaches to installing Linux from CD-ROM. The procedures will be similar to most other Linux distributions that are available on CD-ROM; consult the documentation for those distributions to determine the differences.

From CD-ROM

If you have an IDE/ATAPI CD-ROM drive and a computer with a fairly recent BIOS, it is possible to boot your computer from the Linux CD-ROM to start the installation process.

To check this, consult your computer's or main board's manual, or enter the BIOS setup of your computer while it is booting and see if you can switch the default boot device to your CD-ROM drive. If you can boot from the CD-ROM drive, insert the Red Hat Linux 7.1 Installation CD-ROM and attempt to boot your system. You should see an Installation menu and a boot prompt that says boot:.

NOTE

Even though an installation CD may be designed to boot from the CD-ROM, it still may not boot in all PCs that support bootable CD-ROMs. If you experience difficulty booting Linux, try installing from a floppy disk and CD-ROM as described in the "From Floppy Disk and CD-ROM" section of this chapter.

From Floppy Disk and CD-ROM

If you have a CD-ROM drive but can't boot from it, the next best thing is to install Linux from a combination of floppy disk and CD-ROM. In this scenario, you boot from one or more floppy disks to start the installation process and then install the actual Linux software from the CD-ROM.

Some preparation is necessary to do this. For most distributions of Linux, you need to prepare a boot floppy disk and maybe one or more supplementary disks. Everything you need to do this should be included on the CD-ROM containing your Linux distribution.

If you need a boot disk and any supplementary disks, you can build them off most Linux installation CD-ROMs from DOS or the Windows DOS prompt.

On the Red Hat 7.1 CD-ROM, the Images subdirectory contains two files, boot.img and bootnet.img, that are disk images of the floppy disks used for installing Red Hat Linux 7.1 from files on the local computer or through a network. It also includes various driver disks for PCMCIA cards (pcmcia.img and pcmciadd.img), drivers for older CD-ROMs (oldcdrom.img), and other drivers (drivers.img). Each of these images requires a blank, formatted, high-density 1.44MB floppy and the rawrite.exe utility.

For instance, assuming that your CD-ROM drive is drive D, you use `rawrite.exe` as follows to create the Red Hat boot install disk:

```
C:\>d:\dosutils\rawrite.exe
Enter disk image source file name: d:\images\boot.img
Enter target diskette drive: a
Please insert a formatted diskette into drive A:
and press -ENTER- :
```

Similarly, you enter **d:\images\bootnet.img** as the source filename to create the network boot installation disk.

When this is done, you can boot from the boot install disk to start the installation process.

From Hard Disk

If you have plenty of disk space, you may want to copy the entire contents of the CD-ROM to your hard disk and install from the hard disk. Starting with Red Hat Linux 7.1, hard disk–based installation requires the use of ISO images, which is a single file that contains all of the files in a Red Hat Installation CD-ROM.

There are two basic ways to get the right ISO images. First, you can download them directly over the Internet from a source such as `ftp.redhat.com`. The ISO file for each Red Hat Linux 7.1 CD-ROM is as large as the CD-ROM itself—in other words, about 650MB. Alternatively, you can create an ISO image from a Red Hat Linux 7.1 Installation CD-ROM, using the `mkisofs` command. More information on this process is available in Chapter 3, "Special Installations."

Of course, if you have access to a CD-ROM drive to create an ISO image, then you don't need to install from a hard disk. The only time this should really become necessary is if the Linux installation software won't recognize your CD-ROM drive. With the drivers available on the previously mentioned `oldcdrom.img` file, this should rarely be necessary.

ARRANGING YOUR HARD DISK

When it comes time to install Linux, you are going to have to make some fundamental decisions regarding where to place the operating system on your hard disk(s). If you are extremely lucky, then one of the following two situations applies to you:

▶ You have a blank hard disk, or one you can reformat, available on which to install Linux.

▶ You have a blank partition, or one you can reformat, available on which to install Linux.

Unfortunately, most users who are looking at installing Linux for the first time want Linux to coexist with their current Windows and DOS installations and do not want to reformat an existing partition or hard disk to do this.

Partitioning Concepts

In order to install Linux into an existing system with no free partitions or hard disks, you need to find sufficient disk space and then carefully adjust your system's partitioning to free up a partition to work with during the Linux installation. Generally, if you want to install a fairly complete Linux system, you should free up at least 2GB of disk space. The space you free up should be on a single partition. (In Windows, each partition appears as a separate drive letter such as C, D, or E, so you need to find a drive with 2GB or more of free space.)

A Simple Partition Scheme for a Windows 98 System

Let's look at a simple example. You have a computer with a single 12GB hard disk divided into two 6GB partitions as drives C and D under DOS. You are able to free up 3GB of disk space on drive D, and you want to use this to install Linux.

There are two steps to be taken before you are ready to install Linux:

1. Defragment the drive to ensure that you have a large, continuous area of free space at the end of the partition.

2. Repartition the drive to make the space available for the Linux installation.

Defragmenting a Drive

Defragmenting a drive under Windows 98 is fairly simple. Just follow these steps:

1. Back up the data on your drive.

2. In My Computer or Windows Explorer, right-click the Drives icon.

3. Select Properties from the drop-down menu.

4. Choose the Tools tab at the top of the Properties window.

5. Click the Defragment Now button. Wait until defragmentation is complete and then proceed to the next section.

Partitioning Your Disk

Once you have defragmented a drive with sufficient space to install Linux, you need to create a new partition out of the free space. Most Linux distributions, including Red Hat Linux 7.1, come with a free DOS tool called fips.exe, which is in the dosutils subdirectory or in a subdirectory of that directory.

WARNING

Red Hat does not support FIPS. It is covered under the General Public License, which means that the people behind FIPS have no liability even if you use it correctly and it destroys your data. While I've used FIPS a number of times and have never had a problem, be warned: Use it at your own risk. There are alternative commercial partition-splitting programs, including System Commander (www.v-com.com) and Partition Magic (www.powerquest.com).

This tool enables you to adjust the size of an existing partition, making it smaller by removing empty space at the end of the partition. This empty space is then converted into another partition.

To use fips.exe, you first need to be in MS-DOS mode. To do this, select Shut Down from the Start menu and choose Restart In MS-DOS Mode. Windows 98 should shut down and switch to a full-screen DOS environment.

WARNING

This is a critical step. You shouldn't use a program like FIPS inside a DOS window or full-screen DOS environment while Windows 98 is running. Unlike DOS, Windows 95 and above allow multiple programs to run simultaneously, so it is possible for other programs to try to access the partition being worked with by FIPS. If this happens, your data may be corrupted and irretrievable.

Once in DOS mode, run `fips.exe` from your CD-ROM. If your CD-ROM drive is drive E, use the command

```
C:\>e:\dosutils\fips20\fips.exe
```

The program first presents your partition table. In the previous example of a two-partition drive, this will look something like the following:

```
Partition table:

      |         |  Start        |      |  End          | Start   |Number of |
Part.|Bootable|Head Cyl. Sector|System|Head Cyl. Sector| Sector  |Sectors   |   MB
-----+--------+----------------+------+----------------+---------+----------+----
1    |  yes   |  1   0    1    | 06h  | 254 222  63    |     63| 3582432 |1749
2    |  no    |  0  223   1    | 05h  | 254 286  63    | 3582495| 1028160 | 502
```

On most systems, identifying your partitions is easy because drive C is partition 1, drive D is partition 2, and so on. If you have trouble, use the size of the partition in megabytes in the last column to help.

You are then prompted to choose a partition. In this case, choose 2, since you want drive D to be adjusted. Once you choose, the partition will be scanned, and summary information about the partition, similar to the following, will be presented:

```
Bytes per sector: 512

Sectors per cluster: 8

Reserved sectors: 1

Number of FATs: 2

Number of rootdirectory entries: 512

Number of sectors (short): 0

Media descriptor byte: f8h

Sectors per FAT: 145

Sectors per track: 63

Drive heads: 16
```

```
Hidden sectors: 63
Number of sectors (long): 141057
Physical drive number: 80h
Signature: 29h
```

Assuming you have free space at the end of the partition you have chosen, you are asked which disk cylinder to use as the line where the partition is cut and split. You can use your arrow keys to change the selected cylinder. As you do this, the size of the partitions in megabytes is shown so that you can make sure that the new partition is large enough. The FIPS program handles the job of making sure that you can't choose a cylinder to split that would leave some of the data from your current partition on the new partition.

Finally, a revised partition table appears, and you are asked to confirm that everything looks okay. In this example, you should now have three partitions, with the third being your new partition and the second being smaller in size than it was originally.

TIP

To protect against mistakes, copy `fips.exe`, `restorrb.exe`, and `errors.txt` from your Linux Installation CD-ROM to a bootable floppy disk. These files are usually located in a subdirectory such as `dosutils`. When asked if you want to write backup copies of your boot and root sectors to a floppy disk, answer **Yes**. Then, if you need to recover from a mistake, you can boot from the floppy and run `restorrb.exe` to restore your original boot and root sectors.

WHAT'S NEXT?

In this chapter, you conducted the basic preparation needed to install Linux. Now you are ready for the actual installation.

In Chapter 2, "Installing Red Hat Linux 7.1," you will run through a basic installation of Linux, examining each screen of the installation program and learning how to decide what choices to make.

In Chapter 3, "Special Installations," you will look at special cases, such as how to install Linux on multiple hard drives and how to install Linux onto an existing DOS partition.

Chapter 2

INSTALLING RED HAT LINUX 7.1

Y ou're finally here: You are going to install Linux. By now you should be able to boot the Linux installation CD-ROM, or you should have produced a set of Linux boot floppy disks. You should also have determined where you will be installing Linux and made the space available.

Now you can begin. Although the installation program may ask questions unfamiliar to you if you have not used a Linux-like operating system before, in reality the whole process is quite simple, and many of the tough decisions are made for you by the installation software.

In fact, for the average user who is installing Linux as a second operating system in a Windows 97/98/Me system, the process is generally straightforward, with a few odd turns required. This chapter is based on installing Red Hat Linux 7.1, but the principles are the same for the latest version of most Linux distributions.

Adapted from *Mastering Red Hat Linux 7.1*
by Arman Danesh
ISBN 0-7821-2927-7   1008 pages $49.99

STARTING THE INSTALLATION

This chapter looks at a straightforward installation: installing Linux from the CD-ROM onto a nonnetworked, stand-alone PC.

To do this, you need to have selected which media to boot from to start the installation. As outlined in the previous chapter, your two options are as follows:

▶ Booting directly from the Linux installation CD-ROM. This requires that your computer's BIOS support booting from your CD-ROM drive.

▶ Booting from a set of boot floppy disks and then installing from the CD-ROM.

In either case, insert your boot disk (floppy or CD-ROM) and boot your computer. When the computer starts booting from a Red Hat Linux 7.1 floppy disk or CD-ROM, you will be presented with an initial welcome screen, as shown in Figure 2.1.

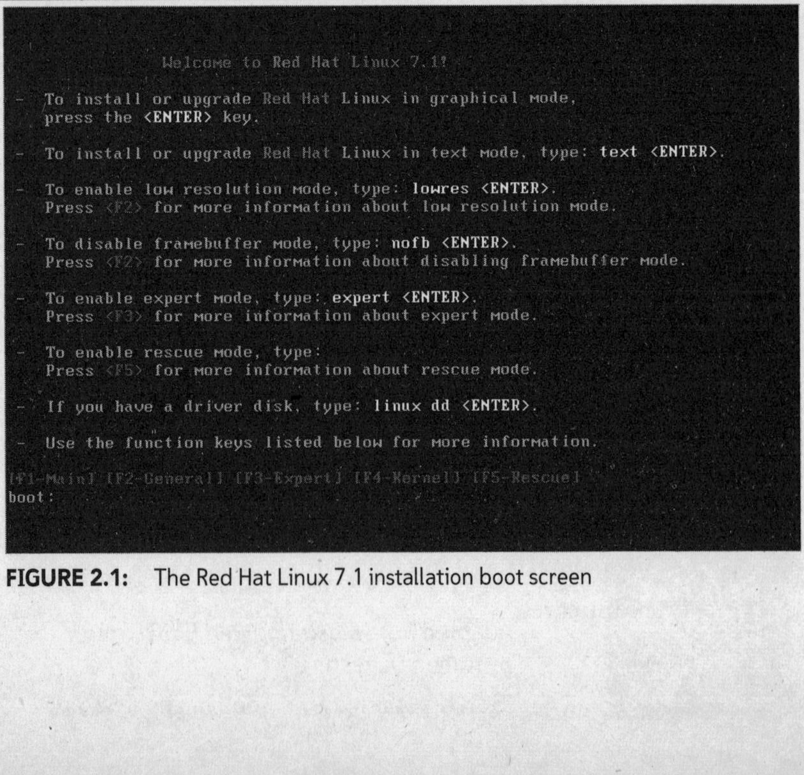

FIGURE 2.1:   The Red Hat Linux 7.1 installation boot screen

Here you have seven main installation options:

▶ Press Enter to start the normal graphical installation process.

▶ While this item is not explicitly shown on the menu, you can type in boot parameters that enable the installation software to detect some types of obscure hardware, and then press Enter to start the normal installation process. (Most hardware is detected automatically during installation.)

▶ Type **text** and press Enter to boot in text mode. (In text mode, installation starts in a screen that is less graphically demanding. If Linux is having trouble detecting your video card, text mode may be a viable option. You might recognize the text-mode screen graphics from Red Hat Linux 6.0 and below.)

NOTE

Compared to the text mode of installation just described, the next two installation modes are closer to the normal graphical installation process.

▶ Type **lowres** and press Enter to boot in low resolution mode. In this mode, graphical installation starts in a 640×400 screen, instead of the standard installation 800×600 screen. If you have a video card that does not have enough memory to support 800×600 graphics, low resolution may be a viable option.

▶ Type **nofb** and press Enter to boot in no frame buffer mode. In this mode, graphical installation starts without the frame buffer associated with accelerated graphics cards. If your graphics card does not support 2D or 3D accelerated graphics, then no frame buffer mode may be a viable option.

▶ Type **expert** and press Enter to boot in expert mode. (In expert mode, hardware detection is not performed, and you will need to provide configuration parameters for all your hardware during the installation. You should revert to this option only if your hardware is not being detected properly and you are fairly confident of the parameters to enter.)

▶ Type **linux rescue** and press Enter to boot a generic Linux rescue disk. This can help you recover from some system failures. It allows you to access your computer as the root user with basic editors and tools that let you reconfigure damaged or lost configuration files. Generally, you should create a dedicated rescue floppy with critical configuration files; rescue mode may be an option if you lose that floppy.

▶ The `linux dd` option is not a separate option but an alternate way to start the normal graphical installation process. If you type **linux dd**, the installation program prompts you to insert a driver disk for special equipment. A typical driver disk can be created from the `drivers.img` file on the `images` directory on the installation CD-ROM.

NOTE

Generally, most users will find that all of their hardware will be successfully detected if they choose the first option, so simply press Enter to start the boot process. If you fail to press any key within 60 seconds, the installation automatically starts as if you had pressed Enter without providing any options. To disable this timer, press one of the help keys (F1 to F5). Then you will have all the time you need to decide how to start the installation program.

Configuring Your System for Installation

The installation process has several steps, which we will consider in turn. However, before we do that, you should learn how to use the keyboard to work in the installation program.

Keyboard Controls

As shown in Figure 2.2, there are several elements to the typical installation screen. These elements include text input fields, check boxes, and buttons.

This screen contains the following elements:

▶ Text input fields (IP Address, Netmask, and so on)

▶ Check boxes (Configure Using DHCP and Activate On Boot)

▶ Buttons (Hide Help, Back, and Next)

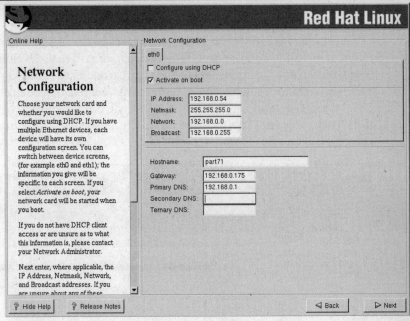

FIGURE 2.2:   A typical Red Hat Linux 7.1 installation screen

You can move between these elements using the Tab key (or the Shift+Tab combination to move backward), or you can use your mouse. The arrow keys can also be used to move between fields.

To toggle the state of a check box, move to the check box and press the spacebar. To press a button, move the cursor to the button using Tab or the arrow keys and then press the spacebar or the Enter key. With a Next button, the F12 key generally works the same as pressing Enter or the spacebar. Of course, if the installation program detects your mouse, you can left-click your selections as well. Just in case, the remaining descriptions in this chapter assume that your mouse doesn't work in the Linux installation program.

Choosing a Language

After you start the installation program at the boot screen as described earlier in this chapter, a welcome screen appears, followed by the first screen of the installation process: Language Selection. This affects only the language that you see during the installation process. To change the language shown on Red Hat Linux 7.1 after installation, see the "Language Support Selection" section later in this chapter.

As you can see in Figure 2.3, the Language Selection screen has a selection list field and a Next button. When the cursor is in the selection list field, you can use the arrow keys or the Page Up and Page Down keys to move through the available languages until the desired one is selected. This selection determines the language that will be used during the installation process. (This is distinct from the language of the actual operating system and the keyboard layout, both of which are selected later.)

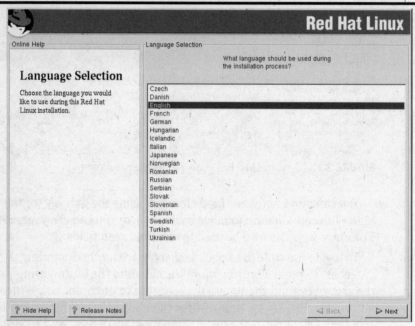

FIGURE 2.3:   Choosing a language

Choosing a Keyboard Type

The next screen presents selection list fields for choosing a keyboard model and layout. If you don't see your keyboard in the model list, the default is Generic 104-key PC. The layout generally corresponds to different languages or dialects (for example, French or Swiss French). In the United States, the correct layout will almost always be U.S. English. Other common models and layouts include those listed in Tables 2.1 and 2.2.

TABLE 2.1: Typical Keyboard Models

MODEL	DESCRIPTION
Dell 101-key PC	For certain Dell PC keyboards
Japanese 106-key	With Japanese characters
Microsoft Natural	Microsoft Natural (split) keyboard
Winbook Model XP5	Winbook Special Model XP5 keyboard

TABLE 2.2: Typical Keyboard Layouts

LAYOUT	DESCRIPTION
Brazilian	Brazilian Portuguese keyboard
Canadian	Canadian English keyboard
German	German keyboard
Swiss German	Swiss German keyboard

You can test your selection at the bottom of the screen, in the Test Your Selection Here text box. You should test your selection especially if you have doubts about your choice of keyboard.

NOTE

If you have a special keyboard and don't see it in the standard mode of the Red Hat Linux 7.1 installation program, start the installation program again in text mode. Red Hat Linux 7.1 includes nearly 80 different keyboard types in this mode.

Configuring Your Mouse

After you configure your keyboard, the next step is to configure your mouse. First, the installation software attempts to detect your mouse. Then you are presented with a list of possible mouse types from which to select (if automatic detection was successful, then the appropriate mouse type is preselected). If you cannot find your specific brand of mouse on the list, choose a generic mouse most similar to yours. Consult your mouse's documentation to determine the type of mouse you have.

If yours is a two-button mouse, make sure that you check the box for three-button mouse emulation. Linux expects a three-button mouse, as do all Unix operating systems. This emulation allows you to click the left and right mouse buttons together to simulate clicking the middle mouse button. This feature, while not absolutely necessary, will enhance X Windows functionality.

NOTE

If you have a mouse with a center wheel, press it. If you hear a click, Linux may be able to recognize it as a three-button mouse. In this case, you may not need to select three-button mouse emulation.

You also need to set up the mouse port, which is typically PS/2 (with a round connector), serial (trapezoidal connector with nine holes), or USB (small rectangular connector). If you have a serial mouse, you also need to set up or confirm the mouse port, usually COM1: or COM2:.

Installing or Upgrading?

Once you have selected and configured your mouse, the next menu allows you to install Red Hat Linux in four different ways. Alternatively, if you already have Linux on your computer, you can just select the Upgrade option. If you want to upgrade without overwriting your configuration files, you generally need to upgrade with the same branded distribution. Most Linux distributions allow you the same options, but the organization of the install screens can differ.

If you are installing Red Hat Linux 7.1 for the first time on your computer, there are four possible ways to install it:

Workstation   Performs a default installation for a Linux workstation. This option automatically erases all existing Linux partitions on your system, and it requires at least 1.2GB of free space on your hard drive.

Server   Performs a default installation for a Linux server. This option automatically erases all existing partitions on your system, including any other non-Linux operating systems and data on your computer. It requires at least 650MB of free space on your hard drive.

Laptop   Similar to a Workstation installation, this option performs a default installation for Linux on a laptop computer. It includes packages typically required by a laptop computer, such as PCMCIA drivers. This option automatically erases all existing Linux partitions on your system. It requires at least 1.2GB of free space on your hard drive.

Custom   Provides complete control over all aspects of the installation process. The default Custom installation requires just over 700MB of free space on your hard drive.

In order to learn the details of installing Red Hat Linux 7.1, you will work with the fourth option, Custom, throughout this chapter and in Chapter 3, "Special Installations."

Setting Up Your Disk Partitions

After you select an installation class, you face a decision about how to allocate disk space for your Linux installation. This is a crucial step in the process because a mistake can erase existing data on your system.

Let's assume that you have a single hard drive in your system, that—as directed in Chapter 1, "Getting Ready to Install Red Hat Linux 7.1"—you created an area of free space (preferably larger than 1GB) using the techniques described there, and that the space is now ready to be used.

The first question you are asked is which tool you want to use to set up your partitions. The two choices in Red Hat Linux are Disk Druid and fdisk.

fdisk is the standard Linux tool for configuring disk partitions and is available for every Linux distribution. However, it is difficult to use and can be especially daunting for first-time Linux or Unix users.

WARNING

If you don't know what you're doing, fdisk can cause you to lose all of your data. Also, the Linux fdisk tool is quite different from the MS-DOS fdisk tool, in that Linux fdisk includes a large number of options, as discussed in Chapter 3.

To help ease this process, Red Hat Linux 7.1 provides its own tool for disk partition management: Disk Druid. This section focuses on using Disk Druid because it eases the initial installation process for users new to the Linux environment. If you select the Disk Druid button, the main Disk Druid screen appears, as shown in Figure 2.4.

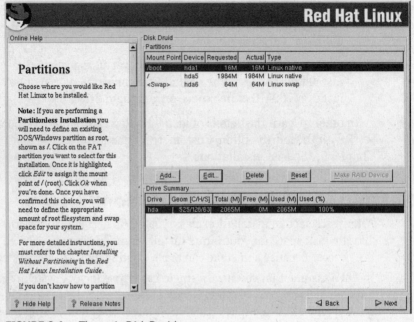

FIGURE 2.4:   The main Disk Druid screen

This screen has three main sections: the Partitions section, the button row, and the Drive Summary section.

In the Partitions section, a single row is displayed for each existing disk partition on your system. The following information is presented about each partition:

Mount Point   This indicates where the partition appears in your Linux directory structure. Linux directories all appear as subdirectories of the root directory. The root directory is /, and all subdirectories start with /, such as /home, /opt, and /usr/X11R6. At a minimum, you need to have a partition mounted as / and a swap partition. If you mount additional partitions as subdirectories, this will spread your Linux distribution across additional directories. For instance, if you mount a partition as /usr, any content stored under this subdirectory is stored on the /usr partition, while all other data is on the root-mounted (/) partition. If you want to limit or dedicate a certain amount of space to a directory, you can mount that directory in a limited amount of space. The primary roles of the standard top-level Red Hat Linux directories are as follows:

/bin   Standard system utilities are stored here.

/boot   The kernel, boot loader, memory maps, and module details are stored here. Commonly set up in a separate partition.

/dev   Device files are stored here.

/home   Users' home directories are stored here.

/mnt   Temporarily mounted filesystems, such as /mnt/cdrom and /mnt/floppy, are normally stored here.

/opt   Optionally installed software is stored here.

/root   The home directory of the root user. Do not confuse this with the root-mounted (/) partition.

/sbin   Standard system administration files are stored here. Typically, these files should be accessible only to the root user.

/usr   Additional system software and administration tools are stored here.

/var   Log files and print spools are stored here. This is commonly mounted separately in limited space on web servers, as the log files from a website can otherwise easily crowd out any other information on that Linux computer.

/etc   Administrative files and configuration files are contained here. Other commands formerly in this directory should be moved to /bin or /sbin.

Device   This indicates the Linux device name for each partition. For IDE disks, the drives are labeled hdx, where x is a letter designating a drive (a for the primary master drive, b for the primary slave, c for the secondary master, and d for the secondary slave). Thus, if you have a single IDE hard disk, it is disk hda. SCSI disks are labeled sdx, with x again designating a drive. Partitions on the disk are then numbered consecutively starting with hda1 and moving up. Generally, partitions 1 through 4 are primary partitions, and 5 and above represent the logical partitions common on many DOS systems. In Figure 2.4, you see Linux partitions associated with the boot directory (hda1), the root directory (hda5), and the Swap partition (hda6).

Requested   This indicates the minimum size of the partition in megabytes.

Actual   This indicates the actual space allocated for a partition. Disk Druid allows the creation of growable Linux partitions, which increase in size as free space is available on the hard disk and space runs out in the partition. DOS partitions should have matching actual and requested values.

Type   This field indicates the type of partition that you can create with Disk Druid. Possible values include Linux native, Linux swap, Linux RAID, DOS 16-bit<32M, and DOS 16-bit>=32M. (While you can't create FAT32 or NTFS partitions here, Disk Druid now recognizes these common Microsoft Windows partitions.)

The next main section of the screen is the set of five task buttons. Use the Add button to create the necessary Linux partitions for your installation and the Edit button to make sure your existing DOS and Windows data is accessible in Linux or to change previous settings. You can delete an individual partition with the Delete button. If you want to start over, use the Reset button. If you need more speed and security with your data, the Make RAID Device button lets you distribute files over a series of independent partitions.

Finally, there is the Drive Summary section. This presents one line for each hard disk on your system and includes the following information about the drives:

Drive   This is the device name for the hard drive, discussed previously.

Geometry   This indicates the number of cylinders, heads, and sectors (in that order) for the drive.

Total This indicates the total available space on the drive, in megabytes.

Free This shows how much of the drive is available, in megabytes, for additional partitions.

Used This indicates the total used space on the drive, in megabytes. This number actually reflects how much is used in the sense of how much has been allocated to partitions. These partitions may not be full, but the space is no longer available to be allocated to other partitions. The number associated with the main Linux-native partitions must be more than zero and should be more than 1GB before proceeding, because you need to use this space to install Linux in. If you don't have any free space, consult the discussion in Chapter 1, which describes how to allocate space for your Linux installation.

Used (%) This indicates the percentage of space on the drive allocated to partitions. If this number is less than 100%, you can add more partitions.

Finally, the button bar across the bottom of the screen has Hide Help, Back, and Next buttons. You can use the Hide Help button to hide the explanation screen on the left side of the page. You can use the Back button to return to the previous menu. Use the Next button when you want to continue to the next menu. The Next button will be available only after partitions are configured correctly for Linux to be installed.

Adding New Partitions

To add a new partition, you simply press the Add button on the main Disk Druid screen. A screen appears asking for the following main information:

- ▶ Mount point
- ▶ Size in megabytes
- ▶ Whether the drive can grow to use unallocated disk space as needed (through the Use Remaining Space check box)
- ▶ Partition type (from a selection list field)

▶ Which drives the partition can be created on. If more than one drive is indicated as allowed and all allowed drives have sufficient space to create the partition, Disk Druid will decide which disk to use. If you want to create the partition on a specific disk, make sure that only that disk is checked.

You should use the Add button to create at least the following partitions:

A swap partition   Linux needs a separate partition to use for swapping. This is necessary when you use up all your physical RAM and the operating system must draw on virtual memory (disk space masquerading as RAM) to keep functioning. Subject to the limitations in the following note, you generally should at least match the amount of physical RAM you have on your system; if you have plenty of free disk space, make the size of the swap partition as much as double that of your physical RAM. For example, on a 32MB system, create a swap partition of between 32MB and 64MB. The partition type should be set to Linux Swap, and no mount point should be indicated. To save room for other partitions, the Use Remaining Space check box should be unselected.

NOTE

In Red Hat Linux 7.1, swap partitions need to be at least 32MB. If you selected a Workstation or a Laptop-class installation, the Red Hat 7.1 installation program allocates 64MB for your swap partition. Alternatively, if you chose a Server-class installation, you'll get a 256MB swap partition.

A root partition   In this chapter, you are going to install Linux in two partitions. (The next chapter discusses the use of multiple partitions or drives for the installation of Linux.) To do this, you need to add another partition. You will probably want the partition to be at least 1GB to give you room to work once Linux is installed. This partition should be type Linux Native, should have a mount point of /, and can be marked with the Use Remaining Space option if there is unallocated free space on your drive that you want to use if the partition grows larger than its initial size.

A boot partition   When you let Red Hat Linux 7.1 partition your drive automatically, it sets up a boot partition by default. Boot partitions include the key components required to boot Linux: the kernel, system map, and hardware module locations. On most Linux systems, a boot partition has to be located below the 1024th cylinder on a hard drive. However, if you've set up your partitions with `fdisk`, Red Hat Linux 7.1 allows you to bypass this limitation by adding `lba32` as a kernel parameter when you set up LILO later.

Editing a Partition

You can edit existing partitions by selecting them from the list of current partitions and then clicking the Edit button. This brings up a window like the one you used when adding a new partition, except that here all the fields are filled in to match the settings of the partition you are editing.

If you have pre-existing DOS partitions, you can make them available to Linux by specifying a mount point for them. To do this, select the partition you want to make accessible in Linux, press the Edit button, and then fill in a mount point for the partition.

If you have a single DOS partition, you could mount it as `/dos`, for instance. If you have two DOS partitions, which are drives C and D in DOS and Windows, you could choose `/dosc` and `/dosd` (or `/c` and `/d`), respectively, as the mount points.

Deleting a Partition

If, in the process of creating your Linux swap and root partitions, you make a mistake (maybe the swap partition is too large or your root partition too small), you can delete the partitions and then re-add them. To do this, select the partition in the list of current partitions and then press the Delete button.

WARNING

Take care when deleting a partition. Don't accidentally delete any partitions that existed before you started installing Linux and that contain important data or software you want to keep.

Reset

If you feel the need to start again while creating your Linux partitions, click the Reset button. This restores the partition table to its state before you started Disk Druid.

Make RAID Device

If you are setting up Linux as a server, you are setting up a computer for multiple users. The programs and data on that server become even more important. You can protect the data by spreading it out among multiple hard drives, known as a Redundant Array of Independent Disks (RAID). If you set up a series of RAID partitions, you can then configure them with the Make RAID Device option.

Moving On

Once you have finished creating and configuring your partitions, you are ready to move on. You can do this by pressing the Next button.

Formatting Your Linux Partitions

The next step is to format your Linux partitions in preparation for installing Linux. A list of partitions of type Linux Native appears with indications of the mount points they have. Any newly created partitions should be marked for formatting by selecting the check box next to the drive.

If you have additional partitions of type Linux Native, they should be formatted if they are new partitions. If they already existed (this is unlikely for new Red Hat users) and you want to retain the data they hold, don't mark them for formatting.

You can also indicate that a bad-block check should be performed during formatting. This is a good idea, especially for new hard drives.

Setting Up LILO

LILO is the Linux boot loader. In order for your system to boot properly, you need to configure and install LILO. LILO also provides the dual-boot features that can enable you to choose which operating system to launch at boot time, providing you with access to your existing Windows or DOS system as well as Linux.

There are four parts to this process, as shown in Figure 2.5. First, you need to decide where to install LILO: on your hard drive or on a boot disk.

Next, if you choose to install LILO on your hard drive (as you should), there are two viable locations: on the Master Boot Record (MBR) or on the first sector of the boot partition. You should install LILO on your MBR unless you are running an operating system with a boot loader such as OS/2 or Windows NT/2000 or have set up another boot loader such as Partition Magic or System Commander. If you already have one of these other boot loaders, you don't need LILO in the way; you should therefore install LILO on the Linux boot partition.

WARNING

You need to either install LILO or create a boot disk during this step in order to boot your Linux system. It is highly recommended that you install LILO during this initial installation.

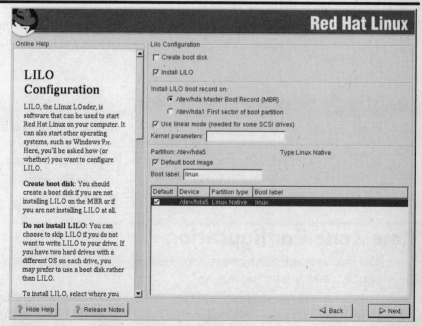

FIGURE 2.5:   Configuring the Linux boot loader

Most hard drives can be accessed in linear mode. Unless your hard drive does not use logical block addressing (LBA) mode (check your BIOS), keep the Use Linear Mode option selected.

In the next part of the screen, you can see all partitions with operating systems. When you set Default Boot Image, you set the operating system (usually Linux or Microsoft Windows) that starts by default when you boot your computer. The Boot Label setting is the name you use (linux in Figure 2.5) to select which operating system will boot when you start your computer.

Network Configuration

The next item to be configured is your network. Because you are installing a stand-alone system in this chapter, choose not to configure your network.

Firewall Configuration

Your firewall is the next item to be configured. But again, because you are installing a stand-alone system in this chapter, choose not to configure your firewall.

Language Support Selection

Here, you can set up the language that you see on your Red Hat Linux system after installation is complete. Red Hat Linux 7.1 gives you a choice of 104 different languages and dialects. If disk space is scarce, choose only the language(s) that you will use; if you choose all 104 options, that will require an additional 135MB of disk space.

Time Zone Configuration

The next step is to configure your computer's clock and time zone. You need to make two decisions.

First, you need to indicate whether you want your system's clock set to your local time or to Greenwich mean time (GMT), also known as Coordinated Universal Time, which is known by its French acronym, UTC. If you run only Linux on your computer, set the clock to UTC. Linux then converts it to the current time for your time zone. If you also run other operating systems on your PC, don't select this option.

Second, you need to choose from the list of available time zones.

Account Configuration

As a multiuser operating system, Linux needs at least one user to exist in order for it to be used. On all systems, you have to have a root user, so you are prompted to provide a root password (twice, for confirmation). The root user is the all-powerful system administrator. When logged in as the root user, you can view all users' files, perform all system administration tasks and, if you want to, delete all files on your system. This is a powerful account, so you need to keep this password secure if other people are going to have access to your system.

You can then set up individual accounts, based on a desired account name and password. Enter a descriptive name in the Full Name text box.

Authentication Configuration

Next, you are prompted to make authentication configuration selections. There are five options on this screen, and each can be selected individually. They are not mutually exclusive. The options are shown here:

Enable MD5 Passwords Typically, Unix systems have used a relatively weak encryption scheme for storing passwords. This option makes Linux use a more rigorous encryption scheme for storage of user passwords. By default, this option is selected.

Use Shadow Passwords Using shadow passwords is a technique designed to make it harder for an attacker or a regular system user to steal the user database and then attempt to crack the system administration password at leisure. By default, this option is selected.

Enable NIS This is a type of network authentication common in many Unix networks, especially those with Sun Solaris–based servers. You can specify the domain name of the group of computers on this network or specify a server where NIS usernames and passwords are stored. By default, this option is not selected.

Enable LDAP The Lightweight Directory Access Protocol is set up for special directories of users. If you know the name of an LDAP server on your network, you can enable LDAP. By default, this option is not selected.

Part i

Enable Kerberos   Kerberos is a secure means of encrypting passwords that are transmitted across a network. Kerberos requires access to a server that grants Kerberos tickets, which includes the encryption scheme. Do not enable Kerberos unless you plan to set up all Linux services to use this protocol. By default, this option is not selected.

Unless you are familiar with these options and have compelling reasons to alter them, leave the default selections the way they are and move on.

Selecting Packages

Now that your hard disks are configured and your Linux partitions are formatted, you are ready to begin installing the actual software. The default installation includes all the necessary core software, but several optional components are also available, including those shown in Figure 2.6.

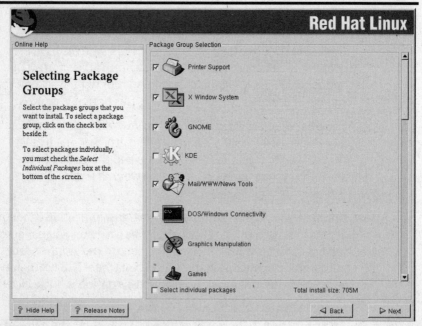

FIGURE 2.6:   Selecting additional components

Each component is a collection of related packages for specific tasks such as dial-up connections, web surfing, and others. You can choose the packages individually by marking their respective check boxes, or you can choose the Everything option, which is the last entry in the list.

The Select Individual Packages option that appears below the list field indicates that you want to select individual packages within each component. However, if you are a first-time Linux user, it will be hard to choose the packages. Leaving this option unselected means that each component is installed in its entirety.

If you have plenty of disk space (more than 3GB; 4GB is preferable), then select everything so that you have a complete Linux installation. Note the Total Install Size shown at the bottom of Figure 2.6. If your space is limited, consider installing the following components at a minimum:

- ▶ Printer Support (If you don't have a printer, then this is unnecessary.)
- ▶ X Window System
- ▶ GNOME
- ▶ Mail/WWW/News Tools
- ▶ DOS/Windows Connectivity
- ▶ Multimedia Support

If you choose to install X Windows, you next get to configure your video card and monitor. Otherwise, you are taken directly to installation, as described at the end of the next section.

Configuring X Windows

X Windows is Linux's graphical user interface (GUI). Chapter 5, "An Overview of X Windows," discusses configuring X Windows in detail. For now, let's quickly run through the configuration process. Configuration can be quite complex, and a whole chapter is devoted to it, so any problems will be left to that chapter for resolution.

First, a list of monitor types appears. If you find an exact match for your monitor, choose it; otherwise, select Unprobed Monitor. An incorrect configuration can cause damage to the monitor. The match should be exact.

Next, an attempt is made to determine what type of video card you have. If this fails, a list of available video cards appears; select the one that most closely matches your card. If none match, select Generic Standard VGA. Select the amount of video memory available on your video card. Consult your video card's documentation for this information. Once you've made your selections, you can click Test This Configuration to make sure that the chosen settings work for your system.

If you see and choose a Customize X Configuration option, you can customize the resolution of X Windows on your monitor (a.k.a. Video Modes). With the Use Graphical Login option, you can set up a graphical login screen. If you want to configure graphics after installing Linux, select the Skip X Configuration option.

NOTE

In some distributions, including older versions of Red Hat, a list of clock chips appears. If your card doesn't have a clock chip or you don't know if it does, choose No Clockchip. Do not guess on this question.

Now you've completed the basic configuration requirements. When you click Next, you're warned that the actual installation is about to begin. Most distributions create a log of your installation process. Red Hat Linux 7.1 saves this as the file /tmp/install.log. Several other distributions create their installation logs in the same file. Click Next, and installation begins.

THE INSTALLATION PROCESS

The installation proceeds automatically, and no input is required during this process. On the screen, you'll see a timer that indicates how long you need to wait before the installation is finished. During the installation of the software, the screen also displays the current status of the installation, indicating which package is currently being installed, how many packages and how many megabytes remain, and the overall progress of the installation.

Creating a Boot Disk

Once the Linux software has been successfully installed, the installation proceeds to the final step: creating a boot disk. Creating a boot disk is wise because it enables you to boot your system in case of an emergency. You can then attempt to resurrect a sick system. Insert a blank (formatted) floppy disk as directed in Figure 2.7, then click Next.

The Red Hat Linux 7.1 installation program copies the boot files to your floppy disk. After this process is complete, the installation program is finished.

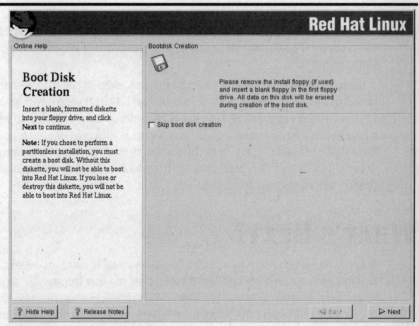

FIGURE 2.7:   Creating a boot disk

Rebooting Your System

Finally, you are prompted to remove any floppy disks from the computer and reboot. Some Linux distributions eject the CD-ROM automatically. If this doesn't happen, remove the CD-ROM before you reboot. If you left Linux as the default operating system, the system boots into Linux, giving you five seconds at the graphical prompt during startup to select an alternate operating system.

In Red Hat Linux 7.1, if you have more than one operating system on your computer, use the up and down arrow keys to choose an operating system. If you choose Linux and all goes well, a Red Hat Linux login prompt appears. You can log in here as the root user with the username root and the password you provided earlier. A command prompt appears, similar to the following:

```
[armand@localhost armand]$
```

You will learn about commands later, but the premise is simple: Type the command and press the Enter key to execute it. Type **exit** and press Enter to log out.

Linux allows you to log in more than once, even in the initial character-based mode. Using the combinations of Alt+F1 through Alt+F6, you can switch between as many as six virtual consoles. You need to log in separately in each virtual console. You can log in as different users and perform different tasks or log in to different virtual consoles as the same user—this is one of the features of Unix and Linux that make them such flexible environments to work in.

WHAT'S NEXT?

By now you should have a working Linux system. If you are one of the few readers who have special circumstances that made it impossible to get your Linux system running by following the steps in this chapter, then take a look at Chapter 3, "Special Installations," which discusses some special-case installations:

> ▶ Installing from a hard drive partition. (This is important if, for some reason, you cannot get Linux to install from your CD-ROM drive.)

> ▶ Installing to multiple partitions or hard disks. (This is useful if you have lots of disk space spread over multiple disks or need the performance gain from splitting Linux in this way.)

▶ Using fdisk instead of Disk Druid to configure your partitions. (Disk Druid is useful but not standard for Linux; using fdisk allows you to learn the workings of this standard tool and provides access to the more powerful tools desired by the expert user.)

If any of these special installations are useful, turn to Chapter 3. If your system booted correctly, though, you are ready to move on and learn about X Windows. Skip to Chapter 4, "Working with Linux Commands and Files," and continue from there.

Part i

Chapter 3

SPECIAL INSTALLATIONS

In Chapter 2, "Installing Red Hat Linux 7.1," you learned how to take the straightforward approach to installing Linux: from a local CD-ROM to a single hard disk partition.

This chapter looks at a few installation variations that are not uncommon. First among these is installing from a hard disk partition. There are cases in which installing from the local CD-ROM drive is not practical. For instance, you may have one of the few CD-ROM drives that the Red Hat installation software can't recognize, or you may have only temporary access to a CD-ROM drive. In these cases, one option is to copy the contents of the Red Hat CD-ROM to blank space on a hard drive and then install from the hard drive.

In addition, with the lower cost of hard drives today, you may have available multiple partitions or hard drives that you can use for your Linux installation. In those cases, you can maximize the performance of your system by spreading your Linux system across multiple partitions and drives.

Adapted from *Mastering Red Hat Linux 7.1*
by Arman Danesh

ISBN 0-7821-2927-7   1008 pages $49.99

Finally, this chapter looks at how to use the fdisk program instead of Disk Druid for configuring your hard disk partitions. fdisk is standard with all distributions of Linux; Disk Druid is available only with Red Hat Linux.

INSTALLING FROM A HARD DISK PARTITION

For some users, there are compelling reasons to install Linux from a different hard disk partition than the one they plan to run Linux from. Possible reasons include the following:

- ▶ A CD-ROM drive that the Linux installation program fails to recognize

- ▶ Lack of a permanent CD-ROM drive, but access to a CD-ROM drive to copy the CD-ROM to a hard disk

- ▶ A notebook computer with a switchable floppy drive and a CD-ROM drive that cannot be booted from the CD-ROM drive

In all these cases, the process of installing from a hard disk partition is basically the same:

1. Create an ISO disk image from the Red Hat CD-ROM on a dedicated hard disk partition. If you copy both Red Hat CD-ROMs, be sure to copy them to the same directory.

2. Make sure you have the correct installation floppy disks ready.

3. Start the installation process by booting from an installation floppy disk created from the boot.img file.

NOTE

If you want to install extra packages such as Linuxconf, you'll need both Red Hat installation CDs. You can purchase the full Red Hat Linux 7.1 package from many major computer stores or online from www.redhat.com, or you can download the CDs online. You can also purchase downloaded CD-ROMs from vendors such as Cheap Bytes (www.cheapbytes.com) or Linux Mall (www.linuxmall.com).

Copying the CD-ROM to a Hard Disk Partition

In order to install from a hard disk partition, you need a dedicated partition available to store the contents of the Linux installation CD-ROM. This partition should contain at least 650MB of free space in order to accommodate the complete contents of the standard Red Hat Linux 7.1 installation CD-ROM. If you're installing more than the standard packages, this partition needs twice that amount of space.

To create ISO image files from the Red Hat Linux CD-ROM, you need to create a package from the contents of the CD-ROM in a file such as cd1.iso. One way to do this is with the following commands in root user mode, which first mount the CD-ROM and then create the ISO image:

```
# mount -t iso9660 /dev/cdrom /mnt/cdrom
# mkisofs -J -r -T -o /tmp/cd1.iso /mnt/cdrom
```

NOTE

Place the CD ISO image file in a subdirectory such as /tmp or /home/mj. This makes it easier for the installation program to identify the location of the image. If you're making ISO images for both installation CD-ROMs, place them in the same directory.

If your CD-ROM device is different, substitute accordingly for /dev/cdrom. In the mkisofs command, the -o switch comes before the filename of the ISO image that you want to create. The -T switch adds a TRANS.TBL file in each directory to preserve long filename information for operating systems that can't handle them, such as MS-DOS. The -r switch uses "Rock Ridge" extensions to allow long filenames, and the -J switch uses "Joliet" records to make this ISO usable on Microsoft Windows computers.

If you have the second Red Hat Linux 7.1 installation CD-ROM, you'll want to create a second ISO image in the same directory.

Because of its size, it can take several minutes to create an ISO. To check the result on a cd1.iso file, you can mount it in a similar fashion to mounting a regular CD-ROM:

```
# mount -t iso9660 -r -o loop /tmp/RedHat/cd1.iso /mnt/cdrom
```

The result should be just like mounting a regular CD-ROM. You can then compare the files on the ISO against the Red Hat Linux 7.1 installation CD-ROM.

Part i

Preparing the Installation Floppies

Chapter 1, "Getting Ready to Install Red Hat Linux 7.1," discusses how to create the necessary installation floppy disks. Refer to the section "From Floppy Disk and CD-ROM" in that chapter for all the details.

In order to install from a hard disk partition in some distributions, you may need both the primary boot installation floppy disk and a driver or supplementary floppy disk, so it is best to have the appropriate disks prepared before starting the installation process.

The Actual Installation Process

To begin the installation, boot from the boot floppy. Follow the steps used for a normal installation from CD-ROM (set out in Chapter 2). The boot disk takes you to a text mode screen, which is really a graphical screen that is less demanding than the standard installation screens shown in Chapter 2. After selecting an installation language and keyboard, you are taken to an installation method screen. In this screen, select Hard Drive instead of Local CD-ROM.

After selecting Hard Drive, you are prompted to indicate the partition and directory with your Linux hard disk images, as shown in Figure 3.1. Based on the example shown earlier, you would type **/tmp** in the Directory Holding Images text box.

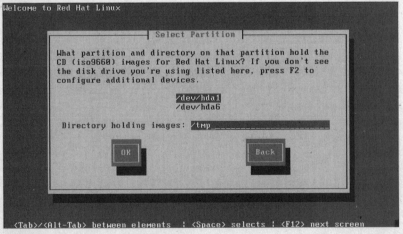

FIGURE 3.1: Selecting a partition and directory

WARNING

As of this writing, these instructions are slightly different from those shown in the documentation for Red Hat Linux 7.1. What you're reading here was tested against a downloaded version of this operating system.

NOTE

Refer back to Chapter 2 for a discussion of Linux device names for disk partitions. If you aren't sure which partition contains the Linux installation image, try each partition in turn. If you make the wrong choice, the prompts bring you back to the screen in Figure 3.1, where you can try again.

The rest of your installation should proceed in much the same way as outlined in Chapter 2.

INSTALLING LINUX ON MULTIPLE PARTITIONS

The title of this section is something of a misnomer. After all, for the typical Red Hat Linux 7.1 installation, you are using at least three partitions: one for your boot files, one for storing the rest of your operating system, and one for your swap space. There can be compelling reasons to use more than one partition for storing Linux.

One obvious reason for this would be if you have a disk that has two available partitions that are not physically contiguous. It is difficult to create one contiguous volume from two different physical partitions. In that case, it is often better to divide your Linux installation across the two partitions. For example, installing Linux on multiple partitions can increase speed and data flexibility. There are several ways to take advantage of having more than one disk for your Linux installation.

Putting Swap on a Separate Physical Drive

If you have a large partition on one drive and a smaller partition (of anywhere from 32MB to 200MB) on a second physical drive, you may want to consider putting your swap partition on that second drive. This can noticeably improve performance if you find yourself swapping frequently.

Consider this scenario: Your Linux installation and your swap partition are on the same physical drive. You are running many applications, and your system has already been swapping a lot. You attempt to launch a new application, but in order for it to be launched, it needs to be loaded from disk into memory—and at the same time, existing data in memory needs to be swapped out to disk. Since the drive can perform only one operation at a time, your one physical drive suddenly becomes a bottleneck as the operating system tries to perform both actions at nearly the same time.

But if your swap partition is on a separate physical drive, there is less of a bottleneck: One disk can be reading data from the disk into memory while the other is finishing the process of moving data from memory onto the disk. Even though the computer can't perform two instructions at the same time, the fact that the slow disk operations are spread over two disks helps minimize the time the CPU is left waiting for the disks to finish their work.

NOTE

When you have two physically separate disk drives, they can both send data to the rest of your computer simultaneously. You can reduce data bottlenecks further by physically connecting each drive to its own disk controller.

Splitting Linux across Multiple Partitions

Another way to use two or more partitions for your Linux software is to split the storage of your Linux software across the partitions in a logical manner. This can provide two benefits:

▶ Expanding the disk space available in critical Linux directory trees such as the /home directory tree

▶ Improving performance by splitting disk accesses across multiple hard disks if the available partitions are on more than one disk

Let's consider how you might want to split your Linux distribution across two partitions. As mentioned in Chapter 2, in the discussion of how to specify the mount point for an existing DOS partition, you use your additional disks by specifying their mount points.

For example, if you want to store all users' home directories on a separate partition, then you would make the mount point for that partition /home while leaving the mount point for your main Linux partition as /. Then, when you write to or read from any subdirectory under /home, you are actually accessing a different partition than when you access other directory trees outside /home.

There are several other popular ways to split your Linux installation across two partitions:

▶ If you plan to install a lot of your own software (including commercial software such as word processors, web browsers, and Windows emulation software), you will find that much of it is installed in the /opt directory tree. If your main Linux partition has plenty of room for the operating system plus user data, then consider mounting your additional partition as /opt. This will give you a separate area for all of your applications, and when you launch applications, the main system disk will still be free for accessing data or running the system utilities and background tasks that Linux is always performing.

▶ If you expect to have many users or plan to store a large amount of data in users' home directories, then consider mounting your additional partition as /home. That way, you can separately monitor user disk use, and you will get a performance gain when many users are accessing their data while other users are trying to launch applications, because these two actions will require access to separate disk partitions.

▶ If you find that neither partition on its own can contain your complete Linux installation, you may want to choose a fairly large directory tree such as /usr/X11R6 (the X Windows directory tree) and install that to a separate partition so that you can install your complete Linux system.

▶ Although many new packages are installed in /opt, if you install much software, you will find that /usr might also fill up quickly, making it a good candidate for a separate partition.

▶ If you are using Linux as a busy mail server or a heavily used, multiuser server, consider giving /var its own partition, since mail spool queues and system logs sit in this directory and can grow quickly in these types of servers.

Using *fdisk* instead of Disk Druid

In Chapter 2, you used Disk Druid to configure your disk partitions when installing Red Hat Linux 7.1. Disk Druid, however, is a program that is available only in the Red Hat installation process. Normally, Linux users use fdisk to configure their disk partitions, both during the installation process and later when they need to adjust their disk geographies.

In fact, fdisk is so familiar to Linux power users that Red Hat acknowledges its predominance as a tool for configuring disk partitions by offering it as an alternative to Disk Druid.

Although fdisk is an extremely complex and powerful tool (and a potentially dangerous and destructive one if misused), the job of performing basic tasks such as displaying a partition table, creating a new partition from free space, and assigning types to partitions is fairly simple.

When you select fdisk instead of Disk Druid during the installation process, first a screen appears and asks you which disk you want to work with. Unlike Disk Druid, fdisk works with only one physical disk at a time. After you select a disk to work with, you temporarily leave the now-familiar Red Hat installation program and are presented with the initial fdisk screen shown in Figure 3.2.

Using /dev/hda as default device!

Command (m for help):

FIGURE 3.2: The fdisk welcome screen

NOTE

The fdisk figures in this chapter are based on starting the installation with the boot.img installation floppy, as discussed in this chapter. If you enter fdisk from the regular graphical Red Hat Linux installation screen, you'll see the same content, except within the graphics of the standard Red Hat installation program.

fdisk operates using simple commands, each a single character long. To issue a command, simply type the command and press the Enter key. If the command needs additional information to perform its task, it prompts you for the missing information.

The simplest command is m or ?. Either of these characters causes fdisk to display the help screen shown in Figure 3.3. This screen lists all the common fdisk commands, including all the commands described in this section.

```
Using /dev/hda as default device!

Command (m for help): m
Command action
   a   toggle a bootable flag
   b   edit bsd disklabel
   c   toggle the dos compatibility flag
   d   delete a partition
   l   list known partition types
   m   print this menu
   n   add a new partition
   p   print the partition table
   q   quit without saving changes
   t   change a partition's system id
   u   change display/entry units
   v   verify the partition table
   w   write table to disk and exit
   x   extra functionality (experts only)

Command (m for help):
```

FIGURE 3.3: The fdisk help screen

NOTE

You can start the Linux fdisk utility after installation with the /sbin/fdisk command. Some users find the alternative /usr/sbin/cfdisk utility easier to use.

Displaying the Partition Table

One of the most useful fdisk commands, p, displays the current partition table for the active disk being worked with. This looks like the table in Figure 3.4.

```
Command (m for help): p

Disk /dev/hda: 255 heads, 63 sectors, 525 cylinders
Units = cylinders of 16065 * 512 bytes

   Device Boot    Begin    Start     End    Blocks   Id  System
/dev/hda1    *        1        1     223   1791216    6  DOS 16-bit >=32M
/dev/hda2           224      224     287    514080    5  Extended
/dev/hda3           288      288     515   1831410   83  Linux native
/dev/hda4           516      516     525     80325   82  Linux swap
/dev/hda5           224      224     287    514048+   6  DOS 16-bit >=32M

Command (m for help):
```

FIGURE 3.4:   The partition table

For each partition on the current disk, the device name, start and end blocks, partition size in blocks, and system type are displayed.

Adding a Partition Using Free Space

To add a new partition using existing free space on your hard disk, use the n command. As shown in Figure 3.5, you are prompted for a partition type. Generally, you should choose Primary as the type.

```
Command (m for help): n
Command action
   e   extended
   p   primary partition (1-4)
p
Partition number (1-4): 2
First cylinder (224-525):
```

FIGURE 3.5:   Adding a new partition

NOTE

With Linux fdisk, you can create four primary partitions as compared to DOS's single primary partition.

Once the partition type is selected, you assign the partition number and finally the start and end disk cylinders. To use all remaining space (assuming all available space is at the end of the drive), take the default first and last cylinders for your partition.

Changing the Partition Type

By default, all new partitions created with fdisk are assigned the type Linux Native (type number 83). To change the type of a partition, use the t command.

You are prompted for a partition to work with, which you can select numerically, as shown in Figure 3.6, and then you are prompted for the type ID. To view a list of type IDs, use the L command at this point to see the list shown in Figure 3.6.

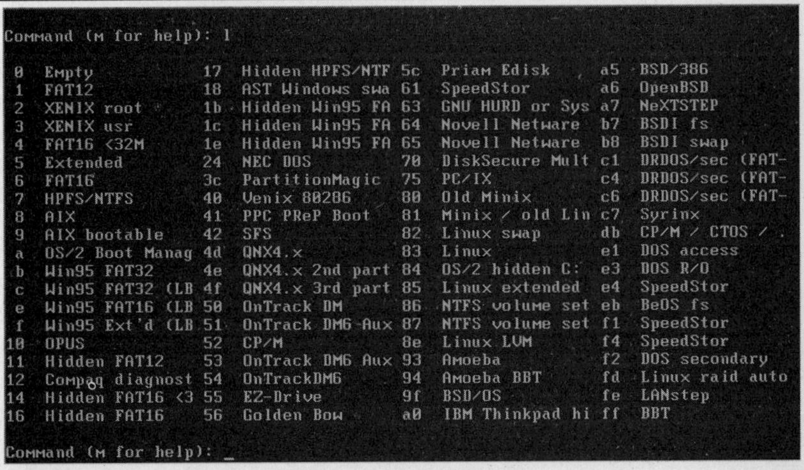

```
Command (m for help): l

0   Empty             17  Hidden HPFS/NTF 5c  Priam Edisk      a5  BSD/386
1   FAT12             18  AST Windows swa 61  SpeedStor        a6  OpenBSD
2   XENIX root        1b  Hidden Win95 FA 63  GNU HURD or Sys  a7  NeXTSTEP
3   XENIX usr         1c  Hidden Win95 FA 64  Novell Netware   b7  BSDI fs
4   FAT16 <32M        1e  Hidden Win95 FA 65  Novell Netware   b8  BSDI swap
5   Extended          24  NEC DOS         70  DiskSecure Mult  c1  DRDOS/sec (FAT-
6   FAT16             3c  PartitionMagic  75  PC/IX            c4  DRDOS/sec (FAT-
7   HPFS/NTFS         40  Venix 80286     80  Old Minix        c6  DRDOS/sec (FAT-
8   AIX               41  PPC PReP Boot   81  Minix / old Lin  c7  Syrinx
9   AIX bootable      42  SFS             82  Linux swap       db  CP/M / CTOS / .
a   OS/2 Boot Manag   4d  QNX4.x          83  Linux            e1  DOS access
b   Win95 FAT32       4e  QNX4.x 2nd part 84  OS/2 hidden C:   e3  DOS R/O
c   Win95 FAT32 (LB   4f  QNX4.x 3rd part 85  Linux extended   e4  SpeedStor
e   Win95 FAT16 (LB   50  OnTrack DM      86  NTFS volume set  eb  BeOS fs
f   Win95 Ext'd (LB   51  OnTrack DM6-Aux 87  NTFS volume set  f1  SpeedStor
10  OPUS              52  CP/M            8e  Linux LVM        f4  SpeedStor
11  Hidden FAT12      53  OnTrack DM6 Aux 93  Amoeba           f2  DOS secondary
12  Compaq diagnost   54  OnTrackDM6      94  Amoeba BBT       fd  Linux raid auto
14  Hidden FAT16 <3   55  EZ-Drive        9f  BSD/OS           fe  LANstep
16  Hidden FAT16      56  Golden Bow      a0  IBM Thinkpad hi  ff  BBT

Command (m for help): _
```

FIGURE 3.6: Changing the partition type ID in fdisk

The most commonly used partition types are shown in Table 3.1.

TABLE 3.1: Commonly Used Partition Types

ID	TYPE
5	Extended
6	DOS 16-bit (larger than 32MB)
7	OS/2 HPFS
b	Windows 95 FAT32
c	Windows 95 FAT32 with Logical Block Addressing (LBA)
82	Linux Swap
83	Linux Native

Deleting a Partition

Sometimes you want to delete an existing partition to create one or more new partitions for your Linux installation. To do this, simply use the d command and, when prompted, enter the number of the partition you want to delete.

Committing Your Changes

While you are working with fdisk, none of the changes you make are actually made to the physical disk. This is a safety precaution so that if you accidentally delete a partition with important data, you will be able to revert to your previous configuration before permanently deleting the partition containing the data.

For that reason, the changes you make are not actually processed until you explicitly ask fdisk to do so at the time of quitting. Therefore, before you quit from fdisk, take care to view the partition table to be sure you have done exactly what you want. If you exit and commit the changes, they are permanent, and going back is not really an option. (In theory, you can save the partition table of your disk to a floppy disk before working with fdisk and then recover from a serious mistake by replacing the new partition table with the saved one; however, this is a complicated procedure and not foolproof. You are better off taking care and making sure that the changes you make to your partition table are exactly the way you want them before committing the changes.)

The two alternative commands for quitting from fdisk are shown in Table 3.2.

TABLE 3.2:   Alternative Commands for Quitting from *fdisk*

COMMAND	EFFECT
q	Quits from fdisk without processing or saving any of your changes.
w	Processes and saves all your changes and then exits from fdisk. This is a permanent action, so take care.

WHAT'S NEXT?

Finally, you are ready to get into the business of actually using Linux. As your first step on that path, you will learn how to work with Linux commands and files in Chapter 4, "Working with Linux Commands and Files."

Chapter 5, "An Overview of X Windows," shows you what X Windows offers and how it compares with the Microsoft Windows environment. Then it will move on to the configuration and use of X Windows and take a look at some common X Windows applications.

PART II
LEARNING THE BASICS

Chapter 4

WORKING WITH LINUX COMMANDS AND FILES

This chapter explores the Unix command-line environment. The command-line environment is where the heart and power of Linux lies. You have seen that X Windows provides quick and easy access to graphical applications that can make most users productive immediately. What is missing, though, is the ability to fully manipulate and work with your Linux system. This ability emerges when you begin to experiment with commands.

Here you'll learn to use some of the more common commands such as `ls`, `find`, and `grep`. Since these commands are found in most distributions, Unix users should immediately know what these and similar commands can do and what power they can provide in the hands of a knowledgeable user.

Adapted from *Mastering Red Hat Linux 7.1*
by Arman Danesh

ISBN 0-7821-2927-7   1008 pages $49.99

In this chapter, you are also going to take a detailed look at the commands used to further manipulate files and directories, including copying, deleting, moving, renaming, and creating. This chapter wraps up with a quick look at filename expansion—that is, wildcards like the commonly used asterisks in DOS and Windows.

NOTE

For this chapter, you need to be using a Linux command line. You can get a command line in two ways: When your system boots, log in to one of the Linux virtual consoles, or, from X Windows, launch a terminal window such as xterm, the GNOME terminal, or KDE's Konsole.

What Is a Linux Command?

Before looking at specific commands, you need to understand exactly what is meant by the term *command*.

Users coming from the DOS environment are probably familiar with the concept of commands that encompass core features of the operating system, such as DIR, COPY, and ATTRIB. These commands provided the basis on which more complicated actions could be built and from which sophisticated batch files could be written.

But in the DOS world, as in the world of many operating systems, the number of available commands is limited and generally static: Users don't add new commands.

In the Unix world, and by extension in Linux, the concept is different. A *command* is any executable file. That is, a command consists of any file that is designed to be run, as opposed to files containing data or configuration information. This means that any executable file added to a system becomes a new command on the system.

Executing a Linux Command

From the discussions of launching X Windows applications, you probably already have a sense of how to execute a command. From the command prompt, simply type the name of a command:

```
$ command
```

Or, if the command is not on your path, you type the complete path and name of the command, such as

$ **/usr/bin/**command

USING PATHS IN LINUX

The concept of *paths* needs a little bit of explanation. Every user, when they log in, has a default path. Find your default path with the following command:

$ **echo $PATH**

The output should look something like this:

$ /usr/local/bin:/bin:/usr/bin:/usr/X11R6/bin:/
home/mj/bin

The $PATH is a list of directories separated by colons. If a command is typed without a path, then all the directories in the default path are checked, in order, for the file associated with the command. In the above example, if there is a command named guess in both the /usr/local/bin and the /home/mj/bin directories, the one in the /usr/local/bin is executed. If you'd rather use the guess command in the /home/mj/bin directory, then you'll need to use the full path, i.e., type the /home/mj/bin/guess command.

COMMON LINUX COMMANDS

The number of Linux commands that are available in a common Linux distribution such as Red Hat Linux 7.1 is quite large. But on a day-to-day basis, even an advanced user will take advantage of only a small selection of these commands.

This section presents some of the most frequently used Linux commands. These commands cover a range of tasks, from moving around your directories to finding out what is running on your system to finding that file you thought was lost. The commands discussed in this section are:

▶ su

▶ pwd, cd, and ls

▶ more and less

- find, locate, whereis, and grep
- tar and gzip
- man

su

The su command is one of the most basic and is useful in many different tasks. The su command is generally used to switch between different users. Consider an example: You are logged in as user1 and you need to switch to user2 to perform some work and then switch back to working as user1.

You could log out, log in as user2, do the work, log out again, and then log back in as user1, but that seems a bit time-consuming. Alternatively, you could log in as user1 in one virtual console and as user2 in another and switch back and forth. The problem with this is that you need to work with—and switch between—different screens.

A third option is to use the su command. If you are logged in as user1 and want to become user2, you simply type

```
$ su user2
```

and you are prompted for user2's password:

```
$ su user2
password:
```

When you finish working, enter the exit command to return to user1:

```
$ exit
```

Put together, a complete session should look like this:

```
[user1@localhost user1]$ su user2
Password:
[user2@localhost user1]$ some commands
[user2@localhost user1]$ exit
exit
[user1@localhost user1]$
```

A common use of the su command is when you need to become the root user, called the *superuser*, to perform many administrative tasks, including creating and managing user accounts, performing network configuration, and configuring printers.

If you issue the su command with no username, you are prompted for the root password and, once this is provided, you are switched to working as the root user:

```
[user1@localhost user1]$ su
Password:
[root@localhost user1]#
```

If you are logged in as the root user, you can use su to become any user on the system without a password (hence the importance of keeping your root password safe from prying eyes). This is particularly useful for the system administrator, who may need to become different users to debug problems but won't necessarily know other users' passwords. Note in the following example how using su to become user1 doesn't cause a password prompt to display when the root user issues the command:

```
[root@localhost/root]# su user1
[user1@localhost/root]$
```

The su command offers many other powerful features often used in advanced system administration tasks. You can learn about these from the su man page. See the section on the man command later in this chapter to learn how to read the su man page.

pwd, cd, and *ls*

When put together, the pwd, cd, and ls commands provide the basic tools you need to work with your directories and files.

The pwd command (which stands for present working directory) is the most basic of the three commands. By typing the command and pressing Enter, you will be informed of which directory you are currently in:

```
$ pwd
/home/armand
```

In this case, the pwd command returns /home/armand as its answer. This tells you that you are in the home directory of the user armand.

The cd command does more than simply look at the current state of things: It actually changes the state. The cd command allows you to change your current directory to any accessible directory on the system.

For instance, consider the previous example where the current directory is /home/armand. Using the cd command, you could change to a subdirectory of the armand home directory called wordfiles:

```
$ cd wordfiles
$ pwd
/home/armand/wordfiles
```

Typing the pwd command after you change directories confirms that you ended up where you wanted to be.

Similarly, you could change to the system's temporary directory, /tmp, with the following command:

```
$ cd /tmp
$ pwd
/tmp
```

The difference is in the forward slash (/) in front of the directory. The first command, cd wordfiles, did not have a forward slash, so the change is relative to the current directory. If you ran the same command from Mike's home directory, /home/mike, you would end up in the /home/mike/wordfiles directory.

The second command, cd /tmp, has a forward slash. You could run this second command from any directory and always end up in the same location.

Finally, the ls command can be used to view the contents of the current directory. For instance, if you use the ls command to view the contents of the armand home directory, the result looks like this:

```
$ ls
2341ch11a.doc              dead.letterscmp-jpc.bak
DISKCOPY.COM               foo        svgalib-1.2.11-4.i386.rpm
DRWEBDEM.IMG               foo.html     test.txt
Xconfigurator-3.26-1.i386.rpm  mail          wabi
Xrootenv                   nsmail     xserver-1.1-1.i386.rpm
armand                     scmp-jpc
```

Notice how the files or directory names are displayed in multiple columns and the width of the columns is determined by the width of the longest name.

In addition to listing the contents of the current directory, it is possible to list the contents of any accessible directory on the system.

For instance, to list the contents of the directory /usr, you enter the command ls /usr:

```
$ ls /usr
X11      doc               i486-linuxaout   lib        sbin
X11R6    dt                ibase            libexec    share
X386     etc               include          local      spool
bin      games             info             man        src
dict     i486-linux-libc5  interbase        openwin    tmp
```

As mentioned above, notice how the number and width of columns in the listing depends on the length of the longest name being displayed.

Of course, you probably are wondering what use a list like this really is. There is no information to tell you which names indicate files and which names indicate subdirectories or what size the files are.

This information can be determined by using an extension of the ls command: ls -l. (To understand the command's structure, refer to the complete discussion of the ls command later in this chapter.) Used in the armand home directory, ls -l produces these results:

```
$ ls -l
total 1807
-rw-r--r--    1 armand   armand     52224 Apr 24 23:00
    2341ch11a.doc
-rw-r--r--    1 armand   armand     24325 May  9 16:06
    DISKCOPY.COM
-rw-r--r--    1 armand   armand   1474979 May  9 16:06
    DRWEBDEM.IMG
-rw-r--r--    1 armand   armand     52313 Jan 21 18:04
    Xconfigurator -3.26-1.i386.rpm
-rw-r--r--    1 armand   armand       396 May 19 23:09 Xrootenv
drwx------    2 armand   armand      1024 May 17 09:55 armand
-rw-------    1 armand   armand     10572 May 18 22:29 dead.
    letter
-rw-------    1 armand   root        1455 Apr 24 21:38 foo
-rw-r--r--    1 armand   armand      2646 May  7 07:32 foo.html
drwx------    2 armand   armand      1024 Jun  4 07:12 mail
drwx------    2 armand   armand      1024 May 17 09:56 nsmail
-rw-r--r--    1 armand   armand      4288 May 14 22:17 scmp-jpc
```

Part ii

```
-rw-r--r--    1 armand   armand      4289 May 14 22:12
  scmp-jpc.bak
-rw-r--r--    1 armand   armand    195341 Mar 25 17:32
  svgalib-1.2.11 -4.i386.rpm
-rw-rw-r--    1 armand   armand        94 May 17 11:44 test.txt
drwxr-xr-x    5 armand   armand      1024 May 19 23:07 wabi
-rw-r--r--    1 armand   armand      4493 Feb  4 15:31
  xserver-wrapper-1.1-1.i386.rpm
```

Note that each file contains reference information. The most important pieces of information are to the immediate left of each filename: the date of last modification of the file or directory and, in the case of files, the size of the file in bytes to the left of the date (so, for instance, a 1024-byte file is a 1KB file).

At the far left of each line, you will also notice that directories are indicated by the letter d while files are generally indicated with a simple hyphen (-). For instance, scmp-jpc is a file:

```
-rw-r--r--    1 armand   armand      4288 May 14 22:17
  scmp-jpc
```

While mail is a directory:

```
drwx------    2 armand   armand      1024 Jun  4 07:12 mail
```

more and *less*

The more and less commands are closely related and provide similar functionality, and the great irony is that less provides more capabilities than more.

The basic purpose of both commands is to display long files or lists of text one screen or window at a time, allowing users to page down through the text and, in some cases, move back up through the text. Both also provide capabilities to search the text being displayed.

This is useful in many instances, including when you want to look quickly at a long text file without having to open it in an editor such as xedit and to view particularly long directory listings.

more

Let's start with the more command. The more command is fairly basic, allowing users to move forward a line or a screen at a time through a large body of text as well as search that text.

For instance, if you have a large text file called `textfile`, you could view it a page at a time with the following command:

```
$ more textfile
```

After pressing Enter, you see the first screen of the file with the text–More–(xy%) displayed on the last line of the screen, where xy represents the percentage of the file passed on the screen. Pressing the spacebar jumps you forward a full screen length, while pressing the Enter key moves you forward one line at a time. When you reach the end of the body of text, you are returned to the command prompt.

To search forward through the file, enter a slash (/) followed by the word or phrase you want to search for and then press Enter. The display jumps forward to the first occurrence of the word or phrase being searched for and displays the occurrence near the top of the screen. You can repeat the same search by entering **n** after the first search, avoiding the need to type the same word or phrase repeatedly.

In addition to using `more` to view the contents of a file, you can pass along the results of another command to `more` using piping.

For instance, on my system, using `ls -l` to view the contents of the /tmp directory produces results 237 lines long—many more lines than my largest `xterm` window can display. In order to be able to view the results of my `ls -l` command a window at a time, I need to pass the results to `more`:

```
$ ls -l /tmp | more
```

This command connects the `ls -l` command to the `more` command with a vertical pipe (which usually corresponds to the double-vertical dashes above the backslash on most U.S. keyboards). The use of the pipe character is the source of the term *piping*. The result of this piping is that `more` is used to display the results of the `ls -l` command, which means you can move down a screen or line at a time or search the results, just as you did earlier with the contents of a file.

NOTE   Complete directions for using `more` are found in the `more` man page. Using a man page is discussed later in this chapter in the section on the `man` command.

less

For all intents and purposes, the `less` command is a vastly improved version of the `more` command. In addition to the basic functions described previously (moving forward a screen or line at a time and searching), the following are some of the other actions that can be performed on a body of text:

- ▶ Jumping directly to a line
- ▶ Jumping directly to the beginning or end of the file
- ▶ Moving backward through a file
- ▶ Searching backward through a file

To jump directly to a line in a file, type the line number followed by the letter **g**. If you don't specify a line number and simply enter **g**, you will be jumped to the first line in the file. Entering the uppercase **G** works in much the same way except that without a line number specified, entering **G** jumps you to the last line of the body of text.

It is easy to move backward through a file using less. The up arrow moves up one line of text at a time and the down arrow moves down one line at a time. You can use Ctrl+B to jump backward one screen at a time.

Finally, entering a slash (/) followed by a word or phrase and then pressing Enter will search forward through the text being displayed, and entering a question mark (**?**) followed by a word or phrase and then pressing Enter will search backward through the text.

NOTE
As some of you may have noticed, these commands correspond to options in the vi text editor.

As with the more command, you can look at the less man page for details on all the features of the command. Using the man pages is discussed later in this chapter in the section on the man command.

find, locate, whereis, and grep

The find, locate, whereis, and grep commands are powerful tools for searching for files. This section discusses only their most basic uses because it would be easy to devote a full chapter to using these commands. If you want a full discussion of the commands, check their man pages once you learn to use the man command later in this chapter.

While all these commands are used for searching, their purposes differ: find is used to search for files by any number of criteria, including name or date of creation, while grep is used to search the contents of files.

find

If you used computers prior to buying this book, then you have probably faced the situation where you know you have created a file but can't remember where you put it. The find command is the Unix answer to this dilemma.

The command can be used to search for files by name, date of creation or modification, owner (usually the user who created the file), size of the file, and even type of the file. This section describes the most frequent use: searching for files by name.

The basic structure of the find command is

```
$ find starting-directory parameters actions
```

The starting directory specifies where to begin searching. For instance, specifying /home means only subdirectories of /home will be searched (in other words, only the user's home directories will be searched), while specifying / means everything will be searched.

The parameters are where you specify the criteria by which to search. In this case, you use the command switch and argument -name filename to specify the file you are searching for.

The actions section indicates what action to take on found files. Generally, you will want to use the -print action, which indicates that the full name and path of the file should be displayed. Without this, the find command will perform the search indicated but will not display the results, which defeats the purpose.

Putting this together, if you want to search for all files named foo on your system, you could use the command

```
$ find / -name foo -print
```

In this case, the results look like this:

```
$ find / -name foo -print
/tmp/foo
/home/armand/foo
/home/tdanesh/foo
```

Part ii

TIP

Notice that you attempted to search the entire system in the previous command. To do this effectively, you need to log in as the root user so that you can access all the directories on the system. If you don't, you will get `permission denied` errors every time `find` tries to search a directory for which you don't have permission.

It is also possible to search for partial filenames. For instance, if you know that the file you are looking for begins with `fo`, then you can use the expression `fo*` to indicate all files beginning with `fo` and ending with any combination:

```
$ find / -name 'fo*' -print
/tmp/foo
/var/lib/texmf/fonts
/usr/bin/font2c
/usr/bin/mh/folders
/usr/bin/mh/folder
/usr/bin/mh/forw
/usr/bin/formail
/usr/bin/fontexport
/usr/bin/fontimport
/usr/bin/fold
etc.
```

Notice the use of the single quotation marks around `fo*`. When you use the `*` character, it is important to place the single quotes around the entire expression. Otherwise, `find` will give you an error:

```
$ find / -name fo* -print -mount
find: paths must precede expression
Usage: find [path...] [expression]
```

If the results being produced by the `find` command are too numerous to fit in one screen, you can use piping and the `more` command just as you did earlier with the `ls -l` command:

```
$ find / -name 'fo*' -print | more
```

locate

If the find command takes too long, you may be able to use the alternative, the locate command. This command searches a database of files on your system, created nightly. It works slightly differently from the find command, since it returns every file and directory with your search string in its name. For example, the locate xauth command would give you these results:

```
$ locate xauth
/home/mj/.xauth
/home/mj/.xauth/refcount
/home/mj/.xauth/refcount/root
/home/mj/.xauth/refcount/root/testlinux
/lib/security/pam_xauth.so
/usr/X11R6/bin/mkxauth
/usr/X11R6/bin/xauth
/usr/X11R6/man/man1/mkxauth.1x.gz
/usr/X11R6/man/man1/xauth.1x.gz
/usr/share/doc/pam-0.72/txts/README.pam_xauth
/usr/share/man/man8/pam_xauth.8.gz
```

Observe how this command gives you the full path to all files and directories that include the text string "xauth," including the /home/mj/.xauth directory and the /usr/X11R6/bin/mkxauth and /usr/X11R6/bin/xauth commands.

This works a lot more quickly than the corresponding find command. The drawback is that locate works from a database file that is updated generally only once every 24 hours; therefore, the results may not reflect the current location or even the existence of a recently moved or created file.

whereis

If you're looking for a known command, you can use whereis to find the directory with the command, the source code, and the relevant man page. Unlike with find or locate, you need the exact spelling of the command. For example, the whereis fdisk command gives you the following results:

```
$ whereis fdisk
fdisk: /sbin/fdisk /usr/share/man/man8/fdisk.8.gz
```

Part ii

This output specifies the location of the fdisk command (/sbin/ fdisk), along with the location of its man page. Since the location of the fdisk source code is not shown, you can assume that it isn't installed.

The drawback to the whereis command is that since it looks through a specified set of directories, it may not find a new command or manual page that you just installed.

grep

Where find searches for a file by its name, type, or date, locate searches through a file database, and whereis identifies command locations, grep is used to look inside the contents of one or more files in an attempt to find the occurrence of a specific pattern of text inside the files.

Consider an example: You know that you created a text file that contains the word *radio* and stored it in your home directory. However, you have forgotten the name of the file and want to quickly check which files contain *radio*. This is where grep comes in handy.

Assuming you are in your home directory, the following command searches for the word *radio* in each file in your home directory and produces results as follows:

```
$ grep radio *
ab.txt:This is a test of searching for the word radio.
pop.txt:On another radio station, he found that
```

Notice how the grep command returns one line for each occurrence of the word *radio* in a file. The name of the file is shown followed by a colon, which is followed by the complete text of the line where the word appeared.

In general, the pattern for the grep command is

```
$ grep text-pattern file-list
```

The text pattern can be a simple word or phrase or a more complicated regular expression. (The use of regular expressions—a powerful method for searching for text patterns—with grep can be found in the grep man page.) The file list can take any form allowed by the shell.

Generally, though, you want to either check the contents of a single file, which takes the form

```
$ grep text-pattern file-name
```

or check the contents of all files in a directory using the command

```
$ grep text-pattern *
```

where the * is an expression indicating that all files in the current directory should be searched.

In its simplest form, the text pattern is a single word or part of a word containing no spaces. If you want to search for a phrase, such as "is a test," you need to enclose the text pattern in quotation marks, as in the following example:

```
$ grep "is a test" *
ab.txt:This is a test of searching for the word radio.
```

Just as it is sometimes useful to pipe the results of a command through the more or less commands, the same is true for grep. Consider the situation where you want a listing of all files in the current directory with the modification date of May 12. You can find this information by piping ls -l through a grep command:

```
$ ls -l | grep "May 12"

-rw-r--r--   1 root      root        19197 May 12 21:17 rfbprotoheader.pdf

-rw-r--r--   1 root      root       110778 May 12 21:20 rfprotoA.zip

-rw-r--r--   1 root      root        17692 May 12 23:03 svnc-0.1.tar.gz

-rw-r--r--   1 root      root        25222 May 12 19:58 vnc-3.3.1_javasrc.tgz

drwxr-xr-x   2 root      root         1024 May 12 21:49 vncjava
```

COMMANDS AND QUOTES

There are three different types of quotes that you can use with a command: a single quote ('), a double quote ("), and a back quote (`). The difference is in how they affect embedded commands such as date and variables such as $LOGNAME. Any pair of matched quotes sends the whole phrase to the command. For example, assume that $LOGNAME=mj and review the following commands:

```
echo Welcome $LOGNAME, the date is date
echo 'Welcome $LOGNAME, the date is date'
echo "Welcome $LOGNAME, the date is date"
echo "Welcome $LOGNAME, the date is `date`"
```

CONTINUED ➡

Linux may or may not run the date command or translate $LOG-NAME, depending on the quotes. These commands include different combinations of quotes and result in the following:

```
Welcome mj, the date is date
Welcome $LOGNAME, the date is date
Welcome mj, the date is date
Welcome mj, the date is Mon June 14 10:45:20 EDT 2001
```

The first example has no quotes. $LOGNAME is translated as mj, but the date command is not run. The second example uses single quotes. $LOGNAME is not translated, and the date command is not run. The third example uses double quotes. While the result is the same as the first command, double quotes are useful with commands such as grep. The final example includes back quotes around date inside double quotes. As you can see, the back quotes make Linux run the subject command.

tar and *gzip*

Most users of other operating systems, including Windows 98/2000 and the Mac OS, are familiar with the concept of *compressed archives*. A compressed archive is a single file that contains one or more files in a compressed form.

Compressed archives are often used to distribute software on the Internet, as is the case with the Zip files common on the Internet. While Linux provides the unzip command to access the contents of Zip archives, in the Unix world, tar archives are generally used to distribute software. These archives are then compressed using the gzip compression program, which compresses individual files.

tar

The tar program was originally used to create system backups on tapes (or tape archives, hence the name *tar*). In its current form, it is widely used for creating archives of files for distribution.

Creating a tar archive is easy:

```
$ tar cvf tar-file-name file-list
```

This command creates a new archive specified by the filename `tar-file-name` (generally, `tar` files have a `.tar` extension) and then stores all the files from the file list in this archive. It is important to remember that this process copies the files into the archive, so there is no danger that the original files will be deleted in the process.

Notice that the `tar` command is immediately followed by a series of options, in this case, `cvf`. Each of these options is used to control different aspects of the behavior of the `tar` command:

▶ specifies that you are creating an archive, as opposed to viewing an existing archive or extracting files from the archive.

▶ indicates that the command should be run in verbose mode, which means that each filename will be displayed as it is copied into the archive.

▶ means that you are archiving to a file, as opposed to a tape drive.

For instance, if you want to archive all the `.txt` files in the current directory into an archive called `text.tar`, use the following command:

```
$ tar cvf text.tar *.txt
ab.txt
pop.txt
```

Notice how the filenames are listed as they are copied to the archive.

Sometimes you want to copy the entire contents of a directory into an archive. Luckily, `tar` copies all files and subdirectories in a directory into an archive if the directory is part of the file list. So, if you have a directory called vnc and you want the entire contents of that directory to be copied to a new archive called `vnc.tar`, you could use the command:

```
$ tar cvf vnc.tar vnc
```

and get the following results:

```
$ tar cvf vnc.tar vnc
vnc/
vnc/LICENSE.TXT
vnc/README
vnc/README.vncserver
vnc/Xvnc
vnc/classes/
```

Part ii

```
vnc/classes/DesCipher.class
vnc/classes/animatedMemoryImageSource.class
vnc/classes/authenticationPanel.class
vnc/classes/clipboardFrame.class
vnc/classes/optionsFrame.class
vnc/classes/rfbProto.class
vnc/classes/vncCanvas.class
vnc/classes/vncviewer.class
vnc/classes/vncviewer.jar
vnc/vncpasswd
vnc/vncserver
vnc/vncviewer
```

Notice that the first line indicates the creation of the vnc directory in the archive and then the copying of the files in that directory into the archive.

If you have an existing archive, you will generally want to either view a listing of the contents of a file or extract the contents of a file.

To view the contents of an archive, you replace the c option with a t. So, to view the list of files in the vnc.tar archive you just created, you could use the following command:

```
$ tar tvf vnc.tar
drwxr-xr-x root/root             0 2001-05-16 23:55 vnc/
-rw-r--r-- root/root         18000 2001-01-23 16:52
  vnc/LICENCE.TXT
-rw-r--r-- root/root          6142 2001-01-23 16:53 vnc/README
-r--r--r-- root/root           601 2001-01-23 16:28
  vnc/README.vncserver
-r-xr-xr-x root/root       1286834 2001-01-23 13:00 vnc/Xvnc
drwxr-sr-x root/root             0 2001-01-23 16:24 vnc/classes/
-r--r--r-- root/root          7143 2001-01-23 16:24
  vnc/classes/DesCipher.class
-r--r--r-- root/root          1329 2001-01-23 16:24
  vnc/classes/animatedMemoryImageSource.class
-r--r--r-- root/root          2068 2001-01-23 16:24
  vnc/classes/authenticationPanel.class
-r--r--r-- root/root          1761 2001-01-23 16:24
  vnc/classes/clipboardFrame.class
```

```
-r--r--r-- root/root       3210 2001-01-23 16:24
  vnc/classes/optionsFrame.class
-r--r--r-- root/root       8309 2001-01-23 16:24
  vnc/classes/rfbProto.class
-r--r--r-- root/root       7092 2001-01-23 16:24
  vnc/classes/vncCanvas.class
-r--r--r-- root/root       7100 2001-01-23 16:24
  vnc/classes/vncviewer.class
-r--r--r-- root/root      20564 2001-01-23 16:24
  vnc/classes/vncviewer.jar
-r-xr-xr-x root/root      11433 2001-01-23 13:00 vnc/vncpasswd
-r-xr-xr-x root/root      10795 2001-05-17 00:17 vnc/vncserver
-r-xr-xr-x root/root      49685 2001-01-23 13:00 vnc/vncviewer
```

Notice how the listing of files is in a complete form, similar to the way in which `ls -l` lists the contents of a directory.

To extract the contents of an archive into the current directory, replace the c or t with an x:

```
$ tar xvf vnc.tar
vnc/
vnc/LICENSE.TXT
vnc/README
vnc/README.vncserver
vnc/Xvnc
vnc/classes/
vnc/classes/DesCipher.class
vnc/classes/animatedMemoryImageSource.class
vnc/classes/authenticationPanel.class
vnc/classes/clipboardFrame.class
vnc/classes/optionsFrame.class
vnc/classes/rfbProto.class
vnc/classes/vncCanvas.class
vnc/classes/vncviewer.class
vnc/classes/vncviewer.jar
vnc/vncpasswd
vnc/vncserver
vnc/vncviewer
```

Part ii

gzip

While `tar` is useful for archiving files, it doesn't perform any compression in the previous examples. Compression in Linux is generally achieved with the `gzip` command.

Unlike Windows Zip archives, which compress many files into a single compressed archive, `gzip` simply compresses individual files without compressing them into an archive.

For instance, if you have a particularly large file called `test.pdf` that you won't use for some time and you want to compress it to save disk space, use the `gzip` command:

```
$ gzip test.pdf
```

This command compresses the file and adds a `.gz` extension to the end of the filename, changing the name to `test.pdf.gz`.

Before compression, `ls -l` shows us that the file size is 110,778 bytes:

```
-rw-r--r--   1 root     root         110778 Jun  5 16:54
   test.pdf
```

After compression, the size has dropped to 83,729 bytes:

```
-rw-r--r--   1 root     root          83729 Jun  5 16:54
   test.pdf.gz
```

As with most commands described in this chapter, you can use any valid shell file expression to list more than one file. For instance,

```
$ gzip *
```

compresses all files in the current directory (but not those in subdirectories).

Uncompressing *gzip* Files   To uncompress a `gzip` file, you can use the `gzip` command with the `-d` option:

```
$ gzip -d test.pdf.gz
```

This uncompresses the file and removes the `.gz` extension, returning the file to its original uncompressed state with the name `test.pdf`.

An alternative command, `gunzip`, eliminates the need to use the `-d` option:

```
$ gunzip test.pdf.gz
```

Combining *gzip* and *tar*   Because early versions of the `tar` command did not compress archives, this was typically done using `gzip`, as shown in the following example:

```
$ tar cvf text.tar *.txt
```

```
ab.txt
pop.txt
$ gzip text.tar
```

This produces a compressed archive called text.tar.gz.

To access the contents of this archive, uncompress the archive and then use tar:

```
$ gunzip text.tar.gz
$ tar tvf text.tar
-rw-r--r-- root/root        48 2001-06-05 16:13 ab.txt
-rw-r--r-- root/root         6 2001-06-05 16:13 pop.txt
```

Recent versions of the tar command, including those shipped with all current distributions, provide a method for directly accessing and creating gzip-compressed tar archives.

By simply adding a z option to any of the tar commands discussed earlier, you can create a compressed archive without the need for a second command. For instance,

```
$ tar czvf vnc.tar.gz vnc
vnc/
vnc/LICENSE.TXT
vnc/README
vnc/README.vncserver
vnc/Xvnc
vnc/classes/
vnc/classes/DesCipher.class
vnc/classes/animatedMemoryImageSource.class
vnc/classes/authenticationPanel.class
vnc/classes/clipboardFrame.class
vnc/classes/optionsFrame.class
vnc/classes/rfbProto.class
vnc/classes/vncCanvas.class
vnc/classes/vncviewer.class
vnc/classes/vncviewer.jar
vnc/vncpasswd
vnc/vncserver
vnc/vncviewer
```

creates a compressed version of the `vnc.tar` archive,

```
$ tar tzvf text.tar.gz
-rw-r--r-- root/root          48 2001-06-05 16:13 ab.txt
-rw-r--r-- root/root           6 2001-06-05 16:13 pop.txt
```

displays the contents of the compressed `text.tar.gz` archive, and

```
$ tar xzvf text.tar.gz
ab.txt
pop.txt
```

extracts the contents of the archive.

NOTE

Full details of the `tar` and `gzip` commands and their options can be found in the man pages for those commands.

man and *xman*

Throughout this chapter, you have seen references to *man pages*. These are manual pages that are provided in a standard format with most Linux software. Almost all the commands that ship with various Linux distributions include man pages.

Using the man command in its most basic form, you can read any existing man page:

```
$ man command-name
```

This displays the man page for the specified command and allows you to scroll through it and search it the same way as when you are using the `less` command to display text.

If the specified man page cannot be found, you get the following error:

```
$ man non-existent-man-page
No manual entry for non-existent-man-page
```

Since you already are familiar with X Windows, you have an alternative to using the man command to view man pages: the xman program.

To launch xman, use

```
$ xman &
```

or

```
$ /usr/X11R6/bin/xman &
```

This will display the initial xman window like the one in Figure 4.1.

FIGURE 4.1:   The initial xman window

From here, you can press the Manual Page button to display the main xman window, shown in Figure 4.2.

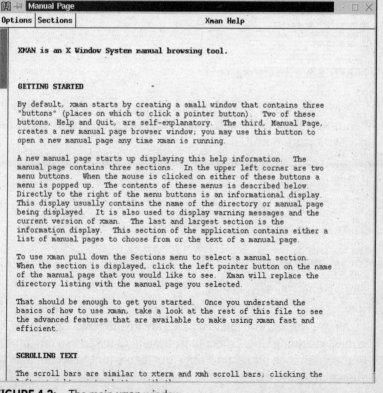

FIGURE 4.2:   The main xman window

Part ii

The main area of the window is used to display the text of the currently selected man page. Initially xman's help file is displayed. The window has two menus: Options and Sections.

The Options menu, shown in Figure 4.3, allows you to switch between listings of man pages (Display Directory) and the contents of the current man page (Display Manual Page), in addition to searching the contents of the current man page. The Help option displays the complete help file for xman, which provides detailed instructions on using xman. If you want to review a specific man page, select the Search option, then type the name of the command in the text box that appears.

FIGURE 4.3:   The Options menu

You are probably more interested in the Sections menu, shown in Figure 4.4, since this is where you begin the process of finding the man page you want to read.

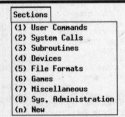

FIGURE 4.4:   The Sections menu

As you can see, the manual pages are divided into eight main categories, including User Commands, System Calls, and so on. Choosing one of these sections brings up a directory listing for the section like the one shown in Figure 4.5.

By double-clicking any of the command names, you can read the man page for that command.

Options	Sections			Xman Help
:		ImageMagick	Magick++-config	Magick-config
Mail		SuperProbe(x)	Win32	XF86_SVGA(x)
XFree86(x)		Xconfigurator(x)	Xmark(x)	Xserver(x)
a2p		a2ps	addftinfo	afmtodit
ali		alias	animate	anno
answer		anytopnm	apacheconf	apm
apmsleep		appres(x)	apropos	arch
ascii-xfr		asciitopgm	ash	asn1parse
at		atktopbm	atobm(x)	atq
atrm		attraction	audiocompose	audiosend
aumix		autoexpect	autorun	autovbox
awk		balsa	basename	bash
bashbug		batch	bdftopcf(x)	beforelight(x)
bg		bind	bioradtopgm	bitmap(x)
blitspin		bmptoppm	bmtoa(x)	bouboule
braid		break	brushtopbm	bsh
bsod		bubbles	builtin	builtins
bunzip2		burst	bzcat	bzip2
bzip2recover		c2ph	ca	cal
cancel		captoinfo(m)	card	case
cat		cd	cdda2wav	cdp
cdparanoia		cdrecord	chage	charset
chattr		checkalias	chfn	chgrp
chmod		chown	chroot	chsh
chvt		ciphers	cjpeg	cksum
clear		cmp	cmuwmtopbm	col
colcrt		colrm	column	combine
comm		command	comp	consoletype
continue		convert	cp	cpio
critical		crl	crl2pkcs7	crontab
csplit		cut	cxpm(x)	date
dbmmanage		dd	ddate	deallocvt

FIGURE 4.5:   A directory listing

Now that you've gotten more comfortable using the Linux command line, we'll move into how to use it to manage your files and directories.

COPYING AND DELETING FILES

Probably the two most common file-manipulation tasks are copying and moving files. You will regularly find yourself replicating files all over your disk drive or copying files to floppy disks, the latter for backup purposes or to "transmit" files using the cheapest of all networking methods: your feet. Similarly, the average PC user at some point will run short of disk space and will strike out in search of files to delete in order to free up precious disk space and avoid investing in a new hard drive.

Part ii

Copying Files

Anyone with even brief experience using DOS or the DOS prompt in any version of Windows is probably aware that clicking, dragging, and dropping is not the only way to copy files. In fact, DOS's copy command offers additional features, such as wildcards, that can make it quicker, easier, and more powerful to use than File Manager or Windows Explorer.

Similarly, in the Linux world, the cp command (normally found at /bin/cp) is used for copying and provides a powerful tool for copy operations.

Basic Copying

Obviously, the most basic uses of the cp command are to copy a file from one place to another and to make a duplicate file in the same directory. For instance, if you want to copy a file (ThisFile) in the current directory to a second file (to be called ThisFile-Acopy) in the same directory, enter the following command:

```
$ cp ThisFile ThisFile-Acopy
```

Using ls -l to look at a directory listing of the files, you would find two files with identical sizes but different date stamps. The new file has a date stamp indicating when the copy operation took place. It is a new, separate file. Changes to ThisFile-Acopy do not affect the original ThisFile file.

Similarly, to make a copy of ThisFile in the /tmp directory (perhaps to share the file with another user), use the following command:

```
$ cp ThisFile /tmp
```

And if you want to copy ThisFile to /tmp but give the new file a different name, enter

```
$ cp ThisFile /tmp/NewFileName
```

DON'T OVERWRITE THAT FILE

The scary thing about Linux distributions is that it is easy to accidentally overwrite a file by copying over an existing file. Consider the situation where ThisFile and NewFile both exist and you issue the command

```
$ cp ThisFile NewFile
```

CONTINUED ➡

Using this command, the contents of NewFile are overwritten by a copy of ThisFile and lost forever (unless you are disciplined about backing up your system).

To avoid this difficulty, you can use the -i flag of the cp command, which forces the system to confirm any file it will overwrite when copying. Then, you see a prompt like this when attempting to copy:

```
$ cp -i ThisFile NewFile
cp: overwrite 'ThisFile'?
```

If you want to protect yourself, you can create an alias for the cp command. By issuing the command

```
$ alias cp='cp -i'
```

you are defining an alias so that any time you issue the cp command, you are in fact issuing the command cp -i. In this way, you are always prompted before overwriting a file while copying. You can configure the Bash shell using the .bashrc file to ensure that every time you log in, this alias is set. (The shell controls the command-line environment in which you work.)

Luckily, this alias is set by default in Red Hat Linux 7.1 when you log in as the superuser, or root. This is especially important because making a small mistake as the root user can have drastic consequences for the whole system. Using this default can help prevent major disasters.

Part ii

Copying Multiple Files in One Command

One of the drawbacks of the DOS copy command is that it could copy only one file or file expression at a time. For instance, use the command

```
$ copy file /tmp
```

to copy a single file to /tmp, or enter the command

```
$ copy *.txt /tmp
```

to copy all text files in the current directory to /tmp. But if there are three separate files you want to copy, you need to use three commands; similarly, if you want to copy all text files and all executable files in the current directory, you need to use two commands.

The Linux cp command, however, makes this process a bit easier. The cp command can take more than the two arguments in the DOS version of the command. Instead, you can pass multiple arguments to the command, and the last argument is treated as the destination and all preceding files are copied to the destination.

Let's look at an example. Suppose you want to copy the files `FileOne`, `FileTwo`, and `FileThree` in the current directory to `/tmp`. Obviously, you could issue three commands:

```
$ cp FileOne /tmp
$ cp FileTwo /tmp
$ cp FileThree /tmp
```

However, you can bundle this all together into one command, making the process easier:

```
$ cp FileOne FileTwo FileThree /tmp
```

Similarly, you can add wildcards to the mix and copy large numbers of files in one command. For instance, the command

```
$ cp *.txt *.doc *.bak /tmp
```

copies all files with any of three extensions in one command.

NOTE

When copying multiple files in this way, it is important to remember that the last argument must be a directory, since it is impossible to copy two or more files into a single file. If you forget to make the last argument a directory, then you will get an error message like this one: `cp: when copying multiple files, last argument must be a directory. Try 'cp -help' for more information.`

If you want to copy an entire directory and all its subdirectories, you can use the -R flag of the `cp` command. This command indicates that you want to recursively copy a directory. If a subdirectory called `SomeDir` exists in the current directory and you want to copy `SomeDir` in its entirety to a subdirectory in `/tmp`, then use the command:

```
$ cp -R SomeDir /tmp
```

to create a directory `/tmp/SomeDir` as a copy of the `SomeDir` subdirectory in the current directory.

Advanced Copying

The `cp` command offers several advanced features that extend it beyond simple copying of files and directories. These capabilities include preserving the state of original files in their copies and alternate methods to protect existing files while copying.

Making Copies As Close to the Originals As Possible   Take a close look at the copies you make. Notice that certain characteristics of the copied files bear little resemblance to the original files. These characteristics include the file ownership, permissions, date stamps, and symbolic links. Let's consider these one by one.

When you copy a file, the resulting file is normally owned by the copier as opposed to the creator of the original file. Let's say that user1 has created a file called TheFile and put it in /tmp for user2 to copy to their home directory. If you look at the file listing, the file looks something like this:

```
-rw-r--r--  1 user1    users     16992 Apr  5 12:10
   TheFile
```

After user2 copies the file with the command

```
$ cp /tmp/TheFile ~/NewFile
```

the resulting file has a new ownership, that of the copier (user2):

```
-rw-rw-r--  1 user2    users     16992 Apr  5 13:10
   NewFile
```

Similarly, when a file is created in a directory, it has a set of default permissions assigned to it. When copying a file, the copy will have the permissions set to the default for the destination directory rather than retain the permissions of the original file. Notice in this example the change in permission between the original file and the new copy. The original file was only group readable but the copy is also group writable. A change has also occurred to the date of the copy, reflecting the date and time when the copy was made instead of the date stamp of the original file.

There are times, however, when you want to retain the original owner, date, and permissions of files when they are copied. Let's say, for example, that the root account is being used to copy a set of files to a removable hard disk for storage in a vault. Unlike a regular tape backup, which requires other tools, this type of backup can be done with the cp command. However, it is important that a backup like this match the original as closely as possible. Luckily, the cp command provides the -p flag, which preserves these attributes. Using the previous example, if the command used was

```
$ cp -p /tmp/TheFile
```

Part ii

then the resulting file would match the original quite closely:

```
-rw-r--r--    1 user1    users         16992 Apr  5 12:10
   TheFile
```

Another sticky problem in copying files is how to handle symbolic links. A symbolic link provides a pointer to a file from another location. In this way, you can pretend that a file is in more than one place at once. If you try to access the link, Linux actually accesses the file that the link points to.

Normally, when you copy a symbolic link, the resulting file is a copy of the file pointed to by the link instead of a new link to the same file. For instance, if TheFile had been a symbolic link as in this example

```
lrwxrwxrwx    1 user1    users         16992 Apr  5 12:10
   TheFile OtherFile
-rw-r--r--    1 user1    users             1 Apr  5 11:10
   OtherFile
```

then issuing the following cp command

```
$ cp /tmp/TheFile ~/NewFile
```

results in a file that is a copy of OtherFile:

```
-rw-rw-r--    1 user2    users         16992 Apr  5 13:10
   NewFile
```

But what if you want to copy the link instead of the file itself? What if you want the result to appear as follows:

```
lrwxrwxrwx    1 user2    users             2 Apr  5 13:10
   NewFile /tmp/OtherFile
```

Well, once again the cp command has a flag to address the situation: the -d flag, which preserves the link to the original file. Simply use the command

```
$ cp -d /tmp/TheFile ~/NewFile
```

to get the desired result.

Having said all this, it is time to put it all together. What if you want to use the cp command to create a useful backup copy of an existing directory and all its subdirectories? Using the combination of these two flags and a recursive copy, you can do this. For instance,

```
$ cp -pdR TheDirectory /backups
```

creates an exact copy of TheDirectory in the directory /backups/ TheDirectory. But the cp command provides a simplified way to achieve this: the -a flag, which indicates that you want an archive of a directory. It is a quick way to indicate the three flags -pdR:

```
$ cp -a TheDirectory /backups
```

Preventing Mistakes   As you saw earlier, one way to prevent mistakes is to use the -i flag, which forces interactive prompting before overwriting occurs in the course of copying files or directories. Other methods are available to provide different degrees of protection.

One method is to use the -b or –backup flag to cause the cp command to create a backup copy of any file about to be overwritten. By default, the backup copy has the original filename with a tilde (~) after it. So, if you copy FileOne to FileTwo using the command

```
$ cp -b FileOne FileTwo
```

and FileTwo already exists, then a backup is made of the original FileTwo called FileTwo~.

It is possible to alter the way in which the cp command names the backup files with the -S flag. The -S flag allows you to change the character used in backup names from the default tilde to something else. For instance,

```
$ cp -b -S _ FileOne FileTwo
```

results in a backup filename FileTwo_.

Alternatively, you can specify one of three types of backup naming schemes with the --backup flag:

t or *numbered*   Create sequentially numbered backups. If an existing numbered backup file exists, then the new backup file created is numbered sequentially after the existing backup file; the resulting filenames look like FileTwo.~*Number*~ (for example, FileTwo.~2~ or FileTwo.~11~).

nil or *existing*   If a numbered backup file already exists, then create a numbered backup; otherwise, create a regular simple backup file.

never or *simple*   Create a simple backup file using the default tilde or alternative character indicated by the -S flag. This overwrites any previous backup with the same name.

For instance, to create a numbered backup in the example above, use the command

```
$ cp --backup=t FileOne FileTwo
```

Part II

or

```
$ cp --backup=numbered FileOne FileTwo
```

Similarly, both of the following commands create simple backup files:

```
$ cp --backup=never FileOne FileTwo
```

and

```
$ cp --backup=simple FileOne FileTwo
```

The -b switch does not work in Red Hat Linux 7.1 with these options.

NOTE

In Red Hat Linux 7.1, you can still use the -V switch to control backup naming schemes; however, you won't be able to use this switch in future releases of cp.

Alternative Flags

You may have noticed that this section covered a lot of flags for the cp command. Sometimes it is difficult to remember the flags. Fortunately, there are long forms for most of these flags that may make them easier to remember:

Short Form	Alternate Long Form
-I	–interactive
-R	–recursive
-p	–preserve
-d	–no-dereference
-a	–archive
-b	–backup
-S	–suffix

While the long forms may seem more intuitive at first, ultimately any regular Linux user will use the short forms. The long forms involve too much typing for frequent use. For instance, consider the following complex cp command:

```
$ cp -i -b -V simple -S _ -R ThisDir /tmp
```

If you use the long form of these flags, you end up with the following command:

```
$ cp --interactive --backup --version-control simple
  --suffix _--recursive ThisDir /tmp
```

Sure, this command is more readable at first glance, but do you really want to type this simply to copy a directory?

Deleting Files

Just as it does for copying files, Linux provides a powerful command for deleting files: rm, found at /bin/rm.

In its simplest form, rm allows you to delete one or more files in the current directory. The command

```
$ rm ThisFile
```

deletes the file ThisFile in the current directory, and

```
$ rm *.txt
```

removes all files with the .txt extension in the current directory.

As with copying, it is possible to provide multiple arguments to the rm command, and all referenced files will be deleted. For instance,

```
$ rm ThisFile *.txt
```

performs the same action as the previous two commands combined.

Like the cp command, this can be extremely useful and potentially dangerous. After all, what happens if, wanting to delete a backup of a document, someone accidentally issues the command

```
$ rm thesis.doc
```

instead of

```
$ rm thesis.bak
```

This is a potential nightmare, and as unlikely as it sounds, it happens all the time, resulting in unnecessary work and headaches.

For this reason, it is wise to use the same -i flag for the rm command because it provides the prompts to avoid disastrous mistakes:

```
$ rm -i thesis.doc
rm: remove 'thesis.doc'?
```

You can also create an alias for rm, making this the default behavior:

```
$ alias rm='rm-i'
```

Deleting Whole Directories

Users frequently want to delete entire directories. Consider, for instance, a directory created after unzipping a software archive downloaded from the Internet. After you have finished installing and testing the software, you will probably want to delete the entire directory. This is done using the -r flag. For instance, to remove a directory called TempInstall, you would use

```
$ rm -r TempInstall
```

Of course, if you have been following along in this chapter, you probably have an alias for the rm command, forcing it to prompt you for every deletion. This can become very tedious for big directories:

```
$ rm -r TempInstall
rm: descend directory 'tempInstall'? y
rm: remove 'TempInstall/File1'? y
rm: remove 'TempInstall/File2'? y
...
rm: remove directory 'TempInstall'? y
```

Just imagine if there were hundreds of files. Responding to prompts for each one would be impractical. In these instances, when you are absolutely certain that you want to delete a whole directory, you should use the -f flag of the rm command. This flag forces deletions, even when you have already indicated interactive operation with the -i flag in your alias:

```
$ rm -rf TempInstall
```

A REMINDER...

Care needs to be taken when using the −f flag. While it is powerful, it can be extremely dangerous.

In Red Hat Linux 7.1, the superuser's account is configured so that the default alias for the rm command is rm -i. This is critically important, because even a seemingly small mistake can be disastrous. If the alias weren't being used, just consider what would happen if, in attempting to delete the /tmp directory, a space made its way in between the / and tmp:

```
$ rm -r / tmp
```

CONTINUED ➡

This would actually delete all the files and directories on the disk. This is why the alias for rm -i is so essential.

Similarly, using the -f flag requires great care when working as the superuser and underscores the need to limit your use of the superuser account to only essential tasks. After all,

```
$ rm -rf / tmp
```

would be just as dangerous if you did have the right alias in place.

MOVING AND RENAMING FILES

Moving files and renaming files are closely linked, and therefore they are treated together in this section. Unlike the DOS/Windows and Macintosh worlds, where renaming and moving are distinct actions, in the Linux environment renaming a file is just a special case of moving a file.

The Basic Move Operation

Let's start by considering the basic move operation:

```
$ mv FileOne /tmp
```

This command moves the file called FileOne from the current directory to the /tmp directory.

Moving and Renaming

Similarly, it is possible to move the file to the /tmp directory and change the name of the file using the following command:

```
$ mv FileOne /tmp/NewFileName
```

By using this concept, you can rename a file. Simply move a file from its existing name to a new name in the same directory:

```
$ mv FileOne NewFileName
```

See how moving and renaming are one and the same?

Part ii

Moving More Than Just One File

As when copying files, it is possible to move multiple files in one step because the mv command can accept more than two arguments and the last argument serves as the destination directory of the move. (As with copying, you can't move multiple files to a file; the last argument must be a directory.) Consider the situation where you want to move all files in the current directory with the extension .bak, .tmp, or .old to /tmp. Use the command

```
$ mv *.bak *.tmp *.old /tmp
```

This simple command moves all the specified files to the destination (/tmp) in one operation.

It is also possible to move entire directories with the mv command without using any special flags. If there is a subdirectory named TheDir in the current directory and you want to move it so it becomes a subdirectory under /tmp, you would use the mv command just as you did earlier for files:

```
$ mv TheDir/ /tmp
```

Similarly, if you want TheDir to become a subdirectory under the directory called NewDir, you can use the following command:

```
$ mv TheDir/ /NewDir
```

NOTE

As with cp and rm, it is wise to set an alias for mv to mv -i to ensure that you don't accidentally overwrite files when moving. You can do this with $ alias mv='mv -i'. In Red Hat Linux 7.1, this is set by default for the cp, rm, and mv commands for the superuser account.

CREATING FILES

You have already learned several ways to create files. After all, you create files when you copy files. You create files when you move files. Other obvious ways of creating files include creating a word processing document, saving an e-mail attachment, or making a screen capture.

However, there are cases where it is necessary to create a new file, even if the file is empty and has a length of zero. The most obvious instance of this would be in cases where a script needs to create a file to indicate a special state. The best example of this is a programming technique called *file locking*. If a script opens a file to make changes, it also creates a special file called a *lock file* that indicates to other programs and scripts that the current file is opened for editing and is therefore unavailable to be changed. Once the script closes the file, it deletes the lock file to make the file once again available.

In order to be able to create these lock files quickly and efficiently without exacting excessive disk space requirements, you need a shortcut method to signify an empty file of a specified name. This is achieved with the touch command. This command creates a file. For instance,

```
$ touch NewFile
```

creates a new file of zero length with the name NewFile:

```
-rw-rw-r--  1 armand    armand       0 Apr  6 21:06 NewFile
```

Another common use of the touch command is to change the modification date stamp of an existing file. Many programs depend on the date stamp of files they are working with to determine what action to take. The touch command lets you change the modification date of a file without opening and editing the file.

Creating Directories

One type of special file in Linux is the directory. A directory is just a special file that contains other files. You can set permissions for a directory that allow or prevent other users from seeing what is in that directory. Directories are as simple as the top-level root directory (/) or your personal home directory (e.g., /home/mj).

But you can't create a directory with the same commands as you might use to create a file. The key commands are mkdir and rmdir. If you wanted to create a directory of documents in your home directory, you might run the following command:

```
$ mkdir documents
```

But this would not work if you were not already in your home directory. To be sure, you can also specify the full desired path to that directory with a command such as

```
$ mkdir /home/mj/documents
```

Whether this command works or not depends on the privileges associated with your username and the permissions on the higher-level

Part ii

directory. For example, as a regular user, you probably wouldn't be able to create a new /golf directory, but as a root user, you could do this.

Of course, you can also remove directories. For example, the following command removes the directory created earlier:

```
$ rmdir /home/mj/documents
```

Whether this command works depends on the permissions in the /home/mj directory and whether this directory is empty. Of course, you could use the rm -r command discussed earlier in this chapter to delete a directory even if it is full of files.

CREATING SYMBOLIC LINKS

In addition to creating files, there are times when it is necessary to create symbolic links. *Symbolic links* (which are simply pointers to a real file in another location) are usually used by system administrators and application developers. Consider a programmer who has several versions of a program that is under development. The current version for testing may be prog5, prog8, or prog10, depending on how far along the development is. In order to ensure that the latest version is always being executed during testing, the programmer can create a symbolic link from prog to the latest version. By doing this, executing prog always executes the desired revision of the application.

There are two possible approaches to creating a symbolic link. The first is to use the ln command with the -s flag to indicate a symbolic link. This command takes two arguments: the file to be linked to and the location and name of the symbolic link to that file.

For instance, to create a link to /bin/cp in the current directory, MyCopy, you use the command

```
$ ln -s /bin/cp MyCopy
```

Using ls -l to see the listing of MyCopy shows us a symbolic link:

```
lrwxrwxrwx   1 armand    armand          7 Apr  6 22:50
  MyCopy -> /bin/cp
```

Another, far less common way to create a symbolic link is to use the cp command with the -s flag:

```
$ cp -s /bin/cp MyCopy
```

A Quick Introduction to Filename Expansion

Before closing out this chapter, you need to take a quick look at an important subject: *filename expansion*. This section will put filename expansion in context.

Filename expansion refers to a special syntax that can be used to expand a compact expression into a list of one or more file or directory names. The simple examples you have seen in this chapter involve the use of the asterisk (*) to represent zero or more characters. For instance, the expression *.txt could match any of the following filenames:

- .txt
- a.txt
- file.txt
- txt.txt

The default Bash shell provides a rich syntax for filename expansion. This book will explore the Bash shell later, but two of the more useful symbols are outlined below:

?   Matches any single character, so file.? would match file.c but not file.txt.

[CharacterList]   Matches any single character in the character list, so file.[abc] would match file.a, file.b, and file.c but not file.d or file.txt. Alternatively, file.[x-z] would match file.x, file.y, and file.z.

What's Next?

In this chapter, you've taken your first big step toward becoming a real Linux user by delving into the world of the command line. You learned about some of the major programs available in the command-prompt environment and are able to manipulate files in sophisticated ways using concise and powerful commands.

In the next chapter, you will move from the command line to the X Windows interface that is more akin to Microsoft Windows, in terms of look and feel.

Part ii

Chapter 5
AN OVERVIEW OF
X WINDOWS

Now that you have succeeded in installing Linux, you will start your learning process by diving straight into the X Windows environment. Many Linux diehards will shudder at our considering X Windows before mastering the intricate details of the Linux command line and the Linux configuration. But it is X Windows that makes Linux an acceptable alternative to Windows and to the Mac OS as a productive operating system for everyday tasks such as word processing, desktop publishing, and browsing the World Wide Web.

This chapter starts by describing exactly what X Windows is. X Windows offers a graphical user interface (GUI) to the Unix world. X Windows provides a way to deliver all the now-commonplace user interface paradigms such as windows, dialog boxes, buttons, and menus. It is X Windows that enables the creation of the sophisticated graphics that make Unix-based workstations the system of choice for many engineering and design applications, and it is X Windows that has made it possible for Linux to emerge as a strong contender in the PC operating system market.

Adapted from *Mastering Red Hat Linux 7.1*
by Arman Danesh
ISBN 0-7821-2927-7   1008 page $49.99

To fully understand what X Windows is all about, this chapter provides a detailed comparison of Microsoft Windows and X Windows, including changes based on X Windows 4. The chapter wraps up by looking at some key components of X Windows, such as X servers, window managers, desktop environments, and Motif.

WHAT IS X WINDOWS?

Put in its simplest terms, X Windows is a complete graphics interface for Unix—and by extension, for Linux. But this doesn't say it all. X Windows is a highly configurable environment that provides a broad range of flexible options for both the user and the application developers producing software to run under X Windows.

The core X Windows concept is the client-server framework. What this means in practical terms is that X Windows provides an environment that is not bound to a single processor. Applications can run on different servers and machines on a network, and applications can display to X Windows terminals and workstations elsewhere on the network.

This separation between where an application runs and where it is displayed is a concept missing in the Windows and Macintosh environments, which tie the application to the display. The benefit of this separation is that in a networking environment, it is possible to have sophisticated graphics desktops displaying applications that are running on well-maintained, powerful, and easy-to-manage central application servers. In fact, this very capability is what gives Unix/Linux and X Windows such a good reputation among professional system administrators of large networks.

Another concept introduced in the X Windows environment is the separation of windowing from the interface. On an X Windows system, two applications must run to provide a complete GUI. The first is the X server, which sets up the graphics display (in other words, resolution, refresh rate, and color depth), displays the windows, and tracks mouse movements, keystrokes, and multiple windows. But an X server does not provide menus, window borders, or mechanisms for moving, switching, minimizing, or maximizing windows. If you look at Figure 5.1, you can see how an X server screen appears without a window manager.

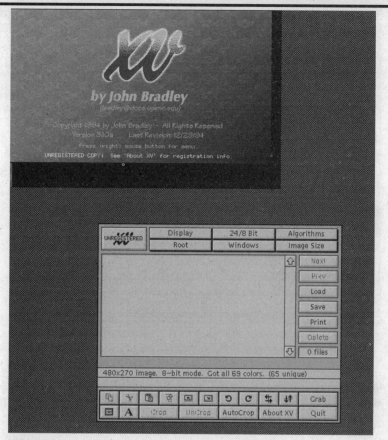

FIGURE 5.1: An X server display with no window manager

Notice the bare simplicity in Figure 5.1. There is no fancy color background, no sophisticated window borders or menu controls, and no other features that make a complete GUI. All these features are provided by a second application called a *window manager*. Figure 5.2 shows a complete X Windows desktop running the fvwm95 window manager. Notice the features of the window frames, the control buttons, and the control menus, as well as a Taskbar and a virtual desktop system. The window manager provides all of these.

Part ii

FIGURE 5.2:   An X Windows display running a window manager

The window manager talks to the X server in a standard, predefined way, as does the X server to the X applications. This means that different window managers with different interface features can all talk in this standard way to the X server. Likewise, the variety of X servers that are available, which offer support for different graphics cards, monitors, and other performance features, can also talk in a standardized way to applications.

MICROSOFT WINDOWS VERSUS X WINDOWS

Given some of the descriptions of X Windows you've seen, it would be natural to assume that Microsoft Windows and X Windows are pretty much the same thing. The reality, though, is that they are fundamentally different beasts.

For example, Microsoft Windows is a complete operating system, with everything from a kernel to a shell to a windowing environment and more. X Windows is just one piece of that operating system puzzle: the windowing environment. Another contrast is in the interface: The Microsoft Windows interface is fairly rigid, while the X Windows interface has an amazingly flexible and customizable design.

Similarities

What is similar about X Windows and Microsoft's current operating system? The main similarities are that they both provide graphical interfaces and make it possible to work with multiple windows. On top of this, they enable the user to interact with information using more than a keyboard and plain characters. Users can utilize a mouse as well as a keyboard and can create interfaces that combine menus, forms, windows, and dialog boxes.

Differences

There are numerous differences between the two windowing systems. The main differences are in the following areas:

- ▶ Flexibility of the interface
- ▶ Fine-tuned control over the interface configuration
- ▶ Client-server technology

Flexible Interface

The flexibility of the X Windows interface is one of the joys of this environment for many users. As discussed already, the separation of the user interface layer from the basic windowing layer makes it possible to create multiple interfaces for X Windows through the creation of different window managers.

Multiple interfaces don't simply provide subtle differences in appearance, as some customization tools for the Microsoft Windows interface offer. Rather, they allow complete redesigns of the user interface from window manager to window manager.

By way of example, Figure 5.3 shows a sample window interface running a window manager that resembles the user interface of the NeXT operating system. Compare that to Figure 5.4, running on the same system and displaying the same applications, which shows a user interface that resembles none of the popular PC or Macintosh operating systems.

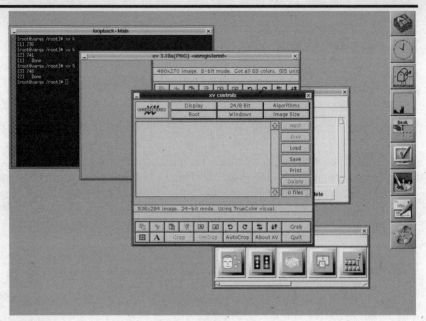

FIGURE 5.3: The AfterStep window manager

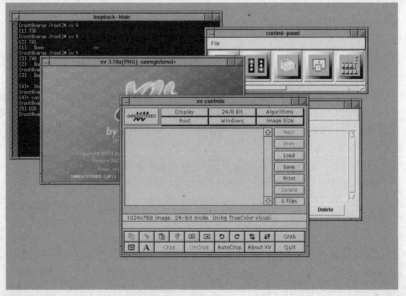

FIGURE 5.4: The LessTif window manager

These examples represent just two of the many look-and-feel designs offered by X Windows window managers. The better-known window managers are discussed briefly later in this chapter.

Fine-Tuned Control

Another advantage of the X Windows environment is that it offers fine-tuned control over all aspects of the windowing environment and the interface. By setting any of dozens of settings, it is possible to control all aspects of the environment, from the background and foreground window colors to cursor color, default font, and default window size. Users can also define modes of interaction. For instance, it is possible to use the mouse pointer to make a window automatically jump to the foreground or to change cursor focus to a background window.

In addition, these and other features can be defined on a per-application basis, creating different settings for each application so that each application launches in the most convenient way possible.

It is also possible to define which windows and applications open each time the X environment starts, as well as to have the system make logical choices about which window manager to use when starting X Windows.

Client-Server Environment

As mentioned previously, the X Windows world works on a client-server model in which applications are clients to an X server that drives the physical display. This has made X Windows well adapted to network environments, allowing applications to run on one machine on the network while displaying their output on another.

Microsoft Windows lacked this capability until very recently and now has it only in a limited and expensive fashion through its Terminal Server services on high-end multiuser Windows NT and 2000 systems. In the Linux, Unix, and X worlds, even the lowliest system is capable of playing either the client role or the server role in this X Windows client-server model.

X Servers, Window Managers, and Desktop Environments

Now that you have a sense of where X Windows fits into things, you need to understand the fundamental components of X Windows: X servers,

Part ii

window managers, and desktop environments. It is these components and the modularity they represent that provides the power and flexibility of X Windows.

X Servers

As you have already seen, the core of the X Windows system is the X server. The X server handles several tasks:

- ▶ Support for a variety of video cards and monitor types
- ▶ Resolution, refresh rate, and color depth of the X Windows display
- ▶ Basic window management: displaying and closing windows, tracking mouse movements and keystrokes

Multiple X servers with these basic capabilities have sprung up. In the Linux world, there are three main choices: XFree86, Metro-X, and Accelerated-X.

XFree86

XFree86 is the default X server with almost every noncommercial Linux distribution because it is available free under the same sort of terms as Linux. Full source code is available, users are free to change the code to meet their own needs, and anyone can redistribute it. Red Hat Linux 7.1 ships with XFree86 4.0.3. Minor updates are released every few months and can be downloaded from the XFree86 website at `http://www.xfree86.org`.

The XFree86 web server is designed to provide broad support for common hardware in the Intel-compatible *x*86 PC, as well as computers with the Compaq Alpha, PowerPC, Sparc, and MIPS processors. While its performance is not always stellar, XFree86 is the norm for X servers in Linux and other Intel-based Unix variants and therefore is the X server that most people are familiar with.

TIP

While MIPS support is not complete at the time of this writing, according to the XFree86 Project website, considerable documentation is available with the MIPS HOWTO at `http://oss.sgi.com/mips/mips-howto.html`.

Among the popular graphics card chipsets supported by XFree86 are Tseng's ET3000, 4000, and 6000, the full range of Trident chips, most of the Cirrus Logic line, Chips and Technologies graphics chips, and many others. You can find a full list of supported hardware on the Driver status page of the XFree86 project at `http://www.xfree86.org/4.0.3/Status.html`. If you are using a later version, substitute accordingly for `4.0.3`.

Although the XFree86 4 X server goes a long way toward making Linux a complete, free, Unix-like operating system, it does suffer from some drawbacks that make it less than attractive for corporate or mission-critical environments. XFree86 sometimes requires painstakingly difficult configuration and installation, has less-than-stable or imperfect support for some graphics cards and monitors, and often will not take advantage of the accelerated features of a graphics card.

Luckily, Red Hat Linux 7.1 ships with an excellent utility called Xconfigurator, which greatly eases the job of configuring XFree86, even to the point of auto-detecting some hardware and suggesting the best options for that hardware. Other distributions ship with utilities of similar quality. This works great unless you present the tool with one of those rare problematic hardware combinations, in which case you will be right back to configuring XFree86 manually.

What's New about XFree86 4?

Version 4 of XFree86 includes a number of new features not found in earlier versions. Some of these new features borrow functionality from the commercial X servers. These features include the following:

- ▶ One unified X server Modular Architectural Design
- ▶ Support for multiple graphics cards
- ▶ Independence from the operating system
- ▶ 3D rendering
- ▶ FreeType support

With one unified X server, XFree86 4 allows the use of different types of graphics cards without reconfiguration. With a runtime loader donated by Metro Link, XFree86 4 no longer depends on the driver libraries of Linux (or any other Unix-based operating system). With GLX extensions, XFree86 now supports 3D rendering through Silicon Graphics' OpenGL

Part ii

3D graphics language. With FreeType support, XFree86 can now manage TrueType fonts.

XFree86 now enhances and adds support for more platforms, including computers based on the Alpha, MIPS, and PowerPC processors. It is expected to be ready for the Intel Itanium IA 64-bit platform when that is released.

NOTE

As of this writing, XFree86 version 4 does not support the older XF86Setup tool. Alternate utilities such as Xconfigurator and xf86config are more than adequate alternatives.

Commercial X Servers

In addition to the XFree86 project, which is a vital part of making Linux a complete and free solution, there are two leading commercial X servers for the Linux world: Metro-X and Accelerated-X.

These products offer the advantage of broader support for various graphics chips and cards and generally take full advantage of the accelerated features of those chips and cards. In addition, Metro-X and Accelerated-X offer more intelligent configuration and can usually be installed and working in a matter of minutes.

Metro-X   Metro-X from Metro Link is a high-performance X server option. Among the many benefits of Metro-X are a well-designed graphical configuration interface like the one in Figure 5.5, support for multi-headed displays (the standard configuration supports four different monitors), support for some brands of touch screens, and more.

Complete information about the Metro-X server, including supported graphics cards, is available on the Metro Link home page at http://www.metrolink.com/. Metro-X costs US$39 for Linux.

Accelerated-X   X-Inside offers a range of X servers for Linux. These include the Accelerated-X server for Linux, a 3D Accelerated-X server, a multi-head Accelerated-X server, and a specialized Laptop Accelerated-X server. The Laptop Accelerated-X server is significant because the chipsets found on laptops are different from those in desktop graphics cards and because LCD screens have their own set of requirements that are ignored by desktop drivers.

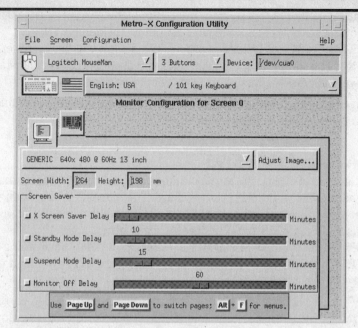

FIGURE 5.5: Metro-X's Configuration window

In fact, support for laptop displays is quite limited in XFree86, and a small mistake can mean that your LCD will be damaged. If you plan to use a notebook full-time as a Linux system, look at the list of systems supported by the Laptop Accelerated-X server to see if yours is there.

Accelerated-X offers support for more than 400 graphics cards from over 60 manufacturers. The Multihead Accelerated-X server supports up to 16 screens and offers all the features of Accelerated-X on each screen.

Overall, X-Inside's servers are competitively priced. Accelerated-X costs US$99.95, the Laptop server is $149.95, and the Multihead server is $199.95. Complete information is available on the X-Inside website at http://www.xinside.com/.

Window Managers

Window managers fill out the niceties of the GUI not provided by X servers. Among other features, window managers include window decorations (which provide the means to resize, move, close, and minimize windows) and mechanisms for launching applications (such as desktop menus, control panels, and button bars).

The remainder of this section takes a brief look at some of the main window managers that are available for Linux, including FVWM, FVWM95, TWM, OLVWM, and others. The default window manager with Red Hat Linux 7.1 is Sawfish, but any reasonably complete installation will include FVWM and other alternative window managers.

An overview of window managers for X Windows is available online at http://www.plig.org/xwinman/.

FVWM and FVWM95

During the mid-1990s, the most common window manager for Linux was FVWM or some variation of that package. The name FVWM is strange because no one is sure what the "F" stands for in the name. Some say it stands for "Feeble" Virtual Window Manager; others argue that it is "Fine" Virtual Window Manager; still others argue that the meaning of the "F" has long been forgotten and isn't important anyway. (I tend to agree with the latter.)

FVWM is a lightweight window manager that provides a flexible, customizable windowing environment designed to look a bit like the Motif Window Manager (MWM, a commercial product). FVWM provides multiple virtual desktops and a module system for extending the window manager and, in the more recent version 2.2.5, allows on-the-fly configuration changes and window-specific feature customization. The FVWM home page is at http://www.fvwm.org/. Figure 5.6 shows a sample FVWM desktop.

FVWM ships with almost every Linux distribution and is known for its usefulness as the basis for newer window managers with their own look-and-feel, including the following:

FVWM95   Designed to look like Windows 95

AfterStep   Designed to look like the NeXT environment

SCWM (Scheme Constraints Window Manager)   Configurable using the Scheme language

Figure 5.7 contains a screen of FVWM95 in action.

FVWM95 is based on version 2 of FVWM and retains the flexible, easy configuration of that release. It continues to support FVWM modules but adds the modules needed to implement Windows 95–style features such as the Taskbar. FVWM95 information is available on the Web at http://www.plig.org/xwinman/fvwm95.html.

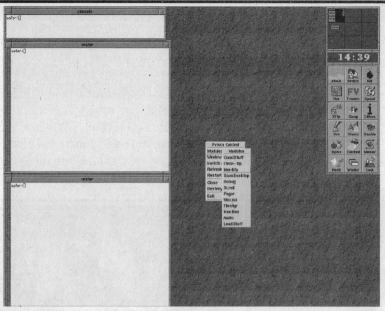

FIGURE 5.6:   A sample FVWM desktop

FIGURE 5.7:   FVWM95 provides a Windows 95–like environment.

NOTE

The FVWM2 package is available on the second Red Hat Linux 7.1 installation CD-ROM.

TWM

The Tab Window Manager (TWM), often called Tom's Window Manager after the name of its primary developer, is a basic, functional environment that is included with Red Hat Linux 7.1 as an alternative window manager. Figure 5.8 shows a typical TWM desktop.

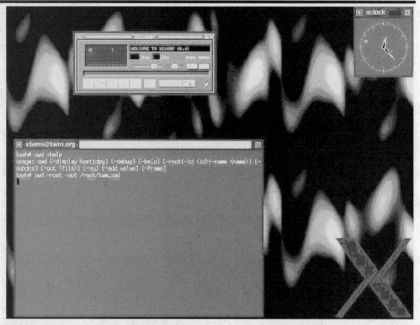

FIGURE 5.8: The TWM desktop

The TWM window manager offers many key features that users expect in an X Windows window manager, including click-to-type or pointer-driven keyboard focus and user-defined key and button bindings. However, the interface is visually simple, and some would see it as limited. VTWM, a version of TWM that includes a virtual desktop, is also available and can be downloaded from `ftp://ftp.x.org/R5contrib/vtwm-5.3.tar.gz`.

OLVWM

OLVWM, the OpenLook Virtual Window Manager, is an extension of the OpenLook Window Manager (OLWM), which was the standard window manager on Sun systems for many years. Although Sun systems now sport Motif and the Common Desktop Environment (discussed later in this chapter), the unique OpenLook interface is still popular with many users. OLVWM adds support for virtual desktops to the OpenLook package. Figure 5.9 shows a sample OLVWM desktop.

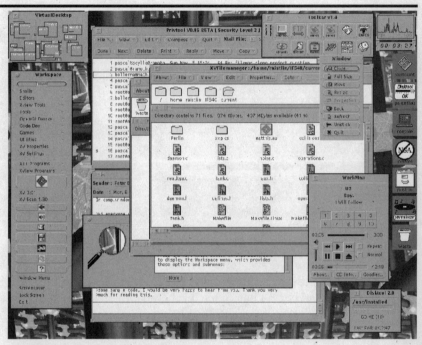

FIGURE 5.9: The OLVWM interface

The interface used in OLVWM will feel awkward to many users, especially in terms of the way in which menus and windows respond to mouse buttons. This is one reason why OpenLook didn't gain huge popularity outside the Sun world. OLVWM can be downloaded from `ftp://ftp.x .org/R5contrib/olvwm4.tar.Z`.

AfterStep

AfterStep is another variant on the original FVWM code. This product is based on an earlier window manager called Bowman and is designed to provide the look-and-feel of the NeXTSTEP window manager from the NeXT platform. Figure 5.10 shows a sample AfterStep desktop.

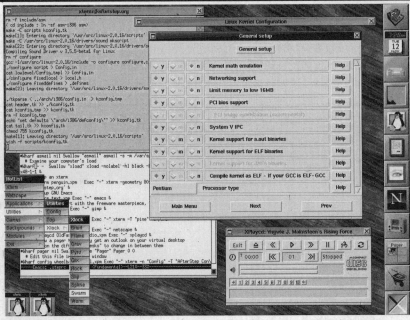

FIGURE 5.10:   The AfterStep desktop

Major features drawn from NeXTSTEP are the look of title bars, buttons, and borders, the appearance of the style menu, and the NeXTSTEP-like icons and button bar. Since it is based on FVWM version 1 code, any modules from that version of FVWM should continue to work with After-Step. Unlike some window managers, such as FVWM95 and OLVWM, organized development work on AfterStep continues today.

The AfterStep home page is at http://www.afterstep.org/.

AmiWM

If you are a former user of the Amiga computer and fell in love with its interface, then AmiWM may be the window manager for you. AmiWM emulates the Amiga workbench, as shown in Figure 5.11. With support for multiple screens such as that found on the Amiga, AmiWM can ease the move to X Windows for former Amiga users.

You can learn about AmiWM and download the software from the AmiWM home page at `http://www.lysator.liu.se/~marcus/ amiwm.html`.

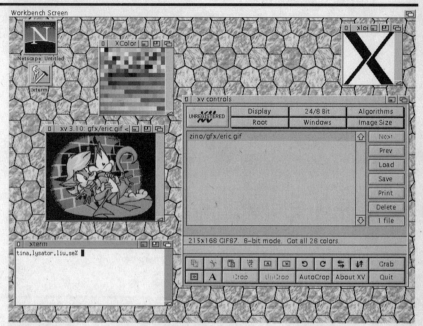

FIGURE 5.11:   The AmiWM window manager

Enlightenment

Enlightenment is a grand project, attempting to develop a window manager that goes beyond the conventional. It provides a useful but also visually attractive environment and allows the user to define everything from functionality to the appearance of the window manager. Figures 5.12 and 5.13 show just two possible configurations of the Enlightenment environment. Among the many features that help Enlightenment stand out are the capabilities it gives users to handcraft the look-and-feel and to embed new features easily.

FIGURE 5.12:   The Enlightenment window manager

FIGURE 5.13:   Users can fully customize the Enlightenment environment.

Although Enlightenment is an ambitious project and offers visually stunning interfaces, installation can be a bit of a challenge for the novice user, often requiring the user to compile and install new libraries. The Enlightenment home page is at http://www.enlightenment.org/. Note also that the authors consider Enlightenment to be in an early pre-release stage (the current version as of this writing is 0.16) and therefore warn of bugs and the potential for crashes. Still, this is an interesting project and a unique concept among window managers.

Sawfish

The Sawfish window manager is the new default with the GNOME desktop environment. Like Enlightenment, Sawfish maximizes the capability to configure each window, in this case, through tools that use the LISP programming language. As part of the GNOME desktop, Sawfish controls are integrated with the GNOME Control Center, as shown in Figure 5.14.

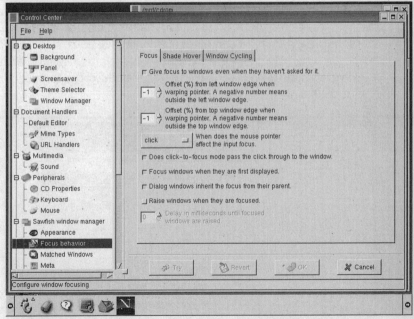

FIGURE 5.14:   Users can fully customize the Sawfish environment.

Like Enlightenment, Sawfish is also a work in progress. The current version as of this writing is 1.0. For more information, go to the Sawfish home page at www.sawfish.org.

Desktop Environments

Desktop environments are more than just window managers. Desktop environments aim to provide a complete, cohesive GUI. With simple window managers, there is no guarantee of consistency of look-and-feel between applications and features found in other operating systems, such as drag-and-drop between applications and cross-application data embedding.

There are different desktop environments for Linux that provide robust, integrated GUIs and provide a target platform for application developers to build software with a common look-and-feel and include integration features such as drag-and-drop.

Two of these desktop environments, the K Desktop Environment and GNOME, are freely available and have emerged as competitors for the *de facto* standard Linux desktop environment.

The K Desktop Environment

The K Desktop Environment (KDE) is an attempt to provide a free alternative to the Common Desktop Environment (discussed later in this section). In this effort, KDE combines a set of applications, such as a file manager, terminal emulator, and display configuration system, with a window manager to create a consistent look-and-feel for X applications. Figure 5.15 shows a typical KDE desktop.

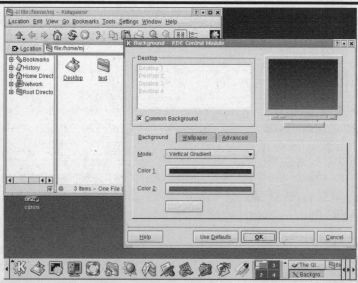

FIGURE 5.15: A KDE desktop

KDE is the default desktop environment for a number of Linux distributions, including Caldera, SuSE, and Corel. It is an alternative desktop environment for most of the other distributions.

Part of the planning behind KDE is that standards be specified and the development environment be such that developers can create applications that are consistent in features as well as appearance. KDE provides an attractive, professional-looking environment in which to work, and if the necessary applications are developed for KDE, it will become a likely prospect for the business desktop. The KDE website is `http://www.kde.org/`.

GNOME: The GNU Network Object Model Environment

GNOME is the result of an alternative effort to develop a comprehensive, free, desktop environment for Linux. Unlike KDE, which includes a built-in window manager, GNOME is window manager—independent. It provides a programming interface that enables a window manager developer to integrate full support for GNOME in his window manager.

Red Hat Linux 7.1 ships with GNOME as the default desktop environment, using the Sawfish window manager.

MWM

MWM, the Motif Window Manager, is a commercial window manager that is part of the Motif distribution. Motif as a complete environment is discussed in more detail in the next section of this chapter.

The Common Desktop Environment

The Common Desktop Environment (CDE) is an ambitious project to standardize the graphical environment and development arena on various Unix platforms, including AIX, Compaq Unix, HP/UX, and Solaris. Now CDE is also available for Linux as the DeXtop graphical interface from X-Inside (`http://www.xinside.com/`). This commercial application, which costs US$49.95, requires X-Inside's Accelerated-X server.

In addition to a consistent graphical environment based on Motif, CDE offers a set of cohesive tools and applications to standardize administrative procedures and ease the configuration and management of a user's graphical work environment. Among the enhancements brought to the X environment by CDE are drag-and-drop capabilities and the types of folders and icons found in other GUI operating systems.

## Part iii

WHAT IS MOTIF?

If you begin to look around the Web for X Windows applications to install on your Linux system, you will inevitably come across applications that refer to the fact that they use the Motif library or the Motif toolkit.

Motif is a development environment for X Windows that was introduced by the Open Software Foundation (OSF) in the late 1980s to provide a consistent policy for X Windows applications. Motif provides a toolkit of widgets that developers can use in developing their applications. With these widget libraries, Motif developers produce applications that adhere to Motif policies for a consistent look-and-feel.

Motif was recently re-released under an "open" license, which means that developers who want to build and distribute applications based on the Motif libraries no longer need to pay for the privilege. However, the Open Group, the organization behind the new Open Motif, still sells the documentation behind this language and set of libraries. Many Linux developers read the Motif license to mean that it cannot be used to develop software for free operating systems such as Linux.

NOTE

The Open Group is an industry organization dedicated to software standards. It is not related to the sponsors of the Open Source license. In fact, it admits that its Motif license does not meet Open Source requirements.

In addition to the toolkit and libraries, the Motif distribution includes its own window manager, MWM, after which the original FVWM look-and-feel was patterned. Figure 5.16 shows a sample MWM desktop.

Do I Need Motif?

For most Linux users, there is probably no need to use Motif. Users who should consider Motif include the following:

▶ Developers who want to develop applications using the Motif toolkit.

▶ Users who want to run applications that require the presence of the Motif libraries. Most commercial applications that use the Motif libraries either embed the necessary Motif code in the application (so it is not necessary for the user to own the license) or include a complete version of the runtime Motif libraries.

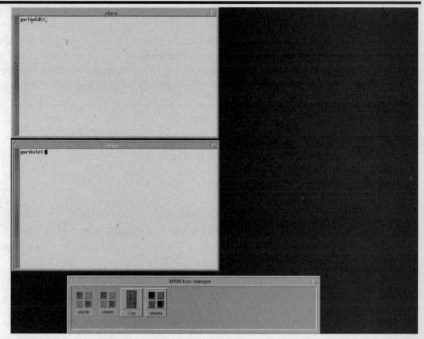

FIGURE 5.16: An MWM desktop

You can download Open Motif from the Open Group website at
http://www.opengroup.org/. Metro Link currently sells a package with
several different versions of Motif tools starting at $99.

An Alternative to Motif

Like so many things in the Linux world, efforts are under way to produce
a freely available alternative to Motif so that Linux developers and users
don't have to purchase Motif. The LessTif Project has developed a product that is compatible with Motif version 1.2 and available under the
GNU Public License.

LessTif hasn't reached full maturity yet (the version at the time of this
writing is 0.92.26), but LessTif can already be used to develop some
applications and run some software. The LessTif FAQ on the LessTif
home page (http://www.lesstif.org/) is quick to point out that Less-
Tif is still not complete. Even so, some of the applications that use Motif
can work with LessTif 0.92.26, including Mosaic 2.7 and the GNUCash
personal finance manager.

NOTE

You can download Motif for free, thus the question "Why use LessTif now that Motif is free?" The Free Software Foundation believes that the new Motif license prohibits its use on most current Linux distributions and that therefore Motif isn't really free. Thus, there is still a need for LessTif as an alternative to Motif.

WHAT'S NEXT?

This discussion of X Windows is your first step toward hands-on use of the Linux operating system.

In the next two chapters, you will master the basics of the X Windows interface using the default desktop environment for Red Hat Linux 7.1: GNOME. You will learn to install X Windows and begin to experiment with using some of the most common X Windows and GNOME applications.

Chapter 6

GNOME FOR THE FIRST TIME

When you've finished installing Linux, you're ready to start your system and take a look at GNOME. Since you'll be logging in as the root user, the operative word is "look"; you shouldn't spend much time with GNOME or perform any file management tasks until you've defined an ordinary user and logged in with your user account. You'll find out how to create an ordinary user in Chapter 7, "Setting System Configuration Essentials with GNOME." For now, take a look around—but remember, it's easy to mess up your system while you're logged in as the root user.

If you're using Linux as well as GNOME for the first time, please bear in mind that there's much more to say about how Linux works. For example, when you start your system, you'll see dozens of text-based messages fly past at high speed—too fast to read, in fact. The focus here is on GNOME, not Linux. Happily, GNOME shields you from most of the underlying complexity of Linux and, assuming all goes well, you can cheerfully ignore the technical details.

Adapted from *Mastering GNOME* by Bryan Pfaffenberger
ISBN 0-7821-2625-1   880 pages $34.99

LOGGING IN

Just what happens when Linux finishes loading depends on how your system has been set up. However, Red Hat Linux 7.1 defaults to the GNOME Display Manager (GDM), so this section first describes the GDM login process.

Logging In with the GNOME Display Manager

If you've installed Red Hat Linux 7.1, you'll see GDM on-screen after Linux finishes booting. Like the X Display Manager (XDM), GDM provides a graphical login interface for Linux users that displays your computer's hostname (see Figure 6.1).

FIGURE 6.1:   When the GNOME Display Manager starts, you'll see a dialog box similar to this one. If you're logging in for the first time, you'll use the username root and the root user's password, but you should create an ordinary user account for your personal use.

These features closely resemble XDM, the default on previous versions of Red Hat Linux, but GDM offers additional functionality, as you'll see when you click on one of the items from the menu bar above. The items on the menu bar, Session, Language, and System, enable you to choose a default language, desktop environment, window manager, or even halt or reboot the system. Just which options you'll see depends on how you installed and configured GNOME.

To log in with GDM, do the following:

1. To choose a default language, click the Language menu item and choose a language from the list. Your language choice will affect the text displayed in terminal windows, GNOME, GNOME applications, and KDE applications.

2. Move the cursor (a big X) to the Login box, until the cursor changes to an I-beam (text) cursor. Type **root**.

3. Press Enter.

4. Carefully type the password you created for the root user account.

5. Press Enter.

   Assuming that your password is accepted, you'll see GNOME start. The Panel appears, along with a Gnome Hint box, and so does the Warning dialog box shown in Figure 6.2. This message is worth taking very seriously; you shouldn't do anything of substance while you're logged in as root. A brief tour is OK, and you'll take one in this chapter—but please create an ordinary user account as Chapter 7 describes.

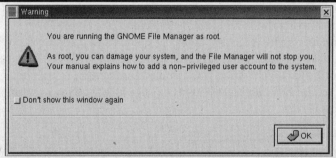

FIGURE 6.2:   This dialog box warns you that it's not safe to use your system while you're logged in as the root user. Take this message to heart, and create an ordinary user account for your own use.

6. Click OK to accept the warning.

TIP

If GDM rejects your password, and you're sure you're not making a typing mistake, check to make sure you haven't accidentally pressed the Caps Lock key. Linux usernames and passwords are case sensitive.

TIP

If you've some experience with Linux, and you know what's involved in editing configuration files, here's a neat tip. On Red Hat Linux 7.1 systems, GDM's configuration file (gdm.conf) lives in /etc/X11/gdm—and it's deliciously customizable. Just by replacing the default filenames, you can specify your own background picture and icons for GDM's display. You can even change the message shown on the login dialog box.

Additional Login Options

If you installed GNOME in some way other than installing Red Hat Linux 7.1, your system may be set up to start differently.

XDM   If your system has been set up to start with the X Display Manager, you'll see a graphical welcome screen. You'll be asked to type a username and password; supply the root username and password and click the button to log in.

Terminal mode   If your system has been set up to start without starting the X Window System, you'll see a text-only prompt asking for a username. Type **root** and press Enter. You'll next see a prompt for the root password. Type the password you created when you installed Linux and press Enter. To start the X Window System (and GNOME), type **startx** and press Enter.

WARNING

If GNOME doesn't start after you log in and start the X Window System, you need to configure X so that it starts GNOME, too. Just how you accomplish this depends on which Linux distribution you're using. In general, you place an executable configuration file in your home directory (.xinitrc or .Xclients) that contains the command exec gnome-session. The specifics depend on which version of Linux or Unix you're using.

Putting GNOME through Its Paces

After you've accepted the login warning, GNOME starts in earnest. The Panel, File Manager, and Help Browser will appear on-screen (see Figure 6.3). Let's take a closer look at how these features work. The rest of this chapter introduces topics that will give you a good taste of how GNOME works, and you'll learn some fundamental concepts that will come in handy later on.

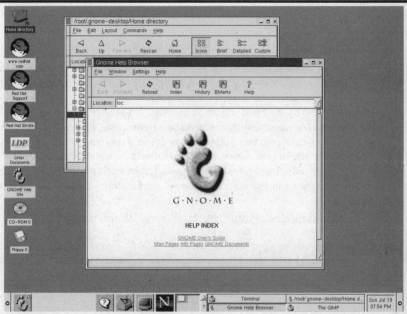

FIGURE 6.3: The default GNOME screen displays the Panel, the File Manager, and the Help Browser.

NOTE

You may have more or fewer default icons on your desktop, depending on the choices you made while installing.

DEVELOPING YOUR MOUSE TECHNIQUE

Coming to GNOME from Microsoft Windows and MacOS, you'll find much that's familiar in terms of mouse maneuvers. All the standard techniques you've learned apply. However, you'll quickly discover that GNOME does show the influence of the Unix world, a strange universe in which mice have three buttons.

TIP

You can use GNOME with a two-button mouse, but you'll appreciate the ability to emulate a three-button mouse by clicking both buttons at once. To find out whether your two-button mouse supports three-button emulation, point to the window background and press both buttons at once. You should see a pop-up menu (the last menu item should be a Help menu). Just click outside the menu to close it. If your two-button mouse doesn't have emulation, you can use a Red Hat utility to configure your mouse. Open a terminal window (see the section "Using Windows" later in this chapter), type **mouseconfig**, and press Enter. Select your mouse type. Be sure to check Emulate 3 Buttons and then click OK.

Standard mouse techniques, familiar to Windows users, are the following:

Click   Point to a screen object and click the left mouse button.

Right-click   Point to a screen object and click the right mouse button.

Double-click   Point to a screen object and click the left mouse button twice in rapid succession.

Drag   Point to a screen object, hold down the left mouse button, and move the mouse.

TIP

Keep in mind that right-clicking an object often displays a context-sensitive menu, one that shows just those options that are relevant to the object.

Here are some new techniques that you'll want to learn:

Middle-click   Point to a screen object and click the middle mouse button. If you're using a two-button mouse with three-button emulation, press both buttons at the same time.

Right-drag   Point to a screen object, hold down the right mouse button, and move the mouse.

Middle-double-click   Point to a screen object and click the middle mouse button twice in rapid succession. If you're using a two-button mouse with three-button emulation, you can try pressing both buttons at the same time, but this is quite difficult to do. Happily, this maneuver is implemented only rarely, and there's usually some other way to accomplish the action linked to middle-double-clicking.

Alt+left-click   Hold down the Alt key, point to a screen object, and click the left mouse button.

Alt+right-click   Hold down the Alt key, point to a screen object, and click the right mouse button.

Mouse-copy   Hold down the left mouse button and drag to select text.

Mouse-paste   Move the mouse pointer to the place you want the mouse-copied text to appear and click the middle mouse button to paste the copied text at the pointer's location. If you're using a two-button mouse with three-button emulation, press both buttons at the same time.

I'll use this nomenclature to refer to mouse maneuvers throughout this chapter.

TIP

Are you left-handed? You can configure a left-handed mouse using the GNOME Control Center. To do so, click the Control Center launcher; it's the toolbox icon on the Panel. In the Control Center, click Mouse in the left panel. (If you don't see this option, click the plus sign next to Peripherals.) In the Mouse buttons area, check Left Handed. Click OK to confirm your choice.

USING WINDOWS

GNOME's windows look like a cross between their counterparts in Microsoft Windows and MacOS—and for good reason: They are. GNOME's designers quite deliberately borrowed good ideas where they could find them—and as you'll see, they added many of their own.

In the upper-right corner, you'll see controls that mimic the controls found in Microsoft Windows 98/NT. The look is similar to the Macintosh, especially the horizontal ribs at the left edge of the title bar. But it's the functionality that will remind Macintosh users of their previous systems. Try double-clicking the title bar; this maneuver "rolls up" the window (like a shade) so that only the title bar is visible. To roll down the shade, just double-click the title bar again.

Understanding Window Controls and Features

Let's take a closer look at the default Red Hat Linux 7.1 GNOME/ Sawfish window controls and features, which are illustrated in Figure 6.4.

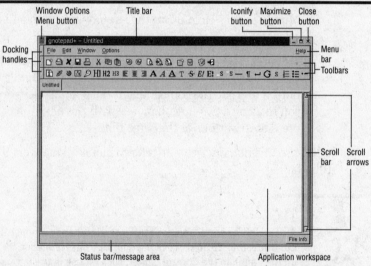

FIGURE 6.4: The default GNOME and Sawfish themes produce windows with this appearance.

Title bar This bar runs across the top of every window. When the window is in the foreground (active), the title bar is highlighted.

Window Options Menu button Located at the left edge of the title bar, this icon looks like a box with a row of horizontal lines.

If you click this icon, you'll see a menu that provides access to all window features. Chapter 7 thoroughly explores these features.

Iconify button   This button, which looks like a dash or minus sign, minimizes the window. It's located near the right edge of the title bar. After you click this icon, you can bring the window back by clicking the window's button on the Pager.

Maximize button   This button, which looks like a square, zooms the window so that it fills the current desktop area.

Close button   This button, which looks like an "X," closes the current window.

Scroll bar and scroll arrows   If the window content is larger than the window size, you'll see scroll bars. To scroll the window, click the scroll arrows or drag the scroll bar.

Docking handles   You can drag these handles to move the menu bar or toolbars to different automatic docking positions within the window. You can also drop the toolbars on the desktop.

Menu bar   On the menu bar are the commands you can use with this application. The menus are organized in a way that will feel familiar to Microsoft Windows and MacOS users.

Toolbars   Like the menu bar, application toolbars are fully dockable, both within and outside the application window.

Status bar/message area   This space is used by the application to display messages.

Application workspace   This is where you'll create and edit the data you're working with.

Essential Window Maneuvers

GNOME's windows will prove sufficiently familiar to Windows and Macintosh users that you won't have any trouble figuring out how they work. Table 6.1 provides a quick guide just in case something isn't obvious.

TIP

To see what a window feature does, move the mouse pointer over the feature and leave it there for a few seconds. You'll see a Tooltip explaining what the feature does. If you don't see the Tooltips or find that the Tooltips get in your way, you can disable them. To do so, click the Main Menu button (the one with the GNOME footprint icon), point to Programs, point to Settings, point to Desktop, and choose Window Manager. Click Run Sawfish Configuration Tool. In the Sawfish Configuration Editor's left panel, click the Miscellaneous tab. In the Tooltips ON/OFF area, check or uncheck the Enable box and click OK.

TABLE 6.1:   Basic Window Management Skills

To:	Do This:
Zoom (maximize) the window	Click the Maximize button with the left mouse button.
Restore the window to its previous size	Click the Maximize button again with the left mouse button.
Size a window	Drag a window border. If you drag one of the lower corners, you can size in two directions.
Move a window	Drag the title bar or right-drag a window border.
Iconify (minimize) a window	Click the Iconify (minimize) button.
Restore a minimized window to the screen	In the Pager, click the window's button.
Shade the window so that only the title bar is visible	Double-click the window's title bar.
Unshade the window so that the entire window is visible again	Double-click the window's title bar again.
Close a window	Click the close box.
Kill a window if the application isn't responding	Right-click the close box.

USING MENUS

GNOME's menus are organized according to the standards used in the Macintosh and Windows worlds, so you'll learn how to use them quickly.

Although all applications have their own unique menus, some of them—
such as the File, Edit, and Help menus—appear in most applications.

Displaying Menus

To display a menu, click the menu's name on the menu bar or hold down
the Alt key and press the menu name's underlined letter. You don't have
to type a capital letter. For example, Alt+F selects the File menu. The
menu appears on the screen (see Figure 6.5).

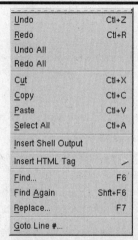

<u>U</u>ndo	Ctl+Z
<u>R</u>edo	Ctl+R
Undo All	
Redo All	
Cu<u>t</u>	Ctl+X
<u>C</u>opy	Ctl+C
<u>P</u>aste	Ctl+V
<u>S</u>elect All	Ctl+A
Insert Shell Output	
Insert HTML Tag	
<u>F</u>ind...	F6
Find <u>A</u>gain	Shft+F6
<u>R</u>eplace...	F7
<u>G</u>oto Line #...	

FIGURE 6.5:   GNOME menus list the available options. You can choose one by
clicking it, by typing its underlined letter, or by highlighting with
the arrow keys and pressing Enter.

Choosing Menu Options

Note the following ways you can choose options:

▶ On the menu, click the option. You can also type the underlined
letter or use the arrow keys and Enter.

▶ Some options have keyboard shortcuts.

▶ Some options have an arrow, which indicates that you'll see a pop-
up menu when you select the option.

Using Tear-Off Menus

If you'll be making extensive use of a menu, you can "tear it off" so that it appears in a separate, on-screen window (see Figure 6.6).

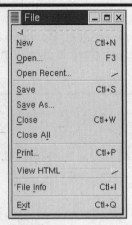

FIGURE 6.6:   A tear-off menu appears in its own separate window. To return the menu to the menu bar, click the left arrow adjacent to the tear marks.

To tear off a menu, right-click the menu tear line (the line of dashes at the top of the menu). You can also Alt+click the menu tear line. You'll see the menu in an independent window.

To restore the menu to the menu bar, click the left button next to the tear marks, or just click the window's close box.

TIP

GNOME-compliant applications can have tear-off menus, but other applications lack this feature.

Moving to the Next Window with Alt+Tab

Microsoft Windows users will feel at home with the Alt+Tab keyboard shortcut, which enables you to display and activate the next window available in the current desktop area. If you press Alt+Tab again, you go back to the previous window.

If you keep pressing Alt+Tab, you'll eventually activate all the open windows in the current area. Note that Alt+Tab doesn't open minimized windows, nor does it open windows on other desktop areas.

USING THE MAIN MENU

GNOME's Main Menu button—the one with the four-toed footprint—provides access to your system's preinstalled applications and utilities. In addition, you can use the Menu Editor to add your own programs to the menu.

Navigating the Main Menu

To display the Main Menu, click the Main Menu button. Options that display submenus are shown with a right arrow (see Figure 6.7).

FIGURE 6.7:   The Main Menu provides access to preinstalled applications and utilities and automatically shows the new ones you'll install. There's also room for your own additions under Favorites.

Just what you'll see depends on the components installed on your system. With a complete Red Hat Linux 7.1 installation, the Main Menu is organized into the following areas:

Program menus   These menus aren't editable; they're automatically generated by system processes. When you install new GNOME-compliant programs, they're automatically added to the appropriate category within the System menus.

Favorites menu   You can use the Menu Editor to add programs here for quick access. Such additions can include X applications that aren't automatically added to the System menus.

Applet menus   The Applets submenu contains the applets installed on your system that can be added to the Panel. Selecting one of these will automatically add it to the Panel.

KDE menus   This option appears only if you installed KDE along with GNOME, as described in Chapter 8, "KDE, Office Applications, and Running Windows Applications in Linux."

Run   This function allows you to quick-run an application if you know the command or command line you'd like to run.

Panel   This option provides access to a number of Panel customization options.

Lock screen   Click this option to start a screensaver. You'll have to type your password to display the screen again.

Log out   Click here to end your GNOME session.

Exploring Default Applications

The version of GNOME distributed with Red Hat Linux 7.1 comes with a variety of GNOME and non-GNOME applications preinstalled.

Here's a quick overview of some of the applications you'll most likely find within the Programs menus:

About Myself (System)   Enables you to specify user information about yourself.

Address Book (Applications)   Allows you to keep contact information.

Audio Mixer (Multimedia)   Enables you to mix sound input from a variety of sources.

Calendar (Applications)   Enables you to schedule appointments and set alarms.

CD Player (Multimedia)   A nifty audio CD player that can automatically access Internet databases of CD information, which enables the player to display the artist's name, CD title, and the title and timing of each track.

Change Password (System)   Enables you to change your password.

Color XTerm (System)   A color version of the popular XTerm terminal emulator program.

Control Center (Settings)   Displays the Red Hat Control Center, which enables you to choose run-level settings, set the system time and date, configure a printer, specify network settings, configure a modem, configure the Linux kernel, search for help information, and launch the Linuxconf configuration utility.

Dia   A diagramming utility that can be used to make flowcharts, network diagrams, and the like.

Disk Management (System)   A utility for mounting, unmounting, and formatting disks.

Electric Eyes (Graphics)   A graphics viewer.

ESD Volume Meter (Multimedia)   Enables you to control system sound output volume.

eXtace Waveform Display (Multimedia)   Displays a graphic rendition of system sound output.

File Manager (Programs)   The GNOME file manager.

Font Selector (Utilities)   Enables you to view the fonts currently available from the X Window System.

GAIM (Internet)   An instant messenger client that supports many different instant messaging formats.

gDict (Utilities)   A dictionary application for obtaining definitions and spelling assistance.

gEdit (Applications)   An easy-to-use text editor that's useful for system-configuration purposes.

gftp (Internet)   A utility for downloading and uploading data from Internet FTP sites.

GIMP (Graphics)   A full-featured photo and graphics manipulation program, compared by many to Adobe Photoshop.

GNOME Color Browser (Utilities)   Displays the colors currently available on the X Window System palette.

GNOME Search Tool (Utilities)   Provides a sophisticated utility for finding files on your system.

GNOME terminal (System)   The GNOME terminal emulation program.

GnoRPM (System)   A utility for installing Red Hat Package Manager (RPM) programs, including Internet search and download programs.

gNumeric spreadsheet (Applications)   A Microsoft Excel–compatible spreadsheet program.

gPhoto   A digital camera application.

GQView (Graphics)   A graphics-viewing program.

Help system (Programs)   The GNOME Help Browser.

Imlib configuration editor (Settings)   Enables you to specify configuration settings for Imlib, the library that provides GNOME with color support.

Linuxconf (System)   The GNOME version of the popular Linuxconf system configuration utility.

Netscape Communicator (Internet)   The full version of the respected web browser package, including e-mail and news-group capabilities.

Pan (Internet)   A Usenet newsreader application that supports posting, multiple servers, binary downloads, and more.

Printer Configuration (System)   Tool to assist with setting up a printer.

Regular XTerm (System)   A monochrome version of the XTerm terminal emulation program.

Simple calculator (Utilities)   A not-so-simple calculator that includes a variety of functions.

System info (System)   Displays information about your system, including the kernel version, operating system version, hostname, disk usage, memory information, and CPU information.

System monitor (System)   Displays running processes (programs) and enables you to terminate them, if necessary.

Text file viewer (Utilities)   A simple viewer for text files.

Time-tracking tool (Applications)   Enables you to keep track of the time you spend on a project.

TimeTool (System)   A utility for setting the system time and date.

Vim   A version of the popular editor vi.

X-CD-Roast An application to copy or burn CDs.

xChat IRC client (Internet) A full-featured client for Internet Relay Chat (IRC).

USING THE PANEL

The Panel is GNOME's answer to the Windows Taskbar, and it offers much of the same functionality. Still, the Panel has a personality all its own, and it's almost infinitely customizable. For example, you can choose background colors and graphics for the Panel, and you can add nifty little utilities called *applets*. Some applets are incredibly useful, such as the free disk space monitor, and others are close to pointless. (My favorite in this category is Wanda the Fish, who gives you a fortune when you click her.)

Hide Buttons and Auto Hide

You'll find Hide buttons at either end of the Panel (see Figure 6.8). Click a Hide button to collapse the Panel into the arrow's corner; what's left is nothing but the Hide button from the other side, which you can click to bring the Panel back on-screen.

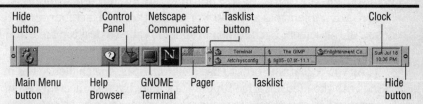

FIGURE 6.8: The default Panel in Red Hat Linux 6.0 installations includes these features.

TIP

By default, GNOME applications are designed to maximize so that they do not obscure the Panel, but this isn't true of non-GNOME applications. If you're using a non-GNOME application, you may need to hide the Panel so you can work with such an application's maximized window.

If you find that the Panel gets in your way too often, try the Auto Hide feature. This feature hides the Panel until you move the mouse pointer to the window edge where the Panel is positioned. To turn on Auto Hide, right-click the Panel background and choose the Panel menu, point to Properties, point to Hiding Policy, and then click on Auto Hide.

Application Launchers

On the Panel, you'll find several application launchers; the version of GNOME distributed with Red Hat Linux 7.1 has launchers for the GNOME Help Browser, the GNOME Control Center, GNOME Terminal, and Netscape Communicator. To launch one of these utilities, just click its launcher button.

You can create your own application launchers. However, application launchers use rather large icons, and you can quickly fill up the available Panel space with these icons. For that reason, you may prefer to use Quick-Launch, a Panel applet that enables you to create much smaller application launcher buttons (much like the small launcher buttons on the Windows Taskbar).

The Pager and Desktop Areas

As you explore GNOME, you'll discover a feature that's completely new to you: desktop areas. By default (in Red Hat Linux 7 distributions), GNOME implements a virtual workspace that is in fact four times the size of the screen. Each screen of space is called a desktop area, and there are four of them: two rows of two areas each.

As you're learning how to use desktop areas, one challenge lies in coping with the mouse's edge-flipping, a somewhat disconcerting event that occurs when you move the mouse pointer close to the screen's edge. If the mouse touches the edge, the screen "flips" to the adjacent desktop area. Often, the flip occurs when you don't want it—for example, when you're trying to click a scroll arrow in a maximized window.

Another challenge presented by desktop areas is figuring out which desktop area you're viewing. That's where the Pager comes in. (In more recent versions of GNOME, the Pager is called the Desk Guide.) Providing a visual representation of the workspace created by desktop areas, the Pager highlights the current desktop area. What's more, the Pager gives you a way to navigate among desktop areas: Just click one of the areas within the Pager to move to that area.

The Tasklist and Task Button

To the right of the Pager is the task button, which has an arrow and a question mark. If you click the arrow, you'll see a list of all the applications in the current desktop area. The question mark button opens the Pager and Tasklist customization options.

Next to the task button is the Tasklist. By default, the Tasklist shows buttons for all the applications running in the current desktop area (but not other desktop areas). Icons on the buttons indicate whether the application is minimized (a larger icon), open but inactive (a smaller icon), or active (a smaller icon with a sunburst).

Panel Applets

To the Panel, you can add applets, mini-applications that perform a variety of useful tasks—and some diverting ones.

The default Panel already contains applets. The Main Menu is actually an applet; you can use additional copies of this applet to create additional menus. The clock at the extreme right of the Panel is also an applet.

GNOME comes with a selection of available applets, which fall into the following categories:

Amusements   This category includes games, cute tricks, and the marvelous Wanda the Fish.

Clocks   A collection of clocks to choose from to display the time.

Monitors   Included are several system monitors, including Battery Charge Monitor for notebooks, CPU load meters, and memory load meters.

Multimedia   Multimedia applets include a mini-CD player and sound control.

Network   Network applets available are an e-mail checker, a modem light utility, an Internet dialer, and a web launcher.

Utility   This category includes a number of alternative clocks, a drive mount utility, and the QuickLaunch applet.

Accessing Disk Drives

When you're using Linux with the command-line (text-only) or X interface, accessing disk drives is a two-step process: You must first mount the drive, and only then can you browse the drive's contents. When you mount a drive, Linux adds the drive's contents to the filesystem at a specified point. Most Linux distributions install the floppy drive so that it mounts to /mnt/floppy, while the CD-ROM is mounted at /mnt/cdrom.

GNOME simplifies disk drive access by enabling a one-step procedure: To access a disk drive, even if it isn't mounted, place a disk in the drive and double-click the disk drive icon. When GNOME starts, it automatically scans your system for mountable drives and creates disk drive icons for the desktop.

WARNING

In Chapter 7, you'll create an ordinary user account for your day-to-day work. However, you won't be able to access disk drives from this account until you modify your system, as that chapter explains.

If you would like to remove the disk from the drive, you must first unmount it. Follow these instructions to unmount a drive:

1. Close all the windows that are showing the drive's contents, including File Manager windows.

2. If you've opened a file on the disk, close the file.

3. Right-click the disk drive icon. A pop-up menu appears.

4. Choose Unmount Device.

Once you've unmounted a CD-ROM disk, you can eject it. To do so, right-click the disk drive icon and choose Eject Device from the pop-up menu.

Exploring GNOME Configuration Options

To configure GNOME, you use the Control Center. This section introduces the Control Center; you'll learn more about the specifics in subsequent chapters.

Accessing the Control Center

To access the Control Center, shown in Figure 6.9, click the Control Center application launcher on the Panel (it's the one with the toolbox icon). You can also click the Main Menu button, point to Programs, point to Settings, and choose GNOME Control Center. Individual pages within the Control Center are also accessible from the Settings submenu of the Programs menu.

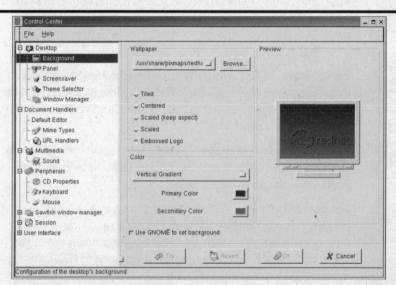

FIGURE 6.9:   The Control Center enables you to choose configuration options for GNOME.

Navigating the Control Center

You navigate the Control Center by clicking options in the left panel. If options are hidden, you'll see a plus sign next to the option's name. Display the hidden options by clicking the plus sign.

Exploring Control Center Capplets

Control Center options are called *capplets* (short for *control applets*). They enable you to configure the following:

> **Desktop**   The Desktop capplets include Background (background colors and images), Screensaver, Theme Selector, and Window Manager.

Document Handlers   This capplet enables you to choose a default text editor as well as enabling you to specify which program handles the various types of Internet data. It also provides a way to associate file data types with the applications installed on your system.

Multimedia   The capplets in this category include Keyboard Bell (which enables you to customize the default keyboard error tone) and Sound (which enables you to assign sound to system and application events). To hear sound with GNOME, you'll need to configure sound on your system, as explained in the next chapter.

Peripherals   The Keyboard capplet enables you to specify auto-repeat and click settings. With the Mouse capplet, you can select left- or right-handed mouse layouts, and you can specify mouse motion speed.

Sawfish Window Manager   This caplet allows you to specify the appearance or look-and-feel of Red Hat's default Sawfish Window Manager.

Session Manager   This capplet enables you to configure session-management options. You can also add non-session-managed programs so that they start automatically when you log in to GNOME. In the more recent versions of GNOME, this option is called Startup Programs.

User Interface   This capplet enables you to choose options for menus, status bars, toolbars, dialog boxes, and GNOME's Multiple Document Interface (MDI), which enables you to tab between multiple open documents in MDI-compatible applications. For example, you can turn off toolbar docking, if you wish.

LOGGING OUT AND SHUTTING DOWN

This section will explain how to log out of your root user account and shut down your system.

WARNING
Never quit Linux by skipping the shutdown procedure and shutting down the power. You may scramble the data on your hard drive.

To log out, do the following:

1. Click the GNOME Main Menu button and choose Log Out. You'll see an alert box with the message, "Really log out?"

   When you are logged in as the root user, you can choose any of the following from this alert box:

   Logout   Choose this option to log out of the root user account. You'll see the Welcome screen again, which enables you to log in using your new user account.

   Halt   Choose this option to shut down your Linux system.

   Reboot   Choose this option to restart your Linux system.

   Note that this alert box also contains an option that enables you to save your system settings, including GNOME applications you've left open. Activate this option if you would like to save your settings.

2. Click Halt and then click Yes. GNOME exits, and you'll see messages from Linux as the system shuts down. If your computer's BIOS supports automatic shutdown, your computer will turn off automatically. Switch off the power manually if automatic shutdown does not occur, but be sure you see the message, "Power down."

WHAT'S NEXT?

In this chapter, you've learned the fundamentals of GNOME. I'm sure you're eager to try out some applications, but before you do, you need to perform a few system configuration tweaks, discussed in the next chapter. These changes will enable you to use GNOME safely, and they'll help you avoid a great deal of frustration.

Part ii

Chapter 7

SETTING SYSTEM CONFIGURATION ESSENTIALS WITH GNOME

You've installed GNOME successfully, and you've already taken an in-depth look at the GNOME interface, but you're not yet ready to work with GNOME. You need to set up an ordinary user account so that you can work with GNOME without fear of damaging your system. Also, you need to enable user access to disk drives.

As your knowledge of GNOME and Linux grows, you'll occasionally need to perform system configuration tasks by editing configuration files. Since you'll need to learn how to use a text editor to perform this task, this chapter shows you how to configure and use a default text editor, gEdit—a GNOME text editor that's very easy to use. In case you're having trouble with your X server, you'll get a chance to test your new text-editing skills by fixing some common problems in the X configuration files.

Adapted from *Mastering GNOME*
by Bryan Pfaffenberger

ISBN 0-7821-2625-1   880 pages $34.99

This chapter walks you through the steps you need to take to configure your system for GNOME. At the end of this chapter, you'll be working safely with your user account, you won't have trouble accessing your disk drives, and your screen will have the color depth that you want.

INTRODUCING LINUXCONF

GNOME contains a version of the popular Linuxconf utility for system administration. Linuxconf provides a menu-based system for performing critical system configuration tasks such as creating user accounts, defining network settings, and controlling access to disk drives. What's especially neat about Linuxconf and Linux in general is the system's capability to restart the services you reconfigure. Thanks to this feature, you don't have to reboot your system after you've reconfigured your system.

TIP

You need to be logged in as the root user in order to use Linuxconf.

To start and explore Linuxconf, do the following:

1. Choose Main Menu ➢ Programs ➢ System ➢ Linuxconf.

2. The first time you run Linuxconf, you'll see the Introduction page. Just click Quit to close this window. The main Linuxconf window appears (see Figure 7.1).

WARNING

Don't make any changes within Linuxconf other than the ones you're told to perform in this chapter! Linuxconf is a powerful application; if you make changes without knowing what you're doing, you could ruin your system configuration.

Take a moment to examine the Linuxconf interface. As you can see, the left panel enables you to browse for configuration options. They're grouped according to category, such as Networking. If options are hidden under a category, you see a plus sign next to the category's name. To show the options, click the plus sign.

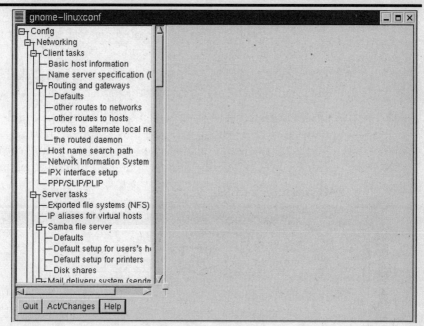

FIGURE 7.1: Linuxconf is a GNOME version of a popular system administration utility. To change system settings, select a setting in the left panel.

You'll use Linuxconf to create a user account for yourself. You'll also use Linuxconf to grant user access to disk drives. Both of these procedures are discussed in the following sections, so keep Linuxconf on-screen.

CREATING AN ORDINARY USER ACCOUNT

As you've learned, it's unwise to perform day-to-day work with Linux when you're logged in as the root user. You need to create an ordinary user account for yourself, even if you're the only person who will ever use the system.

When you create an account for yourself, you'll specify a username and password for the account. You'll also create your home directory.

To create a user account for yourself, follow these steps:

1. Start Linuxconf, if necessary. To do so, choose Main Menu ➢ Programs ➢ System ➢ Linuxconf.

2. In the left panel, scroll down to User Accounts and click the plus sign, if necessary, to display the hidden options.

3. Under Normal, select User Accounts. If the subtopics under Normal are not visible, click the plus sign next to Normal. You'll see the list of default user accounts, including root (see Figure 7.2). The other user accounts are built-in accounts that are used to configure your system.

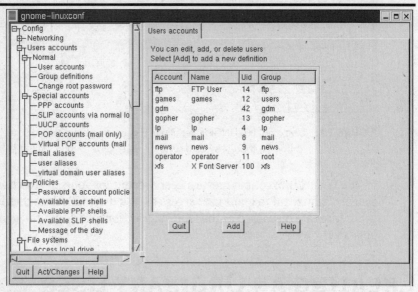

FIGURE 7.2: The User Accounts page shows a number of predefined users. Ignore these and add a new user account for your own use.

4. Click Add. You'll see the Add page, shown in Figure 7.3.

5. In the Login Name text box, type the login name that you want to use. You can use your first name, if you want.

6. In the Full Name area, type your full name. This is optional.

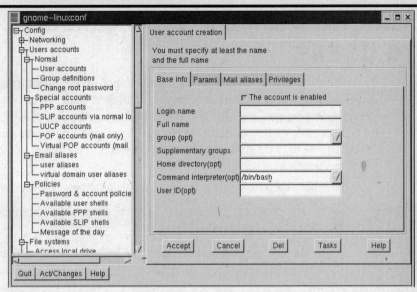

FIGURE 7.3: You can skip most of these options. The ones that are important are Login Name and Home Directory.

7. Important: In the Home Directory text box, type **/home** followed by a forward slash and your login name (the one you just typed in the Login Name text box). If you choose the login name suzanne, you would type **/home/suzanne**.

8. Click Accept. You'll see the Changing Password page.

9. In the New UNIX Password box, type the password you want to use and click Accept. If your password breaks any of several rules concerning password quality, you'll be notified that you've supplied a bad password. Linuxconf doesn't stop you from creating the password, but you should consider changing it to one that meets basic security standards.

10. Type the password again and click Accept. If you typed it incorrectly, you'll need to repeat steps 9 and 10.

11. Click Dismiss in the User Accounts area.

12. In the main Linuxconf window, click File ➢ Accept Changes.

13. Click File ➢ Quit.

Part ii

Making Disk Drives Accessible to Users

By default, Linux doesn't enable ordinary users to access disk drives. Although this seems ridiculous to people coming to Linux from consumer operating systems, this restriction makes a great deal of sense for multiuser operating systems. In such systems, one user could cause others to lose data if a disk drive were unmounted in the midst of a data transfer operation.

Follow these steps to give users access to disk drives:

1. Start Linuxconf, if necessary. To do so, choose Main Menu ➤ Programs ➤ System ➤ Linuxconf.

2. In the left panel, scroll down to File Systems. If the options are hidden, click the plus sign.

3. Click Access Local Drive. You'll see the Local Volume screen, illustrated in Figure 7.4. This screen displays the current settings for all the partitions and disk drives on your system. Depending on how your system was set up, you'll see somewhat different settings on your screen.

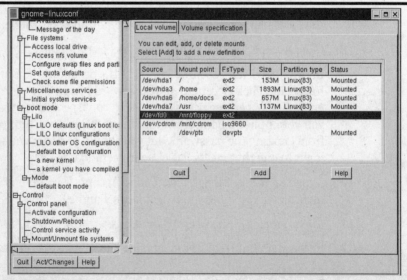

FIGURE 7.4: The Local Volume screen shows the current settings for all the partitions and drives available on your system.

4. In the Source column, locate /dev/fd0. This is your floppy drive (called drive A in Windows). If you have two floppy drives, the second one (drive B) will be called /dev/fd1.

5. Click /dev/fd0. You'll see the Volume Specification screen for this drive, shown in Figure 7.5.

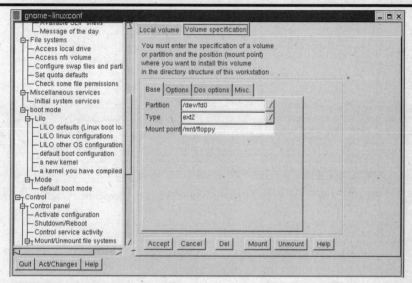

FIGURE 7.5: The Volume Specification screen shows the base specifications for a specific drive or partition.

TIP

If you would like to configure your floppy disk drive so that you can access MS-DOS disks, click the arrow next to the Type box and choose msdos from the drop-down menu.

6. Click Options. You'll see the options available for this drive, shown in Figure 7.6.

7. Check User Mountable. Leave the other options untouched.

8. Click Accept.

9. If your system has a second floppy drive, repeat steps 4 through 8 for /dev/fd1.

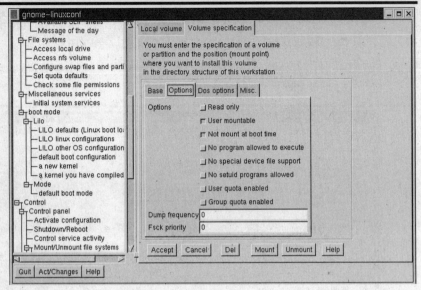

FIGURE 7.6: This page shows the options you can choose for the selected drive or partition.

10.   To give users access to your CD-ROM drive, repeat steps 4 through 8 for /dev/cdrom.

11.   When you are finished activating the User Mountable option for your disk drives, click the Dismiss button on the Local Volume screen.

12.   Click Dismiss. Your changes will be automatically activated.

ACCESSING YOUR WINDOWS PARTITION

If you created a two-OS installation that includes Microsoft Windows, as Chapter 3, "Special Installations," describes, you can access the data in your Windows partition. However, you can't run Windows programs.

To access the data on your Windows partition, do the following:

1.   Start Linuxconf, if necessary. To do so, choose Main Menu ➢ Programs ➢ System ➢ Linuxconf.

2. In the left panel, scroll down to File Systems. If the options are hidden, click the plus sign.

3. Click Access Local Drive. You'll see the Local Volume page.

4. In the Source column, locate the partition that has the VFAT (Windows) file system. This is probably /dev/hda1, but this location could vary, depending on how your system is set up.

5. Click the partition that contains your Windows data. You'll see the Volume Specification screen.

6. In the Mount Point area, type **/mnt/windows**.

7. Click Options.

8. Check User Mountable so you can access your Windows data from your user account.

9. Click Accept.

10. Click Dismiss.

11. Click File ➤ Act/Changes.

When you exit Linuxconf, right-click the desktop background and choose Recreate Desktop Shortcuts. You'll see a new hard disk icon on the desktop. You can double-click this icon to access your Windows data.

SELECTING AND USING A TEXT EDITOR

One of the cornerstones of the Unix philosophy lies in the preferred means of specifying configuration information: Everything should be stored in simple text files, which anyone can edit. As a result, you'll soon find that you'll need to make changes to such files in order to get your system working correctly. Remember, though, that you should do so only under an expert's direction. In this chapter, I'll instruct you to make such changes now and then, but please don't experiment with changes of your own until you know what you're doing.

In this section, you'll get started with a default text editor. It's an appropriate thing to do while you're still logged in as the root user. Most configuration files are stored in directories that aren't accessible from user accounts. In order to edit these files, you'll need to exit your user account and log in as the root user.

Choosing a Default Text Editor

Your first step is to choose a default text editor. By default, GNOME uses Emacs, a complex, difficult utility that's little loved by Linux beginners. You're well advised to configure GNOME so that it works with a friendlier text editor that's actually installed on your system. The only game in town is gEdit, a GNOME text editor that's exceptionally easy to use. In this section, you'll learn how to make gEdit your default text editor. To choose a default editor, you use the GNOME Control Center.

NOTE

You're still logged on as the root user, so bear in mind that the configuration choice you're about to make will affect GNOME only when you're logged in as the root user. After you log out and log in using your ordinary user account, make the same change there so that you can use gEdit to edit files within your home directory.

To choose a default text editor:

1. Choose Main Menu ➢ Programs ➢ Settings ➢ Document Handlers ➢ Default Editor. You'll see the GNOME Control Center, with the Gnome Edit Properties page displayed (see Figure 7.7).

2. Click the arrow next to the Gnome Editor text box and choose gEdit.

3. Click OK.

As you'll quickly discover, gEdit is almost ridiculously easy to use. Take a moment to explore gEdit's basic features. It has some nifty capabilities, including a spell-checker, printing, a simple encryption utility, and the capability to split the screen so that you can view two parts of a document simultaneously. This section explores the basics of using gEdit for editing configuration files.

NOTE

In keeping with the GNOME application design philosophy, gEdit is designed to work with plug-ins, external programs that work with gEdit and extend its capabilities. You'll find many plug-ins already installed; they're accessible from gEdit's Plug-ins menu.

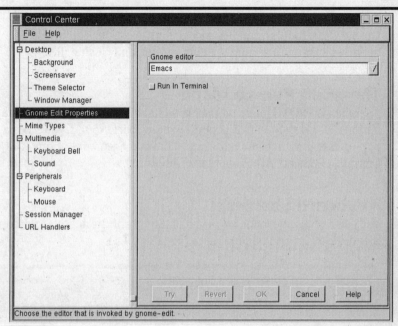

FIGURE 7.7:   In this Control Center page, you can choose a default text editor.

Starting gEdit

To start gEdit, choose Main Menu ➢ Programs ➢ Applications ➢ gEdit.

TIP

Since you'll often use gEdit when you're running your system in root user mode, why not drag gEdit to the desktop? Click the Main Menu button, point to Programs, point to Applications, and drag the gEdit icon to the desktop. As you drag, you'll see that the mouse pointer changes shape to indicate that you're "carrying" an icon. When you've positioned the mouse pointer where you want the icon to appear, release the mouse button. You may now start gEdit by double-clicking the desktop icon.

Exploring the gEdit Window

A fully compliant GNOME application, gEdit has all the goodies discussed in Chapter 6, "GNOME for the First Time," including tear-off menus, dockable toolbars, and keyboard shortcuts. It has some special features too, which are discussed in this section.

The gEdit Toolbar

On the gEdit toolbar, you'll see icons for the actions you'll most frequently perform, including opening, saving, and closing files.

The gEdit Pop-up Menu

As in most GNOME applications, you can right-click to see available options. If you right-click the gEdit window background, you'll see a pop-up menu with useful editing and file management options (Cut, Copy, Paste, Select All, Save, Close, and Print).

Keyboard Shortcuts

You can also use keyboard shortcuts for many of the actions found in the menus, toolbar, and pop-up menu (see Table 7.1).

TABLE 7.1: gEdit Keyboard Shortcuts

TO:	USE THIS KEYBOARD SHORTCUT:
Open a file	F3
Save a file	Ctrl+S
Close a file	Ctrl+W
Quit gEdit	Ctrl+Q
Cut text to the Clipboard	Ctrl+X
Copy text to the Clipboard	Ctrl+C
Paste text from the Clipboard	Ctrl+V
Find text	F6
Find again, with the same settings	Shift+F6
Replace text	F7

Document Tabs

A nifty gEdit feature is the Document Tabs area (see Figure 7.8), which enables you to switch among the documents you're editing. Figure 7.8 shows how gEdit looks with three documents loaded. To switch to a different document, just click its tab.

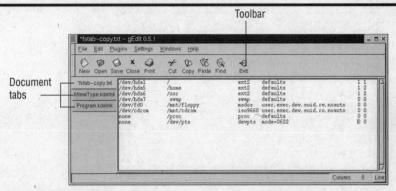

FIGURE 7.8:   gEdit is the ideal tool for editing configuration files.

If you wish, you can position the Document Tabs area at the top, right, or bottom of the screen. To move the Document Tabs area, click Settings, point to Preferences, point to the Documents tab, and choose a position with the Notebook Tab Position drop-down menu. You can also hide them, if you wish. To hide the Document Tabs area, click Settings, point to Preferences, point to the Documents tab, and select Modal from the Mode drop-down menu.

Document Display Options

Often used to edit configuration files, text editors have special features that aren't commonly found in word processing programs. You'll find the following options in the Preferences menu under the Settings menu:

Enable Auto-indent   Check this option to line up text in columns automatically.

Enable Wordwrap   Check this option so that when you're typing, lengthy lines wrap down to the next line instead of going beyond the right edge of the window.

By default, gEdit is set up to work with Wordwrap enabled. If you size the window so that some lengthy lines are hidden, gEdit will wrap them to the next line. You'll see twisty arrows showing where the wrap occurred (see Figure 7.9).

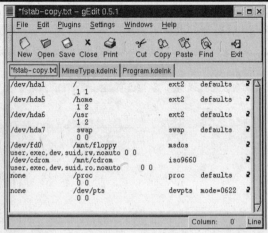

FIGURE 7.9: The twisty arrows show where gEdit wraps lengthy lines so that they remain visible.

If you uncheck Enable Wordwrap, you may not be able to see lengthy lines in their entirety. To indicate that part of a line is hidden, gEdit uses arrows pointing to the right (see Figure 7.10).

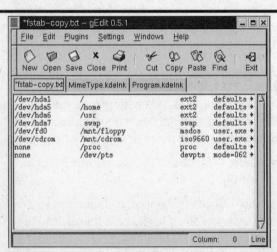

FIGURE 7.10: The arrows indicate that parts of the line are hidden by the window's right border. To see the whole line, enlarge the window or enable Wordwrap and Linewrap.

You should work with gEdit so that all the lines are in view without wrapping, if possible. The files look neater and there's less chance of misreading the text or making an editing error.

To bring all the lines into view, drag the right window border until all the arrows disappear or click the window background.

Searching for Text

If you need to make a change in a lengthy file, you'll find gEdit's search capabilities helpful.

To search for text, follow these steps:

1. Do one of the following:

   ▶ Press F6.

   ▶ Click Edit on the menu bar and click Find.

   ▶ Click Find on the toolbar.

   The Search dialog box, illustrated in Figure 7.11, appears.

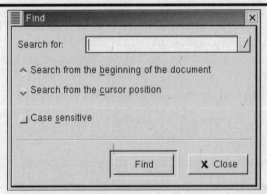

FIGURE 7.11: Save wear and tear on your eyes; let gEdit search a document for matching text.

2. In the Search text box, type the text you want to match.

3. Choose one of the following options:

   Search from the Beginning of the Document This is the default and best option for most searches. It ensures that gEdit will search all of the text.

Search from the Cursor Position This search proceeds from the cursor's current position. If the text occurs above the cursor, you won't find it.

4. To match the capitalization you typed, check Case Sensitive.

5. Click Find to begin the search.

If gEdit finds a match, the program highlights the matching text in the main gEdit window, and the Search dialog box stays on-screen. To search again, click Find Next. When no more matches are found, the Search dialog box closes and an Information box will pop up saying Text Not Found.

TIP

Once you've performed a search, you can search again with the same settings without having to open the Search dialog box. To do so, click Edit on the menu bar and click Find Again. You can also press Shift+F6.

Replacing Text throughout a File

Like a word processing program, gEdit's search and replace capabilities can find text throughout a file and replace that text with substitute text. However, it isn't a good idea to use search and replace on configuration files. The utility may make unanticipated changes that could lead to configuration errors.

To search and replace text throughout a file, follow these steps:

1. Click Edit on the menu bar and click Replace or Press F7. You'll see the Replace dialog box, shown in Figure 7.12.

2. In the Search for box, type the text you want to match.

3. Choose one of the following options:

Search from the Beginning of the Document This is the default and best option for most searches. It ensures that gEdit will search all of the text.

Search from the Cursor Position This search proceeds from the cursor's current position. If the text occurs above the cursor, you won't find it.

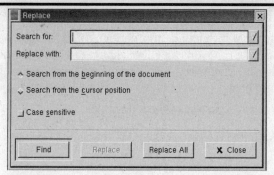

FIGURE 7.12: Although gEdit can search and replace text throughout a file, you shouldn't use this option on configuration files.

4. To match the capitalization you typed, check Case Sensitive.

5. In the Replace With text box, type the text you want to substitute.

6. Click OK to begin searching and replacing.

If gEdit finds a match, the Find button will change to Find Next and the Replace button will become available, as shown in Figure 7.13. Click Replace to make the change or Find Next to skip this instance. Click Cancel to stop searching. When gEdit finds no more matches, the Search and Replace dialog box closes, and an Information box pops up telling you Text Not Found.

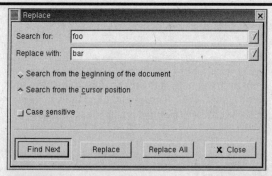

FIGURE 7.13: Don't click Replace unless you're positive you want to make the change.

Saving Your Changes

When you've finished making changes to a configuration file, you need to save the changes. Note that you can't save changes to configuration files unless you're logged in as the root user; you can't save changes to any file that you don't own.

To save changes to a file, do one of the following:

▶ Click Save on the toolbar.

▶ Click Ctrl+S.

▶ Click File on the menu bar and click Save.

▶ Right-click the window background and choose Save from the pop-up menu.

REPAIRING YOUR X CONFIGURATION

If all went well with your Linux installation, X is configured to your liking. Unfortunately, it's all too commonly the case that things don't go well. With Red Hat Linux 7.1, you may be in for trouble if the X probe utility couldn't detect your video card properly. If you had to select video settings manually, you may not be happy with the results you're seeing. Specifically, you may be looking at an 8-bit (256-color) default color depth, which will make images look terrible. In addition, X may have configured your system so that the desktop area is larger than the screen, forcing you to scroll to bring the Panel into view. The following sections show you how to cure these problems.

TIP

To solve these problems, you'll need to edit configuration files while you're logged in as the root user. If you haven't already done so, please read the preceding section, entitled "Selecting and Using a Text Editor."

Increasing Color Depth

The Linux newsgroups are full of messages from people complaining about Linux's lousy on-screen appearance. They've got sophisticated video adapters and expensive monitors, but they're looking at 8-bit (256-color) video.

Here's the reason: XFree86, the version of the X Window System that works with Linux, defaults to an 8-bit color depth when the installation utility (Xconfigurator) fails in its attempt to probe your video adapter's capabilities. This is actually a good thing. If XFree86 defaulted to a higher color depth, it could actually harm or ruin some older monitors that lack protection circuitry. Chances are, though, that you're working with a monitor that can easily handle millions of colors at high resolution, such as 1280×1024.

To solve this problem on GNOME systems, you can make a simple modification to the configuration file used by the GNOME Display Manager (gdm), the graphical utility that springs into action when your system starts. This utility starts X. By making a very simple addition to gdm's configuration file, you can start X with a command option that forces the color depth you want.

WARNING

Do not follow these instructions unless you know that your video adapter and monitor are capable of displaying greater color depths and higher resolution. In general, if you have a recent multisync monitor and a video adapter with at least 4MB of video memory, you should be able to display 16-bit color.

To increase the color depth, do the following:

1. If necessary, log in as root user.

2. Choose Main Menu ➣ Programs ➣ Applications ➣ gEdit. You'll see gEdit on-screen.

3. Do one of the following:

    ▶ Click F3.

    ▶ On the toolbar, click the Open icon.

    ▶ Click File on the menu bar and click Open.

    You'll see the Open File dialog box, shown in Figure 7.14.

4. You need to navigate to the directory where gdm's configuration file, gdm.conf, is stored. On Red Hat Linux 7.1 systems, gdm.conf is stored in /etc/X11/gdm.

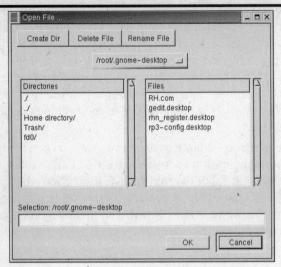

FIGURE 7.14: To browse to a different directory, you can use the Directory Browser. To view the next directory up, double-click the parent directory symbol (..).

To navigate to /etc/X11/gdm, do one of the following:

▸ Use the Directory Browser to go to the top-level directory (/), and use the Directories window to open /etc, then /etc/X11 and /etc/X11/gdm.

▸ In the Selection box, type **/etc/X11/gdm/** and press Enter.

5. When you've located the directory that contains gdm.conf, select the file in the Files window and click OK. (You can also open the file by double-clicking the file's name.) The file appears in gEdit's window (see Figure 7.15).

6. Scroll down and locate the [servers] area. You'll see a line that looks like the following:

```
0=/usr/bin/X11/X
```

This is the command that starts the X server.

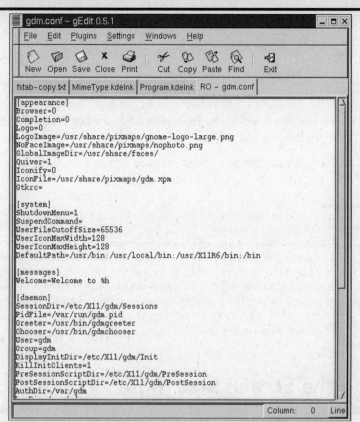

```
[appearance]
Browser=0
Completion=0
Logo=0
LogoImage=/usr/share/pixmaps/gnome-logo-large.png
NoFaceImage=/usr/share/pixmaps/nophoto.png
GlobalImageDir=/usr/share/faces/
Quiver=1
Iconify=0
IconFile=/usr/share/pixmaps/gdm.xpm
Gtkrc=

[system]
ShutdownMenu=1
SuspendCommand=
UserFileCutoffSize=65536
UserIconMaxWidth=128
UserIconMaxHeight=128
DefaultPath=/usr/bin:/usr/local/bin:/usr/X11R6/bin:/bin

[messages]
Welcome=Welcome to %h

[daemon]
SessionDir=/etc/X11/gdm/Sessions
PidFile=/var/run/gdm.pid
Greeter=/usr/bin/gdmgreeter
Chooser=/usr/bin/gdmchooser
User=gdm
Group=gdm
DisplayInitDir=/etc/X11/gdm/Init
KillInitClients=1
PreSessionScriptDir=/etc/X11/gdm/PreSession
PostSessionScriptDir=/etc/X11/gdm/PostSession
AuthDir=/var/gdm
```

FIGURE 7.15: The GNOME Display Manager configuration file, `gdm.conf`, is neatly organized into sections. Don't make any changes other than those discussed in this section.

7. To force the X server to start at a color depth greater than 8 bits, you need to add one of the following options to this command:

-bpp 16   Thousands of colors

-bpp 24   Millions of colors

-bpp 32   Millions of colors (high resolution)

Important: Try the 16-bit setting first. Do not try the higher settings unless you are absolutely certain your video adapter and monitor are capable of them.

8. To add the option, carefully position the cursor after the X, press the spacebar, and type **–bpp 16**. Note that there's a space between –bpp and 16.

9. On the toolbar, click Save.

10. On the toolbar, click Exit.

11. Click the Main Menu button and choose Log Out. Logging out stops the X server.

12. Log in to your root user account again. The X server will restart in the higher resolution mode.

TIP

Chances are that more than one screen size is available for a given color depth. For example, the screen sizes for 16-bit color may include 640×480, 800×600, and 1024×768. To find out whether more than one screen size is available, press Ctrl+Alt+keypad plus (+) and Ctrl+Alt+keypad minus (–). These keys enable you to cycle among the available screen sizes on-the-fly, without having to restart X. If these keys don't do anything, only one screen size has been defined for the color depth you're using.

Getting the Screen Size Right

If you must move the mouse pointer within a desktop area in order to bring portions of a single desktop area into view, your X server has been configured to display a virtual desktop area that's larger than your screen display. If your X server has been set up this way (see Figure 7.16 for an example), you'll surely find this annoying.

NOTE

I'm not talking about desktop *areas* here. As you've learned, GNOME sets up four virtual desktop areas by default. Rather, I'm talking about the problem of a *single* desktop area that's too large for the screen.

To solve this problem, try pressing Ctrl+Alt+keypad minus (–) and Ctrl+Alt+keypad plus (+). These keys enable you to cycle among the available screen sizes for the color depth you're using. If one of the screen sizes fits your monitor perfectly, you may want to make the change permanent.

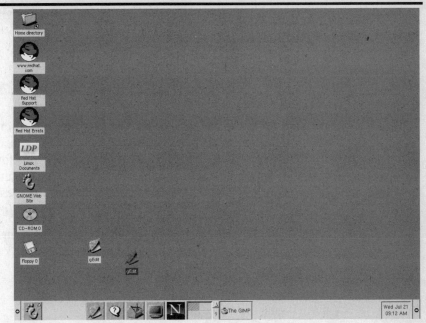

FIGURE 7.16: This X server has been set up so that the virtual screen size is larger than the actual size. Note that you can't see the Panel. To bring the Panel into view, you'd have to move the mouse pointer down.

To make the setting permanent, you'll need to edit /etc/XF86Config, a complex file that's used to configure your X server. Understanding everything that's in XF86Config is quite a job. Fortunately, you can make just this one change without having to learn all about this file.

Follow these steps to select a default screen size that matches your monitor's display:

1. If necessary, log in as the root user.

2. Choose Main Menu ≻ Programs ≻ Applications ≻ gEdit. You'll see gEdit on-screen.

3. Do one of the following:

    ▶ Click F3.

    ▶ On the toolbar, click the Open icon.

    ▶ Click File on the menu bar and click Open.

    The Open File dialog box appears.

4. You need to navigate to the directory where XF86Config is stored. On Red Hat Linux 7.1 systems, XF86Config is stored in /etc/X11. Use the Directories Browser or the Directories window to select this directory.

5. In the Files list, select XF86Config and click OK. You'll see the configuration file in gEdit.

6. Scroll down to the Screen section and find the subsection called Display. Note that these sections are organized by color depth. You should see two or three settings for the color depths of which your monitor is capable. Within each color depth section, you'll find one or more modes, which define the screen size (such as 1024×768 or 800×600).

7. Look for any lines that start with Virtual, as in the following:
    Virtual 1280 1024

    This command creates a virtual screen size of 1280×1024. If the largest display size is 1024×768, you would have to move the mouse to see all of the screen.

8. Carefully place the cursor in front of Virtual and type a pound sign (#), so that the entry looks like this:
    #Virtual

    The pound sign comments out the line to follow, so that its contents do not take effect.

9. If you don't find Virtual, look at the Mode line for each color depth. By default, most X servers automatically set the screen size to the largest size they find in this line. For example, suppose you see this Mode line:
    Modes "1280x1024" "1024x768" "800x600"

    The X server will display a screen size of 1280×1024. If that's too big, delete "1280x1024" so that "1024x768" is the largest size in the line.

10. On the toolbar, click Save.

11. On the toolbar, click Exit.

12. Click the Main Menu button and choose Log Out. Logging out stops the X server.

13. Log in to your `root` user account again. The X server will restart in the higher resolution mode.

LOGGING OUT

When you're finished with the configurations you performed in this chapter, you should log out of your `root` user account. Since you've created a user account for yourself, why not try logging in with your new user account? You'll do so in this section. You'll also learn how to shut down your system from within your user account. Say goodbye to the `root` user account, because you won't be using it again unless you absolutely must.

Logging Out of Your *root* User Account

When you're finished using your `root` user account, you should log out. When you do, you'll have the option of logging out so that you can log in with your ordinary user account. You can also halt or reboot the system. For now, you'll log out so that you can log in with your new ordinary user account.

To log out, do the following:

1. Choose Main Menu ➤ Log Out. You'll see an alert box with the message, "Really log out?"

2. When you are logged in as `root` user, you can choose any of the following from this alert box:

    Logout   Choose this option to log out of the `root` user account. You'll see the Welcome screen again, which enables you to log in using your new user account.

    Halt   Choose this option to shut down your Linux system.

    Reboot   Choose this option to restart your Linux system.

Part ii

Note that this alert box also contains an option that enables you to save your system settings, including GNOME applications you've left open. Activate this option if you would like to save your settings.

3. By default, the Logout option is selected. Click Yes to log out.

Logging In with Your Ordinary User Account

After you've logged out of the root user account, you'll see the Welcome dialog box again. Try logging in with your ordinary user account. Type your username and press Enter, then type your password and press Enter to log in. You'll see GNOME on screen, and File Manager will open—this time, without any warning message. You'll see that File Manager is automatically positioned at your home directory (see Figure 7.17).

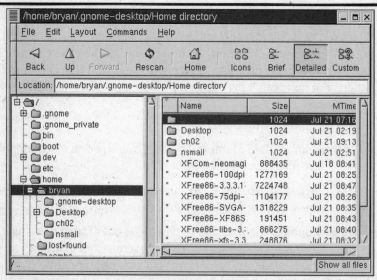

FIGURE 7.17: When you log in to your ordinary user account, File Manager opens automatically and displays the contents of your home directory.

Shutting Down from Your Ordinary User Account

When you choose Log Out from your ordinary user account, you'll see the same alert box with the message, "Really log out?" that you saw when you logged out of the root user account. However, you can't reboot or halt your system from an ordinary user account.

To shut down or reboot your system from your user account, do the following:

1. Choose Main Menu ➤ Log Out. You'll see the alert box with the message, "Really log out?"

2. If you would like to save your session so that the same applications are open the next time you start GNOME, check Save Session.

3. Check Logout, if necessary.

4. Click Yes. The Welcome dialog box appears again.

5. Click System and click Reboot to restart your system or click Halt to shut down your system.

WHAT'S NEXT?

In this chapter you learned how to configure the GNOME environment using both Linuxconf and the GNOME text files. In the next chapter you will learn about the K suite and how to use these productivity tools for such tasks as word processing and graphics. You will also learn how to run Windows applications inside the Linux operating system.

Part ii

Chapter 8

KDE, Office Applications, and Running Windows Applications in Linux

The rumor for years now has been that Microsoft has a team working on Microsoft Office for Linux. Maybe that made for good press during all the Microsoft antitrust lawsuits with the U.S. government. But while we're waiting for MS Office for Linux to materialize, Linux has its own collection of very good office suites that are available today. Most are commercial; one is free. All of them include some level of capability to exchange files with Microsoft Office.

The real benefit for many users who consider adopting one of these office suites is their cross-platform nature. For example, you can run the same office suite, with identical file formats and user interfaces, on Linux, several UNIX platforms, and Windows. This is a great solution for offices where different users prefer different platforms.

Adapted from *Linux! I Didn't Know You Could Do That...*
by Nicholas D. Wells
ISBN 0-7821-2935-8   448 pages $24.99

Use a UNIX Standard: ApplixWare

The ApplixWare suite has been around in the UNIX world for years. A few years ago, a Linux version was developed and distributed in demonstration form for free via download. More recently, the Linux division of the ApplixWare suite was split off into a separate company called VistaSource. Now the office suite for Linux is a commercial product, just as it is for all the other platforms that ApplixWare supports.

VistaSource supports several Open Source projects for Linux enthusiasts, but these projects are of interest mainly to software developers. Their high-quality end-user products are available only commercially. VistaSource actually sells two Linux office suites: ApplixWare Office, which is based on VistaSource's long-popular ApplixWare product, and AnywhereOffice, which attempts to mimic the look-and-feel of Microsoft Office, including the capability to work in Microsoft file formats. Both office suites include the following components:

- ▸ Word processor

- ▸ Spreadsheet

- ▸ Presentation graphics

- ▸ E-mail client

- ▸ HTML authoring

You can find more information about them on the website www.vistasource.com. The latest release of ApplixWare Office 5 for Linux includes features such as these:

- ▸ Dockable toolbars

- ▸ Integration with GNOME themes

- ▸ The capability to open, save, save as, import, and export from a single dialog box

- ▸ A graphical font installer

- ▸ Drag-and-drop support from compatible file managers (such as GNOME)

- ▸ Improved import and export filters, with support for over 100 file formats

- On-the-fly spell-checking

- Autosum spreadsheets

- HTML Spreadsheet Export Wizard

- A native gateway for MySQL

- Bundled drivers for Postgresql and MySQL

DOWNLOAD A CROSS-PLATFORM OFFICE CLONE: STAROFFICE

Another complete commercial office suite for Linux is StarOffice, created by StarDivision in Hamburg, Germany, and now owned by Sun Microsystems. StarOffice attempts to clone Microsoft Office in functionality and look-and-feel and go beyond MS Office to add more features and Internet integration. Frankly, it comes pretty close to succeeding.

StarOffice can be downloaded for free on the Internet for personal use. Visit www.sun.com/staroffice to register yourself and download the StarOffice 5.2 package.

The real power of StarOffice lies in two elements: First, it is a cross-platform solution. You can run an identical version of StarOffice on Windows, Linux, Solaris, OS/2, and other platforms. Second, StarOffice integrates all sorts of features into a common desktop from which you can start new documents, embed and share files, and access all types of Internet resources. The Internet resources include FTP sites, e-mail, newsgroups, and web page authoring, in addition to basic browsing directly from the StarOffice desktop.

NOTE

The part you may like best about StarOffice is that many of its menus and dialog boxes look a *lot* like Microsoft Office, and it works with the latest Microsoft Office file formats.

The latest release of StarOffice includes the following features, all accessible from a single window (see Figure 8.1):

- Text documents (word processing)

- Spreadsheet

- ► HTML document creation

- ► Web page browsing on the Internet

- ► E-mail (creating and receiving)

- ► Presentation graphics

- ► Vector-based drawing

- ► Bitmapped drawing

- ► A daily planner/organizer (similar to Outlook)

- ► Access to FTP and newsgroup sites

- ► A basic (nonrelational) database

- ► StarBasic programming to customize all parts of the system

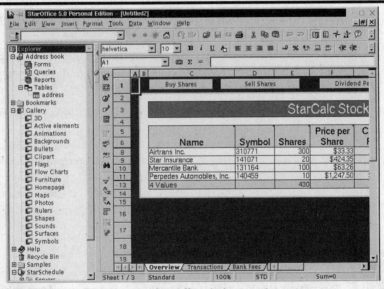

FIGURE 8.1:   The integrated StarOffice desktop environment

A special tool called an Autopilot helps you create new documents in key areas, and access to Internet resources is tightly integrated into the other features. For example, when you view a web page with StarOffice as a browser, you can immediately save that page and begin to edit it as you would any other StarOffice document.

StarOffice does use a lot of system resources—you should have 64MB of memory for decent performance. It also requires about 150MB of disk space, although a networked installation uses only about 10MB in additional space for each user on the system.

TRY THE FREE KOFFICE SUITE

One of the truly impressive parts of release 2 of KDE is the KOffice suite. This suite of applications has been in development for several years and, with the release of KDE 2, it is really beginning to come into its own, with enough good looks and features to make any Linux fan happy. Not that it's *done*, but it's certainly worth exploring and following up on.

NOTE
Remember that KOffice works only if you have upgraded your system to KDE 2. It relies on all the latest libraries and functionality of KDE 2.

KOffice includes the following components, all available from the KDE main menu, under Office:

KChart   A drawing tool that can create charts from spreadsheet or database information

KIllustrator   A vector-based drawing program (try to say Kay-illustrator rather than killustrator)

KOffice Workspace   A management area from which you can work with all the KOffice applications and use documents between multiple applications.

KPresenter   A presentation tool similar in function to Microsoft PowerPoint

KSpread   A full-feature spreadsheet

KWord   A powerful word processor

All of the KOffice components (and KDE 2, in general) use a shared object system called KParts that allows documents to be embedded in each other, something like OLE in Windows or the Object Request Broker (ORB) in many systems. For example, a KSpread spreadsheet can be embedded live in a KWord document.

Part ii

WARNING

KOffice does still crash occasionally. Check www.kde.org for information about the latest updates to the KOffice package.

You can start a single KOffice application such as KWord from the Office menu in KDE, but typically you'll want to start with the KOffice workspace, which provides a list of applications and documents on the left side of the screen. This workspace makes it easy to move between multiple documents and document types, accessing them and pasting them into each other as needed.

You can begin a new document by clicking one of the component icons such as KWord or KSpread. A dialog box then lets you choose to use a template or blank document, or to open an existing file (see Figure 8.2).

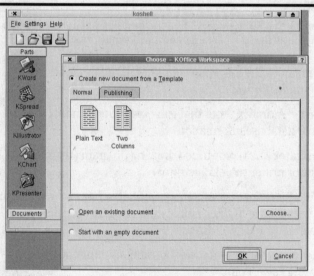

FIGURE 8.2:   Creating a template in KOffice

It would fill an entire book to go into all the features of KOffice, but I can explain how to navigate around the application a little and list some of the great features that each component of KOffice includes. For the rest, you'll enjoy experimenting a little yourself.

NOTE

One thing to know immediately about KOffice is that the authors haven't worried yet about file sharing with systems like StarOffice or Microsoft Office. The KOffice applications support basically their own proprietary format, plus plain ASCII text and, occasionally, HTML.

Once you've started a new text document, the KWord word processor is somewhat similar to FrameMaker in that it is frame-oriented rather than page-oriented (see Figure 8.3). You can add and break apart frames using the icons on the far left of the window or Tools menu.

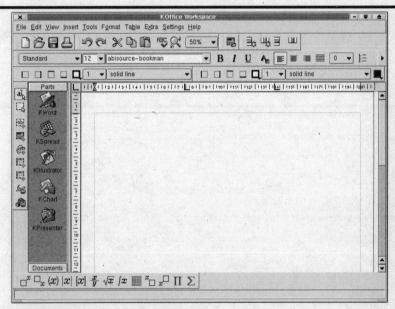

FIGURE 8.3: A blank KWord document

Some of the formatting and other tools that are visible in the default KWord window include the following (holding your mouse pointer over a part of the screen causes a tooltip explanation to be displayed):

▶ Frame border controls let you set different border sides, weights, and line types.

▶ Icons on the left side let you insert and manage different types of frames for formulas, text, pictures, clip art, tables, and so on.

▶ Standard formatting icons control font and type size, bold, italic, font color, centering, and other related features.

▶ The main toolbar includes Undo/Redo, Copy/Cut/Paste, spell-check, Find, and a zoom-control drop-down box.

▶ Picture insert icons and table row/column insertion icons allow easy control of these features.

▶ Rulers with different tab stops and margins show your working area.

▶ Complex formulas can be created using the formula toolbar below the document.

KWord includes complete spell-checking facilities, including user-defined auto-correction options (such as changing *hte* to *the*). It also has the capability to define paragraph styles via the Extra menu (see Figure 8.4).

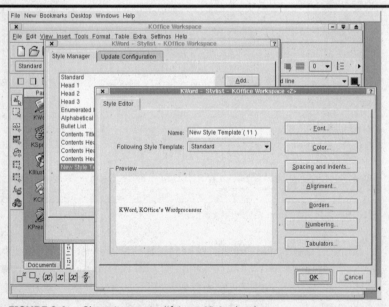

FIGURE 8.4:   Changing or modifying a KWord style

If you need to work on a spreadsheet or presentation, click on the KSpread or KPresenter icon to the left of the document. A dialog box lets you choose to open a new item or an existing file. Many of the toolbars are similar between document types, making it easier to learn how to use them.

KSpread adds more toolbar icons (beyond those of KWord), including numeric precision adjusters and cell alignment tools (see Figure 8.5).

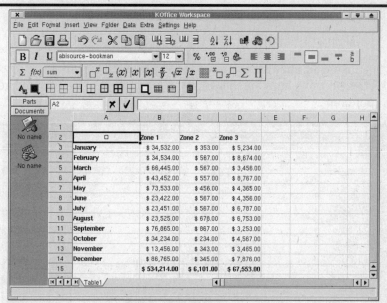

FIGURE 8.5:   The KSpread screen layout

Notice on the left side of the window that the Parts icons no longer appear. The Parts button remains, but below it is a Documents button. When you have multiple documents open, they can be viewed from this Documents list. You can change between them by clicking on an icon. Clicking again on the Parts button returns you to the list of KOffice components. Some additional KSpread features include the following:

- ▶ Cell formatting based on conditional cell attributes
- ▶ Per-cell comments (pop-up yellow notes)
- ▶ Embedded objects and charts
- ▶ Hyperlinks to websites
- ▶ Multiple sort functions

KIllustrator provides a vector-based drawing environment to create images that you can use in KWord or other KOffice documents, as well as in other graphics formats. Unlike most KOffice tools, KIllustrator lets you export images in several formats, including:

- GIF
- XPM
- EPS
- PPM

Figure 8.6 shows the main window of KIllustrator with three objects: stretched text, lines that have non-default properties, and a standard polygon.

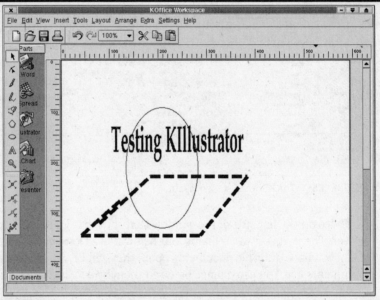

FIGURE 8.6: Using KIllustrator to draw a simple polygon

To draw in KIllustrator, you choose a tool from the vertical bar on the left side of the window. These tools can also be selected from the Tools menu.

Some of the features available in this program include the following:

- An Outline view to speed work on complex drawings
- Support for multiple layers

- ► Insertion of clip art or bitmapped images
- ► Multiple page layout options
- ► An optional grid to guide you as you work
- ► Multiple transformations, including mirror, rotation, and scaling
- ► Quick movement between layers or front to back and vice versa
- ► Grouping of multiple items
- ► Aligning text objects to a path
- ► Converting text objects to curves
- ► Blending and additional palette loading

Each object that you create has a Properties dialog box associated with it. The tabs provided in the dialog box depend on the type of object, but in general you can change the width of lines or outlines, the type of fill in the object, or the font characteristics for text objects. Once you have selected an object, you can view its Properties dialog box by right-clicking and choosing Properties or by choosing Edit ➤ Properties (see Figure 8.7).

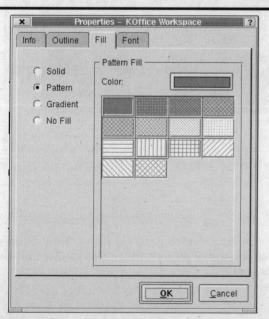

FIGURE 8.7:   Changing fill colors and patterns

Part ii

I'll let you explore KChart on your own; now we'll move on to KPresenter. When you click on KPresenter in the Parts list, you can choose from a set of screen presentation templates to begin your presentation slides.

Although the KPresenter screen looks terrific (see Figure 8.8), it isn't nearly as easy to use as something like StarOffice, ApplixWare, or, yes, even PowerPoint. The KPresenter window has dozens of useful control icons on all four sides of the main image. (The font control items are at the bottom of the screen by default, not above the document as they are in the other KOffice tools.)

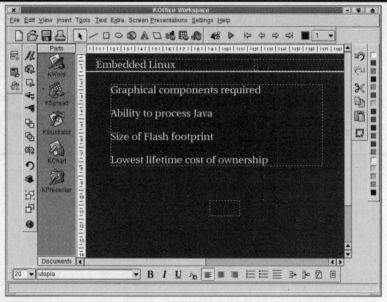

FIGURE 8.8:   A simple slide in KPresenter

NOTE

KPresenter almost seems more like a vector-drawing tool than a business presentation tool. You can do great graphical things, but it's tedious to create a lot of text-filled slides with it.

Although the program isn't the easiest one to use, some of the features you may be interested in include the following:

- ▶ Automatic creation of HTML slideshow presentations
- ▶ Lots of powerful drawing and charting tools
- ▶ Special transition effects
- ▶ Layers and grouped objects
- ▶ Easy insertion of clip art and bitmapped images

RUN OTHER OFFICE PROGRAMS ON LINUX

If you don't need a full suite, many word processors, spreadsheets, and other simple office-type packages are available free for Linux. Try some of the programs described in this section, including the WordPerfect for Linux package.

The Powerful WordPerfect for Linux

Corel Corporation, which owns WordPerfect, made a strong commitment to Linux in the past couple of years. At the moment, the fruit of that commitment is available for download from the website `http://linux .corel.com`. It includes the WordPerfect 9 word processor, Corel Presentations 9, the Paradox database, and the Quattro Pro 9 spreadsheet.

Unfortunately, as of this writing, the future of these products is uncertain. Microsoft invested heavily in the ailing Corel Corporation. This is seen by many Linux enthusiasts as the reason behind the sale of all Corel Linux assets to Linux Global Partners. Although one would assume that the development and sale of these products will continue, that is by no means certain at this point.

Currently, all of these programs are commercial software that is available for free download. For a fee, you can purchase an upgraded version of the software with additional features or add-on files (such as fonts and clipart) and a printed manual. For example, the for-purchase version of WordPerfect 9 for Linux includes features such as these:

- A library of several thousand clip art images
- Printed documentation
- A character-based version of WordPerfect for use in host server environments
- Server license management

All three versions (the free download, the commercial workstation, and the commercial server products) include the following:

- Cross-platform compatibility (the same file format used on WordPerfect for all platforms)
- Document management and revision control
- Complex tables with 90 built-in spreadsheet functions
- Internet publishing
- Charting and drawing tools
- Comprehensive grammar and spelling tools

Use the AbiWord Free Word Processor

AbiWord is a very nice word processor that is completely open source. It has been in development for several years and has definitely reached the point of being a truly useful tool.

AbiWord doesn't try to be a clone of Microsoft Word; its ambitions are simpler than that. But it does provide a clean interface and all the features that most of us use in those expensive commercial word processors we're accustomed to.

To download AbiWord, go to `http://www.abisource.com/free.phtml`.

In the main window of AbiWord, you can see a standard toolbar and drop-down lists for the paragraph style, font, and type size of the current paragraph. A Page view is presented by default, with rulers and a zoom tool to help you adjust the viewing size of the page (see Figure 8.9).

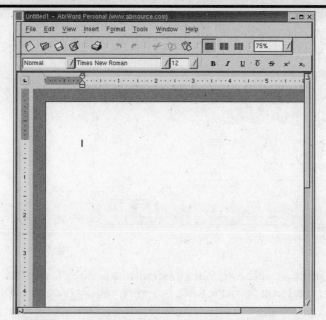

FIGURE 8.9: AbiWord has a clean and easy-to-use interface.

Apart from the nicely done interface, some of the features in AbiWord that you'll appreciate include the following:

- ▶ Capability to save in several formats, including RTF and LaTeX
- ▶ Find and replace with case sensitivity
- ▶ Insert symbol (a very useful dialog box)
- ▶ Insert graphics file (choose Insert ➣ Picture)
- ▶ Paragraph formatting dialog box
- ▶ A fairly complete spell-checking facility
- ▶ Word count with auto-updating

An Options dialog box is also provided via the Tools menu (see Figure 8.10). It most likely will expand in the months to come as additional options configurations are added.

FIGURE 8.10: The AbiWord Options dialog box

An amusing part of the AbiWord program at this point is what it doesn't include. I won't provide a list, but when you choose an item such as File ➤ Page Setup, you see an interesting dialog box that in effect tells you "This feature isn't done yet. If you want to, write it, put it in this source code file, and send it to us at this address." Needless to say, this is a distinctly non–Microsoft Word dialog box. Because AbiWord is open source, the authors are completely open about what parts are not yet completed (see Figure 8.11).

FIGURE 8.11: Those features of AbiWord not yet completed invite you to help.

Although parts of AbiWord are not complete, the program is well thought-out in its design, and it is stable and ready for use right now.

View Your Word Files in Linux

Despite all the talk about alternative office suites and word processors, the most-used word processor at the moment remains Microsoft Word, which isn't available for Linux. Many word processors can read and write Word files, but this section describes an easier way to access those files.

Suppose you have received a Word 97 or Word 2000 file from a colleague. Rather than open a suite such as StarOffice or ApplixWare, a faster and easier solution is to use a Word file-viewing utility to quickly view the contents of the Word file. Several of these tools are available for Linux.

The best tool for quick viewing is catdoc. This program can be downloaded from `http://www.fe.msk.ru/~vitus/`.

catdoc operates much like the cat command. It reads data from the filename you provide and writes a translation of that file to STDOUT (to the screen or to a redirected output). Because most files are longer than a screen, you'll probably want to use the command in one of these forms:

```
$ catdoc wordfile.doc | less
$ catdoc wordfile.doc > wordfile.txt
```

By default, catdoc wraps lines for easy reading on-screen. catdoc does include a -w switch that causes long lines not to be wrapped. Use this switch if you want to import the text into another word processor.

Several other options are available to help you process various character sets that might be used in your Word documents or to map characters. You can also process files that don't seem to have the correct Word file signature.

An interesting feature of Word is that it may save text as hidden when the author of a document thinks the data has been erased. This hidden text is displayed by catdoc. The result is that a person using catdoc may see information that the person providing the document did not intend as part of the document. This may include older edits or even private information that remains from a previous document template.

WARNING

This hidden text problem is especially dangerous when you start a new document by altering or erasing a company-confidential document, rather than starting from scratch and just copying and pasting text that you need from a previous file.

If you send out any Word files to Linux users, the safest way to prevent anyone from seeing private or proprietary data that Word has left (hidden) in the original Word document is to save the document to Plain Text format and then re import it into Word.

Another tool very similar to catdoc is AntiWord. This is also a command-line utility that you can use in this simple format:

```
$ antiword wordfile.doc | less
```

AntiWord can be downloaded at `http://antiword.riscos .org.uk`.

AntiWord includes different options than catdoc. AntiWord isn't as good at handling diverse character sets, but it does include options to view hidden text explicitly (use -s), to alter the width of wrapped text (use -w with a column width), and to output PostScript files (use -p). Enter the `antiword` command without any parameters to see a full list of options.

Finally, the WordView program (recently renamed wv) is intended to provide a much more powerful viewer for Word documents, with many related tools. Unfortunately, I haven't found this program to be very reliable.

With WordView installed, you have a number of programs at your disposal. These include the following:

wvText   Converts a Word file to plain text.

wvPS   Converts a Word file to a PostScript file.

wvMime   Views your Word documents using Ghostview instead of acting as a conversion engine.

wvPDF   Converts a Word file to PDF format.

wvAbw   Converts a Word file to AbiWord file format.

wvHtml   Converts a Word file to HTML 4.

wvLatex   Converts a Word file to LaTeX format.

wvWml   Converts a Word file to Wml format.

wvDvi   Converts a Word file to a DVI file.

wvWare   Converts a Word file to various formats using the above programs.

Although this list is very impressive, when I have used these programs to convert files, the Word View package has been full of errors. If you need one of the features in this list, I recommend exploring this powerful package more fully. Otherwise, stick with catdoc to dump the text from a Word document to the screen for easy reading.

RUN YOUR WINDOWS APPLICATIONS ON LINUX

If the native Linux applications described so far in this part don't meet all your needs, try running your existing Windows applications on Linux using the tools described in this section. It can take a little effort to set up some of these tools, but the results are impressive.

Run Windows Apps with WINE

For years I've been talking to people about the WINE project. WINE is more or less an attempt to clone Windows on Linux. Technically, it's a huge, complex project. However, the simple fact is that, after years of effort, WINE has reached a point where you can run some useful applications on it. I consider it a stop-gap measure for those who prefer to use only Linux but still require a few applications that are available only on Windows.

I used to demonstrate WINE by showing the Windows Solitaire program running on Linux. That was about all it could run a few years ago. My latest test, however, was running a full-blown copy of Quicken Deluxe 99, and it came up without a hitch. That's not to say that every Windows application can run without bugs, but it's a good indication of the power of WINE.

You can obtain more information about WINE at http://www. winehq.com/.

You're ready to launch a couple of Windows programs! To begin, change to the directory where the Windows application is located on your system. For example, use this command on a standard Windows 98 installation:

```
$ cd "/mnt/win/Program Files/Accessories"
```

The MS Paint application is located in this directory. To launch it in Linux, use this command:

```
$ wine ./mspaint.exe
```

Launching a program takes a few moments. WINE is a resource-intensive application, and I recommend having at least 32MB of memory (64MB is much better) if you want to use it regularly. Although WINE may display a couple of messages on your command-line window as it opens, the MS Paint application should appear on-screen after a minute. This isn't very interesting unless you realize that this figure was captured in the middle of a GNOME desktop! (See Figure 8.12.)

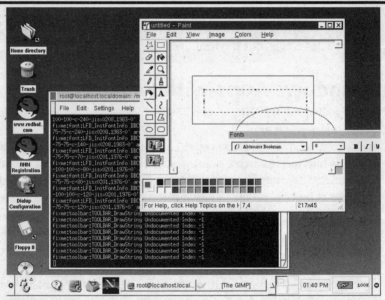

FIGURE 8.12:   The Microsoft Paint program running in a Linux GUI

NOTE

WINE places a couple of files in your home directory as you run applications.

If you're a software developer, you can use some of the developer tools that are part of the WINE project to more easily port applications from Windows to native Linux. To learn more about the WINE project, including details about technical support and some commercial companies that are affiliated with the project, visit www.winehq.com.

Run Linux and Windows with VMWare

In addition to WINE, which acts as a Windows binary emulator (with additional developer tools for Windows-to-Linux porting), you can use a virtual machine emulator to run native Windows on Linux, including Windows 98 or Windows NT.

The idea behind a virtual machine is that the operating system (Windows, in this case) actually thinks that it's running all by itself on a dedicated Intel-based computer.

The program that provides this functionality is VMWare, a commercial product for Linux. You can download a 30-day trial of VMWare from www.vmware.com. One of your operating systems (I'd suggest Linux) acts as a host for VMWare. You then load Windows into the VMWare virtual machine. Applications run within this environment.

Once you have VMWare set up, you can switch between Windows and Linux with a couple of keystrokes, never rebooting your system. You can also copy and paste information between the operating systems using special Clipboard buffers that VMWare provides.

Using VMWare with Linux and Windows obviously requires more system resources than either operating system alone, but the performance on a well-equipped machine is actually very good. To me, the most interesting thing about VMWare is that both operating systems are actually *running* at the same time, rather than just sitting in the background waiting to be activated. I've had people describe a Linux application communicating over the network with a NetWare server, when Linux, Windows, and NetWare 5 were all running at the same time on the same CPU using VMWare.

VMWare is a commercial product. You can download a 30-day trial from the VMWare.com website, or you can purchase the product directly. The Linux version sells for $299 electronically or $329 if you want a boxed product. VMWare also comes in a Linux Express edition for $79 or $99.

WHAT'S NEXT?

In this chapter, you learned how to use Linux to run office and Windows applications. You have seen that Linux is beginning to hold its own in the business world, but what about Linux for recreation? In the next chapter, you will learn about using Linux to play video, audio, and even games. With its open source environment, Linux is very attractive to hardcore game players.

Chapter 9

MULTIMEDIA AND GRAPHICS

Those who strive to use Linux as the desktop system for all their work might think that giving up Windows means giving up all multimedia capabilities with it. Admittedly, Linux isn't as tightly integrated with auto-launching accessories for every new sound format that appears.

However, a surprising number of Linux developers are heavily into music and video. The result is a nice set of audio and video programs that run on Linux. This chapter describes some of the best ones available. A few are standard fare on Linux systems; others are new or unexpected. Programs that require KDE, GNOME, or their libraries (Qt or GTK+) are noted in each section.

Adapted from *Linux! I Didn't Know You Could Do That...* by Nicholas D. Wells

ISBN 0-7821-2935-8   448 pages $24.99

Make Linux Your Personal Video Player

Thousands of video clips are available on the Web, from movie previews and promotional pieces to videos created by individuals. Linux has several utilities that let you view these video clips on-screen.

Use Simple Linux Video Players

There are two popular methods of playing video clips on Linux. The first method uses the XAnim program, which can be used either alone or with a frontend for GNOME or KDE. XAnim itself runs on any version of Linux that uses the X Window System. It supports the following video formats:

- MPEG video (Type I only, with no sound, and no support for Type B or Type P MPEG files)
- QuickTime animations (MOV files)
- AVI animations
- FLI and FLC animations
- IFF animations
- GIF89a animations
- DL animations (formats 1, 2, and most of 3)
- Amiga MovieSetter animations
- Utah Raster Toolkit RLE images and animations
- SGI Movie format files

NOTE
MPEG is currently the most popular format for web-based video clips.

XAnim is included with most recent Linux distributions, but it isn't installed by default. Once you have the XAnim package installed, you can immediately begin viewing movies in MPEG, MOV, or the other formats I just listed.

View video clips with XAnim using a command such as the following from any graphical command line:

```
$ xanim hurricane.mpg &
```

Figure 9.1 shows XAnim playing an MPEG file; XAnim includes separate windows for controls and pictures.

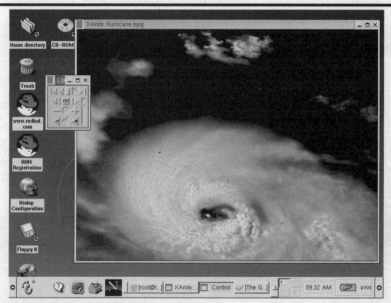

FIGURE 9.1: XAnim playing an MPEG file

Controls for XAnim include play, pause, fast forward, reverse, and volume (though XAnim can't play sound from MPEG files). The controls are not highly attractive, but XAnim has the advantage of running on all Linux systems, with no requirements for additional packages or specific desktop environments. In addition, though not all of its features are part of the graphical interface, XAnim provides dozens of interesting controls for your video clips.

Part ii

The XAnim man page includes descriptions of each supported format and dozens of audio and video options. These include things such as the following:

- ▶ Creating a colormap from a frame of video and remapping other frames to that frame.

- ▶ Converting TrueColor animations such as AVI files (which use separate RGB color channels for each pixel) into a global indexed colormap.

- ▶ Converting TrueColor animations to grayscale.

- ▶ Adjusting gamma or other color settings for the animation.

- ▶ Resizing animation automatically or allowing the user to resize on-the-fly.

- ▶ Scaling an animation vertically or horizontally.

- ▶ Defining frame loops, ping-pong animation, and various frame delays while displaying a clip.

You can also use a number of keys while an animation is playing in XAnim. For example, you can toggle the spacebar to pause and restart an animation or press **Q** to quit.

NOTE
If you don't have sound working yet on your Linux system, skip ahead to see a few hints on Linux sound.

Because XAnim supports so many video file formats and is freely available on Linux, it has been used as the basis for other video players for the popular Linux desktops. Other developers have started with XAnim and created more attractive interfaces or additional features for viewing video clips within the graphical interface.

The GXAnim program is built around the GNOME desktop and the GTK+ library. It relies on XAnim as the engine to display video files. GXAnim is similar to XAnim, but it has a more attractive interface, designed to blend with your GNOME desktop. It includes a control panel and a separate window where the video is displayed, as shown in Figure 9.2.

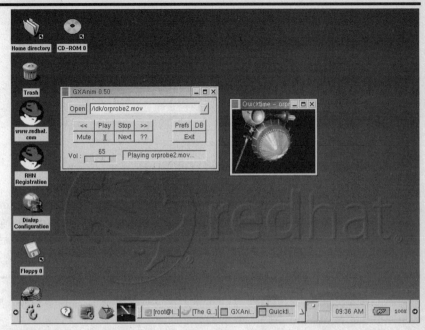

FIGURE 9.2:   GXAnim's control and content windows

The control panel for GXAnim includes an Open button that you can use to select a movie to view. Previously viewed video clips (from the current session) are available using the drop-down list arrow to the right of the Open field. The Next button plays the next video in a series of clips that you have selected for loading.

By clicking on the Prefs button in the GXAnim control panel, you open a dialog box in which you can set up several options for playing clips (see Figure 9.3). These include sizing (Scaling), color correction (Gamma Correct), and other settings. Most of these settings reflect options provided by the XAnim binary as described previously (see the XAnim man page). Not all XAnim capabilities are supported by the GXAnim program—in fact, most are not. Even so, if you're just playing clips you've downloaded from the Web, GXAnim makes a nice player.

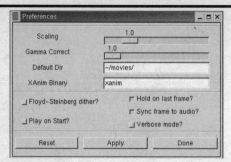

FIGURE 9.3:   The Preferences page of GXAnim

A similar package for KDE is aKtion. Like GXAnim, aKtion requires the XAnim package as a video engine. aKtion has a single window with both controls and video playback, as shown in Figure 9.4. A full-screen mode is available as well.

FIGURE 9.4:   The aKtion video window

The aKtion package uses a command such as the following to launch:

```
$ aktion orprobe1.mpg &
```

aKtion includes a number of nice features for video playback, such as:

▶ Full-screen playback mode

▶ A video "widget" (KXanim) that can be used to add video to other KDE programs if you're writing your own KDE programs

▶ A frame capture (press **C** during video playback to save the current frame to a file)

▶ Documentation in many languages

The controls at the bottom of the aKtion window include a bar showing how much of the current video clip has played and a volume slider (in the lower right of the window). Standard controls for opening a clip, play, stop, forward, and reverse are augmented by a Setup icon (a check mark). The Setup dialog box (shown in Figure 9.5) includes six fairly full tabs of options, taken from those provided by the underlying XAnim engine.

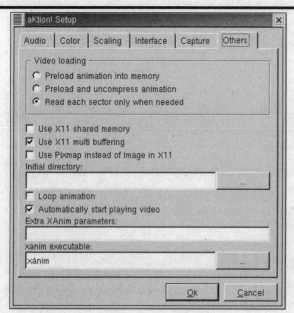

FIGURE 9.5: The aKtion Setup dialog box

If you don't have KDE or GNOME on your system, but you want to explore something beyond XAnim, try MpegTV. MpegTV is commercial software, distributed as shareware. If you intend to use it for commercial purposes, you must register and send a fee to the program owners. Visit the website www.mpegtv.com to register.

The MpegTV program has a nicer-looking interface than XAnim, but its real draw may be that it supports more MPEG features than XAnim (and thus more than aKtion or GXAnim) currently does. (Recall that XAnim supports only one type of MPEG file, and it doesn't support sound in MPEG video clips.)

MpegTV has some nice configuration options available, though not as many as XAnim has. It's a nice-looking program, though you'll likely be too annoyed by the "unregistered" messages to use it much until you register. Use a command such as the following to launch the program:

```
$ mtv hurricane.mpg &
```

In Figure 9.6 you can see the full screen with the Mpeg*TV* controls, the playback window, and the Video Options dialog box.

FIGURE 9.6:   The Mpeg*TV* windows

In addition to the programs mentioned so far, the Red Hat distribution includes a couple of default packages, plaympeg and gtv, that let you play MPEG files without installing anything additional. These are in the SMPEG package, which requires the SDL package. Both are installed by default as part of a workstation installation.

You can run the plaympeg program from any graphical command-line window. This program only plays a video clip—no controls are provided. The gtv program adds a simple control window with play, pause, and speed controls. Figure 9.7 is a view of the gtv program with its control window and a video clip playing:

FIGURE 9.7:   The gtv windows

Both plaympeg and gtv have man pages that you can refer to for information on the available command-line options for these tools.

NOTE

The plaympeg program is installed by default in a way that Netscape uses it (via the plugger package) to play any video clips that you click within a web page.

Use the RealPlayer for Linux

You may have noticed that the programs in the previous section don't support the RealNetworks video and audio formats. RealPlayer is the second method of playing clips in Linux. These streaming formats are proprietary, but of course they are very popular right now.

To get it, you'll need to visit www.real.com and look for the download of the latest basic player. This is a free product that they state quite explicitly is not supported officially by RealNetworks. Instead, they provide a link to an online forum where we can all help each other.

The Real.com website promotes the $29.95 version 8 player quite heavily, but it's not available on any Linux or Unix platform. You may have to explore a little to find the link to the free download. Go to the download page for RealPlayer and look carefully for the small link to RealPlayer Basic, what the site calls "our free player." You'll need to enter a few personal details and your e-mail address before completing the download. (But you can uncheck the box about receiving notices of promotions, events, products, and so on.)

Figure 9.8 shows RealPlayer running on Red Hat 7.

FIGURE 9.8:   RealPlayer from RealNetworks

TUNE IN TO RADIO OR TV WITH LINUX

Several types of expansion cards exist for PCs that provide a radio or television tuner and output the signal to the PC. There are several programs available to take advantage of these cards within Linux.

These programs all rely on a feature of the Linux kernel called Video4Linux. This feature enables Linux to capture incoming data from a video device such as a television tuner card. The home page of the

Video4Linux project is `http://roadrunner.swansea.uk.linux.org/v41.shtml`. Video4Linux is installed by default in Red Hat.

NOTE

A new version of Video4Linux, called Video4Linux 2, is on its way. The applications described here do not require this later version to work.

Some of the hardware devices that are supported by Video4Linux include the following:

- ADS Technologies radio card
- Aztech radio card
- Miro PCTV
- STB TV PCI boards
- Diamond DTV2000 boards
- PCI cards based on the Intel BT848 chip
- VideoLogic Captivator PCI
- 3Com/US Robotics Big Picture capture card/camera
- Iomega Buz

A KDE application that lets you watch television while you're working is KwinTV. This program includes a separate viewing window with dialog boxes to control various items, including the following:

- Scanning the TV tuner for available stations and programming
- Selecting a station from a separate dialog box list
- Using a mixer window to adjust audio quality
- Setting the video image size and input source
- Controlling the selected channel using a programmable infrared remote control that interacts with your Linux PC

Installing the KwinTV RPM is simple, but you'll also need to set up your video hardware (your TV tuner card) with Linux driver support. The KwinTV home page describes how to do this for various hardware components that you might own. The page is `www.mathematik.uni-k1.de/~wenk/kwintv/`. Several of the links refer to pages in German, but you can still learn a lot by exploring this site.

The Links page on the KwinTV site contains a list of other applications for Linux that rely on the Video4Linux system. These include various video capture utilities, several web cam tools, and numerous radio tuner–type utilities, including some designed specifically for the GNOME desktop.

NOTE

Most TV tuner cards include radio tuning as well.

One of the GNOME radio tuner programs is called gtuner. The gtuner program lets you listen to the radio as you work via an interface similar to the CD players described previously.

You can install gtuner using a standard `rpm` command. After you've installed the package, start the program by choosing Programs ➢ Multimedia ➢ gtuner on the GNOME desktop main menu.

The interface of gtuner is somewhat like a car stereo, as you can see in Figure 9.9.

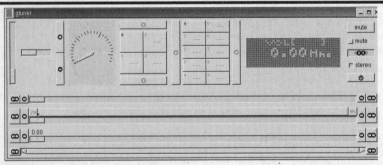

FIGURE 9.9:   The gtuner interface

You can select the band, frequency, and volume of the radio. If you prefer, you can use the slider to select a station and watch the music graphically as you listen.

gtuner includes a set of configuration dialog boxes where you can set up features such as the following:

▶ Sleep timer and wake-up alarm

▶ Mute on exit options

- ▶ List of stations (memory)
- ▶ Support for multiple radio tuner cards
- ▶ A plug-in interface for expandability

Another broadcast-related program for Linux is icecast. icecast is a streaming server for MPEG3 audio (mp3 files). Using icecast, you can broadcast an audio file from your computer (acting as a server) to any other system on your network (or the Internet, if you have sufficient bandwidth) for others to listen to. In effect, you can become a digital DJ by providing a streaming audio signal using the icecast server.

The icecast project is open source software, with a home page at http://icecast.linuxpower.org/. This page includes lists of "netcast" audio (see Figure 9.10). You can visit one of the pages listed and listen to music provided by an icecast server on the Internet.

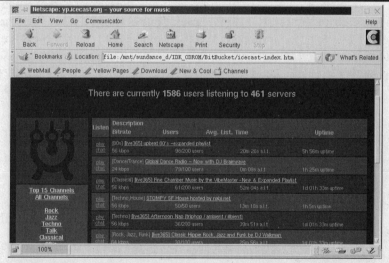

FIGURE 9.10:   The icecast home page showing streaming music feeds

You should consider setting up an icecast server in the same vein as setting up a web server—it takes a little preparation and an ongoing maintenance effort to make something that people want to continue using.

CREATE A LINUX-BASED MUSIC STUDIO

Linux has dozens of great audio tools. These tools begin with a number of CD players, some of which run under any graphical Linux environment. Other programs play audio files that you download from the Internet in popular formats. Synthesizers, sound editors, and mixers are also available. Other tools convert formats or help you create music.

Set Up Your Sound Card in Linux

Playing any type of sound file involves first configuring the sound hardware in your computer. This isn't especially difficult, but it often isn't done automatically when you install Linux.

To make a sound card function in Linux, the correct kernel modules must be added to your system. At least one of these modules must indicate how to access your sound card. Although many sound cards are supported on Linux, the SoundBlaster® card is the most popular sound card in PCs, and many other cards can emulate the SoundBlaster, so I'll describe how to make it function in Linux. Other sound cards will probably use a procedure very similar to this one:

1. Log in as root.

2. Enter this command to load basic sound support:

   ```
   # modprobe sb io=0x220 dma=1 mpu_io=0x330 irq=5
   ```

   This loads the SoundBlaster module and all the modules that go with it. If you see a warning about the sound module already being loaded, you can safely ignore it. However, if you see an error message about the interrupt number, use the command cat/proc/interrupts to examine the interrupts being used on your Linux system and check the documentation for your sound card. Then try the above command again with appropriate parameters.

Red Hat users should try running the sndconfig utility that comes with Red Hat systems. This program is text based but includes an easy-to-use interface. You can start it from any command line, but you should not run it on a graphical desktop (switch to text mode by pressing Ctrl+Alt+F2 first):

```
$ sndconfig
```

The sndconfig utility provides screens where you can then configure your sound card (see Figure 9.11).

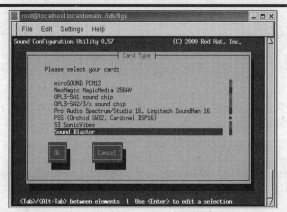

FIGURE 9.11:   Configuring a sound card in Red Hat 7

This utility will either auto-detect your sound card hardware or let you select the right hardware from a list of about 50 sound cards. You then must choose the correct parameters to operate the card (for example, the interrupt number and DMA channel). See your computer's documentation for information on locating the required numbers.

The easiest way to test that your sound hardware is functional is to play a music CD. Both KDE and GNOME (and many other Linux window managers) include a basic CD-playing application.

In both KDE and GNOME, you can choose CD Player from the Multimedia menu. The KDE version is shown in Figure 9.12. After playing a CD, you can use a program such as Kscd to play a sound file. This shows that your sound drivers are correctly loaded and configured.

FIGURE 9.12:   The Kscd interface for playing CD audio

Of course, if you don't hear any sound, several other things could be wrong. If you use a dual-boot system and sound works fine in Windows, try using a different kernel module or different parameters. If sound doesn't work in Windows either, check the following conditions before fiddling with Linux commands:

- ▶ Is the sound card installed tightly into the slot on your system board?

- ▶ Are the speakers plugged into the correct jack (not the microphone jack) on the sound card?

- ▶ Is the power connected to the speakers (many require an AC adapter or batteries)?

- ▶ Are the speakers turned on?

- ▶ Do you have several devices on your system (scanner, sound mixer, sound card, and so on) that might be using conflicting IRQ-interrupt numbers?

Try the OpenSoundSystem

If you're really interested in using sound features on Linux, consider trying the OpenSoundSystem. This is a commercial sound-driver package for Linux. It features:

- ▶ Support for Linux-x86, AlphaLinux, and LinuxPPC

- ▶ Technical support, including ongoing support for the latest Linux kernels

- ▶ A menu-based interface to configure your sound card

- ▶ Automatic detection of sound card kernel parameters

- ▶ Support for PnP (plug and play) sound cards

- ▶ Support for sound cards that are not otherwise supported in Linux because the drivers for them contain proprietary information (that the sound card vendor has not permitted to be included in free sound card drivers)

- ▶ Auto-detection of certain sound cards plus manual configuration tools to change sound card parameters on-the-fly

- ▶ Full-duplex support for Creative Labs SoundBlaster 16/AWE32/ AWE64

You can download an evaluation copy of this $20 product from the 4Front Technologies website at www.opensound.com. The download is free after you enter some personal information. This project and the company that created it are very supportive of Linux—new drivers are released regularly for Linux. The company also sponsors the free Xmms project, which is described later in this chapter.

Play Audio Files on Linux

Audio CD players have been around on Linux for years, and they seem to be getting better all the time. Both KDE and GNOME include default CD players that launch automatically when you insert an audio CD into your system. You can open the Track Editor using the pen-on-paper icon in the lower-left corner of the block of buttons. Figure 9.13 shows the GNOME CD player, gtcd, with the Track Editor window opened for viewing.

FIGURE 9.13:   The GNOME CD player with the Track Editor window

By using Track Editor (a feature of most Linux CD player software), you can enter information about your CDs, such as the artist and song name for each track. Then the next time you insert a particular CD, a code is read from the CD that enables the CD player to display the artist and track titles automatically.

You can also launch the gtcd player by selecting Programs ➤ Multimedia ➤ CD Player in the GNOME menus. You also can insert miniature

CD player controls in the GNOME Panel by choosing Applets ➤ Multimedia ➤ CD Player.

The middle button on the bottom row in gtcd opens the Preferences dialog box, where you can configure many settings for the GNOME CD player, including access to CDDB. CDDB is a shared database of CD titles and track information on the Internet. By accessing CDDB servers around the world, you rarely have to enter information about your own CDs—the information is pulled from a server based on each CD's identification number. Figure 9.14 shows the CDDB Settings tab of the gtcd dialog box.

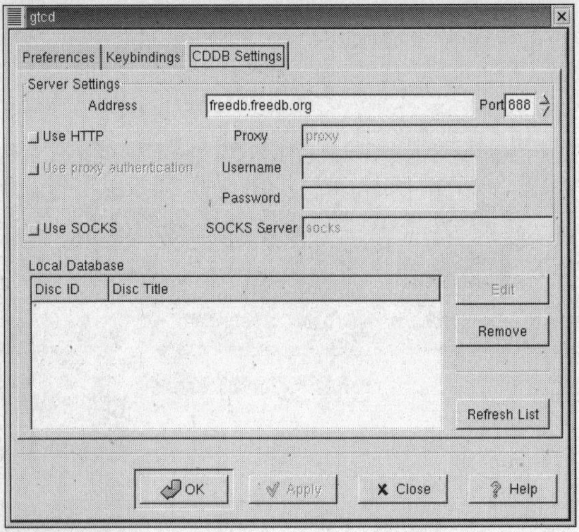

FIGURE 9.14:   Configuring CDDB to detect audio CDs

The CD player provided by KDE, shown in Figure 9.15, is similar in design to the GNOME CD Player. It also starts automatically when you insert an audio CD (if you're running KDE as your desktop). You can start it by choosing Multimedia ➤ CD Player from the KDE menu.

FIGURE 9.15:   The KDE CD player

The KDE CD player includes a configuration button (the little hammer and screwdriver) and a button to access the CDDB setup (the file cabinet drawer). You can also use the "i" button to access websites with CD sales, concert dates, and similar music-lovers information.

In addition to the default players included with KDE and GNOME, other CD players let you enjoy your audio CDs while working within any Linux graphical environment.

A very nice CD player that you can use in any Linux graphical environment is xmcd. This program resembles the KDE CD player, but I'm not sure who was first. It requires the openmotif package.

After I installed these packages, the xmcd program still couldn't find its application defaults. Use the following commands after installing the Xmcd package to merge the graphical resources for xmcd into the X Window System files, then start the program:

```
$ xrdb -merge /usr/X11R6/lib/X11/xmcd/app-defaults/XMcd
$ xmcd
```

Figure 9.16 shows the xmcd interface, which is quite nice. For this figure, I've opened the Options dialog box by clicking the hammer and screwdriver button, the keypad (for access to specific tracks or time points on a CD) using the little grid button, and the CDDB/Track Editing dialog box using the file cabinet button. This gives you a good idea of some key features, in addition to showing the standard display and control buttons.

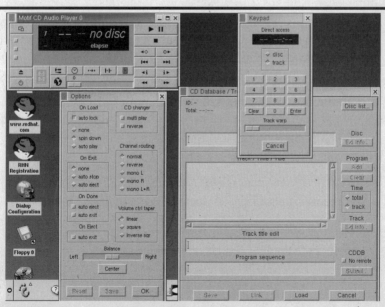

FIGURE 9.16:   The xmcd Options dialog box

Of course, CDs aren't the only way to collect digital music. Websites such as www.mp3.com and many others provide sample tracks or let you create and download personalized music collections. Most of these are likely to be in MPEG3 audio (.mp3 files). Linux supports these and other audio formats, including the following:

▶ MPEG3 (.mp3 files)

▶ WAV

▶ .au files

▶ MIDI (.mid files)

One important distinction to know in digital music is that MIDI format is a description of musical properties, while WAV and MPEG formats are digital recordings (compressed, of course). Another way to explain the difference between these formats is that MIDI is like a piece of sheet music, while WAV and MPEG are like a CD of the orchestra playing it.

It's important to know the difference between these formats because a MIDI player (such as the one included with KDE) must be able to interpret the "instruments" described in the MIDI file in order to create sound waves, while the other formats require (in the broadest sense) dumping the audio data to the sound card. Thus, different utilities may have very different capabilities with various audio formats.

If you want to play one of your MPEG3 audio files without even being in X, you can use the mpg123 command-line program to start a file playing in the background as you work:

```
$ mpg123 chopin5.mp3
```

Red Hat installs the mpg123 program by default. The mpg123 command-line program has many features; just enter the mpg123 command without any filename after it to see a summary of them. For example, with this program you can do the following:

▶ Adjust audio hardware gain (volume).

▶ Repeat frames of the audio a specific number of times.

▶ Shuffle or randomly select and play from among multiple files.

▶ Mix both audio channels into a mono output.

▸ Downsample the audio file to 22 KHz (from the 44KHz standard).

▸ Use a URL as an input parameter to select an audio file to play.

The man page for mpg123 includes more detailed information.

For those with the GNOME desktop, GQmpeg provides an attractive interface similar to a CD player. GQmpeg plays MPEG (.mp3) audio files using the mpg123 command as an underlying tool. You can open GQmpeg's Configuration dialog box using the tiny wrench button above the Playlist button on the lower-right corner of the GQmpeg interface. Figure 9.17 shows some of the types of options that the GQmpeg MP3 player provides.

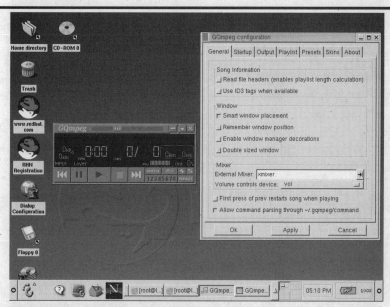

FIGURE 9.17:   The GQmpeg MP3 player

In addition to being able to play files in several popular audio formats (including MPEG3 and WAV), Xwave is an audio editor. With Xwave, you can cut and paste to edit an audio file. Figure 9.18 shows Xwave linearly tracking a digital audio file as it is being played.

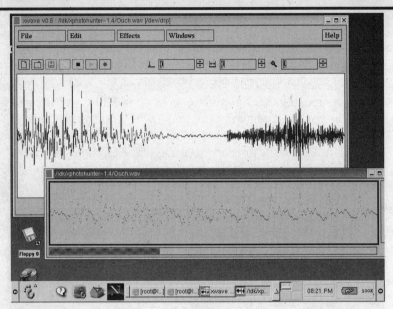

FIGURE 9.18:   The Xwave audio clip editor

Some of the things you can do with an audio clip in Xwave include the following:

▶ Change the frequency of the sampling for the clip

▶ Add echoes

▶ Reverse clips

▶ Cut, copy, and paste portions of a clip

An ambitious project for playing audio files is the Xmms project, formerly the x11amp project. Xmms has the capability to accept plug-ins in the form of libraries designed to perform various operations on audio files. Xmms is installed by default on Red Hat with plug-ins to support the following actions:

▶ Playing audio CDs

▶ Playing MPEG audio files

▶ Playing WAV audio files

▶ Generating tones

▶ Displaying a spectrum analyzer and oscilloscope

▸ Separate volume and balance controls

▸ Support for streaming audio servers, including icecast

Figure 9.19 shows Xmms with the equalizer and playlist editor (to help manage a list of audio files). You can right-click anywhere on the control window to select control and configuration options from a long pop-up menu.

FIGURE 9.19: The Xmms equalizer and playlist

The home page for the Xmms project is www.xmms.org. You can run Xmms using the xmms command from any graphical command line in Red Hat Linux. You'll notice that the image you see doesn't match exactly what I've shown in the figure. That's because Xmms allows you to load skins—or interface designs—to suite your preferences. By default, Xmms displays a mostly black background. By loading the xmmsskins package, you can select from almost 30 different looks.

I chose the skin titled Ultrafina for the figure because I thought it would work for our black-and-white printout. To choose a new skin after you've installed the xmmsskins package, right-click the main Xmms window and choose Options ➤ Skin Browser. A dialog box appears in which you can select the skin you want to use. When you click a skin in the dialog box, you immediately see how it looks on the main Xmms interface.

Another package, the X mixer, Xmmix, has a similar name to Xmms, but not a similar look.

The Xmmix program, shown in Figure 9.20, enables you to mix incoming audio channels from several sources and adjust their volume for the outgoing sound that you hear on the computer's speakers.

FIGURE 9.20:   The Xmmix audio mixer program

Manage Your Sounds

Several synthesizers are available that enable you to create your own music in Linux. SynaesGthesia is a basic music synthesizer package. A more advanced project is the Analog RealTime Synthesizer (ARTS). ARTS is intended to simulate a modular analog synthesizer, creating sounds using various modules to create waveforms that can be graphically combined. Many different filters or modules are included to create different sounds. After you use the graphical interface to create a piece of music, the synthesizer executes the modules that you have created, sending the waveforms to the sound card.

A complete home page for the ARTS project can be found at www .arts-project.org/. Figure 9.21 shows how modules can be seen in the graphical display of the ARTS synthesizer.

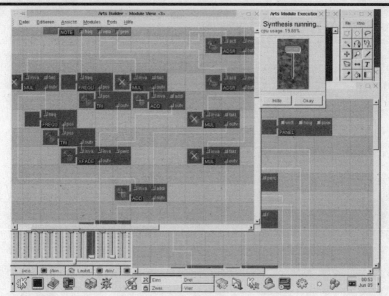

FIGURE 9.21:   The ARTS synthesizer modules

The interesting thing about the ARTS project is that ARTS was chosen as the sound system for KDE 2. If you're using KDE 2, you're using the ARTS system (in its basic form) to produce all the sounds of KDE programs. The KDE documentation and website have additional information about this powerful suite of audio tools.

If you have many files in MIDI format and need to play them or convert them to WAV format for use on another type of player (such as Xmms), you can use the TiMidity++ package.

This is a command-line program that takes a MIDI file as input and creates a WAV file using the name you supply. TiMidity++ includes a very extensive man page describing all of its features.

SoundTracker is more like what you're probably expecting when you hear the words *music synthesizer*. Figure 9.22 shows the main window of this program.

In SoundTracker, you can create instrumental sounds and combine them into music files, adjusting things such as tempo and volume mix of each instrument. Once you have a piece of music you like, you can render it as a WAV file so that you can distribute it or in order to play it yourself using simpler player programs such as those I've already described.

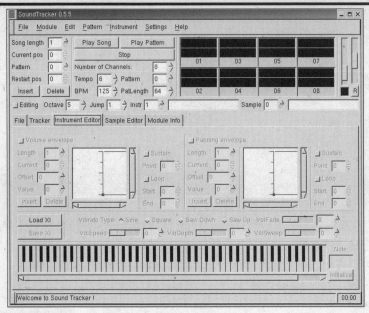

FIGURE 9.22:   The SoundTracker window

SoundTracker includes oscilloscope displays, an automatic transposition dialog box, and dozens of configuration options for loading new capabilities as modules or setting up the keyboard, audio options, and others. Unfortunately, SoundTracker doesn't have as much documentation as you might like if you're new to this type of program. You can learn a lot by visiting the website for SoundTracker at www.soundtracker.org.

A similar type of sound editing program is SoundStudio. SoundStudio includes a visual plot of an audio clip and gives you the capability to copy, cut, and paste segments of a clip. In addition, SoundStudio provides the following effects (from the Effects menu) to alter a digital sound clip:

- ▶ Echo
- ▶ Vibrato
- ▶ Fade
- ▶ Reverse
- ▶ Volume
- ▶ Tempo
- ▶ Reverb

- ▶ Flanger

- ▶ Phaser

- ▶ Chorus

Volume sliders at the bottom of the SoundStudio window let you adjust the volume of input and output channels independently. Figure 9.23 shows the main SoundStudio window with an information dialog box on the right. You can open the File Information dialog box by choosing File ➢ Information on the SoundStudio menu.

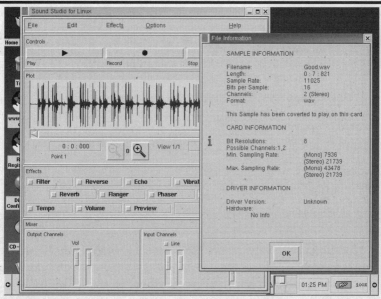

FIGURE 9.23: The main SoundStudio window with File Information box

SoundStudio includes an Options menu where you can select settings for colors, display options, and other parameters. In addition, you can choose Help ➢ User's Guide to open a complete hyperlinked description of how to use SoundStudio.

NOTE
SoundStudio is a tcl/Tk scripted program.

SoundStudio can be downloaded from http://www.tcc-chemnitz .de/firmen/ceres/ss10linux/.

Other Sound Tools

If you're more interested in listening to music than in making new music, you're probably already familiar with Napster. This program's future is up in the air, but without getting into that I'll just explain that Napster is a graphical program designed to help you easily share music files across the Internet with any other users who also want to share their music files.

Using Napster, you can "publish" a list of songs that you have and are willing to make available. You include information such as the artist and song title, as well as how fast your connection to the Net is.

WARNING

Be certain to read the warnings printed in software and on the Napster website about distributing copyrighted material. Don't do it!

You can then search for music files that you're interested in, using the Napster servers to locate someone who has the song files you want to download. Most music files are in MP3 format, so you can use any of the players such as mpg123, GQmpeg, or Xmms to play the files.

NOTE

You can download an official client at www.napster.com.

To begin using Napster, use the Connect icon to set up an account. You'll need to select a username and password, as well as enter your e-mail address and connection speed. After you set up this information, you won't have to enter it again to connect. The program searches for a Napster server and then lets you enter searches or download the music files that you've located, as shown in Figure 9.24.

If you already have a CD and want to turn it into a digital audio file on your Linux PC, use the DAGrab package. This command-line utility lets you specify detailed information about an audio CD and pull digital data into a WAV-formatted audio file.

You need to learn a little about each CD before grabbing digital audio files from it. A couple of sample commands to help you get started are shown here. To see a listing of the tracks on an audio CD, insert the CD and use the dagrab command with the -i option (for index). The output is shown with the command here.

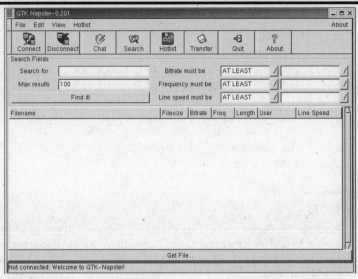

FIGURE 9.24: Napster for Linux

NOTE

The DAGrab program attempts to locate detailed information on your CD by contacting a CDDB server. The CD I used for this example couldn't be located on a CDDB server, so I'll have to enter the track names myself.

```
$ dagrab -i /dev/cdrom
dagrab: error retrieving cddb data
```

track	start	length	type	duration	MB
1	150	2160	audio	00:00:28	4
2	2310	4632	audio	00:01:01	10
3	6942	8365	audio	00:01:51	18
4	15307	7561	audio	00:01:40	16
5	22868	8008	audio	00:01:46	17
6	30876	14309	audio	00:03:10	32
7	45185	9002	audio	00:02:00	20
8	54187	11712	audio	00:02:36	26
9	65899	11390	audio	00:02:31	25
10	77289	7998	audio	00:01:46	17

Part ii

11	85287	7113	audio	00:01:34	15
12	92400	10882	audio	00:02:25	24
13	103282	10836	audio	00:02:24	24
14	114118	8935	audio	00:01:59	20
15	123053	6240	audio	00:01:23	13
170	129293	-	leadout		

CDDB DISCID: 8b06b90f

Done!

NOTE

I include the device name in my example commands. If you don't include a device, DAGrab assumes that it should use /dev/cdrom. If your system is set up to use that standard device, the command dagrab -i works fine without the device name.

The far right column, labeled MB, tells how many megabytes of disk space will be required to grab each track. If I wanted to dump all of the tracks to my hard disk, I would use this command:

```
$ dagrab -a /dev/cdrom
```

The default filename of trackx.wav is used, where x is the track number of each track's file. You can also include an -f option to specify a different filename. Use %02d as a variable for the track number, for example:

```
$ dagrab -a -f song%02d.wav
```

In the same vein, you can dump a single track by indicating the track number. The filename trackx.wav is used by default, or once again you can specify a filename using the -f option. For example, to capture only Track 7 after reviewing the CD index, use this command:

```
$ dagrab 7 -f mozart7.wav
```

NOTE

The DAGrab program includes several options to control the use of local and remote CDDB data when working with your audio CDs. See the man page for details.

Another interesting command-line utility is the Festival speech synthesizer. Festival is a general purpose text-to-speech system. It uses a command-line interface (with a `festival>` prompt) to accept commands or to translate text to spoken sounds.

Start the program with the command **festival**. When the `festival>` prompt appears, you can start by entering **help** to see a list of initial options.

The Festival program includes a client and a server program, plus numerous other binary files as well as support for American, British, and Spanish (generic) speech. To learn more about the system, study the man page. The package includes an empty doc directory; visit the site `www.cstr.ed.ac.uk/projects/festival/manual` to learn more.

CREATE A GRAPHICS WORKSTATION

Linux has terrific support for hundreds of video graphics cards. These enable Linux users to play games and have fancy interfaces such as a 1600×1200 high-resolution KDE 2 desktop.

With all that power, Linux developers have also created tools specially designed for graphics work—things that we used to reserve for SGI or Macintosh computers. While we don't have any official Adobe products (such as Photoshop or Premiere) on Linux, we do have a wide range of tools that I'll describe briefly in this section.

The first thing to be aware of for graphics work in Linux is the range of basic viewers and tools that are installed by default or are easily available on your system. Table 9.1 provides a quick list.

TABLE 9.1

PROGRAM NAME (EXECUTABLE NAME)	COMMENTS
The Gimp (`gimp`)	The most powerful graphics tool commonly available on Linux; hundreds of filters, plug-ins, and so on; installed by default on most systems; see `www.gimp.org`.
XV (`xv`)	An old standby and favorite of many Linux users. Great for image viewing and basic manipulation, though not extensible like the Gimp.
KIllustrate (Use KDE 2 menus)	Part of the KOffice package that you can install with KDE 2 (see Chapter 8). A vector-based drawing program that shows great promise but isn't as complete or stable as other tools.

Part ii

TABLE 9.1 continued

PROGRAM NAME (EXECUTABLE NAME)	COMMENTS
CorelDRAW for Linux	A great vector-based drawing program from Corel, recently sold to Linux Global Partners. See `linux.corel.com`, but expect changes in its status.
Electric Eyes (`ee`)	A basic image viewer included with GNOME on the Programs ➢ Graphics menu.
GQView (`gqview`)	A slightly more advanced image viewer included with GNOME on the Programs ➢ Graphics menu.
Paint (`xpaint`)	A basic bitmapped drawing program, included on the GNOME Programs ➢ Graphics menu and on the KDE menus of some distributions (but often not because of KPaint).
KPaint (`kpaint`)	A basic bitmapped drawing program for KDE, included on the KDE Graphics menu. More attractive but not necessarily more functional than XPaint.
Image Viewer (`kview`)	A basic image viewer supplied with KDE via the Graphics menu. Provides a cleaner layout than GQView and has many simple transformation tools (rotate, zoom, and so on).
Icon Editor (`kiconedit`)	A special-purpose program for editing and creating icons. Provided with KDE on the Graphics menu but useful for many situations because it uses standard X Window System formats.
KSnapshot (`ksnapshot`)	A good screen capture utility provided with KDE on the Graphics menu. (Also try the Gimp under the File ➢ Acquire menu or the command-line xwd utility.)

Exploring all of these basic tools that come with most Linux distributions isn't within the scope of this book. Some of them are so capable (I'm thinking particularly of the Gimp) that entire books are devoted to them. Use the online help and man pages to learn about these programs.

The programs in the sections that follow do more than just view or draw images. They manipulate, download, and generally make images more useful and interesting on Linux and with other special hardware you might already own.

Access Your Digital Photos

I like film. But a lot of people—including professional photographers—are using digital photos more than ever before. You can get your regular film processed and placed on a photo CD, or you can use a digital camera and skip the film altogether.

The xpcd program is a simple viewer for photo CDs. It lets you view photos in the Gimp or use a basic viewer that's part of the xpcd program. A series of items on the Options menu let you set the JPEG quality level, view thumbnails, view in grayscale, and so on.

Once you have the program running, just choose File ➢ Open Photo CD to get started.

If you're using a digital camera instead of having photos processed onto a photo CD, several programs can help you pull your photos into your Linux system. I'll describe three, moving from the simplest to the most complete.

If you own a Kodak digital camera such as the DC200/DC210/DC260, you can upload pictures for viewing in Linux using the kdcpi package.

The kdcpi program is a Perl script, so you'll need to have Perl installed. After untarring the package, change to the kdcpi-0.0.2 directory and run the command as in the following, using the serial port device name, transfer speed to use, and camera command as shown:

```
$ ./kdcpi /dev/cua0 115200 status
```

Other commands include list (to report the available pictures), dump all, and dump x (where x specifies which particular pictures to upload).

This program is in the early stages of development, but it can still save you from rebooting your system to Windows if you have a Kodak digital camera. The author is also working on a graphical interface to list available pictures and facilitate downloading. Figure 9.25 shows a sample from this enhancement, which he has not yet made available publicly. You can learn more about this project on the home page at www .berkhirt.com/HomerProductions/products/kdcpi/.

A more comprehensive tool than kdcpi is gDC3-Play. This graphical program lets you pull photos from any camera that supports the DC-3 protocol, such as a Ricoh RDC-300.

The basic process for using gDC3-Play is simple:

▶ Retrieve the index of photos from an attached digital camera using the Get Index button.

▶ Select a photo to download and click the Download button.

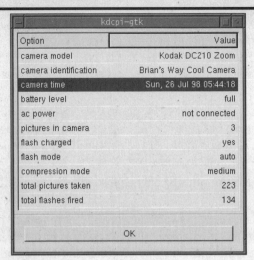

FIGURE 9.25: The kdcpi program

You can choose Settings ➢ Preferences or press the Configure button to open a configuration dialog box where you can set up the device name and baud rate, as well as the filenames to use when saving downloaded pictures. Figure 9.26 shows the basic but effective interface for gDC3-Play.

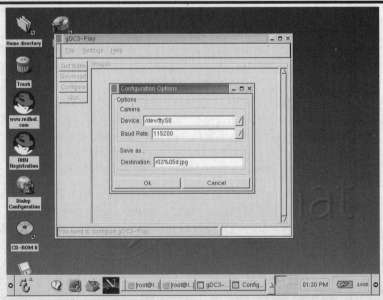

FIGURE 9.26:   The gDC3-Play Configuration Options dialog box

A final option for owners of digital cameras is the gPhoto program. This package is installed by default on Red Hat.

Using gPhoto is similar to using gDC3-Play: You follow the same basic process of reviewing an index of images and then download those you want onto the computer. The difference is that gPhoto is much more advanced in the photo manipulation that it provides via the Image menu (though still very basic compared to the Gimp) and in the flexibility of its features.

The best part of gPhoto, however, is probably the list of about 115 digital cameras that it supports. You just choose Configure ➢ Select Port-Camera Model and pick the camera you're using. You can find this dialog box over the gPhoto main window (see Figure 9.27).

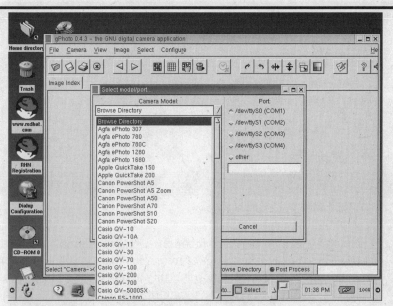

FIGURE 9.27:   The Camera Model dialog in gPhoto

gPhoto also uses a nice multi-tab design to let you quickly switch between the index of photos and the photos themselves.

NOTE

A great feature of gPhoto is the File ➢ Export ➢ HTML Gallery, which creates a web page of thumbnails for easy access to numerous photos via a browser.

Manipulate Your Images

Remember *Terminator 2*? Back then we were all so impressed to see morphing—a smooth computerized transition between two images. Now you can do the same thing on your Linux system.

NOTE

Calculating a morph between images still requires a lot of computer processing power. Be patient.

Xmorph can be used as a plug-in for the Gimp graphical tool, or as a stand-alone program, as shown in Figure 9.28.

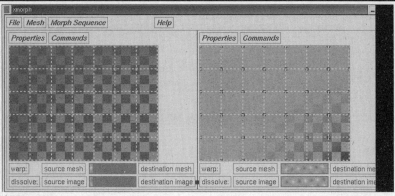

FIGURE 9.28:   The Xmorph program

The Xmorph man page also mentions a command-line tool called morph. Because morphing large or numerous images can be very time-consuming, you can use the morph utility to process morphs on multiple Linux machines (once you have the morph set up) without using the system resources required for a graphical desktop. For more information on this program, visit the home page of the author at http://colorado-research.com/~gourlay/software/Graphics/Xmorph.

Another program that provides more morphing between images is the XMRM package. XMRM provides a complete morphing toolkit for Linux. Figure 9.29 shows the XMRM program in action, with a sample project loaded.

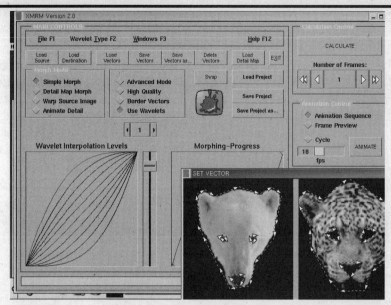

FIGURE 9.29: Setting morph points in XMRM

Creating a great morph requires some effort. You must define certain areas of the images for the program to focus on when creating transitions. You can see from the number of controls in the XMRM program some of the complexities involved. I recommend reviewing both the README.TXT file and the quickstart.html document.

A related image manipulation is the creation of a photomosaic from hundreds or thousands of other pictures. You've probably seen posters of *Star Wars* or something similar done using this technique. When you look at the image from a distance (10 feet or so), you see a single image of a *Star Wars* ship, or of Abraham Lincoln, or whatever. But when you look at the image up close, you see that it is made up of thousands of other images, each related to the main image (for example, frames from a *Star Wars* movie). The location of each smaller image is chosen to reflect the color and brightness of a part of the original image that is being re-created by using many small images.

The Metapixel program will create just such a photomosaic from your own photos or from those that you have downloaded. You need to use the Metapixel-prepare program (actually a Perl script) to prepare all of the component images for use in the mosaic, then use the Metapixel program to create the mosaic itself. Creating a photomosaic from thousands of other photos takes a good bit of computer power. Be patient when you run this program.

If you're interested in mathematical images, KDE includes a basic fractal generator (see Figure 9.30). Fractal generators create complex images by repeating simple structures based on mathematical formulas. You can start the fractal generator from the KDE menus by choosing Graphics ➤ Fractal Generator. Both Mandelbrot and Julia fractals are supported (see the Types menu). You can also set colors, iterations, and zoom factors on the Options menu.

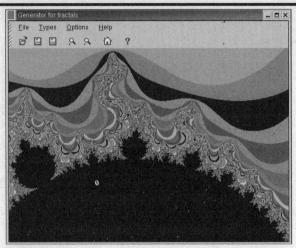

FIGURE 9.30:   The KDE fractal generator

The fun of the KDE fractal generator is to click and drag on a portion of the image and see the program redraw the fractal as a magnified image of the portion that you selected. By choosing File ➤ Save Pic, you can save any image you particularly like as a BMP image.

A more interesting fractal program is Gnofract4D.

NOTE

You can also launch Gnofract4D from the GNOME menu by choosing Programs ➤ Graphics ➤ Gnofract4D.

Gnofract4D differs from a typical fractal generator because it shows you the fractal in four dimensions (as displayed on a two-dimensional screen, that is). The top part of the Gnofract4D window shows you six circles with letters in them. Each circle represents an axis of rotation. To change the view of the fractal image in the main screen, click and drag the tiny circle within one of the six larger circles. The image is immediately redrawn in low resolution, then updated to a new high-resolution image.

You can also click and drag within the image window to zoom in on a portion of the fractal image. As with the KDE fractal generator, you can choose items from the File menu to save a fractal image as a bitmapped file, or to save the parameters for use later.

You can use the Settings ➢ Colors menu to select a colormap for the image. You can see the colormap selection dialog box to the right of the main window in Figure 9.31.

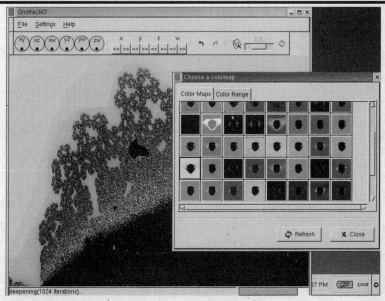

FIGURE 9.31:   Changing the colormap in Gnofract4D

The Settings ➢ Preferences menu includes numerous other configuration parameters that you can adjust for the fractal image. The Fractal Properties dialog box (shown in Figure 9.32) is unusual in its design. You click an arrow to the right of a subtitle (such as Rendering) to display the Rendering options below that item. In the figure, most of the items are open for viewing. When you first open the dialog box, all are closed.

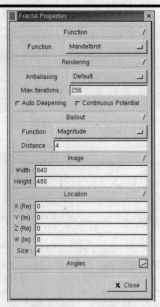

FIGURE 9.32: The Fractal Properties dialog box in Gnofract4D

In the same vein as the other fractal programs is Xmountains, which simply provides a fractal-based image of a mountain scene, scrolling from side to side across your screen.

The Xmountains program is started with the xmountains command. The man page describes a series of 34 options (welcome to Linux) that you can use to control the display from the command line. Figure 9.33 shows a basic Xmountains image.

FIGURE 9.33:   A mountain image created by Xmountains

Try CAD on Linux

QCad is a complete computer-aided drafting system for two-dimensional projects such as home plans, mechanical drawings, and building views. QCad uses the standard .dxf format for its files, so you can work with other drafting programs that use the same format.

NOTE

QCad also runs on other platforms, such as Windows. See www.qcad.org for information.

After you have installed the QCad package, you can use the sample projects included with the package to experiment with this powerful tool. Choose the File ➢ Open menu to open a sample file. In Figure 9.34, you can see one of these sample projects (example03.dxf) in the main window of QCad.

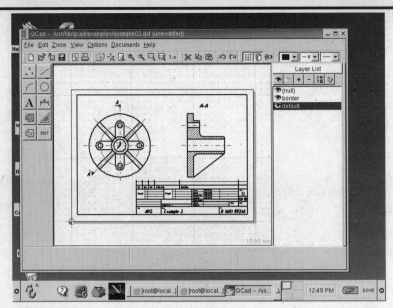

FIGURE 9.34:   A simple CAD image in QCad

The column on the right of the QCad window contains a list of layers in the drawing. You can use the buttons above the list to add new layers or change the properties (such as display color) for existing layers. Buttons on the main toolbar let you select whether to view the layer list or the available libraries. Another part of the toolbar controls the zoom options, which are also available via the Zoom menu.

NOTE
You can view a detailed manual for QCad by selecting Help ➢ Manual or pressing F1.

Choosing Options ➢ General Preferences shows a dialog box where you can select settings for QCad from nine categories such as Dimensions, Printing, and Language. The Options ➢ Current Drawing Settings menu brings up a Preferences dialog box that shows several categories of information that apply to your current project (see Figure 9.35).

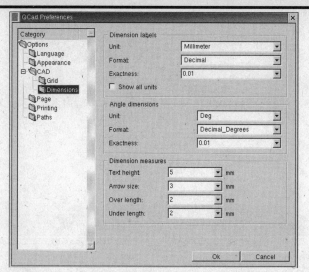

FIGURE 9.35:   Current drawing information in QCad

The toolbar that you see on the right of the window is used to work on the drawing. When you choose certain tools, the toolset updates to reflect your choice. For example, clicking on the Edit button (which appears when you first start the program) causes a new set of tools to appear. If you click the Arc tool, a new set of arc drawing tools appears.

NOTE

Right-click the drawing to back up one level in the displayed toolset.

WHAT'S NEXT?

In this chapter, you have explored many of the ways that Linux can be used to make your time at the computer both productive and fun. As Linux evolves, the graphic and design capabilities will continue to expand. In the next chapter you will learn more about the X Windows environment and how to customize it for your needs.

Part ii

Chapter 10

ADVANCED X WINDOWS CONFIGURATION

As you have already seen in this part of the book, the X Windows environment provides a degree of flexibility and customizability not commonly found in many GUI-based operating systems. Of course, with this degree of flexibility comes some degree of complexity: To fully utilize the X Windows flexibility, you must use configuration methods that are sometimes complex.

This chapter describes in detail the main components of X Windows and how they can be customized. It starts with an XFree86 version 4 `XF86Config` file, which tells the X server how to behave. This file specifies everything from the type of video card and monitor in use (including the desired resolution and color depth) to the input devices (mouse and keyboard) being used.

Once the X server is fully configured the way you like it, you will probably want to control how X Windows starts: what

Adapted from *Mastering Red Hat Linux 7.1* by Arman Danesh

ISBN 0-7821-2927-7   1008 pages $49.99

programs launch at startup, what actions take place before X Windows loads, and how the window manager gets launched. In addition, the X resources database provides a mechanism through which it is possible to control settings such as the colors and fonts used in windows and the behavior of windows in response to certain actions. These settings (and others) can be specified either globally or on a per-application basis.

THE *XF86CONFIG* FILE

The configuration of XFree86 is in the file XF86Config. This file usually can be found at /etc/XF86Config or /etc/X11/XF86Config, depending on your distribution. Red Hat Linux 7.1 places the file in /etc/X11. Alternatively, you can start with a generic configuration file, such as the /usr/X11R6/lib/X11/XF86Config.eg file.

If you don't know where your installation of XFree86 has placed this file, use the locate command to find it:

```
# locate XF86Config
```

The XF86Config file contains information pertinent to the operation of the X server, including keyboard definitions, mouse specifications, and monitor information. This file is generated by XFree86 configuration applications such as Xconfigurator and xf86config.

Sometimes though, fine-tuning your X Windows environment can be achieved only by directly editing the XF86Config file with your favorite text editor.

NOTE

As of this writing, the XFree86 version 4 server does not include drivers for as many graphics cards as XFree86 version 3. Therefore, many configurations include both an XF86Config and an XF86Config-4 file. If you have both files in your /etc/X11 directory, the following instructions apply to your /etc/X11/XF86Config-4 file.

The XF86Config file is broken down into several sections. Not all of these sections are required for a working GUI. With the release of XFree86 version 4, the order of these sections is no longer important.

Files   This section specifies where XFree86 can find its supplementary files, such as fonts, loadable modules, and the color table.

ServerFlags This section is used to enable and disable X server features, such as how to handle certain key sequences.

Module This section specifies runtime-loadable modules loaded during X server startup. These include font rasterizer modules. In most cases, you already have a working X server, and the standard fonts are sufficient, so you may not even have a `Module` section in your `XF86Config` file.

InputDevice This section specifies input devices, including keyboards and mice. Not required if there are `Keyboard` and `Pointer` sections.

Keyboard This section specifies the keyboard protocol that controls how the key map is defined and other keyboard features, such as the repeat rate. Not required if there is an `InputDevice` section for the keyboard. Can work with XFree86 version 4.

Pointer This section indicates the type of mouse being used, the device port occupied by the mouse, and the button behavior of the mouse. Not required if there is an `InputDevice` section for the keyboard. Can work with XFree86 version 4.

VideoAdaptor This section is supposed to support video as a "primitive," in other words, a video adapter that is a component of some larger system. Not used as of this writing.

Monitor This section defines the specifications of your monitor. May incorporate information in the `Modes` section.

Device This section defines available graphic devices (display adapters).

Modes This section defines the refresh rate and the resolution capabilities of your monitor. May be incorporated into the `Monitor` section.

Screen This section links monitors to video adapters. It also defines the behavior of available X servers, such as the generic SVGA server, vendor-specific servers, and the monochrome server. May include multiple `Display` subsections, which correspond to alternate resolutions and color depths.

ServerLayout This section links screens to specific input devices, namely keyboards and mice.

DRI   This section addresses any special settings you might have for the Direct Rendering Interface (DRI), which is more common for graphics-intensive workstations. DRI configuration is beyond the scope of this book. For more information, refer to the following website:

`http://www.xfree86.org/current/DRI.html.`

Vendor   This section will be used for vendor-specific settings. Not used as of this writing.

Files

The `Files` section is used to specify where certain critical files are located on your system. The following is a sample `Files` section without the comments:

NOTE

In the XF86Config file, comments start with a hash mark (#) and continue to the end of the line. XFree86 ignores all the content contained in comments.

```
Section "Files"


    RgbPath  "/usr/X11R6/lib/X11/rgb"


    FontPath "/usr/X11R6/lib/X11/fonts/local/"
    FontPath "/usr/X11R6/lib/X11/fonts/misc/"
    FontPath "/usr/X11R6/lib/X11/fonts/75dpi/:unscaled"
    FontPath "/usr/X11R6/lib/X11/fonts/100dpi/:unscaled"
    FontPath "/usr/X11R6/lib/X11/fonts/Type1/"
    FontPath "/usr/X11R6/lib/X11/fonts/Speedo/"
    FontPath "/usr/X11R6/lib/X11/fonts/75dpi/"
    FontPath "/usr/X11R6/lib/X11/fonts/100dpi/"


#   ModulePath    "/usr/X11R6/lib/modules"


EndSection
```

There are several basic rules to note here that apply to the other six sections as well:

▶ Each section starts with a `Section` line.

▶ Each section ends with an `EndSection` line.

▶ On the `Section` line, the name of the section is specified in double quotes (in this case, `Section "Files"`).

There are three commonly used directives in this section, described in Table 10.1.

TABLE 10.1:   *Files* Directives

DIRECTIVE	EFFECT
RgbPath	This directive specifies the name of the RGB (red-green-blue) database without the `.txt` or `.db` extension. The RGB file specifies the amount of red, green, and blue associated with other named colors. Generally, the default value can be left untouched unless you move or change the name of your RGB database (which is not a good idea, anyway, because several applications make use of the database and expect to find it in its normal location).
FontPath	This directive is used as many times as needed to specify where X Windows can find the installed X fonts on your system. Both scalable fonts and bitmap fonts can be indicated (the bitmap fonts, which can't be scaled, have `:unscaled` appended to the end of the directory). If you add new font directories to your system, you should add a `FontPath` directive for them here.
ModulePath	This directive is used on operating systems such as Linux that support dynamically loaded modules. This directive indicates where to look for modules. With most versions of XFree86, this directive won't appear or will be commented out as in our example. The default path for modules is `/usr/X11R6/lib/modules`, and you need to use this directive only if you need to change this value.

Other font modules are available in the `/usr/X11R6/lib/modules/fonts` directory.

Part ii

ServerFlags

The ServerFlags section allows you to enable and disable some features of your X server. An example ServerFlags section, without comments, appears as follows:

```
Section "ServerFlags"

#  Option  "NoTrapSignals"

#  Option  "DontZap"

#  Option  "DontZoom"

#  Option  "DisableVidModeExtension"

#  Option  "AllowNonLocalXvidtune"

#  Option  "DisableModInDev"

#  Option  "AllowNonLocalModInDev"

#  Option  "AllowMouseOpenFail"

#  Option  "blank time"      "10"
#  Option  "standby time"    "20"
#  Option  "suspend time"    "30"
#  Option  "off time"        "60"

#  Option  "EstimateSizesAggressively" "0"

#  Option  "NoPM" "false"

#  Option  "Xinerama" "true"

EndSection
```

Uncomment any of these directives that you want to activate; leave them commented (the usual default state) if you don't want them activated. Any options specified here are superseded by options in the ServerLayout section.

The directives in this example have the effects described in Table 10.2.

TABLE 10.2:   *ServerFlags* Directives

DIRECTIVE	EFFECT
NoTrapSignals	This directive is used for debugging. When a signal indicating an error is received, the server performs a core dump that dumps the contents of its section of memory to a file on the disk. This can cause instability in your system but is invaluable when debugging problems, particularly with beta and test versions of different X servers. Unless you are troubleshooting or testing an X server, you are best advised to leave this directive commented.
DontZap	Normally, the key combination Ctrl+Alt+Backspace causes X Windows to abort and returns you to the console. With this directive enabled, Ctrl+Alt+Backspace will be ignored, and the key combination will be passed on to the current application for processing. You should uncomment this line only in those rare instances when you are running an application that needs to use this key combination to function properly.
DontZoom	Normally, the key combination Ctrl+Alt+Keypad Plus cycles through available configured screen resolutions for your X server, increasing the resolution each time. Ctrl+Alt+Keypad Minus is similarly used to decrease the resolution. If these key combinations are needed for other purposes by an application, uncomment this line to have X Windows ignore these key combinations and pass them on to your application.
DisableVidModeExtension	This directive prevents tuning of your video display with the Xvidtune client. (Xvidtune isn't discussed in this book; documentation for this program can be found by typing the command **man xvidtune** in an open xterm window.) There is no need to uncomment this entry, and you can leave it commented out by default.

TABLE 10.2 continued: *ServerFlags* Directives

DIRECTIVE	EFFECT
AllowNonLocalXvidtune	Related to the previous directive, this directive allows non-local (in other words, out on the network somewhere) Xvidtune clients to access your X Windows system. For security reasons, it is best to leave this directive disabled.
DisableModInDev	By enabling this directive, it becomes impossible to change keyboard and mouse settings dynamically while X Windows is running.
AllowNonLocalModInDev	Uncommenting this directive allows nonlocal computers to alter your keyboard and mouse settings. It is unwise to enable this directive unless you need to.
AllowMouseOpenFail	Allows the X server to start even if you don't have a working Pointer (mouse).
"blank time" "10"	If there is no activity on your computer for the specified period (10 minutes, in this case), a screensaver is activated. The exact action depends on the specifications of your monitor.
"standby time" "20"	If there is no activity on your computer for the specified period (20 minutes, in this case), your monitor goes into standby mode. The exact action depends on the specifications of your monitor.
"suspend time" "30"	If there is no activity on your computer for the specified period (30 minutes, in this case), your monitor goes into suspend mode. The exact action depends on the specifications of your monitor.
"off time" "60"	If there is no activity on your computer for the specified period (60 minutes, in this case), your monitor goes into off mode. The exact action depends on the specifications of your monitor.
EstimateSizesAggresively	If you have BIOS problems detecting second video adapters, setting this variable to 2 may help. As of this writing, documentation is sketchy on this variable.
NoPM "false"	Disables Power Management.
Xinerama "true"	Precursor for multiple monitors, each with a separate graphics card.

Module

The Module section specifies server and font extensions over and above basic parameters. No modules are required for a working graphical user interface. An example Module section, without comments, appears as follows:

```
Section "Module"

#  Load "dbe"

#  SubSection "extmod"

#    Option "omit XFree86-DGA"

#  EndSubSection

#  Load "type1"

#  Load "freetype"

EndSection
```

Uncomment any of these directives that you want to activate; leave them commented (the usual default state) if you don't want them activated. The directives in this example have the effects described in Table 10.3.

TABLE 10.3: *Module* Directives

DIRECTIVE	EFFECT
Load "dbe"	Loads Double Buffer Extensions, which allows consecutive images to be loaded into different buffers.
Option "omit XFree86-DGA"	Disables the Direct Graphics Access extension.
Load "type1"	Loads the PostScript type1 font module.
Load "freetype"	Loads the named TrueType clone.

Other extension modules are available in the /usr/X11R6/lib/modules/extensions directory.

InputDevice—Keyboard

The InputDevice sections specify pointers (mice) and keyboards. While InputDevice is the default for XFree86 version 4, the legacy Keyboard and Pointer modules can still be used as well. Normally, there are two InputDevice sections: one each for a keyboard and a pointing device.

As you might expect, one InputDevice section specifies information pertinent to the functioning of your keyboard, including the keyboard type and protocol. While this section is no longer used by default, it is still recognized by XFree86 version 4. Even though Red Hat Linux 7.1 uses XFree86 version 4, the Keyboard and Pointer sections (not InputDevice) are part of the default Red Hat Linux 7.1 XF86Config configuration file. A typical InputDevice section, without comments, is shown here:

```
Section "InputDevice"
#  Option  "Protocol"    "Xqueue"

#  Identifier  "Keyboard1"
#  Driver      "keyboard"

#  Option  "AutoRepeat"  "500 5"

#  Option  "XkbDisable"

#  Option  "Xleds"       "1 2 3"

#  Option  "LeftAlt"     "Meta"
#  Option  "RightAlt"    "ModeShift"
#  Option  "RightCtl"    "Control"
#  Option  "ScrollLock"  "Compose"
#  Option  "XkbDisable"
#  Option  "XkbModel"    "pc101"
#  Option  "XkbModel"    "pc102"
#  Option  "XkbModel"    "pc104"
#  Option  "XkbModel"    "pc105"
#  Option  "XkbModel"    "pc106"
```

```
#  Option  "XkbModel"    "microsoft"


#  Option  "XkbLayout"   "us"
#  Option  "XkbLayout"   "de"
#  Option  "XkbVariant"  "nodeadkeys"
#  Option  "XkbOptions"  "ctrl:swapcaps"


#  Option  "XkbRules"    "xfree86"
#  Option  "XkbKeymap"   "xfree86(us)"


   EndSection
```

This looks like a complicated section but, as Table 10.4 describes, it is actually quite simple.

TABLE 10.4:   *Keyboard* Directives

DIRECTIVE	EFFECT
"Protocol" "Xqueue"	The Xqueue protocol is used for various Sun Solaris servers (SRV3, SRV4). If this line is missing, XFree86 defaults to Standard, which works for almost all other systems.
Identifier, Driver	Names assigned by the administrator to the keyboard and keyboard driver.
AutoRepeat	This directive is used to specify how long to wait while a key is pressed down before auto-repeat should start and how often the key should be repeated. All values are in milliseconds. In the previous example, AutoRepeat 500 5 indicates that auto-repeat should start after a key has been held down for 500 milliseconds (half a second), and then the key should repeat every 5 milliseconds.
Xleds	This directive specifies which keyboard LEDs, such as Num Lock and Caps Lock, can be controlled by the user using the xset command.
LeftAlt, RightAlt, Right Ctl, and ScrollLock	X Windows originally ran on Unix workstations that had keyboards distinctly different from the standard PC keyboard. These keyboards included special keys such as Meta, ModeShift, Compose, and ModeLock. If you find that you need these keys for Unix or other applications, then uncomment these directives.
XkbDisable	If this line is uncommented, an extension to X Windows called XKB is disabled. When XKB is enabled (the directive is commented out), XKB determines the keyboard mapping using a series of directives, generally for older X servers.

Part ii

TABLE 10.4 continued: *Keyboard* Directives

DIRECTIVE	EFFECT
XkbModel	This directive is used when XKB is enabled to specify the keyboard model. Standard U.S. keyboards are pc101. The U.S. "Windows" keyboard is pc104. The Microsoft Natural keyboard is microsoft. Most European keyboards are pc102 or pc105. The standard Japanese keyboard is pc106.
XkbLayout	This directive is used when XKB is enabled to specify which keyboard layout to use. It's most common when there is more than one language for a keyboard model; for example, de, for deutsch, corresponds to a German-language keyboard.
XkbOptions	This directive can be used when XKB is enabled to swap the position of your Caps Lock and Ctrl keys. To do this, set the directive to the value ctrl:swapcaps.
XkbRules	Basic ruleset for keyboard layout. Required to use the XFree86 server.
XkbKeymap	This directive is used when XKB is enabled to load a keyboard mapping definition.

TIP

If you are setting up a non-English keyboard, help is available in the HOWTO documents at http://www.linuxdoc.org. A number of language-specific HOWTOs can help you configure keyboards for the specified languages.

InputDevice—Pointer

The second InputDevice section deals with mouse-related configuration. As discussed earlier, you can set up an InputDevice or a Pointer section for mouse-related configuration under XFree86 version 4. The default Red Hat Linux 7.1 XF86Config file includes a Pointer section to configure a mouse. In this section, you set such information as the type of mouse you have, the port the mouse is connected to, and the behavior associated with different mouse buttons.

```
Section "InputDevice"

# Identifier  "Mouse1"
```

```
#  Driver       "mouse"

#  Option  "Protocol"    "PS/2"
#  Option  "Protocol"    "Xqueue"
#  Option  "Device"      "/dev/mouse"

#  Option  "BaudRate"    "9600"
#  Option  "SampleRate"  "150"

#  Option  "Emulate3Buttons"
#  Option  "Emulate3Timeout"    "50"

#  Option  "ChordMiddle"

EndSection
```

Let's take these entries line by line in Table 10.5.

TABLE 10.5:   *Pointer* Directives

DIRECTIVE	EFFECT
Identifier, Driver	Names assigned by the administrator to the mouse and pointing device driver.
Protocol	This directive specifies the protocol used by your mouse. Typical options include Microsoft, Logitech, MouseSystems, BusMouse, PS/2, and Auto (for certain Plug and Play mice that Linux can recognize).
Device	This directive is used to specify which device port your mouse is connected to. If you configured your mouse correctly when you installed your distribution, the device /dev/mouse is linked to your mouse and you can use this. Otherwise, specify /dev/psaux for the PS/2 mouse port, Xqueue for Solaris systems, /dev/ttyS0 for COM1 in DOS and Windows, and /dev/ttyS1 for COM2 in DOS and Windows. Other options are available for pointing devices such as trackballs and touchscreens.
BaudRate	This directive is used for only a few older Logitech-brand mice. Check your mouse's documentation.

TABLE 10.5 continued: *Pointer* Directives

DIRECTIVE	EFFECT
SampleRate	This directive is used for only a few older Logitech-brand mice. Check your mouse's documentation.
Emulate3Buttons	This directive should be used for a two-button mouse. When uncommented, clicking the left and right mouse buttons at the same time will emulate the middle mouse button on a three-button mouse. Because X Windows relies on the presence of three mouse buttons, it is a good idea to enable this for a two-button mouse.
Emulate3Timeout	This directive is used to specify how close in time the two mouse buttons must be clicked to be considered a simultaneous click; this value is relevant only when Emulate3Buttons is enabled. By default, the time is set to 50ms. If you find it hard to get the mouse buttons to click together, lengthen the time by assigning a higher value. This directive assumes that the units are in milliseconds, and you should specify only the numeric value, not the units. In other words, Emulate3Timeout 100 is valid, and Emulate3Timeout 100 ms is not.
ChordMiddle	This directive is used to enable the middle button on some three-button Logitech mice. If you have a Logitech mouse and your middle button is not working, try enabling this directive.

Monitor

So far, the configuration directives you have seen have mostly been self-explanatory and not difficult to use. For every monitor that you attach to your computer, you need a separate Monitor section. Consider the following sample Monitor section:

```
Section "Monitor"


    Identifier   "monitor"
    VendorName   "LG"
    ModelName    "StudioWorks"


    HorizSync    30-70
```

```
VertRefresh 50-160

End Section
```

Table 10.6 describes the various directives for the Monitor section.

TABLE 10.6: *Monitor* Directives

DIRECTIVE	EXPLANATION
Identifier	This directive identifies with a user-assigned name the specifications for the monitor; this is used in other parts of the XF86Config file to refer to the monitor.
VendorName	This directive identifies the vendor of the monitor being defined. This value has no effect on the operation of XFree86, so it is best to assign a meaningful value that will help you identify the definition at a later date.
ModelName	This directive identifies the model of the monitor being defined. This value has no effect on the operation of XFree86, so it is best to assign a meaningful value that will help you identify the definition at a later date.
HorizSync	This directive specifies the horizontal sync range in KHz for your monitor. You may either specify a range as shown in the example or provide discrete values in a list with ranges of values separated by commas (such as 15-25, 30-50). It is essential that you consult your monitor's documentation and provide the correct values for your monitor. If you enter the incorrect values here, you have the potential to destroy or damage your monitor.
VertRefresh	This directive specifies the vertical refresh rates in Hz supported by your monitor. You may either specify a range as shown in the example or provide discrete values in a list with values separated by commas (such as 40-50, 80-100). It is essential that you consult your monitor's documentation and provide the correct values for your monitor. If you enter the incorrect values here, you have the potential to destroy or damage your monitor.

Part ii

Modes

For every monitor that you attach to your computer, you need a separate Modes section. Consider the following sample Modes section:

```
Section "Modes"

Identifier "Modes[0]"
```

```
Modeline "640x480" 46.02 640 656 760 832 480 490 498 522
Modeline "800x600" 71.91 800 808 928 1000 600 612 622 632
Modeline "1024x768" 117.53 1024 1088 1208 1360 768 783 796 829
Modeline "1600x1200" 200 1600 1616 1968 2080 1200 1200 1212 1253
```

EndSection

These Modelines specify possible modes for your monitor. Modes combine a resolution with a refresh, a dot clock, and timings to determine how to display to the monitor. The X server deletes any incompatible modes found in the XF86Config file when it tries to load them. However, getting the information correct for these lines is difficult. Generally, it is best to let your XFree86 configuration software create these lines for you and not alter them.

TIP

If you have multiple monitors, it is best to incorporate Modes information into the corresponding Monitor sections, to avoid confusion.

Table 10.7 describes the function of each number in the first Modeline, from left to right.

TABLE 10.7:   Modeline Items

ITEM	EXPLANATION
640x480	Screen resolution in pixels
46.02	Pixel clock, in MHz
640	Horizontal pixels displayed
656	Horizontal Sync start
760	Horizontal Sync end
832	Horizontal Sync total
480	Vertical pixels displayed
490	Vertical Sync start
498	Vertical Sync end
522	Vertical Sync total

Another way to express the first Modeline in the example

```
Modeline "640x480" 46.02 640 656 760 832 480 490 498 522
```

is as follows:

```
Mode "640x480"
    DotClock      46.02
    HTimings      640 656 760 832
    VTimings      480 490 498 522
EndMode
```

Device

The XF86Config file generally can contain multiple Device sections, to allow for multiple graphics adapters or video cards. The Device sections describe the video cards that can be used by the X server. Usually the server can fill in most of this information, but it is wise to check the result in your XF86Config file. Because this information includes some highly technical specifications about your video hardware, you should let your XFree86 configuration software handle this section unless you really need to make these changes yourself.

A Device section is active only if referenced by a Screen section.

Let's look at two example Device sections:

```
Section "Device"
    Identifier    "Generic VGA"

    VendorName    "Unknown"
    BoardName     "Unknown"
    Chipset       "generic"

#   VideoRam      256

#   Clocks        25.2 28.3
#   BusID         "PCI:1:0:0"
EndSection

Section "Device"
```

```
Identifier   "MGA Millennium I"
Driver       "mga"
Option       "hw cursor" "off"
BusID        "PCI:0:10:0"
```

EndSection

Table 10.8 describes the basic directives used in the Device section.

TABLE 10.8: *Device* Directives

DIRECTIVE	EFFECT
Identifier	As in the Monitor section, this directive provides a name that can be used elsewhere in the XF86Config file to identify the video card.
VendorName	This directive doesn't affect the operation of the X server but helps you identify the hardware later.
BoardName	This directive also doesn't affect operation but is an aid in identifying the device definition.
Chipset	This directive identifies your video chipset. If XFree86 doesn't support your hardware, the generic chipset will be used.
VideoRam	This directive specifies the amount of video memory available, in kilobytes. If you don't provide this information, the server will attempt to ascertain it directly from the video card.
Clocks	This directive specifies the clock settings for your video hardware. Don't edit this line by hand, but rather let your configuration software set it.
ClockChip	This directive specifies the clock chip being used by your video hardware, if it has one. If it does, there is no need to specify a Clocks line, since the clock chip will provide all the information.
Driver	This directive identifies the name of the driver for this particular device.
Option	Some drivers can be further configured. In the example shown, "hw cursor" "off" addresses a particular problem of some graphics cards with cursor placement in the X Window.
BusID	Specifies the location of a PCI or AGP graphics card. Significant when there is more than one graphics card in use.

Screen

The Screen section is used to bring together the information contained in your Monitor and Device sections. You can have multiple Screen sections.

The following is an example section for one Screen:

```
Section "Screen"
    Identifier "Screen L"
    Device     "MGA Millenium I"
    Monitor    "monitor"
    Subsection "Display"
        Depth      24
        Modes      "1024x768"
        ViewPort   0 0
    EndSubsection
    Subsection "Display"
        Depth      32
        Modes      "800x600"
        ViewPort   0 0
    EndSubsection
EndSection
```

The Screen section connects a chosen X server with a device and a monitor and then defines the accessible display modes (combinations of resolution and color depth). Table 10.9 describes the four main directives used in the Screen section.

TABLE 10.9: *Screen* Directives

DIRECTIVE	EFFECT
Identifier	This directive specifies a unique name for the given Screen. If you need a ServerLayout section, you'll need to use Identifier.
Device	This directive specifies the name of a Device identifier. Make sure this corresponds to the appropriate identifier in your Device section.
Monitor	This directive specifies the name of a Monitor identifier. Make sure this corresponds to the appropriate identifier in your Monitor section.

Part II

TABLE 10.9 continued: *Screen* Directives

DIRECTIVE	EFFECT
DefaultDepth	This directive specifies the color depth used when a Depth directive in the Display section is not specified.

Display

In addition to these directives, a subsection called Display is also used in the Screen section. You can use multiple Display subsections to specify available video modes.

Let's analyze the first subsection from the previous example:

```
Subsection "Display"
    Depth       24
    Modes       "1024x768"
    ViewPort 0 0
EndSubsection
```

This Display subsection specifies four directives, as described in Table 10.10.

TABLE 10.10:   *Display* Subsection Directives

DIRECTIVE	EFFECT
Depth	This directive specifies the color depth of the display in the number of bits per pixel. For instance, 8-bit allows 2^8 or 256 colors, 16-bit allows 2^{16} or 65,536 colors, and 24-bit allows 2^{24} or 16.7 million colors.
Modes	This directive specifies the resolution of the display. Common resolutions are 1024×768, 800×600, and 640×480.
ViewPort	This directive specifies the size of a possible virtual desktop. For instance, your 640×480 screen may be a window in a larger 1024×768 virtual display. As your mouse reaches the edge of the screen, the display will scroll to the edge of the virtual display. The ViewPort directive specifies the horizontal and vertical dimensions of the vertical desktop in pixels, but the values are separated by a space rather than by an x. The entry here, ViewPort 0 0, indicates that there is no virtual desktop.
Virtual	This directive specifies a screen size larger than the Modes directive, or the resolution of the display. If you have this directive, you can use your mouse or pointing device to move around this larger virtual area.

ServerLayout

A ServerLayout section completes your configuration by binding the Screen and InputDevice sections. As discussed earlier, the Screen section already brings together information from the Monitor and Device sections. A ServerLayout section is not required for a standard configuration; if it isn't part of your XF86Config file, the active Screen and the keyboard and mouse InputDevice(s) are used.

The following is an example ServerLayout section:

```
Section "ServerLayout"
#   Identifier   "Configuration 1"


#   Screen       "Sony Setup"
#   Screen       "Samsung Setup" RightOf "Sony Setup"


#   InputDevice "Mouse1"      "CorePointer"
#   InputDevice "Keyboard1"   "CoreKeyboard"


EndSection
```

This ServerLayout section specifies three directives, as described in Table 10.11.

TABLE 10.11: *ServerLayout* Section Directives

Directive	Effect
Identifier	Specifies a unique name for this ServerLayout.
Screen	Identifies the Screen sections that you want to use. In this case, there should be two Screen sections, and their Identifier directives should be "Sony Setup" and "Samsung Setup".
InputDevice	Identifies the InputDevice sections that you want to use. In this case, there should be two InputDevice sections, and their Identifier directives are "Mouse1" and "Keyboard1".

Part ii

THE X WINDOWS START-UP SEQUENCE

In addition to configuring your XFree86 server to provide the optimal display quality, you may want to configure the way your X Windows environment starts up. The two main files that allow each user to control his X Windows start-up sequence are .xinitrc and .Xclients. Both of these files sit in the user's home directory. When installed, they override system default files, which in Red Hat Linux 7.1 are /etc/X11/xinit/xinitrc and /etc/X11/xinit/Xclients.

The *.xinitrc* File

xinit is a special program that is used to start the X server and an initial client program, usually a window manager. By default, startx first checks for the existence of the .xinitrc file in the user's home directory and runs xinit based on this file. If the user's .xinitrc file is not found, the system-wide xinitrc file (/etc/X11/xinit/xinitrc in Red Hat Linux 7.1) is used by xinit. If neither of these is found, xinit will open a single xterm window after launching the X server.

The xinitrc or .xinitrc file is an executable shell script. Accordingly, this chapter doesn't go into the details of the shell or shell scripts; rather, it will quickly look at the default xinitrc file from Red Hat Linux 7.1 to see what it does. (The lines are numbered to help make the discussion easier. The line numbers are not part of the actual file.)

```
1:    #!/bin/sh

2:    # (c) 1999, 2000 Red Hat, Inc.


3:    userresources=$HOME/.Xresources

4:    usermodmap=$HOME/.Xmodmap

5:    userxkbmap=$HOME/.Xkbmap


6:    sysresources=/etc/X11/Xresources

7:    sysmodmap=/etc/X11/Xmodmap

8:    sysxkbmap=/etc/X11/Xkbmap


9:    # merge in defaults
```

```
10:   if [ -f "$sysresources" ]; then
11:       xrdb -merge "$sysresources"
12:   fi

13:   if [ -f "$userresources" ]; then
14:       xrdb -merge "$userresources"
15:   fi

16:   # merge in keymaps
17:   if [ -f "$sysxkbmap" ]; then
18:       setxkbmap `cat "$sysxkbmap"`
19:       XKB_IN_USE=yes
20:   fi

21:   if [ -f "$userxkbmap" ]; then
22:       setxkbmap `cat "$userxkbmap"`
23:       XKB_IN_USE=yes
24:   fi

25:   if [ -z "$XKB_IN_USE" -a ! -L /etc/X11/X ]; then
26:       if grep '^exec.*/Xsun' /etc/X11/X > /dev/null 2>&1
             && [ -f /etc/X11/XF86Config ]; then
27:           xkbsymbols=`sed -n -e 's/^[     ]*XkbSymbols
    ]*"\(.*\)".*$/\1/p' /etc/X11/XF86Config`
28:           if [ -n "$xkbsymbols" ]; then
29:               setxkbmap -symbols "$xkbsymbols"
30:               XKB_IN_USE=yes
31:           fi
32:       fi
33:   fi

34:   # xkb and xmodmap don't play nice together
35:   if [ -z "$XKB_IN_USE" ]; then
36:       if [ -f "$sysmodmap" ]; then
37:           xmodmap "$sysmodmap"
```

```
38:      fi


39:      if [ -f "$usermodmap" ]; then
40:          xmodmap "$usermodmap"
41:      fi
42:  fi


43:  unset XKB_IN_USE


44:  # The user may have his own clients to run. If not,
45:  # fall back to system defaults.


46:  # run all system xinitrc shell scripts.
47:  for i in /etc/X11/xinit/xinitrc.d/* ; do
48:      if [ -x "$I" ]; then
49:  . "$i"
50:      fi
51:  done


52:  if [ -f $HOME/.Xclients ]; then
53:      exec $HOME/.Xclients
54:  elif [ -f /etc/X11/xinit/Xclients ]; then
55:      exec /etc/X11/xinit/Xclients
56:  else
57:          # failsafe settings. Although we should never
                get here
58:          # (we provide fallbacks in Xclients as well) it
                can't hurt.
59:          xclock -geometry 100x100-5+5 &
60:          xterm -geometry 80x50-50+150 &
61:          if [ -f /usr/bin/netscape -a -f
    /usr/doc/HTML/index.html ]; then
62:                  netscape /usr/doc/HTML/index.html &
63:          fi
64:          if [ -f /usr/X11R6/bin/fvwm2 ]; then
```

```
65:                        exec fvwm2
66:            else
67:                        exec twm
68:            fi
69:    fi
```

The following steps take place:

1. Lines 3 to 8: The locations of files needed throughout the script are set. Note that these are variables that are used in following lines.

NOTE

The System X Resources file, shown in line 6 as `sysresources`, is located in the `/etc/X11/xdm/Xresources` file in Red Hat Linux 7.1. If you want to set this file as the common default X Windows preferences, as discussed later, change line 6 to reflect the actual location of the file.

2. Lines 10 to 12: If a global .Xresources file exists, apply it. (See the next section for a discussion of X resources.)

3. Lines 13 to 15: If the user has an .Xresources file in his home directory, apply it by merging it with current settings.

4. Lines 17 to 20: If a global X Window keyboard map file exists, apply the rules in the file.

5. Lines 21 to 24: If the user has an X Window keyboard map file in his home directory, apply it.

6. Lines 25 to 33: These lines probably don't apply to you unless you are using a Sun X server for your system.

7. Lines 34 to 43: If there are conflicts with the user- or system-defined X Window keyboard map file, set the keyboard definition to that file.

8. Lines 47 to 51: These lines execute all shell scripts located in the `/etc/X11/xinit/xinitrc.d/` directory.

9. Lines 52 to 69: This is where you actually start running the first clients after the X server starts. First, the script checks whether the user has a `.Xclients` file. If this file exists, it is executed to launch any clients specified in the file. If this file

doesn't exist, the script checks for the existence of the global Xclients file and, if it exists, executes it. Finally, if neither file exists, some default programs are launched, including xclock, an xterm window, a web browser, and, if available, either the FVWM2 or TWM window manager.

The *.Xclients* File

As you noticed in the discussion of the xinitrc file, the user can override the global Xclients file with a .Xclients file in his home directory. In either case, in the Red Hat environment, xinit ends up calling one of these files to launch the initial clients after the X server has started.

Like xinitrc, this file is a shell script and follows all the pertinent rules for shell scripts. To clarify the types of functions that Xclients can be used for, this section will look at the default Xclients file that shipped with Red Hat Linux 7.1 (line numbers have again been added):

```
1:  #!/bin/bash
2:  # (c) 1999, 2000 Red Hat, Inc.


3:  # check to see if the user has a preferred desktop
4:  PREFERRED=
5:  if [ -f /etc/sysconfig/desktop ]; then
6:      if [ -n "`grep -i GNOME /etc/sysconfig/desktop`" ];
    then
7:    PREFERRED=gnome-session
8:      elif [ -n "`grep -i KDE /etc/sysconfig/desktop`" ];
    then
9:    PREFERRED=startkde
10:      elif [ -n "`grep -i AnotherLevel /etc/sysconfig/
    desktop`" ]; then
11:    PREFERRED=AnotherLevel
12:      fi
13:  fi


14:  if [ -n "$PREFERRED" -a "$PREFERRED" != "AnotherLevel" ]
    && \
15:    which $PREFERRED >/dev/null 2>&1; then
```

```
16:       PREFERRED=`which $PREFERRED`
17:       exec $PREFERRED
18:  fi


19:  # now if we can reach here, either they want
         AnotherLevel or there
20:  # was no desktop file present and the PREFERRED variable
         is not set.


21:  if [ -z "$PREFERRED" ]; then


22:       GSESSION=gnome-session
23:       STARTKDE=startkde


24:       # by default, we run GNOME.
25:       if which $GSESSION >/dev/null 2>&1; then
26:          exec `which $GSESSION`
27:       fi


28:       # if GNOME isn't installed, try KDE.
29:       if which $STARTKDE >/dev/null 2>&1; then
30:          exec `which $STARTKDE`
31:       fi
32:  fi


33:  # Last, try AnotherLevel


34:  # these files are left sitting around by TheNextLevel.
35:  rm -f $HOME/Xrootenv.0
36:  rm -f /tmp/fvwmrc* 2>/dev/null


37:  # First thing - check the user preferences
38:  if [ -f $HOME/.wm_style ] ; then
39:     WMSTYLE=`cat $HOME/.wm_style |tr A-Z a-z`
```

```
40:     case "$WMSTYLE" in
41:    afterstep)
42:    exec /usr/X11R6/bin/RunWM -AfterStep
43:    ;;
44:    windowmaker|wmaker)
45:    exec /usr/X11R6/bin/RunWM -WindowMaker
46:    ;;
47:    fvwm95|fvwm|fvwm2)
48:    exec /usr/X11R6/bin/RunWM -Fvwm95
49:    ;;
50:    mwm|lesstif)
51:    exec /usr/X11R6/bin/RunWM -FvwmMWM
52:    ;;
53:     esac
54: fi

55: # Argh! Nothing good is installed. Fall back to fvwm2
    (win95-style) or twm
56: /usr/X11R6/bin/RunWM -Fvwm95 || {
57:     # gosh, neither fvwm95 nor fvwm2 is available;
58:     # fall back to failsafe settings
59:     xclock -geometry 100x100-5+5 &
60:     xterm -geometry 80x50-50+150 &
61:     if [ -f /usr/bin/netscape -a -f
   /usr/share/doc/HTML/index.html ];     then
62:    netscape /usr/share/doc/HTML/index.html &
63:     fi
64:     if [ -f /usr/X11R6/bin/fvwm ]; then
65:    exec fvwm
66:     else
67:    exec twm
68:     fi
69: }
```

Let's break down the steps of the Xclients file:

1. Lines 4 to 13: Set a preferred desktop. You can set your preferred desktop using the PREFERRED variable in line 4. If PREFERRED is not set to any desktop, lines 5–12 check the default desktop shown in the /etc/sysconfig/desktop file against GNOME, KDE, and AnotherLevel.

2. Lines 14 to 18: Make sure the PREFERRED desktop is not AnotherLevel.

3. Lines 21 to 32: If there is no PREFERRED desktop, try GNOME. If GNOME is not installed, try KDE.

4. Lines 35 to 36: Perform some cleanup by removing temporary files that may have been left behind the last time X Windows was run.

5. Lines 38 to 54: Check for a style for the AnotherLevel window manager, launch AnotherLevel with that style, and exit the script.

6. Lines 56 to 69: Attempt to launch AnotherLevel with the FVWM95 style. If that fails, launch xclock, xterm, and Netscape and then attempt to launch FVWM if it exists. If it doesn't exist, launch TWM instead.

If you want to add your own clients to be run every time X Windows is started, you can copy the global Xclients file to your own .Xclients file in your home directory and then edit it. The key to this process is to add the commands for the programs you want to run before the sections where the different window managers might be launched. The reason for this is that the exec keyword used to launch the different window managers causes the script to stop running as soon as the window manager is launched.

X RESOURCES

The X resources database provides applications with preferences information that controls such attributes as colors and fonts, among others. X resources can be used by most X Windows applications to control almost every aspect of behavior that is controlled by command-line flags. With the X resources database, you can specify more suitable defaults than those that are standard for the application. If you are

Part ii

familiar with the Microsoft Windows environment, the X resources database can be loosely compared to the Registry.

How X Resources Work

Every time you start the X Window, different settings are loaded into the X resources database. Default settings are taken from various files listed earlier in the discussion on xinitrc. They are modified by any .Xdefaults file in your home directory. But these settings are detailed and complex.

In order for this all to work, application-related information needs to be categorized so that only the appropriate applications are affected by X resources entries. This is done by grouping applications into classes. Most applications have their own classes; the documentation for the application specifies the class name. For example, xload belongs to the XLoad class, and xterm belongs to the XTerm class. Where a number of similar applications exist, they often are part of the same class (oclock and xclock belong to the Clock class).

NOTE

Observe how capital letters are used to differentiate between applications and classes. For example, xterm is the standard X Window terminal application, and XTerm is the class to which it belongs.

For each class, a standard set of resources allows you to specify such features as foreground and background colors (foreground and background), window size and placement (geometry), and default font (font). In addition, there are resource classes that group related resources. For instance, the Foreground class includes the foreground resource plus any additional foreground-related resources the application may have. Generally, though, you will not need to pay attention to individual resources and will work only with resource classes.

Setting X Resources with .Xdefaults

Setting X resources involves loading entries into the X resources database. These entries take the form

```
<ApplicationClass>|<applicationName>*<ResourceClass>|
    <resourceName> : <value>
```

In Linux man pages and other documentation, the vertical bar (or pipe character: |) is often used to represent "or." Therefore, in the example above, you can use either <ApplicationClass> or <applicationName> for the first entry, and <ResourceClass> or <resourceName> for the second entry.

These values are generally placed into the .Xdefaults file for user-specific resources. Let's look at a sample .Xdefaults file:

```
XTerm*background: Black

XTerm*foreground: Wheat

XTerm*cursorColor: Orchid

XTerm*reverseVideo: false

XTerm*scrollBar: true

XTerm*reverseWrap: true

XTerm*font: fixed

XTerm*fullCursor: true

XTerm*scrollTtyOutput: off

XTerm*scrollKey: on

XTerm*titleBar: false


xclock*Geometry: 100x100+100+100

xclock*Foreground: purple

xclock*Background: mauve
```

This .Xdefaults file sets X resources for both the XTerm class of applications and for the xclock application. For the XTerm class, you find resources setting the colors, the window properties (such as the presence of a scrollbar), and more. For xclock, you see color and geometry being set. The values being taken by these resources match the values that would have been provided to command-line flags such as -fg and -geometry where applicable.

The Database of X Resources

The sources for X resources are the app-defaults files. There are app-defaults files for most X and KDE applications. You can look up these files for settings that you can use in your own .Xdefaults file. In Red Hat Linux 7.1, these files are located in the /usr/X11R6/lib/X11/

app-defaults/ directory. KDE applications have their own special
app-defaults files in the /usr/share/apps/kdisplay/app-defaults/
directory.

Using the *xrdb* Command to Load X Resources

Normally, the .Xdefaults file is loaded when X Windows starts in the
.xinitrc file. However, new values can be loaded into the database
while X Windows is running by using the xrdb command. This is particularly useful for experimenting with values until you find just the combination you want.

If you've set up experimental settings in a file named experiment, you
can load these settings temporarily into the database with the command
$ xrdb -merge experiment. Once you're satisfied with any changes,
you can incorporate them into future X Window sessions by adding the
settings from your experiment file to .Xdefaults.

WHAT'S NEXT?

This chapter wrapped up the focus on X Windows. You will now move on
to an area that is essential to gaining complete mastery of Linux: network
system administration.

PART iii

Basic System Administration and Network Address Services

Chapter 11

CREATING AND MAINTAINING USER ACCOUNTS

Managing users and groups is a large part of your job as a system administrator. Setting up user accounts enables you to provide your users with access while still retaining the ability to track what your users do as well and limit their access as appropriate. It is one of the most visible jobs you'll have. Learning to do it efficiently will save you hours in the long run, and the confidence you'll exude from knowing it well will put you in good standing with your users.

Linux uses two or three files to maintain user and group information. The /etc/passwd file stores information about user accounts, and /etc/group stores information about groups. Most systems also use a file called /etc/shadow to maintain passwords. Later in this chapter, you'll see examples of these files. You'll also see that all the basic administrative tasks of adding, removing, and modifying user and group accounts

Adapted from *Linux System Administration* by Vicki Stanfield and Roderick W. Smith

ISBN 0-7821-2735-5   688 pages $39.99

can be done in any of three ways: by manually editing the account's entry in /etc/passwd or /etc/group, by using Linux command-line utilities that pass the relevant information to those files, or by using a GUI tool such as Linuxconf to enter the same information.

USER ACCOUNTS

Different types of users have different needs and may be assigned different types of accounts. Selecting the right type of account will ensure that the user has the needed access without allowing access beyond his or her scope. Common account types include the following:

▶ TCP/IP network access accounts (PPP and SLIP) to link users to the server (and perhaps beyond) via TCP/IP networking protocols

▶ UUCP network accounts, which allow for networking using older protocols

▶ Normal login accounts (also called *shell accounts*)

▶ Mail accounts (POP, virtual POP, or IMAP) for mail retrieval

The two special account types you'll encounter most frequently are Point-to-Point Protocol (PPP) and Post Office Protocol (POP) accounts. Both of these account types eliminate the need for a user's home directory to exist. Both POP and PPP users never directly log in to a user shell on the system, so such users have no need for a home directory. Using Linuxconf, POP users' login shells are set to /bin/false. That way, even if the user attempted to log in at a console or through a protocol such as Telnet, the session would immediately terminate with an error exit code of -1. In other words, the login attempt would fail, even if the user presented a correct password.

The POP user's Mail User Agent (MUA) authenticates with the mailer system itself. The PPP user does need a login shell of sorts, though. The login shell is effectively the PPP daemon itself, and authentication is performed when the connection is created. Under Red Hat 7.1, Linuxconf creates a home directory for the PPP user at /home/loginname, where loginname is the user's login. (This is the case even if you don't enter anything in the Home Directory field of the User Account Creation screen in Linuxconf.) The PPP user's login shell is set to /usr/lib/linuxconf/lib/ppplogin.

The /etc/passwd File

Information about each user is contained in the /etc/passwd file. As a system administrator, it is critical that you clearly understand this important file. In the excerpt shown in Listing 11.1, you'll notice that root is listed first. The root user is always assigned the user ID (UID) 0 and group ID (GID) 0. Other special users and accounts associated with services and daemons are listed after root and always have UID and GID values below 500. Lastly, regular and special accounts for individual users are listed.

Listing 11.1: An Example of an /etc/passwd File

```
root:x:0:0:root:/root:/bin/bash
bin:x:1:1:bin:/bin:
daemon:x:2:2:daemon:/sbin:
adm:x:3:4:adm:/var/adm:
lp:x:4:7:lp:/var/spool/lpd:
sync:x:5:0:sync:/sbin:/bin/sync
shutdown:x:6:0:shutdown:/sbin:/sbin/shutdown
halt:x:7:0:halt:/sbin:/sbin/halt
mail:x:8:12:mail:/var/spool/mail:
news:x:9:13:news:/var/spool/news:
uucp:x:10:14:uucp:/var/spool/uucp:
operator:x:11:0:operator:/root:
games:x:12:100:games:/usr/games:
gopher:x:13:30:gopher:/usr/lib/gopher-data:
ftp:x:14:50:FTP User:/home/ftp:
nobody:x:99:99:Nobody:/:
xfs:x:43:43:X Font Server:/etc/X11/fs:/bin/false
named:x:25:25:Named:/var/named:/bin/false
marty:x:500:500:Not Feldman:/home/marty:/bin/bash
ernie:x:501:501:Earnest too:/home/ernie:/bin/csh
betty:x:502:502:Ready Betty:/home/betty:/bin/pop
donald:x:503:503:Unka Donald:/home/donald:/bin/bash
```

Looking at the last entry, Donald's record, you can see the following colon-delimited fields:

Username   Donald's username is not capitalized. Typically, initial capitalization is not used in order to avoid uppercase/lowercase confusion. There is no default value for the username field.

Encrypted Password   Technically, this field holds the password for users; however, this particular Linux system is using *shadow passwords*, which are held in /etc/shadow. Therefore, the /etc/password file contains an x in the second field to indicate to login that the actual password is held elsewhere.

User ID   Throughout the system, any file owned or created by Donald will have this number associated with it. It actually is this UID that will be associated with Donald's files, and the human-friendly donald is what is displayed to us, for example by the ls command. Also, every process executing on the system will be associated with a UID. Typically it's the UID of the user who starts up the process.

Default GID   This is Donald's login group. All files are owned by both a user and a group. When Donald creates a new file, it will by default receive his GID value, which will also be associated with the file. It is no coincidence that Donald has a GID equal to his UID, as do all of the other users listed in the password file in Listing 11.1. This is by design under Red Hat Linux, an approach called *user private groups*. We will explore this approach later. Other Linux distributions, for example SuSE, use the traditional approach where all users are default members of one large collective group, typically named users. One of your jobs as a system administrator is to decide whether to use your distribution's default group assignment scheme or use another one.

User Description   This field—called the *comment* field in the command-line utilities such as useradd that we'll describe later—holds descriptive information about the user (Unka Donald in this example). In some organizations, it contains phone numbers, mail stops, or some other contact information. Its contents are included with the Finger utility's report.

User's Home Directory   When the user is authenticated, the login program uses this field to define the user's $HOME variable. By default, in all Linux distributions, the user's home directory will be assumed to be /home/username. If the user's home directory can't be accessed, the user will be defaulted to the root (/) directory. Landing in the root directory when you log in is always an indication that something is awry.

User's Login Shell When the user is authenticated, the login program also sets the user's $SHELL variable to this field. By default, in all Linux distributions, a new user's login shell will be /bin/bash, the Bourne Again Shell. If no shell is specified, it defaults to the Bourne shell, /bin/sh. Special user accounts sometimes require that the user's login shell be set to something other than a shell path. For a POP user or a Virtual POP user, you don't need to assign a shell at all, since they never actually log on to the system. Instead, use /bin/false to prevent the user from getting a login shell if access is attempted while preserving his ability to retrieve mail.

Listing 11.1 reveals over a dozen system accounts (with UIDs of less than 500) in addition to the user accounts (with UIDs of 500 or above). Some of these accounts, such as root, bin, daemon, and halt, are more-or-less required on any Linux system. Others, such as mail, news, games, gopher, and ftp, are associated with specific servers or program collections. Your Linux system can get by without these accounts, but if you install certain programs, they may not work correctly, because they'll assume that these accounts are present. Other accounts, such as nobody, fall in between these two cases; they may be used by several different packages but aren't strictly required for basic functionality.

Some programs add users to /etc/passwd during installation. The qmail mail server, for example, adds several entries for its own use. If you install such a program but then remove its users, the program may fail to operate correctly, if at all. However, you should remove any such accounts if you remove the software that required them.

TIP

It's a good idea to back up the /etc/passwd file (as well as the /etc/shadow file, which stores passwords, and /etc/group, which stores group information) soon after system installation and after adding or deleting users. This can make it easier to recover the system if you ever need to reinstall. It can also help you track down system break-ins, because crackers often create their own accounts. These often have a UID of 0, giving them root privileges even if they use another username on the account. Crackers also sometimes add passwords (revealed in /etc/shadow on most systems) and login shells to normal system accounts, such as ftp.

Part iii

Shadowed Passwords

When a user picks or is assigned a password, it is encoded with a randomly generated value referred to as the *salt*. Using the salt, any password can be stored in 4,096 different ways. The salt value is stored with the encrypted password. When a user logs in and supplies a password, the salt is first retrieved from the stored encrypted password. The supplied password is then encoded with the salt value and compared with the stored password. If there is a match, the user is authenticated.

Because it is used to obtain usernames and group names from the system-held UIDs and GIDs, the /etc/passwd file must be readable by anyone on the system, and this makes it vulnerable to attack. Anyone can pull out a user's encrypted password string and compare it against a generated list of dictionary words that have been encrypted using the same algorithm used to encode the password. A cracker trying to break the password generates the list by encrypting simple dictionary words using all 4,096 salt values. If the password string matches one in the list, the person running the test has that user's password. To combat this security risk, the concept of *shadowing* was adopted.

Shadowing solves the problem by relocating the passwords to another file (/etc/shadow). Only root can read and write to the /etc/shadow file. After shadowing, donald's line in the /etc/passwd file would look like this:

```
donald:x:503:503:Unka Donald:/home/donald:/bin/bash
```

The password is replaced with an x, which indicates that it is shadowed. A line in /etc/shadow contains the encrypted version of Donald's password as well as some other information:

```
donald:HcX5zb8cpoxmY:11088:0:99999:7:0::
```

NOTE   By default, Red Hat Linux 7.1 uses shadow passwords. Listing 11.1 shown earlier reflects this fact; all its password entries are x.

The fields in the /etc/shadow file are as follows:

Username   This is Donald's login name, which matches the one we saw in the /etc/passwd file.

Encrypted Password   This is where the actual encrypted password is stored on a system using password shadowing.

Last Password Change   This number represents the number of days from January 1, 1970, to the day the most recent password change took place.

Days Until Change Allowed   This number represents the number of days until a password change will be allowed. This is typically set to 0, allowing the user to change the password as often as desired.

Days Before Change Required   This number represents the number of days before the user will be forced to change the password. If password changes are not forced, this field is set to 99999.

Days Warning Before Password Expires   This field sets the number of days prior to password expiration you want the user to be notified. Typically the user is notified a week in advance, so this field is set to 7.

Days Between Expiration and Deactivation   This number represents the number of days that an account may be expired before the account is disabled. If inactivation is not intended to be automatic, the field is set to −1 or left empty.

Account Expires   This field shows the date the account will be disabled, represented as the number of days since January 1, 1970. This is particularly useful for temporary employees and students with set graduation dates. If this type of automatic deactivation is not to be used, the field is set to −1 or left empty.

Special Flag   This field is reserved for future use. It typically remains empty.

Shadow passwords were first used in SCO Xenix, but the Shadow Suite was freely distributable. Red Hat Linux doesn't use the Shadow Suite, but instead uses the Pluggable Authentication Module (PAM) system to perform the same function. The utilities involved in maintaining shadowed passwords include the following:

pwconv   Uses the values of PASS_MIN_DAYS, PASS_MAX_DAYS, and PASS_WARN_AGE from /etc/login.defs to add new entries to the /etc/shadow file and removes any entries in /etc/shadow that don't have corresponding entries in /etc/passwd.

pwunconv   Checks the /etc/passwd file against the /etc/shadow file, updating the /etc/passwd entries with corresponding /etc/shadow entries by putting the /etc/shadow password field into the corresponding line in /etc/passwd. The /etc/shadow file is removed upon completion. Some password aging information is lost. This effectively disables shadow passwords. You're only likely to need to do this if you must use some outdated utility that insists on seeing passwords in /etc/passwd, or if you want to manipulate accounts as one file, as when migrating users from another system.

grpconv   Performs the same function as the pwconv utility but on groups from the /etc/group file instead.

grpunconv   Performs the same function as the pwunconv utility but on groups instead.

Adding New Users

To add a new user to the system, you must have root access, and you must follow a series of general steps. The required steps are as follows:

1. Create a record for the user in /etc/passwd.

2. Set the user's password.

3. Specify a login shell for the user.

There are also two optional steps. These help to configure a useful environment, but not all account types require these steps. These additional steps are the following:

4. Create a home directory for the user.

5. Populate the user's home directory with various useful files. (This step isn't described further because it's very system specific. For instance, you might want to add a README file for the benefit of new users.)

You can perform these as single discrete steps, but you can ease your administrative burden by automating the process using either user-creation scripts, which have existed for years, or graphical user interfaces, which have appeared more recently.

Adding a User from the Linuxconf GUI

For the simplest default accounts, many administrators find it best to work from the command line, specifying switches to the useradd and passwd commands, as described in the next section. To create accounts that include some nondefault elements, however, you may prefer to work with a GUI, such as Linuxconf. In particular, creating any of the special accounts mentioned earlier in this chapter from within Linuxconf takes care of the peculiarities of that account's specific authentication sequence. For that reason, creating these accounts is most easily done with the Linuxconf tool. The format of the GUI itself provides excellent cues for the optional fields.

In order to create a user account using Linuxconf under a Red Hat Linux system, simply invoke the utility from the Programs ➣ System menu in GNOME. You can also start Linuxconf from a root shell in either the X Window System or a text console by typing **linuxconf**. If you invoke Linuxconf when you're running X, the program produces an X-based display. You can run it without X, however, in which case the program produces a text-mode display.

Once the Linuxconf screen comes up, you'll need to be certain the Config tab is selected, then select Users Accounts ➣ Normal ➣ User Accounts from the tree menu. Click on the "+" to the left of each item to expand that item. When you select the third menu item, User Accounts, Linuxconf brings up a list of users on the right side of the window, as shown in Figure 11.1. To add a user, click the Add button. You'll then be presented with the User Account Creation screen, shown in Figure 11.2.

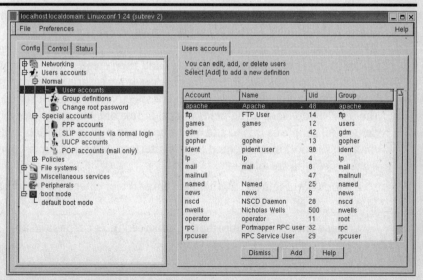

FIGURE 11.1: The Linuxconf Users Accounts module lets you edit existing accounts or add new ones.

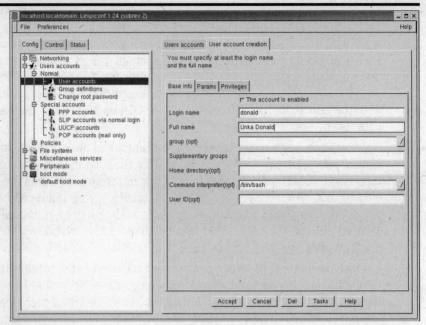

FIGURE 11.2:   The User Account Creation screen has three tabs for entry of assorted information.

The only information you truly *must* enter to add a user is the user-name, entered via the Login Name field. It's also useful to enter something in the Full Name field, however. Once you've done this, click Accept to create an account—Linuxconf asks you to enter a password (twice, to be sure you type it correctly) and then creates the necessary entries in /etc/passwd and /etc/shadow. If necessary, you can enter a nonstandard home directory or group or specify a particular user ID for the user. If you leave these fields blank, Linuxconf will assign default values. As simple as it is to add a new user, you may be tempted to use many of the options presented on the interface, but for the most part the system defaults are adequate.

As shown in Figure 11.2, there are three major categories of information you can add:

Base Info   Basic information provided in /etc/passwd and /etc/group.

Params   Policy enforcement for password aging—the account's expiration date, number of days between enforced password changes, and so on.

Privileges   Special permission management, such as whether the user may use Linuxconf, shut down the computer, and so on.

If you want to change any of these characteristics, do so *before* you click Accept to create the account. Alternatively, you can alter an account's settings after it's been created by clicking the account name in the Users Accounts module seen in Figure 11.1. This brings up the User Information module, which lets you edit a user's account using the same interface as the User Account Creation module (refer to Figure 11.2).

Adding Users from the Command Line

Adding a user from the command line also requires the five steps listed earlier. You can use the `useradd` command to accomplish all of the steps except assigning a password. The `useradd` command accepts the information needed for the individual fields in the `/etc/passwd` file as arguments, as follows:

```
useradd [-D] [-g default_group] [-b default_home]
[-s default_shell]
```

The `useradd` command creates a new user account using the values given on the command line (supplying default values for any items not specified). `useradd` enters data into the appropriate system files. It then creates the user's home directory at `/home/username` by default or at the location specified by the `-b` option. The `useradd` command copies sample configuration files from `/etc/skel`. In Red Hat Linux, a group with the same name as the user is created, and the user is added to that group. (Other distributions may handle groups differently, as explained further in the "The Function of Groups" section later in this chapter, which also describes Red Hat's approach in more detail.)

Next you'll want to give the user a password, using the `passwd` command:

```
# passwd donald
New UNIX password:
Retype new UNIX password:
```

Part iii

The configuration files contained in /etc/skel are intended to be set up for the typical user in that system. The files in this directory include .bash_logout, .bash_profile, .bashrc, .screenrc, .kde/, and Desktop/. You may add any files that will routinely be contained in your users' home directories.

Default values for certain user characteristics may be set in the /etc/login.defs file. The mail directory, which typically is set to /var/spool/mail/*username*, is set via the MAIL_DIR variable in that file. Password aging information is also stored in the login.defs file. The minimum and maximum UID and GID values are stored there for automatic selection by the useradd command.

Migrating Users from Other Unix Systems

Since most Unix variations use the same format for their /etc/passwd files, it is possible to migrate users directly from a Unix platform to Linux. If either the Unix system or your Linux system is using shadowed passwords, you must first run the command to "unshadow" that system— pwunconv. The pwunconv utility requires no arguments. Copy the appropriate user lines from the passwd file of the other machine into the /etc/passwd file on Linux and run /sbin/pwconv to reapply shadowing to each system. Then carefully check or update the passwords for the migrated user accounts.

Modifying User Accounts

Most system administrators make changes to user accounts by editing the appropriate files. It is often easier to use a text editor to edit the passwd file to change a simple configuration detail such as the user's shell than to bring up a GUI utility or use usermod at the command line. We'll show you all three methods, and you can decide which you prefer.

Manually Modifying User Accounts

The most direct way to modify a user's account information is to edit the corresponding entry in /etc/passwd. For example, suppose you wish to change our hypothetical user Donald's shell to the C shell. Use your favorite editor to open the /etc/passwd file. Donald's line looks like this:

```
donald:x:503:503:Unka Donald:/home/donald:/bin/bash
```

Simply change /bin/bash to /bin/csh and save the file. The next time Donald logs in, he will be using the C shell. Of course, other information, including the user's name string, Unka Donald, may be changed as well. You can change the home directory, but you must create the new directory and move any files from the old directory to make it usable. Do not change the UID or GID unless you really know what you're doing. If you change these fields inadvertently, Donald will lose access to his files, since the system sees the owner and group designation numerically and uses the /etc/passwd file to convert them for output in human-readable format to the user.

In principle, it's also possible to edit the contents of /etc/shadow in a similar manner. In practice, though, most of its contents come in a form that's less easily handled by humans. The password is encrypted, so you can't change it by hand unless you're simply copying a password from another system (which is potentially risky). The time information is entered in units of days since 1970, which is awkward to compute. All in all, it's best to leave /etc/shadow alone.

Modifying User Accounts with Linuxconf

To modify any user's account, take the following steps:

1. Start Linuxconf by selecting it from a drop-down menu or typing **linuxconf** at a shell prompt.

2. Open Config ➢ Users Accounts ➢ Normal ➢ User Accounts.

3. Select the account that you'd like to change. You will then be presented with the User information screen, which is essentially identical to Figure 11.2, with any existing values filled in.

4. Change the appropriate fields, and select Accept to accept the modified user information.

5. Click Quit from the User Accounts screen, which follows.

6. Click Act/Changes from the main Linuxconf screen.

7. Click Activate the Changes from the Status of the System screen.

8. Click Quit from the main Linuxconf screen.

Part iii

Modifying User Accounts with *usermod*

To use the usermod utility to alter a field in a user's password record from the command line, use the following command:

```
usermod [-c comment] [-d home_dir [-m]] [-e expire_date]
    ➥[-f inactive_time] [-g initial_group] [-G group[, ]]
    ➥[-l login_name] [-p passwd]
    ➥[-s shell] [-u uid] [-o] [-L|-U] login
```

The important usermod options and their meanings are as follows:

-c *comment* The string that will replace the current comment (also called the user description field—where a full name is normally stored).

-d *home_dir [-m]* New home directory. If –m is specified, move the contents of the old home directory to the new home directory, which is created if it doesn't already exist.

-e *expire_date* The date, in YYYY-MM-DD format, on which the user account will be disabled.

-f *inactive_time* The number of days after password expiration until the account is permanently disabled. Use –1 to turn off the automatic disabling feature and 0 to disable the account immediately upon password expiration.

-g *initial_group* The user's new initial login group. The group must exist.

-G *group* Other groups to which the user should belong. The list is comma-delimited, with no white space. The groups listed must already exist. If the user is currently a member of a group that isn't listed, he will be removed from that group.

-l *login_name* The name of the user will be changed to this login name. This will cause the files owned by this user to show the new login name as owner since the UID will be matched to the entry in the /etc/passwd file. You probably want to change the home directory to use this new *login_name* as well. You may not change the *login_name* of a user who is currently logged in.

-p *password* The user's new password as encrypted by the crypt command. If you pass plain text, it will appear in /etc/passwd as plain text. If you then run pwconv, the /etc/shadow file will contain the plain text password. If the user attempts to log in using the same text string, access will be denied, because the system will attempt to decrypt the text string taken from /etc/shadow before it matches it to the input password string. To change a password, you normally use the passwd command, not usermod.

-s *shell* This is the shell that the user will be assigned at login. Entering a blank for this option causes the system to select the default shell, which in Linux is Bash.

-u *uid* The numeric value of the user's ID. This value must be unique unless you also specify the –o option. System accounts will normally be assigned a UID between 0 and 99. User accounts on most systems begin with 500, leaving 100–499 for other uses. When the UID is updated using usermod, any files owned by the user and existing in the user's home directory will be updated to the new UID so that the /etc/passwd file will assign the correct owner to these files. Files outside the user's home directory will retain the old UID number, meaning that an ls –l of these files will show the numeric version of the old UID or a different user's name if a new user has been assigned the old UID.

-L Lock the user's account by placing an exclamation mark in front of the user's password in the /etc/passwd or /etc/shadow file. This disables the user's ability to log in.

-U Unlock the user's account by removing the exclamation mark from the user's entry in the /etc/passwd or /etc/shadow file, re-enabling the user's password and ability to log in.

login The login name of the user account you want to modify.

Disabling User Accounts

If you need to deactivate an account but believe that the account will be needed again in the future, you'll want to disable it instead of deleting it. A deleted account and a disabled account look exactly the same to a user attempting to log in using that account, but a disabled account does not remove the user's home directory or any files owned by that user.

Manual Disabling

The simplest way to disable an account is to make sure that the user's password has expired. To do this, you can modify the user's entry in /etc/shadow. As discussed earlier, dates in this file are represented as the number of days since January 1, 1970. The third field in an entry is the date the password was last modified, and the eighth field is the date the account will expire. You first want to change the user's password; the third field in the entry will then reflect the current date. Subtract one from that number, insert the new number immediately before the last colon, and save the file.

```
donald:HcX5zb8cpoxmY:11088:0:99999:7:0::
```

Subtracting 1 from 11,088 yields 11,087, so you'd change the entry to this:

```
donald:HcX5zb8cpoxmY:11088:0:99999:7:0:11087:
```

Disabling an Account with Linuxconf

To disable a user's account, follow these steps:

1. Start Linuxconf as previously described.

2. Open Config ➤ Users Accounts ➤ Normal ➤ User Accounts.

3. Select the account that you'd like to disable. You'll then be presented with the User Information screen, which resembles Figure 11.2.

4. Uncheck the Account Is Enabled box.

5. Click Accept to accept the modified user information.

6. Click Quit on the User Accounts screen that follows.

7. Click Act/Changes from the main Linuxconf screen.

8. Click Activate the Changes from the Status of the System screen.

9. Click Quit from the main Linuxconf screen.

Disabling an Account with *chage*

Although you can use the -E option of the usermod command to change the expiration date of a user's account, you should also be familiar with the chage (change aging) command to update the user's password expiration date. chage allows you to input this as the number of days since January 1, 1970, or in the YYYY-MM-DD format as follows:

```
# chage -E 2000-8-12 someuser
```

If the date has passed, the account will be disabled but can be enabled later using the same method. When the user attempts to log in, he will see the following message:

```
Your account has expired; please contact your system adminis-
trator
```

Deleting User Accounts

If you are sure that you will not need a user's account again, you can delete it. Deleting an account basically reverses the steps you took to create it. Those steps were the following:

1. Create a record for the user in /etc/passwd.

2. Set the user's password.

3. Specify a login shell for the user.

4. Create a home directory for the user.

5. Populate the user's home directory with various useful files.

The order in which you reverse these steps is unimportant, however. Of course, you'll need to delete the files you've created in the user's home directory as well as the user's home directory itself. You'll also need to search the system for any other files owned by this user and either remove them or reset their ownership. You must also remove the user's /etc/passwd entry. This may all be done by hand or via tools as before.

Manually Deleting an Account

First you'll want to remove the user's /etc/passwd entry. When pwconv is run again, the /etc/shadow entry for that user will be automatically removed as well. Next, remove the home directory and all of the files contained therein using an rm command such as the following:

```
# rm -r /home/donald
```

The rm command will remove the /home/donald directory and all the files and subdirectories it contains. If you're confident enough and would rather not be prompted, you can add the -f option to the above command (making it rm -rf /home/donald), which instructs Linux not to prompt you about removing files. This is very dangerous, so you might want to just endure the prompts.

TIP

It's a good idea to back up a deleted user's account. You can do this by archiving the files using the tar backup utility and storing the files on floppy disk, high-capacity removable disks such as Iomega Zip disks, CD-R discs, or tape. Keeping a deleted user's files on hand in this way can be handy if you discover you've deleted the wrong account or if you need to recover a particular file from the ex-user's account for some reason.

Next you need to search the computer for other files owned by the deleted user and determine what to do with those files. Use the find command for this as follows:

```
# find / -gid 503 -uid 503
```

Assuming Donald's user ID was 503 and his original group ID had never been changed, this command would generate a list of files by full path that were owned by Donald or had his group ID. You'll then need to look through the file list and determine what to do with each file. If you decide to keep a file but change its ownership, you can use the chown command, as follows:

```
# chown betty.users /opt/somefile
```

This command changes the ownership of /opt/somefile to betty and changes group ownership to the users group. You can omit the period and group name if you don't want to change it, or add an -R parameter before the username to recursively change every file within a directory. For instance, the following command changes the ownership of the /home/samba/sharedfiles directory and all its files and subdirectories to betty, but it doesn't change the group associated with the files:

```
# chown -R betty /home/samba/sharedfiles
```

Deleting an Account with Linuxconf

You can also delete a user using the Linuxconf utility. To do so, follow these steps:

1. Start Linuxconf as previously described.

2. Navigate to Config ➢ User Accounts ➢ Normal ➢ User Accounts.

3. Select the account that you'd like to delete. You will then be presented with the User Information screen, which is similar to Figure 11.2, with any existing values filled in.

4. Click the on-screen Del button to delete the user listed and remove all of the user's files from the user's home directory.

5. Activate the changes as before.

You will still need to locate files owned by this user in other folders and delete or reassign them.

Deleting an Account with *userdel*

The userdel utility will remove a user's entry in the /etc/passwd file and optionally remove that user's home directory and all the files and subdirectories it contains. Any files owned by that user outside the home directory will remain on the system and will appear as owned by the user's ID when displayed via an ls -l command. The userdel command to delete our hypothetical Donald's passwd entry and home directory looks like this:

```
# userdel -r donald
```

You may also choose to delete Donald's /etc/passwd entry but leave all the files in his home directory by omitting the -r.

You may choose to use the find command shown earlier to locate all files owned by Donald or his group.

GROUPS

You saw earlier in this chapter that each user has a default group identity, called a login group, which is assumed upon logging in to the system. Once authenticated by /bin/login, the user assumes the group identity specified in the /etc/passwd file. In Red Hat Linux, a user's default group ID is the same as the user ID; in some other Linux distributions, all users are by default put into a single group, typically called users. Linux administrators can create new groups, associating users for specific purposes such as projects that require certain users to have access to the same set of files. The next sections show how to add and remove groups and how users can become members of different groups.

The Function of Groups

Groups are an integral part of Linux security. Every file has an associated permissions string that specifies the presence or absence of read, write, and execute permission to each of three classes of users: the file's owner, the file's group, and all users on the system (often called *world* permissions). By controlling the group setting for files and by assigning users to particular groups, you can enhance the internal security of your Linux system. For instance, if your system is being used by two different sets of employees, each of which is working on one project, you can create two groups, one for each set of employees. By denying world access to users' files, you can prevent employees in one group from reading files created by members of the other group. If a few users belong to both groups, you can make those users members of both groups, so they can read both groups' files.

Because every Linux installation is unique, it's impossible for a Linux distribution to come with a default group setup that's appropriate for all environments. The packagers of Red Hat can't know what groups you'll need, any more than they can know what users you'll need. Nonetheless, the account-creation tools make certain default assumptions about how you might group your accounts. Different distributions do things in different ways.

In Red Hat Linux, every time a new user is added, a group with the same user ID and numeric group ID as that user is created. Say the user is donald again. A user group called donald would be created, and the user donald would be added to that *user private group*. The umask is set to 002, which means that any file created by donald will have read-write permission for him (the owner) and for the donald group and read-only permission for world. This works well because we know that donald has membership in the group by default. Since donald is the only member of his user private group, only he and the superuser can access files with the group set to donald. Anyone can be added to the donald group and will then have group access to any files that Donald creates with this umask.

Other distributions don't always work this way. Some create a single group (generally called users) and place all users in this group. Thus, both the donald and betty accounts by default belong to the users group. Typically, the umask is 022, so users can read each other's files but cannot write to them. This is a *shared-group* approach.

On small workstations, both these approaches tend to work well because workstations tend to have just one or two users, and the implications of group membership are small. At worst, you may need to add one or two users to each other's groups in the user private group approach or create a couple of new groups and change default group membership in the shared group approach. On larger systems, though, you're likely to need to create a more complex configuration. In an academic environment, for instance, you may need to create groups for different courses; and in a work environment, you may need to create groups for different working groups. The tools to do this parallel the tools used to create user accounts in many respects.

The */etc/group* File

Information about each group is contained in the /etc/group file. Just as with /etc/passwd, it is critical that any system administrator clearly understand this important file. Its structure is fairly simple. Listing 11.2 shows an excerpt from a typical /etc/group file.

Listing 11.2: A Portion of the */etc/group* File

```
root:x:0:root
bin:x:1:root,bin,daemon
daemon:x:2:root,bin,daemon
<  other entries  >
slocate:x:21:
project2038:x:1000:ernie,betty
marty:x:500:
ernie:x:501:
betty:x:502:
donald:x:503:
```

Each entry declares a group name, password, numeric group ID (called the GID), and the group members. Table 11.1 lists the default groups that Linux creates automatically upon installation.

TABLE 11.1: Default Linux Groups

Group	GID	Members	Description
root	9	root	Superuser group
bin	1	root, bin, daemon	Running programs
daemon	2	root, bin, daemon	Running programs

Part iii

TABLE 11.1 continued: Default Linux Groups

Group	GID	Members	Description
sys	3	root,bin,daemon	System group
adm	4	root, adm, daemon	Administrative group
tty	5		Access to terminals
disk	6	root	Access to disk device files
lp	7	daemon, lp	Printing group
mem	8		Kernel memory access
kmem	9		Kernel memory access
wheel	10	root	Users with near-root privileges
mail	12	mail	Used by mail utilities
news	13	news	Used by Usenet news utilities
uucp	14	uucp	Used for UUCP networking
man	15		Used for man page access
games	20		Group for storing game high scores
gopher	30		Used by the Gopher utility
dip	40		Dialup IP group (PPP, SLIP)
ftp	50		Group for FTP daemon
nobody	99		Low-security group
users	100		Default user group on many systems
floppy	19		Group for access to low-level floppy disk devices

Adding New Groups

Just as users can be added manually with a command-line utility or using Linuxconf, groups can also be created in any of these ways. The different methods are explained below so that you can choose the method you prefer. (Once you've created a new group, you presumably want to add users to that group. This process is described in the section "Changing Group Membership.")

Manually Adding a Group

Because the structure of the /etc/group file is fairly simple, administrators typically add groups by editing the file directly. To create a group with an initial set of group members, simply add the usernames of the users to the comma-delimited list at the end of the entry. For instance:

```
cs101:x:101:donald,betty,ernie
```

To check your work, the id command reports all of the groups a user has membership in. The output for the root user looks like this:

```
uid=0(root) gid=0(root)
groups=0(root),1(bin),2(daemon),3(sys),4(adm),6(disk),10(wheel)
```

NOTE

It's normally not necessary to add root to groups you create. root is a very special account that can read and write any file or directory on the computer, so it doesn't need membership in ordinary user groups. root belongs to several system groups as a matter of convenience for handling those groups.

The groups command may be used instead to give the same basic information:

```
root bin daemon sys adm disk wheel
```

Adding a Group with *groupadd*

To add a new group, use the groupadd command, which uses the parameters passed on the command line to create a new group, relying on system defaults for any parameters you don't specify. The new group will be added to the system files as needed. The syntax for the groupadd command is as follows:

```
groupadd [-g GID [-o]] [-r] [-f] group
```

The meanings of the various groupadd parameters are as follows:

-g *GID*   The numeric value of the group's ID. The GID must be unique unless the −o option is given. The value must not be a negative number. The default is to select the smallest remaining ID that is greater than 500 and greater than the ID of any other group. System accounts use the values between 0 and 499.

-r   Designates that the added group will be a system group. The group will be assigned the first available GID under 499 unless the −g option specifies a GID to be used instead.

-f   If a group of the specified name already exists, forces the
groupadd command to leave that group as it exists on the system and continue without returning an error message. (Ordinarily, groupadd would complain about the attempt to reuse a
group name.) Also, this option changes the way that –g
behaves in Red Hat, so that if –g is given without –o, the group
will be added as if neither –g nor –o were specified.

group   The name of the new group being created.

Adding a Group with Linuxconf

You can also use the Linuxconf utility to add new groups. To do so, follow
these steps:

1.   Select Config ➢ User Accounts ➢ Normal ➢ Group Defini-
     tions from the Linuxconf main menu. The result is the User
     Groups Linuxconf module, shown in Figure 11.3.

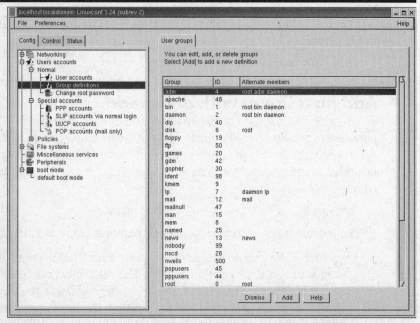

FIGURE 11.3:   The Linuxconf User Groups module allows you to add, remove, or
modify groups in a manner similar to changing user accounts.

2. Click the Add button to add a new group. You will then be presented with a User Groups screen as shown in Figure 11.4.

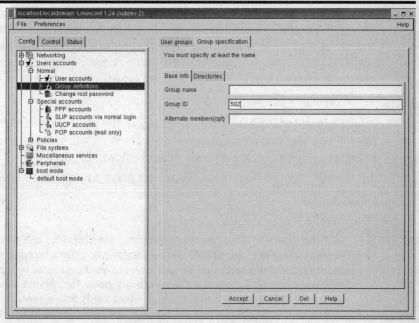

FIGURE 11.4: You can specify user group information using the Group Specification screen.

3. Specify the group's name and any alternate members.

4. Click Accept.

5. Activate the changes as before.

Changing Group Membership

All actions performed by a user are performed under a specific user ID and group ID. Therefore, although a user may belong to more than one group (by adding the username to multiple groups' /etc/group entries, as described earlier), a user may act as a member of only one group at a time. Ordinarily, this is not terribly important, but it can be in some cases. For instance, a user might need to create files that carry a certain group membership, so that other members of the appropriate group can read those files. Every user has a primary group affiliation, specified in the user's /etc/passwd file entry. Upon logging in, the user acts as a member of that group. The newgrp command provides a means for users to temporarily change the group associated with their actions. (The command sg is frequently a synonym for newgrp and is symbolically linked to the newgrp command in Red Hat Linux 7.1.) To use newgrp, type the command, a hyphen (which causes the system to reinitialize the user's environmental variables), and the new group name. For instance, to become a member of the project1 group, type the following:

```
$ newgrp - project1
```

If the user donald has used newgrp to join the group project1, when he creates a new file, such as a project document, it will show up in a long listing (ls -l) with group ownership by the new group:

```
-rw-r--r--  1 donald   project1      10332 Aug 20 16:07 proj_doc
```

NOTE

Although you need to use the newgrp command to *create* files with group ownership other than your primary group (or use chown or chgrp to change ownership after the fact), this isn't necessary to *read* files owned by a group to which you belong, but which isn't your primary group. For instance, if donald is normally a member of the donald group but is also a member of the project1 group, he can read project1 files even without using newgrp, provided the files have group read permissions.

By design, the administrator can configure newgrp to require authentication for group access, but this doesn't seem to work correctly in the Red Hat distribution, so we advise you to avoid assigning passwords to groups.

Modifying Groups

The modification of groups may be done manually, via the command-line groupmod tool, or via Linuxconf. You can modify the group name, the group ID number, and group members. You might need to change a group name or ID number on one system to bring two or more computers' configurations in line with one another or to change your scheme for group layouts. Adding and removing group members are ordinary parts of system administration.

Manually Modifying a Group

To manually modify group information, edit the /etc/group file. Here you can change the group name, GID, and the members. If you wish to change other information, it is much easier to use useradd or the Linuxconf utility.

As an example, consider the following group definition:

```
project1:x:503:donald,betty
```

Suppose you want to give the group a more descriptive name and add a new user, emily. You could change the definition as follows:

```
moonshot:x:503:donald,betty,emily
```

Thereafter, the group ID will appear in program listings and the like as moonshot, not project1. (Even existing files will be changed.) When changing to this group, group members will need to specify moonshot as the group name, and the user emily will be able to use the group's resources.

WARNING

Changing the GID, like changing the UID of a user, will "orphan" files owned by the group. The recovery process is the same as described earlier for altering existing files' UIDs. Unless you have a compelling reason to do so, it's best not to change the GID of an existing group.

Modifying Group Information with *groupmod*

The characteristics of a group may be modified with the groupmod command. All appropriate system files are updated. The syntax for groupmod is similar to that of groupadd:

```
groupmod [-g GID [-o]] [-n group_name] group
```

-g *GID*   The numeric value of the group's ID. This value must be unique unless the –o parameter is specified. As with the groupadd command, group IDs must be nonnegative and should not fall between 0 and 99 unless the group is a system group.

-n *group_name*   The new name of the group.

group   The old name of the group.

Linuxconf

The Linuxconf utility may be used to modify a group. Simply navigate to the Group Definitions option as before. When presented with the group list, highlight the one you wish to modify. You will then be presented with the same Group Specification screen as shown in Figure 11.4, with the existing values filled in. Make changes as needed, and then click the Accept button. Activate the changes as before.

Deleting Groups

Groups may also be deleted using the same three methods as in other account management tasks: manually editing the /etc/group file, using the command line (the groupdel command), or using Linuxconf.

Deleting a Group with *groupdel*

You can delete groups using the groupdel command; this command deletes any entries that refer to the named group:

```
groupdel group
```

However, the groupdel command does not search for files with that GID. That must be done separately with a find command, as in the following example:

```
# find / -gid 503
```

Deleting a Group with Linuxconf

The Linuxconf utility can also be used to delete a group. Simply select the Group Definitions option as before. When presented with the group list, highlight the one you wish to delete. You will then be presented with the same Group Specification screen as shown in Figure 11.4, with the existing values filled in. Click the on-screen Del button, and activate the changes as before.

Manually Removing a Group

Although you can remove a group simply by editing the /etc/group file to delete the line that corresponds to the group you wish to remove, that's not as efficient as the other methods. If you remove the group's entry in /etc/group, you should probably remove the corresponding entry in the /etc/gshadow file (in which shadowed group passwords are stored, if you have elected to use group passwords). If you do not use passwords for your groups, this file will not be automatically updated.

What's Next?

As a multiuser OS, Linux relies upon user accounts and groups to maintain security and keep the system usable to all its users. Over the years, manual methods, text-based tools, and GUI tools have been developed to manage these accounts and groups. However you do it, though, it's important that you understand how Linux handles its accounts and groups—the relationship between usernames and UIDs or group names and GIDs; where passwords are stored; and how users are assigned to groups.

Understanding these topics will enable you to manage your user base effectively, whether it's just one or two people or thousands. These subjects are also critically important for understanding Linux system security. In the next chapter you will learn about setting up and maintaining TCP/IP on Linux to enable network communications.

Chapter 12

TCP/IP LINUX NETWORKING

Perhaps more than any other computer technology, networking has changed our lives. Today it's possible to shop, read newspapers, obtain music and software, do research, correspond with colleagues, and even earn a living entirely online. Although there are costs associated with this new use for computers, society as a whole is rapidly embracing the Internet.

Today's networking protocols began life on Unix systems. At the core of the Internet (and of most local networks) lies a protocol known as the *Transmission Control Protocol/Internet Protocol* (TCP/IP). TCP/IP was first developed on what are by today's standards primitive versions of Unix. As a clone of Unix, Linux has a tightly knit set of TCP/IP networking tools. Indeed, many of Linux's networking tools are the same as those used on "traditional" Unix systems.

This chapter introduces TCP/IP networking in Linux. It begins with an overview of the design of TCP/IP and then launches into the details of TCP/IP configuration in Linux.

Adapted from *Linux System Administration* by Vicki Stanfield and Roderick W. Smith

ISBN 0-7821-2735-5   688 pages $39.99

One very common use of TCP/IP networking is to provide file and printer sharing on a small network, so that users of one system can use files and printers on another directly. This chapter therefore describes this use, although only in broad strokes. TCP/IP is also used for providing many Internet services, such as web and FTP servers, so these topics are touched upon.

UNDERSTANDING TCP/IP NETWORKING

Chances are that you're familiar with how network tools function, at least from the user's point of view. As with so many aspects of our world, however, there's considerable complexity hidden beneath the surface of common network tools such as e-mail and remote printing. Understanding the basic design of TCP/IP networking can be invaluable when you're configuring a system to use these features—and particularly when troubleshooting TCP/IP problems. This section presents an overview of critical design features of TCP/IP and of computer networking in general. If you are already familiar with these concepts, feel free to begin with the "TCP/IP Configuration" section instead.

Network Stacks

The basic goal of networking, from the point of view of high-level software, is to transfer information from a specific program running on one computer to a specific program running on another computer. For instance, when you run a web browser such as Netscape, the goal is to transmit a request for specific documents from Netscape Navigator to a web server program (such as Apache) on a remote computer. Apache responds by returning one or more documents to Navigator. This process of exchanges may repeat many times.

NOTE
The term *server* has two meanings. First, it can refer to a program that runs on a computer. Apache is a web server, for example. Second, it can mean the computer that runs a server program. Likewise, *client* can refer to either a program that requests information of a server program or a computer that requests information of a server computer. When these terms are applied to entire computers, confusion can quickly result in some environments because a single computer can function as both client and server simultaneously.

One of the problems encountered in achieving the goal of data exchange between programs is in controlling access to the network. If programs such as Netscape were allowed to control the network hardware directly, chaos would soon ensue because programs would interfere with one another. At the core of the solution to this problem lies the concept of a *network stack*. This is a set of small software modules, functioning in series, each of which interfaces with two others (or with one other and the network hardware or a human). Network applications—both clients and servers—lie at the top of the network stack. These applications communicate with the layer below them and so on until the bottom layer is reached, at which point the data leaves the computer and traverses the network to the destination system. At that point, the process is reversed, and data travels up the stack to the destination application. This application can then send a reply via the same method. Figure 12.1 illustrates this process.

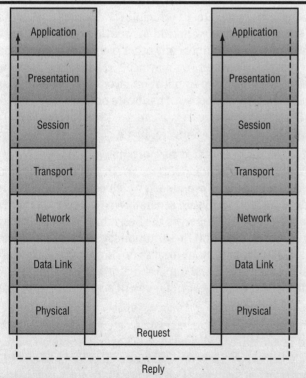

FIGURE 12.1:   Information travels "down" and "up" network stacks, being checked and packed at each step of the way.

At each stage in its journey down a network stack, data is checked or encapsulated in additional information. These "wrappings" function much like an envelope around a letter sent via the Post Office; they help the data reach its ultimate destination. Unlike a physical letter, though, data sent via TCP/IP may be split up into multiple packets. Rather than send a 2MB file in one chunk, TCP/IP breaks it down into many packets of about 1.5KB each. Part of the encapsulation process ensures that the recipient computer is able to reassemble the original file from its many individual packets. TCP/IP was designed to be fault tolerant, so it's possible for the receiving system to request that a specific packet be sent again if it doesn't arrive. Individual packets may travel different routes from source to destination, and the system still functions.

In principle, each layer of a network stack may be swapped out and replaced with an equivalent component without affecting higher or lower layers. For example, the Physical layer in Figure 12.1 corresponds to network hardware, such as Ethernet cards. The Data Link layer consists of drivers for the network hardware. In principle (and sometimes in practice), you can swap out one network card for another or change one driver for another without having to adjust any other components of the network stack. In practice, however, you may need to adjust the driver if you change the network card. At the Application layer, you can change applications without adjusting the network hardware or any of the "invisible" software that lies between the two—you can use Lynx rather than Netscape Navigator for web browsing, for instance.

Figure 12.1 presents an idealized view of a network stack, known as the *Open Systems Interconnection* (OSI) *model*. In practice, TCP/IP is often described in terms of its own model, which contains fewer layers. TCP/IP's model considers hardware separately, so it doesn't extend to the Physical layer, and TCP/IP merges the Session and Transport layers into one and the Application and Presentation layers into one. These differences are unimportant for our discussion, however; the critical points are that data is packed and unpacked as it traverses the network stack, and that the stack helps control network access, including data addressing.

TCP/IP is not the only network stack in existence. Others, such as AppleTalk and IPX/SPX, can also be used. These alternate network stacks can be described by the same OSI model depicted in Figure 12.1, but each has its own idiosyncrasies, so it's normally not possible to swap a layer from one stack for a layer from another stack. (The Physical and to some extent Data Link and Application layers are shared between stacks, however.) TCP/IP is the basis for the Internet and is thus the most common network stack. Linux also includes support for several less-common network stacks, such as AppleTalk and Novell's IPX.

Network Addresses

One critically important component of any network protocol is *addressing*. If you're at one computer and want to use resources located on a server, you must have some method of telling your computer how to reach the server. To a human, the network address most frequently takes the form of a *hostname*, *computer name*, or *fully qualified domain name* (FQDN), such as www.sybex.com. This hostname is sometimes preceded by a code indicating what type of server you want to use on the remote system, such as http:// for a web server (web servers use the *Hypertext Transfer Protocol*, or HTTP). When so used, the hostname is referred to as a *Uniform Resource Locator* (URL).

Hostnames are hierarchical in nature, with each portion of the hierarchy separated by a period (.). The leftmost component of the hostname (such as www in www.sybex.com) is sometimes called the *machine name*. This component identifies a single specific computer. The remainder of the hostname (such as sybex.com) is the *domain name*. It refers to a collection of computers. Domain names are themselves hierarchically arranged. *Top-level domains* (TLDs), such as .com, .org, and .us, contain *domains* such as sybex.com and linux.org, which can be broken down into their own subdomains or have computers assigned directly to them. Thus, the number of levels in the hierarchy is variable. One domain might have many levels (such as a.very.deep.domain.structure.in.the.uk), whereas another can be quite shallow (such as oneroomco.com, which could conceivably point directly to a single computer).

Unfortunately, although hostnames of this form are reasonably easy for people to understand, computers work better with numbers. Therefore, although the Internet includes provisions for using hostnames, at its core it relies upon a different addressing scheme: *IP addresses*. IP addresses are 32-bit numbers that are generally expressed as four decimal numbers separated by periods (.), as in 192.168.204.98. IP addresses are broken into two components: a *network address* and a *machine address*.

This division simplifies the job of *routers*, which are devices that send traffic between networks, because it means the router can be programmed in terms of networks rather than individual computers.

A *network mask* (*netmask* for short) marks the network address portion of an IP address with binary 1s. For instance, 255.255.255.0 places a binary 1 in each bit of the first three bytes of an address, indicating that those first three bytes are the network address and the final byte is the machine address.

An IP or network address can be combined with a network mask using a shorthand form in which the number of leading binary 1s in the netmask follows the IP address, as in 192.168.204.0/24. This is the same as the 192.168.204.0 network with a netmask of 255.255.255.0 (24 ones, expressed in binary).

NOTE

In a hostname, the most significant portion (the machine name) is in the *leftmost* position of the address. In an IP address, the most significant portion (the machine address) is in the *rightmost* position of the address.

Traditionally, the available range of IP addresses is broken up into networks of various *classes*, as indicated in Table 12.1. As indicated by the classes' netmasks, these classes differ in size—each Class A network can contain over 16 million computers; Class B networks can host 65,534 computers, and Class C networks can each have only 254 computers.

More recently, however, networks have been merged or split up in nontraditional ways in order to make more efficient use of the dwindling supply of IP addresses. Each of the three major classes of IP addresses supports a range of *private* IP addresses (shown in Table 12.1), which routers do not route. These IP addresses can be used internally for private networks without acquiring "official" IP addresses. There are also Class D and E networks, which have special meaning and are reserved for future use.

TABLE 12.1:   IP Address Classes and Private Address Ranges

CLASS NAME	RANGE	NETMASK	PRIVATE ADDRESSES
Class A	1.0.0.0– 127.255.255.255	255.0.0.0	10.0.0.0– 10.255.255.255
Class B	128.0.0.0– 191.255.255.255	255.255.0.0	172.16.0.0– 172.31.255.255
Class C	192.0.0.0– 223.255.255.255	255.255.255.0	192.168.0.0– 192.168.255.255

The Internet is fast running out of IP addresses. Although a 32-bit address provides a theoretical limit of about 4 billion addresses, the actual limits are somewhat lower, and the number of Internet-connected computers is growing at a staggering rate.

For this and other reasons, work is underway on *IPv6*, a new means of addressing for TCP/IP networks. IPv6 uses a 128-bit address, which permits roughly 3.4×10^{38} addresses—that's 2.2×10^{18} addresses per square millimeter of land surface on the Earth, which ought to last us a while.

To learn more about IPv6 and its current status in Linux, visit one of these three URLs: `http://www.bieringer.de/linux/IPv6/IPv6-HOWTO/`, `http://www.xelia.ch/Linux/IPng.html`, or `http://www.linuxhq.com/IPv6/linux-ipv6.faq.html`.

As a practical matter, it's necessary to link IP addresses to hostnames and vice versa. This task is accomplished through the *Domain Name System* (DNS), which uses a highly distributed system of DNS servers. Each DNS server is responsible for its own domain or subdomain. These servers are arranged in a hierarchical manner that mirrors the domain name structure.

At the top of this hierarchy are the *root servers*, which know the addresses of the servers that handle the TLDs. Each TLD server knows the addresses of servers that handle each of its domains, and so on. Eventually, a server in this hierarchy is *authoritative* for a domain, meaning that it can say with authority whether a given hostname exists and, if it does, what its IP address is. A similar hierarchy allows *reverse DNS* lookups, so that a name can be found, given an IP address.

Typically, an organization's DNS server performs two tasks:

▶ It fields name queries from computers inside its domain. It queries an appropriate root server and follows the chain of referrals from that server to locate an authoritative server for the requested domain. It then passes the result of this query (typically an IP address or a code saying that the name is invalid) back to the requesting client.

▶ It accepts queries from outside sources regarding the names and IP addresses of systems within its domain.

When you configure a Linux system for networking, chances are you need to know the IP addresses of only from one to three DNS servers. You can then point your Linux system at those DNS servers to let them do the dirty work of traversing the tree of servers to resolve domain names into IP addresses. Linux can function as a DNS server, but configuring Linux in this way is well beyond the scope of this chapter. For that information, consult a book such as Craig Hunt's *Linux DNS Server Administration* (Sybex, 2000).

A final address type is the network card's *hardware address*. The card uses this to tell when packets are addressed to it. Part of the job of the network stack is to find a hardware address matched to any given IP address. The stack does this by broadcasting a query to all the computers on the local network. (For more distant systems, the computer only needs to send the packet to a local *router*, which can then forward the data based on its IP address.) In most cases, you need not concern yourself with the hardware address, although one exception is noted later in this chapter.

Ports

Once a packet has been routed to a destination system, the target computer needs to know what to do with it. This information is conveyed, in part, through the use of multiple *ports*. Each TCP/IP packet is addressed to one of 65,536 ports, which you can think of as being similar to extensions on a business telephone system. By convention, specific server packages listen for traffic on specific ports. For instance, web servers listen on port 80, and mail servers listen on port 25. The file /etc/ services lists the port assignments used by common servers.

As a user, you normally don't need to be concerned with port use, because client programs know which ports to call. As a system administrator, you must occasionally deal with port assignments. For instance, you may need to add an entry to /etc/services if an appropriate entry isn't present.

NOTE

TCP/IP ports are distinct from hardware ports, which are used to link devices such as printers and modems to the computer. An Ethernet card usually has one Ethernet port, but that one Ethernet port (hardware) supports thousands of TCP/IP ports (software).

Client programs also use ports to call *out* of a system. Linux assigns outgoing ports to programs on an as-needed basis, so you don't need to be concerned with this detail. When a server replies to a client, it does so using the port that the client used, so Linux knows to which program it should deliver the return packet. Both client and server programs keep track of the IP addresses with which they're exchanging data, so they can keep packets from different sessions separate.

TCP/IP CONFIGURATION

With the theory of TCP/IP out of the way, it's time to move on to practical Linux TCP/IP configuration. Most distributions, including Red Hat 7.1, allow you to configure TCP/IP at system installation. However, this isn't always practical, because you may need to install hardware or locate new drivers before you can proceed. Even if you use installation-time configuration options or a separate GUI interface, it's helpful to understand the underlying text-mode tools. This chapter therefore emphasizes text-based TCP/IP configuration tools and utilities.

Configuring Network Hardware

The first step in TCP/IP configuration is to set up the hardware. A working network includes a wide variety of network hardware, such as hubs or switches, routers, servers, and so on. The possibilities are so broad, in fact, that it's impossible to cover them all here. Therefore, this chapter focuses on configuring a single Linux system in a network. In this context, hardware configuration consists of locating and installing an appropriate network interface card (NIC) and ensuring that your system contains appropriate drivers for that card.

NOTE

Many isolated Linux systems use the *Point-to-Point Protocol* (PPP) to link the system to the Internet via a telephone modem. This chapter is more concerned with networking via dedicated networking hardware.

Linux supports a wide variety of networking hardware. The most common type of networking hardware today is Ethernet, which comes in several varieties, including 10Base2 (also known as *thin coax*), 10Base5 (a.k.a. *thick coax*), 10Base-T, and 100Base-T. Most of these varieties operate at speeds of up to 10Mbps, but 100Base-T supports 100Mbps speeds. Even faster varieties operate at up to 1000Mbps (1Gbps). The Linux kernel supports most modern Ethernet adapters. To discover what devices

Part iii

your Linux distribution supports, check the configuration options in the kernel compilation interface. Look under Ethernet (10Mbps or 100Mbps) in the 2.2.*x* kernels or Network Device Support ➤ Ethernet (10Mbit or 100Mbit) in the 2.4.*x* kernels (used by Red Hat 7.1).

You can also check with a device's manufacturer to see which Linux drivers to use. Some manufacturers provide Linux drivers for their boards, but these are usually just the drivers from the Linux kernel.

Some networks don't use Ethernet, but instead use other types of networking hardware, such as token ring. Although Linux's support for these more exotic types of hardware isn't as complete as for Ethernet, you can usually find drivers for at least some NICs for most network types. As with Ethernet, you should consult the kernel's configuration options and boards' manufacturers to discover what's supported.

If you compile a driver directly into your kernel, it will automatically load and detect your network card. If your driver is compiled as a module (which is typical of freshly installed Linux systems), you may need to add an entry or two to the /etc/modules.conf file (called /etc/conf.modules on some distributions). Specifically, you may need to set up an alias between eth0 and the name of your NIC's driver. If you have multiple NICs, you may need to add multiple lines to make these associations, as in the following:

```
alias eth0 tulip
alias eth1 via-rhine
```

These lines tell Linux to use the tulip driver for eth0 (the first Ethernet device) and the via-rhine driver for eth1 (the second Ethernet device). Of course, to set up these lines, you will need to have located the appropriate driver for your board, as described earlier. You can see what drivers are present on your system by typing **ls /lib/modules/x.y.z/net**, where **x.y.z** is your kernel version. In Red Hat 7.1, the directory is /lib/modules/2.4.2-2/kernel/net.

TIP

One of the best reasons to configure networking when you install Linux, especially if you're less than intimately familiar with your networking hardware, is that most Linux installation routines include tools that detect the type of network hardware you have installed, so you don't need to figure out this detail.

Once you've configured the hardware and rebooted, Linux should auto-detect the hardware at boot time. When it does, it displays a brief message to this effect, such as the following:

```
eth0: Macronix 98715 PMAC rev 32 at 0xda00,
    00:80:C6:F9:3B:BA, IRQ 9.

eth1: VIA VT3043 Rhine at 0xdc00, 00:80:c8:fa:3b:0a, IRQ 10.

eth1: MII PHY found at address 8, status 0x782d advertising
    05e1 Link➤0000.
```

These lines indicate that Linux has detected two Ethernet cards: eth0 uses a Macronix 98715 (a chip that uses the tulip driver), and eth1 uses a VIA VT3043 Rhine chip (which uses the via-rhine driver). These messages also include the Ethernet devices' hardware addresses—the six-byte hexadecimal values, such as 00:80:C6:F9:3B:BA. These values can be important on some networks, as described later in this chapter. If you don't see such lines at boot time, you should re-examine your configuration to be sure you haven't mistyped a device driver name and that you've correctly identified the NIC's hardware.

TIP

Boot messages scroll by so quickly that you're likely to miss them. After you've booted, you can type **dmesg** to see these messages replayed. Further, you can pipe the results through Grep, as in **dmesg l grep eth**, to isolate just the Ethernet-related messages.

One peculiarity of network hardware under Linux is that these devices don't have the usual device file entries in the /dev directory. Nonetheless, networking devices are named (as in eth0 or eth1). Networking tools communicate these names to the Linux kernel directly, not by accessing device files.

Using DHCP for Configuration

The easiest way to configure most computers for networking is to use the *Dynamic Host Configuration Protocol* (DHCP). This is a networking protocol that allows one system (the *DHCP server*) to maintain information about a network's important characteristics and to feed this information to other systems (the *DHCP clients*). A network administrator maintains the information on the DHCP server, and all other systems need only be told to use a DHCP client program. The client program, when started, sends out a broadcast asking for help from a DHCP server, which then responds with all the important network information.

NOTE

Some DHCP servers respond only to registered clients. The server uses the NIC's hardware address to identify clients. You may need to provide this information to your network administrator or ISP. For Ethernet devices, the code in question is a six-byte hexadecimal value. Linux Ethernet drivers display this value on the screen at boot time, as described earlier.

There are three DHCP clients in common use on Linux systems: dhclient, dhcpcd, and pump. A Red Hat 7.1 Workstation installation includes both pump and dhcpcd. In most cases, you need only to install the appropriate package on the system. When the computer starts, it uses an appropriate startup script to call the DHCP client. In Red Hat 7.1, the /etc/sysconfig/network-scripts/ifup script contains the appropriate call, trying first pump and then dhcpcd. Many other distributions place DHCP client scripts somewhere in the /etc/rc.d directory. If you install a DHCP client and don't want to reboot before using your network, you can call the client program directly, such as by typing **/sbin/pump** on a Red Hat 7.1 system.

Some Linux distributions that rely on GUI configuration tools may require you to set an option in this tool to call the DHCP client automatically at boot time. You can usually bypass this requirement by placing a call in a boot script such as /etc/rc.d/rc.local, but it may be simpler to check the appropriate configuration option. In Red Hat's Linuxconf, it can be found in the Config ≻ Networking ≻ Client Tasks ≻ Host Name and IP Network Devices module, shown in Figure 12.2. Click the Adapter tab for your NIC and select the Dhcp option next to Config Mode.

Unfortunately, although DHCP is supposed to simplify network configuration, it doesn't always work quite the way it should. One particular class of problems relates to servers that use multiple network interfaces, particularly when only one of these should be configured via DHCP. Most DHCP clients allow you to specify an interface to configure. For instance, you could use **pump -i eth1** to tell pump to configure your eth1 interface. You may be able to modify your startup scripts to force your DHCP client to work on only the desired interfaces.

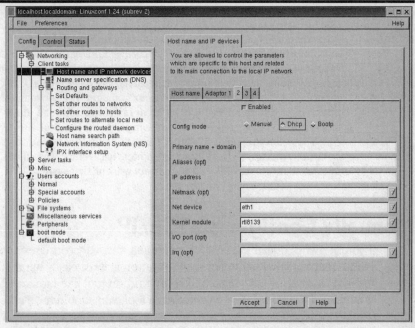

FIGURE 12.2:   In many distributions you can set networking options from a single GUI configuration tool.

Sometimes problems with a DHCP client can be hard to manage. Fortunately, the fact that there are three DHCP clients for Linux provides you with a way out: You can try another client. Before you remove the original client, though, you should locate and back up its configuration file. You may need to restore and modify this file to start a new client, particularly if you use a DHCP client from another distribution, because different distributions use slightly different startup script formats.

DHCP is capable of setting most aspects of a Linux system's network configuration. DHCP cannot, however, install the network drivers. Some DHCP configurations also omit some information—most commonly the hostname—so you may need to do a few manual adjustments even if your system uses DHCP. (The next section describes manual TCP/IP configuration.)

Part iii

NOTE

Some *Digital Subscriber Line* (DSL) installations use an automatic configuration protocol called *Point-to-Point Protocol over Ethernet* (PPPoE). This protocol uses the PPP tools that are normally used over telephone modems, but instead applies them to Ethernet connections. There are several Linux PPPoE clients available, but none is yet the Linux standard. The command-line tool pppoe is installed on Red Hat 7.1 by default. You can read about PPPoE in the pppoe man page or by reviewing the contents of the directory /usr/share/doc/rp-pppoe-2.6. Also check http://www.rodsbooks.com/network/network-dsl.html for pointers to several PPPoE clients. If your DSL installation uses PPPoE, DHCP will *not* work on that system.

Manually Configuring TCP/IP

If your network doesn't use DHCP, you must normally configure your TCP/IP settings manually. This configuration is most easily handled at installation time or using a GUI configuration tool like Linuxconf (Figure 12.2). If you choose to use such a tool, you should have little trouble locating the appropriate options, given the descriptions that follow.

Setting the Hostname

The hostname is most important to computers that want to contact yours as a server. You can't normally set the hostname that's stored on a remote DNS server, however, so you must rely upon the DNS administrator to accomplish this task. You can, however, set the name that your computer believes itself to be. This can be important because some protocols, such as mail, embed the sender's address in outgoing messages. If your hostname is set incorrectly locally, recipient systems may become quite confused or even refuse connections.

You can set your system's hostname using the hostname command. Entered without any parameters, this command reports the system's current name. You can pass a name to the command, however, to set the hostname. For instance, the following command sets the hostname to gingko.oneroomco.com:

```
# hostname gingko.oneroomco.com
```

NOTE

The commands described here for manual TCP/IP configuration can be added to a startup script, such as /etc/rc.d/rc.local, if you want to automate the process. It's usually better to use the distribution's standard network startup scripts for this purpose, though.

Unfortunately, setting the hostname one time with this command does not set it permanently; after you reboot, Linux sets its hostname using values stored in configuration files. Details vary from one distribution to another, but you should pay particular attention to the /etc/HOSTNAME, /etc/hostname, /etc/sysconfig/network, and /etc/hosts files. The first three are common locations for Linux to store the name that it sets using the hostname command when it boots. Red Hat 7.1 uses the /etc/sysconfig/network file.

The /etc/hosts file is a bit different, because it lists mappings of hostnames to IP addresses—it can be used in place of DNS on a small network, and it can augment DNS even on a large network. If you see your IP address in /etc/hosts, be sure it's mapped to your correct hostname.

TIP

If you can't find your system's hostname reference, try typing **grep -r hostname /etc/***. This command should return a list of files in the /etc directory tree that contain the word hostname. One of these is almost certainly the file that sets your hostname. Sometimes this file uses a definition from another file to set the hostname, so you can modify the source file or bypass the definition in another file by modifying the name-setting file directly.

Activating an Interface

To use a network, you must activate an interface. To do this, use the ifconfig command, which tells Linux to begin using a device and to associate it with a specific IP address. The basic syntax for this command is:

```
ifconfig interface [options] [address]
```

Part iii

The meaning of each parameter is as follows:

interface   This is the network interface, such as eth0.

options   You can specify several different options to
ifconfig. The most important are up and down,
which force the system to activate or deactivate an
interface, respectively. (up is the default, so you
can omit it when activating an interface.) You can
also use the netmask *mask* option to set the
netmask—by default, ifconfig uses a netmask
based on the class of network to which the address
belongs, as shown in Table 12.1. You can read
about more options in the ifconfig man pages.

address   This is the IP address to which the computer will
respond on this interface, such as 192.168.203.7.
If you omit the address, ifconfig reports on the
status of an interface, rather than configuring the
interface to use an address.

Various address types can be used with the ifconfig command. Most
users will rely on standard IP addresses, but others, such as the inet6
keyword for IPv6 addresses, are described in the ifconfig man page.

In its simplest form, an ifconfig command can be quite short:

```
# ifconfig eth0 192.168.203.7
```

You may need to add more options. In particular, if your IP address
uses a nonstandard netmask, you may need to specify one, as in:

```
# ifconfig eth0 netmask 255.255.255.128 eth0 192.168.203.7
```

It's a good idea to check on a configuration after setting it up. You can
also use ifconfig to gather useful debugging information even long after
an interface has been activated. For example:

```
# ifconfig eth0
eth0      Link encap:Ethernet  HWaddr 00:A0:CC:24:BA:02
          inet addr:192.168.203.7  Bcast:192.168.203.255
            Mask:255.255.255.0
          UP BROADCAST RUNNING  MTU:1500  Metric:1
          RX packets:7173469 errors:6 dropped:0 overruns:0
            frame:6
```

```
TX packets:6294646 errors:0 dropped:0 overruns:0
    carrier:0
collisions:66163
```

This output shows that eth0 is up and running, using the hardware address 00:A0:CC:24:BA:02 and the TCP/IP address 192.168.203.7. Further statistics include the *Maximum Transfer Unit* (MTU) size of 1500, received (RX) and transmitted (TX) packets (including errors), and collisions. This information can be invaluable when debugging a connection. A huge number of errors or collisions can signal that your network is overburdened or that your hardware is faulty, for example.

NOTE

Some errors and collisions are normal. The preceding example shows a total of 66,163 collisions and 13,468,115 packets sent or received, for a collision rate of about 0.5%. The error rate (6 of 7,173,469 received packets and no transmit errors) is also quite low. It's difficult to specify a threshold above which errors or collisions indicate problems, because these values can vary from one network to another. Collisions occur inevitably on Ethernet networks when two systems try to transmit at the same time. Collision rates therefore go up with total network traffic.

Configuring the Routing Table

It's important that a computer know to which network interface it should send data. When there is just one NIC, this may seem a trivial task, but it's not quite so trivial in Linux, because all Linux systems support a *loopback* (or *localhost*) *interface*, which directs the network traffic back to the Linux system. This interface is very useful in troubleshooting and for some basic Linux features, such as X. It's normally assigned an address of 127.0.0.1 and is configured automatically by default startup scripts. You therefore need not concern yourself about the loopback interface, but you must tell your system how to route all other network data.

This task is accomplished with the route command, which has the following syntax:

```
route [add | del] [target] [gw gateway]
```

Each parameter has a specific meaning:

add | del   Specify add if you want to add an entry to the routing table or del if you want to remove one. When starting up an interface, you use the add parameter.

target   The *target* is the IP address or network address
                       to which the route applies. A network address
                       looks just like an IP address, but it uses trailing 0s
                       in the machine portion of the IP address, as in
                       192.168.203.0. One special target is the default
                       route, which is 0.0.0.0. You can use the keyword
                       default in place of 0.0.0.0, if you like. The default
                       route is the route taken by all traffic that's not
                       matched by more specific rules. You normally
                       specify a gateway system with the default route;
                       traffic to most sites that aren't on your local
                       network then travels through the gateway system.

gw *gateway*   A gateway is a system that knows how to send pack-
                       ets to another network. The terms *gateway* and
                       router carry very similar meanings and are often
                       used interchangeably. Your ISP or network adminis-
                       trator can provide you with the IP address of an
                       appropriate gateway.

NOTE
There's normally no need to specify explicitly the NIC or even the IP address
with which a route is associated, because the route command can discern
this information based on the target or gateway address. If your network is
unusually complex, you can force the route to be associated with a device by
using the dev *device* parameter.

Typically, you specify two routes for traffic passing out of a Linux computer: one for traffic destined for the local network and one for a default
route, which passes through a gateway. You can accomplish this task by
issuing two commands, such as these:

```
# route add 192.168.203.0
# route add 0.0.0.0 gw 192.168.203.1
```

The first of these commands adds a route for local traffic—anything
addressed to the 192.168.203.0 network goes out over the appropriate
NIC. The low-level TCP/IP protocols include routines that enable a computer to locate any other computer that's connected to its local network
segment.

The second command takes over when packets are destined for an
address other than the 192.168.203.0 network (or any other network

defined by an explicit route). In this case, the system directs the packets to 192.168.203.1, which should be a router capable of passing the packets on to the appropriate destination. (In fact, it may pass them on to another router, and so on for quite a few hops on the network.)

If you have configured an interface using an IPv6 address, you can also refer to that interface and address in the route command. Various methods are used to map or route between networks using standard IP and IPv6 addressing. The URLs listed in the text following Table 12.1, earlier in this chapter, provide detailed information on the status and use of this technology.

NOTE

If you're configuring systems on a local network that will not be connected to the Internet, there's no need to specify a gateway route.

You can examine your routing table by issuing the route command without any options (or with the -n option, if you want to see IP addresses rather than machine names). For instance:

```
# route -n
```

```
Kernel IP routing table
Destination     Gateway         Genmask         Flags Metric Ref  Use Iface
192.168.203.0   0.0.0.0         255.255.255.0 U     0      0      0 eth0
127.0.0.0       0.0.0.0         255.0.0.0       U     0      0      0 lo
0.0.0.0         192.168.203.1   0.0.0.0         UG    0      0      0 eth0
```

This output reveals three routes: one for the 192.168.203.0 network, one for the localhost interface (which is actually configured as an entire network), and one for the default route. Most desktop and even server systems will have routing tables that resemble this one. If a computer has multiple NICs, or if its network is unusually complex in any of several ways, the routing table may have additional entries.

Most Linux systems include calls to route in startup scripts. In Red Hat 7.1, /etc/rc.d/init.d/network is responsible for starting networking, including setting up network interfaces and routing, but it calls several other scripts to do parts of these tasks. Ultimately, /etc/sysconfig/static-routes holds the information on routes that are added automatically. (The file /etc/syconfig/static-routes-ipv6 is used for IPv6 networking.) You can therefore modify this file, use Linuxconf to do the job, or add calls to route to some other startup script, such as /etc/rc.d/rc.local.

Specifying DNS Servers

In order to resolve hostnames into IP addresses for arbitrary systems on the Internet, Linux must know the IP address of at least one DNS server. Linux stores this information in the /etc/resolv.conf file, along with information on its own default domain name. A typical /etc/resolv.conf file looks like this:

```
domain room1.threeroomco.com
search room2.threeroomco.com room3.threeroomco.com
nameserver 192.168.203.1
nameserver 192.168.203.20
```

There are three important keywords used in this file:

domain
: This specifies the domain to which the system belongs. Linux tries to resolve names using the specified domain first. For example, if you use the machine name gingko and the above /etc/resolv.conf file, Linux first searches for a computer called gingko.room1.threeroomco.com. This feature allows you to omit the domain name portion of a machine name when a target computer is in the same domain as the source machine.

search
: The search option works much like the domain option, but you can specify several domains to be searched using this parameter, separated by spaces or tabs.

nameserver
: Each nameserver line specifies the IP address of a single DNS server. This must be an IP address, not a machine name—after all, the DNS server is supposed to do name resolution. You can specify as many DNS servers as you like, one per line, but Linux uses only the first three. Normally, only the first is used; but if the first DNS server becomes inaccessible, Linux goes on to the next.

WARNING

Configuring a system to search too many domains or subdomains can increase the time it takes to resolve a domain name. It could also cause you to contact one machine when you meant another, if they bear the same machine names but exist in different domains.

You don't need to do anything special after entering information in /etc/resolv.conf in order to use these DNS servers. Also, Linux remembers these settings when you reboot (unlike some other network configuration options), so you don't need to adjust any startup scripts.

Testing the Setup

With any luck, you now have a working network configuration. You should perform some tests to be sure it's working. If you're impatient, skip ahead to test 6; if you have problems, try the following tests in order:

1. Check the basic Linux TCP/IP stack by pinging the localhost address. Type **ping 127.0.0.1**. You should see a series of output lines similar to the following, indicating that the localhost address is responding:

   ```
   64 bytes from 127.0.0.1: icmp_seq=1 ttl=255 time=0.3 ms
   ```

   Press Ctrl+C to stop this sequence. If this test doesn't work, your configuration is very badly damaged. Every Linux system should pass this test, even immediately after installation.

2. Ping your NIC's external address (as in **ping 192.168.203.7**). This tests the association of the address to a NIC via ifconfig, as well as basic network driver functions.

3. Ping a machine on your local network by IP address. A good system to ping is usually your router/gateway. If this test works, you can be sure that your network hardware and drivers are functioning. If it fails, double-check your ifconfig setup and investigate the possibility of using a more up-to-date driver for your network card.

NOTE

It's possible to configure a computer to ignore pings. Computers can also be offline, or the route to a remote computer can be broken in various ways. It's therefore possible that a ping test will fail despite a flawless configuration of your own system. If this happens, try another system before declaring the test failed.

4. Ping a machine beyond your local network by IP address, as in **ping 198.182.196.56** (this pings www.linux.org, but this address may change in the future; it's best to locate an address using nslookup). If this test works, your gateway configuration is correct. If previous tests succeeded but this one fails, check your routing table, paying particular attention to the gateway.

5. Ping local and remote machines by machine name rather than IP address, as in **ping www.linux.org**. If this test works, your DNS configuration is correct.

6. Use more sophisticated network tools, such as a web browser or Telnet client. It's extremely unlikely that these will fail when pings work, but it's best to be complete.

If the preceding tests are all passed, then your network settings are at least minimally correct. Of course, it's possible you'll run into more subtle problems, such as slow network performance or an inability to reach specific systems. Some such problems can be caused by local configuration problems, such as an incorrect routing table. Network debugging can be a complex task. If you have peculiar problems, you may want to post a message to the comp.os.linux.networking newsgroup.

FILE SHARING

One of the most common uses for networking on small networks is to implement *file sharing*. The idea behind this technology is to allow the users of one computer (the client) to access the files on another computer (the server) as if the server's files were stored on a disk local to the client. The benefits of this arrangement include the following:

▶ Saving on total disk space by storing files needed by many clients on just one system.

▶ Enabling individuals to work from any computer while accessing the same files.

▶ Making collaboration simpler than it would otherwise be, because there's no need to move files around on floppy disks.

Like many networking applications, file sharing requires the use of both client and server software. There are several file-sharing packages available on many OSs. This chapter restricts discussion to just two: the *Network File System* (NFS), which is used by Linux and Unix systems; and *Samba*, which is the Linux implementation of the *Server Message Block* (SMB; a.k.a. *Common Internet File System*, or CIFS) protocol used by DOS, Windows, and OS/2.

NOTE

Both NFS and SMB/CIFS are built at the top level of the OSI network model. Some file-sharing protocols, including SMB/CIFS, optionally can use a variety of protocol stacks, but in Linux both of these use TCP/IP. For more information on Samba server, see Part V, "Samba."

Sharing with Unix or Linux: NFS

NFS is tightly woven into Linux and Unix systems, and it supports the filesystem features (such as ownership and file permissions) upon which Linux and Unix systems depend. It's therefore the file-sharing solution of choice on networks dominated by Linux or Unix computers.

NOTE

For a complete guide to NFS administration in Linux, see *Linux NFS and Automounter Administration*, by Erez Zadok (Sybex, 2001).

Configuring an NFS Server

To configure a Linux system as an NFS server, follow these steps:

1. Install an NFS server package. In Red Hat Linux 7.1, this package is called `nfs-utils-0.3.1-5`.

2. Edit the `/etc/exports` file to share specific directories, as described later in this section.

3. Start the NFS server. On Red Hat systems, you can do this by typing **/etc/rc.d/init.d/nfs start**. (If the NFS daemon is already running, you should use **restart** rather than **start** in this command. You can discover if this server is running by typing **nfsd**.

The NFS "server" includes three daemons: rpc.mountd to manage mount requests from remote NFS clients; rpc.nfsd to handle data transfer requests once a filesystem has been mounted by a remote client; and rpc.rquotad to manage disk space quotas on shared NFS filesystems.

To ensure that the NFS server starts at boot time, check the /etc/rc.d/rc3.d and /etc/rc.d/rc5.d directories for a file called S??nfs, where ?? is a number. These files, if present, should be links to /etc/rc.d/init.d/nfs (or an NFS startup script in some other directory on some distributions). If these files don't exist, you must create them. The following command should accomplish this goal on Red Hat systems, but you may need to adjust the linked-to file on some distributions:

```
# ln -s /etc/rc.d/init.d/nfs /etc/rc[35].d/S60nfs
```

The most critical configuration file for an NFS server is /etc/exports. This file determines which computers may mount an exported directory, as well as various limitations placed on these mounts. Each line in /etc/exports defines one *export*, a directory that's shared. The line begins with the path to the directory and continues with a list of systems that are authorized to use the export, including any client-specific options enclosed in parentheses. Listing 12.1 shows a sample /etc/exports file.

Listing 12.1: An */etc/exports* File Showing Some Common Options

```
/home larch(rw) birch(rw,map_static=/etc/birch.map)
➥gingko.threeroomco.com(ro)
/home/fred 192.168.34.23(noaccess)
/mnt *.threeroomco.com(rw)
/opt 192.168.34.0/24(ro)
```

You can list hostnames in several different ways in /etc/exports, as illustrated by Listing 12.1. These methods include the following:

Individual hostnames You can list the hostnames individually, as in all the systems on the /home export in Listing 12.1. If the clients are part of the same domain as the server, you can omit the domain name, as was done with larch and birch in the example. Alternatively, you can keep the entire hostname.

Individual IP addresses   Instead of using a hostname, you can export a share to a system by specifying its IP address. Using an IP address enhances security slightly. This is the approach used by the /home/fred export in the example.

Domains   You can specify a domain by using a wildcard character, as in *.threeroomco.com, which exports the directory to any computer in the threeroomco.com domain. This approach can be convenient, but it also increases the potential for abuse should a DNS server be compromised.

IP address blocks   You can export a directory to a block of IP addresses by specifying a network address and netmask in abbreviated format, as in 192.168.34.0/24.

WARNING

You can export a share to any computer by omitting the hostname entirely. This may be convenient on a small private network, but it is also quite dangerous, particularly if your computer is accessible to the Internet as a whole.

You should specify one or more options for most exports and clients. You'll do this by specifying the options in parentheses after the client name. Listing 12.1 makes heavy use of the rw and ro options, which provide read/write and read-only access to a share, respectively. (Some NFS servers default to read-only access, while others default to read/write access, so it's best to be explicit on this matter to avoid confusion.) The noaccess option blocks all access to a directory. Listing 12.1 uses this option to prevent the computer at 192.168.34.23 from accessing the /home/fred directory, even if the /home directory is exported to that computer.

One particularly important option is map_static, which is used to specify a file that describes a mapping of client and server user and group IDs. Every Linux or Unix system assigns a user a username, but the username is just a convenient label. Underlying the username is a numeric *user ID*. The same user may have different user IDs on two different systems, even if the usernames are identical on both systems. NFS relies on user IDs, so if map_static is not used, a user might be able to access the *wrong* user's files on a server. The content of the mapping file consists of three columns, separated by spaces: `uid` or `gid` (to indicate whether the code to be changed is a user or group ID, respectively), the ID on the client, and the ID on the server. Listing 12.2 presents a sample mapping file. In this file, user ID 501 on the client is mapped to user 504 on the server, and group 103 on the client becomes group 100 on the server.

Listing 12.2: A Sample NFS Mapping File

```
uid  501  504
uid  503  503
gid  103  100
```

WARNING

If you use a mapping file at all, it's important that it include *all* the users' mappings, even if the user has the same ID on both systems. If you omit a server user ID, then the associated user ID on the client is likely to be gibberish. This may be fine if the user doesn't exist on the client, but it's not OK otherwise.

Various other options exist on some or all NFS servers and may be of interest to advanced administrators. Type **man exports** to learn more about this file and its options.

One thing to keep in mind about NFS is that it operates on a *trusted host* security model. That is, if you list a computer in /etc/exports, you turn over some of your security to that system. NFS exports Linux's username and permission information to the client, but if the remote system's security has been compromised in any way, it's possible that a user of the client might be able to damage files on the server. For this reason, it's generally unwise to export sensitive directories, such as /etc, especially with read/write permissions.

Over the years, there have been several Linux NFS servers. The latest version on most distributions uses special features in the Linux kernel to accelerate the server. You must therefore include NFS server support in your Linux kernel if you recompile your kernel. (All major distributions include this feature in their default kernels.) Unfortunately, this means that an NFS server may break if you upgrade your kernel, particularly from an older 2.2.*x* kernel to a 2.4.*x* or newer kernel. You may therefore need to look for an updated NFS server (or an older one that doesn't use kernel acceleration) if you upgrade your kernel.

Mounting Remote NFS Exports

Linux includes NFS client support in its kernel, and all major distributions compile this support in their standard kernels or as modules. You should therefore have little trouble mounting NFS exports, as long as the server recognizes your system as a valid client. Linux uses its regular mount command for mounting NFS exports. The syntax is as follows:

```
mount [-t nfs] server:/path /mountpoint
```

In most cases, the -t nfs parameter isn't required; Linux can figure out that it's an NFS export you're specifying. server is, of course, the name of the server, and /path is the path to the exported directory on that server. /mountpoint is the local mount point. For instance, the following command mounts the /home share from the server birch on your client at /shared/homes:

```
# mount birch:/home /shared/homes
```

You must normally be root to issue the mount command in this way, but you can add an entry to /etc/fstab to automate this process or allow other users to mount NFS exports. The entries to do this look just like those to mount a local filesystem, except that they include the NFS-style server:/path specification rather than a local device file. They also must specify a filesystem type of nfs.

However it's done, once an NFS export is mounted, you can use it much as you do a local filesystem. Assuming your users have appropriate permissions on the remote system, they may read from and write to remote files. Of course, a network filesystem is not likely to be as fast as a purely local one.

Sharing with Windows: Samba

Ordinarily, NFS is the best choice to share files with other Linux or Unix systems. Windows and related operating systems, however, don't include NFS client packages by default, although they are available as add-ons. Instead, these OSs use SMB/CIFS networking protocols to achieve the same goals. Although NFS and SMB/CIFS serve the same purpose, they differ in many important details. SMB/CIFS was designed with DOS and Windows in mind, so it is the best protocol for file sharing with these systems. Fortunately, all modern Linux distributions include a server for SMB/CIFS: Samba.

Samba is a very complex package—it contains many more options and features than any of Linux's NFS packages. This is largely because Samba must make a Linux computer look like a Windows system, which complicates the file-sharing task. Windows treats filenames and file attributes differently than Linux does, so it's necessary to include workarounds in Samba. Windows networks also include a variety of features that partly replicate functions of normal TCP/IP networking, such as an alternative naming system. These topics go far beyond the scope of this chapter, so if you need to set up a Samba file server, you should consult the chapters in Part V.

Using Samba as a Client

Samba includes two client programs: smbclient and smbmount. The first of these is a program that enables you to perform file transfers in a manner similar to a text-mode FTP client program. By contrast, smbmount enables you to mount a share on the Linux directory tree, much as you can mount an NFS share using the Linux mount command. (In fact, since Samba 2.0.6, you can use mount instead of smbmount.) There are also assorted GUI frontends to these packages, so that you can browse an SMB/CIFS network from Linux much as you can from Windows.

All of the Samba client programs rely upon settings in the [global] section of smb.conf to control aspects of their operation, such as the claimed NetBIOS and workgroup names of the computer. You should therefore be sure these features are set correctly before using Samba as a client.

To use smbclient, you start it and pass the name of the server and the share you want to access:

```
$ smbclient //server/share
```

After you type this command, smbclient prompts you for a password, which should match the password associated with your username on the server. (If your username on the server is not the same as on the client, you can use the -U *username* parameter to specify your username on the server.) The commands available in smbclient are similar to those in the text-mode ftp program, or from a Linux shell—ls to see the available files; put and get to transfer files to and from the share, respectively; cd to move to a new directory; and so on. You can type **?** or **help** to see a summary of commands.

Although smbclient can be a good way to transfer a few files quickly, smbmount is more flexible if you want to be able to directly modify files on the server. You might use this tool to use a Linux program to edit a file that's stored on a server, for instance. To use smbmount, issue the command in the following form:

```
$ smbmount //server/share /mountpoint
```

NOTE

If you don't issue the smbmount command as root, two programs must be used to set the user ID (suid) root for this to work: smbmnt (a helper program to smbmount) and smbumount (used to unmount SMB/CIFS shares). You can issue the command chmod a+s /usr/bin/smbmnt /usr/bin/smbumount to accomplish this task.

Like smbclient, smbmount asks you for a password before it mounts the share. Once a share is mounted, you can access the files on it as if they were on a local disk, with certain caveats. Some filesystems may be shared read-only, so you may not be able to write files to these shares. SMB/CIFS doesn't support Linux-style ownership and permissions, so by default, all files are owned by the individual who issues the smbmount command. When you're done with a share, you can unmount it with the smbumount command; enter it as

```
$ smbumount /mountpoint
```

As mentioned earlier, you can use mount instead of smbmount with Samba 2.0.6 and later. To do so, you call mount with a filesystem type of smbfs:

```
# mount -t smbfs //server/share /mountpoint
```

This procedure works best when the caller is root, unless you create an /etc/fstab entry that allows ordinary users to issue the mount command. When this is the case, you should omit the filesystem type, server, and share names when issuing the mount command (as in **mount /mountpoint**).

Several GUI frontends to smbmount are available. Details of operation differ from one program to another, but as a general rule, these utilities present a GUI view of the local network, as demonstrated by LinNeighborhood (http://www.bnro.de/~schmidjo/), shown in Figure 12.3. When you double-click a share to open it, a dialog box asks for your username and password, and the program then opens a window on the share using the file manager you specify when you configure the program. GUI frontends don't really add fundamentally new functionality to Linux's SMB/CIFS capabilities, but they do make these networks more accessible to those who aren't familiar with Samba's text-mode tools. You may therefore want to install LinNeighborhood or a similar package, such as Kruiser (http://devel-home.kde.org/~kruiser/) or xSMBrowser (http://www.public.iastate.edu/~chadspen/).

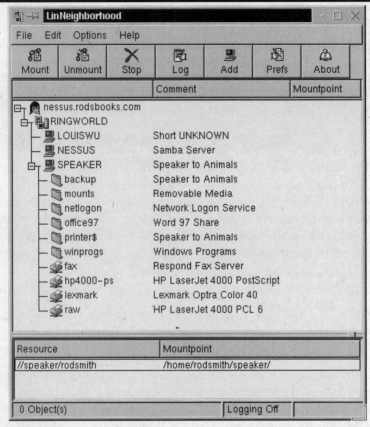

FIGURE 12.3:   LinNeighborhood and other GUI SMB/CIFS browsers provide a user interface similar to that of Network Neighborhood in Windows.

INTERNET SERVERS

If you want to be able to use a computer when you're away from it, you must install some type of server on that computer. Likewise, if you want others to be able to use a computer, a server is necessary. The appropriate server depends on your precise needs. There are some steps common to configuring all servers, but each involves at least some unique aspects, so you should consult the appropriate documentation.

Available Servers

Linux supports a wide variety of Internet server packages. Although these can be used on a local network alone, they're more often used to provide services to various computers on the Internet at large. A few of these servers are discussed to a greater or lesser extent elsewhere in this book. Many are complex enough that entire books are written about them. You can usually find more information in documentation files that come with the servers or on web pages devoted to the servers. A complete list of servers available for Linux would be too long to reproduce here, but the most important server types include the following:

FTP servers   The *File Transfer Protocol* (FTP) is one of the Internet's most important protocols, although it's one of the least flashy. FTP allows individuals to transfer files to or from an FTP server. Links on web pages to program files are often FTP links. Several FTP servers are available for Linux, such as *Washington University FTP* (WU-FTP) at http://www.wu-ftpd.org/ and *ProFTP* at http://www.proftpd.net. Red Hat Linux ships with WU-FTP, but you can install any other FTP server for Linux, if you prefer.

Mail servers   If you want your computer to receive mail addressed directly to it, you must run a *mail server*—a.k.a. a *Mail Transport Agent* (MTA). If your ISP collects and holds mail for you, you may not need an MTA; instead, you can use a mail program that retrieves mail using a protocol such as the *Post Office Protocol* (POP). All major Linux distributions come with an MTA, which is usually configured by default in a reasonable way for a stand-alone workstation. Red Hat Linux ships with sendmail (http://www.sendmail.org), but various alternatives are available and are used by some other distributions. If your system is to be used exclusively as a mail server, you should consider purchasing a book devoted to the topic, such as Craig Hunt's *Linux Sendmail Administration* (Sybex, 2000).

NOTE

For more information on sendmail, see Chapters 27, "Running Sendmail," and 28, "Creating a Basic Sendmail Configuration."

News servers   The *Network News Transport Protocol* (NNTP) controls the transfer of *Usenet news*—a global discussion forum in which users post queries, solutions, and other discussions of topics as diverse as vegetarian cooking, Linux, and the International Space Station. News servers typically exist at ISPs and large organizations such as universities. They exchange articles with each other, resulting in the global span of Usenet news. You can run a news server yourself, either if you're in charge of the news server for a large organization or if you want to run a small news server for internal use or to maintain local copies of the newsgroups in which you're interested. Red Hat Linux comes with *Internet News* (INN), one of the more popular news server packages. Note that you don't need a news server if you just want to read Usenet news. For that, you need a news *reader*, such as tin (`http://www.tin.org`), Knews (`http://www.matematik.su.se/~kjj/`), or Netscape's newsreader component. You also need access to a news server, such as one maintained by your ISP.

Remote login servers   If you want to run programs remotely, you must run some variety of *remote login server*. This is a program that accepts logins from remote locations. A *getty* program is a login server for dial-up connections. The most familiar login server for most people is Telnet, which accepts logins from the Internet at large. (This server comes with all major Linux distributions.) Unfortunately, Telnet sends all information, including passwords, in cleartext, so it's not good from a security point of view. A better alternative in this respect is the *Secure Shell* (SSH), which encrypts all data. One implementation of SSH is OpenSSH (`http://www.openssh.com`), which became a standard part of Red Hat Linux beginning with version 7.0 of the distribution. Red Hat 7.1 includes both client and server packages for OpenSSH, as well as OpenSSL packages for secure browser connections.

Web servers   One of the most visible types of Internet server is the web server, which implements the Hypertext Transfer Protocol (HTTP). On Linux, Apache (http://www.apache.org) is by far the most popular web server. Apache is complex enough that, to do more than basic configuration, you should read a book on the topic, such as Charles Aulds' *Linux Apache Server Administration* (Sybex, 2001).

NOTE

For more information on the Apache web server, see Part VI, "Apache."

X servers   An *X server* is a program that displays the windows created by X-based programs. On an isolated workstation installation of Linux, the X server (typically XFree86) runs on the same computer as the X programs that are being run. However, you can connect to a remote computer (using a login protocol such as Telnet or SSH) and run X programs from that remote system using your local X server. Note that, unlike most servers, the X server runs on the computer that's nearest you; the remote system runs the client programs. This makes sense when you think of it from the program's point of view; to the program, the server and you are at the distant location, and the server provides remote services (a display and input devices). The X server that ships with all major Linux distributions is called XFree86 (see http://www.xfree86.org).

NOTE

For more information on X servers, see Chapters 5 through 10 in Part II, "Learning the Basics."

All servers are security risks. Bugs in servers, misconfigured servers, and flaws in local security (such as poor password selections by your users) make it possible for undesirables to break into your computer.

In addition, some servers provide other possibilities for abuse. For instance, it's easy to misconfigure a mail server so that it can be used to relay mail from anywhere to anywhere. Those who send unsolicited bulk e-mail ("spam") frequently look for open relays to obscure their true locations. Because of the great potential for abuse, you should run as few servers as possible on your Linux computer. Many Linux distributions install many servers by default, so you should check through your inetd.conf or xinetd.conf file (described shortly) and disable anything you're not using.

Using a Super Server

One problem with servers is that when they're running, they consume system resources—primarily memory, but also some CPU time. These resources might be better used by other processes, particularly when the servers are used only occasionally. A system that hosts many seldom-used servers therefore turns to a *super server* to control the servers. A super server is a program that looks for incoming packets addressed to several other servers. When the super server detects such packets, it launches the appropriate server program. When the individual servers aren't needed, they don't run. This approach can save a great deal of memory when you want to run several servers, most of which aren't in use at any given moment.

Another benefit to using a super server is that it's usually possible to implement additional security features with such a server. One approach to this is to use an intermediary package, such as TCP Wrappers, to filter connection requests. TCP Wrappers can examine the IP address of the calling system and allow or deny access based on that address. This can be extremely useful if some servers, such as a Telnet or SSH server, should only be accessible from certain computers.

Using *inetd*

The most common super server in most Linux distributions is inetd. This server was a standard part of Red Hat through version 6.2. With version 7.0, however, Red Hat switched to xinetd, which is described shortly. The inetd server is controlled through the /etc/inetd.conf file. Each line in this file corresponds to a single server. The following example uses TCP Wrappers:

```
ftp stream tcp nowait root /usr/sbin/tcpd in.ftpd -l -a
```

The meaning of each element in this entry is as follows:

ftp	This is the code for the service, as found in the /etc/services file. inetd listens on a particular port for connection requests, and this code— or more precisely, the port number associated with this code in /etc/services—determines to what port number inetd listens.
stream	This is the socket type, which determines some aspects of how the server interacts with the TCP/IP stack. Common options are stream and dgram.
tcp	This is the type of TCP/IP connection—TCP or UDP. Most network servers use TCP, which establishes a lasting two-way connection; but some use UDP, which is less robust but requires less overhead because it doesn't establish a full two-way connection.
nowait	Datagram-based services (those that specify dgram rather than stream) either remain connected to the caller and specify wait here or they are multithreaded and split off a separate thread to handle the connection. The latter type specifies nowait. This entry isn't meaningful for streaming connections, but by convention they specify nowait.
root	inetd launches every server using a particular username. Many servers must be launched as root, but some may be launched under some other username to increase security.
/usr/sbin/tcpd	This entry is the name of the server that's to handle the connection. In this example, the server is tcpd—the name of the TCP Wrappers program. If you want to bypass TCP Wrappers, you would specify the server program directly.

in.ftpd -1 -a   The final entry is any parameters that are to be passed to the server. When the "server" is TCP Wrappers, you pass the name of the real server, along with any parameters that server requires. TCP Wrappers then checks that the incoming request is allowed and calls the real server (in.ftpd in this example), along with whatever parameters you specify (such as -1 and -a).

In the default inetd.conf file, you'll find entries for most common servers. Most of these entries are commented out with pound signs (#), however. You can therefore uncomment the appropriate entries when you add a server of a particular type. Conversely, if you remove a server or want to disable it, you can comment out the appropriate line if it's active.

TIP

One easy first step to securing a Linux server is to comment out all unnecessary lines from inetd.conf. In fact, none of the servers listed in this file are necessary for Linux to boot. Some servers may sound like they're critically important, but they aren't. The login server, for example, is a very low-security remote login server, as described earlier; it is not required for ordinary text-mode logins or even for remote logins via Telnet or SSH. You can go through inetd.conf and comment out all the servers except those you're sure that you need.

After you've made changes to /etc/inetd.conf, you must send the server a SIGHUP signal to tell it to reload its configuration file. You can do this as follows:

```
# ps ax | grep inetd
  468 ?        S       0:00 inetd
# kill -SIGHUP 468
```

The process ID number (468 in the preceding example) will be different on your system. If possible, you should immediately test that your changes took effect. If you added or removed a server, test this by trying to connect to the server.

Using *xinetd*

Although inetd is the most common super server, it's not the only one. One moderately popular inetd replacement is xinetd (pronounced "zi-net-dee"), which can be obtained from http://www.synack.net/

xinetd/. Red Hat 7.1 ships with xinetd rather than inetd. This program's greatest advantage is that it combines many of the features of TCP Wrappers in the super server itself. It's particularly useful on systems that have multiple network cards, because it can block access to particular servers based on the network card.

The xinetd configuration file is /etc/xinetd.conf. Its format is different from that of inetd.conf, but it contains much of the same information. Rather than placing information on a single line, xinetd.conf creates multiple-line entries. Listing 12.3 shows the xinetd.conf equivalent of the sample inetd.conf entry shown earlier. This listing also shows the use of the interface option, which tells xinetd to listen only on the interface associated with the specified IP address. In this example, if the computer has two network interfaces, only one will respond to incoming FTP traffic.

Listing 12.3: A Sample *xinetd.conf* Service Entry

```
service ftp
{
        socket_type     = stream
        protocol        = tcp
        wait            = no
        user            = root
        server          = /usr/sbin/in.ftpd
        server_args     = -l -a
        interface       = 192.168.203.7
}
```

Most of the entries in the xinetd.conf service definition correspond to entries in the similar inetd.conf service definition. One exception is the interface entry, which has no inetd.conf equivalent. Another difference is that there's no call to tcpd in the xinetd.conf definition. This is because xinetd incorporates functionality similar to that of TCP Wrappers. In particular, you can use only_from to specify a list of IP addresses, networks, or computer names that are allowed to use a service, or you can use no_access to "blacklist" computers or networks, blocking them from using a service. You can also block access based on time of day, limit the total number of connections to a service, and so on. These options and many more are detailed in the xinetd.conf man page.

The default Red Hat 7.1 xinetd.conf file is quite short. Instead of listing entries for all services in a single file, Red Hat 7.0 uses a xinetd.conf file that sets only global default options. Files for specific servers appear in the /etc/xinetd.d directory. This configuration makes it easy for server packages to set themselves to run when they're installed. If you're using xinetd on another distribution, you may prefer to maintain a single monolithic xinetd.conf file with entries for all your servers. Both approaches are perfectly valid.

After making changes to your xinetd configuration, you must restart the server. You do this much as you restart inetd, as described earlier.

General Super Server Considerations

Because a super server doesn't keep the real servers loaded at all times, you do *not* normally need to restart the super server if you update the underlying server. You can upgrade your Telnet server, for instance, and the super server will immediately begin using the new version. The exception to this rule is if the updated server needs to be called in a new way—if its name or location has changed, for instance.

The drawback to using a super server is that it necessarily takes some time to launch its child servers. The result is that the server computer won't respond immediately to requests; it may take anywhere from a fraction of a second to several seconds for the system to respond to a request. This can be a major drawback for some servers, such as web servers. You'll have to judge for yourself whether the delay is worth the improvement in memory use and (perhaps) security of using a super server.

Some servers don't work very well, if at all, from a super server. Most installations don't run Samba or sendmail through inetd or xinetd, for instance; although it's possible to run these servers through a super server, the performance penalty is too great. You should therefore not think that you've shut down all unnecessary servers once you've cleared out superfluous servers from /etc/inetd.conf, /etc/xinetd.conf, or /etc/xinetd.d. You may need to clean more from the /etc/init.d directory tree or from other system startup files.

WHAT'S NEXT?

TCP/IP networking is the most popular type of networking today. It's the protocol that's used on the Internet, and many local networking tasks use TCP/IP as well. Configuring Linux for TCP/IP networking involves using a handful of different tools to activate a network interface, tell Linux how to route packets, and so on. Most distributions allow you to configure these options when you install the OS, or you can do it after-the-fact either through a GUI configuration utility or by editing configuration files in a text editor.

File sharing is one of the most popular networking tasks on small networks. This task builds on basic TCP/IP networking features, allowing you to store files on a single computer for use by many systems. This can be a great boon in many work environments, boosting productivity by enabling individuals to work at any computer and to exchange files among themselves easily.

Linux supports a wide variety of TCP/IP-based Internet servers, which can provide private and public services to remote systems. Many of these servers are the topics of entire books. In the next chapter, we will discuss remote connection to serial communications, including modems and terminals.

Chapter 13

SERIAL COMMUNICATIONS, TERMINALS, AND MODEMS

Throughout much of the history of computing, the RS-232 serial port has been an important piece of hardware. The serial port allows you to connect two computers together or to connect a computer to another device, such as a printer or mouse. The general-purpose nature of the serial port has allowed it to be used for a wide variety of tasks. The downside to serial ports is that they're slow. The RS-232 serial port on $x86$ computers is usually capable of a maximum transfer rate of 115,200 bits per second (bps), although some hardware permits higher rates. This compares to 100Mbps (100,000,000 bps) for modern Ethernet devices. For this reason, and because of the development of a variety of specialized interfaces (such as the PS/2 mouse port), the serial port is not as important today as it once was. Nonetheless, there are many jobs for which the serial port is still well suited. This chapter covers those jobs, which include linking "dumb" text terminals to a Linux system, using modems to connect to other systems over telephone lines, and using printers connected via serial ports.

Adapted from *Linux System Administration*
by Vicki Stanfield and Roderick W. Smith

ISBN 0-7821-2735-5   688 pages $39.99

NOTE

Although this chapter emphasizes the traditional RS-232 interface, a new type of serial port has gained in popularity since 1999: the *Universal Serial Bus* (USB). USB is much faster than RS-232 and so lacks many of RS-232's downsides. This chapter points out where RS-232 and USB differ.

Understanding Serial Devices

Before digging into the details of how to use serial ports to accomplish specific goals, it's helpful to understand precisely what a serial port is and how Linux treats the low-level serial port hardware. These details dictate what can and cannot be done with a serial port under Linux and how you communicate with the serial hardware.

Standard Serial Devices

Most *x*86 computers come with two built-in RS-232 serial ports. These devices typically use 9-pin male connectors on the computer, as shown in Figure 13.1, but some serial ports (particularly on older computers and non-computer devices) use 25-pin connectors. The connectors on modems, printers, and other serial devices are usually female.

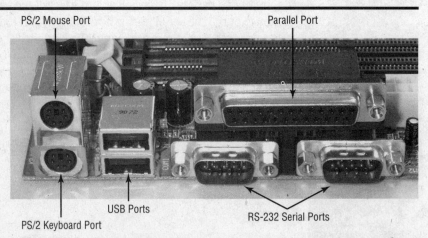

FIGURE 13.1:   Modern *x*86 motherboards include a wide variety of connectors in standardized locations.

USB connectors are physically quite different from RS-232 connectors, as you can see in Figure 13.1. Some of the advantages of USB ports over standard RS-232 serial ports are these:

Higher Speed   USB supports speeds of up to 12Mbps, roughly 100 times as fast as standard RS-232.

Multi-Device Support   RS-232 ports support just one device per port. USB, by contrast, allows you to connect multiple devices to a single USB connector, although you must use a *hub* to do this. A hub simply links several USB devices to a single USB port.

Hot-Swappable Devices   You can attach and detach USB devices while the computer is running. This is risky with RS-232, since a short could conceivably damage the device or the computer.

As a general rule, RS-232 serial devices are well supported in Linux. USB devices, by contrast, are poorly supported in kernels prior to 2.2.18, but USB support in the 2.4.*x* kernels is much better. Therefore, if you plan to use USB devices, you should use a 2.4.*x* kernel or at least 2.2.18. Most Linux distributions shipped in mid-2001 and later include USB support in a patched or late 2.2.*x* or 2.4.*x* kernel.

Enabling Serial Support in the Kernel

Whether you use RS-232 or USB, it's necessary that you understand the kernel configuration options needed to use the devices. You may not need to deal with these options explicitly because most distributions ship with appropriate kernel support enabled, at least for common devices and uses.

For RS-232 devices, kernel configuration options lie in the Character Devices kernel configuration menu (see Figure 13.2). Specifically, to use the standard two serial ports, you should select Y or M to the Standard/ Generic (Dumb) Serial Support option. You don't need to select kernel options for specific RS-232 serial devices, such as modems or printers. Details of communicating with specific devices are handled by appropriate user-level programs, such as pppd or 1pd.

Configuring Linux's USB support is somewhat more complex because you need to select several options in the USB Support kernel configuration menu (see Figure 13.3). Remember that this support is available only in 2.4.*x* kernels or in late 2.2.*x* kernels.

Part iii

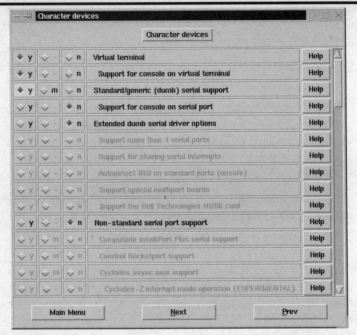

FIGURE 13.2:   The Linux Character Devices kernel configuration menu includes the main RS-232 serial device options.

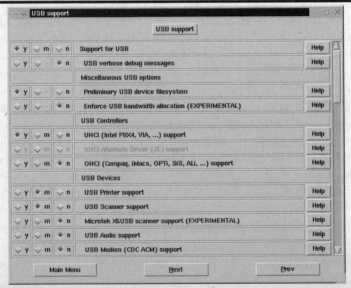

FIGURE 13.3:   USB support requires selecting drivers for specific USB devices.

Specifically, you need to select one or more options in each of three option classes:

Support for USB   This top-level option is required if you want to use any USB device.

USB Controllers   There are two classes of low-level USB controllers: Universal Host Controller Interface (UHCI) and Open Host Controller Interface (OHCI). Select whichever one your motherboard or plug-in USB card supports. If you don't know which your system uses, select both. For UHCI, you have a choice of the main driver or an alternate driver. In most cases, the main driver works well, but if you have problems with it, try the alternate driver.

USB Devices   You must select drivers for specific classes of USB devices, and in some cases even for specific models. The bulk of the USB Support kernel configuration menu is composed of USB device classes, so scan through it to locate your devices. In some cases, you may also need to select options in other kernel configuration menus; for example, some USB cameras require you to enable Video for Linux support in the Character Devices (2.2.x kernels) or Multimedia Devices (2.4.x kernels) menu.

Some computers today use USB keyboards and mice. Modern Linux distributions can use such devices, but there are a few caveats. USB mice use PS/2 mouse protocols, so you can configure X to use a PS/2 protocol over a USB mouse port. USB keyboards should be detected and used automatically if your kernel includes the appropriate drivers, but this support doesn't extend to the LILO boot loader. On x86 computers, you'll have to enable a BIOS option called *legacy USB keyboard support* or something similar to use your keyboard to select different OSs from LILO. Not all BIOSes have such an option, but computers that ship with USB keyboards should include such an option.

Using Serial Device Files

Traditional RS-232 devices use device filenames of the form /dev/ttySn, where n is a number from 0 up. To communicate with a serial device, you (or a program you use) send characters to this device file. For instance, the following command sends the string ATDT555-4321 to a modem attached to /dev/ttyS0, causing the modem to dial 555-4321.

```
$ echo "ATDT555-4321" > /dev/ttyS0
```

NOTE

In the past, the /dev/cuan devices were used as a variant method of accessing serial ports. Use of /dev/cuan is discouraged today, however, and support for these devices may disappear in the future, although it's still present up to at least the 2.4.9 kernel.

Because the serial device interprets the characters, there is no need for cross-device standardization of commands sent over the RS-232 serial port; modems accept different commands than do printers, which use different commands than mice, and so on. There are, however, some Linux commands that can affect how the serial interface works. Of particular importance is the setserial command, which sets the RS-232 port's parameters, such as its speed. This command's syntax is as follows:

```
setserial [-ab] device [parameters] ...
```

The -a and -b options cause the program to display information on the hardware's settings, such as the interrupt request (IRQ) used by the port. -a results in a multiline display, and -b produces a less complete single-line output. You can pass a wide assortment of parameters to the program in order to change how it configures the port. These are the most important parameters:

***port* portnum**   Sets the I/O port number to *portnum*. The I/O port is a hexadecimal number, such as 0x03f8, which indicates where in memory the input to and output from the serial port occur. Unless you're using very unusual hardware, you shouldn't need to adjust this setting.

***irq* irqnum**   You can tell Linux to use an unusual IRQ number with this parameter. As with the port parameter, chances are you won't need to use this option.

***uart* uarttype**   RS-232 serial ports are controlled by *universal asynchronous receiver/transmitters* (UARTs), which come in several varieties. Linux usually detects the UART type correctly at bootup, but if it gets this detail wrong, you can correct the matter by using the uart parameter. (An incorrect UART type is likely to produce unreliable serial port operation.) Most

modern motherboards use 16550A UARTs, so *uarttype* would
be 16550A for these boards. Very old hardware may use earlier
UARTs, such as the 16450; and some devices use more recent
ones, like the 16650.

baud_base **speed**   This parameter sets the speed of the serial
port. The usual value for *speed* is 115200, which is the fastest
speed in bps that most serial ports support.

These options and parameters just scratch the surface of setserial's
capabilities. Read its man page for more information on esoteric features
you can control with the program. This utility is most useful when you
use simple programs and daemons with the serial port. More sophisticated programs and daemons can set the serial port's speed and other
features themselves.

Unlike the RS-232 serial port, there isn't a single device file for each
USB port on your computer. Instead, Linux maps each device to its own
device file. The reason for this arrangement is simple: Using a hub, it's
possible to connect more than one USB device to each USB port. Suppose
a USB port hosts a printer, a mouse, and a modem. Each of those devices
acquires its own entry in /dev or /dev/usb, so you can address each
device appropriately. Precisely how you handle these devices varies from
one device and program to another. For instance, you would normally
reference a USB mouse in your XFree86 configuration file, whereas
you'd reference a printer's file in /etc/printcap.

Table 13.1 summarizes some of the more common USB device files,
including their *major* and *minor* numbers, which define the interface
between the device file and the kernel's drivers. It's important to realize
that the device filenames are largely arbitrary; you can access a device
under any filename you like, so long as that filename identifies a device
file created via mknod with the appropriate type, major number, and
minor number, as described shortly. Some USB devices, such as disk
devices and speakers, are treated as if they were non-USB devices, such
as SCSI disks and ordinary sound cards, respectively. Others use new
major and minor numbers and usually new device filenames.

TABLE 13.1: Methods of Accessing USB Devices in the 2.4.x Kernels

DEVICE	DEVICE FILENAME	TYPE	MAJOR NUMBER	MINOR NUMBER
Disk devices	/dev/sdn	Block	8	0–240
Modem	/dev/ttyACMn	Character	166	0 up
Mouse	/dev/mousen or /dev/mice	Character	13	32 and up or 63, respectively
Printer	/dev/usb1pn	Character	180	0 and up
Scanner	/dev/usbscannern	Character	180	48–63
Speakers	Normal audio devices, such as /dev/audio and /dev/mixer	Character	Varies	Varies
USB-to-parallel adapter	/dev/usb1pn	Character	180	0 and up
USB-to-RS-232 adapter	/dev/ttyUSBn	Character	188	0 and up

If you need to create a device file to access a USB device, you may do so with the mknod command. The syntax of this command is this:

```
mknod filename type major minor
```

In this command, *filename* is the device filename, *type* is either b for block devices or c for character devices, and *major* and *minor* are the major and minor numbers listed in Table 13.1. Be aware that many USB devices' major and minor numbers have changed during the development of Linux's USB code and may change again in the future. These are sometimes documented in files in the /usr/src/linux/Documentation/usb directory, but documentation on this point is still spotty in late 2001.

An experimental feature of the 2.4.x kernels is the /dev filesystem. You can activate this support in the File Systems kernel configuration menu. If active, Linux generates a virtual filesystem for /dev, much like the /proc filesystem. This filesystem automatically creates device files for all devices registered by kernel drivers, including USB devices. Therefore, using this feature obviates the need to create USB device files manually, but you'll have to search the /dev directory to locate the device files. Because this feature is experimental (and hence potentially buggy) in the

2.4.*x* kernel, I recommend you not use it unless you intend to contribute
to its development or have some compelling reason to try it.

Unusual Serial Devices

Some serial devices are rare and nonstandard implementations of RS-232
ports. The problem with the standard implementation of RS-232 serial
devices is that it's difficult to add ports beyond the two included on most
motherboards. Adding third and fourth ports presents only minor
difficulties—most add-on ports come configured to "share" interrupts
with the first two ports, but it's necessary to reconfigure these boards to
use unique IRQs because Linux doesn't normally work well with this
arrangement.

NOTE

Internal modems normally include serial port hardware along with modem
hardware. Adding such a modem works just like adding a serial port. It's
sometimes helpful to disable an unused motherboard serial port before
adding an internal modem, so that the internal modem can take over the identity of one of the first two regular ports. This can normally be done in the
computer's BIOS setup screens. Some internal modems don't have serial port
hardware. These devices are often called *winmodems*, *controllerless modems*,
or *software modems* (although the first term technically applies only to
3Com products). There are Linux drivers for a few such devices—check
http://www.linmodems.org for details. Many don't work under Linux,
however, and so should be avoided.

The problem with using a unique IRQ for each serial port is that the
*x*86 architecture allows for only 15 interrupts, and some are required for
other devices, so it's not possible to assign unique IRQs to more than a
handful of serial ports. To overcome this problem, some companies have
developed *multiport serial cards*, which place several RS-232 ports on one
card and one IRQ. Because these devices use nonstandard hardware, they
require their own unique drivers. If you have need of such a device, check
the Linux kernel configuration area for character devices (refer to Figure 13.2). Depending upon the type of device, you may need to select the
Extended Dumb Serial Driver Options item or Nonstandard Serial Port
Support. In either case, you must select appropriate options for your specific board. You should study these options before buying the hardware
so that you're sure you get something supported in Linux.

CONFIGURING TERMINALS

One of the most common uses for a serial port on a multiuser system is as a port for a terminal. A *terminal* is a device or computer that's used as a means of controlling another computer. Because most *x*86 computers have two RS-232 ports plus their normal keyboard and monitor, it's possible for three people to use a single computer simultaneously if two people access the computer via terminals. (Of course, you can add more serial ports or use networking connections to further increase that number, if you like.) Although most Linux distributions don't come preconfigured to use terminals, it's not difficult to add this capability to a system.

NOTE

Terminal access is almost always performed through RS-232 ports. You can use an RS-232-to-USB adapter, however, to connect RS-232 terminals to a Linux computer via the computer's USB ports.

Understanding Terminals

To understand terminals, it's helpful to think back to the days when Unix systems came in boxes the size of a dishwasher, if not larger. In those days, dozens or hundreds of users accessed a Unix system through dumb terminals—devices that roughly resembled today's iMac computers, at least to the naked eye. Inside these dumb terminals, though, were extremely simple circuitry, no hard disk, and only enough memory to handle the local display and a few extra lines of text. With virtually no processing capability, they were input/output devices, not computers. These devices could take what a user typed at the keyboard and echo it out a serial port, and they could display what was received from the serial port on the screen. These capabilities were very useful when a "real" computer cost millions of dollars and had to be used by many people. Such terminals were the primary means of accessing Unix systems through the 1980s. They were common in corporate and educational settings and are still in use today. (Your local library may use dumb terminals to provide patrons with access to its online book catalog, for example.)

NOTE

Dumb terminals are text-only devices; they cannot be used to run X-based programs such as StarOffice or the GIMP. There is, however, another variety of terminal that can be used with X programs: an *X terminal*. X terminals usually interface through a network port, not a serial port. The NCD X Terminal mini-HOWTO document (`http://www.linuxdoc.org/HOWTO/mini/NCD-X-Terminal.html`) provides information on these devices.

Because of Linux's Unix heritage, Linux includes the software necessary to support dumb terminals; using it is a matter of changing a few default configurations. Once this is done, you can plug in a dumb terminal and use it. Why would you want to do this? For the same reasons large organizations used (and still use) dumb terminals, such as stretching resources and providing access to a computer to more people than would otherwise be possible. If you don't need to run X programs, a dumb terminal can provide perfectly adequate access to a Linux computer.

Instead of a dumb terminal, you can use an outmoded computer. If you have an old 8088-based PC gathering dust in a closet, for instance, you can wipe it off, set it up, link it to a Linux computer, and use a simple DOS *terminal program* to make it work like a dumb terminal. Similarly, specialized devices like palmtop computers often come with terminal programs, so you can access a Linux computer from such devices.

TIP

On rare occasions, X can lock up, leaving Linux unresponsive. Technically, Linux hasn't crashed, and it's usually possible to recover from such problems—if you have some way in other than the system's keyboard. Such a way in is often remote access through Telnet, but this isn't always an option. Using dumb terminal access, even from a palmtop computer, can let you kill or reconfigure X, thus recovering control of the system without using the Reset switch.

When you use another computer as a terminal, you must normally link the two computers through a *null modem* cable. These cables link one computer to another, and they're wired differently than the cables that link a computer to a modem. Most computer stores sell null modem cables.

If you want to use one Linux computer as a terminal for another, you can do so, although it's more common to use Ethernet hardware and the Telnet or SSH program to log in to one computer from another. Linking two Linux computers via serial ports requires you to use a Linux terminal program on one computer, as described later in this chapter, in "Calling a Remote Text-Mode System."

NOTE

Linux uses *virtual terminals* to provide text-mode access to a Linux system from its main keyboard and monitor (which are collectively referred to as *the console*). To configure Linux to use "real" terminals, you extend this configuration to support serial devices as well as the console, as described shortly.

Configuring a getty Program

In most cases, the goal when using a terminal (either dumb terminal hardware or a terminal emulator) is to have the terminal display a Linux login: prompt when the user starts the terminal. Linux normally presents these prompts using a program called getty, or some variant of that, such as mingetty, mgetty, or agetty.

NOTE

The original getty program goes by that name. Various replacements use similar names and do similar things. The word *getty* can therefore refer to either the original getty program or the class of similar programs that fill basically the same role. For the most part, the word is used in the latter sense in this chapter.

Linux runs getty programs from the /etc/inittab file. In Red Hat 7.1, the default /etc/inittab file contains the following lines:

```
# Run gettys in standard runlevels
1:2345:respawn:/sbin/mingetty tty1
2:2345:respawn:/sbin/mingetty tty2
3:2345:respawn:/sbin/mingetty tty3
4:2345:respawn:/sbin/mingetty tty4
5:2345:respawn:/sbin/mingetty tty5
6:2345:respawn:/sbin/mingetty tty6
```

Each line in the /etc/inittab file contains colon-delimited entries that tell the system about certain specific types of services to be run. The preceding entries tell Linux to run the /sbin/mingetty program for each of the first six virtual consoles in run levels 2 through 5. The result of these entries is that you can type Alt+1 through Alt+6 (in combination with Ctrl, if you're currently running X) to shift to any of six virtual consoles. You can log in to any of these to run programs, even under different usernames.

To expand the default configuration to support terminals run over a serial port, it's necessary to add some further entries to /etc/inittab. To do so, follow these steps:

1. Install the mgetty package. On a Red Hat 7.1 system, the package name is mgetty-1.1.25-2.i386.rpm and is on the second CD-ROM.

NOTE

Different distributions use different getty programs by default. The mingetty program used by Red Hat can't handle serial port traffic, but some default getty programs can handle the serial port, so this step may not be necessary with all getty programs. If you use something other than mgetty, however, some of the following details may differ; consult your getty program's documentation for details.

2. To add support for a terminal attached to /dev/ttyS0, add the following line to /etc/inittab just after the existing mingetty lines:

   ```
   S0:2345:respawn:/sbin/mgetty -s 57600 -r /dev/ttyS0
   ```

3. Type **telinit Q** to tell Linux to reexamine the /etc/ inittab file and make appropriate changes—namely, to run mgetty.

You may need to make adjustments to step 2 for your particular needs. In particular, step 2 specifies that the terminal run at 57,600 bps (the -s 57600 parameter) and that it use /dev/ttyS0. The -r parameter indicates that the connection is direct—that is, not via a modem. Modem logins, as described shortly, require a few changes to this configuration.

Once logged on using a terminal, the user can run Linux text-mode programs, including administrative tools such as Linuxconf (assuming the user has sufficient privileges, of course). Some programs, however, rely on text-positioning protocols. These protocols were originally used with particular models of dumb terminals, and so are frequently named after those terminals. Examples include VT-100 and VT-220. In many cases, mgetty can determine the type of terminal that's connected. In other cases, you may need to do this manually by setting the TERM

Part III

environment variable. For instance, if you're using a VT-100 terminal, you could type the following after logging in:

```
$ export TERM=vt100
```

If you find that your display does strange things, type **env | grep TERM** to see what the system thinks the terminal type is, and adjust it as appropriate. Some dumb terminals emulate others, and most terminal programs emulate one or more popular dumb terminals.

Using a Serial-Port Console

Terminals can be very convenient for accessing a Linux system in certain circumstances, but they do have a major limitation: They're useful only after the system has completely booted. There are situations in which you may want to run a computer without a monitor, such as when you place a server in some out-of-the-way location. If you do this, you won't be able to see the computer's boot-time messages or interact with the system when console maintenance is required (as when fsck encounters a problem when rebooting after a crash). Moving a monitor to such an isolated computer and squatting in front of it to perform maintenance can be a pain (sometimes literally!), so Linux provides a solution: a *serial-port console*. In this arrangement, Linux uses the serial port for all console operations. You can then run a null-modem cable to some other computer and use a terminal program on that computer whenever you need to perform console operations on the isolated system.

In order to use a serial-port console, you must do three things:

1. Select the Support for Console on Serial Port option in the Character Devices Linux kernel configuration menu (refer to Figure 13.2).

NOTE   To select this option, you must compile Linux's standard serial support into the kernel by selecting Y to Standard/Generic (Dumb) Serial Support. If you compile the standard serial support as a module, you will not be able to add serial-port console support.

2. Recompile the Linux kernel with this new option enabled.

3. Start Linux while passing it the parameter console=ttyS0 (making an appropriate substitution for the serial port you

use). The usual way to do this is to add a line to your /etc/lilo.conf entry for a kernel and type **lilo** to reinstall LILO. The line reads:

```
append="console=ttyS0"
```

Assuming the new kernel and /etc/lilo.conf entries are the default, Linux uses the specified serial port as its console. You can therefore put the system into single-user mode or recover after a system crash or power outage from a dumb terminal or another computer running a terminal program—even another Linux system. This access does *not*, however, extend as far as letting you select the OS to boot using LILO or modifying your computer's CMOS BIOS settings; these settings rely upon the BIOS, not Linux, for input, and so cannot be redirected by Linux.

WARNING

Some Linux distributions, including Red Hat, use specially formatted text to display startup messages in color. Some terminal programs may misinterpret these codes in various unhelpful ways, as in a request to begin a file transfer. For this reason, you're best off using a very minimal terminal program or disabling terminal program features such as server-requested file transfers.

CONFIGURING MODEMS

One of the most common RS-232 serial devices is the telephone *modem*. This word is an acronym for *modulator-demodulator*, because a modem functions as a way to convert analog data to digital form (that is, *modulate* it) and reverse the process (*demodulate* the data).

Most telephone modems are RS-232 devices, but there are two major exceptions to this rule:

▶ *Internal software modems*—These devices, mentioned earlier, have no serial port circuitry. A few have Linux drivers available (check http://www.linmodems.org for details), but many don't. It's usually best to avoid software modems for use in Linux.

▶ *USB modems*—Modems that interface through the USB port are becoming popular. If a USB modem uses the *Communication Device Class Abstract Control Model* (CDC-ACM) protocol, it should work with the USB support in the 2.4.*x* Linux kernels.

NOTE

Internet access provided by *Digital Subscriber Line* (DSL) and cable TV systems is also often referred to as modem-based. Although these devices do modulate and demodulate data, their use is very different from what's described in this section. Cable and DSL modems are more akin to Ethernet routers and bridges.

Some internal modems—particularly older models—use a serial port in conjunction with conventional modem circuitry. These devices function just like ordinary external modems, which plug into an RS-232 port. No matter what interface the device uses, you can configure a modem in many ways. The configuration details differ depending on who initiates a connection: your computer or a remote computer. When one of your users initiates a connection, you must configure the system to perform *dial-out* access. In order to support remote users calling your system, you must configure your system to accept *dial-in* access of one form or another.

Dial-Out Modem Uses

Small Linux systems, such as desktop workstations, often require dial-out access. The users of such a system may need to contact another via a modem to check e-mail or perform other simple text-based tasks. Moving up in complexity, the modem can be used to initiate a *Point-to-Point Protocol* (PPP) connection in order to allow web browsing, FTP transfers, and so on. Finally, it's possible to send faxes from a Linux computer using a modem. These features are generally most desirable for single-user workstations, but sometimes they're helpful even on multiuser systems. This is particularly true of sending faxes; you can configure a shared printer queue to use a fax modem rather than a printer, thus providing outgoing fax services to an entire network of computers.

Calling a Remote Text-Mode System

One of the simplest types of outgoing modem connection is a text-based link to another computer. The idea behind such a link is similar to that of using a serial port along with a dumb terminal or a computer running a terminal program. The difference is that a pair of modems and the telephone network sit between the two computers. In such a setup, the dial-out computer ordinarily functions as the terminal; the dial-in system runs a getty program and receives the call, as described shortly, in the section "Accepting Text-Mode Logins."

Using modems in text mode is now much less common than it was before the rise of the Internet and PPP connections. It can still be a good way to handle simple access needs, however. Further, some companies still operate *bulletin-board systems* (BBSs), which provide product information, file downloads, and discussion forums for those without Internet access.

To call a remote text-based system, you must use a terminal program. Two popular terminal programs on Linux are the text-based Minicom and the X-based Seyon (shown in Figure 13.4).

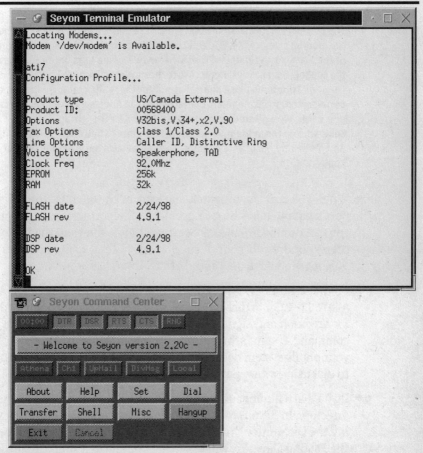

FIGURE 13.4:   The Seyon Terminal Emulator lets you use Linux as if it were a dumb terminal.

Part iii

Details of how to use these programs differ, but the basic principles are the same:

▶ Before you run a program, you may need to create a symbolic link so that /dev/modem points to the device file on which your modem resides (such as /dev/ttyS0). Alternatively, you can configure the program to use the desired device file directly—for instance, by clicking Set in the Seyon Command Center window, clicking Port, and entering the desired device filename.

NOTE

The user who makes a connection must have permission to both read and write the modem's device file. Red Hat Linux's startup scripts change the ownership of the /dev/ttyS*n* device files whenever anyone logs onto the console, so the console user always has access to the modem if it's an RS-232 serial device. Other distributions use a special group for these files, along with 664 or 660 permissions, so all members of that group can access the modem. You can add any users who should have modem access to the group. Use the ls -l command on the modem device for your system to find out how it's configured, and make any necessary changes to the device's permissions or your group configuration.

▶ When you run the program, you may need to adjust the serial port's parameters—most importantly, the port speed. In Seyon, you can do this by clicking Set, then Baud, and then the button corresponding to your desired speed. When using a modern 56Kbps modem, a port speed of 115Kbps is appropriate.

▶ To dial a number, type **ATDT** followed by the number, such as **ATDT555-1234** to dial 555-1234. AT is the standard modem code for *attention* and signals the modem that you're about to give a command. D stands for *dial*, and T refers to touch-tone dialing. (If your phone system doesn't support touch-tone dialing, use **ATDP** to dial using rotary pulses.)

▶ If you dial a number on a regular basis, you can add it to a dialing directory. In Seyon, you can see preconfigured numbers by clicking the Dial button. You can edit these entries by clicking Edit in the Dialing Directory window, which produces a simple text editor showing the configuration file. You can dial a number by selecting it in the Dialing Directory window and clicking Go. This action sends the appropriate AT commands to dial the number.

► When you're done using the program, hang up the modem by logging out of the remote system, turning off the modem, or picking an appropriate option in the program, such as the Hangup button in Seyon's Command Center window.

Seyon stores configuration information in the ~/.seyon directory, so every user may have customized settings. Minicom requires that root run it with the -s parameter to create a configuration file called /etc/minirc.dfl, after which a user can create a custom configuration called ~/.minirc.dfl by changing defaults established by root.

Once you've connected to a remote system using a terminal program, you can use that system according to whatever rules it uses. These rules vary substantially from one system to another. For instance, if you connect to a Linux computer, you typically can use Linux text-mode commands and utilities; but BBSs often use custom menu-based environments in which you type letters or digits to move around the system.

Making a PPP Connection

Today, establishing a PPP link is perhaps the most common use for a dial-out modem. PPP allows you to tie a system to the Internet using full TCP/IP networking features. A PPP-linked system can therefore browse the Web, transfer files via FTP, send and receive e-mail, and so on. Because PPP links are usually transitory and modem links are slow by modern Internet standards, it's uncommon to find servers running on PPP-connected computers. Some Internet service providers (ISPs) do offer accounts that can be used constantly; however, it's usually less expensive to acquire faster service through a cable modem or DSL for always-on connections.

Testing Basic Connectivity   The first step in linking a computer to the Internet via PPP is to acquire an account from an ISP. (If you want to link two computers that you control, such as an Internet-connected server at work and a home system, check the section "Accepting PPP Connections" later in this chapter for information on setting up a system to function as a PPP server.) Fortunately, ISPs are extremely common. You can find listings for them in your local telephone directory, probably under "Internet Services" or some variation of that.

Before you go further in configuring PPP access, you should check that your modem and device files work correctly by trying the instructions in "Calling a Remote Text-Mode System," earlier in this chapter. You can call your ISP's dial-in number with Seyon or Minicom to check basic modem functionality. Depending on how your ISP's system is configured, you may see a `login:` prompt or gibberish when you connect. The main test is that you can get your own modem to dial; if this works, then you can be sure you have no problems relating to your own modem or modem device file permissions.

Connecting via PPP Scripts   Most ISPs today use the PAP or CHAP authentication protocol. These protocols allow you to identify yourself to the ISP in an automated fashion. In Linux, you must configure a file, called `/etc/ppp/pap-secrets` or `/etc/ppp/chap-secrets`, to support these authentication methods. Both files use the same format. Each line contains information for one account and takes this form:

```
client   server   secret   IP address
```

TIP

If you're not sure which system your ISP uses, you can create one file and use a hard or symbolic link to make it accessible under both names. For instance, create `/etc/ppp/pap-secrets` and then type `ln -s /etc/ppp/pap-secrets /etc/ppp/chap-secrets`.

The meanings of each element are as follows:

client   The username on the ISP's system.

server   The name of the ISP's server. This value is normally *, which means Linux accepts any server (because the ISP may change its server's name without notice).

secret   The password to the ISP's system.

IP_address   The numeric IP address or addresses that Linux will accept. This value is normally blank, meaning that the system accepts any IP address.

As an example, the following file can be used to log on to an ISP using the username agb and the password `comehere`:

```
agb  *  comehere
```

WARNING

The PPP secrets file, no matter what its name, is extremely sensitive because it contains your ISP username in an unencrypted form. You should ensure that it's readable *only* by root (that is, that it's owned by root and has 0600 permissions). You should also use a different password on your ISP than you use on any other system, so that if this file is compromised, it can't be used to gain illicit access to other systems.

To initiate a PPP connection using command-line tools, you must have appropriate PPP scripts. Sample scripts are available with the PPP package for most distributions. In Red Hat 7.1, these scripts are in the /usr/share/doc/ppp-2.4.0/scripts directory. Their names are ppp-on, ppp-on-dialer, and ppp-off. The first two are responsible for initiating a PPP connection, and the third breaks a PPP link. You should copy all three scripts to /etc/ppp or to a location on your path, such as /usr/local/bin. You must then modify the ppp-on and ppp-on-dialer scripts to suit your configuration. In particular:

- In ppp-on, locate the lines that begin TELEPHONE=, ACCOUNT=, and PASSWORD= and modify them so that they're appropriate for your ISP and account. (The ACCOUNT and PASSWORD variables may not be required if you use PAP or CHAP, but they should contain dummy variables in that case.)

- Check that the DIALER_SCRIPT variable in ppp-on points to the correct location of ppp-on-dialer. The default location is /etc/ppp.

- Check the call to pppd in the last lines of ppp-on. (pppd is the tool that handles the PPP negotiations; the scripts merely provide it with the information it needs to do its job.) Most of the parameters to this call are quite cryptic, but you should at least be able to confirm that it's using the correct modem device filename and speed (115,200 is appropriate in most cases, but the default is 38,400).

- Check the ppp-on-dialer script. This script includes a "chat" sequence—a series of strings the program expects to see from the modem or remote system in one column, and a series of responses in another column. You may need to log on using Seyon or Minicom and capture to disk the prompts your ISP uses to ask for your username and password and modify the last two lines of the script in order to make it work. Alternatively, you may need to comment out the last two lines by preceding them with pound signs (#) and remove the backslash (\) from the CONNECT line if your ISP uses PAP or CHAP.

NOTE   The chat program expects a single line; its input is formatted in columns in ppp-on-dialer only for the convenience of humans. The backslashes ending most lines signify line continuations, so that chat interprets multiple input lines as a single line. Only the final line should lack a backslash.

When you're done making these changes, type **ppp-on** (preceding it with a complete path, if necessary) as root to test the connection. If all goes well, your system should dial the modem, link up, and give you Internet access. If this fails to occur, check the last few lines of /var/log/messages with a command such as **tail -n 20 /var/log /messages**. There should be some sort of error messages, which may help you to diagnose the problem.

WARNING   Debugging text-mode PPP connections sometimes bears an uncanny resemblance to voodoo. The problem is that there are many minor variant implementations of PPP, both on the ISP side and on the Linux side. Some combinations are incompatible or require unusual pppd parameters. You can read the pppd man pages and try pppd parameters in the ppp-on script if you have problems. You may also be able to find help on your ISP's website if you have some alternate means of accessing it.

Many ISPs send *Domain Name System* (DNS) server information to clients during PPP authentication. If yours doesn't, you'll need to enter this information into your /etc/resolv.conf file. This file should contain one to three lines listing DNS server addresses, as provided by your ISP. For instance:

```
nameserver 192.168.1.1
```

If your PPP configuration doesn't set this information automatically and you don't set it manually, you'll be able to access sites on the Internet by numeric IP address (such as 216.224.70.176) but not by names (such as www.sybex.com). You need to configure DNS information only once, not once per connection.

Connecting Using a GUI Utility   Because of the difficulties associated with establishing a PPP connection using scripts, many users prefer to use a GUI frontend. These tools use the same underlying pppd program as do conventional scripts, but their point-and-click interface makes it easier to enter information on your ISP and account. It's generally possible to dispense with chat scripts when using GUI utilities, which further lessens the possibility of error.

All systems that ship with KDE, including Red Hat Linux, come with a GUI utility called KPPP (shown in Figure 13.5). You can use KPPP even if you don't use KDE. Alternatively, you can use a GUI dialer that's not associated with a specific environment, such as X-ISP (http://users .hol.gr/~dbouras/). Most GUI dialers function in basically the same way, although some details differ.

FIGURE 13.5:   KPPP allows you to enter PPP account information and connect to an ISP using a GUI interface.

To use KPPP, follow these steps:

1. Launch KPPP by typing **kppp** in a terminal window or by launching it from KDE's K menu (usually K ➤ Internet ➤ KPPP). The first time you launch the program, it will have no ISP entries in the Connect To field (Figure 13.5 shows KPPP configured to use an ISP).

2. Click Setup to enter an ISP's information. The result is the KPPP Configuration dialog box, shown in Figure 13.6, but with no accounts defined.

Part iii

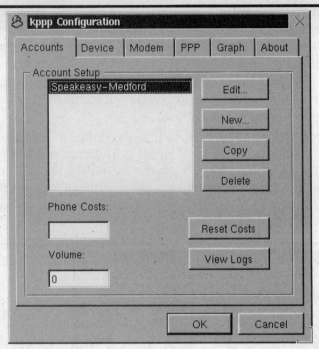

FIGURE 13.6: You can adjust KPPP's settings from the Configuration dialog box.

3. Click New to create a new account. Some versions of KPPP give you the option of using a wizard to simplify account configuration; this tool requires you to enter your country, but it has no entry for the United States. This procedure therefore ignores the wizard; click Dialog Setup if you're asked if you want to use a wizard. KPPP displays the New Account dialog box, shown in Figure 13.7.

4. Enter a name and telephone number in the Connection Name and Phone Number fields, respectively. You can use any name you like; this entry is used to help you identify an account if you have several. The phone number should be one provided by your ISP.

5. Select the authentication method your ISP uses. In most cases, you can leave this set to its default of PAP.

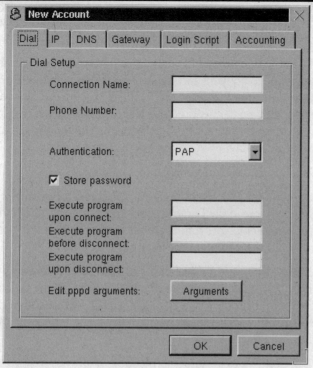

FIGURE 13.7:   The New Account dialog box allows you to enter critical information provided by your ISP.

6. Click through the remaining tabs on the New Account dialog box and enter any information provided by your ISP. The information that's most likely to need setting is the DNS server information. Enter an IP address in the DNS IP Address field and click Add. Repeat this process if your ISP provides two DNS server addresses. In some cases, you may need to create a login script, similar to the one described for script-based PPP dialups.

7. Click OK in the New Account dialog box.

8. In the Configuration window, click the Device tab. Check that Modem Device is set appropriately, and set Connection Speed to 115,200. (You may want to use a lower speed if your modem is particularly slow. In general, you should use a connect speed of at least twice the modem's official speed,

because modems support compression technologies that increase their effective speed when handling uncompressed data.)

9. Check the remaining tabs in the Configuration window. You may want to adjust a setting such as the modem's volume. Many additional settings are useful if you encounter problems making a connection or if you're familiar with the program, your modem, or PPP connections generally and want to enable an advanced option.

10. Click OK in the Configuration dialog box.

11. In the main KPPP window (refer to Figure 13.5), enter your ISP username in the Login ID field and your password in the Password field. Note that these are your username and password on the ISP, not on the local system.

12. The first time you connect or if you encounter problems, it's often helpful to check the Show Log Window item. This results in a window that displays what KPPP sends to the modem and receives back in response; it can be very helpful in diagnosing connection problems.

13. Click Connect to initiate a connection. If all goes well, KPPP displays a Connecting To window that shows the connection status. When a connection is made, another window appears showing the time the system's been connected. You can click the Details button to see assorted statistics on the connection or the Disconnect button to end a connection.

Just as with script-based PPP connections, it's not uncommon to run into problems with a GUI-based PPP tool. A particular ISP may require an unusual set of PPP options, or it may use an odd PPP implementation that cannot be made to work well with Linux. If you encounter problems, your best bet is to use the KPPP menus to experiment with alternate settings. You should also try using a terminal program to log on to the ISP, in order to see if the ISP uses any peculiar login prompts, which might best be handled through KPPP's scripting features (step 6).

Sending Faxes

All modern modems can be used as fax machines. Sending a fax from a computer results in an exceptionally clear fax at the receiving end because the output is generated digitally, rather than scanned from an original (unless of course you use a scanner to create a digital image to be faxed). There are several fax packages available for Linux, including mgetty+sendfax (http://alpha.greenie.net/mgetty/) and HylaFAX (http://www.hylafax.org/). The mgetty+sendfax package is a variant of mgetty, described earlier. This program comes with most Linux distributions. On Red Hat 7.1, the appropriate RPM package is called mgetty-sendfax-1.1.25-2.i386.rpm. You should install it and the regular mgetty package, upon which mgetty+sendfax depends.

In order to use mgetty+sendfax, you must configure it as follows:

1. **Install the package**   Locate and install mgetty+sendfax. It's usually called mgetty+sendfax, mgetty-sendfax, or mgetty, depending on your distribution. (On Red Hat 7.1, it's on the second CD-ROM.)

2. **Configure mgetty+sendfax**   Most distributions place mgetty+sendfax's configuration files in /etc/mgetty+send-fax. You should adjust at least four files:

    fax.allow   This file contains a list of users who are allowed to send faxes. Place one username per line in this file.

    Faxheader   This file contains the header information for outgoing faxes. You should adjust it to list your fax number.

    sendfax.config   This file contains miscellaneous fax configuration information. Most of the items in this file are well commented. Change the fax-id item to your fax number. The fax-devices item is also critically important. It should list your fax device filename (without the leading /dev/), as in ttyS1 or modem.

    faxrunq.config   This file contains additional, miscellaneous fax configuration information. At a minimum, you should set the fax-devices item to point to your fax device filename, the same as you did on the same line in sendfax.config.

3. **Launch faxrunqd**   This is a daemon that watches for faxes to appear in the fax queue directory. Installing the mgetty+ sendfax package normally creates this directory, usually at /var/spool/fax. To use your system to send faxes on a

regular basis, you should configure it to run faxrunqd at system startup, such as by adding it to /etc/rc.d/rc.local or a similar startup file. When you do, be sure to include an ampersand (&) on the startup line, because faxrunqd does not normally start up in the background.

When you've finished configuring mgetty+sendfax, you can send a fax with the faxspool command. The syntax of this command is this:

```
faxspool [options] phone-number file [file...]
```

Options include -n (to set normal resolution, as opposed to the default of fine resolution), -C *program* (to call the specified program to generate a cover page), and -t *hh:mm* (to send the fax at the specified hour and minute). *phone-number* is the number to which the fax is to be sent. faxspool recognizes several file types, including .ps (PostScript), .t (ASCII text), .dvi (TeX DVI output), and .g3 (preformatted fax G3 files). The program uses the filename extension to identify the file type, so it's imperative that the filename extension match what faxspool expects for the file type.

It's possible, but somewhat tricky, to implement a print queue that sends output via a fax modem. One package that can help in this respect is GFax (http://www.gmsys.com/gnome-gfax.html). This program sets up a print queue that displays an X-based dialog box in which you can enter the destination fax number. One utility that allows Windows computers to send faxes via a Linux server that runs Samba is Respond (http://www.boerde.de/~horstf/). This program works much like GFax, but on Windows clients. Both programs rely upon an underlying fax-sending mechanism, such as mgetty+sendfax.

Dial-In Modem Uses

In a dial-in configuration, you set up your modem to accept incoming calls. Typically, the modem either reports to the computer that it's detected a ring, and the computer then commands the modem to answer the call; or the modem answers the call automatically and then reports to the computer that it's received a call. In either case, you must configure Linux to accept the call and perhaps to process the incoming data in different ways according to what *type* of call it is.

Accepting Text-Mode Logins

One of the simplest cases is that of a text-mode login. Suppose you want to set up a system so that employees can call the computer from home to check their e-mail using text-mode programs such as pine or mutt. The configuration for such a system can be very similar to that for a terminal, described earlier. In that configuration, it was necessary to add a line to /etc/inittab to link a serial port to a getty program, so that the getty program could process input from a dumb terminal. The only conceptual difference between that situation and a dial-in modem is that the modem (a pair of them, actually, but the Linux system deals directly with only one) sits between the terminal and the Linux computer. You should follow the steps outlined in "Configuring a getty Program," earlier in this chapter, to set up a modem for dial-in text-mode access. The only difference is in step 2 of that procedure, which requires a slightly different modification to /etc/inittab:

```
S0:2345:respawn:/sbin/mgetty -s 57600 /dev/ttyS0
```

This line differs from the one presented earlier only in the absence of the -r parameter. The mgetty program was designed for use with modems (hence the *m* in *mgetty*), so the -r parameter disables some normal mgetty functionality. Specifically, mgetty normally sends command codes to the modem to prepare it to receive calls, and mgetty responds to a modem's connect messages by passing it the Linux login: prompt. Removing the -r parameter from the /etc/inittab line re-enables these features.

Accepting PPP Connections

It's sometimes desirable to configure a Linux system to accept PPP logins. So configured, an Internet-enabled Linux computer can function as a gateway between a remote computer running any of several operating systems and the Internet. This setup can be convenient if you have a system at work with always-on Internet access and a modem, and you want to provide yourself or your employees with Internet access at home or when you or they are on the road. Many ISPs use Linux systems running PPP servers to handle dozens, hundreds, or more users.

Part III

NOTE

56Kbps modems operate with a speed asymmetry — upload speeds are slower than download speeds. This condition exists because the high upload speeds require that one system (the ISP's computer in a normal configuration) have a special connection to the telephone network. Unless you acquire such a connection, your dial-in PPP system will be limited to 48Kbps speeds, even if you have a 56Kbps modem.

There are many ways to accept PPP connections. The method described here is comparatively simple to set up, but it requires that the calling system use a connection script or manually enter authentication information. No matter how you do it, there are several configuration features you must set. In essence, a PPP link requires that the Linux computer function as a router between the dial-in systems and the rest of the network. Therefore, these systems require router support in the Linux kernel (which is standard in most Linux distributions, including Red Hat 7.1). You must also be able to assign an IP address to the dial-in systems. Normally, this is done on a static basis according to the serial port, as you'll see.

To configure a Linux system as a PPP server, follow these steps:

1. Configure the computer to accept a remote login via a getty program, as described in the previous section.

2. Modify the /etc/ppp/options file so that it contains the following entries (you may need to modify netmask to conform to your network; this value should be the same as the netmask of the PPP server):

```
asyncmap 0
netmask 255.255.255.0
proxyarp
lock
crtscts
modem
login
```

3. Create a file called /etc/ppp/options.*port*, where *port* is the port file, such as ttyS0 for the first serial port. This file contains the IP address or hostname of the PPP server followed by a colon (:) and the IP address or hostname of the PPP client. You should be sure that the PPP client hostname is available for use on the network. For instance:

```
192.168.1.3:192.168.1.200
```

4. Create a /etc/ppp/pap-secrets file entry for any users who should be able to use the PPP link. This entry is similar to the one for dial-out PPP access, but it lists a local username and password. For instance, the following allows the user abell to connect to a PPP server using the password watson:

```
abell  *  watson
```

5. Check the permissions on the pppd file. You should set it to uid root by typing **chmod u+s /usr/sbin/pppd**, if necessary. When you've done this, typing **ls -l /usr/sbin/pppd** should reveal the following permissions:

```
-rwsr-xr-x  1 root  root  140656 Mar  7 10:25
➥/usr/sbin/pppd
```

6. To run pppd, users dialing in must normally type a slightly cumbersome command—it's not very complex by Linux system administration standards, but it's a bit of an annoyance. You can reduce the annoyance factor by setting up a global alias to run this command. Once set up, a user need only type ppp to launch pppd on Linux. You can set this up by entering the following line in /etc/bashrc (assuming your user's account is configured to use Bash as the default shell):

```
alias ppp="exec /usr/sbin/pppd -detach"
```

With these steps, a user should be able to use PPP to connect to the computer and any network to which it's attached. The PPP server requires manual login via a standard Linux login: prompt, after which the client must send the ppp command to start pppd on the Linux system. This can all be handled in a login script or by a manual procedure from some PPP dialers, such as KPPP or the one that comes with Microsoft Windows.

Receiving Faxes

If you've configured your system to accept dial-up text-mode logins using mgetty, as described in the section "Accepting Text-Mode Logins," earlier in this chapter, your system is automatically configured to receive faxes. When a call comes in on the line to which the modem is attached, the modem determines whether the call is a data call or a fax call. If it's a data call, mgetty passes over control of the serial line to appropriate programs to handle data transmission. If the modem detects an incoming fax, mgetty initiates fax reception and places incoming faxes in the /var/spool/fax/incoming directory.

Part iii

Incoming fax files use the standard G3 fax file format. You can view these files with several programs, such as KDE's KFax (shown in Figure 13.8). Such programs are typically quite simple; they allow you to view or print the file, but not much else.

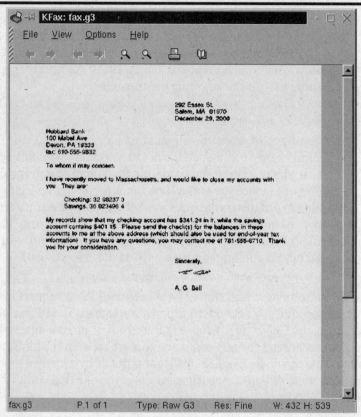

FIGURE 13.8:   KFax includes options to zoom in and out, change to a new page in a fax, or print a fax.

TIP

mgetty includes options to send configuration strings to the modem so that it functions as *only* a data modem or as *only* a fax modem. These options are –D and –F, respectively. They can be added to the appropriate lines in /etc/inittab.

CONFIGURING SERIAL PRINTERS

Most printers connected to Linux computers use the parallel interface. The parallel interface offers one great advantage over the traditional RS-232 interface: speed. Modern parallel ports are theoretically capable of transferring 2MB/s, compared to the 0.014MB/s of an RS-232 serial port. This hundred-fold speed difference is important for printers—especially modern color printers, which often take massive bitmaps as input.

Despite the advantages of parallel ports, some printers use RS-232 serial ports. This interface is least problematic when the printer understands PostScript, because most Linux programs that can print can create PostScript output, which is more compact than the bitmap output that GhostScript creates.

Since 1999, USB printers have started to become popular. The USB interface is capable of 1.5MB/s speeds—roughly comparable to a parallel port. If you want to use a USB printer in Linux, you'll need a 2.4.*x* kernel, or at least a 2.2.18 or later kernel.

Special Considerations for Serial Printers

For an RS-232 serial printer, the configuration details that differ from a parallel-port configuration are in the /etc/printcap file. Specifically:

▸ You must specify an appropriate serial port, such as /dev/ttyS1, on the lp= line.

▸ You must set the speed of the port using the br# line. (The pound symbol is used in place of an equal sign with this option.) For best results, you should set the speed as high as your serial port and printer allow—ideally 115,200 bps (br#115200).

To use a USB printer, you must specify the appropriate USB printer device file on the lp= line—probably /dev/usblp0 or something similar, as described in Table 13.1. You do *not* set the port speed for USB printers as you do for RS-232 serial printers.

In the case of both RS-232 and USB printers, you must have appropriate support in the Linux kernel for the port in question. All major Linux distributions include RS-232 support, but you may need to add this support for USB printers, as just described.

Part iii

When to Use a Serial Printer

If you have a choice, use a parallel printer in Linux, or one that uses an Ethernet interface if you have a network. These interfaces provide the best speed, particularly when printing graphics—and GhostScript converts text into graphics when printing to non-PostScript printers, so unless the printer supports PostScript, most Linux printing is graphics printing.

The USB interface is almost as fast as the parallel interface and so can be a good choice in this respect. If you're using an older distribution such as Red Hat 6.2 that includes no USB support by default, adding the necessary USB support makes USB printers a second choice. Because USB printer support is so new, you should check http://www.linux-usb.org for compatibility information on specific models.

The RS-232 interface is decidedly sluggish, so it should not be used for a printer if you can avoid it. Modern printers that include RS-232 support also invariably support parallel or USB interfaces, so there should be no trouble using these printers via more capable interfaces, at least from the printer's side of things. There are two situations in which you might be forced to use an RS-232 port:

Port Depletion on the Computer   Most *x*86 computers have just one parallel port. If you're using it for one printer, you may need to use an RS-232 port for a second printer. You can buy add-on parallel-port cards for such situations, however, so unless you want to connect many printers to one computer or cannot add a card for some reason, you can usually work around a lack of parallel ports.

Old Serial-Only Printers   A few printers don't include parallel, USB, or Ethernet ports. Fortunately, such printers are usually PostScript models, so they're not as badly affected by RS-232's speed problems as are non-PostScript models.

What's Next?

The RS-232 serial port is a low-speed but very flexible means of interfacing computing equipment. It can be used to link two computers together (directly or through a modem), to connect dumb terminals to a computer, or to interface a printer to a computer. Linux's support for these functions is quite good, but it relies on a large number of additional software packages, such as pppd for PPP links, getty for login access, and the printing system for printers. Understanding these tools is vital for using RS-232 serial ports under Linux.

USB is a recent serial port standard that surpasses the old RS-232 standard in many ways, including speed and flexibility. Many devices are available in USB interfaces, ranging from mice to scanners to disk drives. Linux's support for USB is still new, but with the 2.4.x kernels it is good enough to allow you to use many of these devices. If you're using an older Linux distribution that lacks USB support, however, you'll need to upgrade the kernel to use USB devices.

In the next chapter, you will learn more about connecting your computer to the Internet. Much of what you learned in this chapter will be expanded upon.

Part iii

Chapter 14

CONNECTING TO THE INTERNET

The subject of connecting a Linux system (or any computer system, for that matter) to the Internet is a complex one and a subject that can require a thorough knowledge of that system's network environment.

Still, for many users, this process is simple enough that both X Windows and Linux work on the first attempt.

This chapter starts with a quick look at PPP and its role in the Internet world. It reviews the hardware and software requirements for connecting to the Internet and then walks you through the mechanics of manually making a PPP connection. Finally, this chapter wraps up by explaining how to automate these connections.

Adapted from *Mastering Red Hat Linux 7.1*
by Arman Danesh
ISBN 0-7821-2927-7   1008 pages $49.99

WHAT IS PPP?

Most Internet users are probably familiar with the acronym PPP, simply because the type of account they have with their Internet service provider (ISP) is a PPP account. Many users, though, really don't understand what PPP is all about.

PPP stands for *Point-to-Point Protocol* and is designed to provide a method by which TCP/IP is extended across an analog modem connection. In this way, when you are connected to the Internet using PPP, you become part of your ISP's network, you are an actual host on the Internet, and you have an IP address.

Traditionally, dial-up Internet connections were done using terminal software and Unix shell accounts on central servers. In this environment, the terminal software on the client system merely acted as a display for the server, and only the server had an IP address on the Internet. This contrasts sharply with today's PPP connections, which bring the Internet right up to your modem.

The great flexibility of Internet connection technologies allows a wide variety of PPP connection types. You can have PPP connections with fixed or dynamic IP addresses. Connections can use special authentication protocols such as PAP (Password Authentication Protocol) or CHAP (Challenge Handshake Authentication Protocol). They can even use standard cleartext-based prompt and response mechanisms. Connections can be made manually or can be made automatically as needed.

This chapter discusses the most common Internet connection scenario: connecting by modem to an ISP that offers PPP connections with dynamically assigned IP addresses.

NOTE

"PPP" and "ISP connections" are used interchangeably in this chapter. However, PPP connections are not limited to connections through ISPs. In fact, PPP is also a common way to connect to corporate or educational networks.

REQUIRED HARDWARE AND SOFTWARE

In order to make PPP work properly, some preparation is needed. Hardware and software need to be in place and configured before you can get PPP to work properly. Three key components need to be considered:

- ▶ A modem needs to be installed, configured, and working.
- ▶ PPP support needs to be compiled into the Linux kernel.
- ▶ PPP software needs to be installed.

The Modem

Because PPP is designed for dial-up connections, a modem is an essential piece of the PPP puzzle.

To configure PPP, you need to know the speed of your modem connection and which device it uses in Linux (probably /dev/modem or one of /dev/ttyS0 through /dev/ttyS3).

PPP in the Kernel

The Linux kernel is designed to be highly flexible. It can be compiled to include (or exclude) support for numerous technologies ranging from serial mice right up to networking facilities such as PPP.

In order to make a PPP connection with Linux, it is necessary for the kernel to include PPP support. You can check to see if support is there by watching the messages that scroll by while the operating system is booting. If you see a series of lines like these, PPP is compiled into your kernel:

```
PPP generic driver version 2.4.0
PPP Deflate Compression module registered
PPP BSD Compression module registered
```

If you find that the messages scroll by too quickly, you can use the dmesg command to see the part of the startup messages that should include the PPP messages:

```
$ dmesg | less
```

Part iii

Installing PPP Software

Red Hat Linux 7.1 installs PPP software with a complete or default installation. Two programs are used to establish a PPP connection: /usr/sbin/pppd and /usr/sbin/chat. In Red Hat Linux 7.1, these are part of the ppp-2.4.0-2 package, and you can see if these are installed by using the rpm command:

```
$ rpm -q ppp
ppp-2.4.0-2
```

If you find that you are lacking either pppd or chat, you need to install a new set of PPP software before continuing. Mount the Red Hat CD-ROM at a suitable location (such as /mnt/cdrom) and then install the package ppp-2.4.0-2.i386.rpm:

```
$ rpm -i /mnt/cdrom/RedHat/RPMS/ppp-2.4.0-2.i386.rpm
```

Alternatively, you can download the latest sources for PPP from the PPPD home page at the Samba download mirror site at ftp://ftp.samba.org/pub/ppp/. The current version of PPP is 2.4.1, and the filename is ppp-2.4.1.tar.gz.

You need to expand the archive in a suitable location such as /tmp with the following command:

```
$ tar xzvf ppp-2.4.1.tar.gz
```

Then read through the README.linux file carefully. Installing a new PPP package involves not only compiling the software but also upgrading your Linux kernel source files and recompiling the Linux kernel to match the version of the PPP software being installed.

Describing the details of this process would take a whole chapter, so it is best left to the documentation.

TIP

Comprehensive sources for downloading Linux software can be found on numerous websites, including those for your distribution, as well as the Tucows website at http://www.tucows.com. If you prefer RPM packages, a comprehensive source of these packages is located at http://www.rpmfind.net.

GRAPHICAL PPP CONNECTIONS

There are two major tools available to help you make a PPP connection, designed to help you get on the Internet with your Linux computer: RP3 for GNOME and KPPP for KDE. RP3 on Red Hat Linux 7.1 keeps the human interface as simple as possible. KPPP enables you to configure every part of your Internet connection.

The following sections assume a basic Internet connection where you need few special settings. However, some ISPs do require additional special settings. Both RP3 and KPPP can accommodate special settings as well as diagnostic checks. More information on these optional settings is available later in this chapter, in the sections on PPPD and Minicom.

RP3

RP3 is the Red Hat graphical PPP management tool. If you have an ISP that can handle Linux connections, you can be set up and connected to the Internet in three easy steps. You can make more sophisticated configuration changes later; you can even set up a terminal to troubleshoot any connection problems you might have, but RP3 is easy to use. First, you configure it as the root user, and then any regular user on your system can connect to the Internet.

Configuring RP3

By default, access is configured right on the desktop. To start RP3, double-click the Dialup Configuration icon on your desktop or simply run the /usr/bin/rp3-config command from a terminal in the X Window.

Enter the root password if prompted. If this is the first time you've used RP3, the Add New Internet Connection Wizard will start. Click Next to continue. If you do not yet have a modem configured, you will see a Select Modem dialog box. Plug your modem into a telephone line. Click Next to continue. As you can see in Figure 14.1, RP3 then checks every device that could be connected to a modem.

TIP

If you do not see the Add New Internet Connection Wizard but you see an Internet Connections dialog box, click the Add button. Otherwise, you may not have the RP3 package installed.

Part iii

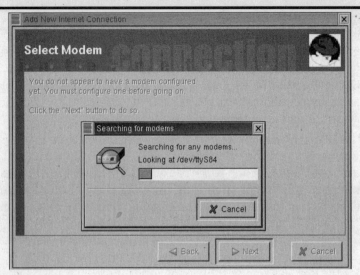

FIGURE 14.1:   Checking for modems

When RP3 finds a candidate device, it checks automatically for a dial tone. After it runs through each device file, it gives you a result such as that shown in Figure 14.2.

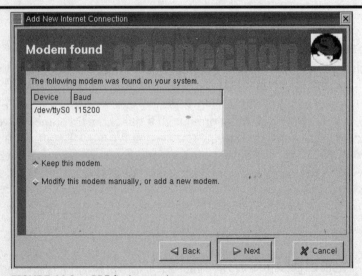

FIGURE 14.2:   RP3 finds a modem.

If it doesn't find a modem, you'll see the window shown in Figure 14.3. This screen enables you to edit the various settings shown to help Linux find and use your modem. Even if Linux found your modem, you can still access this window by selecting the Modify This Modem Manually... option shown in Figure 14.2.

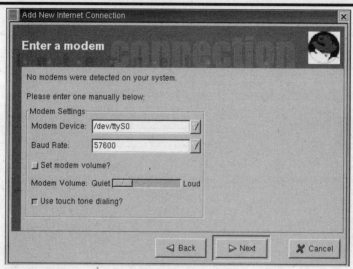

Add New Internet Connection

Enter a modem

No modems were detected on your system.

Please enter one manually below:

Modem Settings

Modem Device: /dev/ttyS0

Baud Rate: 57600

☐ Set modem volume?

Modem Volume: Quiet ☐ Loud

☐ Use touch tone dialing?

◁ Back   ▷ Next   ✗ Cancel

FIGURE 14.3:   Manual modem configuration

NOTE

The baud rate is not identical to the speed of your modem. It should typically be four times the speed of your modem, up to 115,200 baud. However, you can set a lower speed to reduce data loss from outside factors such as noise.

Once you have the modem configured, click Next. The next step is to set up the basics of your Internet connection, as shown in Figure 14.4:

▶ Account Name is the name of your ISP.

▶ Prefix is the number dialed on your telephone for outside access. You can leave this blank if no prefix is required.

▶ Area/Country Code is the numbers required to access the local telephone exchange of your ISP's access number. If you can reach the ISP through a local telephone call, depending on the rules set by your local telephone company, you may want to leave this entry blank as well.

▶ Phone Number is the local access number for your ISP.

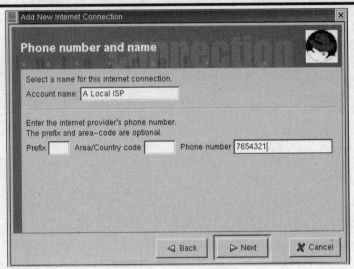

FIGURE 14.4: Entering ISP access information

Click Next, enter the username and password that you use to log on to your ISP, and then click Next again. In the Other Options window, select Normal ISP or AT&T Global Network Services and click Next. When you click Finish in the next window, you're ready to get connected.

Using RP3

Once a PPP connection is configured, any regular user on your system can run it. From the GNOME Main Menu button, choose Programs ➤ Internet ➤ RH PPP Dialer. The Choose window opens, as shown in Figure 14.5. Select the name you assigned to the ISP then click OK, and Linux connects to the Internet through your ISP.

FIGURE 14.5:   Selecting an ISP

KPPP

The other major Linux GUI way to access the Internet is through KPPP, the KDE PPP dialer. If you're in the KDE desktop, click the KDE Main Menu button, then choose Internet ➤ Internet Dialer. In another desktop such as GNOME, open up a command-line window and enter the /usr/bin/kppp command. This brings up the KPPP window, shown in Figure 14.6.

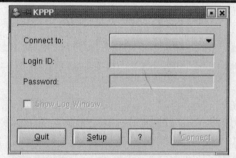

FIGURE 14.6:   The KDE PPP configuration tool

Click Setup in this window. When you see the KPPP Configuration window, choose the Accounts tab if necessary, and then click New. This opens the Create A New Account... window, which is customized primarily for European ISPs. Unless you use an ISP in Europe or New Zealand, click Dialog Setup. This brings up the New Account window, shown in Figure 14.7, where you can set up a connection to your ISP. In most cases, you need to set up only the items shown in Figure 14.7.

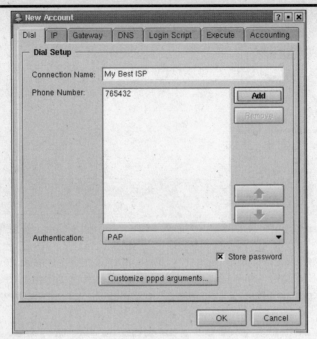

FIGURE 14.7: Setting up an ISP

If you have trouble with your connection, come back to this window. You can configure a number of options under the other tabs shown in Figure 14.7:

Dial   Besides the phone number, you can configure the type of password authentication as well as the programs to execute at various points during your connection.

IP   If your ISP assigns you a static IP address, enter it here.

Gateway   If your ISP doesn't automatically set up a gateway on its network to the Internet for you, you can enter the associated gateway IP address here.

DNS   If your ISP doesn't automatically set up its DNS servers for your connection, you can enter the associated DNS IP addresses here.

Login Script   If your ISP requires the use of a login script, you can enter the associated commands here.

Execute This allows you to set up programs or commands to run at different stages of the connection process.

Accounting If you have to pay for local telephone access on a per-minute basis, you can enter the associated accounting rules here.

Once everything you need is configured, click OK to return to the kppp Configuration window, shown in Figure 14.8.

NOTE

In many countries, local calls are charged by the minute, which creates different requirements for Internet access.

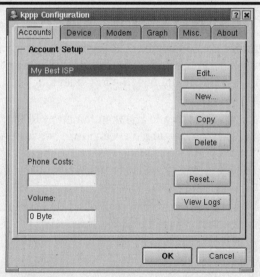

FIGURE 14.8: KPPP configuration options

If you have trouble with your modem setup, come back to this window. A number of helpful tools are available under the various tabs shown:

Accounts Besides showing the name of your ISP account, this tab lets you get to the log files, which often contain useful messages to help you identify whatever problems may arise.

Device Sets up the hardware parameters associated with your modem.

Part iii

Modem   Enables you to test or monitor the modem in various ways.

Misc   Determines the behavior of the PPP daemon when you connect, disconnect, or shut down the X Window.

If you need to enable access by regular users, you can set up suid permissions, which allow all regular users to run either program without giving everyone full access. When you change the permissions on the /usr/sbin/kppp file as follows:

```
# chmod u+s /usr/sbin/kppp
```

all regular users can then run the associated command, /usr/sbin/kppp, to access this utility.

MANUAL PPP CONNECTIONS

The RP3 and KPPP utilities are enough for most users. But if you have problems or want to understand the inner workings of PPP connections in Linux, it is important to understand how the PPP daemon (pppd) and other connection utilities work.

In Linux, the PPP connection is made and maintained by PPPD. But PPPD assumes that a connection has already been made between your modem and your ISP's modem, that all the necessary logging in has taken place, and that the ISP's system is also trying to establish a PPP connection on top of the same modem connection.

This sounds like a lot of conditions, but it really isn't that bad. On almost every ISP, the connection process goes like this:

1.   The modem connection is made.

2.   The login process occurs.

3.   Once the user is authenticated, the ISP begins to try to make a PPP connection by sending the IP address of the client to the client system.

The PPPD program requires steps 1 and 2 to have occurred before step 3 gets under way.

Given this process, it is necessary to make a modem connection to the ISP before attempting to run PPPD. Once the connection is made, the PPP connection can be established with PPPD.

Making a PPP Connection

Fortunately, the PPPD software is designed to bring things together and work with the chat program to handle the entire connection process. Before attempting to connect, you need to gather some information:

▶ Are you assigned an IP address each time you connect, or do you have a permanently assigned IP address? Because most ISPs work on the basis of assigning a dynamic IP address with each connection, you will also work on this basis.

▶ How do you log in to your ISP? One option uses plain-text prompt-and-response logins; another uses a special authentication protocol called Password Authentication Protocol (PAP). A few use another authentication protocol known as Challenge Handshake Authentication Protocol (CHAP). If you attempt to dial in to your ISP with Minicom or other terminal software and are presented with a login prompt of some sort, then you are logging in with plain-text prompts. If you see random characters or no characters at all after connecting, then you are probably using PAP or CHAP authentication.

NOTE

All the examples in this section assume that you are working as the root user on your machine. Because the process of connecting via PPP requires manipulation of interfaces and creation and deletion of network routes, the configuration programs involved need to be run by the root user.

TIP

Information on permanent IP addresses as well as authentication protocols can also help you configure RP3 or KPPP. Talk to your ISP if you aren't sure about or don't already have this information.

Connecting with Plain-Text Prompts

Let's start with plain-text prompts because they are a little easier to work with.

Because PPPD by itself can take control of your modem device but cannot perform the actual dialing or logging in, you need a way to issue commands to the modem and provide the necessary login information.

Part iii

This is achieved with the chat program. The chat program allows you to create a conversational exchange.

For instance, the normal dialing process on a modem is to run a terminal editor and, in an empty terminal window, type a dial command such as **ATDT555-7757**. The response to this is usually a connect string such as CONNECT 115200, to which the user doesn't respond.

NOTE

If you expect a response to an ATDT command, connect your modem. Substitute the number of an ISP or other server that can handle terminal connections for 555-7757.

This exchange can be turned into a simple chat script:

```
"" ATDT555-7757 CONNECT ""
```

This script is made up of two *expect-send pairs*: "" ATDT555-7757 and CONNECT "". An expect-send pair contains two pieces of information separated by a space. In the first pair, chat is told to expect nothing (the first pair of double quotes) and in response to send back the string ATDT555-7757. In other words, as soon as the script starts processing, the ATDT command dials the selected number. Next, the second pair is processed, and chat is told to expect the string CONNECT and in response to do nothing (the second pair of double quotes). If this were the complete script, chat would finish at this point and exit.

Of course, your chat script needs to be a bit longer. In order to complete your chat script, you need to find out exactly what your login session looks like. You can do this by logging in with regular terminal software such as Minicom.

Login prompts at most ISPs generally take this form:

```
Username:
Password:
```

or

```
Login:
Password:
```

or even

```
ogin:
ssword:
```

Use the first case as the example for this chapter. If you find that your login prompts are different, substitute accordingly as you work through the section.

NOTE

Instead of Login: and Password:, some ISPs are set up to send your computer ogin: or sername: and ssword: to accommodate different operating systems.

What is the next expect-send pair? After connecting, you are presented with a Username: prompt, in response to which you provide a username (let's say your username is testuser). The expect-send pair for this interaction would be Username: testuser.

Once a username is provided, you get a Password: prompt, to which you provide a password (let's assume this is testpassword). This produces the expect-send pair Password: testpassword.

For many ISPs this is sufficient, and PPP starts on the ISP's system after the correct password is entered. On a smaller number of systems, the ISP's computers present you with a command prompt at which you have to type a command to start PPP. In this case, you need to create an additional pair.

For this example, the complete chat script looks like this:

```
"" ATDT555-7757 CONNECT ""
Username: testuser Password: testpassword
```

To use this with the chat program (which normally is in /usr/sbin), you simply provide the script as an argument to chat:

```
/usr/sbin/chat "" ATDT555-7757 CONNECT ""
Username: testuser Password: testpassword
```

Note, however, that you don't want to type this at the command line and press Enter. Without being integrated with PPPD and provided access to the modem through that program, chat attempts to chat through the shell. You can use this to test your script, though. Simply type the command at the command prompt. When you see ATDT555-7757, type **CONNECT** and then type **Username:**. You should see *testuser* in response. Follow this by typing **Password:**, and you should see *testpassword* in response.

NOTE

If you need to work out problems with your chat script, try adding the -v flag to your chat command. This sends the output of the script to the system log, where you can analyze the results to find problems.

Once you have a working script, you need to integrate it with PPPD. You are going to use a handful of PPPD options to do this. (The PPPD application takes many additional options, which can be found in the PPPD man page.) The options you will use are the following:

connect   This option specifies a program or command used to establish a connection on the serial line being utilized. In this case, you use the connect option to specify the chat program and its script.

noipdefault   The default behavior of PPPD is to determine the IP address of the local machine on the basis of its hostname. If the ISP assigns a dynamic IP address, which is more common, then the noipdefault option is used to tell PPPD to get the IP address from the remote machine to which it is connecting.

defaultroute   This option tells PPPD to add a default route to the system's routing table, using the remote system (your ISP) as the default gateway. The entry is removed when the connection is broken.

The structure of the pppd command is

```
$ pppd device speed action chatcommands pppdoptions
```

If you are connecting with the device /dev/modem and the modem has a top compressed speed of 115,200bps (in this case, a 56Kbps modem), then you use the following command to connect with the chat script:

```
$ pppd /dev/modem 115200 connect '/usr/sbin/chat "" ATDT555-7757
  CONNECT     ""
Username: testuser Password: testpassword'
noipdefault defaultroute
```

When this command is issued, the modem should dial. After connecting, it will authenticate and establish a PPP connection. If this process is successful, two things should happen.

First, issuing the command /sbin/ifconfig with no flags or arguments should return a list of interfaces, including a PPP interface similar to this one:

```
ppp0        Link encap:Point-to-Point Protocol
            inet addr:194.209.60.101  P-t-P:194.209.60.97
Mask:255.255.255
            UP POINTOPOINT RUNNING  MTU:1500  Metric:1
            RX packets:10 errors:0 dropped:0 overruns:0
            TX packets:11 errors:0 dropped:0 overruns:0
```

Second, entries should be added to the routing table to create a default route through the remote machine (check for this using the /sbin/route command with no flags or arguments):

```
Kernel IP routing table
Destination  Gateway   Genmask          Flags Metric Ref   Use Iface
du1.paus.ch  *         255.255.255.255  UH    0      0       0 ppp0
default      du1.paus.ch 0              UG    0      0       0 ppp0
```

In this example, du1.paus.ch is the remote machine in the PPP connection and is serving as the default gateway.

Connecting with PAP Authentication

Connecting with PAP authentication follows the same basic principles as the text-prompt example you just worked through, except that the method of providing the username and password differs.

The first major difference is that you don't provide the username and password on the command line as part of a PAP script. Instead, you create entries in a special secrets file that is used during the PAP authentication process. In Red Hat Linux 7.1, this file is /etc/ppp/pap-secrets. By default, the permissions on this file make it readable and writeable only by the root user. Other users do not have read access to this file.

The format of entries in the secrets file is normally as follows:

```
username servername password
```

Since you connected to a server through a telephone modem, the second entry is not required. For instance, if you use the test username and password from the previous section, the entry might be this:

```
testuser * testpassword
```

Part iii

The * indicates that this password can be used for connections on any interface.

Once your username and password are in the file, you need to write a new chat script. For most ISPs, as soon as the modem connection is established, PAP authentication can begin. Therefore, your chat script gets simpler:

```
"" ATDT555-7757 CONNECT ""
```

This script dials the ISP and makes sure that a connect message is received before ending the chat program and proceeding on to authentication.

Finally, you need to introduce one more option for PPPD: user. The user option indicates which PAP user from the pap-secrets file is to be authenticated. The end result is the following pppd command:

```
$ pppd /dev/modem 57600 connect '/usr/sbin/chat "" ATDT555-
7757 CONNECT'
noipdefault defaultroute
user testuser
```

As with the earlier text-login example, you can check that everything is in order using ifconfig and route.

Once You Have a Connection

Once you have an Internet connection, you need to make sure that you can fully connect to the Internet. To do this, you need to verify that your DNS services are properly configured to point to your ISP's DNS server, also known as a *nameserver*.

This is done by editing two files: /etc/host.conf and /etc/resolv.conf. This section covers just the necessary basics of the files so that you can get online quickly.

The file /etc/host.conf should contain the following two lines:

```
order hosts,bind
multi on
```

Next, /etc/resolv.conf should contain at least two lines:

```
search
nameserver 100.100.100.100
```

In your case, replace the IP address 100.100.100.100 with the IP address of your ISP's nameserver. Your ISP can provide this information. If your ISP provides you with more than one nameserver, create a separate line for each one as follows:

```
search
nameserver 100.100.100.100
nameserver 200.200.200.200
```

Once this is done, you should be able to resolve names and thus access the Internet. You should also be able to run Internet software such as Netscape and FTP.

Hanging Up

When you have finished using the Internet, you should hang up to reduce phone costs and online charges. To do this, you need to kill the PPPD process.

You can find out the process ID of the PPPD program by using the ps command as the root user:

```
$ ps x | grep pppd
```

The entry for PPPD should look something like this:

```
1316  ttyS0 S    0:00 /usr/sbin/pppd /dev/modem 115200
connect    /usr/sbin/chat "" AT
```

The first number is the process ID. You can kill this process with the kill command:

```
$ kill 1316
```

When PPPD is killed, the modem should hang up.

AUTOMATING MANUAL INTERNET CONNECTIONS

While it is great to be able to establish PPP connections to the Internet, if you have to type the long pppd and chat commands each time you connect, the practicality of using Linux to connect to the Internet will be limited.

Part iii

To improve the situation, you can create two scripts: one for dialing and one for hanging up. These two scripts are going to be called dial and hangup. You will want to place these files in a directory on your path such as /usr/local/bin.

Because you haven't learned about scripting yet, these two scripts are presented here with a brief discussion so that you can get right down to using them. These scripts can be created in any text editor. It is important to make sure that lines that appear as one line here stay as one line in your files.

For the dial script, let's assume that the PAP example earlier in the chapter is the way you want to connect to the Internet.

Once you have created the scripts, you will want to make them executable with the chmod command:

```
$ chmod 700 dial hangup
```

The permission 700 makes the script readable, writeable, and executable by the root user and no one else. If you want to make the script usable by others in the same group as yours, substitute 750 for 700. If you want to make the script usable by anyone who accesses your Linux system, substitute 755 for 700.

TIP

You don't have to create these scripts from scratch. If you have the ppp rpm package installed, preconfigured scripts are available in Red Hat Linux 7.1 in the /usr/share/doc/ppp-2.4.0/scripts directory. For example, you can set up the ppp-on and ppp-off scripts like the dial and hangup scripts described in the following sections.

The *dial* Script

The dial script should look something like this:

```
#!/bin/sh
/usr/sbin/pppd /dev/modem 115200 connect \
'/usr/sbin/chat "" ATDT555-7757 CONNECT' \
noipdefault defaultroute user testuser
```

The first line tells Linux to process the script through the Bourne Shell, which is at /bin/sh. The other lines were covered earlier. Be sure to substitute the number of your ISP for 555-7757. If necessary, substitute your modem device file for /dev/modem and speed for 115200.

Notice that the pppd command is split across three lines. It is still one command. The backslashes at the ends of the first and second lines of this command indicate that the line breaks shouldn't be treated as line breaks and that the command continues on the next line of the file. This is done to make the script more readable.

The *hangup* Script

The hangup script should look like this:

```
#!/bin/sh
kill `cat /var/run/ppp0.pid`
```

As with the dial script, you start by specifying that the script should be processed with the Bourne Shell. Next, you kill the process in a slightly different way than you learned before.

You are relying on the fact that the PPPD process writes its process ID to a file that usually sits in /var/run on most modern Linux systems. The filename consists of the device name followed by a .pid extension. If you have only one modem and one PPP connection active at a time, you can assume that the device is ppp0 and type **/var/run/ppp0.pid** directly into your script.

The cat command simply displays the contents of the ppp0.pid file on the standard output. You put the cat command in back quotes to pass the result of the cat command (which is the process ID of the PPPD process) to the kill command.

NOTE
You can find the back quote under the tilde (~) in the upper-left corner of a standard U.S. keyboard.

But what happens if you have multiple PPP interfaces and want to be able to specify which one to hang up? A quick modification of the hangup script makes this possible:

```
#!/bin/sh
kill `cat /var/run/$1.pid`
```

Part III

Here, you have replaced ppp0 with $1. The $1 indicates that the value of the first argument to the script should be placed in this location. Now you can pass the interface name to the script as an argument. The command

```
$ hangup ppp1
```

hangs up the modem that is being used for the ppp1 interface. Remember, the first modem is on ppp0, so you may need to run the hangup ppp0 command instead.

WHAT'S NEXT?

In this chapter, you took a big step. You brought your Linux system from the isolation of a lone computer on a desktop and connected it to the world with a PPP connection.

The next part of this book covers Linux security. It starts off with an overview of security terms, technologies, and important issues to consider when developing your own security plan.

PART iV

SECURITY

Chapter 15

UNDERSTANDING LINUX SECURITY

Information security has become a topic of increasing interest, not only in the Linux community but in all other areas of information technology. As potential threats materialize and become headline news, network and systems administrators are forced to wear other hats, as part-time police officers, as investigators and, in a few unfortunate instances, even as forensics experts. As the Internet continues to experience mind-boggling growth, fueled by the ubiquity of Linux servers, among other factors, so grows the number of published Linux vulnerabilities and the complexity of defending your network and Linux servers against malicious attacks and so-called benign intrusions.

Adapted from *Linux Security* by Ramón J. Hontañón
ISBN 0-7821-2741-X   512 pages $49.99

While the mission is a challenging one, it is by no means impossible. A Linux administrator has access to a wide variety of tools and techniques to protect against *most* types of intrusions. It is indeed true that there is no such thing as a completely secure system, but it is just as true that by increasing the security measures in your server network, you are making your system a much more difficult target. With the right implementation of these features, your chances of becoming a victim are going to decrease dramatically.

This is the first of three chapters that introduce some basic Linux security concepts.

An Information Security Primer

There is nothing mystical about information security. Rarely well understood and at times overly glorified, the concept of information security cuts across many other disciplines, including network and systems administration, programming, configuration management, and even documentation, auditing, and training. As a Linux server administrator, you will find that securing your network is an exercise in versatility. Very few corporations are large enough to justify the expense of having an information security expert on staff, yet practically any corporation would be adversely affected by even the most casual intrusion.

This section starts by defining a set of working terms commonly used when discussing information security. Then it moves on to define the process of information security, detailing each of the steps that make up this process.

Security Terminology

This discussion will use several terms that are often not well understood or that are open to interpretation. This section provides working definitions for these security-related concepts.

Bastion Host

While the general aim of securing your network is to keep unauthorized personnel out of your servers, there is an increasing need to allow public access to some of those servers. At the very least, you will be asked to maintain a public web and FTP server, and perhaps even a publicly available DNS server. A *bastion host* is one that should be publicly available enough that you don't feel comfortable placing it in the same segment as your private servers. It's a fortified host, hence the name. A bastion host is typically designed and maintained by systems administration staff members who are knowledgeable about the security issues involved in setting up public servers such as these.

Think of the bastion host as the mailbox in front of a house, next to the curb. It's available to anybody, but it is at a safe distance and it is physically separated from the house. You might also think of a bastion host as a scout in a military unit, securing the route ahead of the main group. Figure 15.1 shows the typical placement of a bastion host.

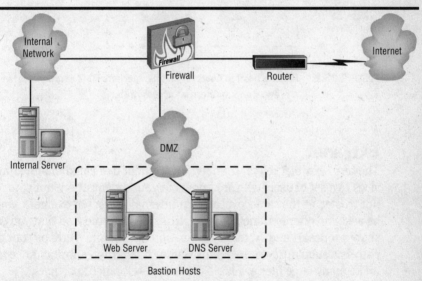

FIGURE 15.1: Placing bastion hosts on a dedicated firewall segment

Demilitarized Zone (DMZ)

You want to establish a network segment that is under your administrative control but physically separate from your protected network. This segment is referred to as a *demilitarized zone* (DMZ). The DMZ is typically a small network, comprising up to a half-dozen or so bastion hosts. Note that a DMZ is often connected to a separate network interface through a firewall, as shown in Figure 15.1. However, a DMZ can also be positioned as an intermediate segment between the firewall and the Internet access router. Figure 15.2 shows this configuration.

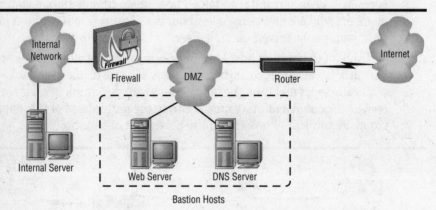

FIGURE 15.2:   Placing bastion hosts on an intermediate DMZ segment between a firewall and an Internet access router

Extranet

The term *extranet* refers to a network segment dedicated to providing services to a set of users who are known to your organization, but who are not trusted at the same level as your internal users. For example, you may be asked to offer extranet services to business partners so that you can share proposals and system-specification documents. Perhaps your company is a subcontractor in a multivendor integration effort and needs to make many large files available to other development partners.

Access to extranet servers often requires some form of authentication, although the appropriate access control measurements should be in place to ensure that extranet users do not gain access to internal network services. Note that it is perfectly acceptable to place extranet servers in the same DMZ segment as the more public bastion hosts. By doing this, you allow outside people access to the material they need to see, but they do not gain access to the internal information of the company that needs to be kept confidential. Figure 15.3 shows the placement of extranet hosts on a DMZ.

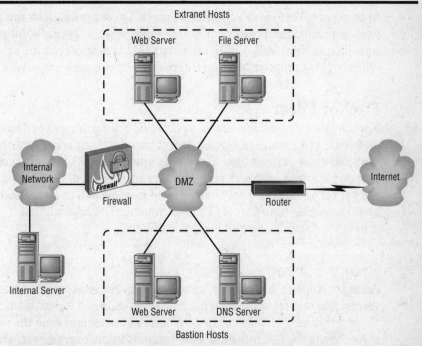

FIGURE 15.3:   Placing extranet hosts on a demilitarized zone (DMZ)

Firewall

In general, a *firewall* is a logical entity or physical device that controls public access to a private network. This is often accomplished by deploying a computing device with physical connections to both the private and public networks. This device can run either special-purpose software or a common operating system with the appropriate packages needed to support the firewall feature. While its primary purpose is to grant or deny network access into and out of the private network, a firewall can also log traffic statistics, authenticate users, and even detect intrusions by identifying suspicious use patterns. This is a very important part of securing your network.

Intranet

The term *intranet* means a private network. When we speak of an intranet, we're referring not only to the physical network segment, but also to a collection of servers (web, mail, multimedia) that are meant to be accessed exclusively by internal users. These are different and physically separated from the extranet and public servers. Typically, intranets include content that is confidential, data that is mission critical, or data that is appropriate only for internal use by company employees.

Packet Filter

Running on a firewall appliance, a *packet filter* program makes decisions on whether to forward or block a packet based on the packet's source, destination, or payload type. The most popular packet filters are those that operate at the network (IP) layer and act on a set of rules based on the packet's source and destination IP address, as well as on the source and destination transport (TCP) layer number. The original, first-generation firewalls were simple packet filters.

Proxy Server

Acting as a specialized type of firewall, a *proxy server* accepts Internet connection requests from internal network clients and forwards them to the target Internet host as if the originator of the request were the proxy server itself. The Internet host then responds to the proxy server, which then forwards the response to the appropriate internal network client. Proxy servers typically operate at the transport (TCP) layer and above and can be used for enforcing access rules, logging connection requests, and even for caching commonly accessed public content.

Security by Obscurity

Security by obscurity is the practice by which internal services are not protected from the public network, but their access is purposely obscured by cryptic addresses, resource identifiers, or both. For example, you may choose to make sensitive information available to your business partners using an anonymous FTP server, but you name the file with a leading period (.) so that the name does not show up on a regular directory listing. This is a questionable practice. Intruders are not easily deterred by obscurity, and automated scanning tools are especially good at finding this type of hidden information. Security by obscurity keeps only the least experienced hackers out of your system.

The Process of Information Security

How much effort you put into protecting your organization's resources is determined by how much it would negatively affect the operation of your organization to have those resources compromised. You need to decide what data *must* be secured and, if you have the resources, what data *should* be secured. You also need to know what the cost to the company will be if the network is cracked and the data is stolen or maliciously changed.

Some organizations' public Internet presence is meant to complement the information available through other means, and a compromise of this information would not have any serious consequences for its operation. For example, it would not be a good use of security resources to ensure the privacy of the transmission of weather data for a free Internet portal, or the integrity of a streaming video feed to a website displaying several traffic cameras.

However, we are in the Information Age, and an increasing number of companies are built exclusively on the integrity and availability of information that needs to be exchanged over the public network. Those organizations rely on their Internet-exchanged data as much as on their bricks-and-mortar presence. This includes online banks, investment and benefits management firms, and the overwhelming majority of business-to-business transactions conducted over the Internet. These enterprises must spare no expense to ensure that the data on their servers is always private and available, and that the integrity of its data is beyond reproach.

Security is not a product. It is not software, and it is also not simply an excuse for a consulting engagement. It is a discipline that needs to be taken into consideration in any decision that you make as a network and systems administrator. Security does not start or stop. You cannot install security, and you can't even buy security. Security is training, documentation, design decisions, and appropriate implementations. The most important aspect of security is monitoring and honing your security policies as needed.

The fundamental steps in the process of information security are described in the next subsection.

Security Policy Development

A security policy is your master document, your mission statement, and the ultimate source that tells the rest of your co-workers *what* you're

protecting and *how* you intend to protect it. While some companies might hire an outside consultant to draft this policy, this often lands in the lap of the network administrator. There are several good online sources for help on this topic:

- The Internet Engineering Task Force's (IETF's) *Site Security Handbook* (RFC 1244) is a comprehensive guide to security policy and procedure development.

- Purdue University's COAST Project offers a number of sample real-life security policies at `ftp://coast.cs.purdue.edu/pub/doc/policy`.

- A good website with general security policy information is `www.sans.org/newlook/resources/policies/policies.htm`.

The basic building blocks of a security policy are as follows:

Version   The revision number and date of the policy.

Introduction   Briefly describes the company's history, its purpose, and its mission, including references to the company's current Internet service provider (ISP), and the provider of any managed or outsourced security applications and mechanisms, such as firewalls, virtual private networks (VPNs), or content filters.

Network Diagram   Shows the basic building blocks of both the intranet and the extranet (if any). Make sure that the diagram clearly shows the border where the internal network connects to the Internet service provider's edge router.

Physical Security   Defines the areas that are off-limits for general employees and the roles and identities of employees who are allowed to enter them. This should include physical specifications for server platforms, such as front panel configuration, power connections, UPS systems, and console access. This section should also address the type of access control used to enter data centers and network closets.

WARNING

It is critically important to restrict unauthorized and inexperienced people from gaining access to the data center or server room. To do otherwise is to invite damaging and expensive accidents or sabotage.

Intranet and Extranet Services   Services allowed *in* and *out* of the intranet/extranet, including service type, source, destination, time of day, and user authentication. Include allowable content for electronic mail exchanges, as well as for HTTP and FTP downloads.

TIP

You may want to know the ports for the services you would like to allow and the ports for the services you do not want to allow here, so that you can reference them later on.

Remote Access   Special restrictions for remote users (via dial-up or dedicated VPN) who gain access to the Intranet using dial-up or encryption clients from the Internet.

Firewall Configuration   Detailed configuration reference of your perimeter defense devices, including access control rules, logging facilities, and authentication methods.

User Account Policy   User account creation and maintenance policy, including choice of usernames, password expiration/termination rules, and disk and process quotas.

Data Use Policy   This section should cover the types of user and data files on the server and how they should be handled. It should include initial permissions, access control, and group creation criteria.

Auditing, Monitoring, and Enforcement   A security policy is useless if it's not actually enforced. In this section, you should clearly define the tools and methodology you'll employ to monitor servers and network resources to ensure that the policy is being followed. Be sure to clearly include the types of punitive or corrective actions to be imposed on violators.

NOTE

You must follow through on the auditing part of the policy document; otherwise it is pointless to create it. It may sound obvious, but you cannot have a secure network if you are not monitoring it for security.

Official Assent   This is the section where you clearly state who is directly responsible for the writing and continued enforcement of the policy. It should include signatures from IT officers, corporate counsel, and the developer or developers of the policy itself. Be sure to date the signatures.

Even the most clear, concise, and complete security policy will be ineffective if it is not accessible to employees. Be sure to include a hard copy of this policy with the new employee orientation packet, and remind your employees periodically of its location online so they can consult it as it evolves. In addition, conduct periodic training sessions on its use and compliance, and set up a mechanism by which users and IT staffers alike can submit suggestions for improvement.

Security Mechanism Implementation

Once you have agreed upon a security policy, it's time to implement the mechanisms necessary to enforce it. This is often a combination of system configuration changes, tool installation, user procedure development, and monitoring. To implement mechanisms for the policy outline used in the previous section, you need to perform the following tasks:

Physical Security   Install UPS devices, combination locks, and physical environment alarms in the data center if they are not already provided for you. Configure Linux servers so root access is allowed only at the console.

Intranet and Extranet Services   Install and configure a perimeter defense device (firewall, router with access lists, and so forth) to enforce restrictions on extranet and intranet services.

Remote Access   Install and configure a virtual private network endpoint and/or a network device to support strong remote authentication and authorization.

User Account Policy   Configure the /etc/login.defs configuration file to force users to change their passwords periodically. I recommend that you set PASS_MAX_DAYS to a maximum of 90, which forces your users to change passwords every three months. This amount of time keeps users on their toes and reminds them that the password is a very important part of network security, even though changing it every 90 days may be viewed as a hassle. Write a script that periodically executes the `last` and `finger` commands to find out how long users have been inactive and inserts an asterisk (*) in their /etc/passwd entries if appropriate. In addition, you should train your users in the art of choosing a good, unpredictable password, one that includes alphanumeric characters and is not related to the user's environment, such as the name of his spouse, the street he lives on, or the car he drives.

Data Use Policy Use the right global `umask` permissions for initial file creation and execute a script periodically to ensure that you have no rogue `setuid/setgid` executables. (See Chapter 16, "System Installation and Setup," for a full discussion of system security configuration and monitoring.)

Auditing, Monitoring, and Enforcement Install an auditing and monitoring tool such as Satan, COPS, or PortSentry and use it periodically to ensure that your network defenses still comply with your security policy.

Periodic Policy Editing and Security Auditing

Much like the Internet, your network is probably changing all the time. Make sure you review your security policy to ensure that it still reflects the needs of your network. Have you added any new servers recently? Has your user population grown substantially as a result of your company's latest merger? Has there been a recent round of layoffs, with a lot of disgruntled employees leaving? Even if your network hasn't changed significantly, you need to play the part of an intruder and try to break into your server from the outside. Make sure you're a step ahead of the real bad guys, who are constantly trying to do the same thing.

An area of your security policy that deserves special attention is remote access. With the recent advent of VPN technology, it is easier than ever to provide universal access to traveling users with a simple Point-to-Point Tunneling Protocol (PPTP) or Internet Protocol Security (IPSec) client installed on their laptops. It is important to realize the implications of allowing this type of access. While you used to be able to physically see the bounds of your network, remote access extends the perimeter of your intranet to places that you may not necessarily want to trust completely. You may want to retool your security policy to include restrictions on such areas as the following:

- ▶ Version of the IPSec/PPTP client to use.

- ▶ Timeout setting of the client. A user who has been idle for 15 minutes typically does not mind re-establishing the remote connection.

- ▶ Type of authentication used. Username/password is no longer enough for secure remote access.

- ▶ Type of screensaver and idle timeout length. Demand the use of screensavers that password-lock after the idle timeout is reached.

The Goals of Information Security

You can map all the security needs for your Linux server into one of four basic goals:

- ▶ Data confidentiality
- ▶ Data integrity
- ▶ User authentication and access control
- ▶ Data and service availability

The ultimate purpose of your security policy, tool and policy implementation, and configuration management is to address each of these goals. The following sections examine each goal in more detail.

Data Confidentiality

In this increasingly public world, maintaining the confidentiality of the data in your Linux servers is a full-time task of its own. Because your users rely on network servers for more aspects of their everyday work routines, they also trust more confidential and private information to these services. The advent of cryptography has provided the Linux systems administrator with an invaluable tool to ensure confidentiality by enabling users to encrypt sensitive data stored on the servers. Linux supports both private-key and public-key encryption, the two primary types of encryption.

Private-Key Encryption

Also referred to as *symmetric-key* encryption, private-key encryption allows users to select a secret key that can then be used to seed an algorithm that converts the sensitive data (plaintext) into scrambled, or encrypted, data (cyphertext). This process is reversible, so the same user can then decrypt the cyphertext into the original plaintext, provided that he can produce the original encrypting key. The longer the key, the harder it is for an attacker to derive the plaintext from the cyphertext.

The *de facto* standard for private-key encryption is the Data Encryption Standard (DES), developed by IBM for use by the U.S. government in 1977. Although its 56-bit key was believed to be more than adequate at the time, the DES algorithm has been cracked several times. This has prompted the National Institutes for Standards and Technology (NIST) to coordinate the development of the next-generation DES, called AES (Advanced Encryption Standard), which uses much longer key lengths and is substantially more robust.

There are several Linux security applications that make use of private-key encryption, including the Kerberos suite of authentication tools.

Public-Key Encryption

Although private-key encryption is an effective way to protect sensitive data, it lacks the versatility necessary to protect data exchanges between two parties, especially when those two parties have no prior knowledge of each other. This led Martin Hellman and Whitfield Diffie to develop the concept of public-key encryption, announced in their landmark 1976 paper, "New Directions in Cryptography," *IEEE Transactions on Information Theory*. The idea is surprisingly simple: The sender encrypts a message with the well-known public key of the receiver. The receiver (and nobody else) can then decrypt the message into the original plaintext. This ensures confidentiality of the message without the need for sender and receiver to share a common private key. Not surprisingly, public-key encryption is a common technique used to protect the content of electronic mail messages as they travel over the Internet.

Part iv

The Linux-supported Pretty Good Privacy (PGP) package and its open-source equivalent, GNU Privacy Guard (GPG), offer two examples of public-key–driven security applications.

Data Integrity

Once an attacker has gained access to your information as it is being transmitted over the Internet, he can do any of the following:

- ▶ Use the content for nefarious purposes, such as extortion or competitive advantage.

- ▶ Modify the content before it reaches its intended destination.

- ▶ Destroy the data altogether.

Preserving the integrity of the data as it travels via the Internet is often a priority even when confidentiality is not. For example, consider a web-driven service through which your customers can download security patches to your company's software products. Although the patches themselves can be downloaded in the clear, it is critical that the customer be assured that the patch has not been maliciously modified.

Once again, cryptography comes to the rescue. By using *digital signatures* attached to the patch distribution, your users can verify the validity of the software that they're about to install. Before making the patch available, the digital signature tool obtains a *digest*, a summary of the data that composes the patch. You then sign this digest with your private key and make your public key available to your users. They can then reverse the process by verifying the signature of the digest using your public key. If a single bit has been modified during transmission, the signature fails verification and your users know that tampering has occurred.

A popular application of data integrity checking in Linux systems security is found in the Tripwire suite of file integrity tools.

User Authentication and Access Control

The need for authentication is as old as mankind itself. As long as there have been groups with different rights and privileges, people have been required to authenticate themselves as legitimate members of those groups. The most basic form of authentication is visual inspection (you look like the Alice I know, therefore, you must be Alice). A slightly more sophisticated form of authentication relies on the subject's possession of a token that is unique to the subject's identity and that only the subject should be able to produce (for example, a secret word or a driver's license). In Internet terms, this translates to simple username/password authentication, which remains the primary means of online authentication.

However, there are two fundamental vulnerabilities inherent in this type of authentication:

▶ People tend to choose easy-to-guess passwords when they're forced to memorize them, and they tend to write them down when they're forced to choose good passwords.

▶ Passwords are easy to sniff. Every time a password is used, it is sent out over the network, typically in the clear, which exposes it to a malicious intruder who is simply monitoring the public medium.

▶ To address the first vulnerability, you should make use of the npasswd utility, which forces users to choose good passwords. You should also use the crack tool, which attempts to guess poor passwords that your users may have chosen. To protect passwords from being sniffed, you must ensure that all remote access takes place either via Secure Shell (SSH) or using one-time passwords through an S/KEY login session.

The advent of e-commerce on the Internet has brought about the need for a way to authenticate truly anonymous parties—those who are totally unknown prior to the transaction. Public-key cryptography once again provides a solution to this problem. By using certificates carrying the digital signature of a well-known *certificate authority* (CA), anonymous parties can be authenticated based on the transitive nature of trust in the CA. That is, if I trust the CA and the CA can vouch for the fact that this person is whom he claims to be, then I should believe it.

The Linux implementation of *Secure Sockets Layer* (SSL) includes the tools necessary to implement a simple *Public Key Infrastructure* (PKI) that you can use to provide strong authentication of anonymous subjects.

Data and Service Availability

It has been said that, in the age of networking and wireless communications, the only truly secure system is a brick—nothing goes in and

nothing comes out. While this may be true, Linux administrators don't have the luxury of taking this radical approach. In fact, the performance of most systems administrators is often measured by their ability to keep the systems always up and accessible from the public network. There are obvious reasons why you would want to make sure that your Linux servers are up all the time (your corporation does want to make a profit, right?), but there are more subtle reasons why high availability is important to information security.

Chances are that your users rely on your online systems for authentication and private communication of sensitive data. In the absence of these systems—that is, if they're not available—users are likely to use less-secure methods to transmit and store data, which often results in compromising the company's security policy. For example, consider a user who needs to send an encrypted proposal to the legal department in the next five minutes. If the PGP key server is down and the user is faced with a substantial delay, the user is more likely to send the document unencrypted rather than face a potential loss of an important sale.

The next section examines the types of vulnerabilities that are often found in Linux servers, including a specific type of vulnerability that can open the door to *Denial of Service* attacks, which aim to disrupt the availability of your Linux server.

LINUX SECURITY

Linux is no more susceptible to attacks than any other Unix variant. Because Linux is an open-source product, it's up to the development and user communities to ensure that whenever a vulnerability is found, it is made public and a fix is made available in a timely manner. Linux has an outstanding track record in this regard. This, along with the constant scrutiny to which the source code is subject every day, makes Linux an excellent platform for the security-conscious systems administrator.

Even so, the cold reality is that no matter how diligently you go about securing your Linux server, chances are that you're going to get attacked. The following sections dig into the character of the typical malicious attacker and provide a comprehensive list of the types of attacks you're likely to be subject to, as well as the consequences of each one. We'll also look at ways you can protect your server installation from these attacks.

Types of Attackers

Just as there are varying types of security incidents, there is also a variety of perpetrator types. Although they come from all sorts of backgrounds, there are four broad groups that can be used to typify the attacker population as a whole. Let's take a closer look at each of these categories.

Joyriders

Often high school or college students, joyriders have time on their hands. They choose their victims at random, and they have no reason to focus on a specific target other than easy availability. Joyriders get discouraged relatively easy, don't use confidential information, and are not likely to tamper with its integrity. Joyriders confide the details of a successful attack only to their friends.

You can protect yourself from joyriders by making sure your Linux server is not subject to any obvious vulnerability and by keeping up with the security patches available for your distribution of Linux. The joyrider is the easiest attacker to defend against.

Cult Members

The Internet has proven to be fertile ground for semi-organized groups that share a common interest in orchestrating network attacks. These groups often conduct themselves as cults, use cryptic names for their members, and communicate through a characteristic jargon that is often hard for the uninitiated to decipher. The most prevalent cults embrace particular sociopolitical causes and pick their victims from those whom they perceive to be the enemy of such causes. Not surprisingly, a number of federal government websites have been the target of these cults, who typically deface the site to include a carefully worded protest message.

Cult members are not as easily deterred as joyriders and share a common pool of skills and resources that makes them challenging to defend against. If your company or agency could be the target of a political movement, you should take extraordinary steps to ensure that your hosts, especially your web and file servers, are protected against defacing and content modification.

Part iv

Spies

Unlike joyriders and cult members, corporate spies target their victims very carefully and often gather information about the target for a long period of time before orchestrating the attack. The attack of choice is usually unlawful intrusion into confidential resources for financial or political gain. Spies are very well financed, and they often have an impressive array of skills and resources available. They aim to be as stealthy as possible and will attempt to cover their tracks after a successful break-in.

You should protect your servers against spies by guarding your confidential data with access control as well as intrusion-detection mechanisms. You should also offer decoys (false confidential information) to keep the spies guessing which file contains the real information. This is similar to the presidential motorcade with four identical black limousines, only one of which actually contains the president.

Insiders

Attacks by insiders are by far the hardest attacks to counter because the potential attackers already possess a wealth of information about the target. Insiders do not have to jump through any hoops to gain access to the Linux server. The only challenge for them is to bypass the basic system security mechanisms that keep them from accessing someone else's information.

Not only is this type of attack hard to prevent, but it's also hard to detect once it has taken place. Chapter 16 offers a great amount of detail on how to make sure that users stay within their bounds and that permissions and access controls are not violated.

Common Attacks against Linux Servers

So now you know *whom* you should be defending against, but *what* is it exactly that you need to be afraid of? You've heard of the most newsworthy security incidents, such as the defacing of the U.S. Department of Justice's website or the widespread disruption of service at E*TRADE and others. But how exactly do they do that? It pays off to dig deep below the headlines and find out exactly how attackers can exploit Linux vulnerabilities in order to wreak havoc on our servers.

The following is a fairly comprehensive list of the types of attacks seen on Linux servers in the last five years.

Web Server Attacks

As the most popular service offered on the Internet today, the HTTP server has become the most vulnerable daemon running on a Linux server today. Note that I'm not implying that web servers are fundamentally weak. It's a simple case of exposure; as the most common service, a web server is also the most frequently attacked. In addition, web servers use a complex set of configuration parameters and are prone to subtle configuration errors, which makes them even more vulnerable. Web server attacks on Linux hosts fall under two categories: common gateway interface (CGI) script intrusions and buffer overflows, as described in the following sections.

CGI Script Intrusions   The `cgi-bin` directory houses executable scripts that can be invoked from the server on behalf of a user. There is nothing inherently insecure about the way web servers handle these scripts, but the fact that you're allowing remote users to execute code in the local server is, by itself, dangerous. When misconfigured, certain web servers even allow remote users to execute these scripts with `root` permissions, which can be used by attackers to grant themselves access to the system via other means at a later time. A recent attack managed simply to gain read-only access to the CGI scripts. Although this sounds like an innocent intrusion, in reality users often keep passwords and other sensitive data hard-coded in the CGI scripts, so the attacker managed to gain access to the system using this information.

In general, you can prevent CGI script intrusions by configuring the web server to prevent the execution of CGI scripts in random locations. You should train your users in proper programming techniques and provide them with plenty of secure sample CGI script code that they can use.

Buffer Overflows   Although buffer overflows have been around since the genesis of the Internet (remember Robert Morris' worm in 1988?), they have become more prevalent with the advent of the World Wide Web and, more important, web browsers. By entering an unusually large URL containing actual computer code, the attacker causes the data structure that was meant to hold the URL to overflow, thereby invading the portion of memory where the actual web server instructions are and replacing them with the instructions included in the URL. This allows the attacker to execute random code with the same permissions as the web server itself.

Make sure that your web server is not being executed with root permissions. Instead, most Linux web servers start as root (so they can listen on TCP port 80, which is a privileged port), but then fork a nonprivileged child process to provide the actual web service. Most servers use the username nobody for this purpose.

root Compromises

This is one of the most devastating attacks on a Linux server and one of the most common. The intruder manages to gain root privileges by using one of the following approaches:

- ▸ Sniffing the root password
- ▸ Guessing the root password
- ▸ Browsing through system logs looking for accidental appearances of the root password
- ▸ Staging a buffer overflow attack on a vulnerable application to gain root access

It's hard to ensure that the root password is kept under lock and key, so you should simply disable root logins, except perhaps on the system console in the data center (see the discussion in the section "Physical Security," later in this chapter). Instead of logging on as root to do administrative work, use the sudo command that allows regular users to assume root privileges temporarily. Chapter 16 discusses sudo and other system security commands.

TIP

It is a good idea to change the root password often and make sure it is not easy to guess. Using a string of random uppercase and lowercase letters with a few numbers thrown in, such as 1RGrh954E45ejh, will make it very hard for someone to hack the root password.

Denial of Service (DoS) Attacks

Denial-of-Service (DoS) attacks have received global attention in the media lately due to the increasing incidence of attacks on high-profile websites. The aim of such attacks is not to steal or modify any private server content, but rather to disabled a public server that offers public content. The preferred method of bringing down a Linux server is to over-whelm it with a large amount of fabricated traffic. A variation on the plain DoS attack is the *distributed DoS* (DDoS) attack, in which a large number of traffic sources are used to generate this bogus traffic. These sources are often hijacked systems belonging to unsuspecting users.

Examples of DoS attacks include the following:

The Teardrop Attack   The attacker floods the victim with a large number of improperly fragmented IP packets.

The Synflood Attack   The attacker opens a large number of TCP connections until the victim's network buffers, which are tied up waiting for the connection to complete, become unavailable.

While there is little that you can do to protect your Linux server from a new DDoS attack, you can prevent it from being hijacked and becoming one of the attackers. By implementing *egress filters* in your Internet routers, you can make sure that the traffic that leaves your network does not have a source address outside of the subnets that make up your private network.

Address Spoofing

This is the attack of choice for packet-filter firewalls. These types of filters are typically configured to ensure that only private—that is, known—addresses are allowed to initiate connections through the device. It is then relatively easy for attackers to forge their source IP addresses to appear as if they were coming from the inside. Although the return packets will not be forwarded to the attackers (they are pretending to have an internal address, and that's where the response will go), attackers can do plenty of damage by sending packets in the blind. In fact, the point of the attack is usually to set up a root compromise or buffer overflow that allows attackers to open up a back door that they can use to access the system later.

To combat IP address spoofing, you should set up *ingress filters* on your packet-filtering device. This ensures that you do not accept packets coming in through the public interface of your firewall with a source that falls within your block of internal addresses. However, this defense is a stopgap tactic at best. The real solution is to avoid using address authentication (packet filtering) and rely on cryptographic authentication instead, such as SSH.

Session Hijacking

In this specialized form of address spoofing, a TCP session hijacker observes the sequence of numbers in a TCP conversation and impersonates one of the participants by providing the other party with the expected sequence number. The attacker stages a DoS attack on the impersonated party in order to prevent it from continuing to take part in the conversation. When successful, the attacker can issue commands on the remote host as if he were the impersonated party.

You should teach your users to recognize the symptoms of a hijacked session so that they can report these incidents. Most often, they should notice that one of their sessions is no longer responding, while other sessions that have been idle for some time are showing unsolicited command output. As with address spoofing, the real solution to the threat of session hijacking is to use an authentication method that is not based solely on IP addresses.

Eavesdropping

One of the most difficult challenges in the expansion of the Internet as a global medium is its public nature, as a result of which the privacy and reliability of communications are never guaranteed. It is surprisingly easy to sniff a network segment and fish for confidential information. In fact, the Linux revolution has exacerbated this problem, because even the most naive user can take advantage of Linux's capability to inspect every packet that it sees on the wire. Not only can intruders capture the payload of network packets flying by, but they can also capture password information that they can use to stage a root compromise of the unsuspecting server.

WARNING

You should never, under any circumstance, allow the root password of your Linux server to traverse the network unencrypted.

To protect your root password, you should:

▶ Disable root logins over the network.

▶ Disable Telnet, rsh, rlogin, and FTP.

▶ Only use Secure Shell (SSH) for interactive logins.

▶ Only use Secure Copy (SCP) to transfer files to and from the server.

In addition, you should make use of Linux's support for VPN technology, which uses strong cryptography to protect the entire conversation between your Linux server and any other host with which you need to exchange confidential information.

Trojan Horses

Everyone has downloaded seemingly useful free software from the Internet, only to find out that its features were largely exaggerated. However, an increasing number of Linux servers are being infected by software that performs a very different task from the one it advertises. These so-called *Trojan horses* are programs that, though disguised as harmless applications, open up a back door through which intruders can exploit the system, often with `root` privileges. The Trojan horse presents itself as a useful tool and is often partially functional, but even as it appears to serve its advertised purpose, it can cripple or destroy your server and often your entire network.

Trojan horses can be extremely difficult to detect. In fact, they are often disguised as security applications, so you can be shooting yourself in the foot while thinking you're improving the overall security of the server. A good example of this surfaced in January 1999, when it was discovered that a widely distributed version of TCP Wrappers was actually a Trojan horse. (See Chapter 17, "Network Services Configuration," for a detailed description of TCP Wrappers.) Although originally designed to monitor and filter Transport layer connections, the Trojan horse version of TCP Wrappers had been modified to provide `root` access to would-be intruders.

Another feature common to most Trojan horse programs is their ability to inform attackers of the intrusion, providing them enough detail about your system so that they can stage a successful attack. The Trojan TCP Wrappers was designed to send an e-mail to the intruder's address that includes information about the infected system and about the unsuspecting user who installed the program.

You can protect yourself against Trojan horses by following these simple recommendations:

- ▶ Download all your software from well-known Internet sites or well-published mirrors of these primary sites.

- ▶ Before you install the software, look for digital signatures or checksums to assure the integrity of downloaded package.

- ▶ Make as much standard software as possible available to your users (as long as your security policy allows it). Keep it up to date.

- ▶ Periodically monitor Trojan horse advisories from the CERT Coordination Center (www.cert.org).

In addition, you should conduct periodic scans of your server and look for suspicious network ports that are active or in LISTEN state. Listing 15.1 shows an execution of the netstat command that shows a server with a suspicious port (555) in LISTEN state. Note that the command has not been able to resolve port number 555 to a well-known number in the /etc/services file. This is an indication that the daemon is not a standard one and should be investigated further.

Listing 15.1: Execution of the *netstat* Command Showing a Suspicious Daemon Running on TCP Port 555

```
[ramon]$ netstat -a
Active Internet connections (servers and established)
Proto Recv-Q Send-Q Local Address        Foreign Address  State
tcp       0      0 *:555                  *:*              LISTEN
tcp       0      0 *:ssh                  *:*              LISTEN
tcp       0      0 *:ftp                  *:*              LISTEN
udp       0      0 *:snmp                 *:*
raw       0      0 *:icmp                 *:*              7
raw       0      0 *:tcp                  *:*              7
Active UNIX domain sockets (servers and established)
Proto RefCnt Flags     Type      State       I-Node Path
unix  0      [ ACC ]   STREAM    LISTENING   491    /dev/log
unix  1      [ ]       STREAM    CONNECTED   985    @0000003d
unix  1      [ ]       STREAM    CONNECTED   886    @00000039
unix  1      [ ]       STREAM    CONNECTED   959    @0000003c
unix  1      [ ]       STREAM    CONNECTED   554    @00000021
unix  1      [ ]       STREAM    CONNECTED   740    @00000035
unix  0      [ ]       STREAM    CONNECTED   117    @00000013
unix  1      [ ]       STREAM    CONNECTED   744    @00000036
unix  1      [ ]       STREAM    CONNECTED   986    /dev/log
unix  1      [ ]       STREAM    CONNECTED   960    /dev/log
unix  1      [ ]       STREAM    CONNECTED   887    /dev/log
unix  1      [ ]       STREAM    CONNECTED   745    /dev/log
unix  1      [ ]       STREAM    CONNECTED   741    /dev/log
unix  1      [ ]       STREAM    CONNECTED   588    /dev/log
```

Cryptanalysis and Brute Force Attacks

Most of the cryptographic algorithms in use today have proven to be robust enough to provide an appropriate level of confidentiality, integrity, and authentication. However, there have been several cases in which some of these algorithms have been found to be vulnerable to attacks or mathematical exploits and in which the keyspace (the average number of combinations before the algorithm can be cracked) has been proven to be much smaller than initially thought. (By "mathematical exploits," I mean those that take advantage of flaws in the functions used by the algorithm designers to derive prime numbers, generate keys, add entropy, and so on.)

In 1998, we saw a highly publicized case of cryptanalysis in which renowned security experts Bruce Schneier and "Mudge" discovered a number of security flaws in Microsoft's authentication algorithm for PPTP, a VPN protocol used in the Windows operating system. The MS-CHAP v.1 authentication algorithm was found to be vulnerable to password eavesdropping. In addition, the Microsoft Point-to-Point Encryption algorithm (MPPE) was also found to be much less effective than the 128-bit key strength that the vendor advertised, thereby exposing the user to eavesdropping attacks on the transmitted data. In 1999, Microsoft released MS-CHAP v.2 as an enhancement of the original version. However, a fundamental flaw still remains; the confidentiality of the VPN transmission is only as strong as the passwords that users choose for authentication.

There is a Linux version of PPTP that is fully interoperable with the Microsoft implementation and therefore is subject to the same password-guessing weakness.

This leads to our last type of attack: brute-force guessing of passwords and keys. As the computing power available to the average user increases at exponential rates, so does the potential for an intruder to guess your password or key. By employing a *brute force* approach, attackers use computing power to attempt to guess encryption keys until the correct one is found. These are also called *dictionary attacks*, because the attacker often uses a well-known dictionary to try to guess a password, based on the fact that most users tend to choose real words as their passwords.

The power of brute force attacks on cryptographic algorithms was best illustrated in the summer of 1998 when the Electronic Frontier Foundation (EFF) was able to crack the 56-bit key of the DES algorithm using a computer built for that purpose at a cost of $250,000. The feasibility of these types of attacks has raised the bar for cryptographic strength and has increased awareness of the limitations of even the strongest cryptography in use today.

Now that you've seen who the enemies are and have taken a peek at their weapons of choice, let's take a look at how you can orchestrate an appropriate defense, using some of the layers in the Open Systems Interconnection (OSI) model as a point of reference.

THE LAYERED APPROACH TO INFORMATION SECURITY

A lot of work has been devoted to adding security to the Linux kernel. There is now native kernel support for packet filtering, packet logging, masquerading, and even defense against Denial of Service attacks.

This goes a long way toward securing the system itself, but are you willing to let intruders get all the way into the portals of your servers? An effective security policy is one that starts at the core of the Linux server and keeps moving outward by including protection mechanisms outside of the system itself. Your defense should cover the network configuration of the server, the network applications that run on the server, the perimeter of the corporate network, and even the remote access clients used by road warriors to access corporate resources over the public Internet.

Let's take a closer look at the considerations that apply to each of these layers. Note that this discussion will work its way outward from the Linux kernel toward the Internet.

Physical Security

This is the most fundamental and often the most overlooked type of Linux server security. Physical security starts with the surroundings of the server itself. Is the room to the data center kept under lock and key? If so, who is allowed to enter the room? Are contractors and maintenance workers escorted? If you're building a new installation or moving into a new location, follow this simple set of guidelines when designing the physical layout of your data center:

▶ Install magnetic card readers to access the data center. Review the access logs periodically. Look for unusual patterns of access. Ask users for verification of their log entries.

▶ Escort maintenance workers and field technicians at all times while in the data center.

▶ Change the default passwords on terminal servers, remote control devices, and power distribution units. Create accounts for each administrator. Monitor their use.

▶ Choose Linux servers with a front panel lock to keep intruders from rebooting the machine and from inserting foreign media into the drives.

▶ Avoid using incoming phone lines to console ports unless it's strictly necessary. Use dial-back modems.

▶ Enable password-protected screensavers such as xlock and vlock on the X-displays of Linux servers.

▶ Install a good monitoring device that alerts a person in the event of excessive temperature, smoke, or humidity in the data center.

It's important to keep in mind that the main goal of physical security is to maintain high availability of your server installation. Make sure that your servers are not on the same electrical circuits as receptacles and appliances that are accessible from outside the data center. You would be surprised how much downtime I can create by sticking a screwdriver in an electric receptacle or light socket in the middle of a three-day weekend.

TIP

Providing redundant power supplies is the answer to a lot of these types of problems. If the servers support it, use it!

I don't recommend that you set BIOS and boot-loader passwords, because they will prevent the system from coming up from a reboot without human intervention. This could seriously jeopardize availability unless you have staff available to care for your servers 24/7.

System Security

The most fundamental security requirement of a Linux server is to guarantee that an active nonprivileged user cannot gain access to another user's protected resources or, more important, to areas of the system reserved for privileged system accounts. More subtle vulnerabilities

Part iv

include users' abilities to overextend their file quotas, CPU use, or maximum number of active processes. All these violations could constitute the seed of a DoS attack, which could render the system or some of its parts temporarily unavailable or even permanently disabled.

Network Security

Securing the system from the potential mischief of employees or users who are otherwise in good standing is a great step forward, but it only covers a system that is isolated from the outside world. This is clearly not a realistic prospect, since most Linux servers are deployed to serve the user population over a network that is often public. Thus, the diligent Linux administrator should carefully evaluate the server's physical connection to the network, including all its interfaces, their TCP/IP configurations and, most important, the configuration of the server's active network daemons.

Application Security

Some of the daemons that come standard in today's Linux distributions are actually full-fledged applications with a fairly complex set of configuration files. Unlike simple Telnet and FTP daemons, web, mail, and file servers use complex protocols. To protect these services, network administrators must deploy a security defense particular to each protocol.

Perimeter Security

The firewall is the workhorse of network security. Firewalls are a pivotal part of a complete security solution, protecting the perimeter of the local area network where it connects to the public Internet. Although the main purpose of a firewall is to keep unwanted traffic out of the local network, it is also where you can log all the traffic going into and out of the network. While most firewalls have two network interfaces, some have additional interfaces that you can use to attach bastion and extranet servers, whose access permissions are such that they need to be physically segregated from the local area network.

Remote Access and Authentication

Just about the time systems administrators managed to get a handle on network security, virtual private networks appeared on the scene, and administrators' jobs got a whole lot tougher. The network perimeter now extends to all the systems that connect to it remotely, at least for the duration of the dial-in session. VPN standards such as IPSec and PPTP provide a common framework for data privacy, but they do not completely address the issue of authentication, and they fail to cover the issue of authorization and access control.

Human Security

Regardless of how much time and energy you devote to developing a sound security strategy, people are ultimately at the controls, and they are often the weakest link in the information security chain. The most airtight of perimeter defenses can be rendered totally useless by an insider with an axe to grind, and the strongest password policy cannot cope with users who write their passwords on yellow sticky notes and paste them on their monitors.

Conducting security awareness training and monitoring security policy compliance are steps in the right direction, but as is often the case, there are many other less-tangible factors that contribute to the security of your server installation. Employees who are disgruntled or just bored present a considerable risk to your enterprise, especially those who have access to sensitive information that could be used by a competitor.

There is no substitute for a satisfied employee who is challenged by the work and rewarded for his effort. While ethics and behavior are difficult to monitor and enforce, it is just as effective to ensure employees' good morale and motivation. A yearly company picnic and a generous performance incentive bonus program could be your company's best investment in information security.

WARNING

If you have to fire a disgruntled employee, you or a member of the security staff should escort him out of the building and make sure that he is not permitted to touch any computer before he leaves. Even before you fire the person, you should have his access removed and passwords changed. Otherwise, you are inviting disaster.

WHAT'S NEXT?

Security is often a poorly understood topic. There is often too much emphasis on tools and not enough emphasis on procedures and methods. An efficient security defense should start with a comprehensive security policy upon which you can build an appropriate set of mechanisms. Remember that security is a process.

The goal of information security is to ensure confidentiality, integrity, authentication, and availability of the data on your servers. Cryptography is the only viable way to ensure that data is properly protected as it is exchanged over the Internet.

There is a diverse array of vulnerabilities and types of attacks that you need to be prepared to defend against. The only way to put up and maintain an effective defense is to start with the system and work your way out toward the perimeter, considering each layer separately. Don't forget to account for remote access to your Linux server.

We'll start the detailed discussion of this layered approach by taking a close look at system security in the next chapter.

Chapter 16

SYSTEM INSTALLATION AND SETUP

This chapter discusses the security implications of the following Linux server administration tasks:

- ▶ Choosing a Linux distribution
- ▶ Building a secure kernel
- ▶ User account security
- ▶ File and directory permissions
- ▶ Syslog security
- ▶ Filesystem encryption

Note that you will be taking on these tasks before you even connect your server to the network. Although most of us associate security with Network layer services, a number of important security issues must be decided during the setup and configuration of the system itself. This chapter guides you through the process of choosing the distribution that is best suited for your security needs and goes on to offer specific advice on how to configure your kernel to maximize system and network security.

Adapted from *Linux Security* by Ramón J. Hontañón
ISBN 0-7821-2741-X   512 pages $39.99

Finally, this chapter gives you practical advice on securing the accounts and the filesystem to ensure that you can offer your users an adequate level of protection against attacks from other legitimate—or seemingly legitimate—system users. You'll learn how to minimize the exposure of your root user, and you'll learn about the tools available to implement filesystem encryption on your Linux server.

Let's start by taking a look at the process of selecting a Linux distribution that's right for you.

Choosing a Linux Distribution

A crucial step in building a secure Linux server is selecting the distribution that best fits the needs outlined in your security policy. This decision is going to determine much of your success in installing and maintaining a secure Linux server. What exactly makes a distribution "secure"? Here is a set of criteria to consider before making that decision:

▶ Does the vendor have a well-known mechanism to report security vulnerabilities found in its distribution?

▶ Does the vendor issue periodic security advisories that warn users of vulnerabilities found in its distribution?

▶ How often are security issues resolved? Does the vendor devote a well-delineated portion of its website or FTP site to security information (patches, security updates, and so on)?

▶ How often does the vendor release general distribution upgrades? A slow-moving release schedule is likely to prolong the exposure of known vulnerabilities.

▶ Does the vendor offer an intuitive, easy-to-use tool for installing and updating software packages?

▶ Does the vendor support open-source efforts to improve Linux security or to create vendor-neutral security scripts and tools?

▶ How long has the vendor been in existence?

▶ Have the previous versions been secure and well maintained?

As with any other choice of Linux software, there is no clear winner here, but you can make a more educated decision by finding out the vendor's general stance in these areas. The following sections look at the most prominent Linux distributions and examine the security features of each one.

Red Hat

As the most successful Linux vendor to date, Red Hat has been able to devote considerable resources to the tracking, dissemination, and resolution of security flaws in the packages that it distributes. However, as of the writing of this book, Red Hat's website still lacks a separate security section where Linux administrators can see all of its security patches at a glance. That said, Red Hat seems to keep up to date on the security issues that come up in its versions.

The Red Hat Package Manager (RPM) system is the industry standard, and its release schedule calls for a major revision every six months or so, which ensures that you're always running recent (and often more secure) software packages. This schedule is a good compromise between having up-to-date software and avoiding the "bleeding edge" of the latest (and often unstable) versions of most tools.

Red Hat's numbering scheme seems to use the .0 minor number for an initial major release (such as 7.0) and .1 and .2 for subsequent maintenance updates. If you opt for Red Hat, you should try to upgrade up from a .0 release as soon as the update is available. You may want to wait for the 7.1 or later version to make sure that any critical bugs have been fixed in the previous version.

Caldera

Rivaling Red Hat's success, Caldera's OpenLinux has grown into a major player in the Linux distribution market. Unlike Red Hat, Caldera maintains separate release lines for clients (eDesktop) and servers (eServer). Both of these packages are now in a stable release line, although new versions are usually not available as often as Red Hat's.

Like Red Hat, Caldera offers a mechanism for updating releases by downloading the appropriate packages (also in RPM format) from its FTP site. Caldera seems to be increasingly committed to offering a security-minded distribution, and most vulnerabilities are addressed by software updates within one or two days of being identified.

Security advisories for OpenLinux can be found at www.calderasystems .com/support/security/ (see Figure 16.1). This is the longest-running resource of its kind, and it includes a chronological list of advisories for all OpenLinux packages and all the available patches or solutions.

Part iv

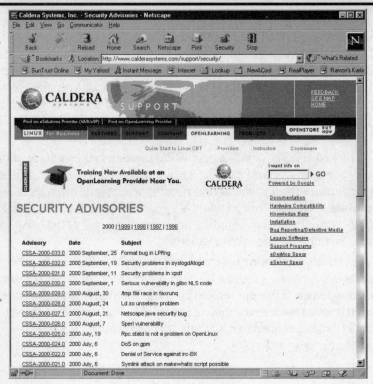

FIGURE 16.1:   OpenLinux security advisories

SuSE

An extremely popular distribution in the European market, SuSE offers a full-featured set of supported packages (six CDs worth) and also uses the RPM system. The release schedule is similar to Red Hat's, with the .0 minor numbers signaling the initial offering of a major release. However, it typically offers up to four minor releases (for example, 6.4) before moving on to another major version. Red Hat, on the other hand, generally has only two minor releases with each version.

One of SuSE's distinguishing characteristics is the inclusion of the seccheck script that can be periodically invoked from cron to test the overall security of the system in a number of areas. The vendor also includes a utility that you can use to "harden" your server installation (harden_suse). This is a sign that this vendor is concerned with security and is willing to spend development and maintenance resources to prove it.

You can find SuSE's security clearinghouse at www.suse.de/de/ support/security/ (see Figure 16.2), including a comprehensive list of advisories and pointers to its two security-related mailing lists.

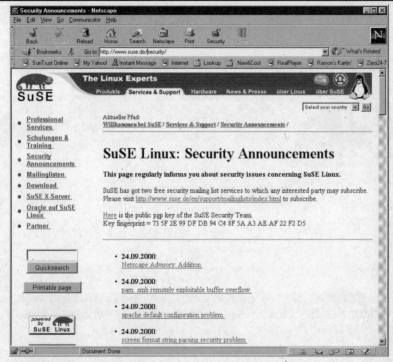

FIGURE 16.2:   SuSE security page on the World Wide Web

Turbolinux

Turbolinux has been in the Linux market since 1992 and has had a great deal of success in the Asian and European markets. Even though it has not been embraced as widely as Red Hat and Caldera in the U.S., it has gained a lot of momentum in recent months, especially in the high-end server application market.

The Turbolinux release schedule is significantly longer than Red Hat's and Caldera's, but it maintains a list of security updates for each release at www.turbolinux.com/security (see Figure 16.3). The vendor also includes a separate security subdirectory for each release update section in its FTP site.

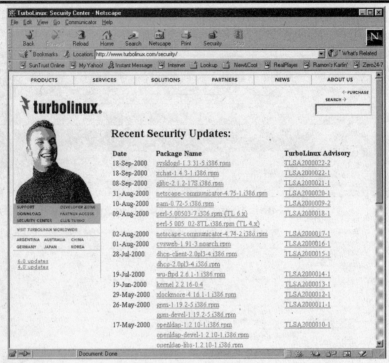

FIGURE 16.3:   Turbolinux Security Center page on the World Wide Web

Debian

This Linux distribution is maintained by a group of about 500 volunteer developers around the world. Because of its nonprofit nature, the release schedule for Debian's Linux distribution is different from most commercial vendors', focusing on small interim minor releases rather than major updates. These small releases are often driven by a number of security fixes and are usually about 100 days apart.

Unlike most commercial vendors, Debian has a clearinghouse for security information at www.debian.org/security/ that you can use (see Figure 16.4). This is one of the most straightforward vendor security sites available. The content is well organized, and the security advisories are easier to find than those of the other vendors. In addition, the page includes links to the archives of the Debian-specific security mailing list, going back at least two years.

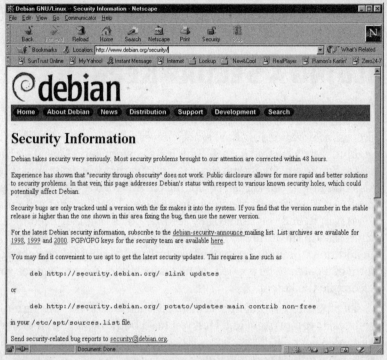

FIGURE 16.4: Debian's security page on the World Wide Web

And the Winner Is...

All Linux distributions can be made secure, and all vendors are making an effort to keep users informed of vulnerabilities and patch availability. Although each vendor seems to excel in a different aspect of security, there are no clear winners or losers.

Your choice of a Linux distribution should depend on your administration style. If you're willing to spend some time every few days catching up with the latest vulnerabilities and you're willing to install incremental patches as needed, Debian is a good choice for you. If instead you prefer to bundle security updates with vendor releases, you should opt for a more actively updated distribution, such as Red Hat, Caldera, SuSE, or Turbolinux.

Part iv

In either case, you should plan to use the security resources of your vendor of choice, including a daily scan through its web page and a subscription to its security mailing list. In addition, you should monitor the BugTraq mailing list (`www.securityfocus.com/forums/bugtraq/`) for vulnerabilities common to all Linux vendors.

BUILDING A SECURE KERNEL

Although most Linux users are content to run the standard kernel provided in the latest distribution, you'll need to become familiar with the process of downloading the kernel sources, modifying its configuration, and building a custom kernel. Building a custom kernel has its advantages: You're specifying the security options that you want, and you're also building a lean kernel, compiling only the driver support that you need. Another benefit of compiling your own kernel is that you know what is in it, and you can see any security holes that may need to be addressed in the future or immediately (if the holes are big enough). In addition, the solution to many security vulnerabilities comes in the form of a patch to be applied to the Linux kernel, which requires you to recompile the kernel.

The first step in building a custom kernel is to obtain the kernel sources. If you're using Red Hat, you need both the `kernel headers` and `kernel-source` RPM packages. To install either of those packages, use one of the following commands:

```
[root]# rpm -q kernel-headers
kernel-headers-2.2.12-20
[root]# rpm -q kernel-source
kernel-source-2.2.12-20
```

These two packages populate the `/usr/src/linux` directory, which should contain all the source and configuration files necessary to compile the Linux kernel from scratch.

TIP

Before you install your new kernel, create an emergency boot disk in case the new kernel has problems booting. On Red Hat, use the command: **mkbootdisk --device /dev/fd0 2.2.12-20** (assuming that your system modules directory is `/lib/modules/2.2.12-20`).

Logged on as `root`, go to the Linux source directory and clean up any lingering configurations from previous kernel builds using the following commands:

```
[root]# cd /usr/local/linux
[root]# make mrproper
```

At this point, you're ready to specify the options that you'd like to build into the kernel using this command:

```
[root]# make config
```

This command prompts you for a series of options that you can add to your kernel (Y), leave out (N), or add as a dynamically loaded module (M). Table 16.1 shows the 2.2.X kernel options that have security implications and should be set to the appropriate value during the make config step.

TABLE 16.1:   Kernel Configuration—Recommended Security Options

CONFIGURE OPTION	DESCRIPTION	RECOMMENDATION
CONFIG_PACKET	Protocol used by applications to communicate with network devices without the need for an intermediate kernel protocol	Y
CONFIG_NETLINK	Two-way communication between the kernel and user processes	Y
CONFIG_FIREWALL	Firewalling support	Y
CONFIG_INET	Internet (TCP/IP) protocols	Y
CONFIG_IP_FIREWALL	IP packet-filtering support	Y
CONFIG_SYN_COOKIES	Protection against synflooding Denial of Service attacks	Y
CONFIG_NET_IPIP	IP inside IP encapsulation	N
CONFIG_IP_ROUTER	IP routing	N
CONFIG_IP_FORWARD	IP packet forwarding (routing)	N
CONFIG_IP_MULTICAST	IP Multicast (transmission of one data stream for multiple destinations)	N

Part iv

The CONFIG_SYN_COOKIES option prevents the kernel from entering a deadlock state whenever its incoming connection buffers are filled with half-open TCP connections. Note that in the 2.2.X kernels, setting CONFIG_SYN_COOKIES simply enables the option but does not actually activate it. You must enter the following to activate SYN_COOKIES support:

```
[root]# echo 1 > /proc/sys/net/ipv4/tcp_syncookies
```

The CONFIG_IP_ROUTER and CONFIG_IP_FORWARD options allow a multihomed Linux server to forward packets from one interface to another. This option should be disabled because there is a possibility that an intruder could use your Linux server as a router, circumventing the normal path of entry into your network (the one you are policing).

The final step before actually compiling the kernel sources is to build a list of dependencies using this command:

```
[root]# make dep
```

Now you're ready to compile your new kernel. Execute the following command to compile and link a compressed kernel image:

```
[root]# make zImage
```

If you have chosen loadable module support during the previous make config step, you'll also need to execute the following commands:

```
[root]# make modules
[root]# make modules_install
```

To boot the new kernel, you must first move it from the source directory to its final destination. Make a backup of the old image first using these commands:

```
[root]# cp /zImage /zImage.BACKUP
[root]# mv /usr/src/linux/arch/i386/boot/zImage /zImage
[root]# /sbin/lilo
```

Rerun LILO every time you update the kernel image on your hard drive. In addition, it is a good idea to create a separate lilo.conf entry for your backup kernel (/zImage.BACKUP), even though you have an emergency boot disk, because planning for disasters is an important part of security. When you are updating your version of Linux, it is always good to be able to go back to the old version if the newer one does not work as it should. See *Linux Network Servers 24seven* by Craig Hunt (Sybex, 1999) if you need more information about LILO and lilo.conf.

You should now restart your system to make sure that you can boot the new kernel. Don't forget to have your emergency boot disk close by in case there are problems.

WARNING

Be prepared for the worst, because if you aren't prepared, the worst is going to happen to you.

USER ACCOUNT SECURITY

Year after year, the CSI/FBI Computer Crime and Security Survey (www.gocsi.com/prelea_000321.htm) shows that the overwhelming majority of successful system attacks come from insiders—that is, disgruntled (or just bored) nonprivileged users who manage to gain root authority through subversive means. Even when the attack comes from the outside, seizing a misconfigured or stagnant user account is one of the easiest ways to crack access to root. It's also important to protect against your own mistakes, since root access can be a powerful and dangerous tool, even in the proper hands.

You should pay special attention to the part of your security policy that regulates the creation and maintenance of user accounts. Here is my recommended set of considerations for managing your Linux server accounts:

> **Disable Inactive Accounts**   Attackers look for accounts that have not been accessed for a while in order to seize them for their nefarious ends. This gives attackers the luxury of being able to "squat" on the account and hide their exploits without being noticed or reported. Most Linux distributions allow you to specify the conditions under which an account should be disabled. I recommend that you disable all accounts as soon as the password expires (more on password expiration later), while allowing users a week to change their passwords before they expire. Red Hat's Linuxconf provides a graphical interface to specify this policy (see Figure 16.5).

> I usually set passwords to expire every four months (120 days) and allow users seven days to change their passwords. The 0 value under Account Expire After # Days simply directs the

system to disable the account if the password expires. The default value of −1 directs the system never to cause the account to expire, so make sure you change this default.

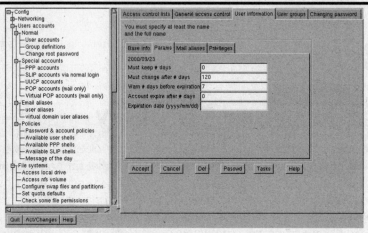

FIGURE 16.5: Setting user account expiration parameters with Linuxconf

Disable *root* Access across NFS Mounts   Pay special attention to the /etc/exports file, where you declare the local filesystems that you'd like to share via Network File System (NFS). By default, the NFS server on most Linux distributions maps user ID 0 (root) to a nonprivileged user, like nobody. However, this behavior can be overridden by the no_root_squash option in the NFS server's /etc/exports file. Avoid this option at all costs. It leaves your entire NFS server at the mercy of a root user on any of your clients.

See *Linux NFS and Automounter Administration* by Erez Zadok (Sybex, 2001) if you have set up your Linux clients to mount remote NFS shares automatically.

Restrict the Use of Your *root* User to When It's Absolutely Necessary   You should resist the temptation to log on as root to execute an administration command and then stay logged on to execute other user-level commands. The longer you're logged on as root, the longer you're exposed to a number of vulnerabilities, such as Trojan horses and session hijacking.

Use a Descriptive *root* Prompt   Sometimes you are your worst enemy. When you have several terminals active on your X-display, it's important to be able to tell at a glance which ones are root terminals. This helps you avoid executing a user-level command on a root window by mistake. Make sure the root prompt is distinctive enough and that it includes a root-specific character, such as a sharp sign (#).

Use a Minimal *$PATH* for Your *root* Account   A common attack on the root account is to place Trojan horse versions of frequently used utilities in a directory that is included in the root $PATH. This is a very subtle attack, and the only way to protect against it is to ensure that you know the contents of your $PATH variable and the contents of the directories included in the variable. To minimize the chance of running a Trojan horse, avoid having directories in your $PATH that are writeable by any user other than root.

Use Special-Purpose System Accounts   An operator who needs simply to shut down the system does not need full root privileges. That's the purpose of default Linux accounts such as operator and shutdown. In addition, I recommend that you install and use sudo, which is described in detail in the section "The Sudo Utility," later in this chapter.

Use Group Memberships   As a Linux administrator, you'll often be asked to make a file or directory available for reading and writing to several users who are collaborating on a single task. Although it is easy to simply make these resources world-writeable, don't do it. Take the time to add a new group, make each of the users a member of this group, and make the resources accessible only to members of the group. Think of files with wide-open permissions as vulnerabilities waiting to be exploited.

Restrict *root* Logins to the System Console   To monitor who is logging in as root, configure the /etc/securetty file to allow direct root access only from the console. This action forces authorized root users to use su or sudo to gain root privileges, thus allowing you to log these events easily. The standard Linux default is to allow root logins only from the eight virtual system consoles (function keys on the keyboard).

Part iv

```
[root]# more /etc/securetty
tty1
tty2
tty3
tty4
tty5
tty6
tty7
tty8
```

Aside from the logging advantage, this is an extra hurdle in the event that the root password becomes compromised. Intruders would have to first gain access to a regular user's account (or to the physical console) to exploit their finding.

Good user account practices are paramount to ensuring the security of your system, but by choosing a poor password, users can undermine all the work you have done to protect their accounts. The next section offers some practical advice on choosing strong passwords and enforcing their use.

Good Passwords

Although stronger modes of authentication are becoming increasingly commonplace, using a username and password remains the most widely used method of authentication for Linux servers. Much has been said and written about the importance of password security, so I'll keep this discussion brief and to the point. There are some very simple rules to follow that can go a long way toward locking down your password policy:

Don't Set Your System to Cause Passwords to Expire Too Quickly   If the period between expirations is too short, users are more likely to feel that they'll forget their passwords, so they will write them down. In addition, users will use cyclic, predictable password patterns. When it comes to password expiration, anything less than three months should be considered too short.

Don't Allow Your Passwords to Get Stale   Conversely, if you allow a user to have the same password for a year, it is exposed for a longer time than is safe. Four months is a good compromise, but six months is not an unreasonably long expiration period.

Avoid Short Passwords   Force your users to pick passwords that are at least six characters in length. Anything shorter than that is too easy to guess using brute force attacks, even if random characters are chosen. Figure 16.6 illustrates how you can enforce a password length minimum using a systems administration tool like Red Hat's `Linuxconf`. Note that in addition to enforcing the six-character limit, this page forces the user to use a minimum of two non-alphanumeric characters.

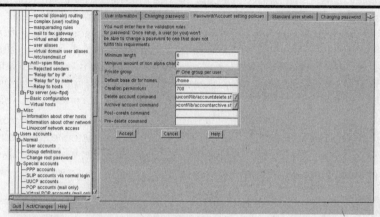

FIGURE 16.6:   Setting password length parameters with Linuxconf

Crack Your Own Passwords   As part of your periodic system security audit, use password-guessing tools to look for weak passwords in your `/etc/passwd` file. Contact the guilty users directly and suggest to them that they use longer passwords with more non-alphanumeric characters and a mix of uppercase and lowercase characters.

Delete Unused Accounts   Most Linux servers don't offer UUCP, PPP, NNTP, Gopher, or Postgres services, yet most Linux distributions ship with these accounts. Completely remove these accounts and any others that don't make sense in your environment.

Avoid Empty Password Fields   Never set up users with no password, even if their shell is highly restricted. Gaining access to any user on your system gets intruders halfway to their destination.

Part IV

An effective way to minimize the risk associated with user passwords is to configure support for shadow password and shadow group files. These are the topics of the next section.

Shadow Passwords

One of the easiest system vulnerabilities to overlook is the ability by any user to *crack* another user's password. This can be done quickly and easily using tools readily available on the Internet. To prevent this, enable *shadow passwords*. Shadow passwords split the password file into two: the /etc/passwd file, which contains a placeholder in the actual password field entries, and the /etc/shadow file, which contains the encrypted password. The /etc/shadow file does not need to be readable by anyone except root, which makes it more difficult for a regular user to attempt to crack another user's password (including root).

Most Linux distributions also support the concept of *shadow groups,* in which the actual members of each group are not listed in the main /etc/group file, but rather in the /etc/gshadow file, which like the /etc/shadow file is readable only by root.

TIP

Some Linux distributions do not have shadow passwords enabled by default. If your distribution is one of these, enable this feature right away.

Listing 16.1 shows how you should look for the existence of the /etc/shadow file. If it does not exist, simply create it with the pwconv command. Note the change in the /etc/passwd file after the conversion.

Listing 16.1: Creating a Shadow Password File

```
[root]# ls -l /etc/shadow
ls: /etc/shadow: No such file or directory
[root]# more /etc/passwd
root:PV/67t9IGeTjU:0:0:root:/root:/bin/bash
bin:*:1:1:bin:/bin:
daemon:*:2:2:daemon:/sbin:
adm:*:3:4:adm:/var/adm:
lp:*:4:7:lp:/var/spool/lpd:
sync:*:5:0:sync:/sbin:/bin/sync
```

```
shutdown:*:6:0:shutdown:/sbin:/sbin/shutdown
halt:*:7:0:halt:/sbin:/sbin/halt
mail:*:8:12:mail:/var/spool/mail:
operator:*:11:0:operator:/root:
ftp:*:14:50:FTP User:/home/ftp:
nobody:*:99:99:Nobody:/:
ramon:aa1g0.pAVx2uA:501:100:Ramon J. Hontanon:/home/ramon:/bin/bash
[root]# pwconv
[root]# ls -l /etc/shadow
-r--------   1 root      root           563 Sep 23 15:27 /etc/shadow
[root]# more /etc/passwd
root:x:0:0:root:/root:/bin/bash
bin:x:1:1:bin:/bin:
daemon:x:2:2:daemon:/sbin:
adm:x:3:4:adm:/var/adm:
lp:x:4:7:lp:/var/spool/lpd:
sync:x:5:0:sync:/sbin:/bin/sync
shutdown:x:6:0:shutdown:/sbin:/sbin/shutdown
halt:x:7:0:halt:/sbin:/sbin/halt
mail:x:8:12:mail:/var/spool/mail:
operator:x:11:0:operator:/root:
ftp:x:14:50:FTP User:/home/ftp:
nobody:x:99:99:Nobody:/:
ramon:x:501:100:Ramon J. Hontanon:/home/ramon:/bin/bash
[root]# more /etc/shadow
root:PV/67t9IGeTjU:11223:0:99999:7:::
bin:*:11223:0:99999:7:::
daemon:*:11223:0:99999:7:::
adm:*:11223:0:99999:7:::
lp:*:11223:0:99999:7:::
sync:*:11223:0:99999:7:::
shutdown:*:11223:0:99999:7:::
halt:*:11223:0:99999:7:::
mail:*:11223:0:99999:7:::
operator:*:11223:0:99999:7:::
ftp:*:11223:0:99999:7:::
nobody:*:11223:0:99999:7:::
ramon:aa1g0.pAVx2uA:11223:0:99999:7
```

The next section of this chapter discusses the sudo utility, a useful tool to minimize the exposure of the root password to your Linux server.

The Sudo Utility

During the normal course of administering my Linux systems, I often go several weeks before actually logging on as the root user. In fact, there have been times when I have come close to forgetting the root password. The sudo utility affords me this luxury, and I recommend that you install this tool on every system that you administer. By allowing the systems administrator to predefine root access for regular users, sudo can be used to execute commands with root privileges in lieu of actually logging in as root and exposing the root password on the network. In general, the less often the root password is actually typed, the more secure it will be.

Installing sudo

You can download sudo in both RPM and source format. I recommend that you use the RPM system to install it, since the default compilation parameters are typically rational, and there is very little need for customization.

Let's start the installation by ensuring that sudo is not already present:

```
[root]# rpm -q sudo
sudo-1.5.9p4-1
```

In this case, you do have a previous installation of sudo, but it's out of date, so delete it and install a more current version using the following commands:

```
[root]# rpm -e sudo
[root]# rpm -i ./sudo-1.6.3p5-1rh62.i386.rpm
[root]# rpm -q sudo
sudo-1.6.3p5-1
```

You now have installed the sudo utility. Make sure you take a look through /usr/doc for the documentation that comes with the source package before you start using the tool.

The *sudoers* File

As with any Linux utility, sudo comes with a configuration file where you can customize its operation. This file is in /etc/sudoers by default and contains, among other things, the list of users who should be allowed to run the sudo command, along with the set of commands that each sudo user is allowed to execute.

The general format used to add users to this file is as follows:

```
user  host(s)=command(s)[run_as_user(s)]
```

For example, if you'd like to grant user alice permission to run the shutdown command, you specify the following:

```
alice ALL = /etc/shutdown
```

Note that the ALL directive can be used as a wildcard for any field in the sudoers file. Let's consider another example where user bob is given access to all root commands, as any user:

```
bob ALL = ALL
```

And finally, let's consider that you'd like user charlie to be allowed to run su to become user operator:

```
charlie ALL = /bin/su operator
```

WARNING

If you're using sudo to grant a user root access to a limited set of commands, make sure that none of these commands allows an "escape" to a Linux shell, because that would give the user unrestricted root access to *all* system commands. Note that some Linux editors (for instance, vi) include this shell escape feature.

Using Sudo

The use of the sudo command is as follows:

```
sudo [command line options] [username] [command]
```

Table 16.2 contains a summary of the most important sudo command-line options.

TABLE 16.2: *sudo* Command-Line Options

Option	Parameter	Purpose
-v	N/A	Prints out the current version
-l	N/A	Lists the allowed and forbidden commands for this user
-h	N/A	Prints usage message
-b	N/A	Runs command in the background
-u	username	Runs the command as the specified username (default is root)

Part iv

For example, to show the contents of the shadow password directory, simply use this:

```
sudo cat /etc/shadow
```

To edit a file in a user's directory preserving his permissions:

```
sudo -u fred vi /export/home/fred/.forward
```

I recommend that you use the sudo command strictly to log the root activity of users who are fully trusted to execute any root command on your Linux server (including yourself), rather than using it to allow certain users to execute a small set of system utilities. It is relatively easy for a user to maliciously extend the privilege of a given command by executing an escape command to the root shell.

The following section describes sudo's logging features, as well as the format of the sudo.log file.

The *sudo.log* file

By default, sudo logs all its activity to the file /var/log/sudo.log. The format of entries into this file is as follows:

```
date:user:HOST=hostname:TTY=terminal:PWD=dir:USER=user:
COMMAND=cmd
```

These fields have the following meanings:

▶ *date*: The timestamp of the log entry

▶ *user*: The username that executed sudo

▶ *hostname*: The host address on which the sudo command was executed

▶ *terminal*: The controlling terminal from which sudo was invoked

▶ *dir*: The current directory from which the command was invoked

▶ *user*: The username that the command was run as

▶ *cmd*: The command that was executed through sudo

For example, Listing 16.2 illustrates a typical sudo.log file showing six entries, all executed by username ramon, invoking commands to be run as root.

Listing 16.2: Contents of the *sudo.log* File

```
Sep 23 14:41:37 : ramon : HOST=redhat : TTY=pts/0 ; PWD=/home/ramon
; USER=root ; COMMAND=/bin/more /etc/shadow
Sep 23 14:43:42 : ramon : HOST=redhat : TTY=pts/0 ; PWD=/home/ramon
; USER=root ; COMMAND=/usr/sbin/pwconv
Sep 23 14:43:51 : ramon : HOST=redhat : TTY=pts/0 ; PWD=/home/ramon
; USER=root ; COMMAND=/bin/more /etc/shadow
Sep 23 14:55:30 : ramon : HOST=redhat : TTY=pts/0 ; PWD=/home/ramon
; USER=root ; COMMAND=/bin/cat /etc/securetty
Sep 23 15:12:27 : ramon : HOST=redhat : TTY=pts/1 ; PWD=/home/ramon
; USER=root ; COMMAND=/bin/linuxconf
Sep 23 15:23:37 : ramon : HOST=redhat : TTY=pts/0 ; PWD=/home/ramon
; USER=root ; COMMAND=/usr/sbin/pwunconv
```

FILE AND DIRECTORY PERMISSIONS

Although it is perhaps one of the most difficult aspects of Linux administration, the use of file permissions is a vital aspect of system security. Linux (like all Unix variants) treats most resources as files, whether they're directories, disk devices, pipes, or terminals. While this makes for straightforward software architecture, it also introduces a fundamental challenge to the Linux administrator charged with ensuring the security of these resources.

Permissions on files and directories have a direct effect on the security of your system. Make the permissions too tight and you limit your users' ability to get their work done. Make permissions too lax and you invite unauthorized use of other users' files and general system resources.

The next subsection of this book examines the specifics of suid and sgid permissions on the Linux operating system.

suid and *sgid*

Linux supports device and file permissions for three distinct groups of users, each of which is represented by three bits of information in the permissions mask, in addition to two special-purpose high-order bits, for a total of 12 bits:

AAABBBCCCDDD

These bits have the following meanings:

AAA   setuid, setgid, sticky-bit

BBB   user (read, write, execute)

CCC   group (read, write, execute)

DDD   other (read, write, execute)

Therefore, if we have a new executable file called report that we want read, written, and executed only by the file's owner but read and executed by everybody else, we set its permissions to the appropriate bit-mask value as follows:

```
[ramon]$ chmod 0755 report
[ramon]$ ls -l report
-rwxr-xr-x   1 ramon     users       19032 Sep 25 19:48 report
```

Note that 7 is the octal representation of the binary number 111. The permissions displayed include only three bits per portion (user, group, other), while in reality, Linux allows you to specify four bits for each of the groups. This is addressed by overloading the representation of the third bit with the following values:

x   execute

s   execute + [setuid or setgid] (applicable only to the user and group portions)

S   [setuid or setgid] (applicable only to the user and group portions)

t   execute + sticky (applicable only to the other portion)

T   sticky (applicable only to the other portion)

Now consider a case in which you'd like this file to be executed with root permissions because it has to read and write to privileged areas of the filesystem, but you would like nonprivileged users to be able to execute it. You can achieve this by setting the first bit of the permissions mask as follows:

```
[ramon]$ sudo chown root:root report
[ramon]$ sudo chmod 4755 report
[ramon]$ ls -l report
-rwsr-xr-x   1 root      root        19032 Sep 25 20:30 report
```

As noted earlier, s in the user portion of the permissions mask denotes that the setuid and execute bits are set for the user (file owner). This means that the file will execute with the user permissions of the file owner (root) instead of the executing user (ramon). In addition, you can set the setgid bit to have the file execute with the group permissions of root, as follows:

```
[ramon]$ sudo chmod 6755 report
[ramon]$ ls -l report
-rwsr-sr-x   1 root     root          19032 Sep 25 20:30 report
```

The third bit in the permissions mask is often referred to as the *sticky bit,* and it is used in directories to signal the Linux kernel that it should not allow a user to delete another user's files, even if the directory is world-writeable. This is most often used in the /tmp directory, which has wide-open permissions:

```
[ramon]$ ls -ld /tmp
drwxrwxrwt   7 root     root           1024 Sep 25 21:05 /tmp
```

Note the final t in the mask. This prevents you from deleting another user's files in that directory unless he explicitly allows you to do so by setting write permissions for others.

In general, use of setuid and setgid should be restricted to those partitions that are only writeable by root. I recommend that you explicitly disallow use of setuid/setgid on the /home directory by specifying the nosuid option in the /etc/fstab file, as shown in Listing 16.3.

Listing 16.3: Contents of the */etc/fstab* File

```
[ramon]$ cat /etc/fstab
/dev/sda8        /            ext2     defaults              1 1
/dev/sda1        /boot        ext2     defaults              1 2
/dev/sda6        /home        ext2     exec,nodev,nosuid,rw  1 2
/dev/sda5        /usr         ext2     defaults              1 2
/dev/sda7        /var         ext2     defaults              1 2
/dev/sda9        swap         swap     defaults              0 0
/dev/fd0         /mnt/floppy  ext2     noauto                0 0
/dev/cdrom       /mnt/cdrom   iso9660  noauto,ro             0 0
none             /proc        proc     defaults              0 0
none             /dev/pts     devpts   mode=0622             0 0
```

Figure 16.7 illustrates how this option can be specified from Red Hat's Linuxconf utility.

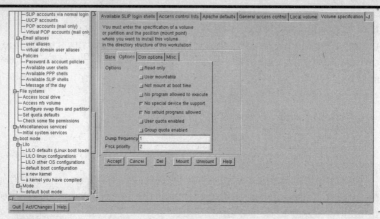

FIGURE 16.7: Setting the *nosuid* option on a local filesystem with Linuxconf

Also, note that the No Special Device File Support option (option nodev in /etc/fstab) is selected. This effectively prevents a user from creating a block device in the /home filesystem, which would be considered a highly suspect action by a nonprivileged user.

Having taken these precautions, you still need to be vigilant of the setuid/setgid present in your Linux server. I suggest that you run this command in cron, piping its output to an e-mail report to your mailbox every morning, as follows:

find / -type f \(-perm -04000 -o -perm -02000 \) -exec ls -l {} \;

This command should report on all the scripts that have either the setuid or the setgid bit set in the permissions mask. Compare the current report with the previous day's report, and ensure that any new files have been created by the administration staff. At the very least, you should have the output of this command written to a separate file within /var/log.

NOTE

The Linux kernel allows you to use setuid/setgid permissions only on binary executables, not on shell scripts. This restriction protects against malicious tampering with shell scripts, a common occurrence that can result in a serious compromise of root.

The *umask* Setting

The default permissions for new files created on your server can have a profound impact on its overall security. Users who create world-writeable files by default are effectively poking tiny holes in your system security. Linux uses the umask configuration setting to control default file permissions. Its use is this:

    umask *AAA*

where *AAA* is the octal complement of a default permissions mask of 666 (777 for directories). For instance, a umask of 022 would yield a default permission of 644 for files (the result of subtracting 022 from 666). Let's look at an example in Listing 16.4.

Listing 16.4: *umask* Configuration Examples

```
[ramon]$ umask 000
[ramon]$ touch example1
[ramon]$ ls -l example1
-rw-rw-rw-   1 ramon    users         0 Sep 25 22:08 example1
[ramon]$ umask 022
[ramon]$ touch example2
[ramon]$ ls -l example2
-rw-r--r--   1 ramon    users         0 Sep 25 22:08 example2
[ramon]$ umask 66
[ramon]$ touch example3
[ramon]$ ls -l example3
-rw-------   1 ramon    users         0 Sep 25 22:08 example3
```

I recommend that you edit your /etc/profile file to assign a mask of 066 to the root user and assign a mask of 022 to your regular users. This ensures that root-created files have no permissions for group and others, while any other files are created with world-read permissions only.

Limiting Core Dump Size

A common means for a local user to gain root privileges is to force a setuid/setgid program to dump a core file (upon crashing) in a specific location within the filesystem. By using this method to overwrite arbitrary files anywhere on the server, including /etc/passwd, /etc/hosts.equiv, or .rhosts, intruders can effectively create for themselves a user with root privileges. With today's servers having gigabytes of physical memory available, these core files could fill an entire

468   **Chapter Sixteen**

disk, which would result in a Denial of Service attack for other users relying on the same filesystem.

There is an effective way to keep core files under control. Using the `ulimit` command, you can control the resource utilization limits of any user, including the maximum size of a core dump file. You should simply set this size to 0, using the following command:

```
ulimit -c 0
```

You can include this command in the global `/etc/profile` configuration file also.

SYSLOG SECURITY

One of the most significant skills of sophisticated intruders is their ability to clean up all evidence that an attack has taken place. This is the electronic equivalent of a criminal using gloves at the scene of the crime, and it's a constant source of frustration for those who make a living out of tracking down the actions of these intruders.

You should go to whatever lengths are necessary to make sure that you can safeguard *some* evidence that your system was tampered with. The problem is that it's very difficult to guarantee that your log files are correct when attackers could be modifying them with their `root` privileges. You should take advantage of the Syslog program's capability to send a copy of all log events to a remote server.

For example, in order to send all your kernel, mail, and news messages to a remote Syslog server (hostname `zurich`), add the following line to your `/etc/syslog.conf` configuration file:

```
kern.*, mail.*, news.*      [TAB]@zurich
```

(Don't forget that the syntax of this file calls for a tab character to be inserted between fields.)

After making this modification, you must send the -HUP (hang-up) signal to the Syslog daemon to force it to read its configuration:

```
[ramon]$ sudo killall -HUP syslogd
```

Keep in mind, however, that some services may not be configured or able to log events via Syslog. You should use `cron` to move those services' log files to a remote server several times throughout the day— the more often the better.

FILESYSTEM ENCRYPTION

However strong your physical and system security measures are, you need to be ready for the time when a user gains access to some other user's files. Cryptography is your last line of defense. By encrypting the contents of sensitive directories, users can protect the privacy of their data even after an intrusion has succeeded.

This section describes two different ways to do this, both of which are based on secret-key technology using standard encryption algorithms. Let's take a look at each of them in more detail.

The Cryptographic File System

The Cryptographic File System (CFS) was developed by Unix pioneer Matt Blaze and constitutes the first full-blown integration of secret-key encryption into the Linux filesystem. One of the most important advantages of CFS is its support of both local filesystem types (such as ext2) as well as remote filesystems such as NFS. This support protects your data as it sits in your server and also as it travels through the network whenever you share an NFS mount point. CFS supports several encryption algorithms, including DES, 3DES, MacGuffin, SAFER-SK128, and Blowfish.

CFS's main drawback, however, is performance. If you elect to use 3DES encryption (which I recommend because DES is barely adequate nowadays), you will pay a price, and you'll see a noticeable delay in your disk access, especially for large files. This is partly due to the fact that CFS operates in user space (outside of the kernel). However, running in user space can actually be an advantage because other cryptographic filesystem modules are offered as patches to particular versions of Linux kernels, and they're often not available for the latest stable kernel.

Let's start by installing the software on our server.

Installing CFS

Although the package can be obtained in source form, it's also available from www.zedz.net (or ftp.zedz.net) in RPM format, as shown in Listing 16.5.

Listing 16.5: Downloading the CFS Distribution in RPM Format

```
[ramon]$ ftp ftp.zedz.net
Connected to ftp.zedz.net.
220 warez.zedz.net FTP server ready.
Name (ftp.zedz.net:ramon): anonymous
331 Guest login ok, send your complete e-mail address as password.
Password: rhontanon@sybex.com
230 Guest login ok, access restrictions apply.
Remote system type is UNIX.
Using binary mode to transfer files.
ftp> cd /pub/crypto/disk/cfs/
250 CWD command successful.
ftp> get cfs-1.3.3bf-1.i386.rpm
local: cfs-1.3.3bf-1.i386.rpm remote: cfs-1.3.3bf-1.i386.rpm
200 PORT command successful.
150 Opening BINARY mode data connection for cfs-1.3.3bf-1.i386.rpm
    (194436 bytes).
226 Transfer complete.
194436 bytes received in 22.7 secs (8.4 Kbytes/sec)
ftp> quit
221-You have transferred 194436 bytes in 1 files.
221-Total traffic for this session was 197280 bytes in 2 transfers.
221-Thank you for using the FTP service on warez.zedz.net.
221 Goodbye.
[ramon]$ sudo rpm -i cfs-1.3.3bf-1.i386.rpm
```

At this point you have installed CFS on your system (note that there is no need to rebuild the kernel or reboot the server). Let's take a look at configuring CFS in the next step.

Configuring CFS

The first step is to make sure your server is configured to run NFS services (statd, portmapper, and mountd). This is a requirement for CFS to work correctly. Since CFS actually protects the privacy of NFS shares, perhaps this is just the tool you were looking for to add NFS back into your security policy. You can verify that NFS is running on your system by looking for the mountd line with the following command:

```
[ramon]$ ps aux | grep mountd
root      5756  0.0  0.7  1132   456 ?   S    19:15   0:00 rpc.mountd
```

Next, create a /null directory. CFS refers to this directory as the *bootstrap mount point*. In addition, you need to create the directory that you want to use as the root for all encrypted data (I chose /crypt for this purpose):

```
[ramon]$ sudo mkdir /null
[ramon]$ sudo chmod 0000 /null
[ramon]$ sudo mkdir /crypt
```

Add the /null directory to the list of exported filesystems using the following command:

```
[ramon]$ echo "/null localhost" >> /etc/exports
```

Add the following commands to the end of /etc/rc.d/rc.local:

```
if [ -x /usr/sbin/cfsd ]; then
        /usr/sbin/cfsd && \
                /bin/mount -o port=3049,intr localhost:/null /crypt
fi
```

That's the end of the installation. You're now ready to try CFS. You can either restart your system or type the commands that you just added in the rc.local file by hand.

Using CFS

There are three commands that support the operation of the CFS package:

```
cmkdir [-1] [private_directory]
cattach [private_directory] [cleartext_directory]
cdetach [private_directory]
```

Start by creating a directory that is going to contain all your confidential information:

```
[ramon]$ cmkdir secret
```

The command prompts you for a passphrase, which is then used to hash out an appropriate secret encrypting key. You'll need this passphrase to be able to get at the data in this directory.

WARNING

Note that, by default, CFS uses the 3DES algorithm for encryption. This is noticeably slower than the DES variant that can be specified using the `-1` switch: (# `cmkdir -1 secret`). I strongly recommend against this option, because the DES algorithm has been known to be vulnerable to brute force attacks. If you're encrypting data that you expect to keep around for a while, you should make it as resistant as possible to cryptanalysis.

The next step is to attach this newly created directory to the master CFS tree:

```
[ramon]$ cattach secret decrypted
```

You are then prompted for the same passphrase that you provided when you created the directory. If you authenticate successfully, the `secret` directory will be available to you as `/crypt/decrypted` in cleartext form. Once you're done working with the cleartext directory, simply make it unavailable using the following command:

```
[ramon]$ cdetach secret
```

As with any other encryption, CFS is only as strong as your ability to protect the passphrase used to encrypt the data. In addition, you should ensure the integrity of the CFS utilities themselves (`cmkdir`, `cattach`, `cdetach`) to be sure that they have not been replaced with Trojan horse versions.

Practical Privacy Disk Driver

A more recent alternative to CFS is Allan Latham's Practical Privacy Disk Driver (PPDD). Unlike CFS, this utility actually creates a disk driver similar to a physical disk device, but its behavior is controlled by the PPDD software. Also unlike CFS, there is built-in support for only one encryption algorithm: Blowfish. This shouldn't be considered a drawback, because Blowfish has fared well so far in the many attempts to crack it via both cryptanalysis and brute force.

The goal of this utility is to provide an encryption device that is totally transparent to the user, who can access the PPDD-protected directories without the need for any special procedures.

Let's take a closer look at PPDD, starting with its installation.

Installing PPDD

As of this writing, there is no RPM package for PPDD, probably because the installation requires a kernel patch and rebuild. You need to download the package in source format from ftp.gwdg.de (see Listing 16.6).

Listing 16.6: Downloading the PPDD Distribution

```
[ramon]$ ftp ftp.gwdg.de
Connected to ftp.gwdg.de.
220 ftp.gwdg.de FTP server (Version wu-2.4.2-academ[BETA-18](1) Mon
    Jul 31 14:25:08 MET DST 2000) ready.
Name (ftp.gwdg.de:ramon): anonymous
331 Guest login ok, send your complete e-mail address as password.
Password:rhontanon@sybex.com
230-Hello User at 204.254.33.77, there are 44 (max 250
230-Local time is: Wed Sep 27 03:00:15 2000
230 Guest login ok, access restrictions apply.
Remote system type is UNIX.
Using binary mode to transfer files.
ftp> cd /pub/linux/misc/ppdd
250 CWD command successful.
ftp> get ppdd-1.2.zip
local: ppdd-1.2.zip remote: ppdd-1.2.zip
200 PORT command successful.
150 Opening BINARY mode data connection for ppdd-1.2.zip (198959
    bytes).
226 Transfer complete.
198959 bytes received in 28.4 secs (6.9 Kbytes/sec)
ftp>
```

Once you have verified that the file has been successfully downloaded (and is the right size), you need to unzip it and extract the tar file, as shown in Listing 16.7.

Listing 16.7: Installing the PPDD Distribution

```
[ramon]$ unzip ppdd-1.2.zip
Archive:  ppdd-1.2.zip
 extracting: tmp/ppdd-1.2.tgz.sig
   inflating: tmp/ppdd-1.2.tgz
[ramon]$ tar zxf tmp/ppdd-1.2.tar
```

At this point you should have a new subdirectory called ppdd-1.2 in your current directory. Since the PPDD distribution will be applying a patch against the current Linux sources, make sure that you have a good set of kernel source and header files in /usr/linux and that you have been able to successfully build a working kernel from these files. Don't forget to make a backup copy of the kernel before patching it.

Next, go into the PPDD source directory and apply the kernel patches:

```
[ramon]$ cd ppdd-1.2
[ramon]$ sudo make apply_patch
```

This results in a modification to the Linux sources, so you should rebuild your kernel and install the resulting boot file at this point. Don't forget to reconfigure LILO and have an emergency boot disk handy.

If the new image boots without any errors, you're ready to create the encryption device. The following command assumes that you'll be using /dev/hdc1 as your encrypted disk partition:

```
[ramon]$ sudo ppddinit /dev/ppdd0 /dev/hdc1
```

It is at this stage that you'll be prompted for a passphrase, whose hash will constitute the secret key used in the Blowfish algorithm.

Next, you need to set up the newly created device, and you need to write an ext2 filesystem on it using the following commands:

```
[ramon]$ sudo ppddsetup -s /dev/ppdd0 /dev/hdc1
[ramon]$ sudo mkfs /dev/ppdd0
```

Using PPDD

To use PPDD, simply mount the encrypted device on a real mount point (I'll use /crypt for consistency):

```
[ramon]$ sudo mount /dev/ppdd0 /crypt
```

From this point on, your users can access resources within /crypt transparently, as if it were a regular filesystem.

Before you shut down the server, you should unmount the /crypt filesystem as you would any other partition, and you should also disconnect the ppdd0 driver, as follows:

```
[ramon]$ sudo umount /crypt
[ramon]$ sudo ppddsetup -d /dev/ppdd0
```

PPDD encrypts an entire filesystem with a key derived from a single passphrase and allows users to access the files within the filesystem using the standard Linux permissions model. This makes PPDD a good candidate for protecting a server's disk from being read by an intruder who has physically seized the system, as well as for protecting backup media that have fallen into the wrong hands.

What's Next?

This chapter examines the issues involved in system-level Linux security and provides a set of recommended configurations and utilities that can aid in protecting your server from unauthorized access by local users. Although all the popular Linux distributions are becoming increasingly security conscious, a staggering number of vulnerabilities are still being reported daily.

It's important to understand the impact of all kernel parameters and recognize which ones can have a direct influence on the security of your server. You should build your own custom kernel for efficiency, but also for security and accountability.

You should protect your server against `root` exploits. One way to do this is by constantly monitoring the permissions of your system files and by guarding against the perils of `setuid`/`setgid` executables. Setting the correct default `umask` for your users ensures that they're creating files with a safe set of permissions. Also, limiting the size of core files with the `ulimit` command can prevent a common type of `root` compromise attack.

When all else fails, filesystem encryption can protect the data that has been compromised. The Cryptographic File System (CFS) provides good granularity for individual protection of user information, while the Practical Privacy Disk Driver (PPDD) is an efficient, transparent method for encrypting filesystems (and backups) in bulk.

In the next chapter, you will continue to learn about security as it relates to establishing and configuring network services.

Chapter 17

NETWORK SERVICES CONFIGURATION

Chapters 15, "Understanding Linux Security," and 16, "System Installation and Setup," described the concepts that you need to master in order to secure your Linux installation and configuration before connecting your server to the public network. It explored the process of choosing a Linux distribution, configuring password authentication, and ensuring the confidentiality and availability of the data kept on the filesystems. In addition, it showed you how to ensure the integrity of system utilities and configuration files.

This chapter takes the discussion one step away from the system itself and deals with connecting a Linux server to a network. Native support for a wide range of TCP/IP services has always been one of the strongest qualities of the Linux operating system. Configuring these services with security in mind, however, is an increasingly difficult challenge for systems administrators as new network services are demanded of their servers.

Adapted from *Linux Security* by Ramón J. Hontañón
ISBN 0-7821-2741-X   512 pages $49.99

This chapter begins by discussing network services configuration on a Linux server. It includes a detailed description of

- ▶ The issues associated with the `inetd` daemon

- ▶ The `/etc/rc.d` startup files

- ▶ TCP Wrappers, a tool for enforcing access control on network daemons

- ▶ The commands that are available to show network activity on your server

Let's start by introducing a simple set of rules to apply when configuring Linux network daemons.

SECURING NETWORK SERVICES

Once you feel comfortable with your system setup, it's time to take the next step: configuring the network interfaces of the server and connecting them to your network. Whether this is an intranet server for internal users or an Internet bastion host for public (and anonymous) use, there are some important issues for you to consider:

- ▶ Which network services are strictly necessary?

- ▶ Should other services be present but inactive?

- ▶ Should I allow any client to connect to the server?

- ▶ Should certain clients be allowed to connect to *all* services?

- ▶ Do I need to maintain a log of service activity?

As always, it's imperative to run the minimum number of services and to ensure that the services that you need to offer don't introduce any of the vulnerabilities described in Chapter 15. The bad news is that there are literally hundreds of network services available on a typical Linux distribution (although they are not always enabled). The good news is that there are only two places to look for these services: the `inetd` daemon and the `/etc/rc.d` directories.

The next section offers a detailed look at the `inetd` daemon and explains the syntax of its configuration file, `/etc/inetd.conf`.

SPAWNING INTERNET DAEMONS WITH *INETD*

All Linux distributions (and all Berkeley-style Unix variants, for that matter) include a central network service utility controlled by the inetd process. This "super-server" acts as the clearinghouse, or central point of administration, for all Internet services running on the server. You can verify that the master inetd process is running on your system by entering the following command:

```
[ramon]$ ps aux | grep inetd
root       421  0.0  0.0  1232   60 ?          S     Sep24
   0:00 inetd
```

The inetd daemon is started by Linux at system startup, and it immediately listens for the network ports listed in the /etc/inetd.conf file, the main configuration file for the inetd daemon (more on that in the next section). If an incoming request matches a network port number specified in its configuration, inetd assigns the appropriate listener application to the incoming socket and continues to listen for future connections. This is done in order to optimize system resources, because having a single process listen for several ports represents a lighter load on the system than having each process listen on its own port.

The only inetd command-line option of interest is -d. This option starts the daemon with debugging enabled, as in the following command:

```
[ramon]$ sudo /usr/sbin/inetd -d
```

Note that you have to stop the inetd daemon manually (because it starts by default), and then reinvoke it with the debug option enabled, as shown in Listing 17.1.

Listing 17.1: Execution of *inetd* with the Debug Option Enabled

```
[ramon]$ sudo killall inetd
[ramon]$ sudo /usr/sbin/inetd -d
ADD : ftp proto=tcp, wait.max=0.40,
user.group=root.(null) builtin=0
server=/usr/sbin/tcpd
ADD : telnet proto=tcp, wait.max=0.40,
   user.group=root.(null) builtin=0
   server=/usr/sbin/tcpd
```

Part IV

```
ADD : login proto=tcp, wait.max=0.40,
    user.group=root.(null) builtin=0
    server=/usr/sbin/tcpd
someone wants telnet
accept, ctrl 3
24257 execl /usr/sbin/tcpd
24257 reaped
someone wants ftp
accept, ctrl 3
24259 execl /usr/sbin/tcpd
24259 reaped
someone wants pop-3
accept, ctrl 3
24261 execl /usr/sbin/tcpd
...
```

Keep in mind that, when invoked with the -d option, inetd displays its diagnostics to the stderr process (the controlling tty by default), making this option useful only when you're trying to troubleshoot a problem. Listing 17.1 shows a debug session during which three requests are received (telnet, ftp, and pop-3).

The next section discusses /etc/inetd.conf, the configuration file used by the inetd daemon.

Configuring *inetd* with */etc/inetd.conf*

As with any Linux facility, the inetd daemon consults a plain-text configuration file upon startup. The /etc/inetd.conf file contains one line for each of the services that inetd is to listen for. Each line contains seven positional fields, separated by tab characters or spaces, as described in this section. Note that each field must be included on each line. These seven fields are as follows:

service name   The *service name* field is the actual name of the service to listen for (telnet, ftp, finger, and so on). These services should correspond to a TCP or UDP port number, and this mapping should be present in the /etc/services file (discussed later in this chapter) or in the /etc/rpc file for RPC-style services. In both cases, service name is the first field in those files.

socket type   The *socket type* field has a value of stream, dgram, raw, rdm, or seqpacket. In a typical Internet Linux server, you should see only `stream` (for TCP sockets) and `dgram` (for UDP sockets).

protocol The *protocol* field denotes the type of Transport layer protocol that the daemon uses. It is one of the choices in the `/etc/protocols` file (for instance, `tcp` or `udp`).

`wait/nowait[`.*max*`]` This field applies only to `dgram` services and refers to the daemon's capability to process incoming requests with multiple threads (`nowait`) or a single thread (`wait`). The optional [`.max`] field is an integer that denotes the maximum number of server instances to spawn in a 60-second interval. You should have no reason to change this from the default of 40. Increasing this value does not enhance the performance of most services and could open the door to a Denial of Service (DoS) attack.

`user [`.*group*`]` The `inetd` daemon can spawn a service with ownership other than the `root` user. You can specify both the *user* and the optional *group* as the service to be run. I recommend that you never run a service as `root` unless strictly necessary (use the nobody username when possible). If running as `root`, be sure to configure `swatch` or `logcheck` to monitor its messages as closely as possible.

server program The *server program* field specifies the actual executable that is spawned when a request is received. Be sure that you specify the entire path to avoid attacks that may change the default `$PATH` variable in the system. Also, apply good integrity-assurance techniques to this executable, in order to avoid Trojan horse attacks. Note that the keyword `internal` can be used if the `inetd` daemon handles this request by itself (for example, `echo`, `time`, `chargen`, and `discard`).

TIP

In a security-minded Linux server, the server program should always be TCPD. (See the section "TCP Wrappers," later in this chapter.)

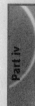

server program arguments The *server program arguments* field is the place to specify arguments that you would like to pass to the server program. Note that you must start with the program name itself (`argv[0]` in Linux programming terms).

inetd Configuration Examples

By default, Linux distributions are shipped with a generous set of daemons in the inetd.conf file. Consider, for instance, the standard /etc/inetd.conf file that is shipped with the SuSE 7.0 distribution, as shown in Listing 17.2. (The comment lines in this etc/inetd.conf file have been removed for simplicity.)

Listing 17.2: A Typical Default */etc/inetd.conf* File

```
[ramon]$ grep -v "^#" /etc/inetd.conf
time    stream  tcp  nowait  root      internal
time    dgram   udp  wait    root      internal
ftp     stream  tcp  nowait  root      /usr/sbin/tcpd
    in.ftpd
telnet  stream  tcp  nowait  root      /usr/sbin/tcpd
    in.telnetd
shell   stream  tcp  nowait  root      /usr/sbin/tcpd
    in.rshd -L
login   stream  tcp  nowait  root      /usr/sbin/tcpd
    in.rlogind
talk    dgram   udp  wait    root      /usr/sbin/tcpd
    in.talkd
ntalk   dgram   udp  wait    root      /usr/sbin/tcpd
    in.talkd
pop3    stream  tcp  nowait  root      /usr/sbin/tcpd
    /usr/sbin/popper -s
finger  stream  tcp  nowait  nobody    /usr/sbin/tcpd
    in.fingerd -w
http-rman stream  tcp     nowait.10000    nobody
    /usr/sbin/tcpd /usr/sbin/http-rman
➥swat    stream  tcp     nowait.400
➥/root   /usr/sbin/swat  swat
```

The systems administrator has some work to do on this file. First of all, very few Linux servers need to provide time services, and the talk/ntalk services are of questionable use for most of today's server installations. The same applies to the Finger service. The pop3 daemon should be present only if your server is meant to house user mailboxes, and I recommend that such a server be dedicated exclusively to that purpose.

Both the shell and login services are RPC-based daemons. Along with the Telnet and FTP services, they should be replaced with a secure equivalent, such as Secure Shell (SSH).

http-rman is a tool that converts Linux man-format manual pages to HTML on-the-fly for real-time perusal via a web server. Finally, swat is the Samba Web Administration Tool (SWAT). If you have a legitimate need for either of these services, be sure that TCP Wrappers is properly configured to restrict their access to authorized clients only. Be sure you see the following response from this grep command:

```
[ramon]$ grep http-rman /etc/hosts.allow
http-rman : ALL EXCEPT LOCAL
```

The syntax of the /etc/hosts.[allow|deny] file is described in the "TCP Wrappers" section, later in this chapter.

XINETD: THE NEXT GENERATION *INETD*

When Panos Tsirigotis of the computer science department at the University of Colorado at Boulder realized that most Linux network administrators were using TCP Wrappers in conjunction with inetd, he set out to develop a tool that would offer the features from both applications. The result was xinetd, the extended Internet services daemon.

On the surface, xinetd works just like inetd, acting as a superserver that inspects all incoming connections and spawns the appropriate server program to handle each connection. Like inetd, xinetd can also be started with a -d option to force more verbose output for debugging purposes:

```
[ramon]$ sudo /usr/sbin/xinetd -d
```

But the real advantage of xinetd over its predecessor is its security features. While inetd with TCP Wrappers can block incoming connections based on source/destination IP addresses and port numbers, xinetd allows the screening of connections based on

▶ Rate of incoming connections (useful to thwart Denial of Service attacks)

▶ Total number of connections for a particular service

▶ Number of incoming connections from specific hosts

▶ Time of the day

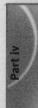

In addition, you can define limits on the size of the log files that the service creates so that a potential attacker can't stage a Denial of Service attack on your server by filling your disk with logging information. Finally, xinetd lets you define a forwarding rule by which incoming connections can be redirected to other hosts in the private network (for example) that need not be reachable from the public Internet.

Installing *xinetd*

Although Red Hat Linux 7.0 includes xinetd as part of the standard distribution, most Linux vendors have not yet bundled xinetd into their products. You can easily obtain the RPM version of the xinetd package from a trusted archive such as www.rpmfind.net. To install xinetd, enter the following command:

```
[ramon]$ sudo rpm -i xinetd-2.1.8.9pre9-6.i386.rpm
```

This package installs the server executable (/usr/sbin/xinetd), as well as the man pages and a startup file (/etc/rc.d/init.d/xinetd).

Configuring *xinetd* with */etc/xinetd.conf*

The xinetd daemon is started by Linux at system startup, and its configuration is obtained from /etc/xinetd.conf, as well as from all the files in the /etc/xinetd.d/ directory. Each file in this directory contains the xinetd configuration for a particular service. (Each file is the equivalent of a single line of /etc/inetd.conf.) For example, the following directory listing of /etc/xinetd.d/ shows that this system has been configured to offer telnet, tftp, and imap services via xinetd:

```
[ramon]$ ls -l /etc/xinetd.d/*
-rw-r--r--    1 root     root         169 Feb  3 17:18 tftp
-rw-r--r--    1 root     root         322 Mar 16 23:28 imap
-rw-r--r--    1 root     root         318 Feb  3 17:18 telnet
```

A typical file in this directory looks like the following:

```
service service_name
{
keyword = value value value ...
```

```
keyword += value value value ...
keyword -= value value value ...


...
}
```

service_name is the actual name of the service to listen for (for example, telnet, ftp, or finger), as defined in the /etc/services file. The *keyword* field defines a set that can be assigned one or more values (=), appended one or more values (+=), or reduced by one or more values (-=). The following are some of the most useful keywords supported by the xinetd utility:

disable   Setting the disable keyword to yes results in the service not starting. Set this keyword to no to enable the service to listen for. This keyword is useful for temporarily disabling a service without having to delete the file from the /etc/xinetd .d/ directory.

socket_type   The socket_type keyword can have a value of stream, dgram, raw, rdm, or seqpacket. In a typical Internet Linux server, you should use only stream (for TCP sockets) and dgram (for UDP sockets).

protocol   The protocol keyword is the type of Transport layer protocol that the daemon uses. It is one of the choices in /etc/protocols (such as tcp or udp).

wait   The wait attribute determines whether the service is single threaded or multithreaded. If its value is set to yes, the service is single threaded; this forces xinetd to start the server and stop handling requests for the service until the server dies. If the value is set to no, xinetd continues to handle new requests after starting the server.

user   The user keyword defines the UID to use for the server process.

group   The group keyword defines the GID to use for the server process.

instances   The instances keyword defines the maximum number of server instances that can be active concurrently for

Part iv

this service. The value can be either a number or the value UNLIMITED (no limit).

server   The server keyword is the fully qualified location of the server program to handle this service.

server_args   The server_args keyword specifies the set of arguments passed to the server. Unlike inetd, the server name itself should not be included in the list of arguments.

only_from   The only_from keyword specifies the remote hosts or networks from which the given service is available. Its value can be a hostname (host.example.com), a domain (.example.com), a single-host IP address (63.75.44.67), a network address (63.75.44.0), or an IP address with a netmask range description (63.75.44.0/24).

no_access   The no_access keyword specifies the remote hosts or networks to which the particular service is unavailable.

access_times   The access_times keyword specifies the time intervals when the service is available. Time periods are specified using the syntax *hour:min-hour:min* (for instance, 09:00-17:00).

log_on_type   The log_on_type keyword defines the destination of the log messages. The value can be one of the following:

► SYSLOG *syslog_facility* [*syslog_level*]: Send the output to the specified syslog facility with the specified level.

► FILE [*soft_limit* [*hard_limit*]]: Send the output to *FILE*. Once the file size has reached *soft_limit*, a message is logged. Once the file size has reached *hard_limit*, logging ceases.

log_on_success   The log_on_success keyword defines the type of information to be logged when the remote client connects to the server and when the connection is torn down. The value can be one of the following:

► PID: Log the server's process ID.

► HOST: Log the remote host address.

► USERID: Log the user ID of the remote process.

▶ EXIT: Log the fact that the service exited, including the exit status.

▶ DURATION: Log the duration of a service session.

log_on_failure   The log_on_failure keyword defines the type of information to be logged when the remote client cannot connect to the server, either because of access control or because of limits imposed on resource allocation. The value can be one of the following:

▶ HOST: Log the remote host address.

▶ USERID: Log the user ID of the remote process.

▶ ATTEMPT: Log the fact that the attempt was made.

bind   The bind keyword specifies the interface or IP address to listen on. This lets you run a server on only the secure interface of a multihomed server, for example.

redirect   The redirect keyword specifies the IP address and port number to which xinetd should forward incoming connections. When a connection is received for the specified service, xinetd spawns a process to forward the connection to the given IP address and an optional TCP port.

xinetd Configuration Examples

The main xinetd configuration file resides in /etc/xinetd.conf and typically contains a defaults section with parameters that affect all services, along with an includedir statement that effectively pulls in all service-specific files in the target directory (/etc/xinetd.d, in this case). Listing 17.3 illustrates a typical /etc/xinetd.conf file.

Listing 17.3: A Typical Default */etc/xinetd.conf* File

```
#
# Simple configuration file for xinetd
#
# Some defaults, and include /etc/xinetd.d/

defaults
{
```

Part iv

```
               instances            = 60
               log_type             = SYSLOG authpriv
               log_on_success       = HOST PID
               log_on_failure       = HOST
        }
   includedir /etc/xinetd.d
```

Note that the file in Listing 17.3 limits the total number of concurrent xinetd instances for a given service to 60. In addition, it requests that logging be performed via the authpriv facility of the standard syslog system. Successful connection attempts log the connecting host and the process ID, and failed connection attempts log the hostname only.

The following excerpt is an example of a Telnet configuration in the /etc/xinetd.d/ directory, included by the main /etc/xinetd .conf file:

```
[ramon]$ sudo more /etc/xinetd.d/telnet
service telnet
        {
                    socket_type      = stream
                    wait             = no
                    user             = root
                    server           = /usr/sbin/in.telnetd
                    redirect         = 10.0.0.2 23
                    bind             = 127.0.0.1
                    log_on_failure  += USERID
                    disable          = no

        }
```

This Telnet service defines the stream (TCP) socket type, specifies multithreaded operation (wait = no), uses the root username as the owner of the service, and logs the user ID when there is an unsuccessful login. Note that this file uses the += operator to add USERID to the set of values already defined for the log_on_failure variable (/etc/xinetd .conf defined log_on_failure = HOST). This file also includes a redirect statement to forward all Telnet connections to host 10.0.0.2 (standard Telnet port 23), while listening for connections only on the loopback interface (127.0.0.1).

Consider a slightly different example:

```
[ramon]$ sudo more /etc/xinetd.d/imap
service imap
            {
                    socket_type    = stream
                    wait           = no
                    user           = root
                    server         = /usr/local/sbin/imapd
                    only_from      = 204.154.22.0/24 localhost
                    disable        = yes

            }
```

In this case, the file defines a listener for the IMAP service (Internet Mail Access Protocol), where only hosts in the 204.154.22.0 class C domain and on the local host are allowed to request service. Note that this file temporarily disables the service by setting the disable keyword to yes.

Let's look at one more example:

```
[ramon]$ sudo more /etc/xinetd.d/tftp
service tftp
            {
                    socket_type    = dgram
                    wait           = yes
                    user           = nobody
                    server         = /usr/sbin/in.tftpd
                    server_args    = /tftpboot
                    access_times   = 01:00-23:00
                    disable        = no

            }
```

This is an illustration of a server (tftpd) that takes a command-line argument (/tftpboot, or the location of the TFTP directory). This is handled by adding the argument to the server_args keyword. Note that this example restricts the access times to this service from 1 A.M. to 11 P.M., perhaps due to the fact that there is a scheduled maintenance period from 11 P.M. to 1 A.M. every day.

Part IV

STARTING NETWORK SERVICES FROM /ETC/RC.D

While most of the core Linux network services are started from inetd, an increasing number of daemons are being configured to start independently upon system startup. This gives application programmers tighter control over the execution of their services and allows them to spawn additional instances of certain daemons, sometimes even in advance of receiving a request. This is especially useful for high-volume and high-overhead services such as WWW, sendmail, SSH, and so on.

It is important, however, to maintain all the startup scripts in a central location within the filesystem, and Linux uses the /etc/rc.d directory as the default for this purpose. Within this directory, there are a number of subdirectories named in a similar manner:

```
[ramon]$ cd /etc/rc.d
[ramon]$ ls -ld rc*.d
drwxr-xr-x   2 root      root           4096 Jul 29 14:30
   rc0.d
drwxr-xr-x   2 root      root           4096 Oct 21 13:42
   rc1.d
drwxr-xr-x   2 root      root           4096 Oct 22 15:40
   rc2.d
drwxr-xr-x   2 root      root           4096 Oct 22 15:40
   rc3.d
drwxr-xr-x   2 root      root           4096 Jul 29 14:30
   rc4.d
drwxr-xr-x   2 root      root           4096 Jul 29 14:30
   rc5.d
drwxr-xr-x   2 root      root           4096 Jul 29 14:30
   rc6.d
drwxr-xr-x   2 root      root           4096 Oct 21 13:41
   rcS.d
```

Each of these directories contains scripts to be executed when the system enters a particular run level (0–6 and S). Table 17.1 shows the significance of each run level. The system's init process (always the first process to be executed) invokes the actions found in the /etc/inittab file, which in turn invokes the appropriate file in /etc/rc.d as the system enters each run level.

TABLE 17.1: The Linux Run Levels and Their Meanings

Run Level	Meaning
0	Halt the system (shut down)
1	Multiuser mode without network
2	Multiuser mode with network
3	Multiuser mode with network and XDM (X Display Manager)
4	Reserved (not used by Linux)
5	Reserved (not used by Linux)
6	System restart (reboot)
S	Single-user mode

Each directory contains both start scripts (filename starts with S) and kill scripts (filename starts with K), as shown in Listing 17.4.

Listing 17.4: Partial Content of the */etc/rc.d/rc3.d* Directory

```
[ramon]$ cd rc3.d
[ramon]$ ls -l
total 0
lrwxrwxrwx 1 root root  8 Oct 21 13:45 K20rwhod -> ../rwhod
lrwxrwxrwx 1 root root 11 Oct 21 13:45 K20sendmail ->
    ../sendmail
lrwxrwxrwx 1 root root 13 Oct 21 13:45 K22wvdial.dod -
    >../wvdial.dod
lrwxrwxrwx 1 root root 12 Oct 21 13:45 K23nfsserver ->
    ../nfsserver
lrwxrwxrwx 1 root root  9 Oct 21 13:41 K23pcnfsd ->
    ../pcnfsd
lrwxrwxrwx 1 root root  9 Oct 21 13:44 K24autofs ->
    ../autofs
lrwxrwxrwx 1 root root 11 Oct 21 13:45 K24ypclient ->
    ../ypclient
lrwxrwxrwx 1 root root  9 Oct 21 13:41 K30random ->
    ../random
lrwxrwxrwx 1 root root  9 Oct 21 13:41 K35routed ->
    ../routed
```

Part iv

```
lrwxrwxrwx 1 root root  9 Oct 21 13:42 K35syslog ->
  ../syslog
lrwxrwxrwx 1 root root  6 Oct 21 13:41 K36nfs -> ../nfs
lrwxrwxrwx 1 root root  8 Oct 21 13:41 K38route -> ../route
lrwxrwxrwx 1 root root 11 Oct 21 13:45 K40dhclient ->
  ../dhclient
lrwxrwxrwx 1 root root 10 Oct 21 13:41 K40network ->
  ../network
lrwxrwxrwx 1 root root  8 Oct 21 13:41 K45dummy -> ../dummy
lrwxrwxrwx 1 root root 17 Oct 21 13:45 K45irda ->
  /sbin/init.d/irda
lrwxrwxrwx 1 root root 11 Oct 21 13:45 K51firewall ->
  ../firewall
lrwxrwxrwx 1 root root 10 Oct 21 13:41 K99kerneld ->
  ../kerneld
lrwxrwxrwx 1 root root  8 Oct 21 13:45 S20rwhod -> ../rwhod
lrwxrwxrwx 1 root root 11 Oct 21 13:45 S20sendmail ->
  ../sendmail
lrwxrwxrwx 1 root root  7 Oct 22 14:54 S20sshd -> ../sshd
lrwxrwxrwx 1 root root  7 Oct 21 13:41 S21cron -> ../cron
lrwxrwxrwx 1 root root  8 Oct 21 13:45 S21smbfs -> ../smbfs
lrwxrwxrwx 1 root root 13 Oct 21 13:45 S22wvdial.dod ->
  ../wvdial.dod
lrwxrwxrwx 1 root root  6 Oct 21 13:41 S30xdm -> ../xdm
lrwxrwxrwx 1 root root 11 Oct 21 13:45 S99firewall_final -
  >../firewall
```

Note that both the start and kill scripts are really just symbolic links to the same script, which lives in the /etc/rc.d directory (in the case of SuSE) or in the /etc/rc.d/init.d directory (in the case of Red Hat and other Linux distributions). When the system is coming up, the S scripts are invoked with a command-line argument of start. When the system is coming down, the K scripts are invoked instead, with a command-line argument of stop. The two numbers after the first letter of the script determine the order in which the script is executed. For example, the S20at script is executed before the S21cron script.

Although the size of the /etc/rc.d directory indicates that there are a large number of daemons started, in reality, most of these scripts check for the existence of a specific configuration before starting the service. This means that unless you have explicitly asked your server to offer a specific service (such as RWHO, for example), the daemon is not started by the script. The S20rwhod script, shown in Listing 17.5, first checks the

/etc/rc.config file and only starts the rwho daemon if it detects that
the $START_RWHOD environment variable has been set to yes.

Listing 17.5: The *S20rwhod* Startup Script

```
[ramon]$ more S20rwhod
#! /bin/sh
# Copyright (c) 1998, 2000 SuSE GmbH Nuernberg, Germany.
➥All rights reserved.
#
# /sbin/init.d/rwhod
#

. /etc/rc.config

base=${0##*/}
link=${base#*[SK][0-9][0-9]}

test $link = $base && START_RWHOD=yes
test "$START_RWHOD" = yes || exit 0

return=$rc_done
case "$1" in
    start)
        echo -n "Starting rwho daemon"
        startproc /usr/sbin/rwhod || return=$rc_failed
        echo -e "$return"
        ;;
    stop)
        echo -n "Shutting down rwho daemon"
        killproc -TERM /usr/sbin/rwhod || return=$rc_failed
        echo -e "$return"
        ;;
    reload|restart)
        $0 stop && $0 start || return=$rc_failed
        ;;
    status)
        checkproc /usr/sbin/rwhod && echo OK || echo No
process
        ;;
    *)
        echo "Usage: $0 {start|stop|reload|restart}"
        exit 1
```

```
esac

test "$return" = "$rc_done" || exit 1
exit 0
```

Note that the S20rwhod script can be used to start and kill the rwho daemon, since it checks for the command-line argument with which it was called.

The first time you boot up your system, be sure to record which daemons get started to ensure that you are not running anything that you don't intend to run. The trusty ps command is the right tool to verify which /etc/rc.d services are running on your server, as shown in Listing 17.6.

Listing 17.6: Looking for Active Network Services in the Process Table

```
[root]$ ps aux
root   1  0.0  0.0   400  280 ?    S  15:02 0:03 init
root   2  0.0  0.0     0    0 ?    SW 15:02 0:00 [powerd]
root   3  0.0  0.0     0    0 ?    SW 15:02 0:00 [kflushd]
root   4  0.0  0.0     0    0 ?    SW 15:02 0:00 [kupdate]
root   5  0.0  0.0     0    0 ?    SW 15:02 0:00 [kpiod]
root   6  0.0  0.0     0    0 ?    SW 15:02 0:00 [kswapd]
root   7  0.0  0.0     0    0 ?    SW 15:03 0:00
    [md_thread]
root  86  0.0  0.2  1384  808 ?    S  15:03 0:00
    /usr/sbin/syslogd
root 190  0.0  0.2  1632 1064 ?    S  15:03 0:00
    /usr/sbin/klogd -c 1
root 270  0.0  0.6  7264 2336 ?    S  15:03 0:00
    /usr/sbin/httpd -f
➥/etc/httpd/httpd.conf -D SUSEHELP
root 292  0.0  0.1  1280  648 ?    S  15:03 0:00
    /usr/sbin/gpm -t sun
➥-m /dev/mouse
root 301  0.0  0.1  1344  704 ?    S  15:03 0:00
    /usr/sbin/inetd
root 341  0.0  0.4  2632 1600 ?    S  15:03 0:00sendmail:
    accepting
➥connections
root 343  0.1  0.3  2376 1184 ?    S  15:03 0:11
    /usr/local/sbin/sshd
```

```
root 352  0.0  0.2  1552  880 ?   S  15:03 0:00
   /usr/sbin/cron
root 398  0.0  0.1  1224  632 tty2 S  15:03 0:00
   /sbin/mingetty tty2
root 399  0.0  0.1  1224  632 tty3 S  15:03 0:00
   /sbin/mingetty tty3
root 400  0.0  0.1  1224  632 tty4 S  15:03 0:00
   /sbin/mingetty tty4
root 01   0.0  0.1  1224  632 tty5 S  15:03 0:00
   /sbin/mingetty tty5
root 402  0.0  0.1  1224  632 tty6 S  15:03 0:00
   /sbin/mingetty tty6
root 420  1.0  2.0 14144 7848 ?    SL 15:03 1:57
   /usr/X11R6/bin/X :0
root 471  0.0  0.6  4024 2328 ?   S  15:05
   0:01 /usr/local/sbin/sshd
root 472  0.0  0.1  1392  736 ?   S  15:05 0:00
   /usr/bin/lpd
root 369  0.0  0.0    0    0 ?   Z  18:14 0:00 [cron
   <defunct>]
```

There are several noteworthy daemons in the process table in Listing 17.6:

- ▶ A sendmail process listening on TCP port 25

- ▶ A line-printer daemon (lpd) listening for network print requests from remote clients

- ▶ A web server (PID 270) listening on TCP port 80

- ▶ A syslogd process accepting remote syslog requests on UDP port 514

- ▶ A Secure Shell (SSH) process listening for client requests on port TCP 22

Let's say that you don't want to run a specific service. In this case, you need to modify the /etc/rc.d directory accordingly. There are several ways to prevent these services from starting, and each Linux distribution has a system tool (Linuxconf, YaST, and so on) that provides you with this capability. Still, it's important to know how to do it "under the hood," because all of these tools are just modifying these script directories anyway.

Part iv

You start by identifying during which run level the service is started; let's use Apache as an example. The following find command walks through the /etc/rc.d directory tree and identifies in which subdirectory the Apache script is present. For example, if you find a startup script in /etc/rc.d/rc3.d, you know that the service in question is being started when the server enters run level 3.

```
[ramon]$ find /etc/rc.d/* -name "*apache" -print
/etc/rc.d/rc2.d/K20apache
/etc/rc.d/rc2.d/S20apache
/etc/rc.d/rc3.d/K20apache
/etc/rc.d/rc3.d/S20apache
```

You can see that the apache daemon is invoked during both run level 2 and run level 3. You can then move to delete these files because they're simply symbolic links to /etc/rc.d/apache:

```
[ramon]$ sudo find /etc/rc.d/* -name "*apache" -exec rm {}
   \;
```

Note that the previous command prevents Apache from coming up the next time you restart the system. To terminate the current process, execute the following command:

```
[ramon]$ sudo killall httpd
```

By cleaning out your /etc/inetd.conf and /etc/rc.d files, you have gone a long way toward keeping your network daemons under control. The next section describes how to go the distance by also controlling some of the configuration files that unwanted daemons tend to leave behind.

ADDITIONAL NETWORK SECURITY CONSIDERATIONS

While most daemons are started from inetd and /etc/rc.d, there are also a number of places within your server that you should be watching. These include mostly configuration files for network services, which should be audited in the event that a service is unintentionally started. For example, special attention should be paid to rhosts authentication, the portmapper daemon, and services started as chroot. The next three sections of this chapter describe these topics in detail.

Disabling *rhosts* Authentication

Although most current Linux distributions no longer come configured for this type of authentication, a few older systems may still be vulnerable. First and foremost, make sure that your inetd.conf file does not include support for the rlogin daemon. The command

```
[ramon]$ grep rlogin /etc/inetd.conf
```

should not return anything. If you do have rlogin enabled, simply delete (or comment out) the offending line and restart the inetd daemon. The r series of remote access commands (rsh, rlogin, rcp) are riddled with security holes and should not be used.

In addition, look for the /etc/hosts.equiv file or an .rhosts file in any /home directory. If there is one, remove or rename it immediately. If this file contains a hostname definition (or IP address), users on that host will be able to rlogin to your server without being prompted for a password if you accidentally leave rlogin running. This is the ultimate vulnerability, and it's the main reason the r commands should never be used.

Use the following command as the root user periodically to weed out all .rhosts files from users' /home directories:

```
[ramon]$ sudo find /home -name ".rhosts" -exec rm {} \;
```

The *portmap* Daemon and RPC Services

The *portmapper* (portmap) is the network service that enables Remote Procedure Call (RPC) facilities such as Network File Systems (NFS) for file sharing and Network Information Services (NIS or "yellow pages") for name resolution. Started from /etc/rc*.d, the portmap daemon listens to local RPC servers, which register their port numbers with the portmap services. (Unlike regular inetd-driven services, RPC programs don't bind to a fixed TCP/UDP port.) Remote clients that wish to use an RPC service contact the portmap first, which then returns the port number where the RPC daemon can be reached.

RPC-based services can be extremely vulnerable to malicious attacks, especially when the intruder registers a bogus RPC service remotely and asks portmap to listen for requests to this service. In addition, it is very difficult to enforce access control on RPC-based services, especially since their associated ports change each time the system is rebooted. This makes the portmap daemon a security liability.

If you are using a Linux distribution that's over two years old, I recommend that you disable it as soon as you build your system and leave it disabled until you come up with an alternative.

TIP

If your Linux distribution is more than three years old, I also recommend that you upgrade your Linux system altogether. Just make sure that you test the upgrade on a practice server and not on a development server; otherwise you could run into a lot of trouble.

In most Linux distributions, portmap is started or stopped from one or more of the following files:

▶ /etc/rc.d/rc2.d/S11portmap

▶ /etc/rc.d/rc3.d/S11portmap

▶ /etc/rc.d/rc4.d/S11portmap

▶ /etc/rc.d/rc5.d/S11portmap

Since 1996, Linux distributions have included a secure version of the portmap service that can enforce access-control rules on the same files as TCP Wrappers (/etc/hosts.allow and /etc/hosts.deny). To find out if you're running this version of portmap, insert the following line into the /etc/hosts.deny file:

```
portmap: ALL
```

In addition, insert the following line into the /etc/hosts.allow file:

```
portmap: <a trusted hostname>
```

Then, proceed to mount an NFS share from the trusted host and from a different host. If you can mount the share from the trusted host but not from the different host, you're running a version of portmap that enforces access control. You can go ahead and enable it by putting the startup script back in /etc/rc.d/rc*.d/S11pormap.

Note, however, that securing the portmap service is only one step toward enhancing the security of your system. If you must use RPC services, make sure that each of them (NIS, NFS, and so on) is secure and up to date, because an intruder can always simply brute force guess which port the service is running on.

Running Network Services as *chroot*

Linux allows you to run a command with a modified root directory such that directory references are relative to the path specified in the chroot command. This allows you, for example, to run several instances of an HTTP server, each with its own set of configurations and executables. The idea is an attractive one: allow the process to believe that it has free reign of the server while confining it to a small "sandbox." However, the chroot protection can be easily circumvented, especially when the application runs with root privileges.

Limit chroot execution of network services to instances when the daemon runs under a nonprivileged user, and ideally to when the daemon operates in read-only mode. chroot is especially useful for non-interactive web servers whose content stays static over time.

TCP WRAPPERS

Developed by Wietse Venema during his tenure at The Netherlands' Eindhoven University, the TCP Wrappers package has quickly become a standard tool included in all of today's Linux distributions. Furthermore, this is arguably the most useful network security tool to come along since the dawning of the operating system.

By interposing itself between the inetd daemon and the server application itself, TCP Wrappers adds a layer of access control to an otherwise wide-open inetd facility. The real beauty of this tool, and the main reason for its popularity, is its simple design. There is no need to recompile (or even modify) either the inetd daemon or the server applications themselves. Instead, you simply modify your /etc/inetd.conf file to include the TCP Wrappers application instead of the real server name. The TCP Wrappers application receives and examines every connection request and decides to grant it or deny it based on a set of criteria specified by the network administrator.

The next two sections describe the TCP Wrappers installation and configuration.

Installing TCP Wrappers

The success of TCP Wrappers has resulted in its widespread use on the majority of production Linux servers today. In fact, most distributions even come outfitted with a default configuration for TCP Wrappers. If you need to install TCP Wrappers on an older Linux installation or you would like to upgrade your existing installation, simply find the RPM distribution of the tool in your favorite archive. Listing 17.7 shows you how to install TCP Wrappers using the RPM facility.

Listing 17.7: Installing TCP Wrappers via RPM (Upgrade Option)

```
[ramon]$ rpm -q tcp_wrappers
tcp_wrappers-7.6-7
[ramon]$ sudo rpm -U tcp_wrappers-7.6-10.i386.rpm
[ramon]$ rpm -q tcp_wrappers
tcp_wrappers-7.6-10
```

Listing 17.7 shows a system that was running version 7.6.7 and has been upgraded to the more recent version 7.6.10.

WARNING

Trojan horse versions of TCP Wrappers were placed on a number of public FTP servers around January 21, 1999. The offending file was labeled as version 7.6, and it introduced a root vulnerability on the systems where it was installed. I strongly discourage you from downloading this file (the TAR archive was named tcp_wrappers_7.6.tar.gz). Obtain it in RPM format from a well-known and trusted repository instead. Refer to CERT Advisory CA-1999-01 for more information.

Once you have verified your TCP Wrappers installation, it's time to look at the configuration files you need to edit. This is the topic of the next section.

Configuring TCP Wrappers

The first step in configuring the TCP Wrappers package is to make sure it is being properly invoked. This is done by ensuring that the service name field in /etc/inetd.conf is set to the location of the TCPD binary (/usr/sbin/tcpd in Listing 17.2). This allows the TCP Wrappers daemon to intercept all incoming requests and to examine them before passing them on to the real server application. The name of this application is specified in the server program arguments field of /etc/inetd.conf.

The real power of the TCP Wrappers tool is the fine-grain level of access control that it provides. The systems administrator can define a set of allowable clients for each network service. To do this, you must edit two configuration files that are typically found in the /etc directory: /etc/hosts.allow and /etc/hosts.deny. These files are already included in most Linux distributions, but make sure that they exist and edit them to reflect your site's security policy.

These two files are consulted by the TCP Wrappers application in that order (first hosts.allow, then hosts.deny) and can contain rules specifying access-control directives. The connection request is granted unless there is a specific deny directive found in one of those files. I recommend that your /etc/hosts.deny file have a catchall rule at the end that denies all requests. This forces you to enter specific allow directives for those services that should be permitted.

The basic syntax for the rules in the /etc/hosts.allow and /etc/hosts.deny files is as follows:

```
daemon_list : client_list [: shell_command]
```

These fields have the following meanings:

- ▶ daemon_list is a comma-separated list of server names.
- ▶ client_list is a comma-separated list of patterns matching one or more clients.
- ▶ shell_command is the action to execute when the rule has found a match.

Table 17.2 describes the types of expressions that can make up one of these rules.

TABLE 17.2: TCP Wrappers Configuration—Access Control List Patterns

PATTERN	MEANING
.example.com	Any hostname that ends with .example.com.
134.33	Any host address whose first two octets are 134.33.
10.0.0.0/255.0.0.0	The class-A network 10.0.0.0.
ALL	A true wildcard (any host).
LOCAL	Hostname that contains no period (.).
KNOWN	Both hostname and address are resolved (via DNS).
UNKNOWN	Both hostname and address are not resolved (via DNS).
PARANOID	Hostname does not match the address (via DNS).

Part iv

In addition, shell commands can use a number of supplied variables whose instance is replaced on-the-fly according to the current context. Table 17.3 summarizes the most significant of these variables.

TABLE 17.3:   TCP Wrappers Configuration—Shell Command Expansion

PATTERN	MEANING
%a	Client host address
%A	Server host address
%h	Client hostname
%H	Server hostname
%p	Daemon process ID
%d	Daemon process name (argv[0])

TCP Wrapper Configuration Examples

The following commands illustrate some of the access-control configurations for TCP Wrappers. This example is a limited setup, where you are denying everything except access to the finger daemon (wide open) and access to the telnet daemon (to local hosts, hosts within the .sybex.com domain, and hosts in the 192.168.0.0/16 block).

```
[ramon]$ more /etc/hosts.allow
in.fingerd:ALL
in.telnetd:LOCAL, .sybex.com, 192.168.
[ramon]$ more /etc/hosts.deny
ALL: ALL
```

The next example is similar to the previous example; it adopts a deny-all stance, but it does allow FTP connections from anywhere except the host badguy.example.com.

```
[ramon]$ more /etc/hosts.allow
in.ftpd:ALL EXCEPT badguy.example.com
[ramon]$ more /etc/hosts.deny
ALL: ALL
```

The following example is a simple configuration with a booby trap. You're allowing all traffic coming from internal hosts to all servers. You're disallowing any external traffic, and a notice of every unsuccessful connection is e-mailed to the `root` account. Note that you're actually mailing the results of the `safe_finger` command, applied against the offending host. This command is supplied with TCP Wrappers, and it acts as a barebones `Finger` client, much leaner (and more secure) than the standard Linux `Finger` client.

```
[ramon]$ more /etc/hosts.allow
ALL:LOCAL
[ramon]$ more /etc/hosts.deny
ALL: ALL (/usr/sbin/safe_finger -l @%h |/bin/mail -s %d-%h
root) &
```

Testing Your TCP Wrappers Configuration

Aside from man pages and documentation, the TCP Wrappers RPM file installs four executables as part of the TCP Wrappers package. You have already seen two of these:

/usr/sbin/tcpd The `tcpd` file is the main daemon executable, which is invoked by the `inetd` daemon before dispatching the appropriate network server application.

/usr/sbin/safe-finger The `safe-finger` file is the `Finger` application often used to obtain information across the network from a client that is attempting to establish an inbound connection.

Two other tools are important for testing your TCP Wrappers configuration. These are `tcpdchk` and `tcpdmatch`, which are described in the following two sections.

Using *tcpdchk*

The executable `/usr/sbin/tcpdchk` is the TCP Wrappers configuration "checker." The `tcpdchk` script examines the configuration files and reports any potential problems they might contain. It reports on the following types of conditions:

▶ Nonexistent pathnames in `/etc/inetd.conf`

▶ Services configured by TCPD but not in `/etc/inetd.conf`

Part IV

▶ Services that cannot be protected with TCP Wrappers

▶ Syntax errors in /etc/inetd.conf and/or the TCPD configuration files

The tcpdchk command can be invoked with the -v option for verbose, tabular output. I strongly recommend that you run this command before you go live with your TCP Wrappers setup and that you don't run it on a production server.

Listing 17.8 contains sample output from the tcpdchk command.

Listing 17.8: Running the *tcpdchk* Utility

```
[ramon]$ tcpdchk -v
Using network configuration file: /etc/inetd.conf

>>> Rule /etc/hosts.allow line 1:
daemons:  ALL
clients:  LOCAL 208.203.255. 153.39. 63.64.73. 204.177.181.
    204.254.33.
access:   granted

>>> Rule /etc/hosts.allow line 2:
daemons:  finger
warning: /etc/hosts.allow, line 2: finger: no such process
    name in /etc/inetd.conf
clients:  LOCAL
access:   granted

>>> Rule /etc/hosts.allow line 3:
daemons:  pop-3
warning: /etc/hosts.allow, line 3: pop-3: no such process
    name in /etc/inetd.conf
clients:  LOCAL 208.255.255.256
warning: /etc/hosts.allow, line 3: 208.255.255.256: not an
    internet address
access:   granted
>>> Rule /etc/hosts.deny line 1:
daemons:  ALL
clients:  ALL
access:   denied
```

In the example in Listing 17.8, the tcpdchk script found two rules in one of the TCPD configuration files that refer to the FTP and POP3 services, neither of which is found in the /etc/inetd.conf file. In addition, the tcpdchk script found a syntax error in our TCP configuration (host 208.255.255.256); an IP address octet cannot go higher than 255.

Using *tcpdmatch*

The /usr/sbin/tcpdmatch script predicts whether a request from a specific client to a given service would be granted or denied. The command syntax of the tcpdmatch script is

```
tcpdmatch service client
```

where *service* is the server name and *client* is an IP address or a hostname corresponding to the host requesting the service. For example, consider the three invocations of the tcpdmatch script shown in Listing 17.9.

Listing 17.9: Running the *tcpdmatch* Utility

```
[ramon]$ tcpdmatch in.ftpd local.example.com
client:    hostname local.example.com
client:    address  10.0.0.2
server:    process  in.ftpd
matched:   /etc/hosts.allow line 1
access:    granted
[ramon]$ tcpdmatch in.ftpd 143.45.22.3
client:    address  143.45.22.3
server:    process  in.ftpd
matched:   /etc/hosts.deny line 1
access:    denied
[ramon]$ tcpdmatch in.telnetd remote.example.com
client:    hostname remote.example.com
client:    address  207.55.44.67
server:    process  in.telnetd
matched:   /etc/hosts.deny line 1
access:    denied
```

In the first two commands in Listing 17.9, you're testing access to the FTP server, first using a local host as the destination and then using an external address as the destination. Given the TCPD configuration, the first request would be granted, and the second request would be denied. The third command example in Listing 17.9 probes access to the telnet daemon from a remote address, which is rightfully denied.

TCP Wrappers Event Logging

One of the most useful features of TCP Wrappers, second to address-based filtering (filtering based on the IP address of the requesting client), is the capability to log every incoming network request, along with the result (grant/deny). As is the case with most Linux applications, TCP Wrappers uses the syslog facility to record events of interest. Examine your /etc/syslog.conf settings and look for the TCP Wrappers log events on the file where the authpriv.* facility is directed (typically /var/log/secure):

```
[ramon]$ sudo tail -f secure
Oct 24 08:05:47 buggs in.telnetd[24257]: connect from elmer
Oct 24 08:06:07 buggs in.ftpd[24259]: connect from elmer
Oct 24 08:07:10 buggs in.rlogind[24261]: connect from elmer
Oct 24 21:04:42 buggs in.ftpd[25220]: connect from
    localhost
Oct 24 21:05:34 buggs in.telnetd[25228]: connect from
    goodguy
Oct 24 21:06:03 buggs in.fingerd[25232]: refused connect
    from badguy
```

Note that each entry in the output from this sudo command contains

▶ A datestamp

▶ The name of the host (buggs)

▶ The name of the network server

▶ The action, whether it was an acceptance (elmer, localhost, goodguy), or a denial (badguy)

It's generally a good idea to configure swatch or logcheck to look for the keyword refused and alert the staff of repeated unsuccessful connection requests, a sure sign of a brute force attack.

THE /ETC/SERVICES FILE

The /etc/services file is found in every Linux installation, and it provides a mapping between a numeric Transport layer port number (TCP/UDP) and a character string used to refer to that service. For example, the /etc/services file is where the system utilities find that

FTP uses port 21/TCP while SNMP uses 161/UDP. The general syntax of the file is

```
service-name    port/protocol    #comment
```

The meanings of these fields are as follows:

- ▶ *service-name* is the string to be looked up (for instance, ftp, snmp, or telnet).

- ▶ *port* is the numeric port number (21, 161, and so on).

- ▶ *protocol* is either TCP or UDP.

- ▶ *#comment* can also be a list of aliases for the given *service-name*.

Listing 17.10 lists the top of a typical /etc/services file found on a Linux system.

Listing 17.10: Partial Detail of a Linux */etc/services* File

```
[ramon]$ more /etc/services
# /etc/services:
# $Id: services,v 1.4 1997/05/20 19:41:21 tobias Exp $
#
# Network services, Internet style
#
# Note that it is presently the policy of IANA to assign a
# single well-known port number for both TCP and UDP;
  hence,
# most entries here have two entries even if the protocol
# doesn't support UDP operations. Updated from RFC 1700,
# ''Assigned Numbers'' (October 1994).  Not all ports
# are included, only the more common ones.


tcpmux          1/tcp          # TCP port service
    multiplexer
echo            7/tcp
echo            7/udp
discard         9/tcp          sink null
discard         9/udp          sink null
systat          11/tcp         users
daytime         13/tcp
daytime         13/udp
netstat         15/tcp
qotd            17/tcp         quote
```

Part iv

```
msp             18/tcp          # message send protocol
msp             18/udp          # message send protocol
chargen         19/tcp          ttytst source
chargen         19/udp          ttytst source
ftp-data        20/tcp
ftp             21/tcp
fsp             21/udp          fspd
ssh             22/tcp          # SSH Remote Login Protocol
ssh             22/udp          # SSH Remote Login Protocol
telnet          23/tcp
```

While it's not a requirement that service names be used, avoid using service numbers in /etc/inetd.conf because they are not as readable, and they are more prone to errors than a character string. Conversely, the netstat command (described in the next section) is much more readable if you create service names for all the service numbers in use.

THE *NETSTAT* COMMAND

The netstat command is one of the most powerful utilities available to you in your quest for a secure network configuration. While the process table shows you which daemons have been started from the command line, and the /etc/inetd.conf file shows you the ones that are inetd-controlled, the netstat command is the ultimate authority on diagnosing which ports your Linux server is listening on.

The netstat command is very broad in function, but it is the –inet and -a options that show you the current state of your network configuration. Consider the sample output in Listing 17.11.

Listing 17.11: Output of the *netstat --inet -a* Command

```
[ramon]$ netstat --inet -a
Active Internet connections (servers and established)
Proto Recv-Q Send-Q Local Address     Foreign Address
    State
tcp        0      0 buggs:ssh          elmer:1186
    ESTABLISHED
tcp        0      0 *:telnet           *:*
    LISTEN
tcp        0      0 *:ftp              *:*
    LISTEN
```

```
tcp         1    0 buggs:2148      226.146.218.1:www
      CLOSE_WAIT
tcp         1    0 buggs:2146      226.148.218.1:www
      CLOSE_WAIT
tcp         0    0 *:www           *:*
      LISTEN
tcp         0    0 buggs:1335      elmer:6000
      ESTABLISHED
tcp         0    0 buggs:ssh       elmer:39470
      ESTABLISHED
tcp         0    0 *:smtp          *:*
      LISTEN
tcp         0    0 *:ssh           *:*
      LISTEN
tcp         0    0 *:socks         *:*
      LISTEN
raw         0    0 *:icmp          *:*
      7
raw         0    0 *:tcp           *:*
      7
```

The `netstat --inet -a` command in Listing 17.11 shows the connections that are currently active (ESTABLISHED) or in the process of being torn down (CLOSE_WAIT), as well as those services that are currently awaiting new connections (LISTEN). You need to focus on this latter category and look for those services that appear after the hostname (and the period) under the `Local Address` column. In fact, I often create a script that e-mails me the output of the following `netstat` command periodically:

```
[ramon]$ netstat --inet -a | grep LISTEN
tcp         0    0 *:telnet        *:*
      LISTEN
tcp         0    0 *:ftp           *:*
      LISTEN
tcp         0    0 *:www           *:*
      LISTEN
tcp         0    0 *:smtp          *:*
      LISTEN
tcp         0    0 *:ssh           *:*
      LISTEN
tcp         0    0 *:socks         *:*
      LISTEN
```

The previous output from the netstat command is the most accurate picture of what your Linux server looks like to a potential intruder. There is a total of six services active, and there are service names for all of them. (I had to add the service name socks to /etc/services by hand; otherwise, I would simply see port 1080.)

The challenge is to make sure that the services listed by this command are those that your security policy currently allows, and to make sure that you have TCP Wrappers configurations for all these services.

Also, be sure to update the daemons that serve these ports with the latest security fixes and monitor their log files several times daily. If you follow these basic guidelines, you'll have a very close grip on the network configuration of your server.

WHAT'S NEXT?

Network security goes a step beyond system security by examining the current configuration of the daemons on the Linux server. This chapter provides a detailed discussion of the configuration of the inetd daemon, as well as the directory structure of the startup network daemons. Both of these must be considered in order to ensure a secure network configuration.

The TCP Wrappers utility is an essential addition to all Linux distributions because it provides a flexible, unintrusive tool to enforce access controls on incoming network connections. In addition, TCP Wrappers affords you the capability to maintain detailed logs of all network activity at the TCP/UDP layer. The netstat command should also be used as an aid in the process of securing the Network layer because it offers a succinct view of the ports that are currently active on the server.

In the next part of this book, we will move from security to access. You will learn about the Samba server and how to use it to allow access from Windows clients to a Linux server.

PART V

SAMBA

Chapter 18

AN INTRODUCTION TO SMB/CIFS

S amba was developed as a means of letting Unix computers offer the types of networking services used on IBM and Microsoft networks. If you're already familiar with Windows networking, you can probably skip this chapter or perhaps just skim it for information specific to Samba. You might not be familiar with Windows networking protocols, though—for instance, you might be a Unix administrator who must suddenly cater to a new group of Windows clients, or you might be trying to set up your first home network. In such cases, you should read this chapter carefully, because it lays down much of the theoretical groundwork for what follows in the next four chapters. Without an understanding of the core protocols and terminology in Windows networking, you'll have a hard time configuring Samba to fit into a Windows network.

Adapted from *Linux Samba Server Administration* by Roderick W. Smith

ISBN 0-7821-2740-1   656 pages $39.99

This chapter describes the history and fundamental technologies behind Windows networking, specifically the *Server Message Block* (SMB) protocol, also called the *Common Internet File System* (CIFS), and its relationship to other network protocols such as TCP/IP. In this chapter you'll learn about the genesis of these protocols and how they've developed over the years. You'll also learn the most common terms used in discussing Windows networks and how these terms correspond to equivalents in TCP/IP networking. Finally, I'll compare and contrast Windows networking protocols with some other common network protocols that you may already know.

NOTE

Because CIFS is the new official name for the SMB protocol, you'll sometimes see the protocol referred to by one name and sometimes by the other. This book uses SMB/CIFS to make it explicit that these two names are largely equivalent. In a few instances, I use one name in preference to the other, as when discussing pre-CIFS SMB development or CIFS as used in Windows 2000.

WINDOWS NETWORKING AND THE DEVELOPMENT OF SAMBA

Windows has its own networking history, independent of the evolution of TCP/IP networking that's familiar to most Unix and Linux administrators. It's important that you know some of this history as you're learning about Samba, because the initial SMB/CIFS design decisions still have an influence today. Since the initial protocols were established, Microsoft and others have expended increasing effort toward making them compatible with the TCP/IP networking that's become dominant. This ongoing effort is part of what makes Samba possible, but merging TCP/IP with Windows networking protocols isn't always elegant.

The Basic Protocols: NetBIOS, NetBEUI, and SMB

In the mid-1980s, IBM wanted to sell networks to businesses. These networks were not the globe-spanning networks that were beginning to emerge on mainframes and minicomputers of the time; rather, they were networks for small offices. These networks offered basic office productivity services, such as file and printer sharing. On such networks, several computers could access files stored on a central server computer or print to a single printer. The goal was to improve productivity by reducing the need for moving files around on floppy disks.

IBM's desktop computer line of the time was the ancestor of today's *x86* computer. Like today's PCs, the PCs of the mid-1980s used a *basic input/output system* (BIOS) to provide application programs and operating systems with access to machine resources. A program or OS could make a BIOS call to read the hard disk, for instance, or to display information on the screen. IBM's engineers saw the network as an extension of the computer's hardware, and so they called the basic protocols they developed *NetBIOS*. This protocol suite was released in 1984. Today, NetBIOS is a series of protocols that can be used in conjunction with various others. It sits in the middle of a stack of protocols used by Windows networking, as described shortly.

NetBIOS by itself is largely inadequate as a networking protocol. Its extension is known as the *NetBIOS Extended User Interface* (NetBEUI) and was released in 1985. Although originally an extension of NetBIOS, NetBEUI today is often considered a lower-level Transport layer in a network stack, as illustrated in Figure 18.1. NetBEUI now competes with the more common *Transmission Control Protocol/Internet Protocol* (TCP/IP) networking stack. The differences between these protocols are discussed later in this chapter in the section "SMB/CIFS and TCP/IP." For now, though, you should know that NetBEUI is a good protocol for use on small networks, but it doesn't scale up well. You can't use NetBEUI for a globe-spanning network such as the Internet because it supports only a limited number of computers (255), among other deficiencies. On the other hand, these very problems can sometimes be benefits. For example, if your Windows network uses only NetBEUI internally, the network is less likely to be invaded from the Internet.

The final core protocol of Windows networking is SMB. In fact, it's from SMB that Samba takes its name. SMB provides high-level constructs atop NetBIOS. If you look at Figure 18.1, you can see that SMB falls between user applications and NetBIOS. This is analogous to the way DOS falls between applications and the BIOS for many functions. DOS provides constructs and services, such as disk files and the capability to access them. Similarly, SMB/CIFS provides file-sharing mechanisms to allow one computer to access another's files.

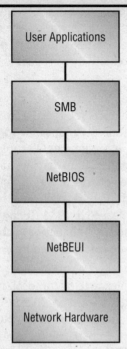

FIGURE 18.1:   NetBEUI resides between NetBIOS and the low-level networking hardware.

To the average end user, these details are largely unimportant. The typical user of Windows XP or Windows 2000 today (or of Windows for Workgroups a few years ago) wants to click on network drive icons and access files. NetBEUI or TCP/IP, NetBIOS, and SMB operate in concert to enable this sort of action. As an administrator, however, you must know something about these protocols in order to evaluate alternatives and select the appropriate protocol and configuration for your network. Only in 2000 has NetBEUI support become available for Linux, from Procom Technology (http://www.procom.com). In most cases, you'll run Samba through TCP/IP rather than through NetBEUI, but you can use NetBEUI if you like. The implications of this configuration are discussed in more detail later in the chapter, in the section "SMB/CIFS and TCP/IP."

The Evolution of SMB Protocols

Windows networking has evolved over time, just as have other computer-related standards. Because any given network might contain a mix of clients and servers that supports variants of the different SMB protocols, the initial connection between computers includes a negotiation of the level of SMB protocol to be used. Specifically, the client sends a list of the protocols it understands to the server, and the server replies with the most advanced protocol it understands from that list. The most important protocol levels are summarized in Table 18.1.

TABLE 18.1: SMB Dialects

NAME	DESCRIPTION
CORE	Original version of SMB. No support for usernames or long filenames.
COREPLUS	A more efficient implementation of CORE.
LANMAN1	Modern implementation with support for usernames and long filenames.
LANMAN2	LANMAN1 with enhancements.
LANMAN2.1	Minor enhancement to LANMAN2.
NT1	LANMAN dialect as implemented by Windows NT.
CIFS1	Minor modification to NT1 protocol, used by Windows 2000.

Samba understands all these SMB dialects, although as of version 2.2.1a, Samba's support for CIFS is incomplete. (CIFS is discussed in the section "SMB/CIFS Terminology," later in this chapter.) You can therefore use Samba to serve shares to the oldest or most recent OSs that understand Windows networking protocols. In the case of very old SMB implementations, though, such as CORE and COREPLUS, you may need to adjust your Samba configuration so that it doesn't require usernames.

The Emergence of Samba

Samba began life in 1991 at the Australian National University in Canberra. A graduate student, Andrew Tridgell, began a reimplementation of the SMB protocol. Tridgell had access to SMB servers running on VMS and Ultrix (a Unix variant for DEC minicomputers and mainframes), and he used packet sniffers and some ingenuity to deduce what the protocols did.

The first release of Samba was in 1992, albeit under a different name (SMB Server). Two years later, interest in Samba began to grow, in part because interest in Linux was accelerating at the same time, and Samba proved to be a useful way to integrate Linux into Windows networks.

Over the years, Samba has grown to support many—but not yet all—of the features of SMB/CIFS as implemented on Windows computers. Samba's capabilities are compared to those of Windows later in this chapter, in the section "Samba's Capabilities."

As I write these words, the current version of Samba is 2.2.1a. If you're using a particularly old Linux distribution that contains a pre-2.0 version of Samba, I recommend you upgrade Samba. Samba versions in the 2.0.*x* range are more usable in many situations, but 2.2.0 and later add enough features, particularly for working with Windows 2000 and later versions of Windows, to make an upgrade worthwhile in many cases. Although much of this section is relevant for Samba 1.9.*x,* some of it isn't. Most of this book's discussion of Samba applies to Samba 2.0.*x* as well as to 2.2.*x.*

There are currently two experimental branches of Samba under development. One is the predecessor to an ultimate 3.0 release of the program and is sometimes called Samba HEAD. The other is a fork from the main Samba project and is known as Samba TNG (for *The Next Generation*). The former can be found at the main Samba website, `http://www.samba.org`; the latter is hosted at `http://www.samba-tng.org`. Both implement features that help Samba operate in a Windows NT or 2000 domain environment. Other changes are being made to the mainstream 2.2.*x* tree, and these are likely to improve Samba's performance and compatibility.

With Windows 2000, Microsoft has changed the focus of its networking protocols. There are a number of new protocols, including *Active Directory Services* (ADS), a replacement that merges *Windows Internet Name Service* (WINS) and NT domains; and the *Distributed File System* (DFS), a replacement for the core SMB/CIFS file-sharing protocols. On a network that contains nothing but Windows 2000 computers, SMB/CIFS as it's known today isn't used. In late 2001, such networks are rare, however, so Samba remains useful. Support for Microsoft's new protocols will no doubt find its way to Linux, either through Samba or some other package.

SMB/CIFS in Various Environments

Today, SMB and related protocols are used mostly on networks dominated by Windows computers. Windows isn't the only OS to support SMB and related protocols, however. You can use these same protocols on a number of OSs, including the following:

Windows   Windows for Workgroups, Windows 9x/Me, and Windows NT (including Windows 2000 and XP) all support SMB "out of the box." Because these OSs are so popular, SMB and related protocols are often referred to as *Windows networking*. Indeed, I frequently use this term in this chapter.

OS/2   IBM's OS/2 4.0 and later come with support for SMB networking. Configuration details differ from Windows, but the basic capabilities of OS/2 are similar. In addition, Samba has been ported to OS/2, so you can set up a Samba server on OS/2 if you don't like the way OS/2 handles the matter or if you're using an older version of OS/2 that lacks SMB networking.

DOS   You can obtain a client for SMB networking on MS-DOS from `ftp://ftp.microsoft.com/bussys/Clients/MSCLIENT/`. You need two files, `DSK3-1.EXE` and `DSK3-2.EXE`, both of which reside in the same FTP directory.

BeOS   BeOS support for SMB exists but is still fairly new. In BeOS 5, you must use a component called WON for a BeOS computer to function as an SMB client. Samba has been ported to BeOS and enables a BeOS computer to function as an SMB server.

MacOS   A third-party utility known as DAVE is available from Thursby Software Systems (`http://www.thursby.com`). DAVE functions for MacOS much as Samba does for Linux, providing both client and server functions. DAVE is available for MacOS through version 9.1, with a limited version for MacOS X available in late 2001. Samba can also be used on MacOS X, although in 2001, client uses are limited.

Amiga   A port of Samba is available for the Amiga OS, providing it with SMB interoperability and particularly server support. Amiga SMB client support is weak, however.

VMS   VMS is an OS used mainly on DEC mainframe and minicomputers. Samba is available for VMS, allowing it to function as an SMB server. VMS client support is more limited.

Unix   Samba runs on just about all Unix computers, allowing them to function as SMB servers. Client operation is a bit spotty. All Unix systems can use smbclient, which is awkward. Some can use a package called smbwrapper, which simulates a filesystem mount.

Samba, of course, also runs on Linux. Building a Samba server under Linux is the focus of the next several chapters. Linux's SMB client support works differently from Unix's SMB client support. As of late 2001, the smbwrapper package has problems with Linux's glibc, and so it doesn't work with Linux. In Linux, the usual way to mount SMB filesystems is through a program called smbmount, described in Chapter 12, "TCP/IP Linux Networking." In most OSs for which Samba is available, a program called smbclient allows you to access Samba shares using an interface similar to that of text-mode FTP clients. The use of smbclient is covered in Chapter 12, as well.

Of course, SMB is not the only network protocol used by these various operating systems. If you're an experienced Linux systems administrator, chances are you're familiar with TCP/IP and probably with file and printer sharing via the *Network File System* (NFS) and the *line printer daemon* (1pd). You may also be acquainted with Novell or AppleTalk networks, both of which use their own network stacks. Using your knowledge of these networks to compare them with SMB should help you understand Samba networking.

SMB/CIFS and TCP/IP

SMB/CIFS can operate over either NetBEUI or TCP/IP. Therefore, SMB/CIFS and TCP/IP aren't really alternates; rather, TCP/IP is one option for operating an SMB/CIFS network. Because NetBEUI has not traditionally been supported on Linux, Samba typically operates *only* over TCP/IP. Recently, however, Procom Technology (http://www.procom.com) has released a NetBEUI protocol stack for Linux. This stack works with Samba and thus allows Samba to participate in networks that use NetBEUI exclusively.

For some time, however, Microsoft has been moving away from Net-BEUI and toward TCP/IP as a protocol stack, so in most cases there's no need to use NetBEUI on Linux. Some security-conscious administrators, however, are concerned that running SMB over TCP/IP might expose the SMB systems to Internet-based attacks. If you want to use a protocol that can't be routed across the Internet, you might want to consider NetBEUI instead of TCP/IP for your SMB/CIFS networking.

The most popular "pure" TCP/IP file-and-printer-sharing protocols, particularly in the Unix and Linux world, are NFS for file sharing and lpd for printer sharing. Following are some of the critical differences between these protocols and SMB/CIFS.

Authentication   Both NFS and lpd operate on a *trusted hosts* model of security. Any computer that appears to be calling from an approved IP address is given a specified level of access to the computer. For instance, you can configure your Linux system to give access to the /home and /opt directories to the computer at 192.168.4.43. Although Samba can be configured similarly, the usual method of authentication in Samba (and in SMB/ CIFS generally) is via username/password pairs—any user who has the correct username and password can gain access to a share. You can apply both methods to Samba, and this can increase Samba's security level. On the other hand, this model often ends up producing passwords stored on a variety of remote computers, which can itself be a potential security problem.

Filesystem Features   SMB/CIFS was created with the needs of DOS and, later, OS/2 and Windows filesystems in mind. As such, it includes features such as hidden and system bits for files but not Unix-style ownership or permission strings. NFS, on the other hand, is a Unix file-sharing protocol by design, so it includes Unix features but not DOS/Windows features. As a general rule, therefore, NFS is the best protocol for file sharing between Unix and Linux computers, while SMB/CIFS is best in a Windows network. Samba goes to great lengths to make Linux work like a Windows system and for the most part succeeds. With filesystem features passing through a DOS/Windows "filter," however, SMB/CIFS is a poor choice for most Unix-to-Unix file-sharing situations.

Monolithic Protocol   SMB/CIFS handles both file and printer sharing. In Samba, it can be configured completely through just one file, smb.conf. (You can also use auxiliary configuration files for various functions, though.) By contrast,

Linux's native file-and-printer-sharing protocols are separate and require separate configuration files. Further, SMB/CIFS supports a few extra network features that require separate protocols in Linux, including messages and a time protocol for clock synchronization.

Implementation Completeness   Samba is a very useful tool, but it's not yet complete. As described in the later section "Browsing," features such as backup master browser functionality are missing from Samba. Linux's support for NFS and lpd is quite complete, however. To be sure, the gaps in Samba's support for SMB/CIFS are comparatively minor, but they might be significant on rare occasions.

Despite these differences, SMB/CIFS and NFS/lpd serve much the same functions. Which works best depends largely on your network. Networks dominated by Windows computers typically work best with SMB/CIFS; those with mostly Unix or Linux computers work best with NFS/lpd. You can mix both protocols, though. Indeed, one server can share the same files and printers via both SMB/CIFS and NFS/lpd. It's even possible to add Novell's IPX/SPX and Apple's AppleTalk to the mix; these protocols don't interfere with each other.

Contrasts to Novell Networks

Novell developed a set of networking protocols at about the same time IBM and Apple did, in the mid-1980s. The result is an entire suite of network tools that competes against NetBEUI, NetBIOS, and SMB/CIFS on the Windows side; and against TCP/IP, NFS, and lpd on the Unix/Linux side. Following are some of the key components of a Novell network:

IPX   The *Internet Packet Exchange* (IPX) is one of the core protocols in Novell networking. It's roughly comparable to the Internet Protocol (IP) of TCP/IP networking.

SPX   The *Sequenced Packet Exchange* (SPX) protocol sits atop IPX, much as the Transmission Control Protocol (TCP) sits atop IP in a TCP/IP network.

NCP   The *NetWare Core Protocol* (NCP) is Novell's file-sharing protocol. Generally speaking, it's similar to SMB/CIFS or NFS.

Novell's networking scheme was developed with DOS in mind and later Windows. As such, it doesn't include support for Unix-style permissions or file ownership. The Novell setup is very efficient; it's often possible to achieve faster file transfers using Novell networking than using SMB/CIFS or NFS.

Linux includes support for Novell networking protocols. To turn a Linux computer into a Novell server, you must use one of two packages: `mars_nwe` or `lwared`, both of which are available from `ftp://sunsite.unc.edu/pub/Linux/system/filesystems/ncpfs/`. Most Linux distributions ship with at least one of these packages. You can use Linux as a client on a Novell network by using the `ncpfs` kernel module. In both configurations, you must also include IPX networking support in the Linux kernel.

It's possible to bind SMB/CIFS to the Novell network stack, but only in Windows. Linux doesn't support this option.

In recent years, Novell—like Microsoft—has adopted TCP/IP as the protocol of choice for Novell networks. Starting in NetWare 5.x, TCP/IP is the default protocol, but NCP is still used. In NetWare 6, released during the latter part of 2001, Novell has made a significant change to its networking model. NetWare 6 (and previous versions, with the correct software loaded) supports a product called Native File Access (NFA), which allows a NetWare server to provide the preferred protocol to whatever client accesses it. For example, if a Windows 2000 machine accesses the NetWare server, it responds in CIFS. For Linux/Unix, it responds in NFS, and for Apple it responds in AFP.

NOTE

For more information on Novell NetWare 6 and Native File Access, see `www.novell.com`.

Contrasts to AppleTalk Networks

In the mid-1980s, Apple developed a networking protocol for its Macintosh computers. Called *AppleTalk,* the protocol was originally designed to allow a network of Macintoshes to share an Apple LaserWriter printer, which was quite expensive at that time. Ethernet hardware was not yet as dominant as it is today, so Apple used custom networking hardware. This hardware is now referred to as *LocalTalk,* although some early documentation used the term AppleTalk for both the hardware and the software. Since then, AppleTalk has been adapted to work over Ethernet hardware—a combination that's often named *EtherTalk*.

AppleTalk is composed of a network stack, much like the other office networking protocols. Its key components include the following:

DDP   The *Datagram Delivery Protocol* (DDP) is at the core of AppleTalk. It's roughly comparable to TCP/IP or NetBEUI.

AFP   The *AppleTalk Filing Protocol* (AFP) is the AppleTalk file-sharing protocol, roughly equivalent to NFS or the file-sharing components of SMB/CIFS.

PAP   The *Printer Access Protocol* (PAP) is AppleTalk's printer-sharing protocol. It's similar to lpd or the printer-sharing components of SMB/CIFS.

In recent years, Apple has adapted AppleTalk to work over TCP/IP, just as NetBIOS can now be used over TCP/IP. Linux supports both the original AppleTalk (over Ethernet or, with rare LocalTalk hardware for *x*86 computers, over LocalTalk) and AppleTalk over TCP/IP. In most cases, you must compile DDP support into your Linux kernel. AppleTalk over TCP/IP works without this support, but you won't be able to browse Linux computers from a Macintosh's Chooser without DDP support, and printing doesn't work at all without DDP support.

You'll also need the *netatalk* package, available from http://netatalk .sourceforge.net or from many Linux distributions. netatalk lets your Linux computer function as a file and print server for Macintoshes and lets you print to AppleTalk printers. As of late 2001, however, support for using Linux as an AppleTalk client is extremely primitive and unreliable. If you need this functionality, you're better off installing NFS or SMB/CIFS support on the Macintosh.

NOTE

MacOS X is built on a Unix core, so it understands NFS natively. If your network includes many Macintoshes and you're considering upgrading them to MacOS X, this upgrade could simplify your file-sharing options, particularly if your servers already support NFS.

AppleTalk's file-sharing capabilities are similar to those of SMB/CIFS. For instance, AppleTalk operates through a username/password security model. Macintoshes also support filesystem features similar to those of

Windows, such as hidden bits, but Unix-style permissions and ownership are new in MacOS X. In addition, MacOS supports two forks for each file: a *data fork* and a *resource fork*. The data fork contains data such as ASCII text or spreadsheet data. The resource fork contains specialized information such as icons or program code. To accommodate forks, netatalk creates a hidden subdirectory in each shared directory. The resource forks go in the hidden subdirectory under a name matched to the data fork file in the main directory.

Like a NetBIOS network, an AppleTalk network is basically two-tiered. AppleTalk supports the concept of *zones,* which are similar to workgroups or domains in NetBIOS. AppleTalk can't be further expanded in a way that's parallel to that of TCP/IP networks, with domains of ever-increasing size. If you use plain DDP-based AppleTalk, those packets won't be forwarded over normal TCP/IP routers, so DDP-based AppleTalk networks are comparatively safe from external attack, just as are pure NetBEUI networks.

To learn more about using Linux as an AppleTalk server, consult the book *Linux: Networking for Your Office* (Sams, 2000).

INTEGRATION OF TCP/IP AND SMB/CIFS

The networking stack previously shown in Figure 18.1 is a fairly basic structure. One of the problems with this picture for cross-OS interoperability is that few operating systems support NetBEUI. Unix-like systems, in particular, traditionally have not supported this network stack. Instead, these OSs use TCP/IP networking, which is the protocol upon which the Internet is built. Because of the popularity of the Internet, Microsoft, Novell, and IBM have added TCP/IP support to their OSs and made it possible to bind SMB and NetBIOS to TCP/IP rather than to NetBEUI. The result is a stack of network protocols that looks much like Figure 18.1, but with TCP/IP used in place of NetBEUI. This is often called *NetBIOS over TCP/IP* (NBT).

Most Internet protocols are defined by standards documents known as *Requests for Comments* (RFCs). NBT is defined by RFCs 1001 and 1002, which outline methods of implementing NetBEUI-like functionality over TCP/IP networks.

One of the most important differences between NetBIOS/NetBEUI and TCP/IP is in the way computers are addressed. TCP/IP uses 4-byte IP addresses to represent computers, as in 192.168.33.12. The hostnames with which users reference computers are converted to IP addresses, and the numeric addresses are used in the data packets sent over the network. NetBIOS, on the other hand, uses names more straightforwardly. In a NetBIOS/NetBEUI network, packets from or to a computer known as LARCH would use the address LARCH literally in the data packets. To run NetBIOS over TCP/IP, the NetBIOS name must be converted to an IP address before the data packet can be sent.

To bridge the gap between these two different and incompatible addressing schemes, NBT can derive an IP address from a NetBIOS name and register a NetBIOS name on a local network. There are actually two ways in which both name resolution and name registration can occur: broadcast and *NetBIOS Name Service* (NBNS). On a broadcast network, a computer may broadcast a name to the entire network, either to register that name or to find out what computer uses the name. This approach is depicted in Figure 18.2.

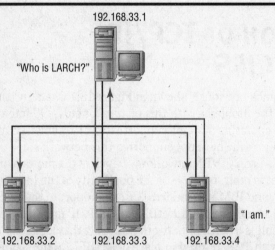

FIGURE 18.2: Broadcast name resolution or registration requires no central authority but consumes a great deal of network resources.

On an NBNS network, a computer can function as an NBNS server and handle all name-resolution functions on a network. This approach is similar to the typical TCP/IP practice of using a machine to handle

Domain Name System (DNS) resolution requests and is illustrated in Figure 18.3.

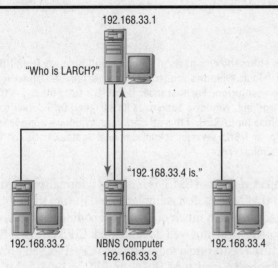

FIGURE 18.3: NBNS reduces the network load associated with name resolution but requires that a computer be devoted to the task.

In both broadcast and NBNS networks, individual computers register their names. That is, rather than assign a computer a name from a central DNS server, the individual computers initiate the process and attempt to use a locally configured name. In a broadcast network, a computer can use the name if no other system responds that the name is already in use. In an NBNS-based network, the NBNS server approves or disapproves use of a specific name.

NOTE

Even with TCP/IP, you configure a name locally on a computer, and the computer may use that name when it identifies itself to other computers in particular protocols. If this locally defined name doesn't match the name on the network's DNS servers, problems may occur. For instance, you might tell a computer that it's larch.threeroomco.com, but threeroomco.com's DNS server might point to another machine as LARCH or might have no entry for that name. In this situation, when another computer tries to make a new connection to LARCH, that connection will fail. However, this problem won't affect data returned to the computer that calls itself LARCH when LARCH initiates the connection.

Microsoft implements NBNS functionality in a service it calls the *Windows Internet Name Service* (WINS). Samba, too, can be configured to function as an NBNS server.

NOTE

Windows 2000 shifts the emphasis of name resolution away from NBNS or broadcasts. By default, Windows 2000 tries to use the computer's Internet hostname in name resolution. For instance, if you try to contact LARCH for SMB/CIFS networking, Windows 2000 uses its assigned DNS server to try to find the IP address for LARCH. If this attempt fails, Windows 2000 falls back on broadcasts or an NBNS server, if it knows of one. Samba can be configured to operate in a similar way.

CIFS, the very latest version of SMB, is basically a formalization of the expansions to SMB that Microsoft has implemented during the 1990s. In the middle of the decade, when much of the initial coding of Samba was done, the SMB protocols were not well documented. CIFS changes this state of affairs and turns SMB into a more official TCP/IP-based protocol than previously. Microsoft submitted CIFS as an RFC in 1997, but it expired before ratification. If you're interested, you can find the submission at www.ubiqx.org/cifs/rfc-draft/draft-leach-cifs-v1-spec-02.html, among other places.

SMB/CIFS TERMINOLOGY

It's important that you understand particular terms when reading about or discussing Samba and SMB/CIFS technology. Some of these terms will likely be familiar if you've worked much with other networking protocols. Others are unique to SMB/CIFS.

Clients, Servers, and Shares

You probably already know the terms *client* and *server* as used in other networking environments. Fortunately, these terms have the same meanings with respect to SMB/CIFS and Samba as they do elsewhere. In case you need a reminder, though, here's a summary:

▶ A *server* is a program that responds to network requests. Servers can either dish out existing data or receive data from a remote source, but as a general rule it's the remote source that initiates the transfer. Most of the functionality provided by Samba is on the server side, although the Samba package does include some client programs.

▶ A *client* stands at the other end of the data transfer from the server. The client initiates the data transfer, often under direct supervision of a human. For instance, in the case of Samba, a person typically uses an application program to load or save a file, print a document, or perform some other action. The SMB/CIFS client then takes that request and passes it on to the Samba server.

Client and server are defined with respect to individual transfers. In the broad scheme of things, two interacting computers can trade these roles or even occupy both simultaneously. For instance, suppose a small network contains two computers, each of which has a printer that's shared via SMB/CIFS. If the user of one computer (let's call it LARCH again) wants to print to the ink-jet printer attached to the other computer (MAPLE), then LARCH functions as the client and MAPLE is the server. If, at the same time, the user of MAPLE wants to print to the laser printer attached to LARCH, then the relationship is reversed. In that case, both computers function as both client and server, simultaneously.

Many small networks are configured in essentially this way—every computer can run both client and server versions of the same protocols. Such a network is known as a *peer-to-peer* network, because each computer is the equal of every other. Other networks are set up in a *client-server* configuration, in which some computers run predominantly client programs and others run mostly as servers.

The servers in a client-server network work as central clearinghouses for data storage, printing, and other functions. This design is superior for large networks because the centralized nature of the design makes administration easier. For instance, suppose a user leaves the company. In a client-server network, you need only remove passwords and accounts on the server computers, which are typically small in number. In a peer-to-peer network, you might need to remove passwords or accounts from every computer on the network.

The other side of client-server networking is that its centralized nature requires you to be extra careful about data integrity on the servers. If a server computer crashes, the problem is much more severe than if a single computer on a peer-to-peer network crashes. For this reason, the reliability of the OS used by server computers on a client-server network is of paramount importance. Fortunately, Linux has developed an excellent reputation for reliability, one of the factors that make it a good choice as a Samba server computer.

When you configure Samba to share resources, you don't give clients complete access to everything on the computer. Instead, you give access to specific directories or print queues. These resources are then called *shares.* (In Unix-style NFS networking, the term *export* is often used in much the same way.) For instance, you might provide access to the directories /home/samba/winprogs and /home/samba/shared-data, each of which is a separate share. The client computers can then access each directory separately. Furthermore, Samba gives you a great deal of flexibility to configure who can access each share. Perhaps everybody needs access to the /home/samba/winprogs directory, but you want only a selection of users or computers to have access to the /home/samba/shared-data directory. Those who have access to the latter share might be separated into two groups: those who can write to the share and those who can't. You can control all of this through the Samba configuration file or through Linux's built-in file permissions.

Workgroups and Domains

Windows networking has traditionally been built around the concept of a workgroup. A *workgroup* is a set of computers linked together to facilitate networking tasks. For instance, you might have a workgroup for your department. Every workgroup has a name, and when you open the Computers Near Me icon within the My Network Places window, Windows automatically shows the workgroup to which your computer belongs. (In Windows 98 and earlier, there is a Network Neighborhood icon on the Desktop rather than the Computers Near Me icon within the My Network Places window.) It's therefore easy to browse shares on your own local network. You can still browse to other workgroups, but it takes a few more mouse clicks to do this; you have to open the Entire Network icon inside Network Neighborhood or My Network Places.

NOTE

Just how widely you can browse depends on a number of factors, such as the arrangement of subnets and routers on your local network, the presence (or absence) of master browser machines, and so on. Some of these factors are described briefly later in this chapter. Even if you can't use the My Network Places icon to browse a computer, you may be able to access its shares by using its Internet address. For this reason, a Samba server should be secured against unauthorized outside access.

A workgroup is a fairly primitive networking structure. Essentially, it is merely a group of computers that announce themselves as having the same workgroup name. For instance, you might have a SALES workgroup on your network, consisting of computers in the sales department. If a couple of these computers are misconfigured with the workgroup name SALS, then you suddenly have a new workgroup called SALS on your network. No special infrastructure or central configuration is required to maintain a workgroup.

A *domain,* by contrast, is a workgroup with at least minimal centralized configuration. Specifically, a domain contains one or more *domain controllers.* The domain controller can be used to control user access to resources on the domain. (You can configure Samba to function as the domain controller.) Figure 18.4 illustrates the role of the domain controller in a NetBIOS domain. Every server hands over the right to perform its own authentication to the domain controller. This approach is quite convenient because it allows for centralized authentication of user accounts and passwords. Otherwise, domains and workgroups are much the same.

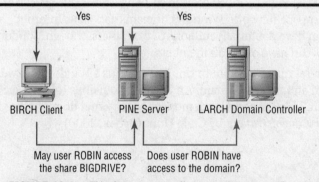

FIGURE 18.4:   The domain controller provides user authentication, but individual servers can still block access to specific shares.

One point of potential confusion is the fact that the same word—*domain*—is used to describe both the Windows networking construct and an Internet construct. Although an Internet domain need not include centralized authentication as a Windows NT domain does, similarities do exist between the two. An Internet domain is, like a Windows networking domain, a collection of computers. An Internet domain is a hierarchical naming system designed to provide unique names to a global network. The Internet domain name must be registered with central authorities, and it ends in an abbreviation such as .com or .net that denotes the domain's central authority. For instance, upenn.edu is the Internet domain associated with the University of Pennsylvania.

NOTE

If you run a TCP/IP network that's not connected to the Internet at large, you may want to create a fictitious domain name to facilitate internal networking tasks. This name should end in a code that's not valid on the Internet as a whole, such as .invalid rather than .com or .net. Be advised, however, that this approach can become unruly if you eventually join the Internet.

Because it is hierarchical, an Internet domain can be broken into *subdomains.* At the University of Pennsylvania, for example, psych.upenn .edu and cis.upenn.edu are the psychology and computer departments, respectively. A Windows NT networking domain cannot be broken into smaller sections or combined into a larger unit. With the introduction of Active Directory, Microsoft added this functionality.

Both Windows and Internet domains can span more than one physical subnet—that is, routers or bridges can sit between various groups of computers on one network. Windows domains as well as Internet domains can have potentially millions of computers, though Windows workgroups can have only 255 members.

As a general rule, a domain in this book means a Windows networking domain, not an Internet domain. An Internet domain is called specifically by that term. If you need to learn more about Internet domains, see *Linux DNS Server Administration,* by Craig Hunt (Sybex, 2000).

TIP

To avoid confusion, you may want to construct your network in such a way that your Windows domains correspond to your Internet domains or subdomains. For instance, suppose you work at the Three Room Company, which has registered the Internet domain name threeroomco.com. You want to configure networking and set up subdomains to modularize your network configuration. You therefore set up three subdomains: room1.threeroomco.com, room2.threeroomco.com, and room3.threeroomco.com. You can reuse these names and configure the machines in the same way for Windows networking, creating Windows workgroups or domains of ROOM1, ROOM2, and ROOM3. An individual computer could then have the Internet address of maple.room2.threeroomco.com and be MAPLE in the ROOM2 Windows networking domain.

Network Browsing

The term *browse* has appeared here and there in this chapter so far, and now it's time to define it. Most people think of NetBIOS browsing in terms of actions taken on a Windows client computer. Specifically, on Windows 9*x* or NT 4.0, you can double-click on Network Neighborhood to see a list of computers in your workgroup, as shown in Figure 18.5. In Windows 2000, Me, or XP, equivalent functionality comes from the Computers Near Me icon in the My Network Places folder. You can then double-click one of these computers to see its shares or double-click the Entire Network icon to see all the workgroups and domains to which your computer has immediate access.

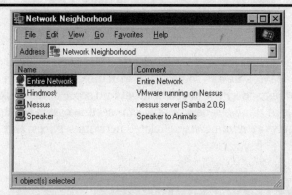

FIGURE 18.5:   Windows' My Network Places or Network Neighborhood lets you browse a network's resources much as you browse a hard disk's directories.

Network browsing works similarly to browsing a hard disk's directories, but there are some important differences:

- ▶ Any given computer may or may not give you access to its shares. In fact, depending on various configuration options, you might be able to use some shares but not others. You might even be unable to see some shares.

- ▶ You can browse to network printers. To use a printer, though, you must install a driver on the client computer.

- ▶ Computers can appear and disappear from the network as they're turned on and off, or as network problems come and go.

WARNING

Don't confuse browsing in Network Neighborhood with browsing the Web using a browser such as Netscape Navigator. Although there are similarities, these two types of browsing are quite different. For instance, file transfers are comparatively awkward and crude in Web browsing. On the other hand, you *can* access a much wider array of computers when you browse the Web using Netscape, assuming your computer has full Internet access. Recent versions of Windows blur the line between the two types of browsing, but the underlying network protocols and capabilities remain quite distinct.

THE STRUCTURE OF AN SMB/CIFS NETWORK

Now that you've covered some of the basic terms and technology underlying Windows networking and some of the structures used in those networks, it's time to go a little deeper and get into some of the pesky but necessary details of Windows networking. This section covers NetBIOS computer and network naming, name-related network services, and domain control.

Naming of NetBIOS Computers and Networks

Just like Internet host and domain names, NetBIOS names have certain restrictions:

▶ NetBIOS names can contain upper- and lowercase letters, numbers, and the following symbols:

```
! @ # $ % ^ & ( ) - ' { } . ~
```

▶ NetBIOS names cannot exceed 15 characters in length.

As a general rule, it's best to avoid symbols in NetBIOS names because they can be confusing to users—especially the period (.), which has special meaning in Internet hostnames. Furthermore, it's generally a good idea to use the same name as both the computer's Internet hostname (without the domain name) and the machine's NetBIOS name. This practice can save a great deal of confusion as you attempt to maintain your network. Because only the hyphen (-) is a valid symbol in Internet names, using the same name for both environments takes all the other symbols out of the running as name components. The same rules apply to workgroup and domain names as apply to NetBIOS machine names.

As with Internet names, NetBIOS names are not case sensitive; LARCH, Larch, and larch all refer to the same computer. Many utilities display NetBIOS names in uppercase letters, although Windows' Network Neighborhood displays only the first letter in uppercase (refer to Figure 18.5). Internet names are generally expressed in lowercase, and that convention is used in this book, as well. (Because some companies promote their website names in mixed case, their URLs are reproduced here that way, too.)

A Named Hierarchy in a Flat Space

A complete Internet machine name (often called a *fully qualified domain name,* or FQDN) consists of several names separated by periods, as in larch.room2.threeroomco.com. The rightmost component (.com in this example) specifies the name of the *top-level domain.* Each top-level domain can have many associated domains. Each of these domains can be (but is not required to be) broken up into subdomains. The subdomains can be further divided and so on, until you reach actual machine names.

This logical hierarchy allows for a huge number of machines that bear the same name but are in different domains or subdomains. For instance, larch.room2.threeroomco.com need not be the only larch in threeroomco.com; there can be a larch.room1.threeroomco.com and even a larch.threeroomco.com. Of course, there may also be machines called larch in entirely unrelated domains, or larch could be a domain name or subdomain name. This structure is part of the reason for the success of TCP/IP, because it's highly extensible. It also allows each domain to administer its own internal structure.

NetBIOS, on the other hand, uses a *flat namespace,* meaning that every machine on a network has one name, and there is no higher-level name construct such as a domain name. If you've read the earlier section on workgroups and domains, you may find this statement surprising, because Windows workgroups and domains were defined as groupings of computers, much like Internet domains. The structure of workgroups or domains is an illusion, however, as illustrated by Figure 18.6. Each computer simply knows to which workgroup or domain it belongs, and a network browser such as My Network Places can use that information to provide the appearance of a hierarchical organization, albeit one with only two levels.

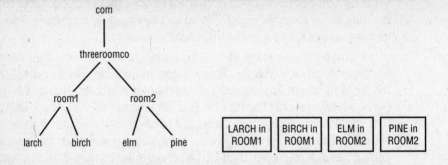

Internet Name Hierarchy   NetBIOS Flat Namespace

FIGURE 18.6:   A truly hierarchical organization like that provided by the Internet (left) is much more flexible than the flat namespace provided by NetBIOS (right).

WARNING

You cannot give the same NetBIOS name to two machines in different Windows workgroups or domains on the same subnet. If you do, you're likely to see only one of the two machines on the network, or you may see a bizarre mixture of the two, such as the comment field for one machine and the shares from the other. If you have an existing TCP/IP network with duplicated machine names in different subdomains, you may need to change one of the duplicated names, at least in NetBIOS.

NetBIOS is largely a local networking protocol, intended for use on small networks. This is particularly true of the NetBIOS naming rules and restrictions. Specifically, you're restricted from using duplicate names in two situations:

On a Single Subnet   When your network uses broadcast name resolution, the broadcasts can reach every computer on a single physical network segment, but no farther. If you use routers or similar network-joining devices between network segments, you can duplicate names on the various network segments. Such an arrangement usually works best when each network segment hosts a different NetBIOS workgroup or domain.

On Networks Served by a Single NBNS Server   Even widely separated networks can share a common NetBIOS workgroup or domain and hence may encounter name conflicts if you use an NBNS server for the domain or workgroup. If you maintain two separate workgroups or domains, however, each of which has its own NBNS server, you can duplicate names for individual machines between domains or workgroups, but not within these structures.

As an example, consider the fictitious threeroomco.com. Suppose each of its three rooms contains a subnet, and the subnets are linked together through a router. In this situation, if the NetBIOS computers are configured to use broadcast addressing, then the same NetBIOS name can appear on computers in each of the three rooms. Each room effectively hosts its own workgroup or domain, even if you use the same workgroup name or domain name. If one computer is set aside as an NBNS server, however, and if all the computers are configured to use that NBNS server, then each computer must have a unique name.

Factors other than naming play a role in this arrangement, as well. Specifically, browsing and domain controllers often require special configuration to function in a routed network environment.

It is the fact that NetBIOS naming protocols require special configuration to be routed that prevents NetBIOS-created chaos from spreading through the Internet as a whole. The fictitious threeroomco.com can have a computer called LARCH, and that computer's name doesn't conflict with a computer of the same name at the fictitious pangaea.edu because these two Internet domains are physically separate and haven't taken steps to join their NetBIOS networks together.

Resource Types

Earlier, in the section "Naming of NetBIOS Computers and Networks," I said that NetBIOS names are 15 characters (that is, bytes) long. This isn't quite entirely correct. In fact, NetBIOS uses 16-byte names—but the 16th byte is used as a resource type code. (If necessary, the computer pads a shorter name to 15 characters by using spaces.) The computer can then use the same (15-character) name several times, once with each resource code that's associated with each resource the computer wants to register. In effect, the network sees the computer as several computers simultaneously, with names that are identical except for their type codes.

Table 18.2 explains the resource types for individual computers. Some of these values aren't used under Samba, as indicated in the table. The most important services are 00 (which is used by all NetBIOS-equipped computers) and 20 (which indicates that the computer offers one or more file or printer shares).

TABLE 18.2:   NetBIOS Resource Types

RESOURCE	VALUE (IN HEXADECIMAL)	FUNCTION
Standard Workstation Service	00	Main computer name.
Messenger (WinPopup) Service	03	Person-to-person text transmission service, similar to `talk`.
RAS Server Service	06	A server that allows remote access to Windows via a modem. Not supported by Samba.
Domain Master Browser Service	1B	A computer that collects other computers' names for use by a client browser.
Master Browser Name	1D	Like a domain master browser, but limited in range to a single subnet.
NetDDE Service	1F	Network Dynamic Data Exchange. Used to share data across networked applications. Not supported by Samba.
File or Print Service	20	File or printer sharing. Described in Chapter 22.
RAS Client Service	21	A remote access client, not to be confused with resource type 06, the RAS server. Not supported by Samba.
Network Monitor Agent	BE	A tool and protocol for monitoring network performance. Not supported by Samba.
Network Monitor Utility	BF	Similar to Network Monitor Agent. Not supported by Samba.

In addition to the resource codes associated with individual comput-ers, codes are associated with workgroups or domains. Because computers register themselves with workgroups or domains, in practice these codes come from individual computers; the codes simply announce the group-related resources offered by the computer. See Table 18.3.

TABLE 18.3: NetBIOS Group Resource Types

RESOURCE	VALUE (IN HEXADECIMAL)	FUNCTION
Standard Workstation Group	00	Domain or workgroup name; used once by each client.
Logon (WINS/NBNS) Server	1C	Server that authenticates user for a domain.
Normal Group Name	1E	Group name used during browser elections.
Group Name	20	Occasionally used as a duplicate of the workstation group value.

Like the resources for individual machines, not all the group resource types are used by all computers. Most computers will use the 00 (Standard Workstation Group) and 1E (Normal Group Name) entries. If a computer serves as a master browser, as described shortly, the 1C entry will be used.

A computer may also register a resource with the name of a user. This usually happens in conjunction with a code of 03 and is used for Messenger (WinPopup) services. When a computer allows Messenger service, it accepts messages that it immediately shows to the specified user.

NOTE
There is overlap in the codes used for machine, group, and user NetBIOS resources. For instance, a computer may register itself twice with the code 00—once to register its presence as an individual computer and again to register its presence in a domain or workgroup.

You can check on these codes in Windows or in Linux by using one of two commands, depending on the OS. You might do this as a trou-bleshooting measure. For example, if you've configured a system to take

Part v

on NBNS server functions but it's not working, you could check it and other systems in this way. Here are the commands you can use for this inquiry:

For Linux:

nmblookup -SR *name*

For Windows:

NBTSTAT -a *NAME*

The output of both commands is similar but not identical. In both cases, *name* is the NetBIOS name of the target computer. For instance, here's how to check the status of SPEAKER, from Linux:

```
$ nmblookup -SR speaker
querying speaker on 192.168.1.255
192.168.1.1 speaker<00>
Looking up status of 192.168.1.1
received 9 names
        SPEAKER          <00> -           M <ACTIVE>
        SPEAKER          <03> -           M <ACTIVE>
        SPEAKER          <20> -           M <ACTIVE>
        .._MSBROWSE__. <01> - <GROUP> M <ACTIVE>
        RINGWORLD        <00> - <GROUP> M <ACTIVE>
        RINGWORLD        <1b> -           M <ACTIVE>
        RINGWORLD        <1c> - <GROUP> M <ACTIVE>
        RINGWORLD        <1d> -           M <ACTIVE>
        RINGWORLD        <1e> - <GROUP> M <ACTIVE>
num_good_sends=0 num_good_receives=0
```

This output shows that the computer called SPEAKER has registered the name SPEAKER three times, using the codes 00, 03, and 20; it's registered ..__MSBROWSE__. once and RINGWORLD five times with codes 00, 1B, 1C, 1D, and 1E. The instances of SPEAKER register the computer itself and tell the network that it can accept Messenger messages and offers file or print shares. (The name ..__MSBROWSE__. is a special name that announces a master browser, described shortly, to a workgroup or domain. The periods in this name are actually nonprinting characters that NBTSTAT and nmblookup display as periods for convenience.) RINGWORLD is the name of the domain to which SPEAKER belongs. The five RINGWORLD codes register the machine as part of the domain (00 and 1E) and advertise it as offering browse services, including both subnet and domain master browser services (1B through 1D).

The Role of PDCs

A *primary domain controller* (PDC) is a computer that's able to handle authentication requests for a domain, as described earlier and shown in Figure 18.4. This term is sometimes restricted to login support for Windows NT networks rather than Windows 9*x* networks. A *backup domain controller* (BDC) serves a similar function but exists, as its name implies, as a backup to the PDC. In an environment with a PDC and BDCs, clients request logon authentication from the BDCs to offload the PDC.

 NOTE

Windows 9*x* and Windows NT use different authentication technologies. Samba supported Windows 9*x* authentication well before it supported Windows NT authentication. As of version 2.0.5a, Samba supports basic PDC functions for both Windows 9*x* and NT. For more complete PDC support, you may need to use more recent versions of Samba. Samba's BDC support does not exist in version 2.2.1a, but it is being added to development versions of Samba (in both the TNG and HEAD branches). If this support is important to you, you should either use Windows NT computers as both PDC and BDC systems or look into the latest (possibly experimental) version of Samba. In addition, Windows 2000 and Active Directory significantly change the purpose of a domain controller and remove the distinctions between primary and backup.

The presence of a PDC is the key feature that distinguishes a domain from a workgroup, as described earlier in this chapter. As a general rule, domains are easier to administer than are workgroups. This is because domains use centralized user databases, so on domains it's easier to add and remove users or change users' passwords than on workgroups—particularly if users routinely use more than one computer. If configured properly, domains can also be more secure, because it's more practical to remove potentially insecure Windows 9*x*/Me password files from client computers. I therefore recommend configuring Samba or a Windows NT or 2000 computer as a PDC in most cases.

Samba's PDC support is rudimentary. It supports centralized logons, but Microsoft has implemented remote configuration tools that are supported poorly, if at all, by Samba. This is a focus of current Samba development efforts, however, so Samba is likely to improve in this area in the near future.

The Role of NBNS Servers

If present, the NetBIOS Name Service (NBNS, also known as WINS) server functions much like a DNS server: It fields requests from client machines for the IP address of a specified computer. NBT actually supports four methods of address resolution. These methods, described below, are called *node types,* in reference to the behavior of a computer (a *node*) that needs to locate another computer.

b-node   The computer sends a broadcast to all the computers on a subnet to locate the target machine. This approach is roughly equivalent to walking up to an office building and using a megaphone to ask for somebody from a specific office to identify that office for you.

p-node   The computer sends a request to the network's NBNS server to ask for the address of a given computer. This is akin to using a directory listing in an office building to locate an office.

m-node   The computer sends a broadcast and, if that approach is unsuccessful, the computer sends a request to the NBNS machine.

h-node   The computer sends a request to the NBNS computer. If the NBNS server doesn't know the name of the target computer, the requester sends a broadcast. Computers that use this approach are also known as *hybrid* nodes.

Most Windows clients are configured as h-nodes. Because broadcasts require every computer to do some work, they tend to be expensive in terms of network resources. Most computers don't actually respond to broadcasts, but they do receive them. Using an NBNS computer, by contrast, reduces the need for system resources because the name discovery process uses point-to-point communication. Particularly if your network uses switches rather than hubs, such point-to-point communication helps to conserve network bandwidth. Broadcasts also don't pass through routers, so you can't use broadcast name resolution if your network consists of several subnets. (There are workarounds possible with Samba, but it's usually easier to use NBNS.)

As with domain controllers, there can be both a primary and a backup NBNS machine for a domain or workgroup. Although Samba can be configured as a primary NBNS, currently it cannot function as a backup NBNS. (Both domains and workgroups can host NBNS computers.)

NetBIOS Browsing

Browsing may seem quite simple from a user's point of view when everything works as expected, but it can actually be quite complex from a network point of view. In order for browsing to function properly, one computer must serve as the *master browser*. This computer is responsible for maintaining a list of the other computers on the network, known as the *browse list*. The browse list contains only machines that are available, not each machine's shares. For instance, suppose a user wants to browse to the JENNIE share on the computer TURRILL. The client computer consults the master browser to obtain a list of computers, including TURRILL. When the user clicks on TURRILL, the client system consults TURRILL directly for a list of available shares, which presumably includes JENNIE. This approach minimizes network traffic and reduces the load on the master browser.

In fact, there are different types of master browsers available—specifically, *domain* and *local* master browsers. The local master browser handles browse requests on a specific subnet. A domain master browser handles browse requests for an entire domain, even if that domain includes multiple subnets. When a domain spans multiple subnets, each local master browser must be told about the other subnets in order to synchronize browse lists across subnets.

You don't normally specify a master browser explicitly. Rather, the computers in a network follow certain rules to determine which one is to serve as the master browser. This procedure is known as an *election;* elections take into consideration factors such as the OS on each machine, the amount of time each computer has been running, and (as a last resort) the name of each machine. You can rig a Linux computer to win (or lose) a master browser election. Linux can function as a local or domain master browser but not as a backup browser (the computer that takes over browsing functions if the master browser goes down).

When a computer comes online, it's supposed to announce its presence to its local master browser. Similarly, when a computer shuts down normally, it's supposed to announce its unavailability to the local master browser. Of course, if a computer crashes, the latter notification won't happen, but the local master browser will eventually figure this out and remove the computer from its browse list.

Because of the way browsing occurs, it's possible for a Windows browse list to show inaccurate information, both on the master browser and on individual clients. When a master browser updates its list, it doesn't automatically notify all the clients of that change. Therefore, you may need to select View ➢ Refresh in an open Windows network browser to obtain the latest information from the master browser. When the master browser itself contains outdated information, this action may not be adequate. Even if a computer doesn't appear in a browse list, you can access the computer by typing its name directly into a Windows Address field. For instance, if the computer TURRILL doesn't appear in a browse list, you can still access the JENNIE share on that computer by typing **\\TURRILL\JENNIE** in the Address field.

Samba's Capabilities

Samba can fill most of the major roles available in a Windows network, including the most critical ones of file server and print server (see Table 18.4 for a summary of Samba's capabilities). See Chapter 22 for more information about configuring Samba to function as a file-sharing server.

TABLE 18.4:   Samba's Windows Networking Capabilities

Network Role	Samba's Capability
File server	Yes
Print server	Yes
Local master browser	Yes
Domain master browser	Yes
Backup local browser	No
Primary domain controller (PDC)	Yes (version 2.0.5a or later required; limited but improving capability)
Backup domain controller (BDC)	No
Primary NBNS/WINS server	Yes
Secondary NBNS/WINS server	No

WARNING

A Samba server can sometimes usurp the role of master browser on a functioning network. If that happens, with any luck the network will continue functioning normally. If you experience browsing problems on any computers after adding a Samba server, though, you can add the lines os level = 1, preferred master = No, and domain master = No to the [global] section of your smb.conf configuration file. These options should ensure that Samba will never take on the role of master browser.

WHAT'S NEXT?

The basic structures and protocols for Windows networking resemble but are different from those used by traditional Unix and Linux networking tools. Although it's possible to set up a simple Samba server without understanding the details of Windows networking protocols, it's imperative that you understand these details when your network is complex or when you want the Samba server to take over critical but transparent services such as NBNS/WINS server functions.

The structures and components of a Windows network parallel those of other network types, such as TCP/IP, Novell, or AppleTalk. All networks require some means of name resolution, organization, and so on. Although the names and configuration details differ, your experience in configuring TCP/IP equivalents to NetBIOS structures can be useful in grasping the basics of what a protocol does. Be careful not to draw the parallels too closely, however, because there *are* critical differences. Those differences are discussed in subsequent chapters.

Chapter 19

INTEGRATING SMB/CIFS
INTO LINUX

Linux, modeled after Unix, was not designed as a Windows network server. Although certain aspects of Unix and Windows are similar, the two differ in many details. Samba must therefore overcome these differences in order to serve files to a Windows network effectively. Considered strictly as a Linux package, Samba must integrate itself into the usual structure of Linux servers. This task is less daunting than the task of masquerading a Linux filesystem as a Windows filesystem, but it's still helpful to know something about Samba's internal structure as you configure the system. The mainstream versions of Samba follow one structure, but the TNG branch follows another. Both are covered in this chapter.

This chapter explains the basic principles for getting Samba to work with Linux. These include the integration of SMB/CIFS with TCP/IP networking and an overview of the Samba daemons and the tasks they perform. In addition, we'll look at the differing assumptions about filenames and attributes made by Linux and Windows and how Samba strives to bridge those differences.

Adapted from *Linux Samba Server Administration*
by Roderick W. Smith
ISBN 0-7821-2740-1   656 pages $39.99

SMB/CIFS over TCP/IP

As mentioned in Chapter 18, "An Introduction to SMB/CIFS," the typical method for using Samba in Linux is at the top level of a TCP/IP network stack. In the past, Windows relied on a competing network stack, Net-BEUI, for linking Windows computers. Today, however, TCP/IP is a common—but not universal—network stack for using SMB/CIFS even on the Windows platform. This section describes the advantages and disadvantages of TCP/IP as a transport mechanism for SMB/CIFS and the basics of integrating the two.

Binding SMB/CIFS to TCP/IP in Windows

The default installation of Samba binds to TCP/IP in Linux. Because this is a common configuration in Windows, it's simplest to use TCP/IP for SMB/CIFS networking. If you have strong reasons to use NetBEUI, you can do so with the help of a third-party add-on from Procom Technology (http://www.procom.com). Procom's open-source NetBEUI stack for Linux forces you to recompile both the Linux kernel and the Samba package, making installation of NetBEUI support tedious compared to using the standard TCP/IP-based Samba.

To use the standard server setup with TCP/IP, you need to make sure that the clients are properly configured. SMB/CIFS may or may not be bound to TCP/IP on your Windows computers. This section tells you how to ensure that a Windows computer uses TCP/IP rather than NetBEUI. Incorrect binding of services can result in slow network performance (particularly when opening a share or starting to browse) or, in extreme cases, complete inability to use the network services. It's therefore important that your Windows clients bind SMB/CIFS to TCP/IP correctly.

Windows 9x/Me

Windows 9x/Me automatically binds SMB/CIFS networking to TCP/IP, but this configuration can become undone. Also, if NetBEUI is installed, Windows may attempt to use it instead of TCP/IP, leading to poor performance or even an inability to reach Samba servers on your network. Therefore, I recommend removing NetBEUI when you use NetBIOS over TCP/IP. Because NetBEUI isn't normally used by any other protocol, removing it won't create any problems if your entire network uses TCP/IP rather than NetBEUI.

WARNING

If you use NetBEUI for SMB/CIFS networking, ensure that NetBEUI is installed, but *do not* remove TCP/IP. Doing so disables other networking protocols, including web browsing and FTP.

To remove NetBEUI, open the Windows Control Panel and double-click the Network icon. You'll see a dialog box similar to the one in Figure 19.1. If you see a NetBEUI item, select it and click Remove. Windows immediately removes the protocol. When you click OK, Windows may prompt you to restart the computer.

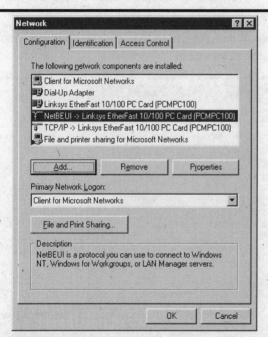

FIGURE 19.1:   Network protocols are listed in the Windows Network dialog box.

NOTE

Figure 19.1 shows that NetBEUI is linked to a Linksys EtherFast 10/100 PC-Card network card, which also appears in the list just above the NetBEUI entry. On your computer, you should see a linkage to whatever network card you have. If the network card's drivers aren't installed, install them. Consult the network card's documentation or a book on Windows for details.

If your Network dialog box shows that the Novell IPX ODI protocol or IPX/SPX-compatible protocol is installed, you can remove either protocol for the same reasons and in the same manner that you remove NetBEUI. Of course, all of these protocols—IPX ODI, IPX/SPX, and NetBEUI— should be removed only if they are not being used.

If your Network dialog box doesn't show a TCP/IP entry like the one below NetBEUI in Figure 19.1, add TCP/IP support to your computer by following these steps:

1. Click Add in the Network dialog box.

2. In the Select Network Component Type dialog box that appears, select Protocol and then click Add.

3. Select Microsoft and TCP/IP in the Select Network Protocol dialog box (see Figure 19.2).

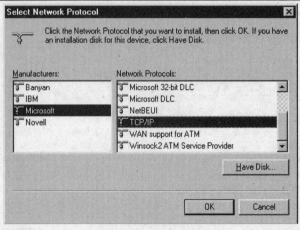

FIGURE 19.2:   You can choose from several network protocols, but only a few are in common use—including TCP/IP.

4. Click OK. Windows may ask for your installation CD. When Windows is done installing the TCP/IP software, it might reboot your computer.

Figure 19.1 shows that the computer hosts both the Client for Microsoft Networks and the File and Printer Sharing for Microsoft Networks protocols. These are SMB/CIFS client and server packages, respectively. If your Windows computer is to be only a client, you can remove the unnecessary package. (Client software is useful even on a server, so I recommend you leave it in place.) If you need to add a package, you can do so in much the same way that you added TCP/IP networking support. Instead of selecting Protocol in the Select Network Component Type dialog box, though, you select either Client or Service. You must then select the appropriate Microsoft packages. Once installed, these services should bind automatically to TCP/IP or NetBEUI.

To ensure that SMB/CIFS is bound to TCP/IP, follow these steps:

1. In the Network dialog box, select TCP/IP.

2. Click Properties to bring up the TCP/IP Properties dialog box.

3. Select the Bindings tab, shown in Figure 19.3. Ensure that the Client for Microsoft Networks item is checked. If your Windows computer is to function as a server, be sure that the File and Printer Sharing for Microsoft Networks item is also checked.

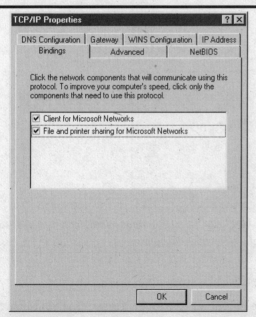

FIGURE 19.3:   Bind clients and servers to TCP/IP from the TCP/IP Properties Bindings tab.

Windows NT 4

Windows NT 4 uses network configuration options similar to those of Windows 9x/Me, but just different enough to cause confusion in some cases. As with Windows 9x/Me, you can avoid several potential problems by removing the NetBEUI protocol, if it's installed and you don't need it. To do so, log on as Administrator and follow these steps:

1. From Control Panel, double-click the Network icon to open the Network dialog box.

2. Click the Protocols tab to open it. It will resemble the one in Figure 19.4.

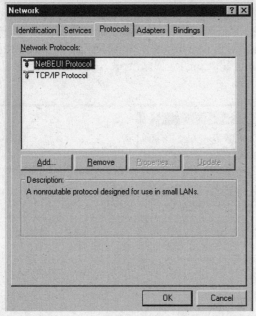

FIGURE 19.4:   In Windows NT, you can add or remove protocols from the Protocols tab of the Network dialog box.

3. Select the NetBEUI Protocol item.

4. Click Remove. Windows asks for confirmation, then removes the protocol. Windows may prompt you to reboot your computer after this step.

If you need to add TCP/IP networking, you can do so from the same Network dialog box. Select the Add button rather than Remove, and pick the appropriate protocol from the list that Windows NT presents.

To ensure that the SMB/CIFS protocols are installed, click the Services tab in the Network dialog box and examine the list of available services. The service called Server provides SMB/CIFS server features; Workstation provides SMB/CIFS client functionality. You can safely omit the former if the computer will be used only as a client. If you need to add a service, click Add and select the appropriate protocol from the list. Windows may prompt you to reboot the computer after installing the new protocol.

If you install TCP/IP but not NetBEUI or IPX/SPX, Windows NT will automatically bind SMB/CIFS to TCP/IP. If you have multiple protocols installed and want to bind only one to the SMB/CIFS features, you can do so from the Bindings tab (see Figure 19.5). Windows NT tries the protocols (TCP/IP or NetBEUI) in the order in which they appear for each service. You can enable, disable, or shift a protocol within the displayed order; select the protocol and click the appropriate button in the dialog box.

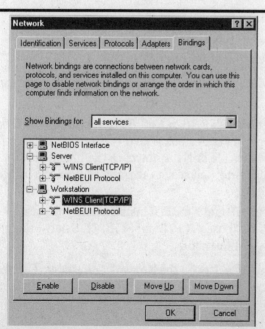

FIGURE 19.5:   Windows NT gives fine control over the order in which the OS tries network stacks with SMB/CIFS clients and servers.

TIP

You can use Windows NT's bindings as a primitive means of access control. For instance, you might want to use TCP/IP under Workstation for accessing a Samba server but disable TCP/IP on the server side to reduce the risk of break-ins from the Internet, while leaving NetBEUI active on the server to allow local NetBEUI-based access.

Windows 2000 and XP

By default, Windows 2000 and XP use TCP/IP for SMB/CIFS networking. If your Windows 2000 computer has been configured for NetBEUI and you want to change this, follow these steps as Administrator:

1. From Control Panel, open the Network and Dial-up Connections window.

2. Right-click the Local Area Connection icon and choose Properties from the pop-up menu. This produces the Local Area Connection Properties dialog box, which is similar to the Windows 98 Network dialog box shown in Figure 19.1.

3. Select NetBEUI Protocol from the list.

4. Click Uninstall. Windows 2000 asks for confirmation. Proceed with removal of the protocol.

5. Windows 2000 will probably suggest restarting the computer. Do so.

If you need to add either TCP/IP or NetBEUI support, use the Local Area Connection Properties dialog box. The procedure is similar to that described for Windows 9x/Me or NT 4; you click the Install button, highlight Protocol, click Add, and select the protocol from the list that Windows 2000 provides.

If you have both TCP/IP and NetBEUI installed and you want to ensure that Windows 2000 uses TCP/IP for SMB/CIFS networking, follow these steps as Administrator:

1. From Control Panel, open the Network and Dial-up Connections window.

2. Right-click the Local Area Connection icon and choose Prop-
    erties from the pop-up menu. This produces the Local Area
    Connection Properties dialog box, which is similar to the
    Windows 98 Network dialog box shown in Figure 19.1.

3. Select Internet Protocol (TCP/IP) and click Properties.

4. In the Internet Protocol (TCP/IP) Properties dialog box, click
    the Advanced button.

5. In the Advanced TCP/IP Settings dialog box, click the WINS
    tab, which will resemble the one shown in Figure 19.6.

6. To use TCP/IP for SMB/CIFS networking, click the radio but-
    ton for Enable NetBIOS Over TCP/IP.

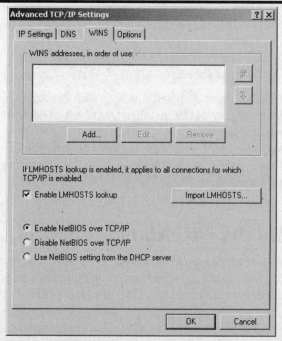

FIGURE 19.6:   The WINS tab primarily controls name resolution but also allows
                    you to enable or disable NetBIOS over TCP/IP.

Linux Features Required for Samba

To use Samba in Linux, you must include certain features and packages. These include the following:

TCP/IP Networking   You must enable TCP/IP networking support in your Linux kernel, including support for your network card. All major Linux distributions' kernels come configured appropriately for TCP/IP networking.

SMB Filesystem Support   If you intend to mount SMB/CIFS shares on your Linux computer, the SMB filesystem support option must be enabled in your Linux kernel. In the Linux kernel configuration, this option appears in the Filesystems menu, in a Network File Systems suboption. All major Linux distributions come with this support enabled by default, but you'll need to attend to this matter if you recompile your kernel. You do *not* need to activate this support if you don't intend to mount SMB/CIFS shared directories or if you intend to use only SMB/CIFS printer shares.

Samba   All major Linux distributions ship with Samba, but the package may or may not be installed by default. If Samba isn't installed, or if you want to use a more advanced version than whatever comes with your distribution, you'll need to obtain and install the Samba software. Chapter 20, "Installing Samba," covers this matter in detail.

THE SAMBA DAEMONS

Linux operates most network servers as *daemons*. The word *daemon* comes from a Greek word meaning *helper,* and Linux daemons help networks by providing services. Daemons typically run unattended in the background. You configure them through special configuration files (smb.conf in the case of Samba) and then set the daemon up to run when the computer starts. Once it's in place, you need not deal with the daemon directly. If it encounters a problem, it typically records the error in a log file, such as /var/log/messages. Most daemons, including Samba, can run for months on end without requiring attention, assuming the initial configuration is good.

Traditionally, Samba has used two daemons, smbd and nmbd, to handle all its server tasks. Samba TNG, however, splits these daemons into several smaller ones. Both schemes are described in this section, which offers an overview of the Samba daemons and their functions.

Instructions for starting and stopping Samba's daemons are not included here. For that information, read the section "Running Samba" in Chapter 20.

NOTE

In addition to the daemons described here, the Samba package includes a daemon called the *Samba Web Administration Tool* (SWAT), which allows for remote or local Samba administration via a web browser. SWAT is described in Chapter 21, "GUI Configuration Tools and the *smb.conf* File."

Samba 2.2.*x*

In late 2001, the current stable release of Samba is 2.2.1a. This version and other 2.2.*x* releases of Samba use two daemons: nmbd and smbd. Earlier versions of Samba also used this configuration, as does the HEAD development tree that's leading towards a 3.0 release. As a general rule, nmbd handles initial computer-to-computer identification, whereas smbd handles the core file-and-printer-sharing functions.

It's possible to run one daemon without running another, but if you do this, your system will lack important functionality. If one daemon crashes or doesn't start but the other works correctly, you may experience some strange connectivity problems. For instance, you might be able to see a computer in the Windows Network Neighborhood but not log onto it; you may be prevented from browsing the computer but be able to access its shares if you connect in some other way. For any such problems, check to see that both daemons are running.

The smbd program typically consumes about 1MB of RAM for each connection it maintains. This amount may go up as the connection is used. For each connection, smbd spawns a new instance of itself, so if you use ps to view your processes, it's not uncommon to see several instances of smbd running. Because of smbd's memory use, it's important that a Samba server have enough memory to service all its clients. In a large network with dozens or hundreds of clients, you may need hundreds of megabytes of RAM in a Samba server. In a small network with just a few clients, a server with 16MB to 32MB may be adequate, although it's probably best to have at least 64MB even for a small server.

nmbd: The NetBIOS Name Browser Daemon

The nmbd program understands the NetBIOS **name b**rowser protocols; hence the program's name. These services are critical if a Samba server is to respond to broadcast NetBIOS name requests or if the computer is to function as an NBNS/WINS server. You can configure many details of nmbd's operation through the main Samba configuration file, smb.conf.

Although nmbd is normally considered a daemon, its default operation is *not* to operate as a daemon. You have to use the -D switch to force nmbd to run as a daemon.

NOTE

nmbd normally listens for connections on UDP port 137. You can override this behavior with the -p switch, but there's seldom any reason to do this because clients won't know to use the unusual port.

Following are some of the services supplied by nmbd:

Response to Name Broadcasts   As described in Chapter 18, when a Windows network does *not* include a NetBIOS Name Server (NBNS), client machines send broadcast messages to all computers on the network in order to locate a specific machine. For instance, if you configure a Windows computer to mount a share from LARCH, the Windows computer sends a broadcast to all the computers asking which one is LARCH. If nmbd is running and is configured to respond to that name, it responds to the request.

By default, nmbd responds to the computer's TCP/IP hostname, but you can configure it to respond to other names. You'll need to edit the smb.conf configuration file or pass the name with the -n parameter to nmbd.

NBNS Duty   You can configure nmbd to function as an NBNS computer and field requests to identify other computers. In this arrangement, if ELM wants to contact LARCH, ELM contacts the computer running nmbd and asks for LARCH's address. Then nmbd responds with LARCH's 4-byte IP address. In addition, when configured in this way, nmbd automatically compiles a mapping of NetBIOS names to IP addresses, so that the daemon can respond correctly when queried about a name.

NBNS Proxy Sometimes you may want nmbd to function as a *proxy* for NetBIOS name broadcast queries. Suppose you have two subnets, as shown in Figure 19.7. Because they're separated by a router, NetBIOS name requests don't reach from one subnet to another. Using nmbd as an NBNS proxy, however, facilitates broadcast NetBIOS name queries by having a system on each subnet respond as a proxy for systems on the other. This feature is most likely to be useful if you have a large subnet that's already configured to use broadcast name queries and you want to add a few machines from another subnet to a workgroup or domain on the main subnet. If the main subnet is configured to use NBNS to begin with, there's no need to set up a proxy.

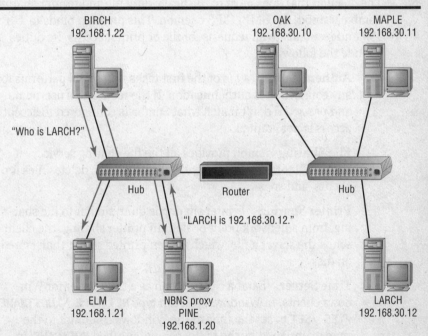

FIGURE 19.7: An NBNS proxy lets you expand a broadcast-based network with minimal fuss.

Master Browser Duty nmbd can function as a master browser, either for the local subnet or for an entire Windows network. When it does so, nmbd maintains a list of SMB/CIFS servers on the network and returns that list to any computer asking for it. This is different from NBNS functions. In NBNS, nmbd returns the IP address of a computer (itself or another computer); in master browser functions, nmbd returns a list of computer names.

Share Browsing   When you browse the shares on a specific Samba server, nmbd on that server is what returns the list of available shares to the client computer. This function is distinct from master browser functions, in which nmbd returns a list of computers on a network.

smbd: The SMB/CIFS Daemon

The daemon that does most of the heavy-duty file and printer sharing in Samba is smbd, the SMB/CIFS daemon. This program binds to TCP port 139 and responds to all requests for file or printer access. Its duties include the following:

Authentication   One of the first tasks that smbd performs for any connection is authentication. If the requestor's username and password don't match what Samba is configured to accept, access is not granted.

File Sharing   smbd provides all the file-sharing services—it accepts files from clients, sends files to clients, deletes files for clients, and so on.

Printer Sharing   Printer sharing is quite similar to file sharing, from a network point of view. In printer sharing, the client sends the server a file, which is then printed rather than stored on disk.

Time Server   Samba can function as a time server for Windows clients. In Windows, you can type **NET TIME ***HOSTNAME* **/YES /SET** to set the time of the Windows computer to the time maintained by the Linux computer called *HOSTNAME*. In Samba's smb.conf file, you must use the time server = Yes option to enable the time server function.

TIP

You can use the xntpd package (http://www.eecis.udel.edu/~ntp/) in Linux to keep Linux's clock synchronized to an atomic clock signal from any of several sites on the Internet. If you then insert the NET TIME command in a Windows startup file, the Windows computers on your network will have reasonably accurate clocks, reset from your local time server every time they reboot.

Samba TNG

The Next Generation (TNG) is the name that's been applied to a variant of Samba devoted to bringing improved Windows NT domain support to Samba. Because this is a development branch, it's not as stable as a mainstream Samba release, so it shouldn't be used in critical environments. Samba TNG competes with the mainstream HEAD development branch that will eventually produce a mainstream 3.0 version of the package. Along with changes to Samba's domain support code, Samba TNG has split the work of the two Samba daemons among several additional daemons:

smbd	The file-sharing server. Run this at all times.
nmbd	The name browser server. Run this at all times.
browserd	The daemon to handle name-browsing functions. Run this if Samba may be a master browser.
lsarpcd	A logon security protocol. Run this if you use encrypted passwords.
samrd	This handles password changes from Windows NT. Run this if you use encrypted passwords.
spoolssd	Spool service for printing from Windows NT clients.
srvsvcd	Server service for browsing. Run this at all times.
svcctld	The service control daemon. Run this to start or stop services remotely.
winregd	Another password-changing daemon. Run this if you use encrypted passwords.
wkssvcd	The workstation service. Run this if you want browsing to work correctly.

In order to obtain full functionality from Samba TNG, you must start all of these daemons. The Samba startup scripts included by most Linux distributions are inadequate, because they only start smbd and nmbd. You must therefore modify your old startup scripts or create new ones to support this explosion of daemons.

Why run Samba TNG? Here are the primary reasons at this time related to integrating Samba into a network with heavy Windows NT, 2000, or XP influences. Samba TNG implements advanced domain control features that let Samba function better as a domain controller for such networks. The development HEAD branch of the mainstream Samba package provides similar functionality, though. If you find that Samba 2.2.*x*'s domain support features are inadequate, you might want to try both the HEAD development version of Samba and Samba TNG. Because both are development packages, it's possible that one will work on your system but another won't. You can obtain Samba TNG from `http://www.samba-tng.org`; the HEAD development version is available from the regular Samba website, `http://www.samba.org`.

Before you try Samba TNG, I recommend you look for a more recent mainstream release. It's possible that Samba 3.0 will be available by the time you read these words. As of late 2001, Samba TNG and the HEAD development branch are both still considered experimental, so I don't recommend you use them on a mission-critical server. If necessary, you can configure a Windows NT 4 or Windows 2000 computer as a domain controller and use one or more Samba 2.2.*x* computers as file and print servers on this domain.

RESOLVING FILESYSTEM FEATURE CONFLICTS

One of the difficulties inherent in using Linux to serve files to DOS, Windows, and OS/2 clients is the fact that these systems use various conventions for file naming and attributes. Linux follows Unix conventions. DOS, Windows, and OS/2 all derive from another tradition and use rules incompatible with Linux. Additional differences exist between these three major Samba client OSs, particularly with respect to filename length limits. Samba must therefore support multiple rules for translating filenames and attributes between filesystems derived from Unix and DOS.

WARNING

People sometimes dual-boot a computer between Linux and Windows (or some other OS) and want to share the same files from both OSs. It's also sometimes desirable to share a Zip disk, floppy disk, or other removable media from Linux, even when the medium uses a *File Allocation Table* (FAT) filesystem. In both cases, Linux filters the FAT filesystem features through its own filesystem features model, so you may lose certain features of the underlying filesystem. For instance, you'll lose the hidden and system bits of a FAT filesystem when you share it through Samba. On rare occasions, this can be a significant problem.

Filename Length and Case Retention

One of the most obvious differences between OSs is in file-naming conventions. Length and case are the two attributes that are important in this respect. Different OSs and filesystems support filenames of various lengths. Linux's `ext2` filesystem is capable of handling filenames of up to 256 characters in length. SMB/CIFS allows up to 127 characters for filenames, but some operating systems (notably DOS) have much more restrictive limits. Samba must find some way to convert long filenames to shorter ones or to simply drop long filenames when the client doesn't understand them.

In terms of case, OSs can treat the upper- and lowercase characters in filenames in one of three ways:

Case-Sensitive   When upper- and lowercase characters are treated as different characters, the filesystem is known as *case-sensitive*. On such a filesystem, the files `BigFile.txt` and `bigfile.TXT` are different files. Both can exist in the same directory, and entering one name when only the other exists produces a "file not found" error. Linux is a case-sensitive OS, although it can behave differently when it accesses files from non-native filesystems, such as FAT. A Samba server normally serves files from a Linux filesystem (usually `ext2fs`, but alternatives like ReiserFS, XFS, and `ext3fs` are becoming increasingly common). Linux always treats filenames from these filesystems in a case-sensitive manner.

Case-Retentive   In a *case-retentive* filesystem, the filesystem preserves the case of filenames but doesn't distinguish between upper- and lowercase characters. For instance, you can save a file as `BigFile.txt` and then retrieve it as `bigfile.TXT`. If one filename exists, you can't create a second file with the same name but in a different case. Windows and OS/2 both use case-retentive filesystems and treat SMB/CIFS shares in this manner, as well.

Case-Insensitive   A *case-insensitive* filesystem treats upper- and lowercase characters identically and converts to one case when saving files. For instance, you might enter the filename BigFile.txt in a File Save dialog box, but the computer will store it as BIGFILE.TXT or bigfile.txt. DOS treats file access in a case-insensitive way, as does OS/2 when it uses a FAT filesystem. In these situations, uppercase is used. When Linux accesses a case-insensitive filesystem (such as a FAT floppy disk or an ISO-9660 CD-ROM), Linux converts uppercase filenames to lowercase by default.

Samba includes a large number of configuration options to control how it converts between Linux's 256-character case-sensitive filesystems and the shorter, case-retentive or case-insensitive filenames expected by its clients. These options are described in Chapter 22, "Configuring File Sharing."

FAT-Style File Attributes

DOS uses FAT as its only filesystem. Operating systems with a DOS heritage, including OS/2 and all versions of Windows, have added the characteristics of FAT filesystems to their more sophisticated filesystems, such as OS/2's *High-Performance File System* (HPFS) and Windows NT's *NT File System* (NTFS). FAT filesystem attributes are each represented by a single bit that's stored as part of the file's description on the disk. Following are some of the attributes supported by FAT and other Microsoft and IBM filesystems. (The specifics of configuring the FAT-style attribute settings are in Chapter 22.)

Hidden Bit

If the *hidden bit* is set, the file is invisible to many programs. Programs actually have a choice of showing or not showing files that are configured as hidden, so a user can easily overcome the hidden bit in many programs. Linux, however, doesn't support the hidden bit. In Linux (and Unix generally), the equivalent effect is achieved by starting a filename with a period (.), as in .bashrc.

Samba can be configured to add the hidden bit to these so-called *dot files* when sharing a directory. (Samba does *not* apply the hidden bit to the . and .. files, which refer to the directory and its parent, respectively.) Samba can also store the hidden bit as the world execute bit in the Unix-style permissions for the file, but this configuration can cause minor problems if the files are ever accessed from Linux. Specifically, if somebody tries to run a randomly selected file that was hidden by a Samba client, an error is likely—albeit not one that will damage the server or its files.

Archive Bit

The *archive bit* is used by the OS to signal when a file needs to be backed up. Normally, a program sets the archive bit whenever it modifies the contents of a file. Backup programs can subsequently use this bit to back up only those files that have changed. There is no equivalent feature in a Unix-style filesystem, but Samba can store the archive bit in the owner execute bit for the file. Like storing the hidden bit, this can cause a file that's not a program to appear to be executable in Linux, which can be confusing or cause error messages to appear if a user tries to execute the file.

System Bit

DOS and related OSs use the *system bit* to identify files that are required or have special meaning to the OS. Chances are you won't store files that use the system bit on a Samba server. If you do, and if you must preserve this bit, you can configure Samba to store it in the Unix group execute bit. As with the hidden and archive bits, setting the group execute bit can cause a file to look like a Linux program file, but trying to run the file just produces an error message.

Read-Only Bit

The *read-only* bit signals that a file can be read but not written to or deleted. This meaning is similar but not identical to the write permission supported by Linux. When the DOS read-only bit is set, the Linux write permission must *not* be set. Samba performs this translation automatically. More importantly, in DOS and its descendants, when the read-only bit is set, you can't delete the file. In Linux, on the other hand, the right to delete a file is a characteristic of the directory in which the file resides.

You can configure Samba to follow DOS-style handling of the read-only bit with respect to file deletions by using the `delete readonly =` `No` parameter in `smb.conf`. This setting is the default. Changing it to `Yes` sets Samba to follow normal Linux standards for file deletions.

Ownership and Permission

Unix systems, including Linux, support two features that aren't supported by DOS or Windows 9x—*ownership* and *permissions*. If you're an experienced Linux administrator, your challenge is to understand how Samba uses these features internally. If you're new to Linux, your challenge is in learning how to use these concepts to increase security on your Samba server.

An Overview of Linux File Security

You can discover the security settings in a Linux file by issuing the `ls -l` command in a directory or on a specific file. The result is something like the following:

```
-rw-r-----   1 philkent users        1846 Oct 23  2000 title.txt
```

For understanding Linux file security, the first, third, and fourth fields of this line are important. The first field, `-rw-r-----`, is the *permissions string* for the file; it represents access rights granted to various classes of users. The third field, `philkent`, is the username of the file's owner. The fourth field, `users`, is the group to which the file belongs. These three strings determine who may access the file and in what ways.

As a general rule, the owner of a file is the user who created that file. The owner usually has superior access rights to the file, as described shortly. The group to which the file belongs is usually the primary group of the file's owner. Both of these characteristics can be changed in Linux with the `chown` command, or with the `chgrp` command in the case of the group. A file can have only one owner and one group.

The permissions string has four parts:

▶ The first character represents any special attributes of the file. For instance, a d as the first character indicates that the file is a directory. In the example string, `-rw-r-----`, the special attributes position is unoccupied (represented by a dash), meaning the file is an ordinary file.

▶ The second through fourth characters represent the read, write, and execute permissions, respectively, assigned to the file's owner. In the example, rw- indicates that the owner has read and write but not execute permission; rwx would indicate read, write, and execute permission. The read and execute permission bits have no counterparts in the FAT filesystem, although all FAT files are assumed to be readable.

▶ The fifth through seventh characters represent the read, write, and execute permissions, respectively, for members of the file's group. In the example string, r-- indicates that members of the group users may read the file but not execute or write to it. Thus, if symmes is a member of the group users, symmes may read the file but not modify it.

▶ The final three characters represent the read, write, and execute permissions, respectively, for all other users of the system (often called *world permissions*). In the example, this string is--, which translates into no permissions—people who are not philkent and who do not belong to the group users cannot access this file at all.

NOTE

One exception to the world permissions rule is root, also known as the *superuser* or *administrator*. The superuser has full access to all files on the computer, no matter what their permissions.

The permissions string can also be expressed as three or four octal numbers, as in 640 or 0640. Each of the final three digits is the octal representation of the three permission bits for the owner, group, and world permissions. For example, rw- is a binary 110, which converts to an octal 6, hence the 6 in 640. Similarly, r-- is binary 100, or octal 4.

In a multiuser environment, it's possible to use Unix-style ownership and permissions to provide security on the system. If a company has half a dozen different projects underway, it can create six groups and assign employees to the appropriate groups. You can then set permissions on files and directories to allow or deny access to files based on group membership. Although a file can belong only to a single group, users can belong to multiple groups, so it's possible to grant members of two or more different projects access to both groups' files.

Using Linux File Security with Samba

At its core, Samba obeys Linux's file security model. Every individual who mounts a Samba share does so as a specific Linux user. Therefore, file accesses follow the permissions allowed to that user. For instance, consider again the example file owned by philkent, which belongs to the group users, with permissions of 0640. If philkent mounts a share, he can read and write the example file. On the other hand, the user symmes, who also belongs to the users group, can read the file but not write it. To symmes, the file appears to be read-only from a Windows computer. To another user who doesn't belong to the users group, the file appears in directory listings but cannot be accessed in any other way—Windows returns an "access denied" message.

An experienced Linux system administrator should have no trouble setting up a basic system of username-based security for a Samba server, particularly if that server is to be used mainly as a repository for individual users' files. Think of Samba as just another user program and you won't go far wrong. If you're less familiar with Unix-style file security, you must familiarize yourself with it to learn what it can do. Table 19.1 summarizes a few permissions and their possible roles.

TABLE 19.1: Linux Permissions and Their Uses

PERMISSION	MEANING AND POSSIBLE USES
0666	Complete read/write access to all users. Useful for low-security shared directories.
0664	Complete read/write access to all users in a given group; read-only access to other users. Useful for collaborative projects in a low-security environment.
0644	Read/write access to the file's owner; read-only access to all other users. Useful in environments with little or no confidential information, and when access to other users' data is beneficial.
0640	Read/write access to the file's owner; read-only access to the file's group; no access to others. Useful in moderate-security collaborative projects.
0600	Read/write access to the file's owner; no access to others. Useful for high-security shared files.
0440	Read-only access to the file's owner and group; no access to others. Useful for shared program files or fixed data.

For the most part, files you save on a Samba server don't need execute bits, at least not from the Linux point of view. (Samba may use these bits to store the archive, system, and hidden attributes, as described in the earlier section "FAT-Style File Attributes.") Directories, however, are a special case. Because it makes no sense to execute directories, Linux uses execute permissions on directories to indicate that you can obtain information about the files in the directory. This access is a practical necessity for using a directory, so when read permissions exist on a directory, execute permissions usually exist, as well.

Samba offers a variety of options for altering the way it uses Linux file permissions. These options allow you to set up security that's more flexible than could be achieved through Linux security alone:

▶ You can set the permissions assigned to files a user creates on a share-by-share basis. For instance, you might set files in a user's home directory to have very restrictive permissions (such as 0600), whereas files in a shared directory might have more permissive permissions (such as 0664 or even 0666).

▶ You can set the permissions assigned to directories a user creates, much as you can set the permissions for files. (Because the execute bit on directories is so important, 0644 becomes 0755, for example.)

▶ You can change the effective username by which a share is accessed. You could, for example, set the same username for all access to a common share in order to avoid having several owners of files in that share. When you set the username in this way, an individual logs on with his normal username. Once he is logged on, Samba creates files with the effective username and gives access using the access rights assigned to the effective username.

▶ You can specify a list of users who may or may not access a share or who may or may not write to a share. This specification is independent of the Linux ownership and permissions restrictions.

▶ You can specify a list of computers that may or may not access or write to a share. This restriction works much like the username-based restrictions.

Chapter 22 covers these security and permissions features in detail.

Windows NT/2000/XP File Security and Samba

Between basic Linux file permissions and Samba's share-by-share enhancements, you can tailor a security scheme to meet most needs. However, these schemes do not integrate well with the security features available in Windows NT (including Windows 2000 and XP). The Windows systems include concepts of ownership and groups that are similar to those of Linux. Rather than a file permissions string, however, these OSs use an *access control list* (ACL).

An ACL is a list of users or groups who may or may not access a specific file. Because an ACL is a *list,* it can contain more than one entry. This characteristic allows ACLs to provide a finer-grained security model than is available in Linux. You can provide similar functionality on a directory basis through Samba's controls, but you can't easily modify these permissions directly from Windows. To address this problem, Samba implements limited ACL support, and that support is still evolving. Samba 2.0.*x* allows you to convert between Linux and Windows users and groups and set the Linux permissions via Windows ACL controls. Samba 2.2.0 supports Windows ACLs on certain OSs and filesystems that include ACL support. Linux doesn't support this natively, but there's a package available at `http://acl.bestbits.at` that you can use to add this support to Linux. This package requires patching the kernel and its `ext2fs` support to handle ACLs. (SGI's journaling filesystem, XFS, also provides ACL support.) Using these advanced ACL features of Samba is currently a tricky proposition, but with any luck it will become easier as ACL support works its way into the standard Linux kernel.

Partitions, Mount Points, and Shares

Most experienced Linux system administrators install Linux on multiple partitions. For instance, `/usr/local`, `/home`, and `/var` might each have their own partitions, in addition to the root (`/`) partition. Samba is completely oblivious to these issues, except for their impact upon Linux's file handling. (For instance, if you unmount a partition, it becomes unavailable to Samba.)

Samba allows you to share any directories you want to share from your Linux computer. You can create multiple shares from the same computer. Each share appears as a separate item to clients. You can even export shares from nested directory trees. For instance, you can share `/winprogs` and `/winprogs/utils` separately. The former share will include the `utils` directory as a directory available from its root. Exporting

/winprogs/utils separately doesn't affect its availability from another share.

TIP

You can use the capability to export nested shares to fine-tune access control. Suppose most of the files in /winprogs require only read access. You can export that directory with read-only permissions. For those occasions when write access is required to the /winprogs/utils directory, you can export it with read/write permissions. Accessing it from the first share most of the time provides just read-only access, which might be desirable as a means of avoiding accidental file deletions or modifications, even when read/write access is available from another share. Similarly, you can restrict access to the /winprogs/utils directory to certain users, while making read-only access to /winprogs available to all.

In the DOS, Windows, and OS/2 worlds, each partition or removable disk device is assigned a unique *drive letter,* starting with C:. (A: and B: are reserved for the first and, if present, second floppy disks.) Depending upon the OS and the options you use to access your Samba shares, you may or may not mount a share on a drive letter. In Windows, there are two ways to access a share: by mounting and by browsing.

When mounting a share, you tie a share to a drive letter by right-clicking a share and selecting Map Network Drive from the resulting pop-up menu. You can then access the drive as if it were a local hard disk. Alternatively, you can use the NET USE command to accomplish the same thing.

With the browsing method, you can locate a share in Network Neighborhood (Computers Near Me in Windows Me and 2000) and access the files on that share without mounting the share. You may also be able to access files by directly specifying their names in the form *HOST**SHARE*\ *PATH**FILE*, where *HOST* is the computer's NetBIOS name, *SHARE* is the name of the share, and *PATH**FILE* is the path to the file relative to the share's root.

TIP

If you mount a share, give it a drive letter that's much later in the alphabet than any drives currently on your computer. For instance, on a computer that has drives C: through E:, give a share a drive letter such as M:. This practice ensures that you won't need to change your share's drive letter should you add or delete local drives. It can also be helpful in standardizing mount points across a network, on which client configurations may not be uniform.

Mounting a share sometimes makes it a bit easier to access files, because you'll do less rummaging about in deeply nested folders. Some older programs—particularly DOS programs—may also require a drive letter, so you may have to mount a share. Nevertheless, browsing can be a convenient and quick way to access a share, particularly if you don't use the share regularly.

NEW SAMBA 2.2.x INTEGRATION FEATURES

With the release of Samba 2.2.0, Samba includes some new features that improve its capability to integrate with Windows networks. Some of these tools let it function better as a file or print server, but others improve its capacity to function as a domain controller. The preceding discussion has mentioned some of these features, but others deserve mention here. These features include the following:

Windows NT Printing Protocols   Windows NT and its derivatives (Windows 2000 and XP) have long supported alternative printing protocols. Although these OSs have long been able to print via Samba, Samba's new support for their expanded printing protocols permits *better* printing. One practical example is that Samba has long been able to deliver printer drivers to Windows 9*x*/Me systems, but not to Windows NT systems. Samba 2.2.*x*, however, can now deliver printer drivers to Windows NT, 2000, and XP systems.

MS-DFS Server Support   Microsoft has been promoting its version of the *Distributed File System* (DFS) as the next-generation file-sharing protocol for Windows systems. Samba 2.2.*x* now supports MS-DFS. (Other vendors also implement DFS, but in a way that's slightly different from what Microsoft uses.)

Improved PDC Capabilities   Samba has long been able to function as a primary domain controller (PDC) for Windows 9*x*/Me systems, and the 2.0.*x* series of Samba has seen increasing PDC support for Windows NT and its derivatives. Samba 2.2.*x* improves this support substantially. For instance, many NT-based administrative programs now work with a Samba PDC, although some only allow you to view data, not change it. Work on this aspect of Samba is ongoing.

Winbind   Although it didn't make it into the initial 2.2.0 release, this feature is expected to arrive with some 2.2.x-series version of Samba and can be used with the experimental HEAD pre-3.0 versions of Samba. Winbind serves as an interface between a Linux system's user authentication methods and a Windows PDC, effectively allowing a Linux computer to offload authentication onto the Windows PDC. This can be extremely useful if you're adding a Linux computer to an existing Windows network; without Winbind, you must add and maintain your Linux users independently or use some cross-platform authentication tool. With Winbind, you can give existing Windows domain users access to the Linux system with relatively little effort.

In sum, Samba's capability to function on a Windows network continues to improve. Samba has long supported serving files and printers, but the new features help in creating seamless user authentication between Linux and Windows systems and in supporting more recent protocols such as MS-DFS.

What's Next?

Samba serves as a bridge between the Linux and Windows worlds, which have differences in networking and filesystem features that Samba must overcome. Some of this work has been done by the integration of SMB/CIFS networking into TCP/IP standards. This step allows Linux computers to use SMB/CIFS without NetBEUI.

Samba's work, however, is still substantial. Its two daemons (more in Samba TNG) must present the illusion of a filesystem that lacks certain features, such as filename sensitivity and Unix-style permissions, while possessing features that in fact it lacks (such as hidden and system attribute bits). In the end, Samba does a remarkably good job of these tasks and even enables you to use Linux's security features and Samba's security extensions for very flexible control of access to shares.

In the next chapter you will move from a theoretical discussion of Samba to the installation of the product on a Linux server.

Chapter 20

INSTALLING SAMBA

The first step to using Samba is to install the software on your computer. Fortunately, this step is usually easy because Samba comes with all major Linux distributions. Nonetheless, there are situations in which you may need to take action to install Samba.

For one thing, although Samba comes with all major Linux distributions, the package might not be installed on any given system. Furthermore, Samba is constantly being improved. If a newer version adds important features or fixes bugs, you may need to update. If you want "bleeding edge" Samba (that is, the very latest version), you must normally obtain source code and compile it yourself. (Note that these development releases are potentially dangerous, however; hence the designation "bleeding edge.")

Adapted from *Linux Samba Server Administration* by Roderick W. Smith
ISBN 0-7821-2740-1   656 pages $39.99

This chapter discusses your options in obtaining and installing Samba. These options range from pulling Samba off your Linux installation CD to obtaining and compiling the source code. Also described here are some of the key Samba configuration files, as well as methods of running Samba once it's installed.

Obtaining Samba

Samba is a very easy package to obtain. It almost certainly came with your Linux distribution, but you may want to look for a more recent version of the package. As a general rule, I recommend using a version of Samba distributed by your Linux distribution's maintainer. Such packages often include startup scripts customized for the distribution, and you're less likely to run into problems such as incompatible support libraries when you stick with a binary created for your distribution.

Alternatively, you can compile Samba yourself. This approach can be beneficial when you need to customize the program in some way, such as adding NetBEUI support (`http://www.procom.com`) or when you want to add or remove unusual Samba compile-time options.

Samba with Your Linux Distribution

Every major Linux distribution comes with one or more Samba package files. Table 20.1 summarizes the names used by many popular distributions. You can check to see if these packages are installed on your system, as described shortly. If not, you can pull out your installation CD-ROM and install the relevant package.

TABLE 20.1:   Samba Package Names in Popular Distributions

DISTRIBUTION	SAMBA PACKAGES
Caldera OpenLinux Server 3.1	`samba-2.0.8-1.i386.rpm, samba-doc-2.0.8-1.i386.rpm, swat-2.0.8-1.i386.rpm`
Corel Linux 1.2	`samba-common_2.0.7-2-cl-1.1_i386.deb, samba_2.0.7-2-cl-1.1_i386.deb, samba-doc_2.0.7-2-cl-1.1_all.deb`
Debian GNU/ Linux 2.2	`samba-common_2.0.7-3.deb, samba-doc_2.0.7-3.deb, samba_2.0.7-3.deb, swat_2.0.7-3.deb`
Linux Mandrake 8.0	`samba-2.0.7-25mdk.i586.rpm, samba-client-2.0.7-25mdk.i586.rpm, samba-common-2.0.7-25mdk.i586.rpm`

TABLE 20.1 Continued: Samba Package Names in Popular Distributions

DISTRIBUTION	SAMBA PACKAGES
LinuxPPC 2000 Q4	`samba-2.0.7-11.ppc.rpm, samba-client-2.0.7-11.ppc.rpm, samba-common-2.0.7-11.ppc.rpm`
Red Hat Linux 7.1	`samba-2.0.7-36.i386.rpm, samba-client-2.0.7-36.i386.rpm, samba-common-2.0.7-36.i386.rpm, samba-swat-2.0.7-36.i386.rpm`
Slackware Linux 8.0	`samba.tgz` (Samba 2.2.0a)
Storm Linux 2000 ("Hail" release)	`gnosamba_0.3.3-2.deb, samba-doc_2.0.7-3.deb, samba-common_2.0.7-3.deb, samba_2.0.7-3.deb, swat_2.0.7-3.deb`
SuSE Linux 7.2	`samba-2.2.0a-0.i386.rpm`
TurboLinux Server 6.5	`samba-2.0.7-11.i386.rpm, samba-client-2.0.7-11.i386.rpm, samba-server-2.0.7-11.i386.rpm, samba-debugtools-2.0.7-11.i386.rpm`
Yellow Dog Linux 2.0	`samba-2.0.7-21ssl.ppc.rpm, samba-client-2.0.7-21ssl.ppc.rpm, samba-common-2.0.7-21ssl.ppc.rpm`

Most of these distributions use fairly standardized Linux package-naming conventions. Specifically, the package names contain the following elements, usually separated by dashes (-), underscores (_), or periods (.):

- ▶ The package name, such as `samba` or `samba-client`.

- ▶ A version number: 2.0.7 in most of the distributions in Table 20.1.

- ▶ A build number, which represents minor revisions that are unique to any given distribution. The build number might be incremented, such as when there's a change in placement of the distribution's documentation files or when a bug in the startup script has been fixed.

- ▶ A code for the distribution, such as mdk for Mandrake. Not all distributions use distribution codes.

- ▶ An architecture code, such as `i386` for Intel 80386 or later CPUs or `ppc` for PowerPC CPUs.

▶ The file type: rpm for a *Red Hat Package Manager* (RPM) file, deb for a Debian package, or tgz for a gzipped tar file (also known as a *tarball*).

As you can see, the distributions split up Samba in various ways. Red Hat and most of its derivatives, for instance, create three packages: samba, samba-client, and samba-common. You should install all three of these packages. (If you don't intend to use client functions, you can omit the samba-client package, however.)

Debian-based distributions split off samba, samba-common, and samba-doc packages. Here again, I recommend installing all three packages. A few distributions split off the *Samba Web Administration Tool* (SWAT) into a separate package, but others fold this into one of the regular packages. (SWAT enables you to administer a Samba system remotely using a web browser.) Some distributions, including Storm Linux 2000, include additional packages that provide Samba-related functionality, such as GUI Samba configuration tools. Such packages are unlikely to cause problems, and they aren't discussed in any depth in this book.

If you have a distribution that's more recent than the ones listed in Table 20.1, chances are that the distribution's base name is the same but the version or build number is higher. If you have a distribution of Linux that's not listed at all in Table 20.1, chances are it has Samba packages named in a way that's similar to those of one or more distributions listed in Table 20.1. You can probably find your Samba package by mounting your Linux installation CD-ROM and searching it with the find command:

```
$ mount /dev/cdrom /mnt/cdrom
$ find /mnt/cdrom -name "*amba*"
```

(You may want to alter the mount point in these commands to match the configuration of your system.)

WARNING

If you have Windows 2000 clients on your network, I strongly recommend that you install Samba version 2.0.7 or later. Samba versions prior to 2.0.5a had serious difficulties with Windows 2000 clients, and even version 2.0.6 isn't perfect in this respect. Samba 2.2.0 adds domain features that are necessary if you want to use a Windows 2000 system as a client on a domain that's controlled by Samba.

Updates from Your Linux Distributor

Even when Samba comes with your Linux distribution, you may want to obtain an updated version of the program. If so, the simplest way is usually to find one from your Linux distributor. Typically there's an updates section on your distribution's web- or FTP site. Updated packages may include bug fixes, improved functionality, better setup routines, and other enhancements.

Should you automatically apply an update if one is available? This is a tough question, for which there are two competing arguments:

- "If it ain't broke, don't fix it." This saying is often applicable to software updates. If your current Samba installation works to your satisfaction, why update? An update always carries the risk of creating new problems.

- "Bug fixes can be important." Updated versions of Samba frequently include bug fixes. Some of these fix serious problems— most notably security weaknesses. It's best to be up-to-date on these bug fixes, to head off problems.

At a minimum, I recommend frequently checking the update web pages for Samba and your particular distribution to watch for security issues that are identified. If a security problem or some other serious bug exists, update. If no such problems are fixed in versions more recent than yours, then an update isn't critical. Decide whether to update based on the description of changes between the versions.

Getting the Most Up-to-Date Samba

Frequently, a distribution maintainer doesn't have the latest version of Samba available in a distribution or as an update. There's often a lag between the release of a new version and the time when it is compiled for a distribution. Consequently, if you need the latest version of Samba, you may need to look somewhere other than on the Linux vendor's website.

TIP

As mentioned earlier in this chapter, Samba packages compiled for a specific distribution typically include features to help Samba work properly with that distribution—specifically, startup and shutdown scripts that are tailored for a particular distribution. If you use a recent Samba package that wasn't built with your distribution in mind, start by installing a package that *was* built for your distribution. You can then save the startup and shutdown scripts (described later in this chapter, in the section "Common Distribution Startup Scripts") and remove the package. When you install the updated Samba, use the startup and shutdown scripts taken from the distribution-specific Samba package. (This procedure may not work with Samba TNG, because it uses more daemons than mainstream Samba versions.)

Following are some sources for updated Samba packages:

RPMFind   The RPMFind website, `http://rufus.w3.org/linux/RPM/`, is an excellent resource for locating software packages in RPM format. Most of the RPMs available through this site are designed for specific Linux distributions, but some are more general in nature. You might discover a more up-to-date Samba package designed for a distribution other than the one you use, or a more general-purpose Samba RPM.

The Debian Package Site   Debian maintains a database of packages at `http://www.debian.org/distrib/packages`. These are primarily from the current stable and beta-test Debian releases. In most cases, Debian packages work on other Debian-derived distributions, such as Corel Linux or Storm Linux, without modification.

Other Distribution Maintainers   You can check the websites devoted to other Linux distribution maintainers that use the same package format as your distribution. For instance, Red Hat users can check Mandrake's website. In most cases, the RPMFind site is a more efficient way to locate such packages for RPM-based distributions.

Freshmeat   The Freshmeat website (`http://freshmeat.net`) is a good spot to locate recent software releases in a variety of formats.

The Samba Site   Ultimately, the single best resource for Samba is the Samba website, `http://www.samba.org`. (This site actually presents a list of mirror sites around the world;

pick the one closest to you.) You can obtain source code or precompiled binaries for any of several popular Linux distributions. The very latest versions—and particularly development packages—may be available only in source code form.

No matter what the source, you ultimately have to choose the form of your package. The easiest packages to install are binaries compiled for your Linux distribution (or at least for the correct architecture, such as Intel x86 or PowerPC). Most precompiled binaries come in RPM or Debian packages, but you can also get Samba as a tarball. Alternatively, you can obtain Samba as source code—again, as either a package file or a tarball. Descriptions of all these options are coming up.

INSTALLING A BINARY PACKAGE

Installation procedures for Samba vary substantially from one Linux distribution to another. Most distributions today use RPM files or Debian packages, but Slackware uses tarballs. A few others, such as Stampede Linux, use their own proprietary formats. As a general rule, if you get a binary package, get one that uses the package format favored by your distribution. If necessary, you can often convert from one format to another with the alien program, or you can install a tarball. (All Linux distributions can read tarballs.) It's always cleanest to start with the correct package format.

Installing an RPM

Most modern Linux distributions use the RPM format, although Debian packages are becoming more popular. Fortunately, installing RPMs is a simple process. (For more on RPM files and how to install them, see Chapter 4, "Working with Linux Commands and Files".)

WARNING

Upgrading an RPM package sometimes wipes out your configuration files. Back up your smb.conf and smbpasswd files (generally located in /etc or /etc/samba.d) *before* upgrading a working Samba installation. If you're upgrading to a version of Samba that wasn't designed for your distribution, you should also back up your Samba startup scripts, which are described later in this chapter in the section "Common Distribution Startup Scripts."

Using Text-Based Tools

To install or upgrade Samba at the shell prompt, issue a command such as the following:

```
# rpm -Uvh samba-2.0.7-36.i386.rpm
```

Either issue the rpm command once for each package you're upgrading or list multiple packages, separated by spaces, on the command line. rpm should respond by displaying a series of hash marks (#) to represent the command's progress; then the job is done.

The -U parameter to rpm specifies a package upgrade, which causes rpm to automatically remove the old package before installing the new one. If you're replacing a set of packages from one distribution with their equivalents from another, manually remove the old packages before installing the new ones. This reduces the likelihood that you'll run into conflicts because of differing package names and contents. Here are typical commands for this situation:

```
# rpm -e samba
# rpm -Uvh samba-2.0.7-36.i386.rpm
```

When the rpm -U command encounters no existing package, it installs the package without complaint. You could also use rpm -ivh in place of rpm -Uvh in this situation.

Verify that the package is installed by typing **rpm -qi**, which displays information such as when and on what computer the binary package was built. Listing 20.1 demonstrates this command.

Listing 20.1: *rpm* Query Output

```
$ rpm -qi samba
Name        : samba      Relocations: /usr
Version     : 2.2.0      Vendor: (none)
Release     : 20010417   Build Date: Tue 17 Apr 2001 03:47:02
              PM EDT
Install date: Thu 19 Apr 2001 11:01:39 AM EDT Build Host:
              jeremy1
Group       : Networking  Source RPM: samba-2.2.0-
              20010417.src.rpm
Size        : 22576520    License: GNU GPL version 2
Packager    : John H Terpstra [Samba-Team] <jht@samba.org>
Summary     : Samba SMB client and server
```

This command also displays an extended plain-English summary of what Samba is, which has been omitted from Listing 20.1. Some packages may include additional information, such as a URL for Samba or the packager's site.

Using GUI Tools

Many Linux distributions include GUI tools to help you install, remove, update, and query RPM packages. Red Hat and Mandrake, for instance, come with GNOME RPM (see Figure 20.1).

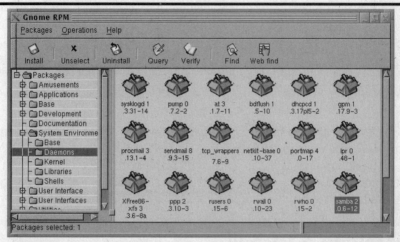

FIGURE 20.1: GNOME RPM is one of several GUI tools used for manipulating packages installed on an RPM-based Linux computer.

To add a package using GNOME RPM, follow these steps:

1. As root, start GNOME RPM by typing **gnorpm** in an xterm window.

2. In the main GNOME RPM window, click the Install button. GNOME RPM displays an Install dialog box in which you can select RPMs.

3. Click the Add button in the Install dialog box. In the file selection dialog box that appears, locate and select the RPM files you want to install. Note that you can select multiple files. When you've selected all your files, click Cancel.

4. Make sure that the check boxes next to all of the packages you want to install are checked in the Install dialog box, and then click the Install button. GNOME RPM installs the packages.

You can use GNOME RPM in a similar manner to update, delete, or query RPM packages. GUI configuration utilities in other distributions, such as Caldera and SuSE, differ in details but have similar functionality.

Installing a Debian Package

Debian packages are incompatible with RPM packages, but the basic principles of operation are the same for both package types. You use the dpkg command to install a Debian package, as in the following:

```
# dpkg -i samba_2.0.7-3.deb
```

This command installs the samba_2.0.7-3.deb package.

Before you run this command, you may need to remove an old package. To do this, use the -r option to dpkg, as in the following:

```
# dpkg -r samba
```

Some Debian-based Linux distributions, such as Storm Linux, include GUI frontends to dpkg similar to the GNOME RPM program for RPM-based systems. If you're more comfortable with GUI tools than with command-line tools, you can use these frontends in a similar way to ease administration.

Installing a Tarball

If you have Slackware Linux or another distribution that uses tarballs for distribution, you can install Samba by using the standard Linux tar utility. You can also use this method if you want to install a tarball on a Linux distribution that ordinarily uses a package management tool. However, I recommend using an RPM or Debian package if your distribution supports one of these file formats.

WARNING

When installing a new version of Samba over an older one on Slackware Linux, the new files will most likely overwrite the old ones. If you install a tarball on a system that normally uses packages, however, or if you install a tarball that was created using a different directory structure than what your current system uses, you may end up with duplicate Samba files. This can cause substantial confusion, because you might end up continuing to use the old binaries even after installing the new ones. You should therefore remove the old package as well as you can before installing a Samba binary via a tarball. Check the directory structure contained within a tarball first, by using the tar command, as in tar tvfz samba.tgz. This command displays all the files in the tarball, including their complete paths.

Tarball installation is a fairly straightforward matter. As the root user, you issue commands similar to the following. These commands install the files from the samba.tgz file, located in the /root directory:

```
# cd /
# tar xvfz /root/samba.tgz
```

Note that the first command (cd /) is critically important; without it, you'll install the files under whatever directory you're currently in, not in the usual directory tree. (It is possible, however, that the tarball you obtain might have to be installed under some directory other than /, in which case you should follow the directions that come with the package to install it.)

COMPILING THE SOURCE CODE

In some cases, a binary installation isn't adequate. For instance:

▶ If you need to modify the source code in any way—including applying unusual compilation options—you must compile the source code yourself unless you can locate a binary that includes those exact modifications.

▶ You may need to install from source code if you've installed updated libraries that are incompatible with the default binaries. (Such a situation is unlikely, however, for two reasons: because such updated libraries would most likely break packages other than Samba, and because you can install multiple versions of most support libraries.)

▶ If you're running Linux on an unusual CPU architecture, you won't be able to use the Intel x86 binaries that are most common. You may be able to find precompiled binaries for your computer's architecture, but if not, you can compile the source code yourself.

There are two primary ways to compile Samba from source: Use source code packaged as an RPM source package, or obtain the source code in a tarball. When you compile from a packaged form, making changes to the source code is comparatively difficult, so I don't recommend this approach if you need to alter the source code. Compiling the source code manually from a tarball allows you to make customizations.

Compiling a Source RPM

If you want to compile your own copy of Samba because you've replaced standard libraries or are running on an unusual architecture for which you can find no binary packages, one of the easiest ways to install Samba on an RPM-based distribution is to use a *source RPM*. This contains the original source code, patches, and installation scripts in a single file. It can be distinguished from a binary RPM in that the source RPM contains src rather than i386, ppc, or some other architecture code as part of the filename.

To create a binary RPM from a source RPM, issue a command similar to the following:

```
# rpm -rebuild samba-2.0.7-36.src.rpm
```

This command builds a binary package from samba-2.0.7-36.src.rpm. The resulting binary package will have a similar filename, but with an architecture code in place of *src* near the end of the filename. The binary package appears somewhere in the /usr/src directory tree, usually in a directory named after the distribution. For instance, in Caldera Open-Linux 3.1, the binary appears in the /usr/src/OpenLinux/RPMS/i386 directory. You can then change to that directory or move the file to another directory and install it as you would any other binary RPM.

NOTE   Building a binary RPM from a source RPM is not a foolproof process. If you're missing a critical development tool, the build process will fail. Something about a computer's architecture, libraries, or environment may occasionally cause a build to fail. Fortunately, Samba is well tested on a wide variety of Linux and non-Linux computers, so you're unlikely to run into problems caused by your host's environment.

Compiling Source from a Tarball

If you need to modify the Samba source code for any reason or use uncommon compilation options that aren't set by default in a source RPM, your best bet is to compile Samba directly from a source tarball. I recommend you download the tarball from the Samba website or from a site that houses source code for your particular Linux distribution.

NOTE

You *can* modify the source code in a source RPM, but the process for doing so is a bit tedious. For a single Samba server, modifying a source RPM is probably not worth the effort. If you want more information on this topic, consult the RPM HOWTO document that comes with all major Linux distributions.

The procedure for compiling Samba from source code is as follows:

1. Obtain the source tarball from your site of choice.

2. Change to the /usr/src directory or some other convenient location.

3. Extract the files from the tarball, with a command such as this:

   ```
   # tar xvfz ~/samba-2.2.1a.tar.gz
   ```

   This command creates a new directory in which the Samba source code resides.

4. Move into the Samba source code directory.

5. Examine the README file in the source code directory. This file may contain important information on the particular version of Samba you've obtained.

6. The actual source code is in a subdirectory called source under the main Samba directory. Move into this directory.

7. Type **./configure** to configure the Makefile and other critical configuration files for your system. (The many configuration options you can specify with the ./configure command are described following this procedure.)

8. Type **make** to build the Samba distribution.

9. Type **make install** to install Samba.

NOTE

Depending on permissions in the /usr/src directory, you may be able to perform steps 1 to 8 as an ordinary user. You *must* perform step 9 as root, however.

Configuration options for Samba are appended to the `configure` command in step 7 of the preceding procedure. For instance, `./configure --with-pam` includes support for the *Pluggable Authentication Module* (PAM), an authentication library that's used on most Linux distributions. Most configuration options come in two forms: one to enable the feature and another to disable it. These generally have the same name, but using `with` or `without` as a prefix, as in `--with-pam` and `--without-pam`. Following are the most important options, specified in their default states:

--without-smbwrapper The `smbwrapper` package is used to mount SMB/CIFS shares. Linux can use the kernel-based `smbfs` instead, and `smbwrapper` has some incompatibilities with glibc, so it's best to leave this option disabled.

--without-afs The *Andrew File System* (AFS) is a network filesystem from Carnegie-Mellon University. You can leave this option disabled unless you plan to share AFS mounts via Samba.

--without-dfs DFS is an updated version of AFS. You can probably leave this option disabled. Note that this DFS is *not* the same as Microsoft's DFS (Distributed File System).

--without-msdfs You can add support for Microsoft's DFS by changing this option. Chances are you don't need it; you probably would use this only when integrating a Samba server into an existing Microsoft DFS tree.

--without-krb4 and --without-krb5 These options disable Kerberos 4 and 5 support, respectively. (Kerberos is a network authentication and security protocol.) If you enable either of these options, you must specify the Kerberos base directory on your system, as in `--with-krb5=`*/path/to/directory*. Unless you use Kerberos on your network, you can safely ignore these options. Learn more about Kerberos at `http://web.mit.edu/kerberos/www`.

--without-automount Automount support lets a computer automatically mount and unmount partitions. Linux distributions increasingly use automounters, so you may want to enable this feature.

--without-smbmount `smbmount` is the program that Linux uses to mount SMB/CIFS shares. I recommend you enable this feature.

--without-acl-support   Access Control Lists (ACLs) are Windows' way of fine-tuning access to files. Samba provides limited ACL support, or full ACL support if your Linux kernel and filesystem support ACLs. (This support currently is rare in Linux.) If you want to enable support for ACLs, change this option to --with-acl-support.

--without-pam   As mentioned earlier, PAM is an authentication method used by most Linux distributions. You should enable this option.

--without-ldap   The *Lightweight Directory Access Protocol* (LDAP) is a means of passing information such as user preferences across a network. This support is largely experimental, so I recommend leaving it disabled unless you want to experiment with it.

--without-nt5ldap   Windows 2000 (originally known as Windows NT 5) includes LDAP support, but Microsoft has implemented the protocol in its own unique way. This option enables Samba to support Microsoft's version of LDAP. As with ordinary LDAP support, it's best to leave this disabled unless you want to experiment with it.

--without-nis   *Network Information System* (NIS) is a method of distributing passwords on a Unix network. If your network uses NIS, you should enable this option.

--without-nisplus   NIS+ is a successor protocol to NIS. Change this option to include support if your network uses NIS+.

--without-nisplus-home   NIS+ includes a feature that enables a system to locate a user's home directory on a distributed network of Unix systems. If you change this option and enable the feature, Samba can automatically mount the correct home directory for users on such a network.

--without-winbind   The Winbind daemon exists in the experimental HEAD (pre-3.0) versions of Samba and may become a standard part of a 2.2.*x* release, but it isn't yet standard as of 2.2.1a. This daemon lets Linux defer its own authentication procedures to a Windows or Samba domain controller. This can serve as an alternative to NIS, NIS+, or Kerberos in many situations. Change this option if you want to compile the Winbind daemon.

--without-ssl   *Secure Sockets Layer* (SSL) is a method of encrypting network connections. Enabling this option allows Samba to use SSL.

--without-syslog   Normally, Samba creates its own log files. If you enable this option, you can use Samba configuration options to send logging information to the system log daemon, `syslogd`, instead of or in addition to Samba's own log files.

--without-netatalk   *Netatalk* is a separate package for serving files to Macintoshes using the AppleTalk protocol. If you enable this option, Samba incorporates experimental support for AppleTalk. I recommend running Netatalk separately from Samba, however.

--without-quotas   Changing this option to `--with-quotas` enables Samba to support user disk quotas better.

--prefix=/usr/local/samba   The directory in which architecture-independent files reside.

--eprefix=/usr/local/samba   The directory in which architecture-dependent files reside.

--bindir=eprefix/bin   The location of user-executable binary files.

--sbindir=eprefix/bin   The location of administrator-executable binary files.

--libexecdir=eprefix/libexec   The location of program executables.

--datadir=prefix/share   The location of architecture-independent, read-only data files.

--libdir=eprefix/lib   The location of program libraries.

--includedir=prefix/include   The location of Samba-related include files.

--infodir=prefix/info   The location of additional information files.

--mandir=prefix/man   The location of Samba's man pages.

--with-sambaconfdir=**prefix**/*lib*   The location of Samba's configuration file, `smb.conf`.

--with-privatedir=**prefix**/*private*   The location of the sensitive encrypted password file (`smbpasswd`).

--with-lockdir=**prefix**/*var/locks*   The location of Samba's lock files, used to implement some file access control features.

--with-swatdir=**prefix**/*swat*   The location of SWAT, used for administering Samba through a web browser.

TIP

You may want to load the `configure` script into a text editor to look for new Samba configuration options that may have been added since these descriptions were written.

By default, Samba installs itself entirely under the `/usr/local/samba` directory. This is the accepted location for packages you build on your own system (that is, locally). It's probably best to leave most or all of these options at their default values. If you're an experienced administrator who has a good reason to move files elsewhere, you may adjust these locations as you see fit.

NOTE

Most Linux distributions compile Samba with nonstandard options in order to match the distribution's available features and common network configurations. For instance, if a distribution uses PAM, its Samba package includes PAM support. Most distributions also change the location for Samba files from the default `/usr/local/samba` to `/usr`, typically. Further adjustments are usually made to other file locations, such as placing configuration files under `/etc`, `/etc/samba.d` or a similar location.

LOCATING IMPORTANT FILES

If you compile Samba from source code, you can control where Samba installs itself by issuing appropriate `configure` options. If you're using a binary distribution, however, file locations are largely out of your control. It's therefore important that you know where to look for critical files—

particularly the smb.conf configuration file, which controls most of Samba's features.

Common Installation Directories

Samba's default installation directory is /usr/local/samba. If compiled directly from source code without changes, Samba installs itself to this directory and creates a variety of subdirectories for storing its files. By default, Samba's binary files go in /usr/local/samba/bin. To run the Samba binaries, you must do one of three things:

▶ Add the Samba binary directory to your path.

▶ Create links to the Samba binaries in a directory that's already on your path, such as /usr/bin or /usr/local/bin.

▶ Include the complete pathname in every reference to a Samba binary, as in startup scripts.

Most Linux distributions don't use the default Samba installation directory. Instead, the Samba binaries and other files are placed directly in conventional directories for daemons, libraries, and so on. If you need to locate your Samba binary files for some reason, there are several ways to do so:

Use the *whereis* Command   You can type **whereis progname** to find the location of the program called *progname*. This command may also return the location of the program's man pages and, if present on your computer, source files. The whereis command works only if the program you're looking for is in a path that whereis searches.

Use the *find* Command   You can locate a program anywhere on the computer by using the find command. For instance, find / -name *progname* will find the file called *progname* anywhere on the entire hard disk, even in an unusual location. This differs from whereis, which doesn't search every directory. The downside is that find takes much more time to return results than whereis does. Read the find man pages for more details.

NOTE

For more information on the whereis and find commands, see Chapter 4.

Consult the Package Listing You can use the package database maintained by RPM or dpkg to locate your files. On an RPM-based distribution, if you know the package name, you can issue a command such as rpm -ql *packagename* to obtain a listing of the files in the *packagename* package. If necessary, you can pipe these results through grep to reduce the clutter, as in rpm -ql samba | grep smbd to locate just the smbd file. On a system that uses Debian packages, the command dpkg-deb -c *package.deb* lists the contents of the package file *package.deb.*

NOTE

Most Linux distributions have documentation files for various packages in the /usr/doc or /usr/share/doc directory. Each package typically has its own subdirectory, as in /usr/share/doc/samba. You can find Samba's own documentation in this directory tree, as well as on the Samba website, http://www.samba.org.

When installed as it is on most Linux distributions, Samba's files are scattered about many directories, such as /usr/bin, /usr/share/doc /samba, and /usr/man. It can therefore be tedious to track down these files individually to update or remove them—but that's what package managers such as RPM are designed to do.

Configuration Files

Samba relies on a handful of critical configuration files. On most Linux distributions, these files reside in /etc, /etc/samba.d or a similar subdirectory of /etc. If you compile Samba yourself and don't change the default location for these files, Samba will look for them in the /usr/local/samba/lib directory. These critical configuration files include the following:

smb.conf This file is the single most important Samba configuration file. You set almost all of Samba's options here— options used by both the nmbd and smbd daemons. The next two chapters are devoted to describing the contents of this file.

smbpasswd Samba doesn't always use this file, but when it does, the file is critically important. It contains encrypted passwords for user accounts. In some ways, this file is equivalent to the standard Linux passwd or shadow file, but the usernames and passwords in smbpasswd are used only by Samba. Samba uses this file only if you configure it to use encrypted passwords.

smbusers   This is another optional file. If present, and if you configure Samba to use it, this file contains a mapping of Windows network accounts to Linux accounts. For instance, you can configure Samba to allow the user with the Windows network name TechnoM to access the Linux account galen.

lmhosts   Similar in concept to the standard Linux /etc/hosts file, lmhosts provides a mapping of NetBIOS names to IP addresses. Options in the smb.conf file can enable or disable use of the lmhosts file.

In addition to these Samba configuration files, you can add your own custom configuration files. It's possible to include one configuration file inside another. For instance, you can create custom configuration files for each user—or for specific users—and include those files in the main smb.conf file for only those specific users.

If your Samba binary is built to expect its configuration files in some location that you don't like, you can use the -s option to force the Samba daemons to look elsewhere for the smb.conf file. You can then use additional options inside smb.conf to force Samba to look in your preferred location for additional configuration files. Suppose you want Samba to look in /etc/samba-configs for configuration files. You could launch the Samba daemons with commands similar to the following:

```
# nmbd -s /etc/samba-config/smb.conf -D
# smbd -s /etc/samba-config/smb.conf -D
```

You would ordinarily include these commands in a startup script. Because most Linux distributions come with Samba startup scripts, you'd likely modify the default Samba startup script to achieve the desired effect.

RUNNING SAMBA

Before you can use Samba, you have to start it. There are several ways to do this. The best way may depend upon your distribution, because most distributions include Samba start up scripts of one sort or another. As a general rule, I recommend using these start up scripts. On occasion, however, you might want to bypass the usual script, either to start Samba manually with unusual parameters for testing purposes or to run it through inetd or a similar super server for security or resource-conservation reasons.

Running Samba Manually

To run Samba manually, start the Samba daemons from a shell prompt as root. Here are the most basic forms of the startup commands:

```
# nmbd -D
# smbd -D
```

Startup Parameters for *nmbd*

Each of the two 2.2.*x* Samba daemons supports several parameters. For nmbd, these parameters include the following:

-D Runs the program in daemon mode. This is the usual way in which to run Samba, but it's not the default.

-a When a new connection is made, appends log messages to the Samba log file for that connection. This is the default behavior.

-o Overwrites the log file for each new connection. This behavior is the opposite of the -a behavior and is not the default.

-h Displays help information for the daemon.

-v Displays the program's version number.

-H filename Uses *filename* as the lmhosts file.

-d debuglevel Sets the debug level to *debuglevel*, which must be an integer from 0 to 10. Increasing the value of *debuglevel* will increase the number of log entries. Useful values for end users are 0 to 3; values above 3 are used mainly by Samba developers. I recommend using a value of 1 for day-to-day operation of Samba. The default value is 0.

-l logfile Sets the log file to *logfile*. In practice, Samba appends .nmb to the *logfile* name you specify. The default value depends on Samba compile-time options. Common values are

```
/var/log/samba.d/smb.nmb
/usr/samba/var/log.nmb
/var/log/log.nmb
```

-n name   Sets the computer's NetBIOS name to *name*. This option overrides the netbios name option in the smb.conf file.

-p port   Sets the UDP port number to which nmbd listens. The default value is 137, and unless you have some specific reason for doing so, you should not change this value.

-s filename   Sets the configuration filename to use. This value defaults to smb.conf in a directory specified at compile time, as described in the section "Compiling Source from a Tarball," earlier in this chapter.

In most cases, you can run nmbd with only the -D option, but in a few cases you may want to add others options. The -s option can be particularly useful if you want to experiment with a variety of different Samba configurations.

Startup Parameters for *smbd*

The second Samba daemon, smbd, sports a variety of startup parameters, most of which are identical to those of nmbd. In particular, -D, -a, -o, -h, -v, -d, -l, -p, and -s have identical meanings for both nmbd and smbd (except that the default log file name uses the .smb suffix for smbd, rather than the .nmb used for nmbd). In addition, smbd supports the following options:

-P   This option enables *passive mode,* in which Samba doesn't send any network traffic. Note: This feature is designed for use only by the Samba developers and should not be confused with the -p (lowercase) option.

-O Socket Options   Socket options affect the details of Samba's operation. Setting specific socket options can some-times improve—or degrade—Samba's performance; the optimal settings vary from one network to another. You can set these options from the smb.conf file by using the socket options settings, or you can set them on the command line. Be sure not to confuse -O with -o; the two options differ in case and meaning.

As with nmbd, you can normally run smbd using only the -D parameter. Other parameters, such as -s and -O, can be useful when you're experimenting with your Samba configuration.

Samba TNG Daemons

A variant version of Samba is known as The Next Generation (TNG), and the Samba TNG package includes several additional daemons. These daemons take over some of the functionality of the nmbd and smbd packages in mainstream versions of Samba and add features needed for support of Windows NT domains. (Similar support also exists in the pre-3.0 development versions of the mainstream Samba branch.) If you want to run Samba TNG or a release derived from Samba TNG, you may need to start these daemons. The daemons accept startup parameters similar to those of nmbd and smbd. Because at this writing Samba TNG is under active development, I recommend you run each daemon with the -h parameter to discover the options accepted by the version you have. The section "Samba TNG" in Chapter 19, "Integrating SMB/CIFS into Linux," tells you more about Samba TNG's features.

NOTE

Aside from the fact that Samba TNG uses several additional daemons, its startup operation and configuration details are the same as for the mainstream version of Samba. You can use the same smb.conf file in Samba TNG that you use in Samba 2.2.x. Future versions of Samba may add a few additional smb.conf parameters, but old configuration files should still work.

Stopping Samba

You can stop Samba using the kill command, just as you can stop any other program. There are two ways to do this:

- Type **killall nmbd; killall smbd** to kill all instances of both nmbd and smbd.

- Type **ps ax | grep mbd** to find all running instances of nmbd and smbd, and then issue individual kill commands on each instance by process ID number.

WARNING

On Linux, the `killall` command kills all running instances of the named program. On some Unix systems, it may have other meanings. Read the `killall` man page before using the program, particularly on non-Linux systems.

It's best to stop the Samba daemons by sending them SIGTERM (15) signals (as in `kill -15 idnum`), rather than SIGKILL (9) messages. The latter may leave shared memory in an inconsistent state. If you want to force the server to load new configuration settings from `smb.conf`, you can do so by sending the server a SIGHUP (1). Doing so protects any connected sessions from disconnection. Existing sessions maintain their current settings, but new sessions use the settings in the newly edited `smb.conf` file.

If your distribution uses a Samba startup script, as described in the following section, you should stop Samba by using the startup script and passing it the `stop` parameter. For instance:

```
# /etc/rc.d/init.d/samba stop
```

The exact location and name of the Samba start/stop script vary from one distribution to another, as you'll see in the next section.

Common Distribution Startup Scripts

Most Linux distributions place startup scripts for daemons and other programs to be run at boot time in the `/etc/rc.d` directory tree. On most distributions, this directory contains a series of subdirectories called `/etc/rc.d/rc1.d`, `/etc/rc.d/rc2.d`, and so on through `/etc/rc.d/rc6.d`. Each subdirectory contains service start/stop scripts corresponding to specific run levels. Each run level corresponds to a specific set of running services. For example, in Red Hat Linux (as well as many other distributions), run level 3 is a text-mode, multiuser boot, whereas run level 5 is a multiuser boot that presents an X-based graphical logon prompt.

The run level in which a computer runs is specified in the `/etc/inittab` file. This file contains a line such as the following:

```
id:5:initdefault:
```

The number (5 in this case) is the run level of the computer. Whenever a Linux system enters a given run level, it runs the startup scripts in the corresponding run level directory under `/etc/rc.d`. Whenever a computer shuts down or shifts to a new run level through the `init` command, the computer runs the scripts in the new run level, which shut down services that are available in the old run level but not in the new one and start services available in the new run level but not in the old one. For more on run levels, see Chapter 4.

Startup Control

In most Linux distributions, the contents of the `/etc/rc.d/rc?.d` directories are actually symbolic links to scripts located elsewhere, such as in `/etc/rc.d` or `/etc/rc.d/init.d`. You can control the startup of Samba in three ways.

Editing the Startup Script   You can edit the startup script in `/etc/rc.d`, `/etc/rc.d/init.d` or wherever it happens to be located. For instance, if you want to add specific startup parameters, as described earlier in the section "Running Samba Manually," you can add them to this startup script. The startup script is likely to be called `samba` or `smb`.

Creating or Deleting Links   If you want to prevent Samba from starting up, you can remove its link in the appropriate `/etc/rc.d/rc?.d` directory. This link is likely to have a name of the form `S??samba` or `S??smb`, where `??` is a number. The shutdown script has the same form but begins with `K` rather than `S`. Likewise, if you want to make Samba start when it doesn't do so, you can create an appropriate symbolic link.

WARNING

Be careful in numbering the Samba startup script; the numbers following the S determine the startup order. Be sure Samba starts *after* your network is brought up.

Editing a Control Script   On occasion, an additional script controls which startup scripts execute. In SuSE Linux, for example, the `/etc/rc.config` file contains variable assignments such as `START_SMB="yes"` that determine which startup scripts run when the system starts. You can edit this control script directly or leave it to GUI configuration tools such as SuSE's YaST.

TIP

If you use a Samba package designed for a distribution other than the one you're using, the Samba package's startup script may not be appropriate for your distribution. You can probably use a startup script from an earlier version of Samba for your distribution or take a startup script designed for another daemon and modify it to run Samba on your system.

Most Samba startup scripts start both the nmbd and smbd daemons. If you use Samba TNG, you'll have to modify the startup scripts to start all the Samba TNG daemons.

You can use the start/stop scripts to start and stop Samba manually by passing the script the parameters start and stop, respectively. Some scripts accept additional parameters, such as restart, which stops and then starts the daemon. If your distribution includes this feature, I recommend using these scripts rather than starting or killing Samba directly. These scripts sometimes perform small but helpful tasks in addition to starting Samba or may pass useful parameters to the Samba daemons.

A few Linux distributions, such as Slackware, use an entirely different method of starting daemons. Rather than individual startup scripts in the /etc/rc.d directory tree, these distributions rely upon one or two monolithic startup scripts. In Slackware, the /etc/rc.d/rc.inet1 and /etc/rc.d/rc.inet2 scripts contain commands to start daemons such as Samba. Other distributions, including those that normally use individualized daemon-starting scripts, also include general-purpose startup scripts (generally called rc.local or boot.local) somewhere in the /etc/rc.d directory tree. You might want to use such a script if you have problems with the individualized Samba startup script—such as if you've compiled Samba TNG yourself and don't want to try to modify the startup scripts to handle this version of Samba. In any event, you can add daemon startup commands similar to those described earlier in this chapter in the section "Running Samba Manually."

Controlling Scripts with GUI Tools

Most Linux distributions include GUI configuration tools to help control what daemons start and stop with the system. For instance, Figure 20.2 shows the Linuxconf tool that ships with Red Hat, Mandrake, and some other Linux distributions. In Linuxconf, you can configure Samba to start automatically by following these steps:

1. In the left pane of the configuration window, expand Control, then Control Panel, then Control Service Activity.

2. Double-click the smb item in the list in the right pane of the window. The result is the display shown in Figure 20.2.

3. Check the Automatic box next to Startup.

4. Click Start if you want to start Samba immediately as well as when you reboot the computer.

5. Click Accept to implement your changes.

WARNING

Linux GUI configuration tools are sometimes quite finicky about the form of their configuration files. It's not uncommon for Linuxconf to crash if you select an option that reads a configuration file you've configured by hand. When you intend to use a GUI tool, it's best if you use *only* that tool for system configuration, to avoid such problems.

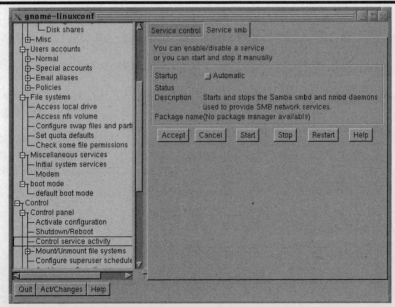

FIGURE 20.2:   Linuxconf and other GUI configuration tools enable you to configure daemons to start and stop without knowing precisely where the startup files are.

The operating details of GUI configuration tools such as Linuxconf vary from one tool to another. The steps you take with another tool, such as SuSE's YaST or Caldera's COAS, differ from those described here. In all cases, though, these utilities configure the system by editing the startup files described in this section or by creating and deleting appropriate links.

NOTE

Some GUI configuration tools, including Linuxconf, can run using text-mode menus in a non-GUI environment, such as a text-mode logon.

Running Samba from a Super Server

It's possible to run Samba from the inetd or xinetd super server. The advantages of running Samba through a super server include the following:

► The server's security is improved. Particularly if you use TCP Wrappers or xinetd, you can improve security for your Samba server by restricting initial connections to the server. Samba includes many security features, however, so this advantage is comparatively small if you take care in establishing your Samba configuration.

► Resources are used efficiently. If your Samba server is used infrequently, running Samba through a super server can minimize the impact on the server's memory. This advantage disappears, however, if it's common for one or more individuals to be connected to the Samba server at all times.

► You get central control. For administrative reasons, you may prefer to use a super server configuration file to control all your servers.

There are also substantial disadvantages to running Samba through a super server:

► You get slower response. When run through a super server, it takes time for Samba to start up when a request is made of it. This can annoy users, who might expect instantaneous or near-instantaneous access to their Samba shares.

▶ Browsing can be unreliable. Samba servers sometimes fail to appear or respond slowly or strangely in browsing when Samba is run through inetd. This problem is even more severe with xinetd, in my experience; nmbd and xinetd simply don't seem to get along very well.

On the whole, I recommend you *not* run Samba through a super server. If the memory of running Samba is so bad that you're tempted to use a super server, it would probably be better to upgrade your system's RAM. The security advantages of running Samba from a super server are fairly minor, and you can otherwise improve system security by using ipchains, iptables, or an external firewall computer. If you try running Samba from inetd or xinetd but encounter unreliable operation, try running Samba directly instead. You might find that your problems disappear.

If you must run Samba from inetd despite the disadvantages of doing so, follow these steps:

1. Disable any Samba startup scripts, such as those in /etc/rc.d/rc?.d. Kill any running Samba processes.

2. Ensure that the /etc/services file contains appropriate entries for all the SMB/CIFS TCP/IP ports. (Most Linux distributions ship with appropriate entries.) Specifically, the file should contain the following entries:

```
netbios-ns      137/tcp   # NETBIOS Name Service
netbios-ns      137/udp
netbios-dgm     138/tcp   # NETBIOS Datagram Service
netbios-dgm     138/udp
netbios-ssn     139/tcp   # NETBIOS session service
netbios-ssn     139/udp
```

3. Edit /etc/inetd.conf to include lines to start Samba. These lines will look something like the following:

```
netbios-ssn  stream  tcp  nowait  root  /usr/sbin/tcpd
➡smbd
netbios-ns   dgram   udp  wait    root  /usr/sbin/tcpd
➡nmbd
```

This example shows Samba called through tcpd, the TCP Wrappers daemon. Some systems call smbd and nmbd directly, however. On the whole, using TCP Wrappers is usually better because it can improve security. If necessary, adjust the path to the tcpd or Samba daemon to match your system's configuration.

4. Find the process ID of the current instance of inetd by typing **ps ax | grep inetd**.

5. Send inetd a SIGHUP to get it to reload its configuration file. You can do this with a command such as this:

   # **kill -SIGHUP** *pid*

   where *pid* is the process ID revealed in step 4.

You can perform similar steps to run Samba from other super servers, such as xinetd (http://synack.net/xinetd/). The details of configuring xinetd differ slightly from the preceding, however. Most importantly, xinetd is configured through the /etc/xinetd.conf file, or individual files for each server in /etc/xinetd.d. An xinetd configuration entry contains the same information as shown in step 3, but it's spread across several lines, thus:

```
service netbios-ssn
{
        socket_type     = stream
        protocol        = tcp
        wait            = no
        user            = root
        server          = /usr/sbin/smbd
}
```

It's uncommon to use xinetd in conjunction with TCP Wrappers, so there's no reference to tcpd in such a setup.

WARNING

nmbd doesn't run well from xinetd, although smbd runs from it acceptably, and nmbd runs fine from inetd. This problem may be fixed with a future version of xinetd or Samba. In the meantime, if you want to run Samba from xinetd, you must run nmbd independently or run it from inetd, while running smbd from xinetd.

What's Next?

For most Linux systems, Samba installation is easy because it's done automatically during Linux installation. If you need to install Samba after the fact, you can do so most easily by using your distribution's package manager. In a few cases, however, you may want to install Samba by compiling it from source code for your own system. Doing this isn't any more complex than compiling and installing most other source code packages, but it's important that you know about critical compile-time options relating to features such as PAM support.

Running Samba is also easy to do if you stick closely to your distribution's default configuration. Many distributions give you the option of whether or not to run Samba at installation time. For others, you can set this option by editing configuration files or by using GUI configuration utilities, as discussed in the next chapter.

Chapter 21

GUI CONFIGURATION TOOLS AND THE *SMB.CONF* FILE

This chapter covers the basics of Samba configuration. Samba is configured in a single file named smb.conf that typically resides in the /etc, /etc/samba.d, or /usr/local/samba/lib directory, although it might exist elsewhere on some systems.

The chapter begins with a description of configuration by direct editing of smb.conf. This is the most flexible means of configuring Samba, but it's also the most error prone. Next are two easier—but less flexible—methods of Samba configuration through GUI configuration tools, Linuxconf and the *Samba Web Administration Tool* (SWAT). Finally, a few of the key general-purpose configuration options are described. These options don't relate to specific file or printer shares but are important for the server as a whole.

Adapted from *Linux Samba Server Administration* by Roderick W. Smith

ISBN 0-7821-2740-1   656 pages $39.99

Editing *SMB.CONF* to Configure Samba

The smb.conf file lies at the core of Samba configuration. It's therefore critically important that you understand how to manipulate this file to achieve the configuration you desire. If you're new to Samba and are more comfortable with GUI configuration tools, you may not want to edit smb.conf directly but instead use a tool such as Linuxconf or SWAT. I recommend you learn at least the basics of smb.conf configuration, though, because doing so can help you understand what the GUI tools do.

In most of this book, configuration options are described in terms of smb.conf features. SWAT uses the same terms, and Linuxconf generally uses similar terms, so you should have no problem locating an option in a GUI tool based on the descriptions in this book—if the option exists in the GUI tool. Bear in mind that Linuxconf, in particular, lacks many features available by direct editing of smb.conf.

Structure of the *smb.conf* File

A very minimal smb.conf file looks like Listing 21.1. This basic file is perfectly functional and produces a usable Samba server, at least on some networks—indeed, it's more than what's needed for minimal functionality. It demonstrates some key features of smb.conf.

Listing 21.1: A Simple *smb.conf* File

```
[global]
        workgroup = RINGWORLD
        hosts allow = 192.168.1. 192.168.2.23

[homes]
        comment = Home Directories
        writeable = Yes
        browseable = No
```

Each share begins with the share name (for example, [global] in Listing 21.1) and ends with the beginning of the next share name ([homes] in Listing 21.1) or the end of the file, whichever comes first. As you'll see, Samba is quite liberal in its handling of the smb.conf file's format. It doesn't care about case, and it's quite tolerant of white space—blank lines, spaces, and tabs. Most people (and most GUI tools for Samba configuration) format shares as it's done in Listing 21.1, with parameters indented for ease of reading.

Types of *smb.conf* Entries

The three main types of entries in the smb.conf file are share names, parameters, and comments.

Share Names   The names in brackets—[global] and [homes] in Listing 21.1—are *share names*. These names mark the beginnings of *share definitions,* each of which sets up a configuration for a single shared resource such as a directory or printer accessible through Samba. The [global] share is special because it sets defaults for all shares and establishes global configuration options that apply to the server as a whole.

Parameters   Each Samba *parameter* is a variable name, such as workgroup or writeable in Listing 21.1. The parameter can be assigned a value, such as RINGWORLD or Yes. Parameters and their values

- ▶ Can contain spaces; the parameter is separated from its value by an equals sign (=).

- ▶ Are case insensitive; workgroup is equivalent to WORKGROUP. There is an exception to this rule: Some values may be case sensitive because the value refers to something that is itself case sensitive. For instance, if the parameter is a pathname or filename on the Linux server, that parameter is case sensitive because Linux treats filenames in a case-sensitive way.

Comments   Comments begin with pound signs (#) or semicolons (;). Any text on a line after one of these characters is ignored by Samba. Comments allow you to document your intent in creating a share or setting an option, particularly if you try something that's subtle and might be misinterpreted later.

You can also use comments to temporarily remove shares or parameters from the smb.conf file. When you comment out a share, you must add a comment character to the beginning of every line of the share—the share name and all its parameters. If

you miss a parameter, it will become part of the previous share's definition.

NOTE
There's also a `comment` parameter, which sets text that can be associated with a share and viewed from client computers.

TIP
A simpler way to disable a share is to use the `available = No` parameter. Doing this makes the share disappear from browse lists and disables access to the share.

Parameter Values

Although the basic format of the `smb.conf` file appears fairly simple, you can create very complex configurations with this file. This is in part because the `smb.conf` file supports a large number of parameters. The values you assign to parameters can themselves add to the complexity of the file, however. These parameters and their values can take several forms, as explained in the following sections.

Strings   A *string* is a set of characters—generally numbers and letters, and sometimes punctuation, spaces, and so on. (You don't need to do anything special to include spaces in a value, but if you like, you can enclose the entire string in quotation marks.) In some sense, all values are strings, but some values are interpreted in special ways.

Some characters carry special meaning, such as quotation marks surrounding a string (which are ignored by Samba) or comment characters (which cause Samba to ignore the rest of the line). The backslash character (\) also merits mention; it allows you to continue a string on the next line. You might use this if you want to include a long list of options, such as computer names, and you want to keep the lines in the file shorter than 80 columns.

Lists   A *list* is a set of several values, separated by commas or spaces. In Listing 21.1, the `hosts allow` parameter is assigned a list of two values: `192.168.1.` and `192.168.2.23`. The `hosts allow` option tells Samba to accept connections only from computers on the `192.168.1.0` network and from 192.168.2.23. The trailing period in 192.168.1. is vital for specifying the entire 192.168.1.0 network, but it's not required to separate items in the list. In some cases, you can use only a comma or only a space, but not either, to separate values in a list.

Booleans   A *Boolean* value can accept either of two values. These can be specified as Yes, True, or 1 for the positive condition; or No, False, or 0 for the negative. The writeable and browseable parameters in Listing 21.1 are both Booleans.

Variables   Samba supports variables in parameter values. Variables can be used to adjust configuration details on a share-by-share or user-by-user basis. In Samba, a variable is preceded by a percent sign (%). Table 21.1 summarizes the variables that Samba supports.

TABLE 21.1:   Variables Recognized by Samba

VARIABLE	MEANING
%a	Client's operating system (architecture); can be OS2 (OS/2), Samba, UNKNOWN, WfWg (Windows for Workgroups or DOS), Win2K (Windows 2000), Win95 (Windows 95, 98, or Me), or WinNT (Windows NT).
%d	Server's process ID.
%g	Primary group of %u.
%G	Primary group of %U.
%h	Server's DNS name.
%H	Home directory of %u.
%I	Client's IP address.
%L	Server's NetBIOS name.
%m	Client's NetBIOS name.
%M	Client's DNS name.
%N	NIS home directory server.
%p	Path to the share's root directory, if automounted.
%P	Path to the share's root directory.
%R	Negotiated SMB protocol level; can be CORE, COREPLUS, LANMAN1, LANMAN2, or NT1.
%S	Share name.

TABLE 21.1 continued: Variables Recognized by Samba

VARIABLE	MEANING
%T	Current date and time.
%u	Effective Linux username.
%U	Requested username (might not be the same as %u).
%v	Samba version.

Some of these variables are undefined at particular points in time. For instance, until you've accessed a share, %u is undefined. That's because this value can be set by, for example, a force user parameter. %U, by contrast, is the username sent when negotiating the session and so is available before accessing particular shares, but not before logging onto the server. You can use variables to achieve many interesting effects:

▶ Create separate log files for each client by using the log file parameter, as in log file = /var/log/samba/log.smb.%m.

▶ Create share options that are customized for specific users, machines, or client OSs by using the include parameter, as in include = /etc/samba.d/smb.conf.%a.

▶ Create shares that are customized for specific users, machines, or groups, by using the path parameter, as in path = /home/samba/%G to create a share for particular groups. (Note that this particular example would not work with the lowercase %g option because that value is undefined until after the share is accessed.)

NOTE

Certain special shares perform such substitutions automatically, as described in the next section, "Privileged Shares."

▶ Display information on the current host in a share's comment or elsewhere, as in server string = Samba server on %h.

Privileged Shares

Samba recognizes a few share names as having privileged status.

[global]   This share, as mentioned earlier in the section "Types of smb.conf Entries," isn't a share in the same sense as most others. Rather, it's a placeholder for default and global configuration options. Some parameters can be used in the [global] share and nowhere else.

[homes]   This share maps to each user's home directory. By default, when viewing a Samba server, a user sees his own home directory and no others. (Users can still access other users' home directories, within the limits of permissions and Samba settings, by directly entering the share name rather than browsing to the share.) File shares are discussed in Chapter 22, "Configuring File Sharing."

[printers]   This share name expands into one entry for each printer defined in the server's /etc/printcap file.

[netlogon]   Windows computers try to access this share when logging onto a Samba server. If the share is present and properly configured, the client tries to run the batch file specified by the logon script parameter. This procedure allows you to create some uniform set of options for all your systems or run logon scripts that are unique for each user (such as by specifying logon script = %U.bat).

All other shares are ordinary file or printer shares. Unless you use variables to restrict access to some users, all users see the same files in these shares or can access a printer share in identical ways.

Keeping Your Configuration File Readable

The smb.conf file can easily become unreadable, particularly if you rely on Samba's willingness to parse files without respect to white space, and if you take advantage of the option to use multiple synonyms for many parameters. Here are a few simple steps you can take to help keep your smb.conf file uncluttered and understandable:

Be consistent   No matter how you decide to format your file, apply your formatting consistently. Inconsistent formatting can make the file difficult to parse.

Indent parameters Follow the usual convention of indenting parameters, but do not indent share names. This practice makes it easy to locate shares when examining the configuration file.

Use comments Although most Samba parameters are designed to be self documenting, you can use comments to describe who should be able to access a share, what a variable means, and so on. It's easy to mistakenly create a share that's accessible by the wrong collection of users or that otherwise doesn't work in quite the way you intended. If you document your intent, it becomes easier to identify errors later.

WARNING

The SWAT GUI configuration tool, described later in this chapter, obliterates any comments you place in the smb.conf file.

Use consistent parameter names Many parameters have synonyms, and some have antonyms (mostly Booleans that can be expressed one way with one parameter and the other way with another). Use just one name. Doing otherwise can cause confusion in the future because it's easy to forget that the two names are synonymous.

Testing Your Configuration File

If you build your smb.conf file by hand, it's easy to make a mistake that renders the file unusable. You can use the testparm program to check that the file is logically correct, as in this example:

```
# testparm /etc/smb.conf
```

If the file is logically correct, testparm responds by displaying output similar to the following:

```
Load smb config files from /etc/smb.conf

Processing section "[homes]"

Processing section "[printers]"

Loaded services file OK.

Press enter to see a dump of your service definitions
```

The testparm program identifies each of the shares in the `smb.conf` file, and you can verify that it's identified all the shares that you think it should. Press the Enter key to see your share definitions (what testparm calls *service definitions*), stripped of comments and unnecessary formatting details.

If there's a problem, however, testparm will identify it:

```
Load smb config files from smb.conf

Unknown parameter encountered: "netbos name"

Ignoring unknown parameter "netbos name"

Processing section "[homes]"

Processing section "[printers]"

Loaded services file OK.

Press enter to see a dump of your service definitions
```

This output tells you that the `smb.conf` file included a misspelling: `netbos name` instead of `netbios name`. The testparm program has identified this misspelling as an "unknown parameter" and has further informed you that it's ignoring the parameter. Of course, you should correct the matter before using the defective file.

USING LINUXCONF TO CONFIGURE SAMBA

Unix was originally configured entirely through text-mode tools, but many Linux distributions include GUI configuration tools. One of these, Linuxconf, is used in many popular distributions, including Red Hat Linux (http://www.redhat.com), Linux Mandrake (http://www.mandrake.com), LinuxPPC (http://www.linuxppc.com), and Yellow Dog Linux (http://www.yellowdoglinux.com/ydl_home.html). Operation details differ somewhat from one distribution to another, but the core of Linuxconf remains the same. It allows you to administer your Linux computer using a text-based, menu-driven tool, an X-based tool, or via a web browser (even from a non-Linux computer). Figure 21.1 shows the main Linuxconf configuration options for Samba, as displayed from Netscape Communicator in Windows 2000.

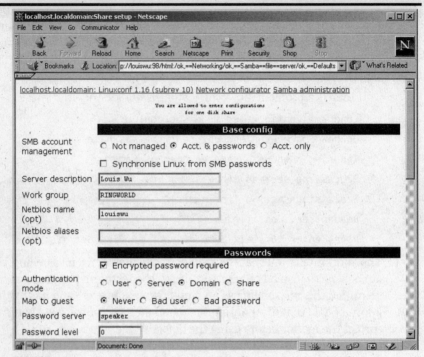

FIGURE 21.1:   You can administer a Linuxconf-equipped computer from any computer that hosts a web browser.

NOTE

Through version 6.2, Red Hat included a Linuxconf module for Samba. This module has been dropped with Red Hat 7.0 and later, however. Red Hat is moving away from the use of Linuxconf and is expected to introduce its own GUI configuration tools in a future version of the distribution. The instructions in this chapter still apply to other distributions that use Linuxconf, including LinuxPPC and Linux Mandrake. You can obtain a Samba module for Linuxconf from http://www.solucorp.qc.ca/linuxconf/modules.hc, but this module may look for the smb.conf file in a location other than the one in which it exists in your system. You can use a symbolic link to work around this problem if you encounter it.

Using Linuxconf Locally or Remotely

If you're already familiar with Linuxconf configuration for your system, you may want to try using it for Samba configuration. To use Linuxconf locally, type **linuxconf** at a shell prompt. If you do this while Linux is running in text mode, you'll get Linuxconf's text-mode interface; if you're running X and you type the command in an xterm or other command-prompt window, you'll get the main GUI version of the utility. You shouldn't need to issue any special configuration commands to make Linuxconf accessible in either of these ways.

To access Linuxconf from a networked computer, first configure the Linuxconf server to accept remote access. To do so, follow these steps:

1. Ensure that the /etc/services file contains a line that defines the port used by Linuxconf:

   ```
   linuxconf 98/tcp
   ```

2. Likewise, a Linuxconf entry must exist in the computer's /etc/inetd.conf file or in a xinetd configuration file (in the /etc/xinetd.d directory). Most distributions that include Linuxconf ship with the appropriate entry enabled, but you should verify that it's there. The relevant entry for inetd.conf is

   ```
   linuxconf stream tcp wait root /bin/linuxconf linuxconf
   ➥--http
   ```

   A xinetd configuration file will have the same information but spread across multiple lines.

3. If you need to add the Linuxconf entry to /etc/inetd.conf or the xinetd configuration, restart the super server. For instance:

   ```
   # ps ax | grep inetd
     379 ?        S        0:00 inetd
   # kill -SIGHUP 379
   ```

4. At this point, Linuxconf should be running and in such a way that it accepts network connections but promptly drops them. In order for this arrangement to be useful, you must add some extra options. The easiest way to do this is to use Linuxconf itself locally. First, start Linuxconf, and select Config ➢ Networking ➢ Misc ➢ Linuxconf Network Access from the expandable menu in the left pane seen in Figure 21.2.

NOTE

Not all Linuxconf utilities look precisely like the one shown in Figure 21.2. Linux Mandrake, in particular, uses a graphical menu system rather than the expandable lists shown here in the left pane. The program's functionality is the same, however.

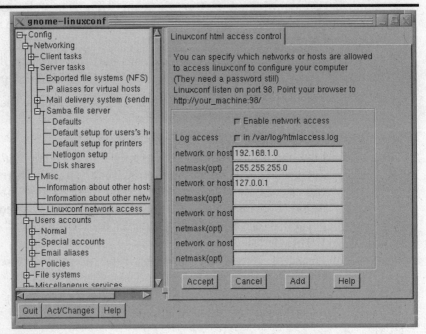

FIGURE 21.2: You can enable remote Linuxconf access through Linuxconf itself.

5. Click the Enable Network Access button in the right pane. Then make the following entries, as shown in Figure 21.2:

   A. In the first Network or Host field in the right pane, enter the IP address of the network to which you want to grant Linuxconf access. Note that this is a network address; it most likely ends in .0.

   B. In the first Netmask (opt) field, enter the network mask of the network to which you want to grant Linuxconf access.

C. In the next Network or Host field, enter **127.0.0.1** (the localhost loopback address). This step grants you access from your own computer, independent of your main network connections.

6. Click Accept in the right panel.

7. Click Quit in the Linuxconf window. The program responds by informing you that the system state doesn't match what you've configured.

8. Click the Activate the Changes button to make your changes current. After a brief pause, Linuxconf disappears.

Instead of entering a network address (steps 5A and 5B), you can enter the IP addresses of specific computers that are to have Linuxconf access. Do this in the same manner as you entered the 127.0.0.1 address in step 5C. As a general rule, the fewer computers to which you grant access, the better.

WARNING

Linuxconf is itself a network server. When accessed from a remote web browser, it requires that you send an administrative password in cleartext across the network. I therefore recommend against using Linuxconf remotely except when absolutely necessary. Ideally, you should do so only from the local network on which the server itself resides.

Once Linuxconf is running and configured to accept remote access, you can use it by typing **http://*servername*:98** into a remote browser's URL entry field, where *servername* is the hostname of the server. You'll first see a general introductory page with a Start button. When you click this button, Linuxconf asks for your username and password. Normally, you can enter **root** and the root password, respectively, for these options. If you've configured your system to allow other users access to Linuxconf, you can type those usernames and passwords instead. At this point, you can browse the Linuxconf menu structure by clicking on links in the browser until you find a configuration page (refer to Figure 21.1).

A Tour of Linuxconf Samba Options

The main Samba configuration options are listed under Config ➢ Networking ➢ Server Tasks ➢ Samba File Server. There are five sets of Linuxconf Samba configuration options: Defaults, Default Setup for Users' Home, Default Setup for Printers, Netlogon Setup, and Disk Shares. They're described briefly in the following paragraphs.

Defaults

Figure 21.1 shows the Defaults options, as seen through a web-based Linuxconf interface. These options relate to the settings in the [global] area of the smb.conf file. Following are descriptions of some critical options.

Server Description   This sets a comment parameter for the [global] share. Unfortunately, the parameter doesn't do much. That's because for servers, it's the server string parameter that must be set to adjust the Comment field as seen from a Windows client. This bug may be fixed in a future version of Linuxconf.

Work Group   This field sets the workgroup parameter. As described in the section "Server Identification," later in this chapter, this parameter is critically important if your computers are to see one another properly.

NetBIOS Name and NetBIOS Aliases   These fields set the primary NetBIOS name and aliases for the computer. By default, Samba takes these values from the computer's hostname, but you can set them here explicitly.

Encrypted Password Required   Check this box if you want to use encrypted passwords on your network. Encrypted passwords are described later in this chapter, in the section "Password Encryption."

Authentication Mode   As a general rule, User is the best authentication mode to employ for a Samba server. If your network uses a domain rather than a workgroup as described in Chapter 1, "Getting Ready to Install Red Hat Linux 7.1," then you may want to use the Server or Domain authentication mode. You must then enter the NetBIOS name of the primary domain controller in the Password Server field. If you want Samba to emulate Windows 9x's share-by-share access controls, you can use the Share authentication method, but this generally creates a lot of administrative headaches.

Allow Hosts and Deny Hosts   In these fields, you can enter the names or IP addresses of hosts to be explicitly allowed and denied.

Show All Available Printers   If you enable this option, Samba creates shares for all the printers listed in your /etc/printcap file. Otherwise, you must create printer shares individually for each printer.

Default Setup for Users' Home

Figure 21.3 shows the Linuxconf configuration panel that is used to configure the [homes] share. As mentioned earlier, the [homes] share defines a file share that changes dynamically for each user. Specifically, it allows each user access to his own home directory. Details you can configure through Linuxconf include the following:

Comment/Description   The string you enter here appears as a comment field when you browse the share in Windows.

This Share Is Enabled   Check this box if you want to enable access to home directories. To disable these shares, leave the box unmarked.

Browsable   Unlike most shares, the [homes] share does *not* need to be browsable. You should therefore leave this item disabled. If you turn it on, users will see two identical shares: one called homes and one with the user's username.

Access Options   In this tab you can apply allow hosts and deny hosts rules to individual shares, just as you can to Samba as a whole.

Users   Click the Users tab to set options relating to individual users. You can set lists of read-only and read/write users, lists of users who may or may not connect to the share, and the maximum number of simultaneous connections Samba accepts to the share.

Scripts   You can configure scripts that Samba runs when a user first connects and when the user disconnects.

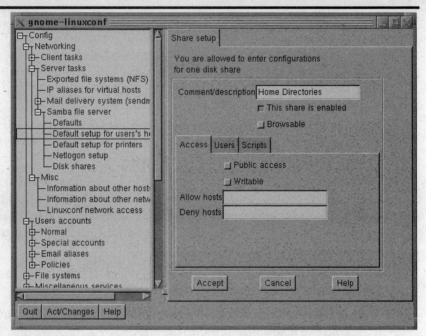

FIGURE 21.3: Linuxconf provides the means to edit users' home shares.

As a general rule, leaving the home accounts' configuration options set at their defaults yields a usable set of shares, one for each user. You may want to edit these options if you need to restrict access to user shares, perform some username or scripting magic, or disable user account access entirely.

Default Setup for Printers

The printer setup options are quite simple, containing only three editable options.

Comment/Description As with home directories, you can enter a string to describe the printer in greater detail. Because this is the default printer setup, which exports all printers in your /etc/printcap file, this field isn't terribly useful for distinguishing one printer from another.

This Share Is Enabled Check this box if you want to share all the printers in your /etc/printcap file. To share some but not all of your printers, you must create a separate share for each printer you want to share.

Public Access   Enable this option if you want to allow anybody to print to your shared printers without requiring a password.

The default options used by Linuxconf set up sharing for all your printers. There is a variety of additional options you can use with printer shares, but Linuxconf doesn't give you access to these options. If you want to configure your printer shares more extensively, you must use SWAT (described shortly) or do manual configuration.

Netlogon Setup

If you want to create a [netlogon] share, Linuxconf can create one for you. Figure 21.4 shows the relevant Linuxconf module.

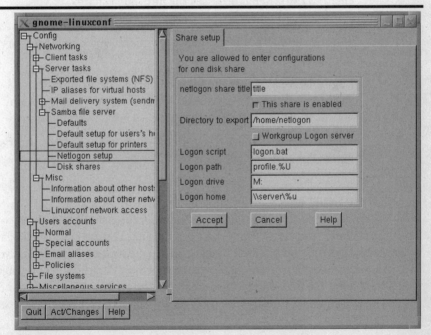

FIGURE 21.4:   Creating basic [netlogon] share information in Linuxconf is easy.

Here are brief descriptions of the options you can set:

Netlogon Share Title   The default name for the share is `net-logon`, but you can change it by specifying another value here.

This Share Is Enabled   Check this box to enable the share.

Directory to Export   Enter the directory you want to use as the `netlogon` directory. This can be any directory on the computer.

Workgroup Logon Server   This option enables the `domain logons` parameter, which lets Samba function as a domain controller. To fully activate this functionality, though, you need to specify additional parameters.

Logon Script   You can specify the name of a script for the client to run when it accesses the `netlogon` share.

Logon Path   You can specify the directory in which Linux stores Windows profiles, which are critical Windows configuration files.

Logon Drive   This is the Windows drive letter (for instance, `M:`) to which the logon home directory is mapped. This option affects only Windows NT clients.

Logon Home   This is the Windows network path to the user's home directory.

Disk Shares

The Disk Shares configuration screen presents a list of the defined disk shares, excluding the `[homes]` definition. You can double-click an existing definition to edit it or click Add to create a new one. When you do so, Linuxconf presents the options shown in Figure 21.5, and you can then enter the definition for a disk share. Normally, you use this panel to create a share for housing the program or data files that will be accessible to a group of people on your network.

Options in the Disk Shares configuration screen include the following:

Share Name   This is the name used to identify the share.

Comment/Description   This is the comment field visible from Windows when browsing a computer's shares.

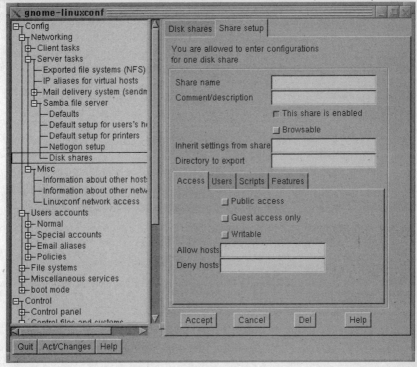

FIGURE 21.5:   More options are available for individual shares than for home shares (compare to Figure 21.3).

This Share Is Enabled   Check this box to make the share usable.

Browsable   If you leave this option turned off, users won't see the share in the list of shares for the computer, although they can still access the share by entering its name directly in the Address field of a Windows file browser.

Inherit Settings from Share   This setting uses the copy parameter to copy parameters from an existing share. You can then modify or add parameters as required to achieve the desired effect.

Directory to Export   Enter the name of the directory that will serve as the root of the exported share.

Access   Use this tab to define which computers can access the share. You can restrict access machine-by-machine with the Allow Hosts and Deny Hosts fields and set options relating to public and guest access. Be sure to check the Writable option if you want users to be able to write to the share.

Users   Set user-by-user access control options on this tab, including a list of the users granted access and the per-user restrictions on read and write access.

Scripts   Use this tab to set scripts that Samba runs when the share is accessed and when the share is closed by the client.

Features   Options here include the capability to force connection as a particular Linux user or group, a per-share guest account specification, and a limit on the allowed number of simultaneous connections to the share.

Tips Concerning Linuxconf Configuration

Using the Linuxconf package is a good way to set up a basic Samba server, but it has its limits. Most importantly, it doesn't provide full access to all Samba options. Therefore, you may find that you have to use another tool, such as SWAT or text-based editing, to create the configuration that's precisely correct for your situation. The Linuxconf printer-share handling is particularly deficient: You cannot use Linuxconf to create printer-by-printer customizations to printer shares, and you don't get access to important printer options such as `postscript`, which can help solve problems created by some Windows PostScript printer drivers.

The Linuxconf Samba configuration module doesn't understand all the synonyms and antonyms provided by Samba. For instance, `read only` is an antonym for `writable`; you can specify that a share be read-only by using either `read only = Yes` or `writable = No`. (Samba also accepts `writeable` as a synonym for `writable`.) If you create a share by hand and use `read only = Yes` or `writable = No`, however, Linuxconf doesn't pick up this option. Instead, it preserves any parameters it doesn't understand, which means you can safely use the utility to adjust the features it does understand—even on shares that use advanced features. The drawback is that you cannot eliminate a feature that Linuxconf does understand if you created it using a form that Linuxconf doesn't understand. You can't remove the `read only = Yes` parameter, for instance. You can, however, select the appropriate option to add a

writable = Yes parameter, which Linuxconf inserts after the existing
read only = Yes parameter. Samba generally uses the last such parameter, so the effect is the same—but the result can be confusing should you
later read the smb.conf file in its raw form. As a result of its preserving
options it doesn't understand, Linuxconf also preserves any comments
you may have inserted into the smb.conf file.

Most Linuxconf installations do not, by default, accept remote logons
via a web browser, and I recommend that you do not change this to enable
remote access. Indeed, you may want to tighten security further by disabling Linuxconf in your super server and restarting it. Doing this will
prevent crackers from exploiting any network access bugs that might be
discovered in Linuxconf in the future. The section "Limiting SWAT
Access" later in this chapter includes information on tightening security
around SWAT. Most of these techniques can be applied equally well to
networked Linuxconf access.

WARNING

Lest you think nobody would bother trying to break into a system through
Linuxconf, consider this: My firewall software has recorded multiple attempts
to access my Linux computer through Linuxconf. Because that particular system
doesn't run Linuxconf at all, these access attempts have been unsuccessful.

Unfortunately, Linuxconf sometimes crashes when it encounters
errors in the configuration files it's designed to manipulate. Occasionally
it crashes even on valid configuration files. For instance, while writing
this chapter, I discovered that Linuxconf on one of my systems (a Macintosh running LinuxPPC 2000 with Samba 2.0.7) crashed whenever I
tried to access the Samba Defaults configuration module—no matter how
simple the smb.conf file. Another computer (an *x*86 machine running
Mandrake 7.0 with Samba 2.0.6) handled this same situation just fine. If
Linuxconf crashes mysteriously, configure Samba manually or use
another tool, such as SWAT.

USING SWAT TO CONFIGURE SAMBA

The *Samba Web Administration Tool* (SWAT) is a standard part of Samba,
although it's not required for normal Samba operation. If you require

remote Samba administration but don't need remote access to other Linux configuration options, management with SWAT is less of a threat to the security of your system than with Linuxconf because SWAT provides direct administrative access to fewer Linux features.

SWAT is a very network-centric configuration tool. In addition, it gives you comprehensive access to Samba features and is less finicky about the state of the smb.conf file. When used as a network administration tool, though, SWAT does allow a possible way in for would-be crackers. There are ways to restrict access to a particular group of machines, however. SWAT also requires an administrative password (such as root's) to function.

Initial SWAT Configuration

Configuring SWAT is similar to configuring Linuxconf for network access. If your system uses inetd, you should first check /etc/inetd .conf. It should contain a line similar to the following:

```
swat  stream  tcp  nowait.400  root  /usr/sbin/swat swat
```

If this line isn't present or is commented out, add it or uncomment it. If your system uses xinetd, you should have a file called /etc/xinetd.d/ swat, which should have an entry resembling the following:

```
service swat
{
        socket_type      = stream
        protocol         = tcp
        wait             = no
        user             = root
        server           = /usr/sbin/swat
}
```

NOTE
Some systems place this entry in the /etc/xinetd.conf file rather than in a file for the SWAT server alone.

In both cases, you should also ensure that the following line is present in the /etc/services file on the server:

```
swat                901/tcp
```

Once both these files are configured correctly, restart inetd or xinetd. You can do this by passing inetd the -SIGHUP signal or xinetd the -SIGUSR1 signal; for instance:

```
# ps ax | grep inetd
 379 ?           S        0:00 inetd
# kill -SIGHUP 379
```

Alternatively, you can use the super server's SysV startup script to restart it:

```
# /etc/rc.d/init.d/xinetd restart
```

When this is done, SWAT will be running on your computer and will be accessible from any system that can access port 901 on the server.

To use SWAT, open a web browser and enter **http://*servername*:901** into the browser's URL field (*servername* is the DNS name or IP address of the Samba server). If all works well, SWAT asks you for a password, as shown in Figure 21.6.

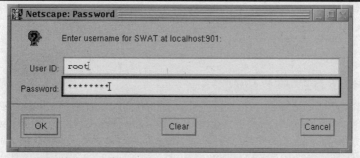

FIGURE 21.6:   SWAT requires a username and password to allow access.

Enter a correct administrative username and password to get SWAT to display its main page (seen in Figure 21.7). From here you can access all the SWAT configuration options, which are described shortly. As with remote access to Linuxconf, you can access SWAT from any OS that supports a web browser—Linux, Windows, MacOS, BeOS, and even DOS.

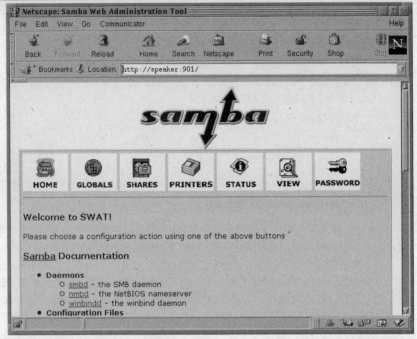

FIGURE 21.7: SWAT configuration options are divided into several groups similar to those used by Linuxconf.

Limiting SWAT Access

I strongly recommend that you take steps to limit access to SWAT. There are several ways to do this, some of which are described in the following sections. As a general rule, TCP Wrappers can be a good starting point for limiting access to SWAT. If your Samba server is accessible from the Internet as a whole, you may do well to add an external firewall to your network; at least use ipchains to block access to the SWAT port (901) from outside your local network. The more barriers you can put up, the better, even if they're redundant—a bug in one security tool can be blocked by another tool that serves a similar function.

Passwords

You must have a Linux password to gain access to SWAT. Normally, you must enter a user ID of root and the root password; however, if permissions on the smb.conf file allow other users to write to that file, these users can use SWAT to modify Samba's configuration. Users without write access to smb.conf can use SWAT to check the server's status, examine the smb.conf file (if it's readable to the user), and change passwords. Take care to protect the root password or any other password that can be used to modify the Samba configuration.

> **WARNING**
>
> SWAT accepts passwords transmitted in cleartext so, depending on your network configuration, your passwords may be sniffed by users of your local network. If you use SWAT from a remote location, packet sniffers on intervening computers might also be able to snatch your password. I therefore recommend *strongly* against using SWAT from remote computers.

You might be tempted to create a special Samba account and change the ownership of smb.conf to that account. You could then use SWAT to edit smb.conf without sending the root password in cleartext. On the surface, this would seem to increase system security. Given the power of Samba, however, this practice isn't much of an improvement over passing the root password in cleartext. A cracker who gains access to the smb.conf file can quickly acquire root access by exporting the /etc directory with root privileges, thus allowing a miscreant to edit the sensitive /etc/passwd and /etc/shadow files. The Samba daemons themselves must be run as root to function fully, so using a non-root user to edit smb.conf affords little protection.

External Firewalls

If your local network has a firewall computer, configure it to block access to port 901. Doing so prevents outsiders from accessing SWAT.

Local *ipchains*

Linux's packet filter tool in the 2.2.*x* kernel series is called ipchains. You can use it to block access to port 901 on the local server computer, except from approved locations. Suppose you want to administer Samba from the server itself (localhost, or 127.0.0.1) and from another computer with an IP address of 192.168.3.23. The following ipchains commands will allow that configuration:

```
# ipchains -A input -p tcp -s 127.0.0.1 901 -j ACCEPT
# ipchains -A input -p tcp -s 192.168.3.23 901 -j ACCEPT
# ipchains -A input -p tcp -s 0/0 901 -j DENY
```

NOTE

For more information on ipchains, read the Linux ipchains HOWTO document.

Local *iptables*

The 2.4.*x* Linux kernels made substantial changes to packet filter firewall capabilities. Although it's possible to compile a 2.4.*x* kernel to use ipchains, the preferred method of setting up a packet filter is with a tool called iptables. In broad strokes, iptables is similar to ipchains, but the former is a more powerful tool. For purposes of blocking access to a single port, though, the two are quite similar. You can achieve the same effect described in the "Local *ipchains*" section using iptables with the following commands:

```
# iptables -A INPUT -p tcp -s 127.0.0.1 --destination-port
➡901 -j ACCEPT

# iptables -A INPUT -p tcp -s 192.168.3.23 --destination-port
➡901 -j ACCEPT

# iptables -A INPUT -p tcp -s 0/0 --destination-port 901 -j
➡DENY
```

In the case of either ipchains or iptables, you may want to add these commands to a startup script of some sort, such as /etc/rc.d/ rc.local. Some distributions include a special firewall script that may already limit access to port 901, so you may need to modify this script to give you access from the computers you need to use to configure the Samba server.

TCP Wrappers

You can run SWAT through TCP Wrappers by replacing the call to /usr/ sbin/swat in the /etc/inetd.conf file with a call to /usr/sbin/tcpd. Then use the usual TCP Wrappers controls in /etc/hosts.deny and /etc/hosts.allow to restrict access to SWAT. Using the same example as for ipchains, to restrict access to SWAT to localhost and 192.168 .3.23, you'd create an /etc/hosts.deny file that contains the following entry:

```
swat: ALL EXCEPT 192.168.3.23 127.0.0.1
```

TCP Wrappers is a flexible tool, and hosts.allow and hosts.deny files can become very complex. Type **man hosts.allow** on a system on which TCP Wrappers is installed to learn more about these files' formats. (The formats are identical, so they share a single man page.)

xinetd

If your distribution uses xinetd instead of inetd and TCP Wrappers, you can restrict access based on the Ethernet card on which a request arrives or apply restrictions similar to those of TCP Wrappers. You can do this with the interface (a.k.a. bind) keyword to bind a server to a specific interface, or via the only_from or no_access keyword, which you use to specify the only clients allowed access to the system or those that are explicitly *not* allowed access, respectively. For instance, you could add the following lines to the definition presented earlier to restrict access to systems on the interface associated with the 192.168.3.7 address and to respond only to two systems on that network:

```
interface      = 192.168.3.7
only_from      = 192.168.3.7 192.168.3.14
```

You can use other features of xinetd to restrict access using other criteria, such as the time of day. Type **man xinetd.conf** on a system on which xinetd is installed to learn more about this super server's options and capabilities.

Logging Out

SWAT contains no explicit means to log out of the tool. It's therefore important that you exit from your web browser when you've finished using SWAT. If you fail to do this and then leave your computer unattended, another individual can use your web browser to reconfigure Samba.

A Tour of SWAT Options

SWAT options are arranged in seven groups: Home, Globals, Shares, Printers, Status, View, and Password (refer to Figure 21.7). Some of these groups control features similar to those controlled by the Linuxconf Samba groups, but SWAT goes beyond Linuxconf.

In all the SWAT configuration pages that allow you to change options, there's a button called Commit Changes. You must click this button to have SWAT write your changes to the smb.conf file.

Home

The Home configuration group (shown in Figure 21.7) is the first view you get through SWAT after entering a username and password. From this page you can jump to Samba documentation, including the Samba man pages and miscellaneous additional files. You can also select any of the six other configuration groups.

Globals

The Globals group allows you to set configuration options that go in the [global] section of the smb.conf file. Figure 21.8 shows the Globals configuration page.

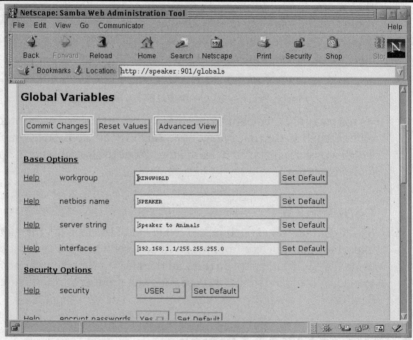

FIGURE 21.8:   In SWAT you use HTML features such as buttons and text entry fields to enter configuration options.

The primary Globals options are the same as those you can set from the Defaults configuration page in Linuxconf: Samba's NetBIOS name, workgroup, security mode, and so on. Other [global] options are described in the section "Important General Configuration Options," later in this chapter.

TIP

By default, SWAT shows only the most commonly used Samba configuration options. On the Globals, Shares, and Printers pages, you can click the Advanced View button to see the more esoteric options.

The Globals page isn't available when you access SWAT as an ordinary user.

Shares

You define file shares from the Shares page. SWAT shows only a handful of options when you first open this page. You must do one of two things to see additional share options:

▶ Type a share name into the text entry field and click Create Share. This creates a new share with the name you've specified and allows you to edit that share.

▶ Select an existing share from the list box and click Choose Share to display the share's present configuration and to edit that configuration.

NOTE

When using the first method, do *not* enclose the share name in square brackets ([]) as you do when editing the smb.conf file in a text editor. SWAT will add the brackets itself.

Linuxconf uses one configuration panel to set up the [homes] share and a different panel for all other file shares. SWAT, by contrast, uses the same Shares page to configure both. The options you can set for file shares are similar to those available in Linuxconf, but they're arranged differently. Chapter 22 covers most of these options in greater detail.

The Shares page isn't available when you access SWAT as an ordinary user.

Printers

SWAT provides much finer control over printer shares than does Linuxconf. In SWAT you can adjust settings of individual printers, not just control all printer shares as a monolithic set. SWAT also gives you access to all of Samba's printer configuration parameters. These allow you to restrict access to printer shares, adjust the commands Samba uses to spool print jobs, and so on.

The Printers page isn't available when you access SWAT as an ordinary user.

Status

The Status page allows you to view and adjust the status of the Samba server. Some key features of this page include the following:

Stop, Start, and Restart Daemons   Depending on the current status of the Samba daemons, you can stop, start, or restart the daemons (see Figure 21.9). SWAT provides this functionality separately for each daemon.

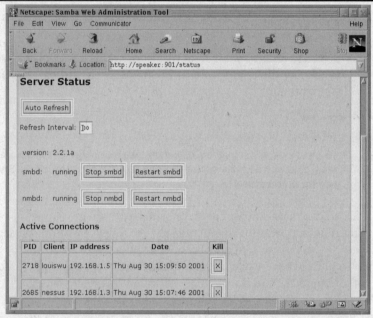

FIGURE 21.9:   You can control the Samba daemons and connections from the Status page of SWAT.

Kill Individual Connections   You can terminate individual connections from the Active Connections table, seen at the bottom of Figure 21.9. This feature is useful when you need to terminate a connection in order to unmount a filesystem.

Active Shares   The Active Shares area (not visible in Figure 21.9) shows the connections to the server. You can also see this information in the Active Connections table but with less information than in the Active Shares table.

Open Files   Also at the bottom of the Status page (again, not seen in Figure 21.9) is a list of open files. This information is helpful when you need to locate the user of an open file, perhaps in order to close the file or terminate the connection because you need to unmount a filesystem. To do so, check the PID column in this table, locate that PID in the Active Connections table, and kill that connection.

When you access SWAT as an ordinary user, you can view all the information presented on this page, but you cannot change any of it; SWAT doesn't give you the necessary buttons to effect changes.

View

The View page displays the smb.conf file's contents as text. Normally, SWAT shows you an edited version of the file; it's missing the commands that are unset—that is, those that rely upon their default values. You can click the Full View button near the top of the page to display the entire file, including all default values. You cannot use this page to modify the smb.conf file, however; if you want to tweak the configuration by hand, you must use a text editor to do the job.

You can use the View page either as an ordinary user or as an administrative user. (You must have read access to the smb.conf file, however.)

Password

Use the Password page (see Figure 21.10) to change your Samba password. When you access SWAT as root, you can also add, delete, enable, and disable users by clicking the appropriate buttons. Essentially, this page is an interface to the smbpasswd program.

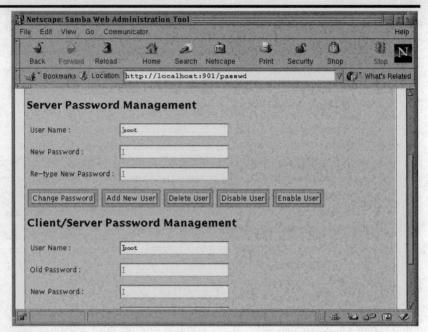

FIGURE 21.10:   The Password page allows easy access to Samba's encrypted password file.

WARNING

The SWAT Password page does not change Linux's regular passwords. If your network is configured to use cleartext passwords for Samba access, the Password page will be useless to you, but SWAT still displays it.

To adjust an account, enter the account name in the User Name field. If you want to change the account's password, enter the password in the New Password field and again in Re-type New Password, then click Change Password. Watch for a notice that the password was changed. If you access SWAT as an ordinary user, enter your old password in the Old Password field, which isn't shown in Figure 21.10.

To add a user, type the desired username and password (twice), and then click Add New User. To delete, disable, or enable a user, you need not type the password.

The section called Client/Server Password Management allows you to run SWAT on one computer to adjust the user information on another server. This other server can be another Samba server (in which case only the Samba server's encrypted password is changed) or a Windows NT, 2000, or XP computer (in which case the Windows computer's login password is changed).

Recommendations for Working with SWAT

SWAT can be an excellent tool for Samba configuration, particularly when you're new to Samba administration and unsure of the names of options. To get the most out of SWAT, however, you'll need to understand the fine points of Samba configuration, such as what variables represent.

SWAT's inherent network nature makes it at least potentially dangerous. As described earlier, in the section "Limiting SWAT Access," I urge you to protect your SWAT server by disallowing outside access as much as is practical. Ideally, if you run SWAT at all, you should use TCP Wrappers, `xinetd`, `iptables`, or some other tool to limit access to only the `localhost` (127.0.0.1) address. Doing this lets you use SWAT locally but not from any other computer. If you must have SWAT access from other computers, restrict it to a limited set of computers on your local network. If you need to configure Samba from a computer that's not on your local network, edit `smb.conf` with a text editor using a secure login protocol such as SSH (_not_ Telnet, which passes all data—including passwords—in unencrypted form).

If you run a Samba server to which your local users do not have regular logon access, you can use SWAT's Password page to allow your network users to change their Samba passwords. This feature can be convenient, but you should measure this convenience against its potential for danger should a miscreant set up a password sniffer on the local network. Another option is to run an SSH server and configure Samba users' shells to call the smbpasswd program. Users can then use SSH to set their Samba passwords. (Note that employing Telnet in this capacity is no more secure than using SWAT; it's SSH's encryption that's a bonus in this situation.)

Whether or not you use SWAT for day-to-day Samba configuration, it's a good idea to learn something about "manual" configuration of `smb.conf`. Fortunately, SWAT uses the same terms to describe configuration options as are used in `smb.conf`, so learning one method of administration helps you with the other. When SWAT reads in an `smb.conf` file, SWAT interprets parameter synonyms and antonyms correctly and may write a changed file using different parameter names. Suppose the original smb.conf file includes a share parameter read only = No; SWAT correctly displays the writeable value as Yes in the web form. If you don't change this value before you commit your changes, SWAT will write an smb.conf file without a read only parameter but with a writeable = Yes parameter. This has the same effect as the original read only = No.

WARNING

Unfortunately, one effect of SWAT's processing of the smb.conf file is that SWAT strips away all comments. Therefore, you should not use SWAT if your configuration file includes important comments.

One feature that SWAT does not handle correctly is the use of variables within include parameters. The include parameter allows you to include one configuration file within another. In Samba you can put variables in this parameter's value to customize Samba's configuration for individual users, clients, and so on. Unfortunately, SWAT corrupts these include directives so that they're useless. You can correct them manually if you only use one or two of them, but if you rely on this feature heavily, you'll probably find it easier to edit your smb.conf file manually at all times.

IMPORTANT GENERAL CONFIGURATION OPTIONS

By now, you have some idea of what sorts of options are in the smb.conf file. We begin with some of the core parameters that go in the [global] section of the smb.conf file.

Server Identification

As described in Chapter 18, "An Introduction to SMB/CIFS," computers on a Windows network are identified by a NetBIOS name. These computers also belong to a workgroup or domain, which in essence is a name shared by several computers on a network. If given no other instructions in the matter, Samba uses the computer's TCP/IP hostname (minus the domain name) as the computer's NetBIOS name. For instance, if a computer is properly configured as gingko.pangaea.edu, Samba uses GINGKO as the NetBIOS name. Samba doesn't know what to use as the workgroup or domain name, however, so you must explicitly configure that. (If you fail to do so, Samba will use a default based on compile-time options—usually WORKGROUP.)

You can also override the use of the TCP/IP name and set a few other name-related options.

workgroup   Use this option to set the computer's workgroup or domain name. The choice depends on the configuration of the network as a whole, although there are some Samba options that influence Linux's recognition of the network.

netbios name   Set or override the computer's NetBIOS name with this parameter. I recommend that you set this option even if you use the same name for both TCP/IP and NetBIOS names, for completeness and to avoid problems should your system's TCP/IP name become misconfigured.

netbios aliases   You can designate two or more names for your Samba server by using the netbios aliases parameter. List all the names other than the main netbios name. Setting this parameter isn't typically necessary, but you might use it if, for instance, you consolidate two or more servers into one. The default value is a null string—no aliases are defined.

NOTE

The %L variable takes on the aliased name for most operations, although not if used as part of the server string. In that case, %L uses netbios name.

server string   The server string parameter sets a short iden-tifying string that appears in the Comment field of a Windows network browser when you enable a detailed view and open a window displaying the servers in a workgroup. This string does not otherwise affect the function of Samba. The default is nor-mally Samba %v (%v being the variable for the Samba version number). I recommend you change this string to remove the version number as a security measure. In Figure 21.11, you can see the effect of the server string parameter, which was set to Samba server on %L for the TEELA server. This server also has netbios alias = TEELAALIAS, so it appears twice in the browse list.

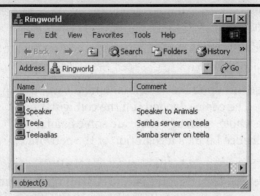

FIGURE 21.11:   The `server string` parameter sets the text that appears in the Comment field in Windows network browse lists.

time server   This Boolean option enables Samba to announce itself as a time server on the SMB/CIFS network. You can then use the `NET TIME` command on a Windows client to retrieve the time as maintained by the Samba server. The default value is No.

include   The `include` parameter, when used in conjunction with the `netbios alias` parameter, customizes an `smb.conf` file for each of two or more aliases. Specifically, you can use the `%L` variable in an `include` parameter to load customized configuration files for each alias. The statement `include = smb.conf.%L`, for instance, loads configuration files that can include shares for each alias, such as `smb.conf.gingko` and `smb.conf.biloba`.

When using an `include` parameter, be careful to place it so that it accomplishes what you want. Essentially, the contents of the specified file will replace the `include` directive. Thus, if the included file contains share definitions, you should place the `include` statement after the end of the [global] section in the main file. Neither SWAT nor Linuxconf handles the `include` parameter well, so if you want to use this feature, edit `smb.conf` and the included files by hand.

NOTE
Samba translates the NetBIOS name to lowercase when used in this fashion, so if you specify `netbios name = GINGKO` and use the `include` parameter specified earlier as an example, you should create a configuration file called `smb.conf.gingko` to match `netbios name`.

As an example, consider the following [global] section of an smb.conf file:

```
[global]
        workgroup = ARBORETUM
        netbios name = GINGKO
        netbios aliases = BILOBA
        server string = Stinky tree
        time server = Yes


include = smb.conf.%L
```

This definition makes the server appear under two names on the Windows network: GINGKO and BILOBA. Both these apparent computers are part of the ARBORETUM workgroup or domain. Viewed in the Details view from a Windows browser, both apparent computers bear a comment of "Stinky tree." The server provides time services to the network. Depending on the contents of the smb.conf.gingko and smb.conf.biloba files and the remaining contents of smb.conf, this computer may have entirely different shares under its two aliases.

Logging Options

If something about your Samba setup doesn't work, one of your best bets for correcting the problem lies with Samba's logging facilities. Ordinarily, Samba sends reports of important system events to log files. The default location of these log files depends on compile-time options but is normally in either the /var/log or /var/log/samba directory. Several log files may be used by Samba:

log.nmb **or nmbd**   These are common default names used by the nmbd daemon. You can change the log name by using the -l runtime parameter to nmbd. When you do so, nmbd appends .nmb to the filename you provide.

log.smb **or smbd**   These are common default names used by the smbd daemon. You can change this name by using the -l runtime parameter to smbd. Unlike nmbd, smbd does not in any way modify the filename you pass through -l. This file stores general information on smbd's operation, such as when it starts and stops.

log.smb. * Most Samba configurations create an entire set of log files, one for each client computer, using the client computer's NetBIOS name as the final part of the log filename. These files store information on connections from particular clients. You can set the name used to create the log files in the smb.conf file, as described shortly.

The logging options in the smb.conf file mostly affect all three of the preceding types of log files, although the log file parameter affects only the last of these file types. The smb.conf parameters are as follows:

log file   Specify the name of the log file with this option. It's not uncommon to see the %m (client NetBIOS name) variable included in a log file parameter. The effect of using %m is to create a different log file for each client, which can help when you're debugging connection problems for particular clients.

debug level   The debug level or log level is a number from 0 to 10 representing the amount of information that's written to the log file. A value of 0 means no information, 1 is the default, 3 is as much as you're likely to ever need as an administrator, and 10 is an extremely detailed log that's useful only to a Samba programmer. The default level of 1 is adequate for most purposes. A synonym for this parameter is log level.

max log size   If the log file exceeds the max log size value (in kilobytes), Samba renames the old file with a .old extension and opens a new log file. This option can keep Samba's log files from overflowing a hard disk's capacity. The default value is 5000—about 5MB.

debug timestamp   Ordinarily, Samba writes in the log file the times at which operations occur. If you set this parameter to No, however, Samba omits the time stamp, which can reduce the size of a log file.

debug pid   Ordinarily, Samba doesn't include the smbd process ID (PID) in the log file. If you use a single log file for all connections, however, including this information can be helpful in tracking which daemon (and hence which connection) belongs to each log entry. Adding debug pid = Yes enables this behavior.

debug uid   If you've configured Samba to run under multiple user IDs (UIDs), you may want to include this information in the log files. Adding debug uid = Yes to smb.conf accomplishes this goal.

syslog   Samba normally logs data itself; however, you can configure it to use Linux's syslog daemon instead of or in addition to its own logging. When you do so, the syslog parameter specifies the log levels sent through the daemon, much as debug level controls logging through Samba's own log files. To use the syslog parameter, you must adjust additional system configuration options:

Compilation Options   Compile Samba with the --with-syslog compile-time option, as described in Chapter 22. Any given Samba binary might or might not have been compiled with this option.

Syslog Configuration   Linux's syslog daemon must be configured to accept logging from other daemons. To do so, add the following line to the /etc/syslog.conf file, making an appropriate adjustment to indicate the file you want to receive daemon-generated messages:

```
daemon.*        /var/log/messages
```

syslog only   If you want to send logging information through the system logger only, set this option to Yes. When you leave this option set to its default value of No, Samba logs information to its own log files, whether or not you use the syslog parameter.

status   Samba maintains a status file that contains information on active connections. You can read this file using the smbstatus command. If you set status = No from its default of Yes, Samba won't be able to report what connections are active. You should therefore not change this parameter.

For most configurations, the default logging options are acceptable. Be careful, however, to specify log file locations that really exist. This is particularly true when using a Samba binary intended for one distribution on another distribution or when copying an smb.conf file from one computer to another. One binary might be compiled with options to use

/var/log/samba as the log file location, for instance, but the target distribution might not have this directory; instead, it might use /var/log/samba.d as the log file location. Correct such mismatches by using the -l runtime parameter and the log file configuration file parameter.

An Overview of Security Issues

Samba includes a plethora of security options. A few security issues are of critical importance from the start, however.

Samba Security Models

Windows OSs use one of two security models: In DOS, OS/2, and Windows 9x/Me, the server requires no username but needs a separate password for access to each resource. In Windows NT and 2000, the server requires a username/password pair that grants access to all of the computer's shares, with share-by-share control implemented using the OS's internal security model. Samba supports a variety of security options to emulate both of these security arrangements. The second model is more natural for a Samba server running on Linux because it closely matches Linux's native security features. Two additional arrangements are extensions of the second model and are used in Windows domains. All four security arrangements are set up with the security parameter. Its allowable values are as follows:

Share This security option attempts to emulate the Windows 9x/Me security model. Samba tries to validate the password against a list of users provided with the username parameter, as well as against a username provided by the client, if the client sent one.

User User-level security fits closely with Linux's native security model and is therefore the preferred security option for use with Samba. It's also the default in Samba 2.0 and later. In this model, Samba requires both a username and password. If the password matches the one stored for the user, Samba grants access to all the computer's shares, provided other security measures don't block access in some way.

Server Server-level security works exactly like User-level security, except that Samba uses another SMB/CIFS server to authenticate users. When using the security = Server option, you must also set the name of the password server using the password server parameter.

WARNING

Never set password server to point to the computer you're configuring. Doing so sets up an infinite loop, which can cause serious problems.

Domain Domain-level security works much like Server-level security, except that the password server is a primary domain controller (PDC), and the Samba server must log onto the domain maintained by the PDC. When using Domain-level security, you can set password server = * to have Samba locate the PDC automatically.

NOTE

When using Server- or Domain-level security, the authenticated user must still have an account on the host Linux server. For instance, if the user lorax is approved by the password server but has no account on the Samba server, then lorax won't be able to access resources except as a guest user. Use of Winbind changes this rule, though; if the server uses Winbind, *all* Linux authentication is deferred to the PDC.

Using Server- or Domain-level security can be convenient, but it slows down authentication slightly. It also poses a security risk. A troublemaker with physical access to your network may be able to remove the password server, set up another computer on that address, and gain full access to any computer that uses the password server for authentication. If you have only one or two Samba servers, I recommend User-level security.

Password Encryption

Password encryption is the source of what may be the single most common problem encountered by new Samba administrators. Windows for Workgroups 3.1, Windows 95 prior to OEM Service Release 2 (OSR2), and Windows NT prior to version 4, Service Pack 3, all sent unencrypted (or *cleartext*) passwords. Windows 95 OSR2, Windows 98, Windows Me, Windows NT 4 Service Pack 3 and later, Windows 2000, and Windows

XP all send passwords in encrypted form. Samba has difficulty with this for two reasons:

- ▶ By default, Samba accepts only cleartext passwords. You have to set the `encrypt passwords = Yes` parameter to have Samba accept encrypted passwords.

- ▶ When set to use cleartext passwords, Samba uses Linux's normal authentication procedures, so the system is automatically configured to accept SMB/CIFS connections from valid Linux users. When set to use encrypted passwords, however, Samba requires a separate password database, which you must create and maintain.

In the long run, it's easier and safer to configure Samba to use encrypted passwords on a network that has a large number of machines that default to encrypted passwords. Here's a brief explanation of how to use this method:

1. Add the `encrypt passwords = Yes` parameter to the `[global]` section of your `smb.conf` file.

2. Create an `smbpasswd` file, which normally resides in the same directory as `smb.conf`. Samba comes with a script called `mksmbpasswd.sh` to create such a file from an `/etc/passwd` file, although all the passwords are invalid, so you must then set them in some way. Alternatively, you can add users one at a time by issuing the **smbpasswd -a *username*** command. If you issue this command before creating an `smbpasswd` file, the command creates the file and adds the user to the new file.

TIP

If you have a large existing user base, you can use the `update encrypted` parameter to automatically update `smbpasswd` entries.

If instead you want to use cleartext passwords, you must reconfigure recent versions of Windows to send passwords without encryption. Samba comes with several files that can help accomplish this. They're normally in a Samba documentation directory such as `/usr/doc/samba-2.2.0/docs` and are named *WinVer*`_PlainPassword.reg`, where *WinVer* is a Windows version, such as `Win95`. Copy these files to a FAT floppy disk, then move the floppy to a target Windows computer. Open the floppy disk and double-click on the appropriate file. When you reboot the computer, it sends cleartext passwords.

WHAT'S NEXT?

Samba configuration is both easy and difficult. Many Linux distributions ship with an smb.conf file that allows the system to function in a minimal way with only minor modifications, such as setting the workgroup appropriately. If you use a GUI configuration tool such as Linuxconf or SWAT, you can probably configure your Samba server in a variety of useful ways without too much difficulty, once you understand the basic principles outlined in this chapter. In fact, you can perform most tasks in SWAT that you can perform by changing smb.conf in a text editor.

In the next chapter, you will learn more about configuring Samba to share files with a variety of Microsoft clients.

Chapter 22

CONFIGURING FILE SHARING

For most installations, the single most important use of Samba is as a file server. It's therefore important that you understand how Samba shares files—how you can specify what directories to share, what permissions to give to Samba users, how Samba handles filenames and FAT-style file attributes, and so on. This chapter introduces the fundamentals of file sharing with Samba.

First you'll see some examples of file shares and the smb.conf parameters to set them up. Following that is a discussion of the critical interaction of Linux-style security with Samba file shares. Finally, you'll examine a number of scenarios that illustrate the use of Samba in specific situations. You may be able to use one of those scenarios as a model for your own Samba configuration.

Adapted from *Linux Samba Server Administration*
by Roderick W. Smith
ISBN 0-7821-2740-1   656 pages $39.99

CONFIGURING FILE SHARES

Basic file sharing is easy to configure with Samba. You normally create a [global] section in the smb.conf file even for a simple one-share server. Once you've configured a rudimentary [global] section, as described in Chapter 21, "GUI Configuration Tools and the smb.conf File," it takes just a few more lines to create a share—even including options to make the share more useful. Let's begin with a simple example and then modify and expand it to demonstrate options.

A Basic File Share Example

The simplest possible file share consists of a single line—a share name in brackets, like this:

```
[test]
```

This definition creates a share that provides read-only access to the Linux /tmp directory (the default values). This sort of access, of course, is of limited utility.

To make this share useful, you add a few more lines to define the parameters you want. For instance:

```
[test]
        comment = Test share on %L
        volume name = TEST
        path = /home/samba/test
        writeable = Yes
```

Each of these parameters adds something to the share, although only the path option is really critical.

> *comment*   The comment parameter isn't critical to Samba operation, but it can help users locate their shares. This parameter adds a comment that's visible when the Details view is used in a Windows file browser, as shown in Figure 22.1. You can include variables in a comment's value, but some won't be usable because they aren't defined until after the share is accessed. (See Table 21.1 in Chapter 21 for a list of variables.)

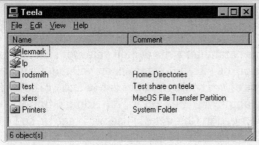

FIGURE 22.1: The comment field is visible only if you use Details view in Windows.

volume name   This parameter, like the comment parameter, is largely cosmetic. If you map a Samba share to a drive letter, the volume name parameter sets the DOS/Windows name used by that volume. This name is unimportant except in rare situations. For instance, if you export a CD-ROM that contains a software installation utility, that utility might work only if the volume name is set correctly.

path   The path parameter specifies what directory tree is to be shared. (A synonym for path is directory.) In principle, you can share any directory that exists on your Linux computer, but some directories aren't good choices for sharing. For example, Windows clients aren't likely to need access to your /usr directory tree. It's common to create one or more subdirectories under /home/samba for Samba shares, but you can also share /mnt (to provide access to removable media), /tmp, or any other directory. If you don't specify a path, Samba shares /tmp.

You can use variables in a path statement, which can be useful if you want to create shares with specific contents for specific users. For instance, path = /home/samba/%g creates a share that accesses a directory named after the user's primary Linux group. This might be useful when creating shares for distinct sets of users. In a university setting, for instance, you could create faculty, staff, grad, and undergrad groups, each with an associated Samba share.

writeable   This parameter controls whether Samba allows users to write to a share. The default value is No, which ensures that users can't damage an exported filesystem. You might want to leave this parameter at its default value for shared program directories or the like, but many shares will require write access. Synonyms of `writeable` are `writable` and `write ok`; `read only` is an antonym. The Samba Web Administration Tool (SWAT, described in Chapter 21) uses `writeable`, so I recommend you do the same to avoid confusion.

You can begin to create useful file shares using only the preceding information, particularly if you use variables as part of `path`'s value. In fact, you may recognize that you can use a username variable (%U or %u) in the `path` value to create a share that's unique for each user. Samba's programmers, however, are one step ahead of you. A special share—[homes]—exists to do just that.

Home Directory Shares

As mentioned in Chapter 21, Samba includes support for a share known as the [homes] share. This share has an effect roughly similar to the following:

```
[%U]
          volume name = %U
          path = %H
```

As explained in Table 21.1 in Chapter 21, %U is a variable for the username of the user who requests the service, and %H is the user's home directory. Therefore, this share definition appears in a network browser under the user's username, has that same username as the volume name, and has the user's home directory as the share's root directory. [homes] is a shorthand way of creating this definition without having to remember the meanings of the variables.

There are a few differences between the foregoing example of a share and a genuine [homes] share, however. These differences include browsing options, naming conventions, and accessibility to other users. As described in the next section, "Browsing Options," the browseable parameter has special meaning in the [homes] share. This parameter has its usual meaning in the [%U] share definition example previously.

A [homes] share is actually accessible under two names: HOMES and the user's username. Suppose the user susani wants to access her home share on the server WARLOCK. She can access it as either \\WARLOCK\SUSANI or \\WARLOCK\HOMES. If marcusc accesses \\WARLOCK\HOMES, he doesn't find susani's files; he finds his own files. If one user enters the share name of another user's [homes] share, access is granted, with restrictions based on additional Samba parameters and Linux permissions. The sample [%U] share, however, is accessible only to the share's owner.

Samba shows the name of only one [homes] share when an individual browses a Samba server from Windows. To access another [homes] share, a user must enter the complete path to that share in an Address field or something similar. For instance, in Figure 22.2, the user is about to access halr's [homes] share, although it's not visible among the shares on the server.

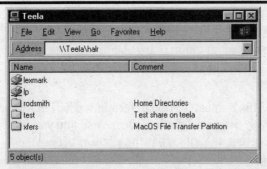

FIGURE 22.2:   Windows 9x/Me allows you to enter a path to a share that's not displayed in the browse list provided by Samba.

Browsing Options

Windows networking is very browser oriented. That is, users frequently locate network resources through the Network Neighborhood icon on their Desktops, which works much like a file manager for local hard disks. Samba includes options that influence the way it interacts with browsers. Some of these options influence "behind-the-scenes" operation of the browser, and others are important when you configure individual shares. These parameters include the following:

>*hosts allow* and *hosts deny*   These are security options that you can apply to an entire server (by placing them in the

[global] section of smb.conf) or to individual shares. Use these parameters to specify lists of hosts or networks to which you want to grant or deny access, respectively. For instance, if a given share holds sensitive data that should be accessible only to a handful of computers, you can list those computers in the hosts allow parameter, and no other computers will be allowed access. These parameters do not make a share disappear from unapproved computers' browse lists, however; any attempt to access the shares is simply unsuccessful. As such, hosts allow and hosts deny can prevent browsing past the list of available shares. Synonyms for these options are allow hosts and deny hosts, respectively.

valid users* and *invalid users   These parameters work much like the hosts allow and hosts deny parameters, but on usernames rather than computers. Often you can use Linux's own permissions settings to achieve similar results, but these parameters are easier to configure when you want to deny share access to a random group of users. For example, if you want to keep taliaw out of a share, you can use invalid users = taliaw.

browseable   This Boolean option determines whether a share appears in browse lists. Its default value is Yes, and you normally want to leave it as Yes so that the share appears in browse lists. Set it to No to hide a share without making it unavailable. Even when a share is set to browseable = No, you can access the share by name. One unusual case is the [homes] shares. When present, a [homes] share is always browseable under its owners' usernames. The browseable option controls whether the share is visible under the name HOMES. To avoid confusion, it's customary to set browseable = No on [homes] shares. A synonym for browseable is browsable.

available   This parameter's default value is Yes. If you set it to No, the share effectively disappears from the server. Use this option if you want to remove a share temporarily more completely than you can with browseable = No.

You can use these browsing options as part of a security plan for your Samba server—especially hosts allow, hosts deny, valid users, and invalid users. The browseable option, aside from its common use in the [homes] share, is helpful mostly for reducing clutter. If you have a server with a large number of shares, many of which are seldom used, and then only by people who know the shares' names, you can set browseable = No in most shares to eliminate potentially confusing shares from the browse list. Similarly, if your clients are all configured to mount a share onto a drive letter at boot time, the share can be configured browseable = No to reduce clutter in the server browse list.

Filename Options

One of the challenges faced by Samba's developers is the fact that Linux (or Unix generally) handles filenames differently from DOS, Windows, and OS/2 (the most common Samba clients). In order to operate effectively as a server for these clients, Samba includes options to present its files as expected by the clients. For many of these options, however, there is no single best way to handle the translation. Furthermore, some of these translation features slow down Samba, so if you don't need the option in question, you might prefer to disable it. Samba provides many smb.conf parameters that you can use to enable or disable these features as you see fit.

The smb.conf filename parameters all fit into one of three categories: filename case options, filename length options, and hidden filename options, all described in the following sections. Most of these options are share-level, so you can set them on a share-by-share basis, or they can go in the [global] section to apply them to all shares.

NOTE

If you use SWAT for Samba configuration, most of these filename options are visible only after you select the Advanced View button.

TIP

Because many of these options are best set to different values for different clients in a mixed-OS environment, you may want to consider using the include parameter with the %a (client OS) variable to set options uniquely for each client OS. A configuration file for a Samba client might set case sensitive = Yes and hide dot files = No. You might simultaneously set up a mangled map (described shortly) to convert *.html files to *.htm for a DOS client. Chapter 21 covers the include parameter.

Handling Case Differences

As explained in Chapter 19, "Integrating SMB/CIFS into Linux," Linux systems use case-sensitive filesystems in which the case of letters is significant. Windows is a case-retentive operating system in which the case of letters is preserved but is unimportant. To further complicate matters, DOS computers use case-*insensitive* filesystems in which filenames are all stored in one case (uppercase for DOS using its normal FAT filesystem). By default, Samba emulates the Windows case-retentive filesystem features. Because this setting works well in most environments with both Windows and OS/2 clients, you can probably leave all the filename options at their defaults. If you want to adjust Samba's handling of these issues, however, you can set several options.

preserve case   By default, this option is set to Yes, which tells Samba to honor the case of files created by a Samba client. For instance, if the client creates a file called MiXEd.uP, Samba stores that file precisely that way. If preserve case is set to No, Samba converts the file's case to all uppercase or all lowercase, depending upon the setting of the default case option.

short preserve case   This option works much like the preserve case parameter, but short preserve case applies only to filenames that are limited to DOS's eight-character-with-three-character extension (*8.3 filename*) format. The default value is Yes.

default case   This parameter specifies the case to which Samba converts files when preserve case or short preserve case is set to No. When default case is set at the default value of Lower, it causes MiXEd.uP to be stored as mixed.up; when set to Upper, the file is stored as MIXED.UP. This option doesn't normally affect your ability to access files, though; its role is mostly to tidy up the appearance of file listings and simplify access from Linux.

case sensitive   This parameter, which defaults to No, controls whether Samba treats filenames in a case-sensitive way. Suppose the server hosts a file called MiXEd.uP. When case sensitive = No, clients can use precisely that name, or they can use MIXED.UP, mixed.up, miXEd.UP, or any other name that varies only in case. When case sensitive = Yes, clients trying to access the file must pass the name in precisely the same case as is used on the server. You might use case sensitive = Yes if the share is to be accessed mostly or entirely from Linux or some other case-sensitive client OS. If DOS, Windows, or OS/2 clients are involved, I recommend you leave this parameter set at the default No. Unfortunately, the default value slows down Samba slightly. A synonym for this parameter is casesignnames.

As a general rule, the case sensitive parameter is the most important of the case options. The other three may be important only for the cosmetic aspect of whether the server preserves the case it's given. Only case sensitive can make a file inaccessible to a client if an application's code changes case between reading a filename from the server and issuing a file open command. This behavior is much more common in DOS programs than in Windows programs.

Handling Length Differences

Windows 9*x*/Me can store filenames of up to 256 characters in length on a local hard disk, and Linux can store files with names of 256 characters as well on its ext2 filesystem. More importantly, DOS can cope only with 8.3 filenames. If you use a Samba server only from DOS clients, this fact doesn't pose a problem. (All the files on the server's shares will have 8.3 filenames, having been created by DOS.) On the other hand, if you use multiple client OSs or if you run DOS programs (which expect 8.3 filenames) in Windows (which can create long filenames), then Samba has a larger task. It must be able to convert filenames between their true long forms and shorter forms—so-called *mangled* or *munged* filenames. Samba includes several parameters that influence how and when Samba does filename mangling.

mangled names   If set at its default value of Yes, this parameter causes Samba to convert long filenames to unique short (8.3) filenames when communicating with DOS and other OSs that request short filenames. For instance, longfilename.txt might appear to a DOS client as LONGF~A7.TXT. If you set this value to No, the file with a long name appears with either a truncated filename (such as LONGFILE.TXT) or not at all, depending on the client OS.

mangling char   This parameter sets the character used for separating the five-character base of a mangled filename from the two-character code at its end. The default is a tilde (~).

mangle case   This option's default value is No, which tells Samba to preserve the case of short filenames when reporting them to clients. If set to Yes, then Samba mangles short filenames that don't conform entirely to the specified default case value. Consider MiXEd.uP again: When mangle case = No, Samba reports this file's name to DOS clients as MiXEd.uP. When mangle case = Yes, Samba reports the file's name as MIXED~F3.UP. As a general rule, you should leave this parameter at its default value.

mangled stack   When a DOS client accesses a file with a long filename on Linux, the DOS client is unaware of the file's true long filename. Therefore, the client may load the file, save it, and load it again, all using the same mangled filename. To speed up such accesses, Samba maintains a list (*stack*) of recently mangled 8.3 filenames. The mangled stack parameter sets the size of this stack, which defaults to 50. If your network hosts a large number of DOS clients, you may want to increase this value. Otherwise, leave it alone or perhaps even reduce it. Increasing the size of the mangled stack can speed up file access using mangled filenames, but doing so increases Samba's memory requirements and slows other file accesses. Unlike the other filename parameters, this one is global in scope; it appears in the [global] section of smb.conf.

TIP

DOS and older 16-bit Windows programs use 8.3 filenames, even when running from Windows 9x/Me, NT, 2000, or XP. You may therefore use the mangled stack even from those OSs. Consider this fact before adjusting the size of the stack.

mangled map   You can specify additional mangling rules with this parameter, which takes the form of a series of filename pattern pairs in parentheses. Samba replaces any filename that matches the first portion of a pair with the equivalent specified by the second pair. Consider the following:

```
mangled map = (*.html *.htm) (*.jpeg *.jpg)
```

This causes Samba to replace any .html extension with .htm and any .jpeg extension with .jpg. Note that these mangling rules apply to *all* filenames, whether or not they would normally be mangled. For instance, if you apply the preceding mangling map, you'll see all .html files as .htm files, even from Windows or Linux clients.

Filename-mangling options can be vitally important if you use DOS clients. The default parameters will work reasonably well with DOS clients, although it's possible some programs will work better if you set mangle case = Yes. You might also want to apply some special rules via the mangled map parameter if your server contains files that might benefit from that treatment. If you use Windows clients, name mangling is less important unless you use a large number of 16-bit programs from Windows.

Handling Hidden Files

Linux shells normally hide files that begin with a dot (.)—that is, *dot files.* These files are still accessible to the user, but they don't clutter most directory listings. In most SMB/CIFS client OSs, the same effect is achieved through a *hidden bit,* which is a flag associated with filenames. Samba includes several options that affect its handling of both Linux dot files and the hidden bit that's supported by SMB/CIFS. In addition, Samba includes options that let you make certain files completely invisible to the client, beyond what a hidden bit can achieve.

hide dot files   By default, Samba sets the SMB/CIFS hidden bit on all the dot files in a share. This behavior is generally desirable because Windows clients don't normally need to see dot files, particularly in home shares. If you use hide dot files = No, however, Samba doesn't set the hidden bit on dot files, so they appear in Windows directory listings. You might want to use this option in non-home shares, particularly if it's important to allow clients to keep dot file clutter from accumulating in a share. You might also set it to No if you have a Windows program that creates dot files but doesn't expect them to be hidden.

hide files   This parameter specifies a list of files that are to be hidden by Samba. You can use wildcards (* and ?) to specify filenames, as well as spaces—and that means you must separate filenames with something other than a space; Samba uses a slash (/) for this function. For example, you might use `hide files = Mail/News/*.rpm` to hide the `Mail` and `News` directories and all Linux `.rpm` files from the client. Samba matches files consistent with the `case sensitive` parameter when applying this option. The default is a null string; no files are hidden (aside from dot files, depending on the setting of `hide dot files`).

veto files This parameter works exactly like the `hide files` parameter, except that vetoed files cannot be accessed at all from the client; it's as if they don't exist on the server. The default is a null string; no files are vetoed. If you set `veto files = *.txt`, no attempt to access files that end in `.txt` will succeed, even if you type a filename directly into a File Open dialog box or at a command prompt on the client.

delete veto files When you remove a directory that contains vetoed files, Samba ordinarily does *not* remove those vetoed files and therefore cannot remove the entire directory. From the client, it appears that the directory is empty but cannot be deleted. If you set `delete veto files = Yes`, however, Samba removes vetoed files when a client deletes a directory containing those files.

File Locking

All multitasking OSs face a potential conflict: Two or more programs may attempt to access a file at the same time. In some cases, this doesn't cause a problem because the accesses are read-only. When two programs write to a file, however, or when one writes to a file while another reads it, errors can occur. The programs may write incompatible changes to the file, or a program reading the file may be unaware of the changes written by another program. To prevent these problems, OSs implement various types of *file locking,* in which one program can "lock" all or part of a file to prevent it from being changed by another program.

Like filenames, the file-locking mechanisms for Windows and Linux are subtly different, so a number of Samba configuration parameters are devoted to bridging this gap.

share modes This option enables Microsoft-style whole-file locking. When enabled, a client program can request a lock on an entire file. The default value is Yes, and it's generally best to leave it set that way.

locking This option enables Microsoft-style partial-file (or *byte-range*) locking. When enabled, a client program can request a lock on only part of the file. The default value is Yes, and it's generally best not to change this setting.

strict locking This option defaults to No, which causes Samba to perform lock checks only when clients request them. Most client programs submit such requests when needed, so the default configuration works well. Some client programs, though, don't submit requests for lock checks when they should, which can result in file corruption. When set to Yes, this parameter causes lock checks prior to any operation, which reduces corruption caused by ill-behaved programs. Setting this parameter to Yes slows down Samba, however.

blocking locks If a client tries to open a file but fails because of a lock, the client may begin *polling*—checking back frequently to try to open the file. A *blocking lock* is a way to avoid this costly practice. When support for blocking locks exists, the client can tell the server how long the client is willing to wait for a file to become available. The server then keeps the request open and, if the file becomes available in the specified time, tells the client. The default value for this option is Yes, but you can disable it if necessary. Normally, you should leave this setting alone.

oplocks An *opportunistic lock* (or *oplock* for short) is a mechanism that enables a client to cache changes it makes to a file locally. This feature can improve performance because the client need not send as many packets back to the server as a file is updated. When an oplock is granted, the server can demand an update from the client at any time, and this feature can be used to force an update should another client try to read the file. Samba enables oplock support by default; you can disable it by setting oplocks = No. When so configured, Samba refuses any request to obtain an oplock on a file. This degrades system performance, but it may be safer if your users regularly access files through Samba as well as from Linux programs (when running a 2.2.*x* or earlier kernel), or through some other server.

level2 oplocks In a traditional oplock, the first client loses the oplock when a second client accesses the file. When `level2 oplocks = Yes`, the oplock is merely downgraded from a read/write oplock to a read-only oplock. This means additional clients can cache their read-only access to the file. If the first client writes changes, all other clients are notified of this change. Employing `level2 oplocks` can improve performance on some types of files, such as program files, so you may want to enable it. This support defaults to `No` in Samba 2.0.7 and to `Yes` in Samba 2.2.*x*.

kernel oplocks Oplocks can be useful to keep a Windows client from stepping on other Windows clients' files, but the 2.2.*x* Linux kernels didn't support oplocks. As a result, Linux programs run from these kernels didn't know about oplocks granted on files served by Samba. The 2.4.*x* kernels add a Samba-compatible oplock option, and with these kernels you can set `kernel oplocks = Yes` to enable this support. This is a highly desirable option because it allows Samba and local programs both to benefit from each other's oplocks.

WARNING

Without kernel oplock support, it's possible for a Linux program to wreak havoc if it opens a file on which Samba has granted an oplock. If you use a 2.2.*x* or earlier kernel, you may want to set `oplocks = No` to avoid this problem or use the `veto oplock files` parameter (described in this section) to deny oplocks only on specific files. A better option is to upgrade to a 2.4.*x* kernel and set `kernel oplocks = Yes`.

fake oplocks Early versions of Samba did not support oplocks. Instead, they supported the `fake oplock` option, which caused Samba to claim that oplocks were available, when in fact they were not. Do not set the `fake oplocks` option to `Yes` on Samba versions later than 2.0.0. This option is unnecessary on modern versions of Samba and may cause file corruption.

veto oplock files With this option, you can specify a list of files that are never granted oplocks. Identify the files with filenames (including wildcards, if desired) separated by slashes (/)

just as you do with the hide files and veto files parameters, described previously in the section "Handling Hidden Files." If only a few files are likely to be accessed from Linux or some other server at the same time they're accessed through Samba, this option is preferable to setting oplocks = No, but again, it's generally better to use a 2.4.*x* kernel, set kernel oplocks = Yes, and not use the veto oplock files parameter.

lock directory   In this directory, Samba stores a variety of housekeeping files related to locking, as well as some other functions such as browse lists. The default is a compile-time option, probably something like /var/lock/samba or /usr/local/samba/locks. You can override the default setting using this parameter.

In most cases, the default locking parameters work well. You may need to adjust these values—particularly those related to oplocks—if you need simultaneous access to files from both Linux and Windows clients. Such adjustments are particularly likely if you upgrade a distribution that ships with a 2.2.*x* kernel to use a 2.4.*x* kernel, because Samba may be compiled to use No as the default for kernel oplocks for such a distribution. Most of these parameters can be applied either globally or share-by-share. The kernel oplocks and lock directory parameters, however, are global options and so must appear in the [global] section of smb.conf.

SETTING OWNERSHIP AND PERMISSIONS

One of the trickier aspects of Samba configuration for many sites—particularly large sites with many users and complex security needs—is integrating Unix-style and Microsoft-style file security models through Samba. As outlined in the section "Ownership and Permissions" in Chapter 19, Linux's security model is different from that of Windows. Compared to Windows 9*x*, Linux's security model is quite sophisticated, so you can do more with a Samba server than you can with a Windows 9*x* server. Windows NT and 2000, however, support *access control lists* (ACLs), which offer an alternative to Linux-style security that's different from Linux's security model and is, in some ways, more flexible. If you're an experienced Windows NT administrator, Linux's security features may take some getting used to. If you're already experienced with Linux or Unix file permissions, you should have no trouble getting your Linux server to do what you want in this respect.

Samba adds to the Linux file permissions repertoire in important ways, some of which I've outlined earlier in this chapter, particularly in the section "Browsing Options." Specifically, the hosts allow, hosts deny, valid users, and invalid users parameters offer a way to fine-tune access to specific shares that is beyond the control afforded through Linux ownership and permissions. For instance, you can deny share access to a particular user or to anybody from a particular computer.

Samba Ownership and Permission Options

Samba provides several options that affect the way Linux filenames and permissions are used by the server. You can use these options to help create a security configuration that works in your network environment.

Controlling Ownership

On a Linux server, every file has an *owner* and a *group*. Every user has rights to read and write files, based on the user's ID and the groups to which the user belongs. You can adjust the owner and group associated with accesses to a share using a pair of smb.conf parameters:

> *force user*   Normally, when you connect to a Samba server, you send your username and password and can then access and create files using the permissions associated with that username. For instance, if you connect as susani, any files you create will be owned by the Linux user susani, and you can read existing files that can be read by susani. The force user parameter changes this. It makes Samba behave as if you logged on using what may be a different username. For instance, if a share includes the force user = marcusc parameter, then any access within that share occurs as if marcusc originated the access, even if susani connected with her username and password. The share may be accessed by any authorized user who supplies a valid username and password.

TIP

The force user parameter is often used to create a share that's accessible to—and writeable by—a group of users. You can create a share under one user's name and then use force user to allow all users to create files in the share, without worrying about the ownership of the created files. I recommend you use a "dummy" account that has little access to the system outside of the target directory when you use this parameter. This reduces the risk of abuse or mistakes that might lead to trouble.

force group   This option works much like force user, but it sets the group for files created when the share is accessed. It also determines what files can be read and written based on group ownership and permissions. You can use force user and force group together to create some unusual effects. For instance, even if the user susani does not belong to the group ranger, you can use force user = susani and force group = ranger to give users connecting to a share the permissions equivalent to susani *and* group ranger.

WARNING

A bug in Samba prior to version 2.0.5 set the group of files created when force user was in effect to the group of the individual who accessed the share. Later versions of Samba set the group to match that of the user whose identity is forced by force user. To be absolutely certain of the group used in a share, use force group.

WARNING

The force user and force group parameters are not set by default. These features are very powerful and thus potentially dangerous. Consider a directory that's world-writeable on Linux but exported with force user = root. If a user logs on through a valid shell account and creates a symbolic link from the share to /etc, then anybody who uses that share can edit the sensitive configuration files in /etc—at least, if Samba allows links to be followed outside of a share (that is, wide links = Yes, which is the default). Even if you specify some other username besides root, damage can occur, because a miscreant might be able to damage other users' files.

Controlling Permissions (Modes)

As described in "Using Linux File Security with Samba" in Chapter 19, any individual user's access to a file is determined in part by the file's permissions (also referred to as the file's *mode*). The mode is represented by a three- or four-digit octal number such as 644 or 0750. Samba can use the execute bits of the file mode to store DOS- and Windows-style file attributes. This is also described in Chapter 19, and discussed again in the section "Storing FAT-Style File Attributes," later in this chapter. Several parameters influence the way Samba treats file permissions:

create mask   You can use the `create mask` parameter to limit the range of permissible modes. This mask is a three- or four-digit number representing the bits that *may* be set in a created file. Any bit that's *not* present in the `create mask` value is stripped from the permissions on any file created by Samba in the share. The default `create mask` is 0744, which allows for read-only access by nonowners of all files. This mask also allows Samba to store the archive bit in the file but not the hidden or system bits. (See "Storing FAT-Style File Attributes," later in this chapter.) The downside, at least if the files are to be read from Linux, is that all newly created files will appear to be executable to the owner. If this fact is a drawback and the presence of the archive bit from Windows clients is unimportant, you can set `create mask = 0644` (or something more restrictive) to eliminate the executable bit. A synonym for `create mask` is `create mode`.

directory mask   This option works like `create mask`, but it applies to directories rather than regular files. In Linux, directories normally have their execute permissions set, so the default `directory mask` value is 0755. A synonym for this parameter is `directory mode`.

NOTE

Both `create mask` and `directory mask` set the *maximum permissions* for a file or directory. For instance, consider `create mask = 0644`, applied to a file that would otherwise have the admittedly odd 0606 permissions. The owner's permissions (the first 6) are unchanged, because the mask contains all the bits in the owner's permission. The group permissions are unchanged from the original 0 because the mask can only unset bits, and 0 has none set. The world permissions are stripped from 6 (rw-) to 4 (r-) because the mask lacks the write bit. The result is therefore 0604.

force create mode   This parameter is similar to create mask, but instead of specifying bits that *may* be present in the final permissions, force create mode specifies bits that *must* be present. In an extreme case, if you set force create mode = 0777, then all files would have 0777 permissions, even if the client tried to create a read-only file. This parameter defaults to 0000. If force create mode specifies greater permissions than does create mask, force create mode's settings take precedence.

TIP

If your users regularly exchange files in a shared directory, but you've config-ured the system to retain users' correct usernames rather than employing force user, you may want to set force create mode = 0660. This configuration ensures that members of the same group can all write to files created by any member of the group.

force directory mode   This parameter is similar to force cre-ate mode, but it applies to directories. The default value is 0000.

restrict acl with mask   This parameter is new to Samba 2.2.0; it determines whether or not the create mask, force create mode, directory mask, and force directory mode parame-ters are used when a client tries to use Windows NT security controls (ACLs). When set to No (the default), the NT ACL mapping features take precedence; when set to Yes, the masks set with other Samba parameters take precedence.

security mask   This parameter controls what Linux security bits can be manipulated by users through Windows NT security controls. If not set explicitly, this value defaults to the same value as the create mask parameter.

directory security mask   This parameter is the equivalent of security mask, but it applies to directories rather than files.

force security mode   This parameter forces Linux security bits on when a user manipulates security options through Windows NT security controls. It defaults to the same value as the force create mode option.

force directory security mode   This parameter is the equi-valent of force security mode, but it applies to directories rather than files.

Part V

inherit permissions   Ordinarily, file and directory permissions are set by options such as force create mode and create mask. The inherit permissions parameter overrides these settings, however, and causes permissions to be inherited from the parent directory. For instance, if a directory has permissions of 0750, then any subdirectory created in that directory has the same permissions. For files, permissions are taken from the parent directory, except that execute permissions are set by Samba's mapping of DOS-style hidden, system, and archive bits. The Linux *set user ID* (*suid*) bit cannot be inherited.

Examples of Usage

You can do some very unusual things with the ownership and permission options. For instance, suppose you want to give one user (perhaps a supervisor) full read/write access to all users' home shares and read-only access to other members of the user's group. You could create a share definition like the following:

```
[homes]
        comment = Home Directories
        include = /etc/samba/smb.conf.%U
        create mask = 0640
        writeable = Yes
        browseable = No
```

Then you'd create an auxiliary configuration file called /etc/samba/ smb.conf.*superv* (where *superv* is the username of the supervisor). This file would contain a single line:

```
        force user = %S
```

The %U variable in the include line in the main smb.conf file causes Samba to search for a file that ends in the username provided by the user of the share. If that file isn't found, Samba ignores the include directive. If the file is present, Samba reads it and includes its contents at that point in the file. When *superv* connects to a user's share, Samba reads the smb.conf.*superv* file, and the force user line it contains makes Samba treat the connection as if it were coming from %S. In the case of the [homes] share, the share name (%S) is the same as the share owner's username. Thus Samba grants *superv* the same permission as the owner of the share.

The `create mask` parameter causes all files to be created with 0640 permissions (except when the client program specifies read-only permissions), so the files are readable from but not writeable by other members of the group. The end result is that *superv* and the share's owner both have full read/write access to the share, while other group members have read-only access to its files. (The home directories must have appropriate permissions themselves, such as 0750.)

> **WARNING**
>
> Tricky configurations such as the one I've just outlined can be convenient, but they're not without their pitfalls. For instance, if ordinary users are allowed to create new files in the `/etc/samba` directory, they could create files to give themselves enhanced privileges or even superuser access! Also, as configured in this example, *superv* can add or delete files, and those changes will look just like those made by the share's normal user—which isn't necessarily desirable from a security point of view.

Interactions with Other Services

When you set (or fail to set) file ownership and permissions through Samba, these options sometimes have effects on other Linux services. For instance, if users can use Telnet or Secure Shell (SSH) to access a Samba server, they can adjust their files' permissions through normal Linux shell commands, such as chmod. Should you configure `force user` to set a shared resource to use a specific user's ID, then that user can access files in that shared directory. This may not be a problem if the shared directory has full write permissions from Samba, but if you use `writeable = No` in Samba, the user will nonetheless have full write access from a Linux shell, where the same user has read-only access from Samba. Similarly, you might use `valid users` or `invalid users` to restrict access to a share, but if the Linux permissions for that share are set permissively, disallowed users may nonetheless be able to access the share from a Linux shell. For these reasons, I suggest you set restrictive Linux ownership and permissions on sensitive data directories. If those directories are to be accessible to a variety of users, you can use `force user` and `valid users` or `invalid users` to open access to those allowed in through Samba.

Similar considerations exist if you use the Samba server in conjunction with other network servers, such as NFS and Appletalk for Unix and Macintosh connectivity, respectively. In these cases, it's generally best to rely primarily on Linux's own security features rather than Samba's to control share access. If you can generate a set of Linux users, groups, and permissions that together produce the desired security effects, that set of rules can work with Samba, NFS, Appletalk, and other network servers. The `inherit permissions` parameter can be particularly useful in this situation because non-Samba servers generally create permissions in a manner that's similar to Samba's behavior when `inherit permissions = Yes`.

Storing FAT-Style File Attributes

As described in Chapter 19, Samba can store DOS-style file attributes using Linux's execute permission bits. (Windows and OS/2 use these same DOS-style attributes.) This feature is controlled through three `smb.conf` parameters:

map archive   If `map archive = Yes` (the default), Linux sets the user execute bit when a client sets the DOS archive bit. Normally, the archive bit is set when a file has not been backed up, so this bit is set when a file is created and removed when a backup program backs up the system.

map system   If `map system = Yes`, Linux sets the group execute bit when a client sets the DOS system bit. Microsoft OSs use the system bit to identify a handful of files that are particularly important to the OS. This parameter defaults to No.

map hidden   If `map hidden = Yes`, Linux sets the world execute bit when a client sets the DOS hidden bit. When the hidden bit is set, most programs don't display the file as being present, although users can still read the file from certain programs. The default value is No.

WARNING

If you export a directory that contains executable Linux programs, such as programs compiled from source code or shell scripts, Samba clients may see these files as being hidden, as system files, or as having their archive bits set. If a client program then modifies those bits (when you use a DOS backup utility on the share, for example), the changes may make the file nonexecutable from Linux. You can easily correct this problem, but it's a nuisance and can in some cases cause other difficult-to-trace errors.

The default values for these file attribute parameters are useful on many configurations but may not always be ideal. It's unlikely that clients will need to store files with their system bits set. The hidden bit is also seldom used. Although the archive bit is commonly used, it's most important when you use Windows-based backup software. Chances are you'll be backing up the Samba server using Linux software and so won't need the archive bit.

The `create mask` parameter can (and, by default, does) remove some or all of these bits. The default `create mask` value of 0744, specifically, is redundant with the default values for these map parameters because it removes the group execute and world execute bits while leaving the user execute bit. If you set `create mask = 0644`, Samba can't set the archive bit, even if `map archive = Yes`. Likewise, `force create mode` can override the map settings. A value of `force create mode = 0755` sets the archive, system, and hidden bits on all files even if you've set their parameters to No.

NOTE

It's rare in Linux to see files with an execute bit set but not the corresponding read bit. You might need to create such files in Samba, however, if you want to store a system or hidden bit but deny read access to users other than the owner or members of the file's group. Suppose you want to store the hidden, archive, and system bits but deny all access to users who don't belong to the file's group; you could use `create mask = 0751`. If you then set the hidden and archive bits in a client but not the system bit, the file will take on permissions of `-rwxr----x` (that is, 0741).

Windows NT, 2000, and XP support ACLs, which provide additional security features. You can create shares with ACL-like security restrictions using the `valid users` and `invalid users` parameters, described earlier in the section "Browsing Options." Windows NT clients can be granted access to Linux's security options by setting `nt acl support = Yes` (which is the default). These clients can then access Linux permission information through the File Permissions dialog box, shown in Figure 22.3. You can't do everything with this access that you can do with native ACLs, but you can control the read and write bits for the owner, group, and all other users of the file.

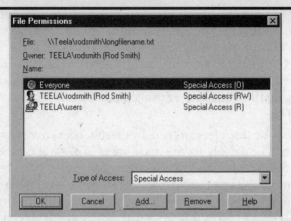

FIGURE 22.3:   Samba can present Linux permissions to Windows NT clients as if they were "special-access" ACLs.

Samba's support for ACLs historically has been rather limited—mapping ACLs onto Linux permissions, which are less flexible than are ACLs. The reason for this is that the Linux kernel and filesystems have not supported ACLs. This is changing, however. SGI's journaling filesystem, XFS, supports ACLs, and there are patches available for ext2fs to add ACL support to it. (See http://acl.bestbits.at for one such implementation.) Samba 2.2.x supports these implementations; if you set nt acl support = Yes (the default), and if the kernel and filesystem on which you store files both support ACLs, Samba stores ACLs as ACLs rather than map them onto Linux permissions. This feature can help greatly in integrating a Samba server into a network with Windows NT, 2000, or XP clients.

TIP

XFS, in addition to supporting ACLs, features a *journal*, which is a data structure that can help a system recover quickly when rebooting after a power failure or crash. If your Samba server has a large disk, using a journaling filesystem can greatly speed recovery in case of a problem. Because of XFS's support for ACLs, it makes an excellent choice for a journaling filesystem for a Samba server. You can obtain XFS from http://oss.sgi.com/projects/xfs/ (you'll need to patch and recompile your kernel). It's likely to make its way into the Linux kernel eventually and may be included with some distributions even before then, in late 2001 and beyond.

A Network Security Preview

Samba includes numerous security features for controlling one user's access to another user's files. If your system has users who need relatively unfettered access to one another's files, you might use `create mask`, `force create mode`, and their equivalent directory parameters to set up a fairly open environment in which all users can read and write each others' files. In a high-security environment, on the other hand, you might want to use strict default security options, such as `create mask = 0600`, to limit access to the files in users' home directories.

Symbolic Links

One network security issue that arises on Samba servers but not on Windows servers has to do with *links,* particularly *symbolic links.* These special files allow one file to act as a stand-in for another file. Let's say you have a file called `report.wpd` located in your `papers` directory. If you want to be able to access this file from the `important` directory, you can create a link so that `important/report.wpd` accesses `papers/report.wpd`. In Linux, you use the `ln` command to create links (`ln -s` creates *symbolic links,* the type of interest to the current discussion). The `ln` command works much like `cp`, used for copying files. This command, for instance, creates a symbolic link:

```
$ ln -s papers/report.wpd important/report.wpd
```

You cannot create Linux links from a client computer through Samba.

NOTE

Windows includes a link-like feature known as *shortcuts*. Because Windows implements shortcuts as ordinary files, you can create shortcuts from Windows clients on Samba servers. These shortcuts can refer to files on the same server, files on the client, or files on other servers. Likewise, shortcuts on a client can refer to files on a Samba server.

Samba's treatment of links is affected by two parameters:

follow symlinks   This Boolean parameter controls whether Samba follows symbolic links. If set to No, any attempt to access a symbolic link fails. This is a useful security precaution to prevent users from setting symbolic links in shared directories to sensitive data in other users' directories or in system directories. Tight security on the Linux computer can also prevent such abuses, but you may want to deploy this option as an added precaution—particularly on shares in which you've set the force user parameter. follow symlinks does *not* affect Samba's handling of *hard links* (those created without the -s parameter to ln).

wide links   This parameter affects links to *directories* that fall outside the export's normal range. Specifically, if wide links = No, Samba won't follow links to directories that lead outside of a share's normal tree, but the links within that tree will still work. If you share the Linux directory /usr/samba/share, for example, then a link from within that share to the /usr/local directory will fail, but a link to /usr/samba/share/somedir/anotherdir will succeed. This parameter does not affect Samba's handling of symbolic links to files that fall outside of the share's directory tree, nor does it apply to hard links.

Both the follow symlinks = No and wide links = No parameters slow file accesses, so you must balance their potential security benefits against their cost in performance. These parameters are share-level and so can be set differently for individual shares.

User-by-User Access Control

You've already examined several parameters that determine who is allowed to access a share. In addition to the valid users and invalid users parameters, as well as hosts allow and hosts deny, the following are a few more that deserve mention.

admin users   You can specify one or more username in this parameter. These users attain what amounts to root privileges when accessing the share. In most cases, this option isn't needed; you can grant specific users greater-than-normal levels of access through other means, such as the write list parameter. I recommend you use admin users sparingly if at all because of its power and, therefore, potential for problems if misconfigured.

write list   When the writeable parameter is set to No, users can't write to a share. You may nonetheless want to grant write permission to one or more users, and you can do so with the write list parameter. For instance, write list = susani grants susani write access to a share that's otherwise marked read-only. In this scenario, however, susani can't overcome her own Linux-based permissions. Without permission to create files in a share (perhaps because the directory is owned by somebody else and has 0750 permissions), susani's presence in the write list doesn't enable her to write in the directory.

read list   The read list parameter is the opposite of write list; it specifies users who are to have *reduced* privileges in a share with respect to creating or modifying files. To users on the read list, the share is effectively the same as one created with writeable = No. Like write list, this parameter does *not* override Linux's normal rules for file permissions.

username   This share-level parameter specifies a list of usernames against which the supplied password is tested. You might use this option when the client computer doesn't send usernames or sends incorrect usernames. Setting username slows down authentication, however, and increases the security risk. You can specify groups of users rather than individual users in one of three ways:

▶ If the username is preceded by an @ symbol (as in @users), then the name is expanded to all users in the Linux group (in /etc/group) or NIS netgroup.

▶ If the username is preceded by a plus sign (as in +users), then the name is expanded to all users in the Linux group of that name.

▶ An ampersand preceding the name (as in &users) indicates that the name is to be expanded to the corresponding NIS group.

Part v

For instance, `username = susani, @rangers` tests passwords against `susani` and all members of the group `rangers`. This parameter is generally used with `security = Share`. Synonyms of this parameter are `user` and `users`.

WARNING

The user list in `/etc/group` must be stated explicitly. Samba does not automatically add users whose `/etc/passwd` entries indicate that they're members of a group if they aren't listed in that group's `/etc/group` line.

Guest Access

SMB/CIFS networking includes the concept of a *guest user*—one who does not have a password, but to whom you may want to grant access to the system. Naturally, it's best to avoid such configurations, but that isn't always possible. In addition, you might want to configure guest access to some low-security shares, such as shared printers on a network that's not connected to the Internet. Having guest access can make life easier for your users because they won't need to remember passwords for these shares. Here are the parameters that control guest access:

map to guest   This global parameter controls the circumstances in which Samba invokes the guest account access. Options are as follows:

- ▶ When `map to guest = Never`, Samba rejects all accesses to shares when invalid usernames or passwords are provided. This is the default. It makes guest access effectively impossible, even if you enable other guest access options.

- ▶ The `Bad User` setting means Samba rejects the access attempt if an invalid password is presented with a valid username. If an invalid username is presented, Samba maps the access onto the guest user.

- ▶ With `map to guest = Bad Password`, if Samba receives an invalid password, it maps the access onto the guest account whether or not the username is valid. This arrangement can be annoying to users who type their correct usernames but mistype their passwords.

guest account   This share-level parameter specifies the name of the Linux account that's used for guest access. In some cases, nobody is a good choice for this account, and in fact nobody is the default guest account. In other cases you may want to create a "dummy" account that has more access than nobody. In the event you need the guest user to have permission to read a particular group's files, for example, you can create a special guest account that belongs to that group.

guest ok   This share-level parameter, when set to Yes, allows guest access to the share. The default value is No, so even if you set map to guest to Bad User or Bad Password, guest access won't work. You must also set guest ok = Yes to allow guest access to a share. A synonym for guest ok is public.

guest only   When guest only = Yes for a share, all accesses to that share are treated as guest accesses. This option requires that guest ok = Yes. If you access the share with a valid username, the access is accepted or rejected according to the accuracy of the password entered and the setting of the global map to guest parameter. If you use an invalid username, access is accepted, assuming that map to guest is not set to Never.

Depending upon your client OS, you may still be asked for a username and password when you try to access a guest share, but depending on how you've set the preceding parameters, you'll be granted access no matter what you type. With the exception of the global map to guest parameter, all of these parameters are share-level, and so can be set on a share-by-share basis.

Consider a share that contains data files that you want to make accessible to all users of your network, even if those individuals don't have accounts on the Samba server. You could set map to guest = Bad User and then create a share like the following:

```
[guest]
        comment = All Users Welcome
        path = /home/samba/guest
        guest account = nemo
        writeable = No
        write list = marcusc, susani
        guest ok = Yes
        guest only = Yes
```

This definition allows everybody equal but limited (read-only) access to the share. All the files in the directory must be readable by the user nemo in order for this definition to be useful. Note also that marcusc and susani are on the write list, so they have read/write access to the share (provided that nemo, the guest user, has write access to the /home/samba/guest directory). These two users can therefore maintain the files in this shared directory. Because of the guest only = Yes line, all other users have read-only access with the permissions granted nemo on the computer. Because the [global] section includes map to guest = Bad User, individuals who have accounts on the system must present valid passwords when using their normal usernames. (If this is the only guest share on the computer, map to guest = Bad Password might be a better choice because it will prevent guest users from being rejected if they happen to try a username that's used by a valid user.)

SOME COMMON FILE-SHARING SCENARIOS

To illustrate many of the parameters described in this chapter, let's examine them in action. This section is devoted to some file-sharing scenarios you may encounter in real life. Each one includes a small but complete smb.conf file that can be used in the stated situation, with descriptions of its effects and consequences.

Shared Program and File Server

Many networks place common programs such as word processors, archiving tools, and graphics utilities on a central server for all to use, while simultaneously allowing users to store their personal files on the server. Though convenient, this configuration is slow compared to an arrangement where program files are stored on individual workstations. You must also be cautious not to violate your programs' license agreements, which may limit the number of computers on which you may use the software.

One particularly onerous problem with this sort of setup is that many Windows programs store program files both in a directory dedicated to the program and in the WINDOWS directory. The result is that you may need to reinstall such programs on every client, despite the fact that the program is stored on the Samba server. These problems can make the configuration awkward but still be useful for programs that are seldom used and don't insist on installing parts of themselves in the WINDOWS directory.

The example smb.conf file for this type of configuration is shown in Listing 22.1.

Listing 22.1: An *smb.conf* File for Sharing Files and Programs

```
[global]
        workgroup = EF
        netbios name = WARLOCK
        server string = Samba server on %L
        encrypt passwords = Yes
        log file = /var/log/samba/log.%m
[homes]
        comment = Home Directories
        writeable = Yes
        browseable = No
        create mask = 0664
        directory mask = 0775
[winprogs]
        comment = Windows Programs
        path = /home/samba/winprogs
        force user = winuser
        write list = susani
        read only = Yes
        create mask = 0600
        directory mask = 0700
```

The definition in Listing 22.1 is fairly straightforward. Note the following:

▶ The [global] section sets assorted configuration options described in Chapter 21. The computer's NetBIOS name is WARLOCK, even if the machine's TCP/IP name is something else. Samba creates a different log file for each client that connects to the computer.

▶ Users' home directories are explicitly set to be writeable but not browseable. This combination lets users write to their home directories and prevents a share called HOME from showing up in Windows clients when browsing the computer. Samba automatically presents a home share named after the user, however, even with browseable = No.

▶ The `create mask` and `directory mask` parameters in the [homes] share set very liberal access policies. This arrangement is suitable for an environment in which users must be able to easily collaborate by reading and writing one another's files. You can create separate Linux groups for each collaborating group. Members can thus read and write files owned by the group's members, but they can only read files from other groups' directories.

▶ The `winprogs` share relies on a user known as `winuser`. The /etc/passwd file on the Linux server must be configured with a user of this name, but the user need not have—and indeed, *should not* have—any login capabilities. Set the user's shell to something like /dev/null so that nobody can log in with that username, and disable the user's password.

▶ `susani` has write privileges in the `winprogs` share, but for everybody else, it's a read-only share. The `create mask` and `directory mask` parameters ensure that the files `susani` creates are readable only by `winuser`, which is fine for this share because it's accessed using `winuser`'s permissions only. If you want users to be able to get to these files from Linux shell accounts, you must modify this aspect of the configuration.

On the whole, the preceding arrangement is a good starting point for many Samba configurations. Of course, you can customize it in various ways to attain the security and other options you require.

User Files on a High-Security Central Server

Some installations require substantial security for user files. Samba's default settings are relatively lax in this respect, and they can be made even less strict (as in the preceding example, by specifying `create mask = 0664` in the [homes] share). To tighten security for user shares, you can use an `smb.conf` file similar to the one shown in Listing 22.2.

Listing 22.2: A High-Security Server Configuration for User File Storage

```
[global]
        workgroup = EF
        netbios name = WARLOCK
        server string = Magic Group File Sever
        encrypt passwords = Yes
        log file = /var/log/samba/log.%m
        hosts allow = 192.168.3. 10.45.23.5 10.48.98.10
[homes]
        comment = Home Directories
        writeable = Yes
        browseable = No
        valid users = %U
        create mask = 0600
        directory mask = 0700
        follow symlinks = No
```

This definition isn't much different from the one in Listing 22.1 in terms of the contents of the [global] and [homes] sections. Here are some key points to note about this configuration:

▶ The server string parameter removes mention of this being a Samba server. There's no point in advertising your server, and hence its vulnerabilities, to would-be crackers.

▶ This server uses encrypted passwords. So did the definition in Listing 22.1, but encrypted passwords are more critical in a high-security environment.

▶ This definition uses a global hosts allow parameter to restrict access to the 192.168.3.0/24 network and to two computers outside of that network. In a real configuration, you should also use measures such as a firewall to deny access to the Samba server.

▶ The [homes] share uses valid users = %U to restrict logins to only the share's owner. Without this parameter, other users could log onto the share, although they'd not be able to read its files because of other aspects of the definition.

▶ The [homes] share sets the masks on files and directories to 0600 and 0700, respectively. This feature prevents other users from reading files created through this share, even using a shell login instead of Samba.

▶ The follow symlinks = No parameter slows access, but it ensures that users can't follow symbolic links out of their assigned directories.

Security doesn't stop with the Samba configuration. On a high-security server, you should disable all unnecessary services, use ownership and permissions to prevent snooping from shell logins, use protocols such as SSH rather than Telnet for shell access, enforce password-change rules, and deploy other security measures as appropriate.

Serving Files to Legacy DOS Systems

A network with a number of DOS computers has file-sharing needs that are different from those of a network of Windows or OS/2 computers. DOS doesn't need long filename support, for instance, and some of Samba's default values work best with computers that understand long filenames. A simple server for individuals' files using older DOS computers might have an smb.conf file similar to the one shown in Listing 22.3.

Listing 22.3: An *smb.conf* File for a DOS Network Server

```
[global]
          workgroup = EF
          netbios name = WARLOCK
          server string = Samba server on %L
          encrypt passwords = No
          security = Share
          log file = /var/log/samba/log.%m
[%m]
          comment = Home Directories
          path = /home/samba/%m
          username = susani, @lurker
          writeable = Yes
          short preserve case = No
          default case = Upper
          create mask = 0775
          directory mask = 0775
```

This definition is substantially different from the preceding ones in some important ways:

▶ encrypt passwords is set to No, because DOS SMB/CIFS clients don't use encrypted passwords by default. One potentially undesirable consequence of this setting is that recent Windows clients won't be able to access the server unless you disable their encrypted password settings, as described in "Password Encryption" in Chapter 21.

▶ security is set to Share because some particularly old clients don't send usernames. If you're dealing with a newer SMB/CIFS implementation for DOS, you can use security = User and a more conventional [homes] share.

▶ Rather than a [homes] share, this definition uses a share called [%m], which creates a unique share for each client computer. It's an effective approach if there's a one-to-one correspondence between client computers and their users, but it's not without its drawbacks. For instance, you cannot access one computer's share from another computer, short of installing symbolic links within the shares. Even specifying the share by name (as opposed to browsing to it) won't work.

▶ The username parameter specifies the users who may access the pseudo-home share. The value of this parameter (susani, @lurker) grants access to the user susani and all users in the lurker group. When the user enters a password on the client system, it's checked against the passwords of each specified user.

▶ The short preserve case = No and default case = Upper parameters force Samba to store short (8.3) filenames using all-uppercase characters. These options help the Samba server's files blend into a DOS environment more consistently than the defaults would do. In most cases, though, these parameters aren't strictly necessary. If the files are to be accessed from Linux as well as from DOS, you might want to omit the default case parameter, which defaults to Lower. This makes the case consistent, but files will have lowercase filenames (more typical in Linux than all-uppercase filenames).

▶ The create mask parameter's value of 0775 allows the DOS clients to set the archive, hidden, and system bits on all files. This option probably isn't required, and there's no reason to think it's more likely to be required for DOS than for Windows clients. You may find a need for it in some cases, though, and it makes a good example.

On the whole, a configuration like that in Listing 22.3 is quite extreme. Many DOS systems work well with a conventional Samba [homes] share, although you might want to use the case options from Listing 22.3. You could use a [%m] share similar to this one in other circumstances, though. For instance, to create shares that map to specific computers (say, to store computer-specific drivers), a [%m] share may fit the bill.

Sharing Files Using Multiple Protocols

One of Linux's strengths as a server platform is that it supports so many protocols. Samba enables Linux to serve files on an SMB/CIFS network, Netatalk supports AppleTalk computers, NFS serves Unix systems, and mars_nwe and lwared support NetWare protocols. To use Samba in such a multiprotocol environment, however, you must ensure that your security measures and file-sharing defaults are appropriate for all the servers. For instance, suppose you create a common directory for file exchange among users. Under Samba, using the force user parameter to force access to that share under a specific username simplifies configuration; you need not ensure that all users have full read/write access to the directory, nor that they all create files that can be read, written, and deleted by other users.

Unfortunately, other file-sharing protocols may not support this option, so in the end you'll need to employ Linux's ownership and permissions to open up access to this directory. You can still use force user on the Samba definition, but you must guarantee that the designated username won't cause problems to the other servers. You may also want to ensure that Windows NT clients can change the permissions on the files through the security mask parameter so that NT users can correct any problems that arise with security on specific files. If your system has kernel and filesystem ACL support, it's possible that clients other than Windows NT, 2000, and XP systems won't have access to the ACL permissions, or they may be interpreted differently by the servers in question than by Samba.

Another challenge that can emerge in a multiprotocol network involves filenames. This problem can be particularly irksome when dealing with Macintosh clients and filenames that contain non-Roman characters, which are common in many European languages. Macintosh users also sometimes include unusual characters, such as bullets (•), in their filenames. Linux servers have various methods for encoding these filenames. Typically, the unusual filenames look fine on the client that created them, but they are ugly or unintelligible on other clients. The best way to handle this usually is to avoid these non-Roman characters in filenames.

Further, filenames longer than what a client can understand often disappear. The most limiting client in this respect is usually the Macintosh, which supports only 31 characters in its filenames—enough for most purposes, but users of other systems (including Samba clients) may accidentally create overlong filenames. One solution is to reduce the number of servers in use. For instance, you can use DAVE from Thursby Software Systems (http://www.thursby.com) to allow Macintoshes to access a Linux Samba server.

Clients and servers occasionally create system-specific files. OS/2 clients, for instance, often create files called WP DATA. SF. Netatalk creates directories called .AppleDouble and Network Trash Folder. You can use Samba's hide files or veto files parameters to hide or remove such files from view. (The WP DATA. SF file will be hidden if you enable the map hidden parameter and set the create mask appropriately, but these settings aren't the defaults. The .AppleDouble directory will be hidden by default but will reappear if you set hide dot files to No.)

It's possible to use a Linux computer as an intermediary between otherwise incompatible network servers. For instance, suppose you have a Windows-dominated network with a small number of Macintoshes. If you want your Macintosh users to have access to shares exported by the Windows computers, you can use the Linux computer as a sort of translator. Use the smbmount utility (see Chapter 12, "TCP/IP Linux Networking") to mount the Windows computers' shares, and then use Netatalk to export them to the Macintoshes. This is a useful trick for limited use. Unfortunately, presently you can't do the opposite because the existing Linux client for AppleTalk file shares is extremely primitive. A better solution on the whole is to create a direct connection between client and server, perhaps by using DAVE to enable the Macintosh computers to use SMB/CIFS directly. Using Linux as a bridge between two otherwise incompatible network protocols results in greater network traffic and more potential for problems than does direct access.

One particularly common cross-platform issue is that of end-of-line characters in text files. DOS, Windows, and OS/2 all use one system—a combination of a carriage return and a line feed (or CR/LF for short). Linux and Unix, by contrast, use only an LF; Macintoshes use only a CR. Short utility programs—dos2unix, unix2dos, mac2unix, and unix2mac— come with many Linux distributions and will handle the appropriate conversions to work around these differences. Also, many editors will convert from non-native end-of-line conventions to the native format for the platform on which the editor runs.

A final issue is file locking. Samba takes great pains to implement SMB/CIFS-style file-locking mechanisms, using Linux's underlying file-locking support along with Samba-specific features to fill in the gaps. When you use Samba with one or more other file servers, however, the other servers can't use Samba's add-on file-locking support for features such as oplocks unless you're using a 2.4.x kernel and have set kernel oplocks = Yes. Even this won't be enough, though; the other server must also support Linux's kernel oplocks (some versions of NFS do, for instance). You can run into problems with file corruption if users try to write the same files from two different platforms without compatible oplocks support. This likely won't be a problem if you use file sharing mainly to export platform-specific files or even users' home directories. If you export shared directories for user-to-user file exchange, however, problems may arise. It's possible that using oplocks = No in Samba will reduce or eliminate these difficulties. Another option is to tell users about the possibility of such issues and suggest that whenever possible they write only new files, rather than overwriting existing files. Of course, this last solution is awkward at best.

WHAT'S NEXT?

File sharing is Samba's primary reason for being. Samba can also be used for printer sharing, but in most cases, a Samba server serves files. Fortunately, configuring Samba to serve files is fairly easy, at least if your needs are close to typical.

This chapter covered the fundamentals of Samba file-sharing configuration, as well as some midlevel topics such as file locking and filename handling. Using the options described in this chapter, you can fine-tune the behavior of your Samba server to best suit your clients' needs. In fact, Samba's many options allow you to configure it in ways that aren't possible with Windows servers. This flexibility is one of Samba's appeals.

In the next part of this book, we will move from sharing information in an internal LAN network to sharing information on the Internet. The next several chapters will discuss Apache, the Linux web server software of choice.

Part V

PART **VI**

APACHE AND
SENDMAIL

Chapter 23

APACHE AND OTHER SERVERS

I generally don't like one-size-fits-all systems, and I try to avoid products that are marketed as the best solution for everyone's needs. Apache is an exception to this rule, largely because it is easily customized, by design. While Apache runs well on commercial Unix platforms and Microsoft Windows NT, it truly shines on the open-source Unix variants. Apache is the number one choice for a web server for both Linux and FreeBSD. In this chapter, I'll tell you why.

The first part of the chapter takes a look at the major web servers in use on the Internet. The chapter continues with a look at the present state of Apache, including its current feature set and features planned for the next release, and ends with a discussion of why Apache is an excellent and exciting choice to run an Internet website.

Adapted from *Linux Apache Web Server Administration* by Charles Aulds

ISBN 0-7821-2734-7   640 pages $39.99

WHO ARE THE MAJOR PLAYERS?

Since a web server can be any software used to implement HTTP, there are far too many different types of web servers in use for me to describe them all. Some are completely homegrown solutions unique to their developers, but most are recognizable and identifiable by a specific name and version. Despite the large number of different HTTP server engines available, a small number of competitors handle the majority of HTTP traffic on the Internet.

In determining what web servers are currently in use on the Internet and in what relative numbers, I first turned to two respected surveys from the consulting firms Netcraft (www.netcraft.com) and SecuritySpace.com (www.securityspace.com). Both surveys are widely accepted as objective, and neither seems to be controlled by commercial interests. The companies don't attempt to profit from the surveys, which they publish to lend credibility to their consulting services. These surveys tend to agree pretty closely, which lends credibility to both.

The July 2001 survey results from Netcraft and SecuritySpace are summarized in the following, showing that the majority of Internet websites today are running Apache.

Server	Netcraft	SecuritySpace
Apache	63.0%	60.2%
Microsoft (IIS)	20.4%	28.5%
iPlanet (Netscape)	6.2%	2.9%
Other	10.4%	8.4%
Total	100.0%	100.0%

ALTERNATIVES TO APACHE

The surveys say that while Apache leads the pack, it is not the only server in widespread use. This section examines the features and architectures of several other web servers.

The Free Servers

Some of the best web server software available is free. Apache itself is free, open-source software. The roots of the Web—its protocols, browsers, and servers—spring from a free and open academic environment. The free CERN and NCSA servers started the Web revolution, and while neither is currently a viable choice, several choices of server software maintain that free tradition to this day.

thttpd

One of the most interesting free HTTP servers is a product called simply thttpd. The thttpd server is the work of one man, Jef Poskanzer, a Berkeley, California-area consultant who distributes freeware through a nonprofit site called ACME Laboratories (`www.acme.com`).

thttpd is one of two HTTP servers I'll mention that are designed to be extremely fast, with small memory footprints, simple to install and manage, highly secure—and almost feature-free. In most environments, thttpd will perform comparably to any other web server. Under extreme loads, however, thttpd will run away from the pack.

It is unlikely that your Internet server has a data pipe large enough to flood a single web server with such a large number of requests that a server like thttpd is needed. If your company has an internal server attached to the network with a Gigabit Ethernet link, you might find you need a super-fast server; the problem is that on an intranet server, you'll almost certainly need features that aren't found in thttpd. High-performance servers such as thttpd are a little like Formula-1 racecars: our highways aren't built for them, and they aren't designed to carry payload.

Mathopd

Minimization is taken to the extreme with Mathopd (available from its author at `http://mathop.diva.nl/`). The number of options and features in Mathopd is deliberately small. The server is made available only for Unix and Linux operating systems.

Why would anyone want to run Mathopd? The code is designed to handle a very large number of simultaneous connections. Like the thttpd server, Mathopd uses the `select()` system call in Unix, rather than spawning a number of processes or threads to handle multiple client connections. The result is a very fast web server, designed to handle the basic functions required by HTTP/1.1 and occupying a very small memory footprint on a Unix machine.

Part vi

A cinch to install and configure and optimized for the maximum possible speed in serving static documents to a large number of connecting clients, Mathopd at first seemed a very attractive alternative to Apache. However, Mathopd offers no user authentication, secure connections, or support for programming. Upon reflection, I realized that, without the capability to add functionality, the server was too limiting for most administrators, and almost no one has data pipes sufficiently large to require the speed of Mathopd. What it does, though, it does better than anyone.

Boa

The last server I'll mention in the free software category is Boa (`www.boa` `.org`), a respectable alternative to Apache for those administrators who are looking for greater speed and system security and are willing to sacrifice some functionality to get it. Boa is another of the nonforking single-process servers that use the `select()` system call to multitask I/O.

Boa turns in very good numbers for CGI scripts, probably some of the best numbers (measured in transactions handled per second) that you'll get on a Linux web server. The performance gain apparently comes from the fact that output from CGI scripts spawned by Boa is sent directly to the client. This is unlike most web servers, which receive data output from CGI programs and send it to the web client (browser).

The Commercial Variety

Commercial web servers are in demand by a certain type of organization. Some organizations have a difficult time accepting that open-source software can have better quality and support than commercial software. These organizations demand commercial software, and several companies have responded to this demand by creating commercial web server software. The following sections discuss several of the best commercial products.

Stronghold

For those sites that require strong security based on the Secure Sockets Layer (SSL), using a commercial server often seems an attractive alternative to open-source Apache. There are good reasons for these e-commerce websites to use commercial software. Probably the best reason to choose a commercial solution is for the support offered by the vendor. If you go the commercial route, you should take full advantage of that product support. You are paying not so much for the product as for that company's expertise in setting up an SSL website. You should expect all the handholding necessary from these companies in getting your site up and running.

If you are seriously considering a commercial SSL web product, Stronghold should be near the top of your list.

Many commercial web products are derived from open-source software, and Stronghold is no exception. Stronghold is Apache server software, specially modified to include strong SSL support and sold as a ready-to-install product, supported by the vendor. There's absolutely nothing wrong with this, and the value added to open-source Apache may be exactly what you need. What you're buying, however, is essentially what you can put together through lots of sweat, trial and error, and time spent in books such as this one. You may well decide that the effort required to "roll your own" pays off rich dividends in education and familiarity with your system. For information on Stronghold, visit C2Net at www.c2.net.

iPlanet (formerly Netscape Enterprise)

Probably the best commercial server available for high-end multiprocessing hardware is iPlanet Web Server (formerly known as Netscape Enterprise Server), a product from the Sun-Netscape Alliance. iPlanet is well suited for large sites with large development staffs who aren't afraid to program in Java. Make no mistake about it, iPlanet is made for Java, and you won't get much mileage from it if you aren't willing to work in that language.

iPlanet is available for a wide variety of operating systems, including Linux. iPlanet for Linux version 6.0 is a fairly new but strong product and bears a price tag of $1,500 per CPU. The product includes add-ons that are not standard with Apache (such as SSL and support for the Java Servlets 2.2 specification and JavaServer Pages 1.1). However, these can be added to Apache.

NOTE

America Online, Inc. (which owns Netscape Communications), and Sun Microsystems, Inc., formed the Sun-Netscape Alliance, which now sells Netscape Enterprise Server as the iPlanet Web Server, Enterprise Edition (www.iplanet.com). A rose by another name?

Many IT managers in the past liked Netscape Enterprise Server because it is backed by Netscape Communications, and the support offered by the company can be valuable. In my opinion, however, the odds of finding documentation that addresses your problem or a savvy techie who's willing to offer truly useful advice or, better still, someone who has overcome the problem before are much better with an open-source application such as Apache. Online resources are often every bit as valuable as technical support for commercial software. As attractive as these commercial servers are, Apache should be the first server you evaluate for Linux.

Roxen

Roxen is actually not a single web server product; the name is used to refer to a line of Internet server products offered by Idonex AB of Link ping, Sweden (www.roxen.com). Roxen WebServer is the web server and is available for free download. Roxen WebServer, however, is part of a larger set of integrated website development tools called Roxen Platform. Roxen SiteBuilder is a workgroup environment that lets a group of website developers collaborate in designing a website. Like most modern development systems, SiteBuilder concentrates on separating site display and content.

At a cost of $11,800, Roxen Platform requires a serious financial commitment even though the WebServer is free. Without the costly developer's tools, Roxen WebServer offers no advantages over Apache, which is far more widely used and, as a result, better supported.

Zeus

The Zeus web server from Zeus Technology of Cambridge, England (www.zeus.co.uk) is an excellent commercial web server for Linux. Zeus consistently turns in superlative numbers in benchmark tests (like the SPECWeb96 web server benchmarks published by the Standard Performance Evaluation Corporation, www.spec.org/osg/web96).

The original version of Zeus was designed for raw speed, with a minimum of overhead (features and functions). That version of Zeus is still available as version 1.0. Subsequent releases of the product include a full list of advanced functions expected in a modern e-commerce web server. Zeus competes well with Apache in nearly every area, including speed, functionality, configurability, and scalability. The one area in which Zeus cannot best Apache is cost. Zeus Web Server version 3 currently costs $1,700, with a discounted price to qualified academic and charitable organizations of $85.

Two features of Zeus that have traditionally appealed to web server administrators are its Apache/NCSA HTTPD compatibility (support for .htaccess files, for example) and the fact that it can be completely configured from a web browser. Zeus is especially popular with web hosting services and ISPs that host customer websites, and the company increasingly targets this market. Zeus is available for Unix and Linux platforms.

IBM

Most of the web servers discovered in my survey that did not fall into one of the big three (Apache, Microsoft, Netscape) were running on some type of IBM hardware, indicated by the response Lotus-Domino. Most of them are really running a special version of Apache. Several years ago, IBM stunned the computing world by announcing its intention to support Apache as a web server included with its Internet Commerce solutions. IBM has since brought Apache to market as IBM HTTP Server, which is bundled with e-commerce solutions such as IBM WebSphere Application Server. IBM markets its server as being "powered by Apache." IBM HTTP Server runs only on IBM hardware.

Microsoft IIS

Microsoft's Internet Information Server (IIS) version 5 is listed here with the commercial servers because, although it is provided free as part of the Windows 2000 server family, you must purchase 2000 Server or 2000 Workstation in order to use it.

The performance of IIS 5 will surprise you. IIS stands as an exception to the oversized, often underpowered, applications that often seem to hog all the resources on a Windows system and cry for more. Microsoft seems to be quite serious about the Web, and for shops that are heavy users of NT, IIS is a very respectable platform for website development. IIS, however, does not run on Linux. Using IIS forces you to run Windows 2000.

The Features of Apache

I've said good things about all of the web servers that compete with Apache for mindshare among Internet website developers and administrators. I even said nice things about Microsoft's IIS. Any one of these servers is capable of adequately supporting a production web server. Why is Apache the most widely used web server on the Internet? This section outlines the most important features.

Standards Compliance   Apache offers full compliance with the HTTP/1.1 standard (RFC 2616). Apache has strong support for all the improvements made to the HTTP protocol in version 1.1, such as support for virtual hosts, persistent connections, client file uploading, enhanced error reporting, and resource caching (in proxy or gateway servers).

Apache also supports sophisticated content negotiation by HTTP/1.1 browsers, allowing multiple formats for a single resource to be served to meet the requirements of different clients. Multiple natural language support is a good example of how this is commonly used.

Scalability   Apache provides support for large numbers of websites on a single machine. Virtual hosting is of particular interest to anyone who needs to host several websites on a single server. Many commercial web-hosting services take full advantage of Apache's low cost and strong support for virtual hosting.

Dynamic Shared Objects   Apache also supports Dynamic Shared Objects (DSOs). This permits loading of extension modules at runtime. Features can be added or removed without recompiling the server engine. Throughout the next few chapters, when explaining how to install a module, I will demonstrate how to compile it as a DSO and enable it for use when Apache is started. There are a few modules that cannot be dynamically linked to Apache and must be compiled into the

Apache runtime, but not many. The DSO mechanism will be preserved in future releases of Apache, and learning to compile and use DSO modules is critical for Apache administrators.

Customizability   Apache can be fully customized by writing modules using the Apache module API. Currently, these can be written in C or Perl. The code to implement a minimal module is far smaller than one might think. Source code is completely available for examination or alteration. The Apache license permits almost any use, private or commercial.

Another important feature is customizable logging, including the capability to write to multiple logs from different virtual servers. Also customizable in Apache are HTTP response headers for cache control and error reporting to the client browser.

Programmability   Apache provides support for server programming using a variety of languages and integration techniques, including PHP, Perl, Java Servlets, JavaServer Pages, Active Server Pages, CGI, FastCGI, and server-side includes.

Potential Use as a Caching Proxy Server   Apache is not designed for general proxy use, but by using a module called mod_proxy, you can make it a very efficient caching proxy server. In other words, Apache can cache files received from remote servers and serve them directly to clients who request these resources, without downloading them again from the origin server. Caching for multiple clients (on a local area network, for example) can greatly speed up web retrieval for clients of the proxy server and reduce the traffic on an Internet connection.

Security   Apache's security features include support for user authentication and the SSL protocol:

> ▶ Support for DBM (and other databases such as Oracle or MySQL) for user authentication allows very large lists of authorized users to be searched efficiently.
>
> ▶ Support for SSL allows the exchange of digital certificates and encryption of data crossing the Internet. Secure Sockets Layer is already a critical component of any Internet-based web server used for commercial

Part VI

purposes. In future years, expect to see reliable server and user authentication becoming more widely used on the Internet. Apache will always support the leading security mechanisms.

Further Benefits

None of the major features outlined for the current Apache release is unique to Apache. The feature set alone, while impressive, is not enough to justify a decision to choose Apache over other excellent alternatives. There are, however, other benefits to Apache.

Apache has been ranked (by Netcraft) the number one web server on the Internet since April 1996, and as this book goes to press, Apache powers an estimated 60 percent of all websites reachable through the Internet. While its popularity alone doesn't indicate its superiority, it does say that a lot of successful, high-volume sites have been built using Apache. That represents a huge vote of confidence in the software. It also means Apache is thoroughly tested. Its security, reliability, and overall performance are demonstrated, documented, and unquestionable.

Apache has unparalleled support from a tremendous group of individuals. Some are programmers; most are end users and administrators. For a software system as widely used as Apache, regardless of the nature of your problems, the odds are that someone, somewhere has encountered it and can offer some insight into its resolution. While it might seem logical to assume that support for no-cost software will necessarily be inferior to that provided by commercial software vendors, I haven't found that to be true at all. As a professional network administrator, the most difficult problems I've had to solve were nearly all related to commercial software (for which I usually paid dearly) and often involved licensing servers and product keys. The usual answer from Tech Support is "you need to upgrade to the next revision level." Trust me, you won't have these problems with Apache.

Apache is under intense active development at all times, and yet many websites continue to operate just fine with Apache engines many revisions behind the current release. I believe it is the not-for-profit motivation of its developers that is responsible for this degree of dependability in each revision. There is simply no reason for Apache developers to rush to market with incomplete, bug-ridden releases. The result is a tremendous benefit to administrators who are already stressed trying to roll out product upgrades on an almost continuous basis.

The most compelling reason to use the Apache web server is that, by design, Apache is highly configurable and extensible by virtue of its support for add-on modules. The Apache application program interface (API) gives programmers access to Apache data structures and the ability to write routines to extend the Apache core functionality. It is possible, of course, to write modifications to any server for which the source code is freely available, but only Apache makes this easy with a well-documented API that doesn't require a module programmer to understand the Apache core source code.

The upshot of all of this is that there is a wide variety of third-party modules available for Apache. You'll learn about the most important of these in relevant chapters throughout the rest of Part VI of this book. From these modules, you can pick and choose the ones you need and forget the rest. Most of the standard modules provided with the basic server as distributed by the Apache Software Foundation are optional and can be removed from the server core if statically linked, or they simply can be not used if they are compiled separately as dynamically loadable modules. It's a great alternative to programs bloated with functions that are never used.

THE ARCHITECTURE OF APACHE

I'll admit that when I saw benchmarks showing that some HTTP servers were significantly faster than Apache, at first I doubted the test results and then wondered why anyone would choose Apache over one of these speed-demon web servers.

Many of these servers do, indeed, outperform Apache at serving static resources to clients, both in response time and in the number of simultaneous clients they can handle. A closer examination of what these super-fast servers are capable of revealed that much of their speed is achieved by stripping them of most of the functionality that is standard in Apache.

Most of the fast, small servers handle all client connections from a single process that is written to use nonblocking synchronous I/O multiplexing. That sounds impressive, doesn't it? Essentially, it means they make use of a call to a function called `select()`, which is available in operating systems like Linux. The `select()` function allows the calling process to be notified of an incoming connection on one or more sockets. In other words, the process is not blocked waiting for connections but can be performing other tasks rather than sitting in a listening state. Using `select()` also allows data to be written and read on multiple sockets (I/O multiplexing); it notifies the calling process of which socket has data waiting in buffers to be written or read.

Apache is an example of a *preforking server*. This means that the main server starts a pool of processes to handle client requests, rather than forking a new process for each incoming request. Having the pooled processes already online and waiting (idle) greatly speeds up the process of serving requests. I find this model more robust than the single-process model using multiplexed I/O, because the main Apache server process is protected (it doesn't talk to any client) and is always available to restart child processes that misbehave or die unexpectedly. In fact, the default behavior of Apache is to kill and restart each client process after it has answered an arbitrary (user-configurable) number of requests. This eliminates the possibility that a small memory leak in any process will grow into a big problem if that process is allowed to run for many days, weeks, or even months.

Apache's use of a preforked process pool rather than a single process making use of `select()` is not a bad design decision, and especially not one that leads to less than adequate performance. Perhaps a more valid criticism of Apache is that it uses a pool, or *swarm*, of multiple processes rather than *threads* to handle requests. Apache provides the administrator with some control over the Apache process storm. However, the benefits that can be achieved from these optimization options are small even in the best cases.

Unix systems traditionally schedule CPU time by process, and Apache has definite Unix roots. Threads, however, are less demanding of resources than processes and are generally much faster to schedule, especially on multiprocessing operating systems with multiple processors that are capable of running multiple threads simultaneously. A move to fully threaded code in Apache should result in significant performance enhancements without sacrificing functionality and versatility. Apache 1.3 for NT is multithreaded (and runs as a single process or *task*, which is an NT service that creates multiple threads to handle connections). A major new feature of Apache version 2.0 (previewed later in this chapter) is the use of *multiple-processing modules*.

The important thing to keep in mind about speed and Apache is just how unimportant raw speed is on most web servers. In fact, most web servers function with less than 10Mbps of bandwidth, and most Internet web servers are at the end of links no faster than a T1 line, which is

1.544Mbps. Apache, on a low-end Pentium workstation running Linux with only 64MB of RAM, can easily fill these data pipes. Anything faster is simply unnecessary, and every administrator needs to balance speed against limited functionality in many of the super-fast servers. A number of criteria should be used to determine the applicability of web server software to the needs of the business, and speed is only one of these.

New Features of Apache Version 2.0

As of mid-year 2001, a public beta of version 2.0 (2.0.16) is available. This release was thoroughly tested and ran on the apache.org website for several weeks before its release. Version 2.0 is primarily of interest to programmers and shouldn't significantly change the way Apache is installed, configured, and administered. Everything in these chapters is accurate for version 2.0. The feature set of version 2.0 is nailed down, and I'll describe the major changes that can be expected. Soon 2.0 will be a production release and will contain the features described in this section to enable work to be performed on the thread/process scheduling layer independently of the Apache core code.

The most significant changes to Apache that will emerge in version 2.0 are intended to increase the portability of Apache, enhance the already strong support for add-on modules, and increase the performance of Apache on all platforms. The first of these changes involves moving the multiprocessing capability of Apache (currently implemented in Unix by one server process per client connection, and in Win32 as one thread per client) into *multiple-processing modules* (MPMs). These are responsible for mapping client requests to either a thread or a process, making it possible for one set of Apache code to work on multiple platforms. Initially, version 2.0 will include MPMs for several different process-forking schemes in Unix and MPMs for NT and OS/2. On Unix systems that support POSIX-compliant threads, there is a new mode of operation for Apache called a *hybrid mode*. This enhancement is designed to improve the scalability of Apache, not necessarily the performance or stability of the server, and will make no difference at the majority of installed Apache sites.

The second change is also intended for programmers and is designed to increase the cross-platform portability of code written to support Apache. Apache 2.0 will be packaged with an application program interface (API) implemented in an Apache Portable Runtime (APR) layer. The APR completely masks fundamental differences in the way platforms

Part vi

handle things like process forking and socket connections. Programmers working on Apache 2.0 and later versions will need only to ensure that they program to the APR to ensure that their programs, or modules, run on all supported platforms. For example, using the APR, a programmer will not really have to know the details of how processes are forked in both Unix and NT, where the system calls are quite different. The programmer will need to learn only how to spawn or fork a process in the APR to produce code that works identically on both platforms.

The third change to Apache in version 2.0, and the one that most affects us as systems administrators, is in the way that Apache modules register *callbacks*, or functions, with the Apache server. Here again, while the details of the changes in 2.0 are germane only to the Apache programmer, the implications of this change directly affect all Apache server administrators because modules written for Apache 1.3 will not work with 2.0 without modification. Before moving your site to Apache 2.0, carefully ensure that you have 2.0 versions of all the Apache modules you'll require. Ports of the core modules will probably be released along with version 2.0, but third-party modules may not be modified immediately.

Apache 2.0 incorporates changes that the Apache Software Foundation and the principal Apache developers consider essential to maintaining the viability of the Apache server in an increasingly commercial Internet. A move to Apache 2.0 will be essential to any Apache site that wants to remain on the leading edge. The question is *when would be the best time to upgrade to Apache 2.0?* As with all software in production use, the answer to that question is determined by the features that will improve your site with added capabilities or increased performance. Simply upgrading to have the very latest version is a time-consuming, frustrating, never-ending exercise. Consider all the angles before making your decision to update.

What's Next?

In this chapter, we looked at what web server software powers the Internet and determined that 60 percent of all Internet-accessible web servers are running Apache. Only on the very largest Internet sites does Apache yield prominence to commercial engines, for reasons that probably have less to do with the suitability of Apache than with the fact that many large firms are still reluctant to rely on open-source software (an attitude that is rapidly eroding). The major web servers that compete with Apache have some strong features, but the features of Apache show why Apache is dominant.

This chapter has served as an extended introduction to Apache and its foundations. Beginning in the next chapter, we'll (metaphorically) roll up our sleeves and start getting our fingernails dirty—that is, we'll install the server on a Linux system. Then, in succeeding chapters, we'll move on to various aspects of configuring Apache.

Part vi

Chapter 24

INSTALLING APACHE

The previous chapter introduced Apache as well as other web servers commonly used on the Internet. The topics of installing, configuring, and administering Apache begin here, in this chapter.

One of the important things to realize about installing Apache is that there are two completely different ways to do it. You can download the source code and compile it on your own machine, or you can take the easier route and download binary files that have already been compiled for your machine and operating system.

Both methods of installation have merit, and both are discussed in this chapter, with step-by-step examples of the procedures that you should use on your own Linux system. The installation of a basic Apache server is a straightforward process. Follow the instructions in this chapter, regardless of which method of installation you choose, and soon you'll have a working Apache server, ready to configure.

Adapted from *Linux Apache Web Server Administration* by Charles Aulds

ISBN 0-7821-2734-7   640 pages $39.99

THE DECISION TO COMPILE

Before proceeding, determine whether it makes sense to compile the Apache code yourself. There are some very good reasons to start with the source code to create your own copy of Apache.

One of the reasons most often cited for the success of open-source software such as Apache and Linux is that the source code is available for inspection and modification. That's certainly an enticement for C code hackers and for companies with the programming resources to customize the code. The vast majority of us, however, don't write customized Apache code. Instead, we benefit from the code improvements made by others.

Compiling Apache from the source code makes it possible to add user-written modifications (or *patches*) to the code. Patches are essentially files that contain changes to a source code base and are usually created by *diffing* modified source to the original; in other words, comparing the modified and original source files and saving the differences in a file distributed as a *patch*. Another user acquires the patch, applies it to the same source code base to reproduce the modifications, and then compiles the altered source.

Patches make it possible for nonprogrammers to make changes (often, quite sophisticated ones) to source code and then compile it themselves. Without the ability to patch the source and compile it yourself, you need to search for precompiled binaries that already include the necessary patches. Depending on your particular platform, it might be difficult to locate binaries that include the patches you require.

Another reason to compile from source code is that it allows you to take advantage of compiler optimizations for your hardware platform and operating system. This consideration is by no means as important as it was once, because chances are you can easily find binaries for your particular system. Table 24.1 shows the binary distributions of Apache available from the Apache Project website for a variety of platforms. In the unlikely circumstance that your operating system is missing from this list, you can always download and compile the Apache source yourself.

TABLE 24.1:   Apache Binary Distributions

NAME	LAST MODIFIED
aix	20-June-2001
aux	06-May-2000
beos	02-Nov-2000
bs2000-osd	23-Jan-2001
bsdi	18-Oct-2000
cygwin	12-Jun-2001
darwin	12-Jun-2001
dgux	12-Jun-2000
digitalunix	12-Jun-2000
freebsd	31-May-2001
hpux	20-Jun-2001
irix	13-Oct-2000
linux	20-Jun-2001
macosx	10-Apr-2001
macsxserver	30-Oct-2000
netbsd	12-Jun-2000
netware	21-May-2001
openbsd	13-Oct-2000
os2	19-May-2001
os390	03-Aug-2000
osf1	12-Jun-2000
qnx	31-May-2001
reliantunix	22-May-2001
rhapsody	30-Oct-2000
sinix	22-May-2001
solaris	20-Jun-2001
sunos	24-Feb-2000
unixware	13-Oct-2000
win32	17-Jul-2001

Part vi

It is not necessary to compile source code on your own hardware to optimize the resulting binary. Most binaries are already optimized for a given type of hardware. For example, to run on an Intel 486 or Pentium system, download an i386 binary or an i686 binary for the Pentium II or Pentium III processor. A compiler designed to optimize code to run on an Intel processor was probably used to create the binary. It is unlikely that your compiler will produce code that performs significantly better. Some companies offer Linux distributions that are optimized for performance on Pentium-class Intel processors (Mandrake Linux is one such distribution: www.linux-mandrake.com). If the fastest possible system performance is your goal, you should consider such a Linux distribution teamed with more or faster hardware.

One word of warning about using binaries is in order. Often, the available binaries lag behind new releases. If you want to stay on the "bleeding edge" of changes, you must use source code distributions, which is not always the best decision for production servers.

In sum:

▶ Use an Apache binary distribution when you need a basic Apache server with the Apache modules included in that distribution. All standard Apache modules are included with these binary distributions, compiled separately from the server as DSO modules. You can pick and choose the ones you want, using only those that you require and disabling the others to conserve the memory required to run Apache. If all the functionality you require is available in the set of standard Apache modules and your operating system is supported, you have nothing to lose by installing one of these. Even if you require a few modules not included with the binary distribution, most of these are easily compiled separately from the Apache server itself without requiring the Apache source. A few, however, require that the Apache source be patched and that you have the source code available on your system. It is impossible to install these modules without the Apache source code; you won't find them in an Apache binary distribution.

▶ Compile the Apache server source code whenever you need functionality that requires patching the original source code (Secure Sockets Layer [SSL] is an example of such a module or server extension). You will also need to compile the Apache source if you intend to write your own modules.

If you can work with precompilcd binaries, feel free to skip the material on compiling Apache. It will always be here if you need it in the future. If you have decided to compile the Apache source code, take a look at the next section; otherwise, you can jump ahead to the "Installing the Apache Binaries" section.

DOWNLOADING APACHE SOURCE

Download the source code for Apache by pointing your web browser at www.apache.org/dist or one of its mirror sites (see Figure 24.1). Download the latest Apache, which will be in Unix tar format, compressed with the GNU Zip (gzip, or simply gz) utility. The latest Apache source code archive is named apache_1.3.20.tar.Z.

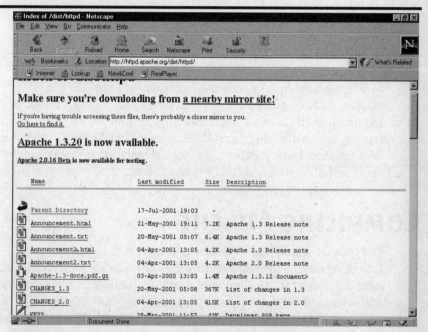

FIGURE 24.1: The Apache source code distribution site

Change directory to where you intend to unpack the Apache source code and compile the server. A common location for source code on Linux systems is the /usr/local/src directory, and that's a pretty logical choice. If you want to place the Apache source in a subdirectory of /usr/local/src, do the following:

```
# cd /usr/local/src
```

From this directory, invoke the Linux tar utility to decompress the archive and extract the files. Tar will automatically create the necessary directories. When the operation is finished, you will have the Apache source saved in the directory /usr/local/src/apache_1.3.20:

```
# tar xvzf /home/caulds/apache_1.3.20.tar.gz

apache_1.3.20/

apache_1.3.20/src/

apache_1.3.20/src/ap/

apache_1.3.20/src/ap/.indent.pro

apache_1.3.20/src/ap/Makefile.tmpl

apache_1.3.20/src/ap/ap.dsp

apache_1.3.20/src/ap/ap.mak

    many files extracted
```

The top-level Apache source directory is /usr/local/src/apache_1.3.12, and I'll refer to this as the Apache source directory frequently in the book. If you install Apache from source, you'll return frequently to this directory, to make changes to your Apache installation. This directory is distinct from the Apache installation directory, where you'll install Apache and from where you'll run it.

COMPILING APACHE

Old (pre-1.3) versions of Apache could only be compiled the old-fashioned way: by manually editing the Configuration.tmpl file, running the ./configure command, and then running the make utility. An editor was used to customize the compiler flags (EXTRA_CFLAGS, LIBS, LDFLAGS, INCLUDES) stored in the template as needed for a given system. Thank goodness there is now a better way.

All recent versions of Apache include the APACI configuration utility. Although some administrators insist that configuring the Apache compilation manually gives them better control over the compiler switches and installation options, I disagree. APACI is the installation method preferred by the Apache development team; it is the easiest way to compile Apache, and it is the best way to maintain your Apache source code, especially if you've altered it by applying source patches and a number of third-party modules (see Chapter 26, "Apache Modules"). It is probably best to learn only one way to configure Apache compilation options. If you're going to learn only one method, it is best to learn the APACI installation method.

Using APACI

With Apache version 1.3, a new configuration module was introduced with the Apache source distribution. The APache AutoConf-style Interface (APACI) is a configuration utility similar to the GNU Autoconf package, although it is not based on that popular GNU utility. APACI provides an easy way to configure the Apache source prior to compilation in order to specify certain compiler options and the inclusion (or exclusion) of Apache modules. Like GNU Autoconf, APACI also performs a number of tests in order to ascertain details about your system hardware and operating system that are relevant to the Apache source compilation.

APACI does not compile the Apache source; its purpose is to create the files that specify how that compilation is performed. Its most important task is to create the *makefiles* that are used by the Linux make utility to direct the C compiler how to proceed, and also where to place the compiled programs when make is instructed to perform an install.

THE NEED FOR ANSI-C

The Apache source code is written in C language that is compliant with the specifications codified by the American National Standards Institute, or ANSI-C. For that reason, you will need an ANSI-C–compliant compiler to complete the install. This is not a big deal, because your Linux distribution includes the GNU C compiler (GCC), which is the ANSI-C compiler recommended by the Apache Software Foundation. If APACI is unable to locate a suitable compiler, you will be notified, and the configuration will abort. You can then install GCC from your Linux CD-ROM or from www.gnu.org. The Free Software Foundation makes binary distributions available for Linux and a large number of Unix platforms, or you can download and compile the source code yourself, although compiling GCC can turn into a time-consuming exercise. Binary distributions of GCC are well optimized, so it is unlikely that you can build a more efficient C compiler.

The *configure* Script

The heart of APACI is a shell script named `configure`, which you'll find in the top-level Apache source directory. This script does not compile the Apache server; its function is to examine your system to identify its capabilities and locate the supporting files it needs. The `configure` script may warn you that it can't build Apache and give instructions on how to correct problems it finds. On most systems running a fairly recent version of Linux, this will not occur. Once `configure` determines that it can build Apache on your system, it then identifies the best possible combination of options for that system. The information it gathers and the decisions it makes about configuring Apache for your system are written into a special file that you'll find stored in `src/Configuration.apaci`. In this file it stores information specific to your system (including build options you specify to `configure`).

The last step that the `configure` script takes is to run a second script, which you'll find as `src/Configure`. This script takes the information from `src/Configuration.apaci` and uses it to create a set of files that control the actual compilation and installation of Apache (using the make utility on your Linux system). You'll find these makefiles created in a number of the Apache source directories.

You will usually run `configure` with a number of options (command-line arguments) to customize your Apache configuration. In fact, if you run `configure` with no command-line arguments, it will report, "Warning: Configuring Apache with default settings. This is probably not what you really want," and it probably isn't. The next few sections will show you how to specify additional options to `configure` or override its default values. This is a procedure you'll return to many times, whenever you need to alter your Apache configuration or change its functionality by adding new modules. The following `configure` statement compiles Apache version 1.3.20. Note that this is a single Linux command with three arguments; the backslash (\) character is used to continue the command on a new line. It's a handy trick for manually entering long command lines and can also be used to improve the readability of shell script files.

```
# ./configure --prefix=/usr/local/apache \
> --enable-module=most \
> --disable-module=auth_dbm \   > --enable-shared=max
```

The --prefix argument in the example above tells Apache to install itself in the directory /usr/local/apache. (This is the default installation location for Apache, so in this case the option is unnecessary.) However, there are many times you may want to install into an alternate directory—for example, if you do not want to install a second Apache version alongside one that already exists (I have five versions of Apache on my server for testing purposes). Another reason you may want to install Apache into an alternate directory is to preserve the default locations used by a Linux distribution. For example, assume the version of Apache that comes with your Linux distribution is installed in /etc/apache instead of the default /usr/local/apache directory. Use --prefix to install Apache in the /etc/apache directory. (For standard file location layouts, see the section "The *config.layout* File," later in this chapter.)

Linux systems can use --enable-module=all to enable all modules in the standard distribution. The --enable-module=most option enables all the standard modules in the Apache distribution that are usable on all platforms supported by Apache. Table 24.2 lists the modules that are not installed when you specify --enable-module=most, along with the reason they are not used. Red Hat Linux 7.0 users will not be able to compile Apache with mod_auth_dbm and should use the --disable-module=auth_dbm directive to disable use of that module. Users of other Linux distributions (or earlier Red Hat distributions) who wish to use the module can omit the directive. Table 24.4 later in this chapter lists all of the standard modules included in the 1.3.20 release of Apache.

TABLE 24.2:   Apache Modules Omitted by *--enable-module=most*

MODULE	REASON FOR OMITTING
mod_auth_db	Some platforms may not support Berkeley DB.
mod_mmap_static	Some platforms do not support memory-mapped files.
mod_so=no	Some platforms do not support dynamic loading of modules.
mod_example	This module is only for programmers and isn't required on production servers.
mod_auth_digest	This module conflicts with mod_digest.
mod_log_agent	This module has been replaced by mod_log_config.
mod_log_referer	This module has been replaced by mod_log_config.

Part vi

On Linux systems, I recommend specifying `--enable-module=most` and then manually adding any modules from Table 24.2 that you require. To enable support for DSOs, for example, add the `--enable-shared=max` option, which causes Apache to build all modules as *dynamic shared objects* (DSOs), with the exception of two, `http_core` and `mod_so`, both of which must be statically linked into the Apache kernel. The `http_core` module provides core directives for managing the Apache server, and `mod_so` enables the server to use DSO modules.

Throughout the book, as I discuss adding modules, I'll describe how to use additional arguments to `configure` to alter the way Apache is built. For Linux systems, I consider the following command line sufficient to build a suitable Apache system:

```
./configure --enable-module=most --enable-shared=max"
```

WHY USE DSOs?

The extension of Apache Server through the use of modules has always been part of its design, but it wasn't until release 1.3 that Apache supported dynamic loadable modules. These dynamic shared objects are available in Apache on Linux and other operating systems that support the necessary system functions for a program to load a module into its address space with a system call. This is similar to the way dynamic link library (DLL) files work in Microsoft Windows; in fact, DLLs are used to provide this functionality in the Windows version of Apache.

The use of DSO modules in Apache has several advantages. First, the server can be far more flexible because modules can be enabled or disabled at runtime, without the need to relink the Apache kernel. The exclusion of unnecessary modules reduces the size of the Apache executable, which can be a factor when many server instances are run in limited memory space.

On Linux systems, the only significant disadvantage to the use of DSO modules is that the server is approximately 20 percent slower to load at startup time, because of the system overhead of resolving the symbol table for the dynamic links. This is generally not a factor unless Apache is run in inetd mode (see Chapter 25, "The Apache Core Directives"), where a new instance of HTTPD is spawned to handle each incoming client connection.

In most cases, Linux administrators should build their Apache server to make maximum use of DSO modules.

A Sample *configure* Run

Using the configure command, the compilation will proceed as shown in Listing 24.1. (The output is far too long to reproduce here, and much of it is repetitive, so it has been edited to suit this text.)

Listing 24.1: Compiling Apache with the *configure* Command

```
# ./configure --prefix=/usr/local/apache \
> --enable-module=most \
> --disable-module=auth_dbm \
> --enable-shared=max
Configuring for Apache, Version 1.3.20
 + using installation path layout: Apache (config.layout)
Creating Makefile
Creating Configuration.apaci in src
 + enabling mod_so for DSO support
Creating Makefile in src
 + configured for Linux platform
 + setting C compiler to gcc
 + setting C pre-processor to gcc -E
 + checking for system header files
 + adding selected modules
    o rewrite_module uses ConfigStart/End
 + using -lndbm for DBM support
       enabling DBM support for mod_rewrite
    o dbm_auth_module uses ConfigStart/End

-- Many deleted lines --

make[2]: Leaving directory
'/usr/local/src/apache_1.3.20/src/support'
<=== src/support
make[1]: Leaving directory '/usr/local/src/apache_1.3.20'
<=== src
```

The configure script essentially creates a set of instructions to the compiler for compiling the source files into a working system. It uses information you provide, along with other information about the capabilities of your system, such as what function libraries are available. The result is primarily a set of makefiles, which instruct the Linux make utility how to compile source files, link them to required function libraries, and install them in their proper locations.

The *config.status* File

Whenever you run the `configure` script, it creates a file with the name
`config.status` in the Apache source directory (or overwrites the file if
it already exists). This file is actually a shell script that contains the last
command line used to successfully run `configure` and typically looks
like the one in Listing 24.2.

Listing 24.2: A Typical *config.status* File

```
# cat config.status
#!/bin/sh
##
## config.status -- APACI auto-generated configuration
   restore script
##
## Use this shell script to re-run the APACI configure
   script for
## restoring your configuration. Additional parameters can
   be supplied.
##

SSL_BASE="/usr/local/src/openssl-0.9.5" \
./configure \
"--with-layout=Apache" \
"--prefix=/usr/local/apache" \
"--enable-module=most" \
"--disable-module=auth_dbm" \
"--enable-module=ssl" \
"--activate-module=src/modules/extra/mod_define.c" \
"--enable-shared=max" \
"$@"
```

There are a few lines here that have been added since I showed the minimal set of options required to compile a full working Apache server. The
SSL_BASE line, which actually precedes the invocation of the `configure`
utility, sets an environment variable that points to the OpenSSL source.
This environment variable will be used later by the Secure Sockets Layer
(SSL) module, which is enabled by the line `--enable-module=ssl`. The
`--activate-module` line is used to compile a third-party module and
statically link it into Apache from a source file previously placed in the
location designated for these "extra" modules. You can also use another
option, `--add-module`, to copy a module source file into this directory

before compiling and statically linking it to the server. This option saves you only the copy step, however, so it isn't terribly useful:

```
--add-module=/home/caulds/mod_include/mod_include.c
```

A great benefit of the config.status file is that it saves your hard-won knowledge.

You can rerun the last configure command at any time simply by ensuring that this file is executable by its owner (probably root) and invoking it as follows:

```
# chmod u+x config.status
# ./config.status
```

Although the config.status file contains many lines, all of them (except for comments and the last line) end in a backslash character, which indicates that the lines should be concatenated and passed as a single command to the shell interpreter. The last line, $@, concatenates to the end of the command line any argument passed to config.status when it is executed. You might run config.status, for example, with an additional option:

```
# ./config.status "--activate-module=src/modules/auth_mysql/
   libauth_mysql.a"
```

In this case, the portion of the command line enclosed in quotes is substituted for $@ in the config.status script and concatenated to the command line passed to /bin/sh for processing.

You can modify config.status and rerun it to add, remove, or change the order of the arguments. This order is often significant. For example, I discovered that, to use the --enable-shared option (which specifies compilation of modules as dynamic shared objects), you must include this option after all --enable-module and --activate-module arguments. I learned this the hard way. But once I did learn how to do it right, I had the config.status file to retain that information for later use. Unfortunately, determining the precedence of configure options is largely a matter of trial and error.

I prefer to copy the config.status file to another filename. This ensures that the file I use to configure Apache won't be accidentally overwritten if I run configure to test other options. After running configure, you may want to do something like the following:

```
# cp config.status build.sh
# chmod u+x build.sh
```

Part vi

This creates a brand-new file (a shell script) named `build.sh`, which can be edited and then executed to reconfigure Apache. I have used the same `build.sh` over and over again during the course of writing this book, with several versions of Apache, modifying it as needed to enable or disable modules or install locations.

The *config.layout* File

The paths that Apache uses to locate files during compilation and to determine where to move files during the installation are stored in a special configuration file named `config.layout`, which you will find in the Apache source directory. This file contains collections of directory paths to be used as defaults on different types of systems. Each of these collections is identified by a system name, and so they are called *named layouts.* When you run `configure`, Apache attempts to guess the operating system using a helper script, `src/helpers/GuessOS`. If its best guess matches the name of one of the named layouts, it uses that layout to determine the correct path information. Otherwise, it uses the Apache default setup, which is defined in `config.layout` as layout "Apache." The Apache layout is shown in Listing 24.3.

Listing 24.3: The Apache Path Layout in *config.layout*

```
#   Classical Apache path layout.
<Layout Apache>
    prefix:        /usr/local/apache
    exec_prefix:   $prefix
    bindir:        $exec_prefix/bin
    sbindir:       $exec_prefix/bin
    libexecdir:    $exec_prefix/libexec
    mandir:        $prefix/man
    sysconfdir:    $prefix/conf
    datadir:       $prefix
    iconsdir:      $datadir/icons
    htdocsdir:     $datadir/htdocs
    cgidir:        $datadir/cgi-bin
    includedir:    $prefix/include
    localstatedir: $prefix
    runtimedir:    $localstatedir/logs
    logfiledir:    $localstatedir/logs
    proxycachedir: $localstatedir/proxy
</Layout>
```

Each line of `config.layout` defines a directory pathname. Some of the paths are derived from others previously defined in the file. You might note from this layout that all the paths are derived from the one identified as `prefix`. Therefore, simply by running `configure` with the `--prefix` argument to change this location, you automatically change *all* of the default paths for the Apache installation.

You can specify a named layout when running `configure` by using the `--with-layout` argument. For example, if you use the same file locations that Red Hat Linux uses, specify `configure` with the `--with-layout=RedHat` argument:

```
# ./configure --with-layout=RedHat
```

It's important to realize that `config.layout` is a convenience and is used to provide a single location in which a number of directory paths are set. Apache will store data in these directories (or expect to find it there).

If you want to change any of these paths, you can modify `config.layout` creating a custom layout as described later, or you can override and change any default with a separate `configure` option. Table 24.3 lists all of the `configure` options used to set Apache's paths.

TABLE 24.3: *configure* Options to Set Apache's Paths

OPTION	SPECIFIES LOCATION FOR
`--bindir=DIR`	User executables
`--sbindir=DIR`	System executables
`--libexecdir=DIR`	Supporting libraries (DSO modules)
`--mandir=DIR`	Apache manual (man) pages
`--sysconfdir=DIR`	Configuration files (`httpd.conf`)
`--datadir=DIR`	Read-only data files
`--iconsdir=DIR`	Image files used by Apache
`--htdocsdir=DIR`	Read-only document files
`--cgidir=DIR`	Read-only CGI files
`--includedir=DIR`	Include files
`--localstatedir=DIR`	Writeable data files
`--runtimedir=DIR`	Runtime data
`--logfiledir=DIR`	Apache log files
`--proxycachedir=DIR`	Proxy cache data

Part vi

The following example uses path variables as configure arguments to install all of Apache's user executables in /usr/bin and all system executables in /usr/sbin, which is where the Red Hat layout puts them. All other layout options are read from the Apache layout in config.layout. The following command accomplishes the same thing as the custom layout shown in Listing 24.5, later in this chapter:

```
# ./configure --bindir=/usr/bin --sbindir=/usr/sbin
```

For those readers who are using the Red Hat Linux distribution, the Apache that is provided as a Red Hat Package Manager (RPM) uses a layout that looks like this:

```
#   RedHat 5.x layout
<Layout RedHat>
        prefix:         /usr
        exec_prefix:    $prefix
        bindir:         $prefix/bin
        sbindir:        $prefix/sbin
        libexecdir:     $prefix/lib/apache
        mandir:         $prefix/man
        sysconfdir:     /etc/httpd/conf
        datadir:        /home/httpd
        iconsdir:       $datadir/icons
        htdocsdir:      $datadir/html
        cgidir:         $datadir/cgi-bin
        includedir:     $prefix/include/apache
        localstatedir:  /var
        runtimedir:     $localstatedir/run
        logfiledir:     $localstatedir/log/httpd
        proxycachedir:  $localstatedir/cache/httpd
</Layout>
```

Note that all paths are altered because the Red Hat layout modifies the Apache prefix variable, and because all depend on prefix. The Red Hat layout actually tries to put files into more standard directories. Rather than storing Apache binaries in a special directory (such as /usr/local/apache/bin), Red Hat places them in the Linux directories that are actually reserved for them, /usr/bin and /usr/sbin. Likewise, Red Hat prefers to keep Apache configuration files under /etc, a directory in which you'll find configuration files for a large number of other Linux utilities, such as FTP, DNS, sendmail, and others.

Viewing the Layout *configure* Will Use

If you're planning to alter the paths that configure will use, you'll want to see which layout configure will choose and then either make a copy of that layout to edit and rename it or simply edit that layout in config.layout. Running configure with the --show-layout argument prints the layout that configure intends to use and the paths it reads from that layout. Listing 24.4 shows typical output.

Listing 24.4: Using *--show-layout* with the *configure* Command

```
# ./configure --show-layout
Configuring for Apache, Version 1.3.20
 + using installation path layout: Apache (config.layout)

Installation paths:
             prefix: /usr/local/apache
        exec_prefix: /usr/local/apache

             bindir: /usr/local/apache/bin
            sbindir: /usr/local/apache/bin
         libexecdir: /usr/local/apache/libexec
             mandir: /usr/local/apache/man
          sysconfdir: /usr/local/apache/conf
            datadir: /usr/local/apache
           iconsdir: /usr/local/apache/icons
          htdocsdir: /usr/local/apache/htdocs
             cgidir: /usr/local/apache/cgi-bin
         includedir: /usr/local/apache/include
       localstatedir: /usr/local/apache
          runtimedir: /usr/local/apache/logs
          logfiledir: /usr/local/apache/logs
       proxycachedir: /usr/local/apache/proxy

  Compilation paths:
           HTTPD_ROOT: /usr/local/apache
      SHARED_CORE_DIR: /usr/local/apache/libexec
```

```
     DEFAULT_PIDLOG: logs/httpd.pid
 DEFAULT_SCOREBOARD: logs/httpd.scoreboard
   DEFAULT_LOCKFILE: logs/httpd.lock
    DEFAULT_XFERLOG: logs/access_log
   DEFAULT_ERRORLOG: logs/error_log
  TYPES_CONFIG_FILE: conf/mime.types
 SERVER_CONFIG_FILE: conf/httpd.conf
 ACCESS_CONFIG_FILE: conf/access.conf
RESOURCE_CONFIG_FILE: conf/srm.conf
SSL_CERTIFICATE_FILE: conf/ssl.crt/server.crt
```

At the very least, --show-layout is a convenient way to find out where Apache puts all the files. Because it expands variables, it is more readable than looking directly in the file. Whether you should use it to modify default settings directly is debatable. Many administrators consider it safer to use the information displayed by --show-layout to build a new layout, as described in the next section. Whether you work with the default layout or a copy, editing a named layout has the advantage that you can change the default path values that configure uses without specifying your changes as arguments to the configure command. All the settings are visible in one place, and since you modify only those you want to change in a given layout, you don't have to do a lot of work in most cases.

Creating and Using a Custom Layout

The best way to modify an Apache layout is to create a custom layout of your own, copying another layout, renaming it, and making your modifications to a custom layout that you will use during the Apache compilation by giving it a name of your choosing. This is what I recommend, and Listing 24.5 shows a custom layout that I have used named MyLayout. I modified the standard Apache layout and made two changes, to put the Apache executables in the same locations as the Red Hat layout shown in Listing 24.4. I'm running a Red Hat system, and this places them where Red Hat's startup files expect to find them.

As noted, many administrators consider it inherently risky to edit the default layout directly; they prefer to leave the original layout values intact and work on a copy. Apache's use of named layouts makes it easy to follow this approach. You might add a layout to config.layout like the one shown in Listing 24.5.

Listing 24.5: A Custom Path Layout

```
<Layout MyLayout>
    prefix:          /usr/local/apache
    exec_prefix:     $prefix
# Use all Apache layout options,
# but install user and system
# executables as Red Hat does
    bindir:          /usr/bin
    sbindir:         /usr/sbin
# end of changes from Apache layout
    libexecdir:      $exec_prefix/libexec
    mandir:          $prefix/man
    sysconfdir:      $prefix/conf
    datadir:         $prefix
    iconsdir:        $datadir/icons
    htdocsdir:       $datadir/htdocs
    cgidir:          $datadir/cgi-bin
    includedir:      $prefix/include
    localstatedir:   $prefix
    runtimedir:      $localstatedir/logs
    logfiledir:      $localstatedir/logs
    proxycachedir:   $localstatedir/proxy
</Layout>
```

To use the new custom layout, run configure with the --with-layout argument, and compile:

```
# ./configure --with-layout=MyLayout
```

The Other *configure* Command Options

You can get a complete list of all configure options by running the command with its --help argument. All of the variables that are used as named layout options are available, as well as all of the configuration options discussed earlier. The options I've shown are probably the only configure options that you'll ever need to use, but there are several others with far more specific purposes. For example, the --enable-rule option is used to enable certain compiler rules to enable Apache to compile on certain systems (Linux users will never need this). There are also a number of options that deal with suEXEC (which is discussed in Chapter 25).

Making Apache

Upon completion of the configuration phase, you have constructed a set of makefiles in various places within your Apache source tree. The make command is used to begin the actual compilation phase of the install:

```
# make
===> src
make[1]: Entering directory `/usr/local/src/apache_1.3.20'
make[2]: Entering directory `/usr/local/src/apache_1.3.20/src'

-- Many lines deleted --
```

The final step of the install is to call make again, this time with the install argument, which moves all the compiled binaries and support files to their default locations (or locations you specified in the configuration step above). Most files are copied into directories relative to the Apache root directory that you specified with the --prefix argument:

```
# make install
make[1]: Entering directory'/usr/local/src/apache_1.3.20'
===> [mktree: Creating Apache installation tree]

-- Lines deleted
+-----------------------------------------------------------+
| You now have successfully built and installed the         |
| Apache 1.3 HTTP server. To verify that Apache actually     |
| works correctly you now should first check the            |
| (initially created or preserved) configuration files      |
|                                                           |
|    /usr/local/apache/conf/httpd.conf                      |
|                                                           |
| and then you should be able to immediately fire up        |
| Apache the first time by running:                         |
|                                                           |
|    /usr/local/apache/bin/apachectl start                  |
|                                                           |
| Thanks for using Apache.          The Apache Group        |
|                             http://www.apache.org/        |
+-----------------------------------------------------------+
```

With the appearance of the message above, you have installed an Apache system that should run after you make a few simple changes to its configuration file.

An optional step you can take is to reduce the size of the Apache executable using the Linux `strip` command. This command removes symbolic information that is used only by debuggers and other developer tools. For a production version of the Apache kernel, this information can be stripped to reduce the memory required by the server. The reduction is slight, but if you are running a number of Apache processes, the savings add up. Running `strip` on a freshly compiled Apache 1.3.20 executable reduced its size by about 14 percent. Be aware that once you `strip` symbol information from a binary file, you can no longer run debugging tools if you have problems running that program.

```
# ls -al httpd
-rwxr-xr-x  1 root     root        461015 Dec  6 11:23 httpd
# strip httpd
# ls -al httpd
-rwxr-xr-x  1 root     root        395516 Dec  6 11:46 httpd
```

If you compile Apache from source code, feel free to skip down to the section "Running the Server." That's where you'll learn to start the server.

Installing the Apache Binaries

Compiling Apache from source code is so easy, especially for Linux, that it should be your choice of installation method if you plan to make any alterations to the out-of-the-box Apache configuration. If you plan to add third-party modules that are not compiled as DSOs or if you plan to modify your server to support SSL, you have no choice; you *must* work with the Apache source code and compile it yourself.

On the other hand, if you need only a simple server, which is used primarily to distribute static HTML pages or other documents and has little if any user input or server-side programming, there are two much quicker ways to get up and running. If you are not concerned with implementing specialized modules that aren't among those provided with the standard Apache distribution, consider using one of two alternatives to compiling Apache. The first of these is to install Apache precompiled binaries using a Linux package manager; the second method is to download binary distributions from a trustworthy source such as the Apache Software Foundation. Both methods are described in the following sections.

Which Modules Are Included?

In deciding whether to install from the RPM or source distribution, you'll probably want to know which modules each one includes. Table 24.4 lists the Apache modules that are provided with the RPM and those included in the binary distribution for Linux made available on the Apache website (`www.apache.org/dist/httpd/binaries/linux`). The first column lists all the standard modules; the second and third columns indicate which of these are enabled as dynamically loadable modules by default when you install Apache. The Red Hat RPM and the Apache binary distribution differ slightly, probably because of differing ideas about what is important to Red Hat Linux users. This list is based on release 1.3.20.

Note that if you install Apache with Red Hat Linux, you'll get some freebies—the last three listed modules are installed from separate RPMs and provide PHP and Perl programming support for your web server.

TABLE 24.4:   Apache Modules Provided with the Red Hat RPM and with the Apache Binary Distribution

MODULE	1.3.20 RPM	1.3.20 BINARY
libproxy.so	X	X
mod_access	X	X
mod_actions	X	X
mod_alias	X	X
mod_asis	X	X
mod_auth	X	X
mod_auth_anon	X	X
mod_auth_db	X	
mod_auth_dbm		X
mod_auth_digest	X	
mod_autoindex	X	X
mod_bandwidth	X	
mod_cern_meta	X	X
mod_cgi	X	X
mod_digest	X	X
mod_dir	X	X

TABLE 24.4 continued: Apache Modules Provided with the Red Hat RPM and with the Apache Binary Distribution

MODULE	1.3.20 RPM	1.3.20 BINARY
mod_env	X	X
mod_example	X	
mod_expires	X	X
mod_headers	X	X
mod_imap	X	X
mod_include	X	X
mod_info	X	X
mod_log_agent	X	
mod_log_config	X	X
mod_log_referer	X	
mod_mime	X	X
mod_mime_magic	X	X
mod_mmap_static	X	
mod_negotiation	X	X
mod_put	X	
mod_rewrite	X	X
mod_setenvif	X	X
mod_speling	X	X
mod_status	X	X
mod_throttle	X	
mod_unique_id	X	X
mod_userdir	X	X
mod_usertrack	X	X
mod_vhost_alias	X	X
mod_php	*	Not incl
mod_php3	*	Not incl
mod_perl	*	Not incl

* installed from separate RPMs by the Red Hat Linux installation program

Red Hat Package Manager

For Linux users, there is probably no better way to install compiled programs than a package manager. The most widely used of these is the Red Hat Package Manager (RPM). RPM was originally developed by Red Hat (www.redhat.com) for inclusion in its Linux distribution. RPM packs a set of files into a single package, usually a file with the .rpm extension. This file can then be transferred to any other system and unpacked to reproduce the files in the exact location where they were found on the source system, creating directories where necessary. Traditionally, this is done with tar in the Unix world, and most source code is still distributed in so-called *tarballs*. RPM is better. It can manage all the packages installed on your system, it can use newer packages to upgrade those already installed, it can cleanly uninstall packages, and it can even verify the installed files against the RPM database. Verification is useful because it detects changes that might have been made accidentally or deliberately by an intruder.

True to the spirit of open-source software, Red Hat donated RPM to the public domain, and many other Linux distributions have the capability to load RPM files. Red Hat, SuSE, Mandrake, TurboLinux, and Caldera OpenLinux are all RPM Linux distributions. Although other package managers exist for Linux, RPM is the most widely used, and more packages are available as RPMs than in any other format.

NOTE

If your Linux doesn't support RPM, you can add that support yourself. In keeping with the spirit of open source, and as a way of encouraging other Linux developers to use RPM, the source is no longer distributed by Red Hat (although you may be able to find it on Red Hat's website). The source files are available from the www.rpm.org FTP server at ftp://ftp.rpm.org/pub/rpm. This site also contains a wealth of information about using the Red Hat Package Manager. You'll find not only the source for all versions of RPM ever released, but also precompiled binary distributions for Intel 386 and Sparc platforms. For most versions of Linux, adding your own RPM support will not be necessary.

The best source for RPMs that I've ever found is the RPM repository on rpmfind.net (http://www.rpmfind.net/linux/RPM). Figure 24.2 illustrates the RPM site after we've chosen the option to view the index by name. There are numerous packages for Apache 1.3.20, so to make a choice we need more information about them. Figure 24.3 shows the detailed display for apache-1_3_20-8_i386.src.rpm.

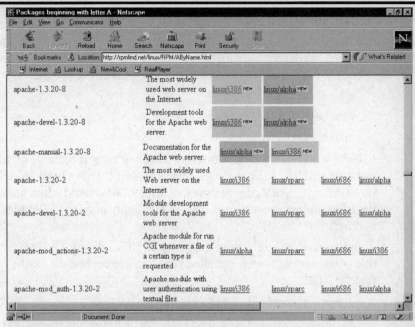

FIGURE 24.2: A sampling from the `rpmfind.net` RPM repository

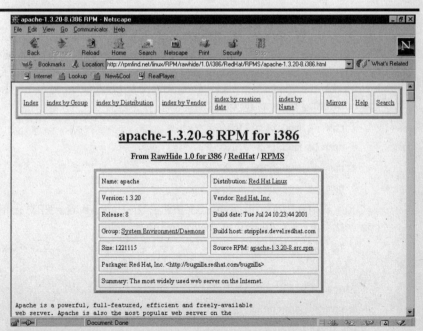

FIGURE 24.3: The `rpmfind.net` display for Apache 1.3.20

Before installing the Apache 1.3.20 RPM on my Linux system, I removed the existing Apache RPM that was installed when I loaded the Red Hat distribution. Run RPM with the -qa argument, which says "query all installed packages," to determine which Apache RPMs are installed. Pipe the output to grep to display only those lines containing the string apache:

```
# rpm -qa |grep apache
apache-1.3.6-7
apache-devel-1.3.6-7
```

The -e argument to rpm erases an RPM package. It removes all files installed with the RPM package, unless those files have been modified. Uninstalling an RPM also removes all directories created when installing the RPM, unless those directories are not empty after the RPM files are removed.

In this example, removing the installed RPMs failed. The error warns that other packages were installed after and are dependent on the Apache RPM:

```
# rpm -e apache-1.3.6-7
error: removing these packages would break dependencies:
        webserver is needed by mod_perl-1.19-2
        webserver is needed by mod_php-2.0.1-9
        webserver is needed by mod_php3-3.0.7-4
```

To remove the Apache 1.3.6-7 RPM, it is necessary to first remove the three RPMs listed as dependent on that RPM, which I did with the following commands (if the package removal happens without error, the rpm command returns no output):

```
# rpm -e mod_perl-1.19-2
# rpm -e mod_php-2.0.1-9
# rpm -e mod_php3-3.0.7-4
# rpm -e apache-1.3.6-7
```

Once all the RPMs are removed, install the new Apache RPM using rpm with the -i argument in the following manner:

```
# ls -al apache*.rpm
-rw-r--r--   1 caulds    caulds      833084
Jan 17 09:41 apache-1_3_20-8_i386.src.rpm
# rpm -i apache-1_3_20-8_i386.src.rpm
```

This RPM is designed to install Apache in the /home/httpd and /etc/httpd directories, which is where you'll find it on standard Red

Hat systems. The RPM installs all the required configuration files, with values that allow the server to start:

```
# cd /home/httpd
# ls
cgi-bin  html  icons
```

The RPM even provides a default HTML page in the default DocumentRoot directory (/home/httpd/html). This page allows your server to be accessed immediately after installation:

```
# ls html
index.html  manual  poweredby.gif
```

A listing of the /home/httpd/html directory shows two files and a subdirectory. The index.html file contains the HTML page the newly installed server will display by default; it is a special filename used to indicate the default HTML page in a directory. The poweredby.gif file is a graphic the server displays on the default page. The directory manual contains HTML documentation for the new Apache server. Access the manual from a web browser using http://localhost/manual.

The Apache configuration files, logs, and loadable modules are all found elsewhere on the file system (in /etc/httpd):

```
# cd /etc/httpd
# ls
conf  logs  modules
# ls conf
access.conf  httpd.conf  magic  srm.conf
# ls modules
httpd.exp          mod_bandwidth.so  mod_include.so     mod_setenvif.so
libproxy.so        mod_cern_meta.so  mod_info.so        mod_speling.so
mod_access.so      mod_cgi.so        mod_log_agent.so   mod_status.so
mod_actions.so     mod_digest.so     mod_log_config.so  mod_unique_id.so
mod_alias.so       mod_dir.so        mod_log_referer.so mod_userdir.so
mod_asis.so        mod_env.so        mod_mime.so        mod_usertrack.so
mod_auth.so        mod_example.so    mod_mime_magic.so  mod_vhost_alias.so
mod_auth_anon.so   mod_expires.so    mod_mmap_static.so
mod_auth_db.so     mod_headers.so    mod_negotiation.so
mod_autoindex.so   mod_imap.so       mod_rewrite.so
```

The RPM also writes the Apache executable `httpd` into a directory reserved for system-executable binaries:

```
# ls -al /usr/sbin/httpd
-rwxr-xr-x   1 root    root    282324 Sep 21 09:46 /usr/sbin/httpd
```

Binary Distributions

The last means of installing Apache is almost as easy as the RPM method. Binary distributions of Apache, compiled for a large number of operating systems and hardware platforms, are available from the Apache Software Foundation and can be downloaded from www.apache.org/dist/httpd/binaries/linux. You may need to look elsewhere if your hardware or OS is quite old (an old Linux kernel on a 486, for example). The page listing Apache for Linux distributions is shown in Figure 24.4.

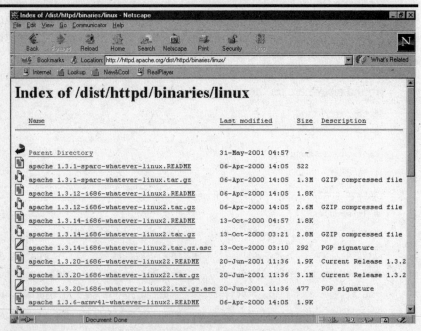

FIGURE 24.4:   Linux binary distributions on the www.apache.org site

When downloading binary distributions for Intel microprocessors, you need to make sure you download a version that was compiled to run on your specific processor family. For example, the i686 family includes the Pentium II, PII Xeon, Pentium III and PIII Xeon, and the Celeron processors. The i586 family includes the Pentium and Pentium with MMX CPUs, and i386 generally indicates the 80486 family. A binary compiled for the i386 family will run on any of the processors mentioned above, including the latest Pentium CPUs, but it will not be as fast as code compiled specifically for a processor generation. If you are downloading a binary distribution for a Pentium II or Pentium III, look for an i686 distribution; if you are downloading for an 80486, you must get the i386 binaries.

There is a handy Linux utility that will query the system's processor and return its hardware family type. Enter **/bin/uname -m** to obtain this information (the **m** is for *machine type*). When this was run on my server machine, which has an old Pentium 200 MMX chip, I got this result:

```
# uname -m
i586
```

For a Pentium PC running Linux, use the following steps:

1. Download the file apache_1.3.20-i686-whatever-linux22.tar.gz, which is the binary tarball, compressed with gzip. This long filename indicates the version of Apache (1.3.20), the CPU for which it was compiled (Intel 686 family), and the operating system version (in this case, any Linux 2.2 kernel).

NOTE

For every binary package on the website, there is a README file to accompany it. You can view or download this file for information about the binary distribution, such as who compiled it and when, as well as what compiler options and default locations for files were built into the Apache executable.

2. Make sure you are in the directory where you downloaded the binary distribution (or move the downloaded file elsewhere and change to that directory). After the installation process is complete, you will probably want to delete the directory that was created to hold the installation files. All the files you need to run Apache from the binary are moved from that directory to their intended locations:

```
# cd /home/caulds
# pwd
/home/caulds
# ls apache*
apache_1_3_20-i686-whatever-linux22_tar.gz
```

3. Uncompress and extract the distribution with tar to create a new directory tree containing all the files from the distribution:

```
# tar xvzf apache_1_3_20-i686-whatever-linux22_tar.gz
```

4. Change the working directory to the directory you just created:

```
# cd apache_1.3.20
# ls
ABOUT_APACHE      Makefile.tmpl        build.log       icons
Announcement      README               cgi-bin         install-
➥bindist.sh
INSTALL           README-WIN.TXT           conf             logs
INSTALL.bindist   README.bindist       config.layout   src
KEYS              README.configure     config.status
LICENSE           WARNING-WIN.TXT      configure
Makefile          bindist              htdocs

# ls bindist
bin cgi-bin conf htdocs icons include libexec logs
  man proxy

# ls bindist/bin
ab        apxs       htdigest  httpd         rotatelogs
apachectl dbmmanage  htpasswd  logresolve
```

5. The binary distribution includes a shell script for installing the files in their proper locations (the locations where the Apache daemon expects to find them). Run the shell script as follows to create the Apache folders. After it runs, you should find everything neatly installed under /usr/local/apache:

```
# ./install-bindist.sh
Installing binary distribution for platform i686-whatever-
  linux22
into directory /usr/local/apache ...
[Preserving existing configuration files.]
[Preserving existing htdocs directory.]
Ready.
  +----------------------------------------------------------+
  | You now have successfully installed the Apache 1.3.20    |
  | HTTP server. To verify that Apache actually works        |
  | correctly you should first check the (initially          |
  | created or preserved) configuration files:               |
  |                                                          |
  |   /usr/local/apache/conf/httpd.conf                      |
  |                                                          |
  | You should then be able to immediately fire up           |
  | Apache the first time by running:                        |
```

```
|                                                          |
|   /usr/local/apache/bin/apachectl start                 |
|                                                          |
| Thanks for using Apache.          The Apache Group       |
|                                   http://www.apache.org/ |
+----------------------------------------------------------+
```

You can actually start the Apache server from the httpd file in the bin directory (the last listing above), but it has been compiled with default values that will not allow it to operate from this location. You can verify that it is operational by entering a command such as the following, which will cause httpd to start, display its version information, and quit:

```
# ./bindist/bin/httpd -v
Server version: Apache/1.3.20 (Unix)
Server built:   Feb 27 2000 19:52:20
```

RUNNING THE SERVER

The Apache daemon is started from a single executable file (httpd), which is usually supported by a number of modules that are loaded by the server after it reads its configuration files. The Apache server is started when httpd is invoked, either manually at the command line or more commonly as part of a startup script.

The normal behavior of httpd is to run as a system daemon or listening server process, waiting for HTTP client connections on one or more sockets, bound to one or more of the system's network interfaces. The httpd file can also be invoked with several arguments that cause it to run, display some information, and quit immediately without going into daemon mode. A few of those arguments are demonstrated below; you can use this to test your Apache executable and display its running environment. In each case, I am invoking httpd from its standard location, although it could be placed anywhere on your file system without affecting its operation. On my systems, I usually place the file in a protected location reserved for system binaries (/usr/sbin/).

I've already demonstrated the -v argument, which displays the version number and compile date of the httpd file.

The -V (uppercase) option provides the same information and also displays all the default values compiled into httpd. The most useful information is the default locations in which the Apache server looks for its supporting files and writes its directories. Most of these locations can be overridden at runtime by special directives in httpd.conf, but this is rarely necessary.

Part vi

```
# /usr/local/apache/bin/httpd -V
Server version: Apache/1.3.20 (Unix)
Server built:    Jun 11 2000 16:51:03
Server's Module Magic Number: 19990320:7
Server compiled with....
 -D EAPI
 -D HAVE_MMAP
 -D HAVE_SHMGET
 -D USE_SHMGET_SCOREBOARD
 -D USE_MMAP_FILES
 -D USE_FCNTL_SERIALIZED_ACCEPT
 -D HTTPD_ROOT="/usr/local/apache1_3_20"
 -D SUEXEC_BIN="/usr/local/apache1_3_20/bin/suexec"
 -D DEFAULT_PIDLOG="logs/httpd.pid"
 -D DEFAULT_SCOREBOARD="logs/httpd.scoreboard"
 -D DEFAULT_LOCKFILE="logs/httpd.lock"
 -D DEFAULT_XFERLOG="logs/access_log"
 -D DEFAULT_ERRORLOG="logs/error_log"
 -D TYPES_CONFIG_FILE="conf/mime.types"
 -D SERVER_CONFIG_FILE="conf/httpd.conf"
 -D ACCESS_CONFIG_FILE="conf/access.conf"
 -D RESOURCE_CONFIG_FILE="conf/srm.conf"
```

The -l argument displays the modules that are compiled into httpd
(also referred to as *statically linked*). One module, httpd_core, is always
statically linked into httpd. A second module (the shared object module,
mod_so) is statically linked when dynamic loading of modules is required.
For this server, all other modules are available to the server only if
dynamically loaded at runtime:

```
# /usr/local/apache/bin/httpd -l
Compiled-in modules:
  http_core.c
  mod_so.c
```

The −t option runs a syntax test on configuration files but does not start
the server. This test can be very useful because it indicates the line number

of any directive in the httpd.conf file that is improperly specified:

```
# /usr/local/apache/bin/httpd -t
Syntax OK
```

Every configuration option for a basic Apache server is stored in a single file. On most standard Apache systems, you'll find the configuration file stored as /usr/local/apache/conf/httpd.conf. If you have Apache loaded from a Red Hat Linux distribution CD or an RPM distribution, you'll find the file in an alternate location preferred by Red Hat, /etc/apache/conf/httpd.conf. When Apache is compiled, this location is one of the configurable values that are hard-coded into it. Unless explicitly told to load its configuration from another file or directory, Apache will attempt to load the file from its compiled path and filename.

This compiled value can be overridden by invoking the Apache executable with the -f option, as shown in Chapter 25. This can be handy for testing alternate configuration files or for running more than one server on the system, each of which loads its own unique configuration.

Finally, you can run httpd with no arguments to start the server as a system daemon. Some simple modifications will probably have to be made to the default httpd.conf provided when you install Apache, although only very minor changes are actually required to start the server. In all likelihood, the first time you start Apache, you'll receive some error telling you the reason that Apache can't be started. The most common error new users see is this:

```
httpd: cannot determine local host name.
Use the ServerName directive to set it manually.
```

If you get an error when starting Apache the first time, don't panic; it is almost always fixed by making one or two very simple changes to Apache's configuration file. In fact, you should expect to make a few changes before running Apache. To do this, you'll modify Apache configuration *directives*, the subject of the next chapter. Chances are that the directives you need to learn about and change are those covered in the "Defining the Main Server Environment" section of Chapter 25. If your server won't start, you need to follow the instructions there.

If Apache finds an httpd.conf file that it can read for an acceptable initial configuration, you will see no response, which is good news. To find out if the server is actually running, attempt to connect to it using a web browser. Your server should display a demo page to let you know things are working. Figure 24.5 shows the demo page from a Red Hat system.

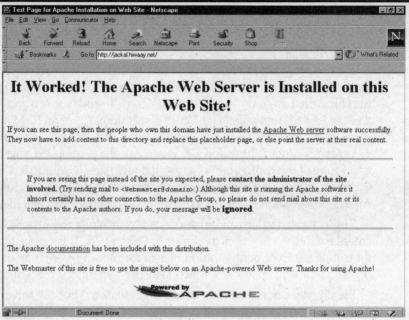

FIGURE 24.5:   The demonstration web page installed with the Apache RPM

You can also determine if the server is running the slightly more com-plicated way and use the Linux process status (ps) command to look for the process in the Linux process table, as shown in the following:

```
# ps -ef | grep httpd
root      8764      1  0 13:39 ?       00:00:00 ./httpd
nobody    8765   8764  0 13:39 ?       00:00:00 ./httpd
nobody    8766   8764  0 13:39 ?       00:00:00 ./httpd
nobody    8767   8764  0 13:39 ?       00:00:00 ./httpd
nobody    8768   8764  0 13:39 ?       00:00:00 ./httpd
nobody    8769   8764  0 13:39 ?       00:00:00 ./httpd
```

This list is more interesting than it might appear at first. I used the e argument to ps to display all system processes, the f argument to display the full output format, and then grep to display only those lines contain-ing the string httpd. Note that only one of the httpd processes is owned by root (the user who started Apache); the next few httpd processes in the list are all owned by nobody. This is as it should be. The first process is the main server, which never responds to user requests. It was respon-sible for creating the five child processes. Note from the third column of the output that all of these have the main server process (denoted by a process ID of 8764) as their parent process. They were all spawned by the main server, which changed their owner to the nobody account. It is these processes that respond to user requests.

Stopping the Apache server is a bit more difficult. When you start Apache, it writes the process ID (or PID) of the main server process into a text file where it can later be used to identify that process and control it using Linux signals. By default, this file is named httpd.pid and is written in the logs directory under the server root. On my system:

```
# cat /usr/local/apache/logs/httpd.pid
8764
```

You'll note that the number saved in the file is the PID of the main Apache server process we saw in the process status listing earlier. To shut down the server, extract the contents of httpd.pid and pass them to the kill command. This is the line that kills Apache:

```
# kill 'cat /usr/local/logs/httpd.pid'
```

Using Apachectl

Apache comes with a utility to perform the basic operations of controlling the server. This utility, called apachectl, is actually a short shell script that resides in the bin directory under ServerRoot. It does nothing more than simplify processes you can perform by hand, and for that reason doesn't require a lot of explanation.

Start the server by invoking apachectl with the start argument. This is better than simply running httpd, because the script first checks to see if Apache is already running and starts it only if it finds no running httpd process.

```
# /usr/local/apache/bin/apachectl start
/usr/local/apache/bin/apachectl start: httpd started
```

Stopping the server is when apachectl comes in really handy. Invoked with the stop argument, apachectl locates the httpd.pid file, extracts the PID of the main server, and then uses kill to stop the process (and all of its child processes). It is exactly what you did earlier using ps and kill, but it is much easier. That's what apachectl is: an easy-to-use wrapper for shell commands.

```
# /usr/local/apache/bin/apachectl stop
/usr/local/apache/bin/apachectl stop: httpd stopped
```

Running Multiple Apache Servers

Many administrators find that they need to run multiple Apache servers on the same physical system. They may want to run a separate server (with its own document space) to provide secure connections using Secure Sockets Layer, or run multiple versions of Apache for testing. My Linux server, for example, has Apache production versions 1.3.6, 1.3.9, and 1.3.12 installed, plus the 2.0 alpha 2 and 2.0 alpha 4 releases. I don't run them all simultaneously (although I could do so, by having each listen for connections on different TCP ports), but I can fire up any one of them at any time.

Apache makes it very easy to install multiple servers on the same box. All you need to do is ensure that each one starts its own unique configuration file. Generally, when you install multiple versions of Apache, you should specify different values for --prefix when running configure. When installing version 1.3.20, I instructed configure to place it in a directory other than the default /usr/local/apache:

```
# configure --prefix=/usr/local/apache1_3_20
```

Now, the newly installed 1.3.20 version will have its own configuration file, its own Apache daemon executable (httpd), and its own set of DSO modules.

If you want to run multiple copies of the same Apache server version but with alternate configurations, you can use the -f argument to httpd. This argument lets you choose a configuration file that is read by the Apache daemon at startup and contains all the settings that define the configuration for each particular server:

```
# httpd -1 /usr/local/conf/test.conf
```

Using Defines to Implement Alternate Configurations

Another way to maintain alternate configurations uses a single configuration file. If there are features that you may want to implement, you can place the directives for those features in blocks that, when the configuration file is parsed, will be either read or ignored conditionally. In the configuration file, the <IfDefine var> directive is a container for directives that should be run only if var has been set. The var argument is a type of variable known as a *define*; on the Linux command line, the -D argument to httpd sets these variables. When the module for SSL is installed, all of

the directives it adds to the Apache configuration file are placed between
<IfDefine> directives:

```
<IfDefine SSL>
    Listen 443
</IfDefine>
```

The directives in this container will be read only if the variable *SSL* is
defined. In other words, you want the server to listen for connections on
TCP port 443 (the standard port for SSL) only if you defined *SSL* when
you started the daemon. Do this by invoking the Apache daemon, httpd,
with the -D argument, like so:

```
# /usr/local/apache/bin/httpd -D SSL
```

You can do the same to store alternate configurations in a single file by
setting your own defines for the different blocks you want to be active.

WHAT'S NEXT?

This chapter has presented three methods of installing Apache:

1. From a package prepared for a Linux package manager, such
    as RPM.

2. From the downloadable binaries available from the Apache
    Software Foundation.

3. By compiling the binaries yourself from the source files.

Although it's more difficult and time consuming, compiling from
source is the way I prefer to install Apache because it permits the greatest flexibility in configuration or customization. Complete instructions
were given on how to obtain, compile, and install Apache from source
code. Many sites will prefer to install ready-made binaries, however, and
these offer the quickest and most painless way to install Apache and
upgrade it when the time comes. Full instructions on using the Apache
Software Foundation's binary archives and third-party RPM packages
were given. In the next chapter, I'll describe the Apache configuration
file (httpd.conf) and the most important of the core directives that can
be used in that file to customize your Apache server. The core directives
are always available in every Apache server, and there is nothing in this
chapter that does not apply to your Apache server.

Chapter 25

THE APACHE CORE DIRECTIVES

We define Apache's behavior and configuration options by using statements called *directives*. Apache directives are rigorously defined in how and where they can be used, and they have a specific syntax, very much like the commands of a programming language. Directives are not commands, though, and using directives is not like programming. Directives are instructions to Apache, telling it how to behave and where to find its resources, but they do not directly control the actions of Apache. Rather, they can be thought of as supplying information to the Apache server engine.

Customizing Apache to meet the needs of your specific website means learning the purpose and use of a number of configuration directives. The most important of these are the core directives. These are the directives that are always compiled into the Apache executable. They are always available and require no special configuration to be used.

Adapted from *Linux Apache Web Server Administration* by Charles Aulds

ISBN 0-7821-2734-7   640 pages $39.99

Apache directives fall into two groups: those that are always available (the so-called *core directives*), and those supplied by optional add-on *modules*. These configuration directives become available to the administrator only when their modules are added to the server and are meaningless until their modules are enabled. You can do this when compiling Apache by statically linking the module to the Apache kernel or at runtime by using the `LoadModule` and `AddModule` directives in `httpd.conf`. The next chapter is devoted to Apache modules and discusses the use of these two directives. Many Apache add-on modules have been adopted by the Apache Software Foundation for inclusion with the Apache distribution, although their use is optional.

Every directive is associated with a specific module; the largest module is the core module, which has special characteristics. This module cannot be unlinked from the Apache kernel and cannot be disabled; the directives it supplies are always available on any Apache server. All of the directives presented in this chapter are from the core Apache module, and all of the most important directives from the core module are covered. Apache's online documentation includes a comprehensive reference to all the modules and directives.

The core module provides support for basic server operations, including options and commands that control the operation of other modules. The Apache server with *just* the core module isn't capable of much at all. It will serve documents to requesting clients (identifying all as having the content type defined by the `DefaultType` directive). While all of the other modules can be considered optional, a useful Apache server will always include at least a few of them. In fact, nearly all of the standard Apache modules are used on most production Apache servers, and more than half are compiled into the server by the default configuration.

In this chapter, we'll see how directives are usually located in a single startup file (`httpd.conf`). I'll show how the applicability of directives is often confined to a specific scope (by default, directives have a general server scope). Finally, I'll show how directives can be overridden on a directory-by-directory basis (using the `.htaccess` file).

USING APACHE DIRECTIVES

The emphasis Apache's developers placed on a modular design has proven to be one of its greatest strengths. From the start, Apache was designed with expandability and extensibility in mind. The hooks that were designed into the program enable developers to create modules to extend the functionality of Apache and are an important reason for its rapid adoption and huge success. Apache modules add not only new functionality to the server but also new directives.

To get the most out of Apache, you need to be familiar with all the standard modules. You may not need or use all of them, but knowing that they exist and having a basic knowledge of what each does are very valuable when needs or problems arise in the future. This chapter is a tutorial that explains when a directive should be used, what it does, and how you can use it in your server configuration.

The excellent Apache help system should be your first stop when you need to know exactly how a directive is used. Apache is documented very well (if not extensively), according to the loosely standardized documentation format used by the Apache Software Foundation. The Apache documentation is always available online at httpd.apache.org/docs. The same set of documentation (without the search features) is also provided with the source distribution of Apache and installed as part of the installation procedure. While the documentation pages provided with Apache are complete, viewing them from your own server is limited in two ways. First, the documentation will not be updated until you install a newer version of Apache. Second, you will not have the search capability of the Apache website. For quick lookups of directive use, though, you'll save time by referencing the documentation on your server.

The All-Powerful *httpd.conf* File

In keeping with its NCSA HTTPd origin, Apache originally used three configuration files:

- ▶ The main server configuration file, httpd.conf
- ▶ The resource configuration file, srm.conf
- ▶ The access permissions configuration file, access.conf

The Apache Software Foundation decided to merge these into a single file, and in all current releases of Apache, the only configuration file required is httpd.conf. Although there are legitimate reasons to split the Apache configuration into multiple files (particularly when hosting multiple virtual hosts), I find it very convenient to place all my configuration directives into a single file. It greatly simplifies creating backups and maintaining revision histories. It also makes it easy to describe your server configuration to a colleague—just e-mail him a copy of your httpd.conf.

Part VI

TIP

To follow along with the descriptions in this chapter, you might find it useful to open or print the `httpd.conf` file on your system to use for reference. On most systems, the file is stored as `/usr/local/apache/conf/httpd.conf`. If you have Apache loaded from a Red Hat Linux distribution CD or a Red Hat Package Manager (RPM) distribution, you'll find the file as `/etc/apache/conf/httpd.conf`. Nearly everything you do to change the Apache configuration requires some modification of this file.

For convenience, the `httpd.conf` file is divided into three sections. Although these divisions are arbitrary, if you try to maintain these groupings, your configuration file will be much easier to read. The three sections of the `httpd.conf` are as follows:

Section 1   The *global environment* section contains directives that control the operation of the Apache server process as a whole. This is where you place directives that control the operation of the Apache server processes, as opposed to directives that control how those processes handle user requests.

Section 2   The *main* or *default server* section contains directives that define the parameters of the main or default server, which responds to requests that aren't handled by a virtual host. These directives also provide default values for the settings of all virtual hosts.

Section 3   The *virtual hosts* section contains settings for virtual hosts, which allow web requests to be sent to different IP addresses or hostnames and be handled by the same Apache server process.

Securing Obsolete Configuration Files

Apache looks for the traditional `access.conf` and `srm.conf` files each time it loads, even though it runs without these files and won't generate an error if it does not find them. This creates a potential security hole. To eliminate the possibility of someone (perhaps intentionally) writing these files into the location where Apache looks for them, you can disable Apache from performing this search. Apache provides two legacy directives to specify the locations of these once-necessary files, which you can use to indicate `/dev/null` as the location for both files:

```
AccessConfig /dev/null
ResourceConfig /dev/null
```

DIRECTIVE SCOPE AND CONTEXT

One of the important things to know about any directive is the context in which it operates. The context of a directive determines not only its scope—in other words, its range of applicability—but also where the directive can be placed. There are four contexts in which Apache directives can operate:

The General Server Context   Directives that operate in the general server context apply to the entire server. Some of these directives are valid only in this context and make no sense in any other. For example, the StartServers directive specifies the number of HTTPd listener processes that are spawned when Apache is first started, and it makes no sense to include this directive in any other context. Other directives (such as ServerName, which is different for each virtual host) are equally valid in other contexts. When used in the general server context, most of these directives set default values that can be overridden when used in narrower contexts, just as a virtual host will override ServerName to set its own value for this directive.

The Container Context   This group includes directives that are valid when enclosed in one of the three containers: <Directory>, <Files>, or <Location>. These directives are applicable only within the scope defined by the enclosing container. A good example is a Deny directive, which prohibits access to resources. When used within any one of the three containers mentioned, it denies access to the resource or group of resources defined by the enclosing container.

The Virtual Host Context   Although a virtual host is actually defined by the container directive <VirtualHost>, for the purpose of defining directive contexts, it is considered separately because many virtual host directives actually override general server directives or defaults. The virtual host attempts to be a second server in every respect, running on the same machine and, to a client that connects to the virtual host, appearing to be the only server running on the machine.

The .htaccess Context   The directives in an .htaccess file are treated almost identically to directives appearing inside a <Directory> container in httpd.conf. The main difference is that directives appearing inside an .htaccess file can be disabled by using the AllowOverride directive in httpd.conf.

For each directive, you need to know the context in which it can be used and the overrides that enable or disable it. This information is provided in the Apache documentation in a standardized format. A list of directives is displayed at http://httpd.apache.org/docs/mod/directives.html. If you click the link for the Action directive, the entry in Figure 25.1 is displayed.

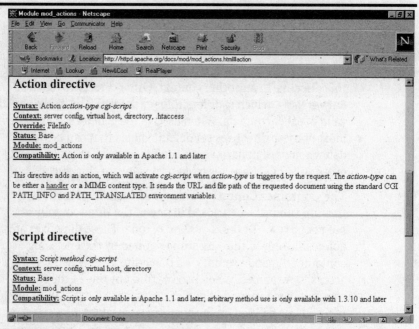

FIGURE 25.1:   Directive documentation

You can see that the Action directive is valid in all four contexts but is subject to being overridden by a FileInfo override when used in an .htaccess file. That is, if the FileInfo override is not in effect for a directory, an Action directive appearing inside an .htaccess file in that directory is disabled. This is because the Action directive is controlled by the FileInfo override.

The Apache server is smart enough to recognize when a directive is being specified out of scope. You'll get the following error when you boot, for example, if you attempt to use the Listen directive in a <Directory> context:

```
# /usr/local/apache/bin/httpd
Syntax error on line 925 of /usr/local/apache1_3_20/conf/httpd.conf:
Listen not allowed here
httpd could not be started
```

DEFINING THE MAIN SERVER ENVIRONMENT

General server directives are those used to configure the server itself and its listening processes. General server directives are not allowed in the other contexts we'll discuss, except for virtual hosts. General server directives also provide default values that are inherited by all virtual hosts, unless specifically overridden.

I changed four directives, all of which were modifications of lines found in the default httpd.conf file, to get my server up and running. Once you've installed Apache, you should be able to get the server running by making only these changes, and you probably won't require all four. The default Apache configuration that you installed in Chapter 24, "Installing Apache," is complete, and you can usually start the server using this configuration. However, before doing that, you should understand the purpose of the four directives in this section. These directives, while simple to understand and use, all have a server-wide scope and affect the way many other directives operate. Because of the importance of these directives, you should take care to ensure that they are set properly.

The *ServerName* Directive

Apache must always be able to determine a hostname for the server on which it is run. This hostname is used by the server to create *self-referential URLs*—URLs that refer to themselves. When more than one virtual host is run on the same system, each will be identified by a unique ServerName directive. For a system that hosts only a single web server site, the ServerName directive is usually set to the hostname and domain of that server.

When I installed Apache and ran it for the first time, I was presented with the error `httpd: cannot determine local host name`. To correct this, I located the `ServerName` directive in my `httpd.conf` file and discovered that the Apache distribution had created the directive, using my fully qualified hostname as the Apache `ServerName` (if no fully qualified domain name can be identified, the default will be the machine's IP address string), but left the directive commented out. The directive was acceptable to me, so I uncommented the line:

```
ServerName jackal.hiwaay.net
```

The *ServerRoot* Directive

The `ServerRoot` directive specifies the directory in which the server lives and generally matches the value of the `--prefix` option that was set during the installation of Apache.

```
ServerRoot /usr/local/apache1_3_20
```

Typically this directory will contain the subdirectories `bin/`, `conf/`, and `logs/`. In lieu of defining the server `root` directory using the `ServerRoot` configuration directive, you can also specify the location with the `-d` option when invoking HTTPd:

```
/usr/local/apache/bin/httpd -d /etc/httpd
```

While there's nothing wrong with using this method of starting the server, it is usually best reserved for testing alternate configurations and for cases where you will run multiple versions of Apache on the same server simultaneously, each with its own configuration file.

Paths for all other configuration files are taken as relative to this directory. For example, the following directive causes Apache to write error messages into `/usr/local/apache/logs/error.log`:

```
ErrorLog logs/error.log
```

The *DocumentRoot* Directive

The `DocumentRoot` directive is used to define the top-level directory from which Apache will serve files. The directory defined by `DocumentRoot` contains the files that Apache will serve when it receives requests with the URL `/`.

It's perfectly acceptable to use the Apache default, which is the directory `htdocs` under the Apache server root, but I usually prefer to change this to the /home filesystem, which is a much larger filesystem reserved for user home directories.

To change the value of DocumentRoot on my system, I commented out the Apache default and added a new DocumentRoot directive of my own:

```
# DocumentRoot "/usr/local/apache/htdocs"
DocumentRoot "/home/httpd/html"
```

Note that a full path to the directory must be used whenever the directory is outside the server root. Otherwise, a relative path can be given. (The double quotes are usually optional, but it's a good idea to always use them. If the string contains spaces, for example, it must be enclosed in double quotes.)

When you change DocumentRoot, you must also alter the <Directory> container directive that groups all directives that apply to DocumentRoot and subdirectories:

```
# <Directory "/usr/local/apache/htdocs">
<Directory "/home/httpd/html">
```

The *ScriptAlias* Directive

The ScriptAlias directive specifies a directory that contains executable scripts, such as CGI programs that can be invoked from a web browser. By default, Apache creates a ScriptAlias for all URLs requesting a resource in /cgi-bin/.

I also changed the ScriptAlias directive for my server. I chose to comment out Apache's default location and add my own, which is located with the web documents on my /home filesystem. There's nothing wrong with the Apache default location (under the Apache server root directory) for the /cgi-bin directory, but you may want to change the location for ease of maintenance:

```
# ScriptAlias /cgi-bin/ "/usr/local/apache/cgi-bin/"
ScriptAlias /cgi-bin/ "/home/httpd/cgi-bin/"
```

Make sure that only users specifically authorized to create executable scripts can write to the directory you name. I usually assign group ownership of my cgi-bin directory to a web administrator's group:

```
# chown -r nobody.webteam /home/httpd/cgi-bin
# chmod 750 /home/httpd/cgi-bin
```

The name of this group is arbitrary, but I use the command shown above to assign ownership of the cgi-bin directory (and all of its subdirectories and files) to a user named nobody and the group webteam. The default behavior of Apache on Linux is to run under the nobody user account. The group name is arbitrary, but it is to this group that I assign membership for those user accounts that are permitted to create or modify server scripts. The second line ensures that the file owner has full read, write, and execute permission, that members of the webteam group have read and write access, and that all other users have no access to the directory or the files it contains.

MORE GENERAL SERVER DIRECTIVES

You may want to modify a number of other general server directives before putting your server into operation. These directives are usually acceptable when left at their default values, but changing them rarely carries a significant risk. In all cases, if you feel that you understand the purpose of the directive well enough to add it to your httpd.conf file (or modify it if it's already there), don't be afraid to make such changes. These directives exist to make Apache as customizable as possible; they're for your use.

The *ErrorDocument* Directive

If Apache encounters an error while processing a user request, it is configured to display a standard error page, which gives the HTTP response code and the URL that caused the problem. Use the ErrorDocument directive to define a custom error response to standard HTTP errors that are more user-friendly and understandable. Using ErrorDocument, you can configure Apache to respond to a particular HTTP error code in either of two ways:

1. You can display custom error text. For example, the following would display a custom message for HTTP Error Code 403 (Forbidden). Note that the text begins with a double quote that is not part of the message itself; it is not a quote-enclosed string. Do not end the message with a second quote.

   ```
   ErrorDocument 403 "You are not authorized to view
   this info!
   ```

2. You can issue a redirect to another URL, which may be external or internal. A fully specified URL that begins with http:// is assumed to be an external redirect. Apache will send a redirect to the client to tell it where to request the document, even if the redirect resolves to a resource on the same server. A relative URL is a local redirect, relative to the server's DocumentRoot, and Apache will serve the request directly without sending a redirect that would require the client to request the document again. Here are examples of each of the possible redirect forms:

```
#HTTP Error 401 (Unauthorized); display subscription
page ErrorDocument 401 /subscription_info.html

#HTTP Error 404 (Not found); redirect to error script
ErrorDocument 404 /cgi-bin/bad_urls.pl

#HTTP Error 500 (Internal error) Redirect to backup
server ErrorDocument 500 http://jackal2.hiwaay.net
```

NOTE

If you attempt to redirect a request with an ErrorDocument 401 directive (which means that the client is unauthorized to access the requested document), the redirect must refer to a local document. Apache will not permit an external redirect for this HTTP error.

The *LogLevel* Directive

Apache provides an error log in which the server records errors, warnings, and unusual conditions it encounters while running. By default, the error log is ServerRoot/logs/error_log, but the location can be changed using the ErrorLog directive.

The LogLevel directive is used to specify which of eight verbosity levels Apache is to use in logging errors. Table 25.1 lists these levels, which correspond to the same error levels used by the Linux system log. To set the LogLevel to error (no lower level of verbosity is recommended), use this directive:

```
LogLevel error
```

Error logging is automatically enabled for all levels in Table 25.1 above the one specified. That is, if you have used LogLevel to set the error logging level to warn, Apache will also write all errors that are defined for levels `emerg`, `alert`, `crit`, and `error`. The default value is the same as specifying `LogLevel error`, which on production servers is generally verbose enough to diagnose most errors. I recommend setting the verbosity level at least one step higher (`warn`), and I usually use `LogLevel info` on my servers. Many of the additional log entries are useful and informative, but not so numerous that they fill the log file too quickly. `LogLevel debug` is usually useful only to programmers, particularly when they have written modules specifically to write debugging messages, and should never be enabled on a production server. Never reduce the logging verbosity level below `LogLevel crit` (in other words, never use the `emerg` or `alert` levels); this will cause you to miss important warning and error conditions that can warn of problems either present or impending.

TABLE 25.1:   Error Logging Levels

LEVEL	DESCRIPTION	EXAMPLES
emerg	Emergency conditions that render the system unusable	No active child processes: shutting down.
alert	Conditions that require immediate action	Child 1234 returned a Fatal error...Apache is exiting!
crit	Critical conditions	Parent: Path to Apache process too long.
error	Error conditions	master_main: create child process failed. Exiting.
warn	Warning conditions	child process 1234 did not exit, sending another SIGHUP.
notice	Advisory conditions that do not indicate abnormal activity	httpd: SIGNUSR1 received. Doing graceful restart.
info	Information only	Shutdown event signaled. Shutting the server down.
debug	Messages displayed only when running in debug mode	loaded module mod_vhost.c

The *DefaultType* Directive

The `DefaultType` directive is very rarely used in the general server scope. It can redefine the default MIME content type for documents requested from the server. If this directive is not used, all documents not specifically typed elsewhere are assumed to be of MIME type `text/html`.

Apache reads its MIME-type-to-filename-extension mappings from a file named `mime.types`, which is found in the Apache configuration directory. This file contains a list of MIME content types, each optionally followed by one or more filename extensions. This file is used to determine the MIME content header sent to the client with each resource.

The `DefaultType` directive is generally used in a directory scope to redefine the default type of documents retrieved from a particular directory. In the following example, the default MIME type for all documents in the `/images` directory under `ServerRoot` is defined to be `image/gif`. That way, the server doesn't rely on an extension (such as `.gif`) to determine the resource type. A file with no extension at all, when served from this directory, will be sent to the requesting user with an HTTP header identifying it as MIME type `image/gif`.

```
<Directory /images>
    DefaultType image/gif
</Directory>
```

Controlling Server Processes

The following directives are used to control the Linux processes when Apache is run on that platform. The first directive is used to determine how Linux processes are created to answer user requests. The remaining three directives all control system settings for the Apache server processes.

The *ServerType* Directive

In Chapter 23, "Apache and Other Servers," I noted that the Linux Apache server usually runs as a pool of listening processes, all of which are under the control of a single main server process that *never* responds to client requests. This stand-alone mode is by far the most efficient way to run Apache on Linux and the default if no `ServerType` directive is specified, but it is not the only way that Apache can be run.

The `ServerType` directive can be used to specify an alternate mode of operation, called *inetd mode* after the Linux process of that name. When the Apache configuration file contains the directive

```
ServerType inetd
```

there will be no HTTPd process that binds itself to network sockets and listens for client connections. Instead, the Linux inetd process is configured to listen for client connections on behalf of Apache and spawn HTTPd processes as required to handle arriving connections. This is similar to the way Linux handles services such as File Transfer Protocol (FTP).

The Apache inetd mode of operation is not recommended for most Apache installations, although it results in a more efficient use of resources if the server load is very light (a few hundred connections per day) or when the available memory is extremely limited (64MB or less of RAM). The Apache server processes spend most of their time in an idle (waiting) state, so not running these processes continuously frees resources (particularly memory) that would otherwise be tied up.

The downside is that, because the system has to create a new listener process for each client connection, there is a delay in processing web requests. The use of dynamically loadable modules increases the time required for Apache to load and begin responding to user requests. This delay is not usually significant when Apache starts its pool of processes in stand-alone mode, but in inetd mode, where Apache starts the processes after the request is received, the delay can be noticeable. This is particularly true if a large number of DSO modules have to be loaded and mapped into the Apache kernel's address space. When using Apache in inetd mode, you should avoid using dynamic modules and instead statically link the necessary modules and eliminate those modules that you aren't using by commenting out or deleting the associated directives in httpd.conf.

NOTE

Some Apache administrators prefer to use inetd and TCP Wrappers for all server processes. The Apache Software Foundation questions the security benefits of this practice and does not recommend the use of TCP Wrappers with the Apache Server.

Setting Up Apache for inetd Setting up Apache to run in the inetd mode is not quite as simple as running the server in the default stand-alone mode. Besides adding the ServerType inetd directive to httpd.conf, you must ensure that the Linux system is configured to respond to web requests and spawn HTTPd server processes as required. The Linux /etc/services file must contain lines for the TCP ports on which Apache requests will be received. For standard HTTP requests on TCP port 80, the /etc/services file should contain the following line:

```
http 80/tcp
```

If you are running Apache with Secure Sockets Layer (SSL), you should also include a line for the default SSL port:

```
https 443/tcp
```

Additionally, for each line in /etc/services that applies to Apache, you must have a corresponding line in the /etc/inetd.conf file. For the two lines above, you would make sure /etc/inetd.conf contains the following lines:

```
http stream tcp nowait nobody /usr/local/apache/bin/httpd

https stream tcp nowait nobody /usr/local/apache/bin/httpd
➥-DSSL
```

The first argument on each line is the service name and must match an entry in /etc/services. These lines give the inetd server process a full command path and optional arguments to run the Apache server for each defined service. The process will be started with the user ID (UID) nobody, which in Linux is UID -1. The user nobody owns the Apache process, so you should ensure that file and directory permissions permit user nobody to access all resources needed by the server.

Before these changes will be effective, it is necessary to restart Apache or send the HUP (hangup) signal to the running inetd process, as in this example:

```
# ps -ef | grep inetd
root        352     1  0 08:17 ?        00:00:00 inetd
# kill -HUP 352
```

The *PidFile* Directive

The PidFile directive defines the location and filename of a text file that contains the process ID (PID) of the running Apache server. Processes that need to know the Apache server process ID—for example, the apachectl utility—read the PID from this file. It is rarely necessary to change the Apache default PID file, which is stored as httpd.pid in the logs directory under the Apache ServerRoot.

This directive changes the default to place the PidFile directive in the location that Red Hat Linux uses:

```
PidFile "/var/run/apache.pid"
```

The *User* Directive

For Apache servers running in stand-alone mode, this directive defines the Linux user that owns the child processes created to handle user requests. This directive is meaningful only when the Apache server is started as `root`. If the server is started as any other user, it cannot change ownership of child processes.

The default behavior of Apache on Linux systems is to change the ownership of all child processes to UID `-1` (which corresponds to user nobody in the standard Linux `/etc/password` file). This is the preferred way to run Apache on Linux systems.

In the following example, I've chosen to run Apace as www, a special web-specific user account that I create on all my web servers. For ease of administration, Apache resources on my server are usually owned by user www and group wwwteam.

```
User www
```

The *Group* Directive

Like the `User` directive, this directive is used to change the ownership of the child processes created to handle user requests. Instead of changing the user ownership of these processes, however, this directive changes the group ownership.

The default behavior of Apache on Linux systems is to change the group ownership of all child process to *group ID* (GID) −1, which corresponds to the nobody group in `/etc/groups`. It often makes more sense to change the group ownership of the Apache server processes than it does to change the user ownership. On Linux servers where I want to give several users read/write access to my Apache configuration files and web resources, I normally set up a special group with a name such as webteam:

```
Group webteam
```

I place all the web developers' accounts in this group and also change the Apache configuration to run server processes owned by this group.

As it must with the `User` directive, a stand-alone Apache server must be started as `root` to use the `Group` directive. Otherwise, the server can't change the group ownership of any child processes it spawns.

Defining How the Server Listens for Connections

Apache provides three core directives that define the IP addresses and TCP port numbers on which it listens for and accepts client connections. If none of these directives is used, the server listens for connections on TCP port 80 (the HTTP default) on every IP address assigned to the server machine.

The *BindAddress* Directive

This BindAddress directive is used to limit the Apache server to listening for client connections on a single IP address. By default, Apache listens for connections on all network interfaces, which is equivalent to including the line BindAddress * in httpd.conf.

WARNING

Always use a numeric IP address as an argument to the BindAddress directive. The directive accepts a fully qualified hostname, but that should be avoided because it forces the server to rely on a successful DNS query to resolve the hostname to an IP address. If the DNS server is unavailable when Apache is started, the DNS query will fail, and the Apache server will not start.

This directive is very limited. It can be used only once in an Apache configuration. If multiple directives exist, only the last is used. It cannot specify port values, nor can it be used to specify multiple IP addresses (other than the special case of * or ALL). For these reasons, the Listen directive (described shortly) is much more flexible and should usually be used instead.

```
BindAddress 192.168.1.1
```

This example of the BindAddress directive (which is always valid only in a server context) causes the Apache server to *bind to,* or listen for, connections on a single network interface (designated by the IP address assigned to that port). By default, Apache listens for connections on all network interfaces on the system. This directive can be used, for example, with an Apache server on an intranet to force it to listen only for connections on the system's local area network address, ignoring connection attempts on any other network adapters that may exist (particularly those accessible from the Internet).

The *Port* Directive

This directive specifies the TCP network port on which Apache should listen for client connections. It does this only if the Apache configuration has no Listen directive that specifies a port number for the main server.

The port number can be in the range from 0 to 65,535. Port numbers below 1,025 are reserved for system services. Each reserved port number is associated with a specific network protocol. The /etc/services file lists the reserved ports on your system. The ports in this range are reserved for services that are owned by the system's root user. This includes the default port for HTTP servers, port 80. To use port 80, Apache must be started as root, although the normal behavior for a stand-alone server is for this primary server to spawn listener processes that run as nonprivileged users but are still bound to port 80.

Like the BindAddress directive, the Port directive is limited to a single TCP port for the server and cannot be used to set different port values for different network interfaces. Also, only one Port directive is used in httpd.conf. If more than one exists, the last one overrides all others. However, while the BindAddress directive should be avoided, using the Port directive is a good practice. This is because the Port directive serves a second purpose: The Port value is used with the value of the ServerName directive to generate URLs that point back to the system itself. These self-referential URLs are often generated automatically by scripts or server side include (SSI) pages. While it is acceptable to rely on the default value of the Port directive (80), if you want to create self-referential URLs that use any port other than 80, you *must* specify a Port directive, such as this:

```
Port 443
```

This directive defines the default port on which Apache listens for connections as TCP port 443, the standard port for Secure Sockets Layer (SSL). Note that subsequent Listen directives can cause Apache to accept connections on other TCP ports, but whenever the server creates a URL to point back to itself, the Port directive will force it to include 443 as the designated port for connections.

The *Listen* Directive

The Listen directive is used to specify IP addresses or ports on which to accept connections. It incorporates all of the functionality of both the BindAddress and Port directives but has several important advantages over them. Listen should be used instead of BindAddress and Port. The Listen directive has a global server scope and has no meaning inside a container. Apache is smart enough to detect and warn if the Listen directive is used in the wrong context. Placing a Listen directive inside a virtual host container, for example, generates this error:

```
Syntax error on line 1264 of /usr/local/apache/conf/httpd.conf:
Listen cannot occur within <VirtualHost> section
```

If Listen specifies only a port number, the server listens to the specified port on all system network interfaces. If a single IP address and a single port number are given, the server listens only on that port and interface.

Multiple Listen directives may be used to specify more than one address and port to listen to. The server will respond to requests from any of the listed addresses and ports. For example, to make the server accept connections on both port 80 and port 8080, use these directives:

```
Listen 80
Listen 8080
```

To make the server accept connections on two specific interfaces and port numbers, identify the IP address of the interface and the port number separated by a colon, as in this example:

```
Listen 192.168.1.3:80
Listen 192.168.1.5:8080
```

Although Listen is very important in specifying multiple IP addresses for IP-based virtual hosting, the Listen directive does not tie an IP address to a specific virtual host. Here's an example of the Listen directive used to instruct Apache to accept connections on two interfaces, each of which uses a different TCP port:

```
Listen 192.168.1.1:80
Listen 216.180.25.168:443
```

I use this configuration to accept ordinary HTML requests on Port 80 on my internal network interface; connections on my external interface (from the Internet) are accepted only on TCP port 443, the default port for Secure Sockets Layer (SSL) connections.

THE *OPTIONS* DIRECTIVE

The Options directive controls which server features are available in a particular directory. The value can be set to None, in which case none of the extra features are enabled, or one or more of the following:

ExecCGI   Permits execution of CGI scripts.

FollowSymLinks   The server will follow symbolic links (symlinks) in this directory. Following symlinks does not change the pathname used to match against <Directory> sections. This option is ignored if set inside a <Location> section.

Includes   Permits server side includes (SSI).

IncludesNOEXEC   Server side includes are permitted, but the #exec and #include commands of SSI scripts are disabled.

Indexes   If a URL that maps to a directory is requested and there is no DirectoryIndex (for example, index.html) in that directory, then the server will return a formatted listing of the directory.

MultiViews   Allows content-negotiated MultiViews. MultiViews are one means of implementing content negotiation— allowing multiple variants of a resource, distinguished by a separate extension, for example, somedoc.html.en and somedoc.html.de for an English and a German version of the source document.

All   Includes all options except for MultiViews. This is the default setting.

SymLinksIfOwnerMatch   The server will follow only symbolic links for which the target file or directory is owned by the same user ID as the link. Like FollowSymLinks, this option is ignored if set inside a <Location> section.

Normally, if multiple options apply to a directory, the most specific one is used, and the other options are ignored. However, if all the options on the `Options` directive are preceded by a plus (+) or minus (–) character, then the options are merged. Any options preceded by a plus are added to the options currently in effect, and any options preceded by a minus are removed from the options currently in effect.

Since the default setting for the `Options` directive is `All`, the configuration file that is provided with Apache contains the following section, which enables only `FollowSymLinks` for every directory on the entire system:

```
<Directory />
    Options FollowSymLinks
</Directory>
```

The following examples should clarify the rules governing the merging of options. In the first example, only the option `Includes` will be set for the /web/docs/spec directory:

```
<Directory /web/docs>
    Options Indexes FollowSymLinks
</Directory>
<Directory /web/docs/spec>
     Options Includes
</Directory>
```

In the example below, only the options `FollowSymLinks` and `Includes` are set for the /web/docs/spec directory:

```
<Directory /web/docs>
   Options Indexes FollowSymLinks
</Directory>
<Directory /web/docs/spec>
   Options +Includes -Indexes
</Directory>
```

Using either `-IncludesNOEXEC` or `-Includes` disables server side includes. Also, the use of a plus or minus sign to specify a directive has no effect if no options list is already in effect. Thus, it is always a good idea to ensure that at least one `Options` directive that covers all directories is used in `httpd.conf`. Options can be added to or removed from this list as required in narrower scopes.

WARNING

Be aware that the default setting for Options is All. For that reason, you should always ensure that this default is overridden for every web-accessible directory. The default configuration for Apache includes a <Directory> container to do this; do not modify or remove it.

THE CONTAINER DIRECTIVES

The scope of an Apache directive is often restricted using special directives called *container directives*. In general, container directives are easily identified by the enclosing <> brackets. The conditional directives <IfDefine> and <IfModule>, which are not container directives, are exceptions. Container directives require a closing directive that has the same name and begins with a slash character (much like HTML tags).

A container directive encloses other directives and specifies a limited scope of applicability for the directives it encloses. A directive that is not enclosed in a container directive is said to have *global scope* and applies to the entire Apache server. A global directive is overridden locally by the same directive when it is used inside a container. The following sections examine each type of container directive.

The *<VirtualHost>* Container

The <VirtualHost> container directive encloses directives that apply only to a specific *virtual host*. A virtual host is a website hosted on your server that is identified by a hostname alias. For example, assume your server is www.aulds.com and that it hosts a website for a local bait and tackle shop. That shop, however, does not want its customers connecting to www.aulds.com for information; it wants customers to use the website www.worms.com. You can solve this problem by creating a virtual host for www.worms.com on the real host www.aulds.com. The format of the <VirtualHost> container directive is this:

```
<VirtualHost address>
    directives
</VirtualHost>
```

The directives you enclose in the <VirtualHost> container will specify the correct hostname and document root for the virtual host.

Naturally, the server name should be a value that customers of the website expect to see when they connect to the virtual host. Additionally, the file served to the customers needs to provide the expected information. In addition to these obvious directives, almost anything else you need to customize for the virtual host can be set in this container. For example:

```
<VirtualHost 192.168.1.4>
    ServerAdmin webmaster@host1.com
    DocumentRoot /home/httpd/wormsdocs
    ServerName www.worms.com
    ErrorLog logs/worms.log
    TransferLog logs/worms.log
</VirtualHost>
```

This example defines a single virtual host. This is a form of virtual host referred to as *IP-based*. The first line defines the Internet address (IP) for the virtual host. All connections to the Apache server on this IP address are handled by the virtual server for this site, which might be only one of many virtual sites being hosted on the same server. Each directive defines site-specific values for configuration parameters that, outside a <VirtualHost> container directive, normally refer to the entire server. The use of each of these in the general server context has already been shown.

The *<Directory>* and *<DirectoryMatch>* Containers

The <Directory> container encloses directives that apply to a filesystem directory and its subdirectories. The directory must be expressed by its full pathname or with wildcards. The following example illustrates a <Directory> container that sets the Indexes and FollowSymLinks options for all directories under /home/httpd/ that begin with user:

```
<Directory /home/httpd/user*>
    Options Indexes FollowSymLinks
</Directory>
```

<Directory> containers are always evaluated so that the shortest match (widest scope) is applied first, and longer matches (narrower scope) override those that may already be in effect from a wider

container. For example, the following container disables all overrides for every directory on the system (/ and all its subdirectories):

```
<Directory />
    AllowOverride None
</Directory>
```

If the httpd.conf file includes a second <Directory> container that specifies a directory lower in the filesystem hierarchy, the directives in the container take precedence over those defined for the filesystem as a whole. The following container enables FileInfo overrides for all directories under /home (which hosts all user home directories on most Linux systems):

```
<Directory /home/*>
    AllowOverride FileInfo
</Directory>
```

The <Directory> container can also be matched against regular expressions by using the ~ character to force a regular expression match:

```
<Directory ~ "^/home/user[0-9]{3}">
```

The <DirectoryMatch> directive is specifically designed for regular expressions, however, and should normally be used in place of this form. This container directive is exactly like <Directory>, except that the directories to which it applies are matched against regular expressions. The following example applies to all request URLs that specify a resource that begins with /user, followed by exactly three digits. (The ^ character denotes "beginning of string," and the {3} means to match the previous character; in this case any member of the character set [0-9].)

```
<DirectoryMatch "^/user[0-9]{3}">
    order deny,allow
    deny from all
    allow from .foo.com
</Directory>
```

This container directive would apply to a request URL such as the following:

```
http://jackal.hiwaay.net/user321
```

because the <DirectoryMatch> container directive looks for directories (relative to DocumentRoot) that consist of the word user followed by three digits.

INTRODUCTION TO REGULAR EXPRESSIONS

Many Apache configuration directives accept regular expressions for matching patterns. Regular expressions are an alternative to wildcard pattern matching and are usually an extension of a directive's wildcard pattern-matching capability. Indeed, I have heard regular expressions (or regexps) described as "wildcards on steroids."

A brief sidebar can hardly do justice to the subject, but to pique your interest, here are a few regexp tags and what they mean:

^ and $ Two special and very useful tags that mark the beginning and end of a line. For example, ^# matches the # character whenever it occurs as the first character of a line (very useful for matching comment lines), and #$ matches # occurring as the very last character on a line. These pattern-matching operators are called *anchoring operators* and are said to "anchor the pattern" to either the beginning or the end of a line.

* and ?   The character * matches the preceding character zero or more times, and ? matches the preceding pattern zero or one time. These operators can be confusing, because they work slightly differently from the same characters when used as wildcards. For example, the expression fo* will match the pattern foo or fooo (any number of o characters), but it also matches f, which has zero o characters. The expression ca? will match the c in score, which seems a bit counterintuitive because there's no a in the word, but a? says zero or one a character. Matching zero or more occurrences of a pattern is usually important whenever that pattern is optional. You might use one of these operators to find files that begin with a name that is optionally followed by several digits and then an extension. ^filename\d*.gif will match filename001.gif and filename2.gif, but also simply filename.gif. The \d matches any digit (0–9); in other words, we are matching zero or more digits.

+   Matches the preceding character one or more times, so ca+ will not match score, but will match scare.

CONTINUED ➡

Part VI

. The period character matches any single character except the newline character. In effect, when you use it, you are saying you don't care what character is matched, as long as some character is matched. For example x.y matches xLy but not xy; the period says the two must be separated by a single character. The expression x.*y says to match an x and a y separated by zero or more characters.

{n} This operator (a number between braces) matches the n occurrences of the preceding character. For example, so{2} matches soot, but not sot.

If you're an experienced Linux systems administrator, you're already familiar with regular expressions from using grep, sed, and awk. And if you're an experienced Perl user, you probably also have some knowledge of regular expressions. The GNU C++ Regular Expressions library and Windows Scripting Host (WSH) even allow expressions in Microsoft's JavaScript or VBScript programs.

The only way to develop proficiency in using regexps is to study examples and experiment with them. Entire books have been written on the power of regular expressions (well, at least one) for pattern matching and replacement.

Some useful resources on regexps are the following:

Mastering Regular Expressions, by Jeffrey E.F. Friedl (O'Reilly, 1997)

http://www.perl.com/CPAN-local/doc/manual/
html/pod/perlre.html

http://www.delorie.com/gnu/docs/regex/regex_toc.html

http://lib.stat.cmu.edu/scgn/v52/section1_7_0_1.html

The *<Files>* and *<FilesMatch>* Containers

The <Files> container encloses directives that apply only to specific files, which should be specified by filename (using wildcards when necessary). The following example allows access to files with the OurFile extension only by hosts in a specific domain:

```
<Files *.OurFile>
    order deny,allow
    deny from all
    allow from .thisdomain.com
</Files>
```

Like the <Directory> container, <Files> can also be matched against regular expressions by using the ~ character to force a regular expression match. The following line, for example, matches filenames that end in a period character (escaped with a backslash) immediately followed by the characters xml. The $ in regular expressions denotes the end of the string. Thus, we are looking for filenames with the extension .xml.

```
<Files ~ "\.xml$">
    Directives go here
</Files>
```

The <FilesMatch> directive is specifically designed for regular expressions, however, and should normally be used in place of this form.

<FilesMatch> is exactly like the <Files> directive, except that the specified files are defined by regular expressions. All graphic images might be defined, for example, using this:

```
<FilesMatch>  "\.(gif|jpe?g|png)$">
    some directives
</FilesMatch>
```

This regular expression matches filenames with the extension gif or jpg or jpeg or png. (The *or* is denoted by the vertical bar | character.) Notice the use of the ? character, which indicates zero or one occurrences of the preceding character (e). In other words, a match is made to jp, followed by zero or one e, followed by g.

The *<Location>* and *<LocationMatch>* Containers

The <Location> container encloses directives that apply to specific URLs. This is similar to <Directory>, because most URLs contain a reference that maps to a specific directory relative to Apache's

DocumentRoot. The difference is that <Location> does not access the filesystem but considers only the URL of the request. Most directives that are valid in a <Directory> context also work in a <Location> container; directives that do not apply to a URL are simply ignored because they are meaningless in a <Location> context.

The <Location> functionality is especially useful when combined with the SetHandler directive. For example, to enable status requests, but only from browsers at foo.com, you might use the following. (Note that status is not a directory; it is a part of the URL and actually invokes a server-generated status page. There is no /status directory on my system.)

```
<Location /status>
    SetHandler server-status
    order deny,allow
    deny from all
    allow from .foo.com
</Location>
```

You can also use extended regular expressions by adding the ~ character, as described for the <Directory> and <Files> container directories. However, a special container directive, <LocationMatch>, is specifically designed for this purpose and should be used instead.

<LocationMatch> is exactly like the <Location> container directive, except that the URLs are specified by regular expressions. The following container applies to any URL that contains the substring /www/user followed immediately by exactly three digits—for example, /www/user911:

```
<LocationMatch "/www/user[0-9]{3}">
    order deny,allow
    deny from all
    allow from .foo.com
</Location>
```

The *<Limit>* and *<LimitExcept>* Containers

<Limit> encloses directives that apply only to the HTTP methods specified. In the following example, user authentication is required only for requests using the HTTP methods POST, PUT, and DELETE:

```
<Limit POST PUT DELETE>
    require valid-user
</Limit>
```

`<LimitExcept>` encloses directives that apply to all HTTP methods except those specified. The following example shows how authentication can be required for all HTTP methods other than GET:

```
<LimitExcept GET>
    require valid-user
</Limit>
```

Perl Sections

If you are using the mod_perl module, it is possible to include Perl code to automatically configure your server. Sections of the httpd.conf file containing valid Perl code and enclosed in special `<Perl>` container directives are passed to mod_perl's built-in Perl interpreter. The output of these scripts is inserted into the httpd.conf file before it is parsed by the Apache engine. This allows parts of the httpd.conf file to be generated dynamically, possibly from external data sources such as a relational database on another machine.

This option absolutely requires the use of mod_perl. For information on mod_perl, see perl.apache.org.

Apache's Order of Evaluation for Containers

When multiple containers apply to a single incoming request, Apache resolves them in the following order:

1. Apache will first evaluate any `<Directory>` container (except those that match regular expressions) and merge any .htaccess files it finds that apply to the request. `<Directory>` containers are always evaluated from widest to narrowest scope, and directives found in .htaccess files override those in `<Directory>` containers that apply to the same directory.

2. Directives found in `<DirectoryMatch>` containers and `<Directory>` containers that match regular expressions are evaluated next. Directives that apply to the request override those in effect from `<Directory>` or .htaccess files (item 1 of this list).

3. After directives that apply to the directory in which the resource resides, Apache applies directives that apply to

the file itself. These come from <Files> and <FilesMatch> containers, and they override directives in effect from <Directory> containers. For example, if an .htaccess file contains a directive that denies the requester access to a directory, but a directive in a <Files> container specifically allows access to the file, the request will be granted because the contents of the <Files> container override those of the <Directory> container.

4. Finally, any directives in <Location> or <LocationMatch> containers are applied. These directives are applied to the request URL and override directives in all other containers. If a directive in a <Location> container directly conflicts with the same directive in either a <Directory> or a <Files> container, the directive in the <Location> container will override the others.

Containers with narrower scopes always override those with a wider scope. For example, directives contained in <Directory /home/httpd/html> override those in <Directory /home/httpd> for the resources in its scope. If two containers specify exactly the same scope (for example, both apply to the same directory or file), the one specified last takes precedence.

The following rather contrived example illustrates how the order of evaluation works:

```
<Files index.html>
    allow from 192.168.1.2
</Files>


<Directory /home/httpd/html>
    deny from all
</Directory>
```

In this example, the <Directory> container specifically denies access to the /home/httpd/html directory to all clients. The <Files> directive (which precedes it in the httpd.conf file) permits access to a single file index.html inside that directory, but only to a client connecting from IP address 192.168.1.2. This permits the display of the HTML page by that client, but not any embedded images; these can't be accessed, because the <Files> directive does not include them in its scope. Note also that the order of the containers within the configuration file is *not* important; it is the order in which the containers are resolved that determines which takes precedence. Any <Files> container directives will always take precedence over <Directory> containers that apply to the same resource(s).

THE .HTACCESS FILE

Although an Apache server is usually configured completely within the httpd.conf file, editing this file is not always the most efficient configuration method. Most Apache administrators prefer to group directory-specific directives, particularly access-control directives, in special files located within the directories they control. This is the purpose of Apache's .htaccess files. In addition to the convenience of having all the directives that apply to a specific group of files located within the directory that contains those files, .htaccess files offer a couple of other advantages. First, you can grant access to modify .htaccess files on a per-directory basis, allowing trusted users to modify access permissions to files in specific directories without granting those users unrestricted access to the entire Apache configuration. Second, you can modify directives in .htaccess files without having to restart the Apache server (which is the only way to read a modified httpd.conf file).

By default, the Apache server searches for the existence of an .htaccess file in every directory from which it serves resources. If the file is found, it is read, and the configuration directives it contains are merged with other directives already in effect for the directory. Unless the administrator has specifically altered the default behavior (using the AllowOverride directive as described below), all directives in the .htaccess file override directives already in effect. For example, suppose httpd.conf contained the following <Directory> section:

```
<Directory /home/httpd/html/Special>
    order deny,allow
    deny from all
</Directory>
```

All access to the directory /home/httpd/html/Special would be denied. This may be exactly what the administrator wants, but it is more likely that the directory exists under the web server root so that someone can get to it with a browser. This can be accomplished by creating an .htaccess file in the Special directory with directives such as the following, which overrides the directives already active for the directory:

```
allow from 192.168.1.*
```

Here, we've used a wildcard expression to specify a range of IP addresses (possibly the web server's local subnet) that can access resources in the Special directory.

The *AllowOverrides* Directive

By default, whenever Apache receives a request for a resource, it searches for an .htaccess file in the directory where that resource resides and in every parent directory of that directory on the filesystem. Remember that this search is not limited to DocumentRoot and its subdirectories but extends all the way up the filesystem hierarchy to the root directory (/). It treats each of these exactly as if it were a <Directory> container for the directory in which it is located. The directives in all .htaccess files found in the requested resource's tree are merged with any other directives already in effect for that directory. Those lower in the filesystem hierarchy override those higher in the tree; this means you can grant permission to access a directory even if that permission was denied to a higher-level directory (and, consequently, all of its subdirectories). After merging all the relevant .htaccess files with all directives from all applicable <Directory> containers, Apache applies them according to the order of evaluation described earlier.

What I've just described is the default behavior of Apache with regard to .htaccess files. You can modify this behavior through the special directive AllowOverride, which controls how .htaccess files are handled. The AllowOverride directive specifies which directives, when found in an .htaccess file, are allowed to override conflicting directives that are already in effect. AllowOverride is used not to enable or disable directives but to specify types of directives that can be overridden in .htaccess files.

The following is a list of all permissible arguments to the AllowOverride directive. Each enables or disables a set of directives when those directives are found in .htaccess files. Consult the Apache documentation at httpd.apache.org/docs/mod/directives.html for the applicable AllowOverride for each directive for which an override can be specified. The AllowOverride directive does not apply to directives that do not provide an override.

All This enables all .htaccess overrides. Therefore, all directives that are permissible in an .htaccess file can be used to override settings in the httpd.conf file.

WARNING

The default behavior of Apache is to search for .htaccess files in each directory in the path of a resource as if AllowOverride All had been specified for all directories. This makes the server hard to secure, because anyone who can write a file into any of the directories from which Apache serves files can create a bogus .htaccess file that can be used to subvert system security. It is always best to use AllowOverride to disable .htaccess files in all directories, enabling the use of .htaccess files only for specific purposes and locations on a case-by-case basis. Disabling the search for .htaccess files also has the added benefit of improving Apache performance.

None   This disables .htaccess overrides. If AllowOverride None is specified for a directory, Apache will not read an .htaccess even if it exists in that directory. If AllowOverride None is specified for the system root (/) directory, no directory will ever be searched for an .htaccess file.

Authconfig   Allows the use of all user/group authorization directives (Authname, Authuserfiles, Authgroupfile, Require).

FileInfo   Allows the use of directives controlling document types.

Indexes   Allows the use of directives controlling directory indexing.

Limit   Allows the use of directives that control access based on the browser hostname or network address.

Options   Allows the use of special directives, currently limited to the directives Options and XBitHack.

SETTING UP USER HOME DIRECTORIES

In nearly every server used to support multiple users, it is useful to provide individual users with their own web home directories. This is a very common practice among Internet service providers that support web hosting for their users. Providing user home directories is similar to virtual hosting in some respects, but it is much simpler to implement. The functionality is provided by a standard Apache module (mod_userdir) that is compiled into the Apache server by default.

Specifying Username-to-Directory Mappings

If you intend to allow users to publish their own web pages, the UserDir directive indicates the name of a directory that, if found in the users' home directories, contains web pages that are accessed with a URL of the form http://serverhostname/~username/. The Apache default is to name this directory public_html. There is absolutely nothing wrong with this default value, but for years, since I first administered a CERN 3.0 server, I have chosen to name this directory WWW. A simple change to the UserDir directive in httpd.conf lets me reconfigure this value for all users on the server:

```
UserDir WWW
```

Once I've added this line to Apache's httpd.conf file and restarted the server, each user on my system can now place files in a /WWW subdirectory of his home directory that Apache can serve. Requests to a typical user's web files look like this:

```
http://jackal.hiwaay.net/~caulds/index.html
```

The UserDir directive specifies a filename or pattern that is used to map a request for a user home directory to a special repository for that user's web files. The UserDir directive can take one of three forms:

A Relative Path This is normally the name of a directory that, when found in the user's home directory, becomes the DocumentRoot for that user's web resources:

```
UserDir public_html
```

This is the simplest way to implement user home directories, and the one I recommend because it gives each user a web home beneath his system home directories. This form takes advantage of the fact that ~account is always Linux shorthand for *user account's home directory*. By specifying users' home directories as a relative path, the server actually looks up the user's system home (in the Linux /etc/passwd file) and then looks for the defined web home directory beneath it).

WARNING

Be careful when using the relative path form of the `UserDir` directive. It can expose directories that shouldn't be accessible from the Web. For example, when using the form `http://servername/~root/`, the Linux shortcut for `~root` maps to a directory in the filesystem reserved for system files on most Linux systems. If you had attempted to designate each user's system home directory as his web home directory (using `UserDir /`), this request would map to the `/root` directory. When using the relative directory form to designate user web home directories, you should lock out any accounts that have home directories on protected filesystems (see the section "Enabling/Disabling Mappings," later in this chapter). The home directory of the `root` account (or *superuser*) on Linux systems should be protected. If someone were able to place an executable program in one of `root`'s startup scripts (such as `.profile` or `.bashrc`), that program would be executed the next time a legitimate user or administrator logged in using the `root` account.

An Absolute Path   An absolute pathname is combined with the username to identify the `DocumentRoot` for that user's web resources:

```
UserDir /home/httpd/userstuff
```

This example would give each user his own directory with the same name as his user account beneath `/home/httpd/userstuff`. This form gives each user a web home directory that is *outside* his system home directory. Maintaining a special directory for each user outside his system home directory is not a good idea if there are a lot of users. They won't be able to maintain their own web spaces, as they could in their respective home directories, and the entire responsibility will fall on the administrator. Use the absolute form for defining user web home directories only if you have a small number of users, preferably where each is knowledgeable enough to ensure that his web home directory is protected from other users on the system.

An Absolute Path with Placeholder   An absolute pathname can contain the * character (called a *placeholder*), which is replaced by the username when determining the `DocumentRoot` path for that user's web resources. Like the absolute path described above, this form can map the request to a directory outside the user's system home directory:

```
UserDir  /home/httpd/*/www
```

Part vi

Apache substitutes the username taken from the request URL of the form `http://servername/~username/` to yield the path to each user's web home directory:

`/home/httpd/username/www`

If all users have home directories under the same directory, the placeholder in the absolute path can mimic the relative path form by specifying:

`UserDir   /home/*/www`

The behavior of the lookup is slightly different, though, using this form. In the relative path form, the user's home directory is ooked up in `/etc/passwd`. In the absolute path form, this lookup is not performed, and the user's web home directory must exist in the specified path. The advantage of using the absolute path in this manner is that it prevents URLs such as `http://servername/~root` from mapping to a location that web clients should never access.

The disadvantage of using the "absolute path with placeholder" form is that it forces all web home directories to reside under one directory that you can point to with the absolute path. If you needed to place user web home directories in other locations (perhaps even on other filesystems), you will need to create symbolic links that point the users' defined web home directories to the actual location of the files. For a small to medium-size system, this is a task that can be done once for each user and isn't too onerous, but with many users, it's a job you might prefer to avoid.

The use of the `UserDir` directive is best illustrated by example. Each of the three forms of the directive described would map a request for

`http://jackal.hiwaay.net/~caulds/index.html`

into the following fully qualified path/filenames, respectively:

1. `~caulds/public_html/index.html`

2. `/home/httpd/userstuff/caulds/index.html`

3. `/home/httpd/caulds/www/index.html`

Redirecting Requests for User Home Directories

A server cannot force a browser to retrieve a resource from an alternate location. It sends a status code showing that the server couldn't respond to the browser's requests and a Location directive indicating an alternate location. The browser is politely asked to redirect its request to this alternate location. In the case of UserDir, the server issues a redirect request to the client, which will in all likelihood request the resource again from the specified alternate location, and the user is none the wiser. The argument to UserDir can also take the form of a URL rather than a directory specification, in which case the mapping is sent back to the client as a redirect request. This is most useful when redirecting requests for users' home directories to other servers. The following UserDir directive:

```
UserDir http://server2.hiwaay.com/~*/
```

would cause a request for

```
http://jackal.hiwaay.net/~caulds/docfiles/index.html
```

to generate a URL redirect request that would send the requester to the following resource, which is on a separate server:

```
http://server2.hiwaay.net/~caulds/docfiles/index.html
```

Enabling/Disabling Mappings

Another form of the UserDir directive uses the keywords enabled or disabled in one of three ways:

```
UserDir disabled <usernames>
```

This disables username-to-directory mappings for the space-delimited list of usernames. For example:

```
UserDir disabled root webmaster
```

WARNING

If you are running a 1.3 version of Apache, it is strongly recommended that your configuration include a UserDir disabled root declaration.

Using the disabled keyword without a username turns off all username-to-directory mappings:

```
UserDir disabled
```

This form is usually used prior to a UserDir enabled directive that explicitly lists users for which mappings are performed.

```
UserDir enabled <usernames>
```

Part vi

This enables username-to-directory mappings for the space-delimited list of usernames. It usually follows a `UserDir disabled` directive that turns off username-to-directory mappings for all users (all are normally enabled):

```
UserDir disabled*
UserDir enabled caulds csewell webteam
```

Using suEXEC with User Directories

Most sites that support user directories also allow users to create and run their own CGI processes. It is easy to see how allowing users to write and run CGI programs that run with the permissions of the web server could be disastrous. Such a script would have the same access privileges that the web server itself uses, and this is normally not a good thing. To protect the web server from errant or malicious user-written CGI scripts, and to protect web users from one another, user CGI scripts are usually run from a program called a *CGI wrapper*. A CGI wrapper is used to run a CGI process under different user and group accounts than those that are invoking the process. In other words, while ordinary CGI processes are run under the user and group account of the Apache server (by default that is user nobody and group nobody), using a CGI wrapper, it is possible to invoke CGI processes that run under different user and group ownership.

There are several such CGI wrappers, but one such program, called suEXEC, is a standard part of Apache in all versions after version 1.2 (though it is not enabled by the default installation). suEXEC is very easy to install and even easier to use. There are two ways in which suEXEC is useful to Apache administrators. The most important use for suEXEC is to allow users to run CGI programs from their own directories that run under their user and group accounts, rather than that of the server.

The second way in which suEXEC is used with Apache is with virtual hosts. When used with virtual hosts, suEXEC changes the user and group accounts under which all CGI scripts defined for each virtual host are run. This is used to give virtual host administrators the ability to write and run their own CGI scripts without compromising the security of the primary web server (or any other virtual host).

Configuring Apache to Use suEXEC

The suEXEC tool is very easy to set up using the APACI installation script. APACI's `configure` script is provided with a number of options that are used to configure suEXEC. The most important of these is `--enable-suexec`, which is required to enable suEXEC. All of the other options have default values that you can find by peeking into the makefile in the top Apache source directory. On my system, I chose to use all the available options when running configure. Even when the default values are acceptable, I include them in my build.sh script, borrowing the default values from the makefile and modifying them where I want. Listing 25.1 shows the complete build.sh script I use to build Apache version 1.3.20 with suEXEC support.

Listing 25.1: A *build.sh* Script for Building Apache 1.3.20 with suEXEC Support

```
CFLAGS="-DUSE_RANDOM_SSI -DUSE_PARSE_FORM" \
./configure \
"--enable-rule=EAPI" \
"--with-layout=Apache" \
"--prefix=/usr/local/apache" \
"--enable-module=most" \
"--enable-module=ssl" \
"--enable-shared=max" \
"--enable-suexec" \
"--suexec-caller=www" \
"--suexec-docroot=/home/httpd/html" \
"--suexec-logfile=/usr/local/apache/logs/suexec_log" \
"--suexec-userdir=public_html" \
"--suexec-uidmin=100" \
"--suexec-gidmin=100" \
"--suexec-safepath=/usr/local/bin:/usr/bin:/bin" \
"$@"
```

To build and install Apache with suEXEC, I enter three lines in the Apache source directory:

```
# ./build.sh
# make
# make install
```

After building and installing Apache with suEXEC support, you should test it by invoking HTTPd with the -l argument. If suEXEC is functional, the result will look like this:

```
# ./httpd -l
Compiled-in modules:
  http_core.c
  mod_so.c
suexec: enabled; valid wrapper /usr/local/apache/bin/suexec
```

Part VI

If Apache is unable to find suEXEC, or if it does not have its user setuid execution bit set, suEXEC will be disabled:

```
# ./httpd -1
Compiled-in modules:
  http_core.c
  mod_so.c
suexec: disabled; invalid wrapper
/usr/local/apache1_3_12/bin/suexec
```

Apache will still start, even if suEXEC is unavailable, but suEXEC will be disabled. You have to keep an eye on this; it is unfortunate that, when suEXEC is disabled, no warning is given when Apache is started, and nothing is written into Apache's error log. The error log will show only when suEXEC is enabled. You can check inside Apache's error log (which is in logs/error.log under the Apache installation directory unless you've overridden this default value). If all is OK, the error log will contain the following line, usually immediately after the line indicating that Apache has been started:

```
[notice] suEXEC mechanism enabled (wrapper:
    /usr/local/apache/bin/suexec)
```

If suEXEC is not enabled when Apache is started, verify that you have the suEXEC wrapper program, owned by root, in Apache's bin directory:

```
# ls -al /usr/local/apache/bin/suexec
-rws--x--x  1 root    root      10440 Jun 28 09:59 suexec
```

Note the s in the user permissions. This indicates that the setuid bit is set—in other words, when executed, the file will run under the user account of the file's owner. For example, the Apache HTTPd process that invokes suEXEC will probably be running under the nobody account. The suEXEC process it starts, however, will run under the root account, because root is the owner of the file suexec. Only root can invoke the Linux setuid and setgid system functions to change the ownership of processes it spawns as children (the CGI scripts that run under its control). If suexec is not owned by root and does not have its user setuid bit set, correct this by entering the following lines while logged in as root:

```
# chown root /usr/local/apache/bin/suexec
# chmod u+s /usr/local/apache/bin/suexec
```

If you want to disable suEXEC, the best way is to simply remove the user setuid bit:

```
# chmod u-s /usr/local/apache/bin/suexec
```

This not only disables suEXEC, but it also renders the suEXEC program a bit safer because it will no longer run as root (unless directly invoked by root).

Using suEXEC

While suEXEC is easy to set up, it's even easier to use. Once it is enabled in your running Apache process, any CGI script that is invoked from a user's web directory will execute under the user and group permissions of the owner of the web directory. In other words, if I invoke a script with a URL such as http://jackal.hiwaay.net/~caulds/cgi-bin/ somescript.cgi, that script will run under caulds's user and group account. Note that all CGI scripts that will run under the suEXEC wrapper must be in the user's web directory (which defaults to public_html but can be redefined by the --suexec-userdir configuration) or a subdirectory of that directory.

For virtual hosts, the user and group accounts under which CGI scripts are run are defined by the User and Group directives found in the virtual host container:

```
<VirtualHost 192.168.1.1>
    ServerName vhost1.hiwaay.net
    ServerAdmin caulds@hiwaay.net
    DocumentRoot /home/httpd/NamedVH1
    User vh1admin
    Group vh1webteam
</VirtualHost>
```

If a virtual host does not contain a User or Group directive, the values for these are inherited from the primary web server (usually user nobody and group nobody). Note that all CGI scripts that will run under suEXEC for such a virtual host must reside beneath DocumentRoot (they can be in any subdirectory beneath DocumentRoot, but they cannot reside outside it).

SIMPLE REQUEST REDIRECTION

For simple redirection, the Alias core directive is very useful. The following gives an example of how Alias permits easy access to HTML documents outside the DocumentRoot directory on my server.

Many applications for Linux include documentation in the form of linked HTML pages. These are ordinarily outside the hierarchy of resources that has the Apache DocumentRoot at its top. Apache documentation is no exception. Some provision should be made to allow access to these pages. On my system, the Apache documentation pages are installed in /usr/local/apache/htdocs. I used the Alias directive to alias two directories outside my DocumentRoot to URLs that appear inside the DocumentRoot resource tree. The first of these is the documentation for the MySQL database, which placed its documentation in /usr/doc/MySQL-3.22.29 when installed on my system.

```
# pwd
/usr/doc/MySQL-3.22.29
# ls
PUBLIC  index.html   manual.ps     manual.txt
README  manual.html  manual.texi   manual_toc.html
```

I first granted ownership of this directory to the user and group that Apache processes run under. On Linux systems, these are both user ID -1, which are both named nobody. (Most Unix systems use the same user ID and group ID as Linux. FreeBSD, which does not provide either of these, is the most notable exception.) I changed the ownership of the directory recursively, so that all subdirectories and files would be accessible to the user and group nobody:

```
# chown -R nobody.nobody /usr/doc/MySQL-3.22.29
```

I symbolically linked the top-level HTML file to one that Apache will read when the requested URL names only the directory and not a particular file (that is, where it matches one of the names specified in DirectoryIndex):

```
# ln -s manual_toc.html index.html
```

Using a symbolic link, rather than copying the file or renaming it, ensures that only one copy of the file exists, but that it can be accessed by either name. The last step was the insertion of two Alias directives into httpd.conf. Place these in a manner that seems logical to you, probably somewhere in the section of the file labeled Main server configuration, so that you can easily locate the directives at a later date.

```
Alias /MySQL/ "/usr/doc/MySQL-3.22.29/"
Alias /ApacheDocs/ "/usr/local/apache/docs/"
```

Any user can now access these sets of documentation on my server using these URLs:

```
http://jackal.hiwaay.net/MySQL/
http://jackal.hiwaay.net/ApacheDocs/
```

PROVIDING DIRECTORY INDEXES

I'm ending this chapter with a discussion of a very important set of Apache directories that are not actually part of the core module, but are such a part of the standard distribution that they are used on every Apache server. You might notice that most web pages are not retrieved by the specific filename. Rather than entering a URL such as this:

```
http://jackal.hiwaay.net/dirname/index.html
```

you generally enter a URL such as this:

```
http://jackal.hiwaay.net/dirname
```

This URL actually maps to a directory on the server (a directory named dirname beneath the directory defined in the Apache configuration as DocumentRoot). It is only through a standard Apache module named mod_dir that a specific page is served to clients that send a request URL that maps to a directory. Without mod_dir, the second form, which does not specify a single resource, would be invalid and would produce an HTTP 404 (Not Found) error.

The mod_dir module serves two important functions. First, whenever a request is received that maps to a directory but does not have a trailing slash (/), such as this:

```
http://jackal.hiwaay.net/dirname
```

mod_dir sends a redirection request to the client indicating that the request should be made instead to this URL:

```
http://jackal.hiwaay.net/dirname/
```

This requires a second request on the part of the client to correct what is, technically, an error in the original request. Though the time required to make this second request is usually minimal and unnoticed by the user, whenever you express a URL that maps to a directory rather than a file, you should include the trailing slash for correctness and efficiency.

The second function of mod_dir is to look for and serve a file defined as the index file for the directory specified in the request. That page, by default, is named index.html. This can be changed using mod_dir's only directive, DirectoryIndex, as described in the next section. The name of the file comes from the fact that it was originally intended to provide the requestor with an index of the files in the directory. While providing directory indexes is still useful, the file is used far more often to serve a default HTML document, or web page, for the root URL; this is often called the *home page*. Remember that this behavior is not a given; mod_dir must be included in the server configuration and enabled for this to work.

The *DirectoryIndex* Directive

The default value of the file served by mod_dir is index.html. In other words, if the Apache configuration contains no DirectoryIndex directive, it will look for and attempt to serve a file named index.html whenever a request URL resolves to a directory. Although this is a default behavior, the standard Apache configuration will create the following line in the httpd.conf file that it installs:

```
DirectoryIndex index.html
```

The last change I made was to add a second filename to the DirectoryIndex directive. I added an entry for index.htm to cause the Apache server to look for files of this name, which may have been created on a system that follows the Microsoft convention of a three-character filename extension. The files are specified in order of preference from left to right, so if it finds both index.html and index.htm in a directory, it will serve only index.html.

```
# DirectoryIndex index.html
DirectoryIndex index.html index.htm
```

Fancier Directory Indexes

I've described the behavior of Apache when a request is received that maps to a directory on the server. Through mod_dir, Apache serves a file from the directory defined in the DirectoryIndex directive (or index.html if DirectoryIndex is not specified). In cases where no such file exists, Apache uses a second module, mod_autoindex, to prepare an index or listing of the files in the directory.

Figure 25.2 shows the default directory index that mod_autoindex will serve to the requesting client.

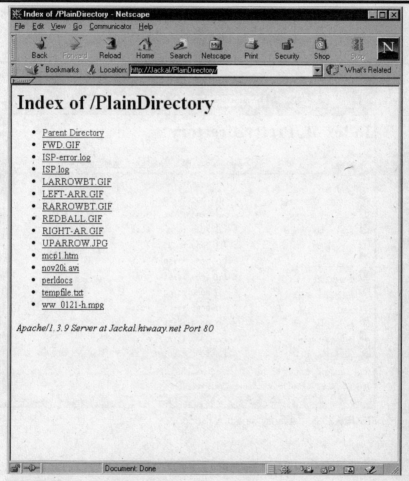

FIGURE 25.2: A plain directory listing

In addition to this plain directory listing, mod_autoindex also allows the administrator full control over every aspect of the directory listing it prepares. This is called *fancy indexing*. You can enable fancy indexing by adding the following directive to httpd.conf:

```
IndexOptions FancyIndexing
```

The default `httpd.conf` file provided with the Apache distribution uses many of the directives that I'll describe in the following sections to set up the default fancy directory for use on your server. Figure 25.3 shows what this standard fancy directory looks like when displaying the results of a directory request.

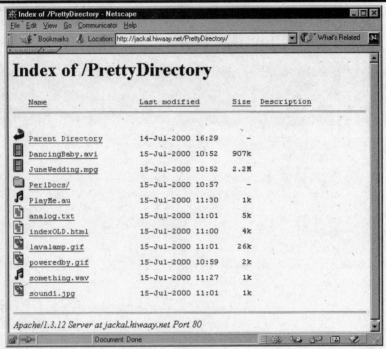

FIGURE 25.3:   A fancy directory listing

The *IndexOptions* Directive

`IndexOptions` can also be used to set a number of other options for configuring directory indexing. Among these are options to specify the size of the icons displayed, to suppress the display of any of the columns besides the filename, and to set whether clicking the column heading sorts the listing by the values in that column. Table 25.2 depicts all possible options that can be used with the `IndexOptions` directive.

TABLE 25.2: Index Options

INDEX OPTION	DESCRIPTION
FancyIndexing	Enables fancy indexing.
IconsAreLinks	Makes icons part of the clickable anchor for the filename.
IconHeight=pixels	Sets the height (in pixels) of the icons displayed in the listing. Like the HTML tag <IMG HEIGHT=n >.
IconWidth=pixels	Sets the width (in pixels) of the icons displayed in the listing. Like the HTML tag <IMG WIDTH=n >.
NameWidth=n	Sets the width (in characters) of the filename column in the listing, truncating characters if the name exceeds this width. Specifying NameWidth=* causes the filename column to be as wide as the longest filename in the listing.
ScanHTMLTitles	Causes the file description to be extracted from the HTML <TITLE> tag, if it exists. The AddDescription directive overrides this setting for individual files.
SuppressColumnSorting	Disables the normal behavior of inserting clickable headers at the top of each column that can be used to sort the listing.
SuppressDescription	Disables the display of the file description.
SuppressHTMLPreamble	Disables automatic HTML formatting of the header file if one is specified for the listing. No <HTML>, <HEAD>, or <BODY> tags precede the header file, and they must be manually placed into the file contents if desired.
SuppressLastModified	Disables the display of the Last Modified column of the listing.
SupressSize	Disables the display of the Size column in the listing.
SupressDescription	Disables the display of the Description column of the listing.
None	Disables fancy indexing.

Part vi

Options are always inherited from parent directories. This behavior is overridden by specifying options with a + or – prefix to add or subtract the options from the list of options that are already in effect for a directory. Whenever an option is read that does not contain either of these prefixes, the list of options in effect is immediately cleared. Consider this example:

```
IndexOptions +ScanHTMLTitles -IconsAreLinks SuppressSize
```

If this directive appears in an `.htaccess` file for a directory, regardless of the options inherited by that directory from its higher-level directories, the net effect will be the same as this directive:

```
IndexOptions SuppressSize
```

This is because as soon as the `SuppressSize` option was encountered without a + or − prefix, the current list of options was immediately cleared.

Specifying Icons

In addition to `IndexOptions`, `mod_autoindex` provides other directives that act to configure the directory listing. For example, you can provide a default icon for unrecognized resources. You can change the icon or description displayed for a particular resource, either by its MIME type, filename, or encoding type (GZIP-encoded, for example). You can also specify a default field and display order for sorting or identify a file whose content will be displayed at the top of the directory.

The *AddIcon* Directive   AddIcon specifies the icon to display for a file when fancy indexing is used to display the contents of a directory. The icon is identified by a relative URL to the icon image file. Note that the URL you specify is embedded directly in the formatted document that is sent to the client browser, which then retrieves the image file in a separate HTTP request.

The name argument can be a filename extension, a wildcard expression, a complete filename, or one of two special forms. Examples of the use of these forms are as follows:

```
AddIcon /icons/image.jpg *jpg*
AddIcon (IMG, /icons/image.jpg) .gif .jpg .bmp
```

The second example illustrates an alternate form for specifying the icon. When parentheses are used to enclose the parameters of the directive, the first parameter is the alternate text to associate with the resource; the icon to be displayed is specified as a relative URL to an image file. The alternate text, IMG, will be displayed by browsers that are not capable of rendering images. A disadvantage of using this form is that the alternate text cannot contain spaces or other special characters. The following form is not acceptable:

```
AddIcon ("JPG Image", /icons/image.jpg) .jpg
```

There are two special expressions that can be used in place of a filename in the AddIcon directive to specify images to use as icons in the directory listing. ^^BLANKICON^^ is used to specify an icon to use for blank lines in the listing, and ^^DIRECTORY^^ is used to specify an icon for directories in the listing:

```
AddIcon /icons/blankicon.jpg  ^^BLANKICON^^
AddIcon /icons/dir.pcx ^^DIRECTORY^^
```

There is one other special case that you should be aware of. The parent of the directory whose index is being displayed is indicated by the .. filename. You can change the icon associated with the parent directory with a directive such as the following:

```
AddIcon /icons/up.gif ..
```

NOTE

The Apache Software Foundation recommends using AddIconByType rather than AddIcon whenever possible. Although there appears to be no real difference between these (on a Linux system, the MIME type of a file is identified by its filename extension), it is considered more proper to use the MIME type that Apache uses for the file, rather than directly examining its filename. There are often cases, however, when no MIME type has been associated with a file and you must use AddIcon to set the image for the file.

The *AddIconByType* Directive   AddIconByType specifies the icon to display in the directory listing for files of certain MIME content types. This directory works like the AddIcon directive described in the previous section, but it relies on the determination that Apache has made of the MIME type of the file. (Apache usually determines the MIME type of a file based on its filename.)

```
AddIconByType /icons/webpage.gif text/html
AddIconByType (TXT, /icons/text.gif) text/*
```

This directive is used almost exactly like AddIcon. When parentheses are used to enclose the parameters of the directive, the first parameter is the alternate text to associate with the resource; the icon to be displayed is specified as a relative URL to an image file. The last parameter, rather than being specified as a filename extension, is a MIME content type. (Look in `conf/mime.types` under the Apache home for a list of types that Apache knows about.)

The *AddIconByEncoding* Directive   `AddIconByEncoding` is used to specify the icon displayed next to files that use a certain MIME encoding. MIME encoding generally refers to file compression schemes and therefore determines what action is required to decode the file for use. Some typical encoding schemes and examples of the use of this directive are

```
AddIconByEncoding /icons/gzip.gif x-gzip
AddIconByEncoding /icons/tarimage.gif x-gtar
```

Specifying a Default Icon   A special directive, `DefaultIcon`, is used to set the icon that is displayed for files with which no icon has been associated with either `AddIconByType` or `AddIconByEncoding`. The directive simply identifies an image file by relative URL:

```
DefaultIcon  /icons/unknown.pcx
```

Adding Alternate Text for Images

When an image is displayed in a web page, the HTML tags used to embed the image in the page provide for an alternate text string that is displayed in browsers that cannot display graphics. This text string is also displayed as pop-up text if the user of a graphical browser right-clicks on the associated image.

Three directives are provided by `mod_autoindex` for setting the alternate text associated with a file in the fancy directory listing. Each of these directives is analogous to one of the `AddIcon` directives and uses the same syntax.

The *AddAlt* Directive   The `AddAlt` directive specifies an alternate text string to be display for a file in text-only browsers, instead of an icon. Like its `AddIcon` counterpart, the directive specifies a filename, partial filename, or wildcard expression to identify files:

```
AddAlt "JPG Image" /icons/image.jpg *jpg*
AddIcon "Image File".gif .jpg .bmp
```

Note that it is possible to use a quoted string with the `AddAlt` directive, which can contain spaces and other special characters. This is not possible when specifying alternate text using the special form of AddIcon as shown previously.

The *AddAltByType* Directive   AddAltByType sets the alternate text string to be displayed for a file based on the MIME content type that Apache has identified for the file. This directive works very much like its counterpart, AddIconByType:

```
AddAltByType "HTML Document" text/html
```

The *AddAltByEncoding* Directive   AddAltByEncoding sets the alternate text string to be displayed for a file, based on the MIME content encoding of the file, as determined by Apache:

```
AddIconByEncoding "GZipped File" x-gzip
```

Specifying File Descriptions

The AddDescription directive is used to specify a text string to be displayed in the Description column of the listing for specific files. AddDescription is normally used to provide a description for specific files. Files can be identified by a partial or full pathname:

```
AddDescription "My Home Page" index.html
```

Note that this example sets a description to apply to all files named index.html. To apply the description to a specific file, use its full and unique pathname:

```
AddDescription "My Home Page" /home/httpd/html/index.html
```

AddDescription can also be used with wildcard filenames to set descriptions for entire classes of files (identified by filename extension in this case):

```
AddDescription "PCX Image" *.pcx
AddDescription "TAR File" *.tgz *.tar.gz
```

When multiple descriptions apply to the same file, the first match found will be the one used in the listing; so always specify the most specific match first:

```
AddDescription "Powered By Apache Logo" poweredby.gif
AddDescription "GIF Image" *.gif
```

In addition to AddDescription, there is one other way that mod_autoindex can determine values to display in the Description column of a directory listing. If IndexOptions ScanHTMLTitles is in effect for a directory, mod_autoindex will parse all HTML files in the directory and extract descriptions for display from the <TITLE> elements of the documents. This is handy if the directory contains a relatively small number of HTML documents or is infrequently accessed. Enabling this option requires that every HTML document in the directory be opened and examined. For a large number of files, this can impose a significant workload, so the option is disabled by default.

Adding a Header and Footer

The mod_autoindex module supplies two directives that enable you to insert the contents of a file at the top of the index listing as a page header or at the bottom of the listing as a page footer.

The HeaderName directive specifies a filename using a URI relative to the one used to access the directory. The contents of this file are placed into the listing immediately after the opening <BODY> tag of the listing. It is usually a good idea to maintain the header file in the same directory it describes, which makes it easy to reference by its filename:

```
HeaderName HEADER.html
```

Files identified by the HeaderName directive must be of the major MIME content type text. If the file is identified as type text/html (generally by its extension), it is inserted verbatim; otherwise it is enclosed in <PRE> and </PRE> tags. A CGI script can be used to generate the information for the header (either as HTML or plain text), but you must first associate the CGI script with a MIME main content type (usually text), as follows:

```
AddType text/html .cgi
HeaderName HEADER.cgi
```

The ReadmeName directive works almost identically to HeaderName to specify a file (again relative to the URI used to access the directory being indexed) that is placed in the listing just before the closing </BODY> tag.

Ignoring Files

The IndexIgnore directive specifies a set of filenames that are ignored by mod_autoindex when preparing the index listing of a directory. The filenames can be specified by wildcards:

```
IndexIgnore FOOTER*
```

NOTE

The default httpd.conf file provided with Apache contains an Index-Ignore directive that prevents filenames beginning with README or HEADER from being displayed in the index listing by mod_autoindex. This makes those filenames obvious (but not necessary) choices for use as headers and footers for directory listings.

Ordering the Index Listing

The IndexOrderDefault directive is used to change the default order of the index listing generated by mod_autoindex, which is to sort the list in ascending order by filename. This directive takes two arguments. The first must be either Ascending or Descending to indicate the sort direction; the second names a single field as the primary sort key and can be Name, Date, Size, or Description:

```
IndexOrderDefault Descending Size
```

The secondary sort key is always the filename in ascending order.

Example of an Ordered Index Listing

In order to illustrate typical uses of some of the mod_autoindex directives discussed, I created an .htaccess in the same directory that was illustrated in Figure 25.3. This file contains the following directives, all of which are used by mod_autoindex to customize the index listing for the directory. The result of applying these directives is shown in Figure 25.4.

```
IndexOptions +ScanHTMLTitles
AddIcon /icons/SOUND.GIF .au
AddDescription "1-2-Cha-Cha-Cha" DancingBaby.avi
AddAltByType "This is a JPG Image" image/jpeg
HeaderName HEADER.html
ReadmeName README.txt
```

The IndexOptions directive is used to enable the extraction of file descriptions from the <TITLE> tags of HTML formatted files (technically, files of MIME content type text/html). In Figure 25.4, you can see that it did that for the file indexOLD.html. If this file had its original name, index.html, the index listing would not have been generated; instead, index.html would have been sent (by mod_dir) to the client.

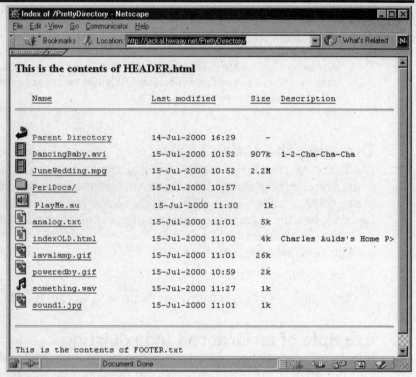

FIGURE 25.4: A customized mod_autoindex listing

I've also provided an example of adding an icon using the AddIcon directive and a file description using AddDescription. The results of these directives can be seen in Figure 25.4. The alternate text for JPEG images (added with the AddAltByType directive) is not displayed in the figure but would be seen in place of the image icon in text-only browsers. It will also appear in a graphical browser in a pop-up dialog box when the cursor is paused over the associated icon. This gives the page developer a handy way to add help text to a graphics-rich web page, which can be particularly useful when the icon or image is part of an anchor tag (clickable link) and can invoke an action.

The last two directives I added to the .htaccess file for this directory specify an HTML-formatted file to be included as a page header and a plain text file to be included as a page footer. Each consists of a single line, also visible in Figure 25.4. The header file contains HTML-formatting tags (<H3> and </H3>) that cause it to be rendered in larger, bolder characters. There is no reason that either the header or footer could not be much longer and contain far more elaborate formatting. Use your imagination.

WHAT'S NEXT?

This chapter has covered a lot of ground because so much of Apache's functionality is incorporated into the configuration directives provided by its core modules. We began with the essential concept of directive *context*, the scope within which particular directives are valid. We then looked at the directives used to configure the basic server environment and how the server listens for connections. These directives are fundamental to Apache's operation, and every administrator needs to be familiar with them.

Later sections of the chapter explored the directives used to create and manage user home directories. These are not only essential functions for any ISP installation of an Apache server, they are also widely used in intranets.

The next chapter moves beyond the core module to the use of third-party modules and the techniques you can use to incorporate them into your Apache server.

Part VI

Chapter 26

APACHE MODULES

I've already discussed the importance of modules to Apache's design philosophy. Without the concept of extension by module, it is unlikely that Apache would have garnered the level of third-party support that directly led to its phenomenal success in the early days of the Web. Apache owes much of that success to the fact that any reasonably proficient programmer can produce add-on modules that tap directly into the server's internal mechanisms. As administrators, we benefit greatly from the availability of these third-party modules.

Adapted from *Linux Apache Web Server Administration* by Charles Aulds

ISBN 0-7821-2734-7   640 pages $39.99

At one time, it was thought that commercial web servers, with the support that "commercial" implies, would eventually eclipse the open-source Apache server. It seemed completely logical that when a company began to get serious about the Web, it needed to look for a serious web engine, a commercial server—not some piece of unsupported free software downloaded from the Internet. But as we've seen, Apache took the top spot from its commercial rivals and has continued to widen that lead, even while most Unix-based applications slowly gave ground to their NT competitors. Apache owes much of its success to a vibrant, innovative, and completely professional community of users and developers that you can be a part of. Apache is as fully supported as any commercial product. Virtually any feature or function you want in a web server is available as an Apache module, usually offered by its author at no cost to all Apache users.

This chapter looks at the types of modules available, how the module mechanism works, how to link modules to Apache as dynamic shared objects (DSOs), and where to find third-party modules. It concludes with a step-by-step example of installing a module.

TYPES OF APACHE MODULES

Except for the very basic kernel code, virtually all of the capability of an Apache server is implemented in modules. Apache modules can be categorized in three groups:

The core module (`httpd_core.c`**)** is the only module that must always be statically linked into the Apache kernel. It is the only module that is absolutely essential to an Apache server. It cannot be removed from the server, and the functions provided by this module are available in all Apache servers. The directives furnished by the core module are always available; they are the only directives discussed so far in this book.

The standard modules are provided as part of the Apache distribution and are maintained by the Apache Software Foundation as part of the Apache server itself. Most of the standard modules are compiled by the standard installation scripts (described in Chapter 24, "Installing Apache") into the Apache code. Unlike the core module, however, any one of the standard modules can be removed at the server administrator's discretion. This might be done for security reasons, but the most common reason for removing a module from Apache is to reduce the amount of memory used by each running instance of the server. (Remember that Apache maintains a pool of server processes to handle user requests. Since each process in the pool requires its own memory space, the amount of space saved by eliminating unused modules can be multiplied by the number of processes in the Apache server pool.)

Third-party modules are modules written, supported, and distributed by sources other than the Apache Group. These modules are not provided as part of the Apache distribution and must be obtained separately.

HOW MODULES WORK

Apache modules are able to register callbacks with Apache for the functions they provide. A *callback* is a function that is registered with Apache so that Apache can call the function at various stages of the request processing cycle. Callbacks are generally registered as handlers for processing specific events. Callback functions registered with Apache are called at specific times, such as when the module is loaded and initialized, when a new Apache child process is started or shut down, and at various stages of the resource request process. Most of the hooks provided by Apache for modules to register callback functions are part of the HTTP request cycle. There are 11 phases of the request cycle currently defined for which modules can register callback functions, and they occur in the following order:

Post-Read-Request Actions in this phase take place immediately after the request header has been read. Although any module can register a callback to run at this phase of the cycle, the phase always includes the determination of which virtual host will handle the request. This phase sets up the server to handle the request. Modules that register callbacks for this phase of the request cycle include mod_proxy and mod_setenvif, which get all the information they need from the request URL.

URL Translation At this stage, the URL is translated into a filename. Modules such as mod_alias, mod_rewrite, and mod_userdir, which provide URL translation services, generally do their main work here.

Header Parsing This phase is obsolete (superseded by the Post-Read-Request phase); no standard module registers functions to be called during this phase.

Access Control This phase checks client access to the requested resource, based on the client's network address, returning a response that either allows or denies the user access to the server resource. The only module that acts as a handler for the Access Control phase of the request cycle is mod_access.

Authentication This phase verifies the identity of the user, either accepting or rejecting credentials presented by the user, which are as simple as a username/password pair. Examples of modules that work during this phase are mod_auth and mod_auth_dbm.

Authorization Once the user's identity has been verified, the user's authorization is checked to determine if the user has permission to access the requested resource. Although authenticating (identifying) the user and determining that user's authorization (or level of access) are separate functions, they are usually performed by the same module. The modules listed as examples for the Authentication phase also register callbacks for the Authorization phase.

MIME Type Checking This phase determines the MIME type of the requested resource, which can be used to determine how the resource is handled. A good example is mod_mime.

FixUp This is a catch-all phase for actions that need to be performed before the request is actually fulfilled. mod_headers is one of the few modules on my system that register a callback for this request phase.

Response or Content This is the most important phase of the request cycle; it is the one in which the requested resource is actually processed. This is where a module is registered to handle documents of a specific MIME type. The mod_cgi module is registered, for example as the default handler for documents identified as CGI scripts.

Logging After the request has been processed, a module can register functions to log the actions taken. While any module can register a callback to perform actions during this phase (and you can easily write your own), most servers will use only mod_log_config to take care of all logging.

Cleanup Functions registered here are called when an Apache child process shuts down. Actions that would be defined to take place during this phase include the closing of open files and perhaps of database connections. Very few modules actually register a callback for this request phase. In fact, none of the standard modules use it.

Incorporating Perl Scripts with *mod_perl*

Modules already exist for most of the common tasks that web servers need to perform, and many administrators will never need to write their own. But if you do plan to write your own modules or even just use modules written by other system administrators, you should know about the mod_perl module. Perl is the scripting language most widely used by system administrators, and mod_perl is the tool that makes it available to Apache.

Before there was a mod_perl, it was not possible to write an Apache module in anything but C, and for production server applications, I'm not sure I would ever have recommended a scripting language for the task, even if it had been possible to use one. The mod_perl module changed that. With its memory-resident Perl interpreter and capability to perform one-time compilation and caching of Perl scripts, it virtually eliminates one of the most valid criticisms leveled at Perl: its lack of speed when compared with binary code compiled from source languages like C.

The mod_perl module provides a built-in handler for each of the 11 phases of the Apache request cycle listed above. This makes it extremely easy to invoke a Perl function at any phase. For example, if you want Apache to call a Perl function that will be performed immediately following the receipt of a user request, you can register the function as a callback by placing the following lines in httpd.conf:

```
PerlModule Apache::MyModule
PerlPostReadRequestHandler Apache::MyModule::myhandler
```

The first line preloads the module into the Apache:: namespace. The second line registers the myhandler function within that module as a callback during the Post-Read-Request phase of the request cycle. When a request comes in, Apache will ensure that myhandler, which has already been loaded and compiled by mod_perl, is called. The function will have access to Apache's internal data structures and functions through the Perl Apache API calls (each of which, in turn, calls a function from the Apache API).

One of the best and most complete sets of online documentation for any Apache module is that available for mod_perl at perl.apache.org/guide/.

INSTALLING THIRD-PARTY MODULES

There is no rigid specification to which Apache modules from third-party sources must adhere. There is no standard procedure for installing and using Apache modules. There are guidelines, however, that define a "well-behaved" Apache module, and most modules are fairly standard and therefore quite simple to install and configure.

The Two Linking Methods

Apache modules can be installed either within the Apache source tree or outside it. Those installed within the Apache source become, essentially, a part of Apache, even if their inclusion is optional. The standard Apache modules (those that are part of the Apache distribution) fall into this category. A limited number of third-party modules must also be installed in this fashion, particularly if they rely on changes made to the Apache source code. When this method is used, the module source code is usually placed in the /src/modules subdirectory with the rest of the Apache source. Special configuration directives are passed to the APache AutoConf-style Interface (APACI) to compile the module with the rest of Apache, link it with the resulting runtime, and make the necessary changes to http.conf to enable the module.

Most third-party modules, though, are better compiled outside the Apache source tree. In other words, they are compiled in a completely separate directory from the Apache source, as dynamic shared object (DSO) modules, and are loaded at runtime by Apache.

Although the module source can be placed inside the Apache source tree and the APACI configuration utility instructed to compile it as a DSO, I strongly recommend against doing this. If you intend to use a module as a DSO, it can be compiled on its own, outside the Apache source tree, using a utility called apxs, which is provided with the Apache distribution. One advantage of compiling with apxs is that the resulting module, which will have the extension .so for *shared object*, is a stand-alone module that can be used with different versions of the server. This allows you to upgrade modules without recompiling Apache, as you must do when a module is compiled within the Apache source tree using APACI. More importantly, using DSO modules compiled with apxs allows you to upgrade the Apache server without having to rerun the configuration for each module, specifying the new Apache source tree.

There are nearly as many installation procedures as there are modules. Some install inside the Apache tree; most can be compiled separately from Apache. Some simply compile a DSO and leave you to manually edit httpd.conf; some configure httpd.conf for you. Read the INSTALL file carefully before compiling any module, at least to get some idea of how the installation proceeds and what options are available. In general, though, the best way to compile and install Apache modules is to use the utility Apache has provided specifically for this purpose, *apxs*. Because most third-party modules are best compiled as DSOs using apxs, that is the method I describe in this chapter. The only modules I recommend installing as statically linked modules are those that come with the standard Apache distribution. These are automatically linked to Apache during the server installation unless at least one --enable-shared argument is passed to configure. Chapter 24 describes how standard modules are chosen and identified as statically linked or DSO modules.

Making the Choice

Virtually all Apache modules can be either statically linked or compiled as a DSO to be loaded at runtime, and the choice is usually yours to make. For most Apache sites, the DSO method provides the most flexibility and easiest maintainability, although you pay a small performance cost for it. Administrators should consider statically linking modules only when they rarely alter their Apache configuration.

Table 26.1 summarizes the characteristics of each method of linking a module.

TABLE 26.1: Static vs. Dynamic Linking

FEATURE	STATICALLY LINKED	LINKED AS DSO
Installed Using:	APACI	apxs
Module Source Location:	Module source resides in the Apache source tree.	Module source resides outside the Apache source tree.
Impact on Size of Apache Executable:	Increases the size of the Apache runtime executable.	Keeps Apache runtime as small as possible.
Loading Speed:	Fastest loading.	Increases load time of the module by about 20 percent.
Module Loaded When:	Module always loaded, even if disabled and unused.	Module loaded only when specified in httpd.conf.
Recommended When:	The Apache configuration is simple, requiring few add-on modules and few changes and when fastest possible loading is important.	Server configuration changes frequently or when modules are frequently changed, upgraded, or installed for testing.

Using Dynamically Linked Modules

DSO modules are loaded as part of the Apache server at runtime, that is, when the server is started. DSO modules are designed to be loaded dynamically into the running server's address space and are able to access and directly modify internal Apache data structures. Loading a DSO module is approximately 20 percent slower than if the module were statically linked into the server kernel. However, a DSO module, once loaded, is in every respect a part of Apache, and there is no performance overhead inherent in running a function in a DSO module rather than as statically linked code.

With two important exceptions, all modules distributed with Apache can be compiled as DSO modules that are loaded at runtime. The first exception is the core module, which must always be statically linked into the Apache kernel. The second module that can never be run as a DSO (for reasons I hope are obvious) is the module that provides the server with the capability of dynamically loading shared objects. No DSO module can be loaded for use by the server without mod_so, and this module must always be statically linked into the Apache kernel when Apache is compiled. When at least one --enable-shared= argument is passed to the Apache configure script (see Chapter 24), mod_so automatically links into Apache when it is compiled. You can see the result of this linking by running httpd with the −1 switch:

```
# /usr/local/apache/bin/httpd -1
Compiled-in modules:
    http_core.c
    mod_so.c
```

This example shows the most basic httpd daemon, which must always have the core module linked into it, and optionally, the mod_so module that provides support for DSO modules. All other module support is dynamically linked at runtime to the httpd process. The mod_so module supplies the server with a new directive, LoadModule, which is used in the Apache configuration file to designate a module for dynamic loading. When the server reads a LoadModule directive from the configuration during its initialization, mod_so will load the module and add its name to the list of available Apache modules. The module does not become available, however, until an AddModule directive specifically enables it. The AddModule directive is a core directive and is not specific to DSO modules. All modules, even those that are statically linked into the Apache kernel, must be explicitly enabled with an AddModule directive. Only DSO modules, however, require the LoadModule directive.

A DSO module exposes an external name for itself that does not necessarily have to match the name of the shared object file. For example, if a module calling itself firewall_module is stored in a file mod_firewall.so in the /libexec directory under the Apache ServerRoot, it is enabled for use by the inclusion of the following two lines in the Apache configuration file:

```
LoadModule firewall_module        libexec/mod_firewall.so
AddModule mod_firewall.c
```

The LoadModule directive (supplied by mod_so) links the named module to the httpd process and then adds the module to the list of active modules. The module is not available, however, until enabled by the AddModule directive, which makes the module's structure, its internal functions, and any directives it supports available to Apache. As noted above, the LoadModule directive has no meaning for statically linked modules, but an AddModule line is required for all modules before they can be used. This permits the disabling of even a statically linked module by simply commenting out or removing its associated AddModule line in httpd.conf.

These two directives do not have to be located together; and in most cases, they are not. Somewhere near the beginning of your httpd.conf file, in the general server configuration, you should find a group of LoadModule directives, followed by a section consisting of AddModule directives. Always remember that when you add a LoadModule directive, you must add a corresponding AddModule directive to enable the loaded module.

If you disable a module simply by commenting out its AddModule directive, you will be loading a module that is never used; of course, that is wasteful. Conversely, if you have an AddModule directive without a corresponding LoadModule directive, the module must be statically linked, or you will get a configuration error when you start the server because you will be attempting to enable a module the server knows nothing about. Generally, you should add and delete the LoadModule and AddModule directives in pairs.

The order in which DSO modules are loaded determines the order in which they are called by Apache to handle URLs. As Apache loads each module, it adds the name to a list. DSO modules are always processed in the reverse of the order in which they are loaded, so the first modules loaded are the last ones processed. This is a very important thing to remember. You will encounter some modules that must be processed in the correct order to avoid conflicts. When a module must be processed before another, make sure its AddModule line is placed after the other module in the httpd.conf file.

The internal list of modules can be erased with the ClearModuleList and then reconstructed with a series of AddModule directives. If you compiled Apache to use DSO modules, you'll find that it does exactly that in the httpd.conf file it created, which begins like this:

```
ClearModuleList
AddModule mod_vhost_alias.c
AddModule mod_env.c
AddModule mod_log_config.c
AddModule mod_mime.c
... lines deleted ...
```

You can refer to this section to see the processing order of modules, but change it only with very good reason; altering Apache's default ordering of the AddModule lines can cause undesirable and unpredictable results. There are times, however, when the processing order of modules needs to be changed. You may, for example, want to use multiple modules that provide the same functionality but in a specific order. There are other cases where some modules fail to function completely if other modules precede them.

If you do venture to change the file, remember the rule of *first loaded, last processed.*

Using apxs

Since the release of Apache version 1.3, Apache has been packaged with a Perl script called apxs (for APache eXtenSion). This relatively simple utility is used to compile and install third-party modules. One important benefit of using apxs rather than placing the module in the Apache source tree and compiling it with the APACI configure script is that apxs can handle modules consisting of more than one source file; configure cannot.

A few modules have special installation requirements; these modules generally come with detailed instructions (usually in a file named INSTALL) that should be followed carefully. Generally, modules that cannot be installed using the procedures detailed in this section are those that must make modifications to the Apache source. The OpenSSL module (mod_ssl) is one such module. During its installation, this module makes extensive patches and additions to the Apache source and requires a recompilation of Apache to work.

With those exceptions, however, nearly every Apache module can be compiled with apxs. apxs is the preferred way to compile most third-party modules, and you should become quite familiar with its use.

You can invoke apxs with combinations of the following arguments to control its actions.

-g Generates a template for module developers; when supplied with a module name (using the -n switch), this option creates a source code directory with that name and installs a Makefile and sample module C source code file within it. The sample C program is a complete module that can actually be installed; however, it does nothing but print out a line indicating that it ran. For example:

```
# apxs -g -n mod_MyModule
```

-q Queries the apxs script for the values of one or more of its defaults. When the apxs script is created during an APACI installation, default values for the following variables are hard-coded into the script: TARGET, CC, CFLAGS, CFLAGS_SHLIB, LD_SHLIB, LDFLAGS_SHLIB, LIBS_SHLIB, PREFIX, SBINDIR, INCLUDEDIR, LIBEXECDIR, and SYSCONFDIR. Examples include the following:

```
# /usr/local/apache/bin/apxs -q TARGET
httpd
# /usr/local/apache/bin/apxs -q CFLAGS
-DLINUX=2 -DMOD_SSL=204109 -DUSE_HSREGEX -DEAPI
➥-DUSE_EXPAT -I../lib/expat-lite
# /usr/local/apache/bin/apxs -q PREFIX
/usr/local/apache
```

TIP

The default value for any apxs hard-coded variable can be overridden by specifying a new value with the –S switch, for example: # apxs –S PREFIX="/usr/local/apachetest" -c -n MyModule.so.

-c Compiles and links a DSO module, given the name of one or more source files (and, optionally, a list of supporting libraries). Using the -c argument to apxs enables the following options:

-o outputfile Specifies the name of the resulting module file rather than determining it from the name of the input file.

-D name=value Specifies compiler directives to be used when compiling the module.

-I directory Specifies a directory to add to the list of directories searched by the compiler for include files.

-l library Adds a library to the list of libraries to be linked into the module.

-L directory Adds a directory to the list of directories to be searched for libraries to be linked to the module.

-Wc, flags   Passes flags to the compiler. Each flag must be specified as it would appear if it were a command-line argument, and the comma is mandatory:

```
# apxs -c -Wc,-O3 MyModule.c
```

-Wl, flags   Passes flags to the linker. Each flag must be specified as it would appear if it were a command-line argument, and the comma is mandatory:

```
# apxs -c -Wl,-t MyModule.c
```

-i   Installs a DSO module that has already been created with apxs -c into its correct location, which is determined by the PREFIX variable hard-coded into apxs, if not overridden with a -S switch. Using the -i apxs argument enables the following two others.

-a   Modifies the Apache configuration file (httpd.conf) to add LoadModule and AddModule directives to enable the newly installed module.

-A   Use this argument to add the lines but leave them commented out so that they don't take effect when Apache is started.

-e   Exactly like -i.

-n   Names a module that is not the same as the DSO file. For example:

```
# apxs -i -a -n mod_MyModule MyModule.so
```

The -c and -i arguments to apxs are usually combined. The following line will compile a DSO from a single source file, install it, and modify the Apache configuration to load it the next time Apache is started:

```
# apxs -c -i -a MyModule.so
```

WHERE TO FIND MODULES

Third-party Apache modules are available from hundreds of sources. However, I have never used an Apache module that wasn't listed with the Apache Module Registry (modules.apache.org). This site does not attempt to maintain a repository of modules for download. It maintains information about all Apache modules, including a brief description of each one's function, along with information about the author and, most importantly, a link to the site where the latest version of the module is maintained for download. Figure 26.1 shows the search form for this site.

TIP

To request a list of all the modules available on the site, simply enter an empty search string.

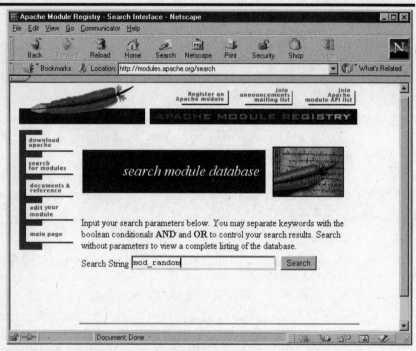

FIGURE 26.1:   The Apache Module Registry

EXAMPLE OF INSTALLING A MODULE

To conclude this chapter, let's work through a complete example of installing, configuring, and using a typical module. The module I chose from those available at the Apache Module Registry is Brian Aker's mod_random (see Figure 26.2), which performs a very simple task.

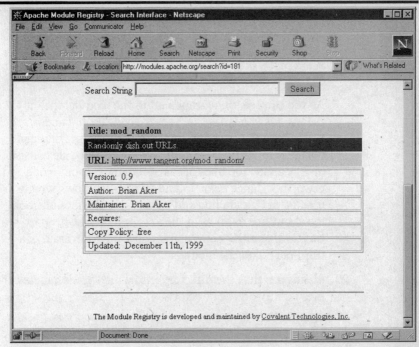

FIGURE 26.2: The Apache Module Registry listing for mod_random

The mod_random module redirects clients to a random URL from a list provided either in Apache configuration directives or in a text file. You could use this module, if you're the serious sort, to implement a simple load-balancing scheme, randomly redirecting clients to different servers. Or, you may (like me) simply use the module for fun.

1. Begin by downloading the module from the author's site (modules.apache.org links to it, but if you need the URL it's http://www.tangent.org). Download the latest archive of the module, which was mod_random-0_9_tar.gz when I snagged it. Unpack the archive into a location such as /usr/local/src:

```
# pwd
/usr/local/src
# tar xvfz /home/caulds/mod_random-0_9_tar.gz
mod_random-0.9/
mod_random-0.9/ChangeLog
mod_random-0.9/INSTALL
```

```
mod_random-0.9/LICENSE
mod_random-0.9/Makefile
mod_random-0.9/README
mod_random-0.9/TODO
mod_random-0.9/VERSION
mod_random-0.9/mod_random.c
```

As you can see, there's not a lot to the module; the only file you really need is the C source code (mod_random.c). Everything else is simply nonessential support files and documentation. This working core of the module consists of only about 100 lines of easy-to-follow C source code and is worth a glance if you intend to write your own simple module in C. Installing and configuring the module took me about five minutes; if the author has done his part, there's absolutely no reason for anyone to be afraid of a third-party Apache module!

2. Make sure that the directory into which you extracted the files is the working directory:

```
# cd mod_random-0.9
# ls -al
total 14
drwxr-xr-x   2 1001     root      1024 Dec 11 17:48 .
drwxr-xr-x  17 root     root      1024 Mar 15 13:24 ..
-rw-r--r--   1 1001     root        30 Dec 11 17:47 ChangeLog
-rw-r--r--   1 1001     root       779 Dec 11 17:47 INSTALL
-rw-r--r--   1 1001     root      1651 Dec 11 17:47 LICENSE
-rw-r--r--   1 1001     root       820 Dec 11 17:47 Makefile
-rw-r--r--   1 1001     root       738 Dec 11 17:47 README
-rw-r--r--   1 1001     root        72 Dec 11 17:47 TODO
-rw-r--r--   1 1001     root         4 Dec 11 17:47 VERSION
-rw-r--r--   1 1001     root      3342 Dec 11 17:47 mod_random.c
```

3. At this point, you should read the installation instructions (INSTALL) and glance at the contents of the Makefile (if one has been provided). The Makefile contains instructions for a command-line compilation and installation, and it probably even contains lines for stopping, starting, and restarting the Apache server. These lines are added by the template-generation (-g) argument to apxs, described in the last section. After demonstrating the manual use of apxs to install mod_random, I'll show how the Linux make utility can be used to simplify the already simple procedure.

4. Although you can break this up into a couple of steps, I found it convenient to compile (-c) and install (-i) the module and configure Apache to use it (-a) all in one command:

```
# /usr/local/apache/bin/apxs -c -i -a -n random mod_random.c
gcc -DLINUX=2 -DMOD_SSL=204109 -DUSE_HSREGEX -DEAPI
-DUSE_EXPAT -I../lib/expat-lite -fpic
-DSHARED_MODULE -I/usr/local/apache/include
-c mod_random.
gcc -shared -o mod_random.so mod_random.o
cp mod_random.so /usr/local/apache/libexec/mod_random.so
chmod 755 /usr/local/apache/libexec/mod_random.so
[activating module 'random' in /usr/local/apache/conf/httpd.conf]
```

5. Make sure that the installation procedure modified httpd.conf to use the new module. I checked using the Linux grep utility to extract mod_random entries from httpd.conf:

```
# grep mod_random /usr/local/apache/conf/httpd.conf
LoadModule random_module      libexec/mod_random.so
AddModule mod_random.c
```

6. Just to be absolutely sure that everything worked, I restarted the server:

```
# /usr/local/apache/bin/apachectl restart
```

7. Then I checked server-info to ensure that mod_random is loaded (see Figure 26.3).

8. One part of any module configuration is always manual, and that is editing the Apache configuration to make use of the module, usually by specifying the module as a handler, and usually by including directives supplied by the module. Our mod_random is no exception. I added the following section to my httpd.conf file to take full advantage of all the module's features:

```
# Brian Aker's mod_random configuration
#
<Location /randomize>
    SetHandler random
    RandomURL http://www.acme.com/
    RandomURL http://www.apple.com/macosx/inside.html
    RandomURL http://www.asptoday.com/
    RandomURL http://atomz.com/
    RandomFile /usr/local/apache/conf/random.conf
</Location>
```

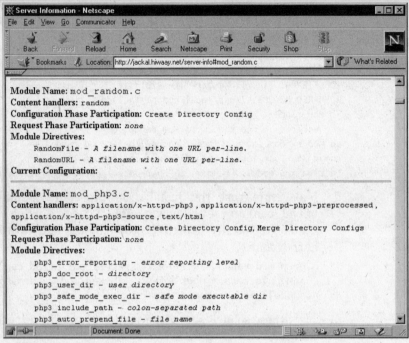

FIGURE 26.3: The Server Information page for mod_random

9. I first created a <Location> container, which applies to a partial URL, /randomize. This is not a directory name; it applies to a request URL. All the directives in the <Location> container apply to any arriving requests to a URL that ends in /randomize.

10. Using the RandomURL directive, I manually added a handful of URLs for random selection by the module and then used the RandomFile directive to point to a file containing a list of URLs (one per line) that are added to mod_random's list of URLs.

11. After creating the necessary <Location> container in httpd.conf, I restarted the server to ensure that it was read and then pointed a browser at my site, using the URL http://jackal.hiwaay.net/randomize.

12. I was immediately redirected to one of the sites I'd specified for random selection in httpd.conf.

You may or may not eventually have a use for the mod_random module. But the basic procedure demonstrated in this example will be the same for any module you decide to add: Download the archived file, extract it into your working directory, compile and install it (after reading the INSTALL file for instructions), check your httpd.conf file to verify that the module has been added, manually edit the configuration file to specify your new module as a handler, and finally, test the configuration.

Using the Included Makefile

Most third-party modules, particularly if the author uses the –g template-generating feature of apxs, will include a Makefile that can be used with the Linux make utility to do many of the tasks I just described. You can use the included Makefile (if one exists) to perform the steps I described above, but the additional convenience it offers is only slight. If you'll examine the Makefile included with mod_random (see Listing 26.1), you'll see that it does nothing but invoke the same commands I demonstrated above, using apxs to do the real work.

Part vi

Listing 26.1: The Makefile Included with *mod_random*

```
##
## Makefile -- Build file for mod_random Apache module
##
# the used tools
APXS=/usr/local/apache/bin/apxs
APACHECTL=/usr/local/apache/bin/apachectl
# additional defines, includes and libraries
#DEF=-Dmy_define=my_value
#INC=-Imy/include/dir
#LIB=-Lmy/lib/dir -lmylib
# the default target
all: mod_random.so
# compile the shared object file
mod_random.so: mod_random.c
	$(APXS) -c $(DEF) $(INC) $(LIB) mod_random.c
```

```
# install the shared object file into Apache
install: all
$(APXS) -i -a -n 'random' mod_random.so
# cleanup
clean:
-rm -f mod_random.o mod_random.so
# install and activate shared object by reloading Apache to
# force a reload of the shared object file
reload: install restart
# the general Apache start/restart/stop
# procedures
start:
$(APACHECTL) start
restart:
$(APACHECTL) restart
stop:
$(APACHECTL) stop
```

The entire process of compiling and installing mod_random, using the supplied Makefile, can be summarized as follows:

Make	Compiles mod_random.so with apxs.
make install	Uses apxs to copy mod_random.so to Apache and modify server config.
make restart	Restarts Apache using apachectl.

NOTE

On the surface, the Makefile appears to be the simplest way to install third-party modules, and it often is, but this method depends on the existence of a properly configured Makefile. The standard Makefile also depends on the values of several environment variables to work properly. If these aren't set on your machine (or if you run multiple Apache configurations), the Makefile will not work as expected. This is a good reason to bypass the Makefile and invoke the proper apxs commands manually.

WHAT'S NEXT?

From the very beginning, the Apache web server was designed for easy expandability by exposing a set of functions that allowed programmers to write add-in modules easily. Support for dynamic shared objects (DSOs) was added with the release of Apache 1.3. DSO allows modules to be compiled separately from the Apache server and loaded by the server at runtime if desired or omitted by the administrator who wants to reduce the amount of memory required for each loaded copy of Apache.

The modular architecture of Apache is an important factor in the popularity of the server. Because of its fairly uncomplicated programmer's interface for extending the server's capabilities, a large number of modules are available (at no cost) from third-party sources.

In the next chapter of this book, you will move from web services to e-mail, using the old Linux standard, Sendmail. You will begin by installing sendmail and then creating a basic configuration from your system.

Part vi

Chapter 27

RUNNING SENDMAIL

S endmail implements the SMTP protocol for Linux systems. It sends and receives SMTP mail for the system, and it acts as an interface between the user's mail program and the Internet. These vital tasks make sendmail a basic component of most Linux systems.

Sendmail is such an essential part of a Linux system that it is usually installed by default and run at startup. If it is not installed on your system, you need to know how to install it. Additionally, you need to know how to compile the sendmail program for those times when you want to install the latest source code distribution of sendmail on an existing Linux system. This chapter covers both of those topics. It also examines how and why the sendmail process runs at startup, and you'll look at the tools used to control whether or not starting the sendmail daemon is part of the Linux boot process on your system.

Adapted from *Linux Sendmail Administration*
by Craig Hunt
ISBN 0-7821-2737-1   480 pages $39.99

RUNNING SENDMAIL AT STARTUP

Sendmail runs in two distinct modes: *real-time mode* for outbound mail delivery and *daemon mode* for collecting inbound mail and queue processing. When a *mail user agent* (MUA) has mail to send, it creates an instance of the sendmail program to deliver that piece of mail. The instance of sendmail lives long enough to deliver that one piece of mail. If it cannot successfully deliver the mail, it writes the mail to the mail queue and terminates. Most sendmail processes have a very short life. The sendmail daemon, on the other hand, runs the entire time the system is running, constantly listening for inbound mail and periodically processing the queue to deliver undelivered mail. The sendmail daemon, like most other daemons, is started at boot time.

The ps command reveals whether or not sendmail is running on your system:

```
[root]# ps -C sendmail
  PID TTY             TIME CMD
  542 ?          00:00:36 sendmail
```

The low process ID (PID) shows that this process was started during the boot. Running this ps command on most Linux systems will show that sendmail is running, because generally sendmail becomes part of the boot process when you first install Linux.

Many systems are running the sendmail daemon unnecessarily. It is not necessary to run sendmail as a daemon in order to send mail. Running the sendmail command with the -bd option is required only if your system receives SMTP mail directly. A Linux mail client can collect inbound mail from the mailbox server using POP or IMAP and can relay outbound mail through the mail relay server without running the sendmail daemon. Deciding which systems should run the sendmail daemon is part of the process of planning your e-mail architecture. Unneeded daemons consume system resources and provide holes through which network intruders can slither. Take care when selecting which systems really need any daemon, including sendmail.

It is possible to enable or disable sendmail after the system is installed, and there are several tools to do this. These tools vary according to the type of start-up procedures used. Some Linux systems use BSD-style start-up procedures, and others use System V–style procedures.

NOTE

For more information on start-up procedures and run levels, see Chapter 4, "Working with Linux Commands and Files."

On Linux distributions that use System V–style boot procedures, the script that starts sendmail is usually found in the /etc/rc.d/init.d directory, where it is stored under a name such as sendmail, mail, or mta. On distributions that use BSD-style boot procedures, the commands that start sendmail are stored in one of the rc scripts. For example, on Slackware 4.0, the commands to start sendmail are found in the rc.M script located in the /etc/rc.d directory. Regardless of the name of the script used for this purpose, some start-up script is used to start sendmail at boot time.

TIP

To locate the sendmail start-up script on your Linux system, go to the directory that holds start-up scripts and run the command grep sendmail * to search every file for references to sendmail. Not sure where the start-up scripts are stored? Go to /etc and look for files or directories that begin with the string rc. Those are start-up files and directories.

On a BSD-Style Linux System

Linux systems such as Slackware that use BSD-style boot procedures start sendmail by executing the sendmail command directly from one of the main start-up files. The code that runs the sendmail daemon in the Slackware Linux /etc/rc.d/rc.M start-up script is very straightforward, as shown in Listing 27.1.

Listing 27.1: Starting Sendmail from a Slackware Boot Script

```
# Start the sendmail daemon:
if [ -x /usr/sbin/sendmail ]; then
  echo "Starting sendmail daemon"
  /usr/sbin/sendmail -bd -q 15m
fi
```

Listing 27.1 shows a Slackware system ready to run sendmail. The first line is a comment, as indicated by the fact that it starts with a pound sign (#). The next lines are an if statement that checks whether or not the sendmail command is available. If the command is found, a message is displayed on the console indicating that sendmail is starting; then the sendmail command is run.

The code in Listing 27.1 runs the sendmail command with the -bd and the -q options. In addition to listening for inbound mail, the sendmail daemon periodically checks to see whether there is mail waiting to be delivered. It's possible that a sendmail process that was started to send a message was not able to successfully deliver the mail. In that case, the process writes the message to the mail queue and counts on the daemon to deliver it at a later time. The -q option tells the sendmail daemon how often to check the undelivered mail queue. In the Slackware example, the queue is processed every 15 minutes (-q15m).

To prevent Slackware from starting sendmail at boot time, comment out the lines shown in Listing 27.1 out from the rc.M script by placing a pound sign at the beginning of each line. To restore sendmail to the boot process, remove the pound signs. These techniques are easy and they work, but they are far from elegant.

Editing a start-up script directly is easy but dangerous. Most systems administrators worry that an editing error will have a major negative effect on the next boot. I have never really had a major boot problem cause by an editing error, but I understand the fear. Distributions that use System V–style start-up procedures alleviate this fear by making it unnecessary to edit the start-up file directly.

On a System V–Style Linux System

Most Linux distributions use a System V–style boot process that allows the system to be initialized in different ways, depending on the run level. All of the service initialization scripts are located in a single directory, usually called /etc/rc.d/init.d on Linux systems that use this style of startup. The initialization scripts are indirectly invoked by links contained in directories assigned to each run level. Caldera and Red Hat are good examples of System V–style Linux systems.

NOTE

A detailed description of the Linux boot process is beyond the scope of this book. To learn more about the boot process, run levels, and start-up scripts, see *Linux Network Servers 24 seven* by Craig Hunt (Sybex, 1999).

The code that Caldera and Red Hat use to start the sendmail daemon is found in the /etc/rc.d/init.d/sendmail script. It is more complex than the code used by Slackware because Red Hat and Caldera use script variables read from an external file to set the command-line options. The file they read is /etc/sysconfig/sendmail, which normally contains these two lines:

```
DAEMON=yes
QUEUE=1h
```

Changing the values in the /etc/sysconfig/sendmail file controls the daemon configuration. The QUEUE variable sets the time value of the -q option. In this case, it is one hour (1h), which is a value that I like even more than the 15 minutes used in Slackware configuration. Don't set this time too low. Processing the queue too often can cause problems if the queue grows very large because of a delivery problem such as a network outage.

If the variable DAEMON is equal to yes, the sendmail command is run with the -bd option. If you are configuring a mail client and don't want to run sendmail as a daemon, you could directly edit the /etc/sysconfig/sendmail file to set DAEMON=no.

TIP

Although changing the DAEMON value is one way to do this, it is generally a better idea to remove the sendmail script from the startup as described below than it is to edit the content of a script.

With a System V–style startup, you don't have to directly edit startup files. One of the advantages of the System V–style boot procedure is that major services have their own start-up scripts, and those scripts are invoked indirectly, which makes it possible to control whether or not a service is started at boot time by controlling whether or not the script is invoked. The sendmail script is invoked indirectly from the run level directories by the S80sendmail script (see Listing 27.2). An examination of that script shows that it is just a symbolic link to the real sendmail script.

Listing 27.2: The Sendmail Link for Run Level 3

```
[craig]$ cd /etc/rc.d/rc3.d
[craig]$ ls -l S80sendmail
lrwxrwxrwx 1 root root 18 Dec 26 1999 S80sendmail -> ../init.d/sendmail
```

To enable or disable the sendmail start-up script for a specific run
level, simply add or remove the symbolic link in that run level's directory.
By itself this would be simple enough, but Linux systems make it even
easier by providing tools to manage the run level directories.

Enabling Sendmail with tksysv

tksysv is an X Windows tool for controlling scripts started at each run
level. Figure 27.1 shows the main tksysv screen.

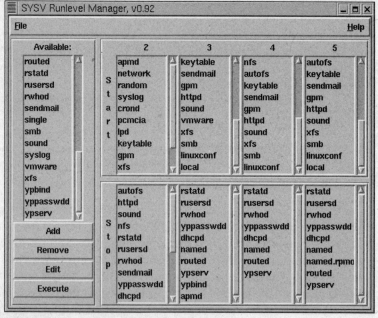

FIGURE 27.1: Enabling sendmail with tksysv

All of the scripts that can be controlled by tksysv are listed on the
left side of the screen. On the right are the services that are started and
stopped for run levels 2, 3, 4, and 5. To disable a service for a specific run

level, simply highlight the service in the Start list for that run level and click the Remove button. For example, to remove sendmail from run level 5, which is traditionally used as the run level for dedicated X Windows workstations, click `sendmail` in the Start list under run level 5 and then click Remove. After that, sendmail will no longer start when the system boots under run level 5.

To add sendmail to a run level, highlight `sendmail` in the Available list and click Add. You'll be asked to select a run level. An example might be run level 3, which is traditionally the default run level for multiuser servers. Select the run level and click Done. You're then asked to select a script number. Use the default, which is 80 for the `sendmail` script. Click Add and the script is added to the startup. The next time the system reboots under run level 3, sendmail will be started.

TIP

Of course you don't want to reboot your system just to run the `sendmail` start-up script. Use the Execute button to run the `sendmail` script immediately.

tksysv has a couple of nice features. First, it comes bundled with different versions of Linux. It runs just as well on Caldera as it does on Red Hat, and it runs just as well under Red Hat 6 as it does under Red Hat 7. Second, a clone of tksysv called ntsysv runs in text mode and therefore doesn't require X Windows. A dedicated e-mail server might not be running X Windows. In that case, you want a tool like ntsysv that runs in text mode.

Enabling Sendmail with ntsysv

ntsysv is even easier to use because it doesn't bother you with lots of questions about run levels. It assumes the current run level as a default unless it is run with the `--level` argument. ntsysv presents you with a list of services that can be automatically started at boot time. One of these is sendmail. The start-up script for every item in the list that has an asterisk next to it will be run during the next boot. Use the arrow keys to scroll down to the `sendmail` entry in the list and then use the spacebar to select or deselect `sendmail`. When the settings are just what you want, tab over to the OK button and press Enter. That's all there is to it. Figure 27.2 shows the main ntsysv screen.

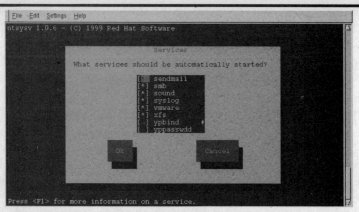

FIGURE 27.2:   Enabling sendmail with ntsysv

Enabling Sendmail with Linuxconf

Another tool that is popular on Red Hat systems is Linuxconf.
Linuxconf is a general-purpose system administration tool. One of the
features it provides is a way to manage the start-up scripts. Figure 27.3
shows the Linuxconf screen.

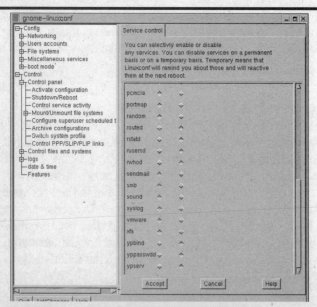

FIGURE 27.3:   Enabling sendmail with Linuxconf

From the menu on the left side of the Linuxconf window, select Control ➢ Control Panel ➢ Control Service Activity. A list of services appears on the right side of the window; it is the same list of services displayed by ntsysv. Again, as with ntsysv, you don't have to worry about run levels. Simply enable or disable the sendmail script by selecting the appropriate button next to the sendmail entry.

Enabling Sendmail with chkconfig

One other tool that can be used to control the scripts that are run at boot time is chkconfig. This is a command-line tool based on the chkconfig program from the Silicon Graphics IRIX version of Unix. The Linux version has some enhancements, such as the capability to control which run levels the scripts run under. The --list option of the chkconfig command displays the current settings:

```
[craig]$ chkconfig --list sendmail
sendmail 0:off 1:off 2:on 3:on 4:on 5:on 6:off
```

To enable or disable a script for a specific run level, specify the run level with the --level option, followed by the name of the script you want to control and the action you want to take, either on to enable the script or off to disable it. For example, to disable sendmail for run level 2, enter the command shown in Listing 27.3.

Listing 27.3: Controlling Sendmail with chkconfig

```
[root]# chkconfig --level 2 sendmail off
[root]# chkconfig --list sendmail
sendmail 0:off 1:off 2:off 3:on 4:on 5:on 6:off
```

Running the Start-Up Script Manually

The previous sections discussed several different ways to do essentially the same thing—enable or disable sendmail at boot time. All of these approaches work. Choose the one that is compatible with the version of Linux you're running and that suits your tastes. Remember, though, that most of the time you will install and enable sendmail during the initial system configuration and will never again need to fiddle with the boot files.

It is far more likely that you will need to stop or restart a sendmail process that is already running on your system. On most systems, this can be done by manually invoking the boot scripts. The `sendmail` start-up script on a Red Hat system accepts five arguments:

- ▶ `stop` terminates the current sendmail daemon process.

- ▶ `start` starts a new sendmail daemon if one is not already running.

- ▶ `restart` terminates the current sendmail daemon and starts a new one. An alternate name for the same command is `reload`.

- ▶ `condrestart` checks first to see if sendmail is running. If so, it terminates the current sendmail daemon and starts a new one. If sendmail is not currently running, it starts sendmail.

- ▶ `status` displays the process ID of the current sendmail daemon.

Listing 27.4 is an example of restarting the sendmail daemon on a Red Hat system.

Listing 27.4: Restarting Sendmail with the Start-Up Script

```
[root]# /etc/rc.d/init.d/sendmail restart
Shutting down sendmail:                                    [  OK  ]
Starting sendmail:                                         [  OK  ]
```

NOTE

If you're running Red Hat 6.0 or higher, an alternative to specifying the full path-name of the `sendmail` start-up script is to enter **service sendmail restart**. On other versions of Red Hat, use the full pathname.

The primary limitation of the start-up scripts is that they all start the sendmail daemon with only the -bd and -q options. This is correct more than 99 percent of the time. There are a few occasions when additional command-line arguments are needed. If the occasion is a test, it is simple enough to run sendmail from the command line. If you need additional command-line arguments for every boot, the only option is to edit the start-up scripts or create your own start-up script to include the arguments you need.

Controlling Sendmail with Signals

Not every Linux system has a script that can be used to start, stop, and restart sendmail. On all systems, though, sendmail can be controlled through signals. The sendmail process handles three different signals—four, if you count the fact that SIGTERM aborts sendmail just as it does most other processes—but there are three signals that have a special meaning to sendmail. These three signals are the following:

SIGHUP The SIGHUP signal causes the sendmail daemon to restart and reread its configuration file. The most common use of SIGHUP is to force sendmail to reload its configuration after the configuration file has been updated. SIGHUP can even be used to terminate the current copy of sendmail and run a new one after the sendmail program has been updated, because SIGHUP causes a true restart, not just a reread of the configuration file.

SIGINT The SIGINT signal causes sendmail to do a graceful shutdown. When sendmail receives SIGINT, it removes the lock files if it is currently processing the queue, it switches back to the user ID that it started under to create a clean log entry, and then it exits without errors. Like most processes, sendmail can be terminated by the kill signal, SIGTERM. However, SIGINT is a cleaner way to shut down sendmail, because unlike SIGTERM, SIGINT will not leave unresolved log entries or unused lock files lying around.

SIGUSR1 Use the SIGUSR1 signal to cause sendmail to write out its current status via syslogd. SIGUSR1 causes sendmail to display information about the open file descriptors, information about its host connection cache, and output from the debug_dumpstate ruleset, if one is defined in your configuration. None of this output is of particular interest to a systems administrator.

Listing 27.5 shows an example of passing a signal to sendmail. In the example, the signal is SIGHUP, but the same technique can be used to send any of the signals to sendmail.

Listing 27.5: Restarting Sendmail with *SIGHUP*

```
[root]# ps -ax | grep sendmail
  542 ?         S       0:00 sendmail: accepting connections
[root]# kill -HUP 542
[root]# ps -ax | grep sendmail
  773 ?         S       0:00 sendmail: accepting connections
```

Listing 27.5 illustrates the effect of the SIGHUP signal by showing that the process ID of sendmail changes after sendmail is sent the signal. Clearly, a process must be terminated and restarted to change process IDs. The kill command used in this example is explained in the next section.

The *kill* Command

The kill command is used to send a signal to a running process. As the name implies, by default it sends the kill signal (SIGTERM). To use it to send a different signal, specify the signal on the command line. For example, specify -INT to send the SIGINT signal. The PID is usually provided on the kill command line to ensure that the signal is sent to the correct process.

As usual on a Linux system, there is more than one way to do this. You can learn the PID of sendmail using the ps command:

```
[root]# ps -ax | grep sendmail
  542 ?        S      0:00 sendmail: accepting connections
```

You can also learn the PID by displaying the sendmail.pid file:

```
[root]# head -1 /var/run/sendmail.pid
542
```

Combining the last command with kill, you can send a signal directly to sendmail. For example, to restart sendmail, you could enter the following command:

```
kill -HUP 'head -1 /var/run/sendmail.pid'
```

The head -1 /var/run/sendmail.pid command that is enclosed in single quotes is processed by the shell first. On our example Linux system, the first line of the sendmail.pid file contains the PID 542. That is combined with the shell's kill command and then is processed as kill -HUP 542.

The discussion of signals, boot scripts, and everything else in this section assumes that you have sendmail already installed on your system. In the next section, we look at how to install sendmail if you don't already have it or if you want to upgrade to the latest release.

INSTALLING SENDMAIL

Sendmail is delivered with every major Linux distribution, and it is normally installed as part of the initial Linux installation. If it is not installed at that time, it can easily be added later using one of the package-management systems available for Linux.

To simplify the task of adding and deleting software on a running server, most Linux vendors have developed package-management systems. Slackware installs software from traditional tar files, but Debian and Red Hat have developed full-blown package-management systems. Debian and systems that are based on Debian, such as Corel, use the dpkg system. Most other Linux distributions use the Red Hat Package Manager (RPM). RPM is the most widely used package manager and the one this book covers in greatest detail. Before getting into RPM, let's take a quick look at the Debian package manager.

Installing Sendmail with *dpkg*

Locating a binary package in the correct format is the first step in installing a new software package with any package manager. Debian packages are found at www.debian.org/distrib/packages. These packages are intended for installation on the current Debian distribution but will usually work on any Debian-based release, such as Corel Linux.

After locating the upgrade package, use the dpkg command to remove the old software. Remove the currently installed sendmail package with the following command:

```
[root]# dpkg -r sendmail
```

Next, use the dpkg command to install the new Debian package. For example, to install sendmail 8.9.3, you would enter the following:

```
[root]# dpkg -i sendmail-wide_8.9.3+3.2W-20.deb
```

NOTE

As of this writing, 8.9.3 is the most recent version of sendmail available as a Debian package.

These dpkg examples are simple and clean. As we'll see in the discussion of RPM, package installations are not always this simple.

Part vi

Locating RPM Software

To install sendmail with RPM, you need to locate an updated sendmail RPM package. If you failed to install sendmail during the initial Linux installation and you just want to correct that oversight, you'll find the sendmail RPM on the Linux CD-ROM. If you want to upgrade an existing installation, you need to search for the latest RPM packages.

www.sendmail.org provides the source code distribution of sendmail, but RPM packages are not available from that site. To find RPM packages, go to your Linux vendor or to www.rpmfind.net.

Searching a Vendor Website

Because e-mail service is so important, all of the major Linux vendors make an effort to update their versions of sendmail when a critical bug is fixed or a major new feature is added. A good place to start looking for updates is at your vendor's website.

Figure 27.4 shows the Red Hat website. Just like the Debian site, it contains a search page that lets you search for a binary package. In Figure 27.4, we ask Red Hat to list all of the available sendmail RPM packages.

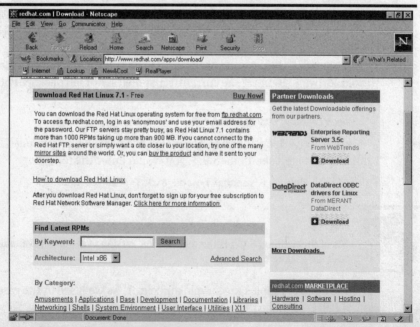

FIGURE 27.4:   The Red Hat RPM search engine

The search produces several matches. At this writing, the latest version of sendmail available as an RPM is 8.11.4, which is the version of sendmail used in the rest of this chapter. The packages returned by a search can be downloaded simply by clicking the name of the package and selecting an appropriate mirror server.

Searching the vendor site will probably provide the RPM package you need. However, I prefer a wider search that checks all the sources of RPM packages to ensure that I don't miss the newest updates.

Using *rpmfind.net* to Locate Sendmail Software

Vendors are not the only ones who make RPM packages available on the Net. To search a wide variety of RPM sources, go to www.rpmfind.net. Figure 27.5 shows the www.rpmfind.net website, which lists several sendmail RPM packages.

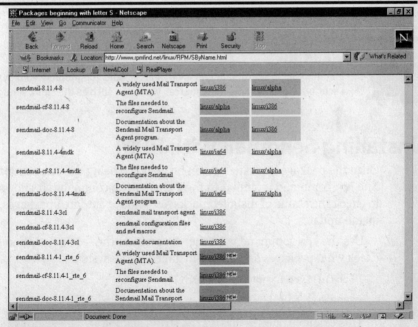

FIGURE 27.5: The rpmfind website

The web page in Figure 27.5 is the RPM repository database indexed alphabetically by name. The database is also indexed by distribution, by vendor, and by time of creation, if those things are helpful for your particular search. In this case, we are looking for sendmail, so we just jump to "s" in the alphabetic listing.

Our example Linux system is running sendmail 8.9.3. Figure 27.5 shows that there are several newer sendmail RPM packages available, with the newest being sendmail 8.11.4-8. This particular sendmail update contains three RPM packages:

▶ `sendmail-cf-8.11.4-8` contains the sendmail configuration files, including the `cf` directory used extensively in this text.

▶ `sendmail-doc-8.11.4-8` contains the sendmail documentation.

▶ `sendmail-8.11.4-8` is the heart of the system, including the sendmail program.

Following the links from the page shown in Figure 27.5 will lead you to detailed information about each package and a link from which the package can be downloaded. All three of the packages should be downloaded. These are the RPM packages that you'll install later in this chapter.

WARNING

Installing an RPM from an unknown source could compromise your system's security. Use RPMs only from sources you trust, such as the Linux vendor.

Installing Sendmail with RPM

Once the package is located, it can be installed using the `rpm` command. The `rpm` command is similar to the Debian dpkg command. It allows you to check the status of installed packages, remove outdated packages, and install updates.

Use the `rpm` command with the `-q` option or the `--query` option to check what packages are already installed in the system.

```
[craig]$ rpm --query sendmail
sendmail-8.9.3-10
```

This example queries rpm for the string sendmail. The response shows that sendmail version 8.9.3 is installed on our example system. At the time of this writing, the latest RPM version of sendmail available from www.rpmfind.net and www.redhat.com is 8.11, so we decide to upgrade the example system.

Before installing a new version of an RPM package, you can remove the old one by running rpm with the --erase option. (See the section "Cleaning Up after RPM," later in this chapter, for an example of this.) Removing the old sendmail RPM package is probably a good idea if you plan to compile and install the sendmail program from the source code distribution. If you plan to install a new RPM version of sendmail, removing the old package is unnecessary. Use the -U option with the rpm command, as shown in Listing 27.6, to update an existing RPM installation with a newer package.

Listing 27.6: Updating Sendmail with *rpm*

```
[root]# rpm -U sendmail-doc-8.11.4-8.i386.rpm
[root]# rpm -U sendmail-cf-8.11.4-8.i386.rpm
[root]# rpm -U sendmail-8.11.4-8.i386.rpm
error: failed dependencies:
        openssl is needed by sendmail-8.11.4-8
        libsfio is needed by sendmail-8.11.4-8
        libcrypto.so.0 is needed by sendmail-8.11.4-8
        libsasl.so.7 is needed by sendmail-8.11.4-8
        libsfio.so is needed by sendmail-8.11.4-8
        libssl.so.0 is needed by sendmail-8.11.4-8
```

The sendmail 8.11 package is composed of three components: the documents, the configuration files, and sendmail itself. In Listing 27.6, the documents and configuration file components install without a hitch. The third component, however, fails to install. RPM informs us that several pieces of software required by sendmail 8.11 are not available on this example system. RPM calls required software *dependencies*. Sometimes other software depends on the package you're installing or removing, and sometimes the software you're installing depends on other software.

This is the worst-case scenario. We had hoped everything would be easy sailing. Now we need to track down all of the packages needed by sendmail 8.11, install those packages, and then attempt to install sendmail-8.11.4-8.i386.rpm all over again. This bit of unpleasantness is a blessing in disguise. If we installed sendmail 8.11 from source code and did not know that openssl and libsfio are required, some of the features of sendmail would not work as advertised. It could take a long time tracking down the underlying problem. RPM makes sure that we know about the problem right from the start. We could force RPM to install sendmail-8.11.4-8.i386.rpm without the dependencies by adding the `--nodeps` argument to the `rpm` command line, but that's just asking for trouble. The best thing to do is track down and install the required packages.

A search of `www.rpmfind.net` informs us that we need three different RPM packages to fix the six dependencies: `openssl-0.9.6-1.i386.rpm`, `libsfio-1999-1.i386.rpm`, and `cyrus-sasl-1.5.24-6.i386.rpm`. The first two packages, `openssl` and `libsfio`, are pretty obvious because RPM lists them as the first two dependencies needed by `sendmail-8.11.4-8.i386.rpm`. An examination of the list of files provided by each package shows that they provide every dependency except `libsasl.so.7`. A search for `libsasl.so.7` tells us that it is found in `cyrus-sasl-1.5.24-6.i386.rpm`. We download the three packages and install them as shown in Listing 27.7.

Listing 27.7: Fixing Dependency Problems for Sendmail 8.11

```
[root]# rpm -i openssl-0.9.6-1.i386.rpm
error: file /usr/man/man1/passwd.1 from install of openssl-0.9.6-1
       conflicts with file from package passwd-0.58-1
[root]# rpm -i --replacefiles openssl-0.9.6-1.i386.rpm
[root]# rpm -i libsfio-1999-1.i386.rpm
[root]# rpm -i cyrus-sasl-1.5.24-6.i386.rpm
[root]# rpm -U sendmail-8.11.4-8.i386.rpm
[root]# rpm -q sendmail
sendmail-8.11.4-8
```

Even this installation didn't go completely perfectly. The `openssl-0.9.6-1.i386.rpm` package creates a new `passwd` man page. The problem is, it doesn't own the old page, which was put on the system by the `passwd-0.58-1.i386.rpm` package. RPM won't let a new package change a file that belongs to another package unless you tell it to. In this case, we want the new `passwd` documentation, so we use the `--replacefiles` argument with the `rpm` command to replace the old `passwd` documentation with the new documentation.

All of the other installations run smoothly. Once the dependencies are resolved, `sendmail-8.11.4-8.i386.rpm` installs without complaint. A quick query to RPM shows that the new package is in place.

Next, restart sendmail to make sure that the newly installed daemon is running, and run a quick test to make sure the new daemon is alive and servicing the SMTP port. Listing 27.8 shows these two commands.

Listing 27.8: Restarting and Testing Sendmail

```
[root]# /etc/rc.d/init.d/sendmail restart
Shutting down sendmail:                    [  OK  ]
Starting sendmail:                         [  OK  ]
[root]# telnet localhost 25
Trying 127.0.0.1...
Connected to localhost.
Escape character is '^]'.
220 wren.foobirds.org ESMTP Sendmail 8.11.4/8.11.4;
    Sun, 13 Aug 2000 18:00:03 -0400
quit
221 2.0.0 wren.foobirds.org closing connection
Connection closed by foreign host.
```

As Listing 27.8 shows, sendmail 8.11 is installed and running. Despite all of the problems encountered in this installation, sendmail is upgraded and running after fewer than a dozen commands. Linux package managers have done much to simplify upgrades.

NOTE

I have never had a problem with dependencies upgrading sendmail before version 8.11. This just turned out to be a lucky break. Normally, things go so smoothly when preparing examples for Linux books that problems have to be described without actual examples. This time we were lucky enough to have a real problem. You might never see dependency problems when installing sendmail yourself, but it is good to know how they are resolved.

X Tools for Installing Sendmail

In the previous section, we used the command-line version of rpm. It is easy to use and easy to explain, and it runs on most Linux systems—even those that don't have X Windows running. If you are using X Windows, there are some graphical tools for running the Red Hat Package Manager. Several systems use a tool named glint. Systems with the KDE desktop environment use a tool named kpackage, and systems with the GNOME desktop environment use a tool called gnorpm. Figure 27.6 shows gnorpm running on a Red Hat 6 system.

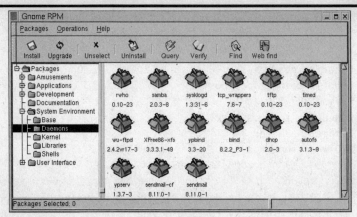

FIGURE 27.6: Installing sendmail with gnorpm

Understanding gnorpm is easy once you understand the rpm command. The icons near the top of the window clearly parallel the -U (upgrade), -q (query), -V (verify), and -e (uninstall) command-line options. Simply highlight the package you're interested in and select the action you want to take. Figure 27.6 shows the test system after sendmail was upgraded.

Even without GUI tools, it is simpler to upgrade an existing RPM package with a new one than it is to delete the package and replace it with software you compile yourself, for a couple of reasons:

- ▶ First, using the rpm command is easier than compiling software.

- ▶ Second, the features of rpm, such as pointing out dependencies and verifying the integrity of the software, are unavailable if you don't use rpm.

The latest software is not always available as a binary package. The Debian example in this chapter illustrates that. Sometimes you must compile your own version of sendmail from the source code to get the latest release. Compiling sendmail is the next topic of this chapter.

Cleaning Up after RPM

We need to digress for a moment from the basics of upgrading with RPM. If you have RPM, and your current sendmail was installed via RPM, you should upgrade with RPM. Take advantage of the tools your Linux system offers. However, if you are forced to upgrade a system that was originally installed via RPM with source code, you should clean out the RPM installation before upgrading.

The following section describes downloading and compiling the latest sendmail source code. Before installing a new version of sendmail that you have downloaded and compiled, remove the old RPM version with the --erase option, as in this example:

```
[root]# rpm --erase --nodeps sendmail-cf-8.9.3-1
[root]# rpm --erase --nodeps sendmail-8.9.3-1
```

The --nodeps option is added to this command line to force RPM to erase the sendmail software, even though other packages are dependent on it. Attempting to erase sendmail without using the --nodeps option results in an error message stating that other software depends on sendmail, and it is not removed, as shown in the following:

```
[root]# rpm --erase sendmail
removing these packages would break dependencies:
       sendmail is needed by sendmail-cf-8.9.3-1
```

Failing to remove the sendmail RPM package before installing a non-RPM version, such as a version that you compile yourself, means that the system will think the old RPM version still is installed. rpm --query will continue to report the old sendmail version number. If the -V option is used to verify the sendmail RPM package, it may report false and misleading errors. Here is an example of what can happen when the components of sendmail are changed or upgraded without using RPM and then are verified by the rpm command:

```
[craig]$ rpm -V sendmail
S.5....Tc   /etc/aliases
missing     /etc/rc.d/rc2.d/S80sendmail
S.5....T    /var/log/sendmail.st
```

The -V option prints out a line for each file in the package that fails verification. Values are printed at the beginning of the line to indicate which tests were failed. Each letter or number indicates a failure, and each dot indicates a test that was passed. The possible values are as follows:

▶ S indicates that the file has the wrong file size.

▶ M indicates that the file is assigned the wrong file permissions or file type.

▶ 5 indicates that the file has an incorrect MD5 checksum.

▶ D indicates that the file is located on the wrong device.

▶ L indicates that the file is improperly a symbolic link.

▶ U indicates that the file has the wrong user ID (UID) assigned.

▶ G indicates that the file has the wrong group ID (GID) assigned.

▶ T indicates that the file has the wrong file creation time.

▶ C indicates that the file is a configuration file that is expected to change.

In the previous example, two files have the wrong checksum and the wrong creation date, and they are the wrong size. These are all things you would expect, because they are not the original files. They are files that were installed over the original files. The file that is missing is the S80sendmail script we deleted in Listing 27.3. All of the other files associated with the sendmail RPM check out. However, even these three errors might set off alarm bells with the system's computer security officer. For this reason, clean out the RPM installation before installing sendmail from source code, as described in the following section.

DOWNLOADING AND COMPILING SENDMAIL

Even if your Linux system comes with its own version of sendmail, obtaining the latest sendmail source code distribution provides useful documentation, tools, and example configuration files. Additionally, there are times when you need a security fix or update, and the latest version of sendmail has not yet been posted as an RPM or other binary distribution.

The latest sendmail distribution is available via anonymous FTP. When you know exactly which package you want to download and where it is located, sometimes FTP can be faster than the Web. Sendmail can be downloaded from ftp.sendmail.org, where it is stored in the pub/sendmail directory, shown in Listing 27.9. When you change to that directory, an informational message is displayed that tells you about the latest version of sendmail. New releases are constantly being created. The following examples are based on sendmail V8.11.4. To compile the sendmail program, download the compressed tar file as a binary file and then uncompress and extract it with the `tar` command as shown in Listing 27.9. User input is shown in bold.

Listing 27.9: Downloading the Sendmail Source Code

```
[craig]$ ftp ftp.sendmail.org
Connected to ftp.sendmail.org.
220 pub2.pa.vix.com FTP server ready.
Name (ftp.sendmail.org:craig): anonymous
331 Guest login ok, send your e-mail address as password.
Password:
230 Guest login ok, access restrictions apply.
Remote system type is UNIX.
Using binary mode to transfer files.
ftp> cd pub/sendmail
ftp> get sendmail.8.11.4.tar.gz
local: sendmail.8.11.4.tar.gz remote: sendmail.8.11.4.tar.gz
200 PORT command successful.
150 Opening BINARY mode data connection for sendmail.8.11.4.tar.gz
    (1356543 bytes).
226 Transfer complete.
1356543 bytes received in 1.5 secs (863.31 Kbytes/sec)
ftp> quit
221-You have transferred 1356543 bytes in 1 files.
221-Thank you for using the FTP service on pub2.pa.vix.com.
221 Goodbye.
[craig]$ cd /usr/local/src
[craig]$ tar -zxvf /home/craig/sendmail.8.11.4.tar.gz
```

NOTE

Remember that things will change for future releases, so always review the README files and installation documents that come with new software before beginning an installation.

Next, change to the sendmail-8.11.4 directory created by the tar file and use the Build script to compile the new sendmail program, as shown in Listing 27.10.

Listing 27.10: Compiling Sendmail with the *Build* Command

```
[craig]$ cd sendmail-8.11.4
[craig]$ ./Build
Making all in:
/usr/local/src/sendmail-8.11.4/libsmutil
Configuration: pfx=, os=Linux, rel=2.2.10, rbase=2,!CA
 rroot=2.2,   arch=i586, sfx=, variant=optimized
Using M4=/usr/bin/m4
Creating ../obj.Linux.2.2.10.i586/libsmutil using ../devtools/OS/Linux
Making dependencies in ../obj.Linux.2.2.10.i586/libsmutil
make[1]: Entering directory
      '/usr/local/src/sendmail-8.11.4/obj.Linux.2.2.10.i586/libsmutil'
cc -M -I. -I../../sendmail -I../../include -DNEWDB
      -DNOT_SENDMAIL debug.c
errstring.c lockfile.c safefile.c snprintf.c strl.c    >> Makefile
make[1]: Leaving directory
      '/usr/local/src/sendmail-8.11.4/obj.Linux.2.2.10.i586/libsmutil'
Making in ../obj.Linux.2.2.10.i586/libsmutil
make[1]: Entering directory
      '/usr/local/src/sendmail-8.11.4/obj.Linux.2.2.10.i586/libsmutil'
cc -O -I. -I../../sendmail -I../../include -DNEWDB
      -DNOT_SENDMAIL -c debug.c -o debug.o
cc -O -I. -I../../sendmail -I../../include -DNEWDB
      -DNOT_SENDMAIL -c errstring.c -o errstring.o
... Many, many, many lines deleted...
cc -O -I. -I../../sendmail -I../../include -DNEWDB
      -DNOT_SENDMAIL -c vacation.c -o vacation.o
cc -o vacation   vacation.o ../libsmdb/libsmdb.a
      ../libsmutil/libsmutil.a -ldb -lresolv -lcrypt -lnsl -ldl
groff -Tascii -man vacation.1 > vacation.0 ||
      cp vacation.0.dist vacation.0
make[1]: Leaving directory
      '/usr/local/src/sendmail-8.11.4/obj.Linux.2.2.10.i586/vacation'
```

Build detects the architecture of the system and builds the correct Makefile for your system. It then compiles sendmail using the newly created Makefile.

According to the documentation, running `Build` is all you need to do on most systems to compile sendmail. It certainly works on Caldera Linux systems, as this example illustrates. However, the installation notes warn of several possible problems that can occur with some Linux systems, which are described in the next section, "Known Problems."

Once sendmail compiles, it is installed by using the `Build` command with the `install` option (see Listing 27.11).

Listing 27.11: Installing the New Sendmail Binaries

```
# ./Build install
Making all in:
/usr/local/src/sendmail-8.11.4/libsmutil
Configuration: pfx=, os=Linux, rel=2.2.10, rbase=2, rroot=2.2,
     arch=i586, sfx=, variant=optimized
Making in ../obj.Linux.2.2.10.i586/libsmutil
make[1]: Entering directory
      '/usr/local/src/sendmail-8.11.4/obj.Linux.2.2.10.i586/libsmutil'
... Many, many, many lines deleted...
Making in ../obj.Linux.2.2.10.i586/vacation
make[1]: Entering directory
      '/usr/local/src/sendmail-8.11.4/obj.Linux.2.2.10.i586/vacation'
install -c -o bin -g bin -m 555 vacation /usr/bin
install -c -o bin -g bin -m 444 vacation.0 /usr/man/man1/vacation.1
make[1]: Leaving directory
      '/usr/local/src/sendmail-8.11.4/obj.Linux.2.2.10.i586/vacation'
```

The `Build` command installs the man pages in the `/usr/man` directory and the executables in `/usr/sbin` and `/usr/bin`. It installs the help file (`sendmail.hf`) and the status file (`sendmail.st`) in `/etc/mail`.

Known Problems

The sendmail documentation lists some problems that are known to affect compilation on Linux systems. The problems fall into several categories, ranging from compiler problems to kernel problems.

Two problems relate to GNU tools that are commonly used on Linux systems. One is an incompatibility detected between GDBM and sendmail 8.8. Later versions of sendmail improved the approximation algorithm to detect GDBM so that the sendmail code can adapt to GDBM. The sendmail release notes suggest using Berkeley DB instead of GDBM.

The other GNU problem is with the gcc compiler. Old versions of gcc, versions 2.4 and 2.5, cannot be used to compile sendmail with the compiler optimization (-0) option set. This was fixed when version 2.6 was released. The Caldera system that generated the example in Listing 27.9 uses the Experimental GNU Compiler Suite version 2.91, which is a follow-up to gcc.

Several problems are described that existed with very old kernels (pre–version 1.0), very old versions of libc (pre–version 4.7), and a very old version of the BIND domain name software (version 4.9.3). No one should currently be running any of this old software.

The sendmail documentation also reports problems that relate to having previously compiled BIND on your system. The symptoms of this problem are unresolved references during the link phase of the sendmail compile. If you have compiled BIND from source code on your system, and BIND wrote header files in /usr/local/lib and /usr/local/include, these files may cause problems when sendmail is compiled. The documentation suggests adding -lresolv to LIBS in the sendmail Makefile to avoid this problem.

Finally, the documentation mentions problems with Linux kernel 2.2.0. This is the most worrisome of the problems reported because the documentation does not provide a workaround. I have never seen this problem, but if I did, I would upgrade the Linux kernel to the highest patch.

Frankly, none of the problems described in the sendmail installation notes has ever struck any Linux system that I have worked with. A far more common occurrence is for something to change in the new distribution that makes your old configuration obsolete. We look at that challenge next.

Configuration Compatibility

New versions of sendmail can have changes that make the old configuration incompatible with the new sendmail program. Watch for these changes and adjust the configuration when they arise.

The /etc/mail directory is a new default location used by sendmail version 8.11. The Build install command places the help file and the status file in this new directory, but the help file and the status file locations are also defined in the sendmail configuration file. If the files are not in the locations your mail server configuration expects, you can do one of two things:

▶ Simply move the files to the locations you want.

▶ Change the sendmail configuration to point to /etc/mail for these files. This is the default location expected by sendmail 8.11, so using these locations actually means removing the define macros that point to the "non-standard" locations for these files. Using the default locations means that you will have a simpler configuration file.

Regardless of what you do, the physical location of the files and the location of the files defined in the configuration must agree.

Sendmail 8.11 has also changed the location of the sendmail configuration file (sendmail.cf). Traditionally, the file was located in the /etc directory, and that is where it is found on most Linux systems. Sendmail 8.11 uses the new /etc/mail directory for the sendmail.cf file. Attempting to run the newly compiled sendmail binary on the example system will fail because Caldera keeps the sendmail.cf file in the /etc directory, and sendmail 8.11 is looking for it in the /etc/mail directory. A simple test shows this:

```
[root]# sendmail -v -t
/etc/mail/sendmail.cf: line 0: cannot open: No such file or directory
```

This needs to be fixed, and again you can either move the file or change the configuration. To change the configuration, provide the sendmail command with the correct path to the configuration file by using the -C command-line option—for example, sendmail -C/etc/sendmail.cf. The sendmail start-up script must also be edited to insert this command-line option so that the correct configuration file is used every time the system reboots. Frankly, this is more trouble than it is worth. Just move the sendmail.cf file to /etc/mail. It is simpler and better because other newly installed mail tools might be looking for the sendmail.cf file at the new default location.

One other thing that should be checked before declaring the installation complete is the sendmail.cf file. New versions of sendmail may add new configuration syntax that makes the older configuration files incompatible with the new release. The sendmail program checks the version (-v) command inside the sendmail.cf file to determine the level of the configuration syntax. The easiest way to check compatibility is to use the sendmail command to send a piece of test mail:

```
[root]# sendmail -v -t -C/etc/sendmail.cf
Warning: .cf file is out of date: sendmail 8.11.4 supports
        version 9, .cf file is version 8
^D
No recipient addresses found in header
```

Running the sendmail command with the -v option tells the program to provide verbose messages, which is just what you want when you're testing. The -t option tells sendmail that the mail will be typed in at the console. In this case, I immediately terminate the session with a Ctrl+D (which is what the ^D illustrates) because I don't want to send mail, I just want to see the warning message. The new sendmail program complains about the version level of the configuration file. In this particular case, mail would not be delivered successfully because too much has changed between sendmail 8.9 and 8.11. This is not always the case. Sometimes you can force mail through an old configuration, but you shouldn't.

This example shows that this configuration is not compatible with the new release. To solve this incompatibility, you need to rebuild your configuration. Understanding basic sendmail configuration is the topic of Chapter 28, "Creating a Basic Sendmail Configuration".

What's Next?

Sendmail runs in two different modes to handle outbound and inbound mail. Sendmail is started in real time to handle individual pieces of outbound mail but runs as a daemon to collect inbound mail. There are several tools that help you control which systems run the sendmail daemon as part of their startup.

Before the sendmail program can be run, it must be properly installed. Sendmail can be installed using a Linux package manager or compiled from source. Despite the complexity of sendmail, it is installed in the same manner as all other Linux packages, and the same tools are used to control the sendmail start-up process as are used with any other Linux start-up process. Installing and running sendmail are two tasks that don't have any special complexity. If you know how to install and run Linux processes, you know how to install and run sendmail on a Linux system.

Once installed, sendmail must be configured. Configuring sendmail is the topic of Chapter 28.

Part vi

Chapter 28

CREATING A BASIC SENDMAIL CONFIGURATION

At the conclusion of Chapter 27, we compiled sendmail 8.11 from the source code distribution. Much to our dismay, we discovered that the new sendmail program would not run even after the `sendmail.cf` configuration file was moved to the `/etc/mail` directory where the new sendmail expected to find it. Sendmail 8.11 complained that the `sendmail.cf` file provided with the Linux distribution was an older version that was not compatible with the new software release. The solution to this problem is to build a new `sendmail.cf` file that is compatible with the new software, and in this chapter that is just what we do.

Adapted from *Linux Sendmail Administration*
by Craig Hunt
ISBN 0-7821-2737-1   480 pages $39.99

Building a new sendmail configuration, even a very basic one, is a multistep process. The sendmail.cf configuration file is built from m4 macros. To build your own configuration, you must

- ▶ Locate the correct m4 macro libraries and files
- ▶ Have a basic understanding of the m4 macro language
- ▶ Select an appropriate macro configuration file
- ▶ Modify the file as necessary
- ▶ Process your newly created macro configuration file through the m4 macro processor

This chapter covers all of these steps while building a very basic configuration file that solves the incompatibility problem encountered when we upgraded to sendmail 8.11 using the source code distribution. Remember that in Chapter 27, "Running Sendmail," we installed sendmail under Linux in two different ways. Before we compiled and installed sendmail from source code, we installed it using RPM. A few problems emerged during the RPM installation, but once the installation finished successfully, everything was ready to run. There was no compatibility problem and thus no reason to build a simple configuration to solve a compatibility problem.

However, even if you use RPM to install sendmail, the topics covered in this chapter will be useful to you. Building this simple configuration provides an introduction to m4 and provides the basis for understanding more complex configurations. This foundation is useful for all sendmail administrators, whether or not you use RPM. Let's begin by locating the m4 macro language source files provided with the sendmail distribution.

THE *CF* DIRECTORY STRUCTURE

m4 is a general-purpose macro processor. It has a wide variety of uses and is not specifically intended for sendmail configuration. m4 macro definitions have been built by the people who maintain sendmail so that we can create a sendmail configuration with m4.

The sendmail distribution contains the m4 source files needed to build the sendmail.cf file. These source files are found in the cf directory located under the top directory created by the sendmail distribution tar file. The top directory created by the tar file always has a name based on the sendmail distribution's version number. The format of this directory name is sendmail-*version*, where *version* is the version number. Thus, the tar file for sendmail 8.11.4 creates a top directory named sendmail-8.11.4, and the configuration files for that release are found in sendmail-8.11.4/cf. All this, of course, is relative to the directory in which you restore the tar file. In Chapter 27, we restored the tar file in /usr/local/src, so the complete path to the configuration files in the example system is /usr/local/src/sendmail-8.11.4/cf. A listing of that directory shows 10 entries.

```
[craig]$ ls /usr/local/src/sendmail-8.11.4/cf
README cf domain feature hack m4 mailer ostype sh siteconfig
```

The cf directory contains a README file and nine subdirectories. The README file provides useful documentation on the m4 language and how that language is used to build a sendmail.cf file. Always check this file for the latest changes and the newest features.

As you'll see later, the names of most of the subdirectories (domain, feature, hack, mailer, ostype, and siteconfig) are clearly identifiable as the names of m4 macro commands used to build a sendmail configuration. Only the cf, m4, and sh directories do not share names with m4 macros. All of the directories, however, are worth exploring.

THE *SENDMAIL-CF* RPM FILES

In this chapter, the cf directory and its subdirectories are described as part of the sendmail source code distribution. These same files, however, are available as part of an RPM installation. In Chapter 27, we installed the RPM version of the cf directory. It was the RPM package identified as sendmail-cf-8.11.4-8.i386.rpm. It contains all of the files that are described in this chapter. The only difference is the location of the files. To find out where the files are stored, run an rpm query and ask for a file listing as follows:

```
[craig]$ rpm -q -l sendmail-cf
```

On our example Red Hat system, this command shows that the cf directory is named /usr/lib/sendmail-cf. A listing of /usr/lib/sendmail-cf shows the following:

```
[craig]$ ls /usr/lib/sendmail-cf
README cf domain feature hack m4 mailer ostype
➡ sh siteconfig
```

CONTINUED ➡

Thus, if you're using an RPM installation, /usr/lib/sendmail-cf is equivalent to cf in these discussions. The same README file and the same nine subdirectories appear in /usr/lib/sendmail-cf on an RPM installation as appear in cf on a source code installation. Everything covered in this chapter applies regardless of how you installed sendmail 8.11.

Little-Used Directories

Three of the directories in the cf directory (hack, sh, and siteconfig) have very little use for most configurations. For two of these directories, this lack of use relates directly to the lack of utility of the macro commands they represent.

The cf/hack directory holds m4 source files built by the local system administrator to solve temporary sendmail configuration problems. Temporary code fixes are called *hacks*, thus the name for this directory and the command that uses it. The HACK command is almost never used, and thus the hack directory is almost never used. An ls of the hack directory shows that it contains just one file.

```
[craig]$ ls hack
cssubdomain.m4
```

The one file contained in the hack directory is an old fix that was used for a few months at Berkeley to handle a domain name transition. The file is there only as an example. It cannot be used by anyone but Berkeley, and it is no longer of any use to them. Even the domain name transition handled by this hack could now be handled more easily with the database features built into the current sendmail. The hack directory and HACK command are still there, but there is simply no good reason to use them.

The cf/siteconfig directory contains files that define the UUCP connectivity for the mail server. The files list the locally connected UUCP sites using a specific sendmail m4 syntax. The siteconfig directory contains four example files:

```
[craig]$ ls siteconfig
uucp.cogsci.m4   uucp.old.arpa.m4   uucp.ucbarpa.m4   uucp.ucbvax.m4
```

The siteconfig directory and the SITECONFIG command are still maintained for backward compatibility. However, this directory is obsolete and should no longer be used to define the UUCP connectivity for a UUCP mail server.

The last little-used directory does not even map to an m4 macro command. It is the cf/sh directory, and it contains only one file.

```
[craig]$ ls -l sh
total 2
-rw-r--r--   1 craig  users     1128 Feb  7 1999 makeinfo.sh
```

Even the name of this file is different. All of the files we have seen so far are m4 macro source files. As such, they all end with the .m4 extension. This file, however, ends with the .sh extension, indicating that it is a shell script. The permission bits show that even though it is a shell script, it is not executable. It is probably not being used. Still, I'm curious. So I change the permissions and run the script:

```
[root]# chmod 744 makeinfo.sh
[root]# ./makeinfo.sh
##### built by root@ibis.foobirds.org on Thu Aug 17 09:36:03 EDT 2000
##### in /usr/local/src/sendmail-8.11.4/cf/sh
##### using as configuration include directory
define('__HOST__', ibis.foobirds.org)dnl
```

The script produces three lines of comments that could be used to identify who built the sendmail.cf file, when they built it, and in what directory. The third line includes the name of the configuration directory when it is actually run by m4. The last line of output assigns a value to a variable. Of course, you don't really run this script. As I said, I was just curious. The script is used by the m4 process when it builds the sendmail .cf file. You never use this script directly, and you never use this directory to store any of your own configuration files.

The *domain* Directory

The cf/domain directory is one of the directories where you are most likely to store your own configuration files. The purpose of the domain directory is to hold m4 source files that define configuration values that are specific to your domain or network. The configuration file you create for your environment is then used in the macro configuration file via the

DOMAIN command. Because the intent is for you to create your own file, the six files shown when you ls the domain directory are all just examples.

```
[craig]$ ls domain
Berkeley.EDU.m4        EECS.Berkeley.EDU.m4   berkeley-only.m4
CS.Berkeley.EDU.m4     S2K.Berkeley.EDU.m4    generic.m4
```

When you create your own domain configuration file, start by copying the example file generic.m4 to a name that is meaningful for your domain or network. For example, if your domain is foobirds.org, you might copy generic.m4 to foobirds.m4. Then edit the new file to set the values needed for your environment.

The *cf* Subdirectory

Most of the work creating a basic configuration takes place in the cf/cf directory. This is the working directory of sendmail configuration. It contains all of the macro configuration files, and it is where you will put your own macro configuration file when you build a custom configuration. Listing 28.1 shows that the cf/cf directory contains more than 40 files.

Listing 28.1: Contents of the *cf/cf* Subdirectory

```
[craig]$ cd /usr/local/src/sendmail-8.11.4/cf
[craig]$ ls cf
Build                    generic-solaris2.cf
Makefile                 generic-solaris2.mc
chez.cs.mc               generic-sunos4.1.cf
clientproto.mc           generic-sunos4.1.mc
cs-hpux10.mc             generic-ultrix4.cf
cs-hpux9.mc              generic-ultrix4.mc
cs-osf1.mc               huginn.cs.mc
cs-solaris2.mc           knecht.mc
cs-sunos4.1.mc           mail.cs.mc
cs-ultrix4.mc            mail.eecs.mc
cyrusproto.mc            mailspool.cs.mc
generic-bsd4.4.cf        python.cs.mc
generic-bsd4.4.mc        s2k-osf1.mc
generic-hpux10.cf        s2k-ultrix4.mc
generic-hpux10.mc        tcpproto.mc
generic-hpux9.cf         test.cf
generic-hpux9.mc         test.mc
generic-linux.cf         ucbarpa.mc
```

```
generic-linux.mc              ucbvax.mc
generic-nextstep3.3.mc        uucpproto.mc
generic-osf1.cf               vangogh.cs.mc
generic-osf1.mc
```

Most of these files—more than 30 of them—are example macro control files. You can identify a macro control file by the .mc extension. Some are examples meant as educational tools, but most are prototypes or generic files meant to be used as the basis of your own configuration. Particularly interesting are the generic files designed for use with different operating systems. Generic files for Solaris, HPUX, BSD, Linux, and several other operating systems are included. For a Linux systems administrator, the generic-linux.mc file is the one that gets the most attention.

Several of the files are identified by the .cf extension. These files are the result of processing macro configuration files through m4 and are already in the proper format to be used as the sendmail.cf file. It is unlikely, however, that you will use one of these files directly. Unless the generic macro configuration file is exactly to your liking, the sendmail configuration file produced from that .mc file will not be what you want. For example, the problem we want to solve is the fact that the /etc/sendmail.cf file on our example system is not compatible with sendmail 8.11. Using the generic-linux.cf file as the sendmail.cf file might solve this problem, but as the test in Listing 28.2 shows, it doesn't work for our example system.

Part VI

Listing 28.2: Testing the *generic-linux.cf* File

```
[root]# sendmail -v -t -C /etc/sendmail.cf
Warning: .cf file is out of date: sendmail 8.11.4 supports version 9,
      .cf file is version 8
No recipient addresses found in header
^D
[root]# sendmail -v -t -C ./generic-linux.cf
./generic-linux.cf: line 66: fileclass: cannot open
      '/etc/mail/local-host-names'
: No such file or directory
```

The first sendmail test illustrates the problem we have with the old sendmail.cf file. It is version 8, and sendmail 8.11 wants a version 9 configuration file. The second test uses the -C command-line argument to specify the generic-linux.cf file as the sendmail configuration file. That test also fails. This time, the configuration is looking for a file named /etc/mail/local-host-names, which does not exist. We can fix the problem by creating the desired file or by simplifying the configuration so that it doesn't need that file. In this chapter we use the latter approach.

The *cf/cf Build* Script

New sendmail configurations are generally built inside the cf/cf directory. Two of the files in this directory are there to aid the build process. These are the Build shell script and the Makefile it uses. Listing 28.3 shows a sendmail configuration file being constructed with the Build script.

Listing 28.3: Using the *cf/cf/Build* Script

```
[root]# ./Build test.cf
Using M4=/usr/bin/m4
rm -f test.cf
/usr/bin/m4 ../m4/cf.m4 test.mc > test.cf ||
    ( rm -f test.cf && exit 1 )
chmod 444 test.cf
```

The Build script is easy to use. Provide the name of the output file you want to create as an argument on the Build command line. The script replaces the .cf extension of the output file with the extension .mc and uses the macro configuration file with that name to create the output file. Thus, putting test.cf on the Build command line means that test.mc will be used to create test.cf.

Despite the simplicity of the Build command, I never use it to build a sendmail configuration, and you probably won't either. The reason I don't use it is that the m4 command line used to build a sendmail configuration is also very simple. For the average sendmail administrator, the Build script doesn't offer any significant advantages. The real reason the script exists in this directory is to make it simple for the people who maintain sendmail to build several .cf files with one command. This helps the source code maintainers because, as we have seen, the sendmail configuration files need to be rebuilt every time sendmail is upgraded to keep the version number of the configuration file compatible with the version number expected by the new sendmail system. Build has four special keyword arguments that construct multiple configuration files with one command:

▶ **generic** The generic keyword builds the .cf files for the eight generic macro configuration files. These are the only .cf files that normally come with the sendmail distribution.

► **berkeley** The berkeley keyword builds the 16 different configuration files that were used at Berkeley. Because the Berkeley configurations are just used as examples, the .cf files for these configurations normally are not built.

► **other** The other keyword builds any configurations listed in the $OTHER variable of the Makefile. In sendmail 8.11, there is only one configuration listed in this variable, and it is not delivered as a .cf file.

► **all** The all keyword builds all of the configurations defined in the $GENERIC, $BERKELEY, and $OTHER variables in the Makefile.

If you need to build multiple configurations, it is possible to edit the Makefile, changing the $OTHER variable so that it contains the names of all your configurations, and to then use Build other to create all of your configurations at one time. It's possible, but unlikely. Most sendmail administrators do not have enough different configurations to bother with this. We won't mention Build again. In the rest of this chapter, the m4 command is used directly to build the sendmail configuration file.

The cf/cf directory and possibly the cf/domain directory are the only two directories to which you are likely to add configuration files. The four remaining directories are all used to build a configuration, but you use the files that are already there. It is unlikely you will add or change files in those directories.

The *ostype* Directory

Every macro configuration file must contain an OSTYPE command to process a macro source file from the cf/ostype directory. The files in this directory define operating system–specific characteristics for the sendmail configuration. Listing 28.4 shows the contents of the ostype directory.

Listing 28.4: The *cf/ostype* Directory

```
[craig]$ ls ostype
aix2.0.m4       bsdi2.0.m4      irix5.m4       qnx.m4          svr4.m4
aix3.m4         darwin.m4       irix6.m4       riscos4.5.m4    ultrix4.m4
aix4.m4         dgux.m4         isc4.1.m4      sco-uw-2.1.m4   unixware7.m4
aix5.m4         domainos.m4     linux.m4       sco3.2.m4       unknown.m4
altos.m4        dynix3.2.m4     maxion.m4      sinix.m44       uxpds.m4
amdahl-uts.m4   freebsd4.m4     mklinux.m4     solaris2.m4
```

```
aux.m4        gnu.m4        nextstep.m4   solaris2.ml.m4
bsd4.3.m4     hpux10.m4     openbsd.m4    solaris2.pre5.m4
bsd4.4.m4     hpux11.m4     osf1.m4       solaris8.m4
bsdi.m4       hpux9.m4      powerux.m4    sunos3.5.m4
bsdi1.0.m4    irix4.m4      ptx2.m4       sunos4.1.m4
```

The directory contains configuration files for more than 40 different operating systems. Solaris, BSD, Linux—they are all here and easily identified by name. In fact, there are many more operating system definitions in the ostype directory than there are generic macro configuration files in the /cf/cf directory. One thing that I find slightly surprising is that there is no redhat.6.2.m4 or slackware.7.0.m4 file. Different Linux distributions are at least as different as AIX 3 is from AIX 4, yet different Linux vendors don't create OSTYPE files. Still, it doesn't matter. You can start with the standard Linux OSTYPE and do all your customization in the macro configuration file you build in the cf/cf directory.

The *mailer* Directory

In addition to an OSTYPE command, every usable server configuration must have at least one MAILER command. MAILER commands process source files from the cf/mailer directory. Each file in the mailer directory contains the definition of a set of mailers. Listing 28.5 shows the mailer definition files delivered with sendmail 8.11.

Listing 28.5: The Contents of the *cf/mailer* Directory

```
[craig]$ ls mailer
cyrus.m4   local.m4    phquery.m4   procmail.m4   smtp.m4    uucp.m4
fax.m4     mail11.m4   pop.m4       qpage.m4      usenet.m4
```

The directory contains definitions for 11 different sets of mailers, all of which are described in this text. In this chapter, we use only the two most basic sets of mailers: local.m4 for local mail delivery and smtp.m4 for SMTP mail delivery.

The *feature* Directory

The feature directory contains the m4 source code files that implement various sendmail features. Listing 28.6 shows that there are more than 40 features available.

Listing 28.6: The *feature* **Directory**

```
[craig]$ ls feature
accept_unqualified_senders.m4      no_default_msa.m4
accept_unresolvable_domains.m4     nocanonify.m4
access_db.m4                       nodns.m4
allmasquerade.m4                   notsticky.m4
always_add_domain.m4               nouucp.m4
bestmx_is_local.m4                 nullclient.m4
bitdomain.m4                       promiscuous_relay.m4
blacklist_recipients.m4            rbl.m4
delay_checks.m4                    redirect.m4
dnsbl.m4                           relay_based_on_MX.m4
domaintable.m4                     relay_entire_domain.m4
generics_entire_domain.m4          relay_hosts_only.m4
genericstable.m4                   relay_local_from.m4
ldap_routing.m4                    relay_mail_from.m4
limited_masquerade.m4              smrsh.m4
local_lmtp.m4                      stickyhost.m4
local_procmail.m4                  use_ct_file.m4
loose_relay_check.m4               use_cw_file.m4
mailertable.m4                     uucpdomain.m4
masquerade_entire_domain.m4        virtuser_entire_domain.m4
masquerade_envelope.m4             virtusertable.m4
```

The *m4* Directory

The last subdirectory in the cf directory is the m4 directory. This is the directory that contains the m4 macro definitions and the sendmail.cf skeleton code needed to build a sendmail.cf configuration file. Remember that m4 is not a language designed to build sendmail configurations. It is a general-purpose macro language. The commands you use to build a sendmail configuration are macros defined by the sendmail developers. This is the directory that contains the definitions of those macro commands. The cf/m4 directory contains only four files:

```
[craig]$ ls m4
cf.m4   cfhead.m4   proto.m4   version.m4
```

Two of these files are very small. The version.m4 file defines just one sendmail.cf variable—the Z variable. The Z variable is assigned the sendmail version number, which in our examples is 8.11.4. Because this value changes with each sendmail release, it is defined in a separate file for easy maintenance.

NOTE

The sendmail version number is not the same thing as the `sendmail.cf` version number. In these examples, the sendmail version number is 8.11.4, but the `sendmail.cf` version number is 9. The fact that both the release number and the configuration file number are called version numbers can be confusing. Furthermore, neither of these has anything to do with the `VERSIONID` macro, which is just used to store configuration control information to help you track the changes you make to your m4 macro configuration file. No wonder systems administrators find sendmail confusing!

The other very small file is `cf.m4`. This is an important file because it is specified on the m4 command line to incorporate the library of sendmail m4 macro commands into the m4 process. The `cf.m4` file does not contain the macro definitions. Instead, it includes by reference the file that contains the macro definitions.

The m4 macros used to configure sendmail are defined in the file `cfhead.m4`. This file includes lots of stuff, but the most important is the definition of many of the commands used to build a configuration.

The last file, `proto.m4`, is the largest. It contains raw `sendmail.cf` data exactly as it appears in the `sendmail.cf` file. The `proto.m4` file is the source of most of the content found in the `sendmail.cf` file.

The commands defined in the `cf/m4` directory and how they are used to build a configuration are the topics of the remainder of this chapter. Let's take a look at the m4 macro language used for sendmail configuration.

The *m4* Macro Language

The sendmail program reads its configuration from the `sendmail.cf` file. The `sendmail.cf` file is a few hundred lines long, and every line is written in a terse syntax that is easy for sendmail to parse but difficult for a human to read and write. As the systems administrator, your job is to create the `sendmail.cf` file. Luckily, you do that not with hundreds of lines of arcane code but with a few lines of macro code. The `sendmail.cf` file is created from a macro configuration (`.mc`) file that usually contains fewer than 20 lines of m4 commands. The m4 commands that you will use to build a basic sendmail configuration are listed in Table 28.1.

TABLE 28.1: Common *m4* Commands

COMMAND	USE
define	Defines a value for a configuration variable.
divert	Directs the output of the m4 process.
dnl	Deletes all characters up to and including the next newline character.
DOMAIN	Selects a file containing attributes for your specific domain.
FEATURE	Identifies an optional sendmail feature to be included in the configuration.
MAILER	Identifies a set of mailers to be included in the sendmail.cf file.
OSTYPE	Selects a file containing operating system–specific attributes.
undefine	Clears the value set for a configuration variable.
VERSIONID	Defines version control information for the configuration.

The commands shown in Table 28.1 are the most commonly used m4 macro commands. All of the commands shown in uppercase are macro commands defined in the cfhead.m4 file. The commands shown in lowercase are built-in m4 commands. The subset of commands shown in Table 28.1 is all you need to build a basic configuration. As such, they all deserve a more thorough explanation.

Controlling *m4* Output

The m4 program is a stream-oriented macro processor. It views the data it handles as a stream of text characters. It collects input data from various files, expands macros embedded in those files, and directs the output stream of characters to another file. Two of the commands in Table 28.1 are used to control the stream of output characters: divert and dnl.

The divert command directs the output stream to different targets. As of sendmail 8.11, there are 11 different targets for the data stream. The 11 possible divert values are listed in Table 28.2.

Part vi

TABLE 28.2: Possible Values for the *divert* Command

Value	Meaning
-1	Discard this output.
0	Send this data through normal processing.
1	Use this data for hostname resolution.
2	Add this data to ruleset 3.
3	Add this data to ruleset 0.
4	Add this data to the UUCP-specific sections of ruleset 0.
5	Use this data to define domain names this server will relay.
6	Add this data to the Local Info section of the sendmail.cf file.
7	Save this data as a mailer definition.
8	Use this data to define a spammers blacklist.
9	Add this data to ruleset 1 or 2.

Most of the values that can be specified with divert are used only by sendmail developers. They are used, in essence, as buffers to hold data for specific parts of the sendmail.cf file. The data is collected in these buffers and then moved to the sendmail.cf file in the final stage of processing. It is possible to use any of these values in a configuration, but it is unlikely and unnecessary because commands exist to send data to the correct buffers without resorting to divert commands. For any reasonable configuration, the divert command is used with only two different settings:

▶ divert is set to -1 to discard the output. Thus, divert(-1) is found at the start of a block of text that is not to be written to the sendmail.cf file. While the block of text could be anything that's not intended for the output file, it is usually the copyright statement that is found at the beginning of many of the example configuration files. The divert(-1) command at the start of the copyright means that the copyright is treated as a large comment.

▶ divert is set to 0 to direct the stream to the output file—sendmail.cf, for example. If the divert(-1) command is used at the start of a large comment, divert(0) is used at the end of the comment to redirect the stream to the output file.

The dnl command is also used to control the output stream. The dnl command accepts no arguments. Its two basic functions are determined by its position on the command line:

▶ If the dnl command occurs at the end of a line after another m4 command, it is used to clean up unwanted blank lines from the output file. For example, dnl on the line OSTYPE(linux)dnl ensures that any extraneous output generated after the linux OSTYPE macro is expanded doesn't get written to the send-mail.cf file.

▶ If the dnl command occurs at the beginning of the line, the line is treated as a comment. For example, the line dnlNext define the domain name is a comment. If the example line did not begin with dnl, m4 would interpret define and domain as m4 commands. Messy! Always start each comment line with dnl unless it is a large comment bracketed by divert commands.

The divert and dnl commands direct m4 output, but they do not define or generate the output data. The other m4 commands are used to generate the actual configuration file.

The Basic Commands

In broad terms, there are two types of files used to build an m4 configuration. One of these is the macro configuration file, which is traditionally identified by the .mc file extension. The macro configuration file is the input file for the m4 command, and its name appears on the m4 command line. The other files are m4 source files that are referenced by the macro configuration file. Traditionally, m4 source files are given the file extension .m4. Almost all m4 macro commands from Table 28.1 can appear in either type of file, although three of the commands are generally found only in the macro configuration file:

OSTYPE   The OSTYPE macro is required, and it is always found in the macro configuration file. The OSTYPE macro command loads an m4 source file that defines operating system–specific information. File and directory paths, mailer pathnames, and system-specific mailer arguments are the kind of information generally found in an OSTYPE file. The sendmail source distribution provides more than 40 predefined operating system macro files, and you can create your own for a specific Linux distribution if you like. The only argument passed to the

OSTYPE command is the name of the m4 source file that contains the operating system–specific information. Here is the command that processes the `linux.m4` OSTYPE source file:

```
OSTYPE(linux)
```

DOMAIN   The DOMAIN macro loads a file that contains information specific to your domain or network. The DOMAIN source file is a perfect place for commands that affect hostnames and domain names and that define values, such as mail relay names, that are specific to your network. Because the information is specific to your domain, you must create your own DOMAIN source file. The sendmail source code distribution provides an example DOMAIN source file named `generic.m4` that you can use as a starting point for creating your own configuration.

Assume you created a DOMAIN source file that you called `foobirds.m4`. The following command, placed in the macro control file, uses `foobirds.m4` to help in building the `sendmail.cf` file:

```
DOMAIN(foobirds)
```

The DOMAIN command is optional. When it is used, it normally appears only in the macro configuration file.

MAILER   The MAILER macros identify the various sets of mailer definitions that should be included in the `sendmail.cf` file. A usable configuration must have at least one MAILER command; almost every Linux configuration has the following two:

> ***MAILER(local)***   The MAILER(`local`) macro command adds the `local` mailer and the `prog` mailer to the configuration. The `local` and `prog` mailers are essential, so any usable configuration will have at least this MAILER command.

> ***MAILER(smtp)***   The MAILER(`smtp`) macro adds mailers for SMTP, extended SMTP, eight-bit SMTP, directed delivery SMTP, and relayed mail. Every Linux system that sends SMTP mail, whether directly or through a mail server, has this MAILER command.

In addition to these two important sets of mailers, there are nine other sets of mailers available with the MAILER command.

Most of them are of very little interest to the average systems administrator.

OSTYPE, DOMAIN, and MAILER are generally found only in the macro configuration file. The other four commands in Table 28.1 are found in both macro configuration and macro source files:

VERSIONID   The VERSIONID macro defines version control information. This macro is optional, but it is found in most m4 files. The command has no required format for the argument. Use any version control information you want. The basic format of the VERSIONID macro is this:

```
VERSIONID('version-control-data')
```

WARNING

A quoted string in the argument field of any m4 macro must begin with ' and end with '. This is important. If other quotation marks are used, you will have errors in your configuration.

FEATURE   The FEATURE macro identifies an optional send-mail feature for inclusion in the sendmail.cf file. A single m4 file can contain several FEATURE commands. The format of the FEATURE macro is this:

```
FEATURE('feature-name'[, 'parameter'[, 'parameter']...])
```

feature-name identifies the requested feature. There are more than 40 sendmail features available, some of which can be configured with optional parameters. Features are documented on the sendmail website at http://www.sendmail.org/m4/features.html. Next to the define command, the FEATURE command is the most heavily used command in the m4 configuration.

define   The define command is used to set the value of a configuration variable for the sendmail.cf file. This file contains hundreds of variables called macros, classes, and options. The define command identifies the variable by name and sets the value for the variable using this format:

```
define('variable-name', 'value')
```

There are hundreds of variable names, most of which you will never use.

undefine   The undefine command is the opposite of the define command. It returns the value of a variable to the system default. Thus, the only argument provided to the undefine command is the variable name:

```
undefine('variable-name')
```

At first glance, the undefine command may seem odd. Why would you define a variable value only to undefine it? The answer is that you didn't define it in the first place—someone else did. Configurations are built by bringing together several m4 source files that already exist. An existing file may have several values you want for your configuration, and a few you don't want. The undefine command lets you use what you want from the m4 source file while resetting the values you don't want.

The basic configuration commands appear in an m4 configuration file in the following order:

▶ VERSIONID, when used, is the first macro in the file.

▶ OSTYPE is defined before the other essential macros.

▶ DOMAIN, when used, comes next.

▶ define commands that affect a FEATURE macro that will be specified in the macro configuration file must come before that FEATURE macro.

▶ FEATURE macros come next.

▶ define commands that specify variable settings for the configuration, other than those that affect a previously identified FEATURE, come after the FEATURE macros.

▶ MAILER macros are the last basic commands in the file.

As you'll see later, there are several more commands that can be used in the m4 configuration files. These commands add complexity to the structure, but the basic structure is as described above.

The nine commands covered so far are used to build most configurations. The syntax and the purpose of the commands have been described, but until you see the commands in the context of a configuration file, it is difficult to imagine exactly how they are used.

An Example Macro Configuration File

The sendmail distribution comes with a large number of example macro configuration files. One that is sure to draw the attention of a Linux systems administrator is the file generic-linux.mc. Listing 28.7 shows the contents of this file.

Listing 28.7: The *generic-linux.mc* File

```
divert(-1)
#
# Copyright (c) 1998, 1999 Sendmail, Inc. and its suppliers.
#       All rights reserved.
# Copyright (c) 1983 Eric P. Allman.  All rights reserved.
# Copyright (c) 1988, 1993
#       The Regents of the University of California.  All rights
#   reserved.
#
# By using this file, you agree to the terms and conditions set
# forth in the LICENSE file which can be found at the top level of
# the sendmail distribution.
#
#


#
#  This is a generic configuration file for Linux.
#  It has support for local and SMTP mail only.  If you want to
#  customize it, copy it to a name appropriate for your environment
#  and do the modifications there.
#

divert(0)dnl
VERSIONID('$Id: generic-linux.mc,v 8.1 1999/09/24 22:48:05 gshapiro
          Exp $')
OSTYPE(linux)dnl
DOMAIN(generic)dnl
MAILER(local)dnl
MAILER(smtp)dnl
```

The example file starts with a divert(-1) command that discards what follows. Because the following text will not appear in the output file, it is provided only as a comment or informational message. In this case, the discarded text includes a copyright notice and some general

information about the file and how it should be used. The block of text ends with a `divert(0)dnl` line that redirects the output to the output file, which in effect turns m4 processing back on. In the future, when we display the contents of a macro control file we will show only the active commands and ignore the block of text at the start of the file for the sake of clearer and shorter listings. However, you should know that most example files start with a similar block of text.

An optional VERSIONID macro is the first macro command in the `generic-linux.mc` file. The version control information is intended for the people who maintain this example file. You can safely ignore it. When you create your own configuration files, you should use version control information that is meaningful to you or to the tools you use to maintain the file.

The example OSTYPE command tells m4 to process the file `../ostype/linux.m4` for operating system attributes. No surprise here. Using Linux operating system attributes is just what you would expect in a file named `generic-linux.mc`. The macro configuration file must have one OSTYPE command, and it must occur before most of the other configuration commands in the file.

The DOMAIN command in Listing 28.7 processes the file `../domain/generic.m4`. The configuration settings in `generic.m4` are examples of the type of commands you might include in your own DOMAIN m4 source file. The DOMAIN command line is included in the `generic-linux.mc` file primarily as an example of how the command is used in a macro configuration file.

The `generic-linux.mc` file ends with two MAILER commands. These are the same two MAILER commands that were described in the preceding section. Almost all Linux sendmail configurations have these two lines. If additional mailers, such as the UUCP mailers, are added to the configuration, they are added after these two MAILER statements.

Let's follow the advice at the beginning of the `generic-linux.mc` file to build our own simple configuration file.

Building a Simple *m4* Configuration File

The problem we want to solve is very straightforward. We have installed sendmail 8.11 on the example system and we want a basic configuration that will work with that release. We aren't concerned yet with building a full-featured sendmail configuration. We just want to get the system running. Let's start with the `generic-linux.mc` file.

Begin by changing to the `cf/cf` directory and copying the `generic-linux.mc` file to `test.mc`. Make sure the file permission for `test.mc` is 644 so that you can edit the file:

```
[root]# cd /usr/local/src/sendmail-8.11.4/cf/cf
[root]# cp generic-linux.mc test.mc
[root]# chmod 644 test.mc
```

Now edit the file to create the new configuration. Our goal is to create the simplest possible configuration in order to get the system running. To do that, remove the DOMAIN(generic) line from the `test.mc` macro configuration file; it is primarily included as an example and has not been customized for our domain. While editing the file, don't forget to update the VERSIONID macro to reflect the fact that this is a new configuration file. The following `tail` command shows the macros in the file after the edits:

```
[root]# tail -5 test.mc
divert(0)dnl
VERSIONID('test.mc, v1.0')
OSTYPE(linux)dnl
MAILER(local)dnl
MAILER(smtp)dnl
```

The new `test.mc` file is even simpler than the `generic-linux.mc` file.

The *m4* Command Line

The new `test.mc` configuration file cannot be used by sendmail directly. The `test.mc` file is an input file for the m4 command. The next step in creating the new sendmail configuration is to process the `test.mc` file through m4 as shown in Listing 28.8.

Listing 28.8: Running *m4*

```
[root]# m4 ../m4/cf.m4 test.mc > test.cf
```

The example shows the m4 command format used to build a `sendmail.cf` file. The pathname `../m4/cf.m4` is the path to the m4 source tree required to build a `sendmail.cf` file. This must be specified on the m4 command line if it is not included in the macro configuration file with an `include` command. Notice that it is a relative pathname, starting with `../`. Older versions of m4 required a relative pathname. Changing to the `cf/cf` directory was not just a convenience; it was a necessary part of running m4 with the correct source tree path. This is no longer necessary on Linux systems. The GNU m4 program used with Linux can accept an absolute pathname for this argument, which means that the macro configuration file can be stored anywhere on the system. Red Hat takes advantage of this fact when installing sendmail via RPM. RPM places a copy of the Red Hat macro configuration file in /etc/mail and includes an absolute pathname to cf.m4 inside the macro configuration file.

The second command-line argument is the name of the new macro configuration file, test.mc. m4 reads the source files ../m4/cf.m4 and test.mc, and outputs the file test.cf. The file output by the m4 command is in the correct format for a sendmail.cf file.

Testing the Configuration File Compatibility

The test.cf file is in the correct format to become the sendmail.cf file, but before moving it to /etc/mail/sendmail.cf, you should make sure it works. A quick test will tell you, as shown in Listing 28.9.

Listing 28.9: Testing Compatibility

```
[root]# sendmail -v -t -C /etc/sendmail.cf
Warning: .cf file is out of date: sendmail 8.11.4 supports
         version 9, .cf file is version 8
^D
No recipient addresses found in header
[root]# sendmail -v -t -C ./test.cf
^D
No recipient addresses found in header
```

As Listing 28.9 shows, the new test.cf configuration file resolves the compatibility problem that appears when we upgrade sendmail by compiling new source code. The test doesn't prove anything else, and I won't pretend this simple configuration is the best possible configuration, but it meets the goal we set of getting sendmail up and running.

Installing the New Configuration

Once you decide to use the new configuration file, move it to the location where sendmail expects to find its configuration file. The name of the configuration file for sendmail 8.11 defaults to /etc/mail/sendmail.cf. On most Linux systems, the configuration file is /etc/sendmail.cf. Put the new file in the appropriate location for your system. In this example, we compiled sendmail 8.11 from source code with the default setting, so we need to move `test.cf` to `/etc/mail/sendmail.cf`, which we do in Listing 28.10.

Listing 28.10: Putting a New Configuration File in Place

```
[root]# mv /etc/mail/sendmail.cf /etc/mail/sendmail.cf.hold
mv: /etc/mail/sendmail.cf: No such file or directory
[root]# cp test.cf /etc/mail/sendmail.cf
[root]# sendmail -v -t
To: craig@wren.foobirds.org
From: craig
Subject: Test
Please ignore this test.
^D
craig@wren.foobirds.org... Connecting to wren.foobirds.org. via
    esmtp...
220 wren.foobirds.org ESMTP sendmail 8.11.4/8.11.4;
    Tue, 29 Aug 2000 20:42:44 -0
400
>>> EHLO ibis.foobirds.org
250-wren.foobirds.org Hello root@almond.nuts.com [172.16.12.1],
    pleased to meet you
>>> MAIL From:<craig@ibis.foobirds.org> SIZE=78
250 2.1.0 <craig@ibis.foobirds.org>... Sender ok
>>> RCPT To:<craig@wren.foobirds.org>
250 2.1.5 <craig@wren.foobirds.org>... Recipient ok
>>> DATA
354 Enter mail, end with "." on a line by itself
>>> .
250 2.0.0 e7U0fRg00818 Message accepted for delivery
craig@wren.foobirds.org... Sent (e7U0fRg00818 Message
     accepted for delivery)
Closing connection to wren.foobirds.org.
>>> QUIT
221 2.0.0 wren.foobirds.org closing connection
```

The first step is to move the current `sendmail.cf` file to a backup file, called `sendmail.cf.hold` in Listing 28.10. In this case, the move is unsuccessful because we just installed sendmail from source files and there was no `/etc/mail/sendmail.cf` file. Still, I always run `mv` first just to make sure I don't overwrite a file that I later want to recover.

Next, we copy the `test.cf` file to `/etc/mail/sendmail.cf` and run a test to make sure everything is working. This time we don't need to use the -C argument with the sendmail command because the sendmail configuration file is in the correct location. Also, this time we run a complete test and actually send a piece of mail. The mail is delivered correctly and is properly formatted.

We have a complete, working sendmail 8.11 system.

More *m4* Commands

This is a chapter about basic configuration, but as you might imagine, the basic commands covered in this chapter are not the whole story. Several other m4 commands must be understood just to read all of the example macro configuration files that come with the sendmail distribution. Table 28.3 identifies and describes the other commands found in the example files. The one command listed in lowercase is a built-in m4 command. All of the other commands, which are listed in uppercase, are macros the sendmail development team created for sendmail configuration.

TABLE 28.3:   More *m4* Commands

COMMAND	PURPOSE
EXPOSED_USER	Overrides masquerading for specific users.
HACK	Processes a file that contains temporary fixes.
include	Incorporates an external m4 file into this file by reference.
LOCAL_CONFIG	Marks the start of a section that contains sendmail.cf commands.
LOCAL_RULE_*n*	Marks the start of a section that contains rewrite rules. The *n*, which must be 0, 1, 2, or 3, identifies the ruleset that the rewrite rules are added to.
LOCAL_RULESETS	Marks the start of a ruleset to be added to the configuration.
MASQUERADE_AS	Defines a domain name that is used to rewrite the host part of sender addresses.
MODIFY_MAILER_FLAGS	Defines mailer flags used to override the current mailer flag settings.
SITE	Identifies the names of UUCP sites connected to the server.
SITECONFIG	Points to the file that contains the SITE commands for the UUCP mail server.
UUCPSMTP	Maps a UUCP hostname to an Internet hostname.

The first and most important thing to realize about the commands in Table 28.3 is that there are some you will never use. Just because a command shows up in an example file doesn't mean it is the correct command for you or even a recommended command. Some of the example files that come with sendmail are very old. Some of the commands used in these files are obsolete and can be ignored. The last three commands in Table 28.3 are good examples. SITE, SITECONFIG, and UUCPSMTP are obsolete techniques for configuring the system to handle UUCP mail. These functions have been replaced by the use of databases.

Another command you can safely ignore is HACK. As the name implies, it is intended to process a file that contains a hack to fix a mail problem. All normal mail problems can be addressed through the normal configuration. A hack is supposed to be something temporary, a fix that needs to be addressed in the configuration but that you know will not be required in the near future. The idea is that the fix can be put in a separate file in the cf/hack directory and then discarded when no longer needed. The problem with hacks is that they tend to develop a life of their own. The duration of a problem is rarely known. A hack that seems temporary soon becomes permanent. Generally it is better to fix all problems permanently in the "regular" configuration instead of creating a hack. A "permanent" fix can be removed as easily as a hack when it is no longer needed.

Use the include command to simplify the m4 command line. In Listing 28.8, the m4 command line begins with the argument ../m4/cf.m4 to ensure that the macro definitions and header files in the cf/m4 directory are available to the m4 process. This argument must be added to the command line every time m4 is run. It is possible to include the cf.m4 file inside the macro configuration file so that it doesn't have to be specified on the command line. If the following line is added to the beginning of the test.mc file:

```
include '../usr/local/src/sendmail-8.11.4/cf/m4/cf.m4'
```

the test.mc file can be processed with the following m4 command:

```
[root]# m4 test.mc > test2.cf
```

Those who use include commands in other languages generally think the include command can be used to separate a complex configuration into several files and then bring those files together for processing. While that is true for m4 in general, it is not true for sendmail configuration. All macro configuration files are short files that do not benefit from being segmented. The only time you'll see include used in the files provided with the sendmail distribution is when cf.m4 itself includes the large and complex `cfhead.m4` file. The only time you will use `include` is when you want to include the `cf.m4` file in your macro configuration file to simplify the `m4` command line.

The `LOCAL_CONFIG`, `LOCAL_RULESET`, and `LOCAL_RULE_n` commands allow you to put raw `sendmail.cf` configuration commands directly in the `m4` source file. These and other related commands mean that everything that can be done in the `sendmail.cf` file can be done in the `m4` macro source files. We use the `LOCAL_CONFIG`, `LOCAL_RULESET`, and `LOCAL_RULE_n` commands several times in this text to define complex `sendmail.cf` configurations.

The `MODIFY_MAILER_FLAGS` command is used to override the flags set for a mailer. The `MODIFY_MAILER_FLAGS` command has two arguments: the name of the mailer and the flag to be modified. The flag is preceded by a + if it is to be added to the existing set of flags or by a - if an existing flag is to be removed.

The `MASQUERADE_AS` and `EXPOSED_USER` commands both deal with masquerading. Frequently, an organization wants all of its outbound mail to appear as if it came from one source. This is done to create clean and consistent e-mail addresses and to hide the names of internal systems that should not be receiving mail directly. *Masquerading* is the name for this type of mail rewriting. `MASQUERADE_AS` defines the hostname that is used as the hostname part for all outbound mail. If `MASQUERADE_AS('foobirds.org')` is set in the configuration, mail from `craig@wren.foobirds.org` goes out as mail from `craig@foobirds.org`.

`EXPOSED_USER` addresses a problem created by masquerading. Assume that mail from `root@wren.foobirds.org` and `root@ibis.foobirds.org` is passed through the server with the `MASQUERADE_AS('foobirds.org')` setting. If both addresses are rewritten to `root@foobirds.org`, you have a problem. There is no way for the recipient to know exactly where the message really originated, and the remote user could not reply to the correct address. Usernames, such as `root`, that are found on every system should not be masqueraded. The `EXPOSED_USER` command is used to define usernames that should not be masqueraded.

The commands in Table 28.1 and Table 28.3 are just the tip of the `m4` iceberg. Many more commands exist. This chapter does not provide exhaustive coverage of the `m4` language. It is an introduction to `m4` that helps you understand the `m4` commands contained in the example files. Understanding these basic commands should help you read the macro configuration file provided by your vendor.

In Conclusion

Sendmail reads its configuration from the sendmail.cf file. However, this file is not directly configured by the sendmail administrator. Instead, the file is constructed indirectly from m4 macros.

The sendmail distribution provides the m4 source files necessary to build a sendmail configuration. The m4 source files are contained in the nine subdirectories of the cf directory. For most configurations, eight of the nine subdirectories can be ignored because either they are unused or they contain source files that are never modified by the systems administrator. The only subdirectory that the administrator needs to work with for most configurations is the cf/cf directory.

The cf/cf directory contains the macro configuration files. The sendmail administrator creates a macro configuration file that selects the source files that provide the features necessary for the sendmail configuration. Most macro configuration files are not built from scratch. The sendmail distribution provides about 20 different example macro configuration files. You select a macro configuration file that matches your needs and only make small adjustments if they are necessary.

The macro configuration file is then processed through m4 to produce the sendmail.cf file. Even this step may not be necessary if you don't need to change the example macro configuration file for your configuration. Several sendmail configuration files built from example macro configuration files are included in the cf/cf directory.

To select and modify the correct macro configuration file, you must have a basic understanding of the m4 sendmail macro configuration language. Use the tables in this chapter to help you read and modify the macro configuration file. Don't bother memorizing the details of the sendmail configuration language; you won't build new configurations often enough to make that skill worthwhile. Instead, learn the basic commands in Table 28.1.

A configuration can be built by starting with an example file and modifying it for your configuration, as was done in this chapter. An even more common way to configure sendmail is to use the macro configuration file provided with your Linux distribution.

Part vi

Appendix

RECOMPILING THE LINUX KERNEL

L inux is one of the few operating systems where you can impact how your computer works at its core. Because Linux includes all of the source code to the kernel of the operating system, anything you can think of can be attempted in Linux. Of course, for most of us, that means reconfiguring the kernel with the tools provided, rather than modifying the C language source code files.

Nevertheless, hundreds of option settings are available as part of the standard kernel configuration utilities. This appendix describes how to use the kernel configuration tools to select options that you want included with your running Linux system and then shows how to recompile the kernel source code based on those options.

Adapted from *Mastering Red Hat Linux 7.1*
by Arman Danesh
ISBN 0-7821-2927-7   1008 pages $49.99

WHY CHANGE THE KERNEL?

If you're new to Linux, you may be asking yourself, "Why on Earth would I want to recompile the kernel?" You may also be thinking that it's a very difficult process.

Linux is much more user-friendly than it was two or three years ago; advancements in the installation process, graphical interfaces, and hardware support have all made Linux accessible to those of us who aren't computer science gurus. In fact, the process of recompiling the kernel, described here, uses a menu-driven configuration interface and a single (long) command line to remake the kernel.

Linux is highly "tunable"; you can refine its capabilities to meet your unique requirements. However, many of the features of Linux are not activated by default in the standard Linux kernel. This is true for several reasons.

The most important thing to understand is that every user makes trade-offs in their software. For example, when using a compression program, you can choose a faster compression time or choose a smaller compressed file.

In the same way, Linux kernels must make trade-offs. For example, you can have a smaller kernel or one that supports more hardware without additional configuration steps. Or you can have a system optimized for routing IP packets or for handling normal workstation tasks.

PROGRAMMING TERMS: MAKING, BUILDING, AND COMPILING

As you read about working with the kernel, you'll see three terms used interchangeably: *remaking*, *rebuilding*, and *recompiling* the kernel. Although you can think of them as being synonymous, it's also helpful to understand what each of these terms really means.

When you develop software in Linux (and in many other operating systems), you use a configuration file for your programming project that describes how the pieces of source code and all libraries fit together. This information is stored in a file called Makefile, which is used by the utility make. (You'll use the make utility several times later in this appendix.)

CONTINUED ➡

The process of actually converting the source code of a project into something the computer can use (a binary) is called *compilation*. The standard C language compilers for Linux, gcc or egcs, are used to compile source code.

However, because a programming project generally has dozens of separate components, the make utility checks the dates and times on each component and recompiles only the components that have been updated since they were last compiled. This saves a great deal of time in creating a new version of a project when only part of the source code has been altered.

When you use the make utility, you can indicate that you want to recompile "from scratch" all of the components of your project. This is called a *build*.

So remaking the kernel, rebuilding the kernel, and recompiling the kernel all do similar things. And with several hundred thousand lines of source code, the process still takes a while to complete, no matter what you call it.

The kernel is configured to provide a good balance between kernel size, speed, and hardware support. This balance seeks to meet the needs of average users as the Linux vendor sees them. In this appendix, you will learn how to make your own decisions about which features are most important to your computing environment.

Learning about Modules

Kernel modules are a critical part of Linux. A kernel module allows you to add functionality to the core of Linux without recompiling the kernel source code. As you'll see later in this appendix, that's a great benefit.

For example, if you discover that you need to work with a special new SCSI interface card, you can load a kernel module to support it with a single command (the insmod command). Previously, Linux would have required you to rebuild the kernel to include support for that SCSI device.

As the number of hardware devices supported by Linux has increased, kernel modules have allowed the Linux kernel to remain relatively small, while still allowing users to easily add support for the hardware that they own.

TIP

A big difference between Linux and some other operating systems is the ability to load or remove support for hardware, file systems, languages, and so forth without ever rebooting the system.

Table A.1 contains a summary of the commands used with kernel modules. You can view the man page for any of these commands to see more information.

TABLE A.1:   Commands Used with Kernel Modules

COMMAND	DESCRIPTION
lsmod	List all of the modules currently installed in the running kernel.
insmod	Insert a module into the running kernel. This command uses the module name and, optionally, additional parameters to define how the module behaves (for example, IRQ and address information for a hardware device).
rmmod	Remove a module from the running system. Be careful that you don't remove modules that are in use by other modules. (See the output of the lsmod command for details on dependencies of currently loaded modules.)
depmod	Create a dependencies file that can be used by the modprobe command to load a set of modules.
modprobe	Load the set of modules defined by the depmod command.

NOTE

All of the noted commands, except lsmod, require the user to be in root mode. In Red Hat Linux 7.1, these commands are in the /sbin directory, which is not on the path by default; therefore, you'll probably need to type the full path to these commands, e.g., /sbin/lsmod, /sbin/insmod, and so on.

Other information about the modules on your Linux system is available by reviewing certain system files.

Because kernel modules are inserted into the running source code, they are stored as object code (already compiled). Each module has the file extension .o.

Check the following files:

- ▶ /boot/module-info-2.4.2-2 contains per-module information that you can alter to reflect any specific settings of your hardware.

- ▶ /lib/modules/2.4.2-2 contains several subdirectories that divide all of the available kernel modules on your system. For example, check the contents of the kernel/drivers/cdrom subdirectory to see all the modules available to support various CD-ROM drives.

NOTE

The kernel version associated with Red Hat Linux 7.1 is 2.4.2. If you are using a different version of Linux or have previously upgraded the kernel, substitute version numbers accordingly.

TIP

All Linux kernels have version numbers in a *major.minor.patch* format. The biggest changes are associated with a new major revision number. Changes to the minor revision number can be quite significant. When the minor revision is an even number, the kernel is considered to be stable. When it is an odd number, it is developmental and should not be used by novices or for production computers. As incremental changes are developed, the changes are incorporated into a patch revision.

Understanding Reasons to Recompile

If you're still wondering specifically why you would need to recompile your Linux kernel, the information in Table A.2 should provide some insight. This table outlines some solutions to common problems you may encounter.

Of course, you may need to rebuild the kernel for only one of these reasons. But understanding why people work with the kernel will show you more about the flexibility of Linux.

TABLE A.2:   Solutions to Problems Recompiling the Linux Kernel

PROBLEM	SOLUTION
You hear that your processor has a bug that could crash your system. Linux has a workaround, but you're using an older version.	Download the patch to the Linux kernel and remake the source code. In 20 minutes, the problem is solved.
You've purchased a new SCSI card that is supported in a Linux kernel module, but you can't boot the system from your SCSI hard disk unless the SCSI module is part of the default kernel.	Remake the kernel, indicating that the necessary SCSI support is built in rather than created as a module.
A security alert appears about problems with a Linux file system driver. A patch is available within hours.	Download the patch and remake your kernel to provide the most up-to-date security for your system.
A new network card driver is available for your system. You download the source code from the vendor's Web site.	Remake the kernel so that the source code version for all modules matches your new network card module.
You purchased a commercial Linux product that had a 2.2.16 Linux kernel, but now you'd like the latest revised kernel.	Download the kernel sources (they're fairly large) and remake the kernel so you have the latest version of the kernel.
Users on your system are complaining that they can't access certain file systems unless they use a bunch of strange commands first (such as insmod, for example).	Remake the kernel with the needed file system support built in so that file systems of that type can be mounted without explicitly adding a kernel module.

Finding Out about Kernel Updates

The Linux kernel can change literally every day. Fortunately, when you're running a stable system, you generally don't care to follow all of those changes. In fact, most of the changes to Linux occur in the development version of the kernel, which isn't something you want to run a production system on anyway.

To keep up-to-date on happenings with the Linux kernel and related topics, plan to visit the following Web sites regularly. These sites are updated several times a day with new information:

> ***www.linuxhq.com***   This site contains a large collection of information about the Linux kernel, with sections on the latest

development and stable kernels, links to information resources, and many useful details about the Linux kernel.

www.freshmeat.net This site is a clearinghouse for announcements about releases of open source software and related topics. This site includes a searchable archive of release information. The Freshmeat site is not focused on the Linux kernel per se, but it includes information about kernel releases.

www.linuxtoday.com This site is a daily news digest about open source software and related topics. This site includes a searchable archive of release information. While the Linux Today site is not focused on the Linux kernel per se, new kernel release announcements are posted here.

CHECKING FOR SOURCE PACKAGES

In order to recompile your Linux kernel, you must have the source code to the kernel installed on your system. The kernel source code on Red Hat Linux 7.1 is located in a single rpm package installed by default. If it isn't installed, the package to check for is

```
kernel-source-2.4.2-2.i386.rpm
```

You can install this package using the rpm command after mounting the Red Hat 7.1 CD-ROM:

```
rpm -Uvh kernel-source-2.4.2-2.i386.rpm
```

NOTE

Red Hat includes the kernel source code in an rpm package that is not marked as a "source code package" with the file extension .src.rpm. The .src.rpm package is not what you need.

NOTE

The kernel source package is not included on the Publisher's Edition of Red Hat Linux 7.1 that ships with this book, but it can be downloaded from http://www.redhat.com.

Checking for Tools

In addition to the source code itself, you must have a compiler available to rebuild the source code. The two tools you need are:

▶ The make utility

▶ The C language compiler, gcc or egcs

The exact versions of these utilities may vary from system to system. It's best if you have a recent version of the compiler, such as gcc 2.96 or egcs 1.1.2.

To check for these utilities on your Linux system, use the following commands (the output from a typical Red Hat installation is shown):

```
# rpm -q make
make-3.79.1-5
# rpm -q gcc
gcc-2.96-81
```

NOTE

The same commands should work on any Linux distribution that uses rpm for software package management.

If you don't see these tools installed on your system, you'll need to use rpm or a similar utility to install them from the Red Hat Linux 7.1 CD-ROM before proceeding with this appendix.

TIP

When you try to install gcc, you may see a failed dependencies message. This message lists other rpm packages that need to be installed first. In this case, the required additional packages are also available on the CD-ROM.

WARNING

If you don't already have a boot disk with your current kernel, you can create one in root user mode with the /sbin/mkbootdisk -device /dev/fd0 2.4.2-2 command.

BACKING UP THE OLD KERNEL

Although the implication here is that rebuilding the Linux kernel is child's play, you should still take a few precautions before diving into the deep end of the pool. That means backing up your kernel and providing a method to reboot to the previous version of the kernel in case of problems.

Backing up the current kernel involves three steps:

1. Back up the source code tree for the kernel so you can re-create the current kernel if the configuration becomes corrupted.

2. Back up the kernel itself so you have a kernel to start your system with that you already know works.

3. Create a new boot loader entry so you can boot from the backup of your kernel.

Backing up the source code tree for your current kernel is simple. Just use a command such as the following cp command, which copies the entire kernel source code tree to a duplicate directory. (You can then copy it back to the original name if you need to use the backup.)

```
# cp -r /usr/src/linux-2.4.2 /usr/src/linux-2.4.2.sav
```

Backing up the kernel itself is almost as simple; use a command like the following cp command. (Change it to match the exact kernel version you're running.)

```
# cp /boot/vmlinuz-2.4.2-2 /boot/vmlinuz-2.4.2-2.orig
```

TIP

When you rebuild the kernel, the existing kernel is saved with the file extension .old. However, that old kernel version is not automatically accessible to boot your system, which is the purpose of these steps.

The LILO boot loader that normally launches Linux from your hard drive is configured by pointing to a kernel file in your root file system. For example, you may see a line like this in your /etc/lilo.conf file:

```
image = /boot/vmlinuz-2.4.2-2
```

This line indicates the path and filename of the kernel to start.

Once you have created a backup of the kernel itself (in the previous step), you should also create another entry in `lilo.conf` so that you can start your Linux system with the old (proven) kernel.

To do this, follow these steps:

1. Open the `/etc/lilo.conf` file in a text editor.

2. Find the section in the `/etc/lilo.conf` file that refers to your kernel image.

3. Make a copy of that entire section (usually about four or five lines of text).

4. In your copy, change two items:

    ▸ Change the name of the kernel to the name of your backed-up kernel (with the .orig ending in the example).

    ▸ Change the label field to something like `linux.original` or `linux-previous`.

5. If there is a line starting with `initrd`, change the name of this to an appropriate backup, such as `initrd-2.4.2-2.orig.img`. You'll create this file later, if required.

6. Save your changes to `/etc/lilo.conf`.

7. Run the command `/sbin/lilo` to add the new entry to your boot loader. As `lilo` runs, you see the different labels on screen as images are added to your boot loader.

The next time you reboot your system, you will see the new kernel entry appear in the graphical LILO boot prompt. If you are using a distribution that does not use a graphical LILO boot prompt, you may have to press Tab to see the additional image you defined as a precaution before rebuilding your kernel.

GETTING A NEW KERNEL

There are a number of ways to get a copy of a new kernel. Two major ways are through the Linux Kernel Archives at `http://www.kernel.org` or through your Linux distribution's Web site. If you're looking for an `rpm` version of the kernel, a central source is located at `http://www.rpmfind.net`. This section covers downloading kernels in the `tar.gz` format, in files such as `linux-2.4.4.tar.gz`.

WARNING

Make sure to back up the previous version of your kernel, as described earlier in this appendix.

Once you've downloaded the relevant kernel package, move it to the /usr/src/ directory. Remember, this section assumes that you've already backed up your current kernel as described earlier in this appendix.

To extract the kernel and associated files (over 8,000 in version 2.4.4), navigate to the /usr/src directory, then run the following command:

```
tar zxpvf linux-2.4.4.tar.gz
```

If your kernel package filename is different, substitute appropriately. Now you can use one of the utilities discussed in the following sections to configure your new kernel.

TIP

If you're upgrading a kernel, make sure that your software is advanced enough to accommodate the upgrade. For the kernel 2.4 series, review the /usr/src/linux-2.4.x/Documentation/Changes file for versions of critical software that you need.

CONFIGURING THE NEW KERNEL

The interesting part of creating a new Linux kernel is setting up the new kernel configuration. This is the step in which you decide what the kernel will include, what it will not include, and so forth. You have a choice between configuring a kernel from new or existing sources. For example, if you're running Red Hat Linux 7.1, you could reconfigure the existing 2.4.2 kernel with new options. Alternatively, you could download and install the newer 2.4.4 kernel. While the detailed configuration options vary, the tools, utilities, and techniques remain the same.

Linux includes three separate configuration utilities. Each one is suited to different preferences:

A command-line interface   A command-line interface asks questions one at a time about what you want to include in the kernel. This interface is convenient for those who are very familiar with the kernel or who may have a script that processes the configuration information using this interface.

The command-line interface is also the choice for those who have very limited control over their screens and therefore can't use the menu-based interface. The greatest disadvantage of the command-line interface is that you can't return to a previous question and review it or change your selection.

A character-based menu interface   This interface uses several levels of menus that you can explore, selecting options as you go, and return to any area. This option is available for computers with some graphics capability, which you can access directly without having to configure or access an X Window interface.

A graphical, X-based interface   This interface is very similar to the character-based menu interface, but it is truly graphical. This is the most attractive interface, but it requires the installation of the X Windows system.

All three methods (command line, menus, and true graphical) create the same configuration file that the make utility uses during the compilation/rebuilding process. All three methods also include copious help information to answer your questions about specific options.

Understanding the Options

As you review the various options presented in any of the configuration methods (command line, menu, or graphical), you need to understand how each option can be applied to your Linux kernel.

The options are identified by different indicators, depending on which tool you use to configure the kernel, but the same options are available in each case. The configuration items fall in two groups:

▶ Module-capable

▶ Non-module-capable

If an option is not capable of being a loadable kernel module, then it must be either

▶ [*]   Part of the kernel, or

▶ [ ]   Not part of the kernel

The bracket indications above show how the selection of an option is shown in the menu-based configuration tool.

If an option is module-capable, you have these choices (again, these are shown as they would appear in the menu configuration tool; similar indications are shown in both of the other tools):

▶ < >   Not included, and not created as a module that can be loaded later.

▶ <*>   Included as part of the kernel, so that it doesn't have to be loaded later as a kernel; it's always part of the system.

▶ <M>   Included as a module, but not part of the kernel itself. Thus, this option can be added or removed from the running kernel at your discretion.

TIP

If you're having trouble changing an option, you may need to set another option first. For example, you must enable SCSI devices in general before you can select specific SCSI device support.

Once you have all the tools (`make` and `gcc`) and the source code installed, you are ready to start one of the configuration tools and configure your kernel.

Remember that you need to use only one of the three interfaces described in the following sections. Review each section briefly and decide which interface you want to use, based on the figures and descriptions given.

TIP

The first time you install and configure a freshly downloaded kernel, check every section. If there is anything remotely "special" about your computer (e.g., it has only one CPU, needs laptop PC Card support, requires USB support), you should change the kernel configuration. Also, keep the options that you activate to a minimum; fully loaded kernels can be so large that they slow down your system.

Starting the Command-Line Interface

To start the command-line interface, follow these steps:

1. Use the su command to obtain root access.

2. Change to the source code directory:

   ```
   # cd  /usr/src/linux-2.4.2
   ```

NOTE

If you downloaded a different kernel to a different directory, substitute accordingly.

3. Execute the following make command:

   ```
   # make config
   ```

Almost immediately, you see the first configuration question. When you use the make config command, you are prompted to respond to a series of questions about the kernel. Figure A.1 shows the first few questions.

```
[root@linux71 linux-2.4.2]# make config
rm -f include/asm
( cd include ; ln -sf asm-i386 asm)
/bin/sh scripts/Configure arch/i386/config.in
#
# Using defaults found in arch/i386/defconfig
#
*
* Code maturity level options
*
Prompt for development and/or incomplete code/drivers (CONFIG_EXPERIMENTAL) [N/y
/?]
*
* Loadable module support
*
Enable loadable module support (CONFIG_MODULES) [Y/n/?]
  Set version information on all module symbols (CONFIG_MODVERSIONS) [Y/n/?]
  Kernel module loader (CONFIG_KMOD) [Y/n/?]
*
* Processor type and features
*
Processor family (386, 486, 586/K5/5x86/6x86/6x86MX, Pentium-Classic, Pentium-MM
X, Pentium-Pro/Celeron/Pentium-II, Pentium-III, Pentium-4, K6/K6-II/K6-III, Athl
on/Duron/K7, Crusoe, Winchip-C6, Winchip-2, Winchip-2A/Winchip-3) [Pentium-III]
  defined CONFIG_MPENTIUMIII
Toshiba Laptop support (CONFIG_TOSHIBA) [N/y/m/?] []
```

FIGURE A.1: The most basic configuration option for the Linux kernel is make config, which asks you questions in a command-line format.

TIP

The exact series of questions that you see depends on how you respond to questions as you go along.

If you want to select the default option for each question, simply press Enter. In each case, the default selection is shown as an uppercase letter. For example, you will see this question about networking:

```
Networking support (CONFIG_NET) [Y/n/?]
```

If you press Enter, the default of Y, for Yes, is selected. For those options that can be defined as built-in or as modules, the options appear as in this example:

```
Kernel support for ELF binaries (CONFIG_BINFMT_ELF) [Y/m/n/?]
```

Many of the device-related questions present only m/n options, for [Module] or [Don't include].

For each question you see, you can enter a question mark, ?, to see a screen of descriptive information. This information is usually very helpful in determining how to use the option.

TIP

The same help information is available in any of the three kernel configuration tools.

Three disadvantages of using this configuration option are:

▶ You have to answer several hundred individual questions (depending on how you respond, the total number will vary).

▶ You can't go back and change a selection you've made without starting over.

▶ You can't easily see an overview of the options in various categories.

The advantages of using this configuration option include:

▶ Except for the Linux kernel source, you need only a very basic Linux installation to configure the kernel.

▶ You can create scripts to feed input to the configuration script for automated configurations.

The menu configuration option described in the next section provides an easier way for most people to review all of the kernel configuration parameters and create a kernel configuration file.

NOTE

If you need to end or cancel the configuration process before answering all of the questions, press Ctrl+C. An error message from the script appears, and no configuration file is created.

Starting the Character-Based Menu Interface

To start the character-based menu interface, follow these steps:

1. Use the su command to obtain root access.

2. Change to the source code directory:

    ```
    # cd /usr/src/linux-2.4.2
    ```

NOTE

If you downloaded a different kernel to a different directory, substitute accordingly.

3. Execute the following make command:

    ```
    # make menuconfig
    ```

NOTE

The menu-based configuration tool requires a package named ncurses. Ncurses is installed by default on most Linux systems, but if you see errors when you run the make menuconfig command, check that the ncurses-devel package is installed.

You'll see a collection of suspiciously confusing lines scroll down your screen as the make command compiles the menu-based configuration utility. You can ignore these lines; they are the output of the compiler and related programs. After a minute or two, you'll see the screen shown in Figure A.2.

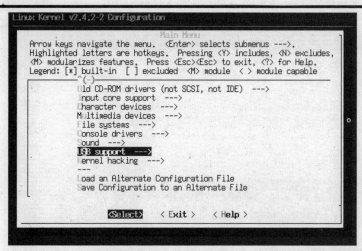

FIGURE A.2:   You can configure the Linux kernel from this character-based menu interface.

The menu configuration option starts with a list of the categories in which you can select kernel options. To navigate this interface, remember the following keystrokes:

▶ Use the up and down arrow keys to move among the options listed in the menus.

▶ Type **M** to select a kernel option as a module (when applicable).

▶ Use the Tab key to move between the buttons shown below the list of kernel options: Select, Exit, and Help.

▶ Press Enter to choose a selected item, such as the Help button.

The three buttons below the option list have the following functions:

Select   Displays the submenu of options associated with the high-lighted item.

Exit   Returns to the previous menu, finishing the configuration if selected from the highest-level menu.

Help   Displays a help screen full of information about the highlighted menu option.

A sample help screen is shown in Figure A.3.

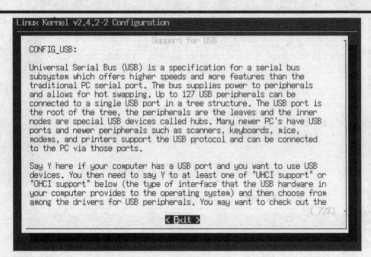

FIGURE A.3:   Help information is available for every kernel option by choosing the Help button.

The kernel configuration tools described in this section are used to create a kernel configuration file that is used to rebuild the kernel. Once you have set up a kernel with all the options you prefer, you can save a copy of the configuration file for repeated use later.

This is done using the last two items on the main menu: Save Configuration To An Alternate File and Load An Alternate Configuration File. Use the down arrow or Page Down key to scroll down to these items.

These last two items on the main menu provide the capability to save your configuration settings or load an existing configuration file:

▶ Use the Save Configuration To An Alternate File option to create a second copy of the kernel configuration file to reuse yourself or to pass on to another person.

WARNING

Don't use the Save Configuration To An Alternate File option until you have completed the selection of all kernel options in the various menus.

▶ Use the Load An Alternate Configuration File option if you have a configuration file that someone has given you or that you have saved previously. Loading such a file sets all the options so that you don't have to select any of the menu items unless you want to make further changes.

Items in the menu list that have submenus of options are displayed with an arrow on the right side of the item; for example, on the main menu you see the following option:

```
USB Support  -->
```

When you view a menu item that actually sets a kernel option, you see the following options displayed to the left of the option, as described previously in this appendix (see also Figure A.4):

▶ [*]   Part of the kernel

▶ [ ]   Not part of the kernel

▶ < >   Not included, and not created as a module that can be loaded later.

▶ <*>   Included as part of the kernel, so that it doesn't have to be loaded later as a module; it's always part of the system.

▶ <M>   Included as a module, but not part of the kernel itself. Thus, this option can be added or removed from the running kernel at your discretion. The relevant option highlighted in Figure A.4, USB Modem, includes this module as part of your configuration. You can confirm this after the new or recompiled kernel is installed; just use the /sbin/lsmod command. Modules like this can be added and removed with the /sbin/insmod and /sbin/rmmod commands, respectively, as discussed earlier in this appendix.

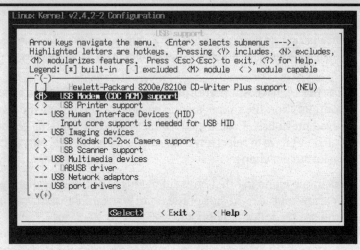

```
Linux Kernel v2.4.2-2 Configuration
                          USB support
  Arrow keys navigate the menu.  <Enter> selects submenus --->.
  Highlighted letters are hotkeys.  Pressing <Y> includes, <N> excludes,
  <M> modularizes features.  Press <Esc><Esc> to exit, <?> for Help.
  Legend: [*] built-in  [ ] excluded  <M> module  < > module capable
    ^(-)
  [ ]    Hewlett-Packard 8200e/8210e CD-Writer Plus support   (NEW)
  <M>    USB Modem (CDC ACM) support
  < >    USB Printer support
  --- USB Human Interface Devices (HID)
  ---    Input core support is needed for USB HID
  --- USB Imaging devices
  < >    USB Kodak DC-2xx Camera support
  < >    USB Scanner support
  --- USB Multimedia devices
  < >    DABUSB driver
  --- USB Network adaptors
  --- USB port drivers
    v(+)

              <Select>    < Exit >    < Help >
```

FIGURE A.4: Individual options in the `menuconfig` tool are shown with selection brackets to the left of each item.

TIP

Depending on the screen on which you're viewing the menus, you should see a bold or different color character as part of each line. You can type that character to select that option rather than using the arrow keys and the Select button.

The current state of each option is shown in the brackets to the left of that option. To change the selected option, type any of the following keys:

- ▶ **Y**   To include the feature in the kernel
- ▶ **M**   To create a module to support this feature (when a possibility)
- ▶ **N**   To not include the feature, nor make a module for it
- ▶ **?**   To display a help screen for the highlighted item

TIP

You can also press the spacebar repeatedly to toggle between the available options for the highlighted item.

When you have reviewed and set all of the kernel options that you want to check, choose the Exit item on the main menu. A configuration screen appears asking if you want to save the updated kernel

configuration file based on your selections (see Figure A.5). Choose Yes
to create the configuration file.

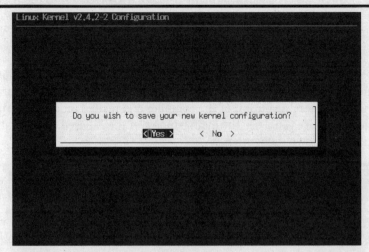

FIGURE A.5:   After choosing configuration options, be sure to save a new
configuration file as you exit the menu-based configuration tool.

Starting the Graphical Interface

To start the graphical (X-based) kernel configuration interface, follow
these steps:

1. Start the X Windows system (using any graphical environ-
    ment or desktop that you prefer).

2. Open a terminal emulator (command-line) window.

3. Use the su command to obtain root access.

4. Change to the source code directory:

    ```
    # cd /usr/src/linux-2.4.2
    ```

NOTE

If you downloaded a different kernel to a different directory, substitute
accordingly.

5. Execute the following make command:

    ```
    # make xconfig
    ```

NOTE

The X-based configuration tool requires a few X Windows system development packages. If you see errors when you run the make xconfig command, check that the appropriate development packages have been installed on your system.

As with the menu-based option, a series of lines scrolls down your screen as the make command compiles the X-based configuration utility. These lines are the output of the compiler and related programs. After a minute or two, you'll see the main window of the X-based configuration utility, as shown in Figure A.6.

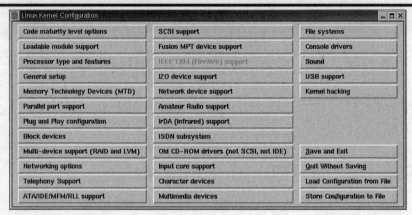

FIGURE A.6:   The graphical kernel configuration tool provides menus and buttons for selecting kernel options.

TIP

Any graphical program is likely to require more system resources than an equivalent character-based program. If your system is short on memory, the X-based kernel configuration tool may be sluggish. Try the menu-based configuration tool in the previous section.

Using the X-based `xconfig` tool is very similar to using the `menuconfig` tool. You choose categories for features that you want to select or deselect. For each category, a dialog box appears in which you can choose to have a feature built into the kernel, created as a loadable module, or not used at all. Figure A.7 contains a sample of one of these dialog boxes.

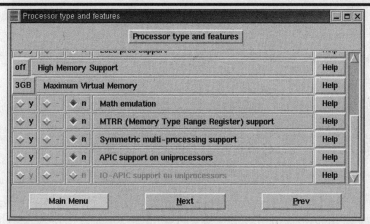

FIGURE A.7:   Dialog boxes similar to this one are used to select features in the X-based kernel configuration tool.

TIP

When you modify kernel 2.4.2 for Red Hat Linux, symmetric multiprocessing support is enabled by default. Change this setting to n unless you actually have more than one CPU on your computer.

As you review different features, you can always select the Help button to the right of an item to see a help screen about that feature. (See Figure A.8.) The information provided in these screens is the same as what you would see in the command-line or menu-based configuration tools.

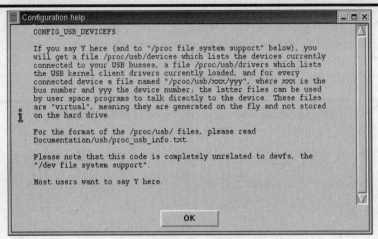

FIGURE A.8:   Help information appears in separate windows when using the X-based configuration tool.

One great advantage of using the X-based configuration tool when you're first working with new kernel configurations is that the graphical interface shows you dependencies between various options. For example, in the Block Devices section, you must enable the Multiple Device Driver Support option before the RAID support options can be built in to your kernel.

The `menuconfig` tool shows a dependency by using indents on the menus, but the graphical tool disables the RAID options until you select the Multiple Device Driver Support option on which RAID depends. As a result, it is easier to understand relationships between modules and features by using the X-based configuration tool.

The options on the bottom of the X-based tool are similar to what you use in the menu-based tool:

Save And Exit   Create the kernel configuration file and close the configuration tool.

Quit Without Saving   Close the configuration tool, but don't create a kernel configuration file.

WARNING

If you don't create a kernel configuration file using one of the three tools described in this chapter, you can't rebuild the kernel.

Load Configuration From File Load a previously saved configuration file (for use later on or to pass to a friend) that was stored under a name that you chose.

Store Configuration To File Save a kernel configuration file (for use later on or to pass to a friend) under a name that you select. You must still use the Save And Exit option to create a kernel configuration file in the default location to be used immediately for kernel rebuilding.

COMPILING AND RUNNING THE NEW KERNEL

Once your kernel reconfiguration is complete, check for a new configuration file (`.config`), probably in the `/usr/src/linux-2.4.2` directory. Remember, to see hidden files, you need to use the `ls -a` command. If `.config` is there, you're ready to use the `make` command to rebuild your kernel.

The preferred commands vary slightly based on your Linux system but are straightforward in every case.

Return to a command line after configuring the kernel and make sure you can leave your system running for a while to let the compilation proceed.

Rebuilding the kernel can take from 15 minutes to several hours, depending on your processor, memory, and other factors. Because of this, most people prefer to combine all of the commands to rebuild the kernel on a single command line, separated by semicolons, so that they execute one after another. By doing this, you can simply return to your system after a while and find the whole process completed.

Starting the Rebuild Process

The commands given here create a new kernel and also rebuild all the kernel modules, placing them in the correct system directories to be accessible to your kernel using standard module commands.

To rebuild the system, use these commands:

```
# make dep; make clean; make bzImage; make modules; make
  modules_install
```

TIP

You can also enter each make command separately, entering the next command after each one has finished. If you don't plan to use modules, you can omit the last two commands. Review the README file where you unpacked the new kernel (/usr/src/linux-2.4.2 in this appendix) for more information.

When you enter these commands, you see lines of information scrolling slowly down your screen as the make program enters different directories, starts the gcc or egcs compiler for various source code files, and links together pieces of the code. Each of these commands may take a substantial number of minutes to complete.

If you have an initrd file in your /etc/lilo.conf file, you should create a new initrd file at this time. First, back up your current initrd file, which is initrd-2.4.2-2.img in Red Hat Linux 7.1. To do so, run the following commands:

```
# cp /boot/initrd-2.4.2-2.img /boot/initrd-2.4.2-2.orig.img
# /sbin/mkinitrd /boot/2.4.2-2.img 2.4.2-2
```

Now you're ready to make a boot disk from your new kernel with this command:

```
# make bzdisk
```

TIP

You'll need to insert a formatted floppy disk in the drive before running this command. Once the boot disk is ready, test it. Reboot your computer with the boot disk in the floppy drive.

Once the commands described previously have completed and you return to a command prompt, you have a new kernel on which you can run your system.

You need to move the newly created kernel to the standard location so it can be used. The command to do this is

```
# cp /usr/src/linux-2.4.2/arch/i386/boot/bzImage /boot/
  vmlinuz-2.4.2-2
```

Finally, to update the boot-loading map you must run the lilo command:

```
# /sbin/lilo
```

TIP

If the name of the copied kernel image has a different kernel version number (or even no number at all), substitute accordingly. Just make sure that it matches the appropriate filename given in your /etc/lilo.conf file, as discussed in the earlier section on backing up the kernel.

Testing the New Kernel

After you have moved your new kernel into the default position (as shown in the lilo.conf file), you can reboot your system to start the new kernel.

Once your Linux system has been rebooted, try the additional features that you specified in the kernel configuration. This might include things like the following:

- ▶ Comparing the size of the new kernel to the previous one. Also try the free command to see how much system memory is used.

- ▶ Mounting a file system or accessing a device without first loading a kernel module to support it (if you had built-in support for that service).

- ▶ Using a networking resource (such as IP aliases) that was not available in your original kernel.

You may also want to try the uname command to see the timestamp of your current kernel. This command verifies that the kernel you're running is the one that you rebuilt. Make sure that the date and time match when you rebuilt your kernel.

```
# uname -v
#1 Tue Mar 9 13:27:39 EST 2001
```

NOTE

If the response from the uname command indicates that you are not running the new kernel, you may have a problem with your LILO boot loader. Check the information in the /etc/lilo.conf file to be sure that the correct kernel has been specified.

INDEX

Note to the Reader: Throughout this index **boldfaced** page numbers indicate primary discussions of a topic. *Italicized* page numbers indicate illustrations.

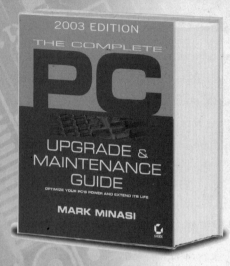

TELL US WHAT YOU THINK!

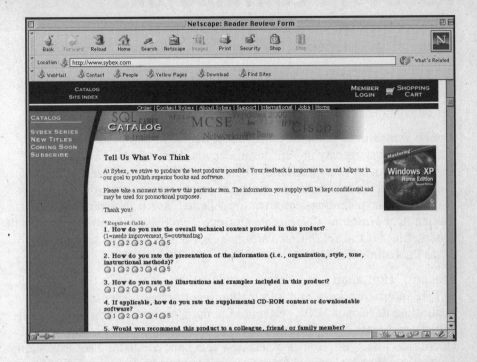

Your feedback is critical to our efforts to provide you with the best books and software on the market. Tell us what you think about the products you've purchased. It's simple:

1. Go to the Sybex website.
2. Find your book by typing the ISBN number or title into the Search field.
3. Click on the book title when it appears.
4. Click **Submit a Review.**
5. Fill out the questionnaire and comments.
6. Click **Submit.**

With your feedback, we can continue to publish the highest quality computer books and software products that today's busy IT professionals deserve.

www.sybex.com

SYBEX Inc. • 1151 Marina Village Parkway, Alameda, CA 94501 • 510-523-8233

ABOUT THE CONTRIBUTORS

Charles Aulds is a programmer/analyst with Epic Data, Connectware Products Group of Richmond, British Columbia. He, his wife, and daughter live on a 22-acre "mini-farm" in north Alabama. Charles has over fifteen years of experience in UNIX systems administration and is now a developer of barcode data collection software systems.

Arman Danesh is pursuing an advanced degree in Computer Science at Simon Fraser University in Vancouver, Canada. Formerly MIS Manager at Landegg Academy in Switzerland, where he was responsible for hundreds of Linux desktop installations and multiple Linux servers, Arman is the author of many books, including *Mastering Corel Linux*, *Mastering Linux*, Second Edition, and *Mastering ColdFusion*, all three from Sybex. He also writes about the Internet for the *South China Morning Post* and is editorial director for Juxta Publishing Limited.

Ramón J. Hontañón has worked for more than a decade in the UNIX, TCP/IP internetworking, and information security fields, serving as UNIX application developer, UNIX systems administrator, information security consultant, and most recently senior manager of security product engineering at UUNET Technologies. He has extensive experience conducting security audits for government agencies and financial institutions and designing UNIX-based security solutions aimed at both internal and customer security.

Craig Hunt is a noted TCP/IP and Linux expert who lectures regularly at NetWorld+Interop, ComNet, and other networking trade shows. His other books include the best-selling *Linux Network Servers 24seven*, published by Sybex.

Bryan Pfaffenberger Linux expert and open-source software advocate, is the author of *Mastering GNOME* from Sybex and numerous additional books on Linux. A regular columnist for *Linux Journal* (linuxjournal.com) and Linux Republic (techrepublic.com), Bryan is a professor in the Media Studies department at the University of Virginia, where he teaches the University-wide computer literacy course.

Roderick W. Smith has used UNIX and Linux systems and networks since 1994. He is the author of five other books, including *Linux Samba Server Administration* from Sybex.

Vicki Stanfield   is a Red Hat Certified Engineer who has worked with Linux since 1994 and with UNIX since 1980. She works for Strictly Business Computer Systems, a Red Hat business partner. Her system administrative experience includes many varieties of UNIX, VMS, and both Slackware and Red Hat Linux.

Nicholas D. Wells   is the former director of Linux vendors Caldera Systems and Lineo. He has written nine books on various topics, including Linux web servers, StarOffice, and KDE. He contributed to *Mastering Linux, Premium Edition* from Sybex, and teaches various Linux topics in Keystone Learning Systems videos.

Dan York   has been teaching, speaking, and writing about UNIX and Internet systems for more than 11 years, focusing in recent years on Linux. He has taught Windows NT classes for three years and continues to speak on integrating Windows and Linux/UNIX systems. He is President of the Linux Professional Institute and is employed by Linuxcare, Inc.

LINUX SAMBA SERVER ADMINISTRATION (CRAIG HUNT LINUX LIBRARY)

BY RODERICK W. SMITH

ISBN 0-7821-2740-1
656 pages
$39.99

Get up to speed on the theory and protocols at the heart of Samba. Begin by mastering Samba's basic functionality then move ahead to advanced techniques and make Samba responsible for critical Windows networking functions. Learn about how to keep your system healthy and secure, perform ongoing maintenance, troubleshoot problem spots, and more.

LINUX SECURITY (CRAIG HUNT LINUX LIBRARY)

BY RAMÓN J. HONTAÑÓN

ISBN 0-7821-2741-X
512 pages
$49.99

This is the most complete, most advanced guide to Linux security you'll find anywhere. Written by a Linux security expert with over a decade of experience, *Linux Security* teaches you, step-by-step, all the standard and advanced techniques you need to know to keep your Linux environment safe from threats of all kinds. Hundreds of clear, consistent examples illustrate these techniques in details.